Navigating the Globally Evolvin
of Sport, Exercise, and Perform.
Psychology

This edited collection brings together global voices on career development within the field of sport, exercise, and performance psychology (SEPP).

Divided into seven sections, this book provides insight into becoming a SEPP professional. It begins by addressing what the SEPP profession is, offering definitions of sport psychology and considers terminology; ethics; diversity, equity, and inclusion; and mental well-being. Section 2 focuses on career development, helping readers navigate topics such as business skills and the global job market. Later sections examine specific roles within the profession, including the SEPP researcher, the SEPP practitioner, the SEPP teacher, and the SEPP mentor. Throughout, professionals from around the world share their perspectives and experiences of working in SEPP, providing a diverse perspective of SEPP as a professional field.

Offering a comprehensive read on the field of sport, exercise, and performance psychology globally, this is the ideal resource for graduate students and early-career professionals. It will also be of interest to professionals already working in the area and looking to continue their professional development.

Andrew P. Friesen is an Associate Professor in the Department of Kinesiology at Penn State Berks, USA, and a Fellow of the Association for Applied Sport Psychology (AASP). His research focuses on emotion regulation in sport and the professional development of practitioners. In addition to his academic role, Andrew runs a private practice providing mental performance services to athletes and performers. He has authored and edited numerous publications in applied sport psychology and actively mentors emerging professionals pursuing certification and careers in the field.

Sebastian Brueckner is a Mental Performance Consultant and Leadership Coach based in Germany whose work bridges applied practice, teaching, and international collaboration. He has served as a consultant to athletes, coaches, and organizations across levels of performance, with an emphasis on evidence-based approaches to mental skills training and professional development. His scholarship and service reflect a global commitment to advancing the profession, with particular interest in practitioner identity and the integration of research into applied practice.

Lauren S. Tashman is the Senior Research Scientist for Mursion, Inc. and Mental Performance Consultant and Leadership Coach based in New York City, USA. As a Certified Mental Performance Consultant (CMPC), she has worked with athletes, coaches, healthcare professionals, business leaders, and performing artists to help individuals and teams consistently perform at their best. She has extensive experience in higher education and professional training, and she is passionate about helping emerging professionals build sustainable, values-driven careers. Her contributions to the field include applied practice, supervision, applying the science of high performance in the business world, and international professional service.

Global Perspectives on Sport, Exercise, and Performance Psychology

This series brings together global perspectives on sport, exercise, and performance psychology (SEPP). Books cover becoming a SEPP professional, navigating the field of SEPP, and applied practice within sport, exercise and performance domains.

Titles in the series:

Becoming a Sport, Exercise, and Performance Psychology Professional
A Global Perspective
Edited By J. Gualberto Cremades, Lauren S. Tashman

Navigating the Globally Evolving Field of Sport, Exercise, and Performance Psychology
Edited by Andrew P. Friesen, Sebastian Brueckner, and Lauren S. Tashman

Contextually Competent Applied Practice Across Sport, Exercise, and Performance Domains
Edited by Andrew P. Friesen, Sebastian Brueckner, and Lauren S. Tashman

For more information about this series, please visit: https://www.routledge.com/Global-Perspectives-on-Sport-Exercise-and-Performance-Psychology/book-series/GPSEPP

Navigating the Globally Evolving Field of Sport, Exercise, and Performance Psychology

Edited by
Andrew P. Friesen, Sebastian Brueckner, and Lauren S. Tashman

Routledge
Taylor & Francis Group
NEW YORK AND LONDON

Designed cover image: Getty Images

First published 2027
by Routledge
605 Third Avenue, New York, NY 10158

and by Routledge
4 Park Square, Milton Park, Abingdon, Oxon, OX14 4RN

Routledge is an imprint of the Taylor & Francis Group, an informa business

Library of Congress Cataloging-in-Publication Data
Names: Friesen, Andrew P. editor | Brueckner, Sebastian editor |
Tashman, Lauren S. (Lauren Saenz), 1980- editor
Title: Navigating the globally evolving field of sport, exercise, and performance psychology / Edited by Andrew P. Friesen, Sebastian Brueckner, and Lauren S. Tashman.
Description: New York, NY : Routledge, 2027. | Series: Global perspectives on sport, exercise, and performance psychology | Includes bibliographical references.
Identifiers: LCCN 2026007614 (print) | LCCN 2026007615 (ebook) |
ISBN 9781041319528 hardback | ISBN 9781041319498 paperback |
ISBN 9781003781479 ebook
Subjects: LCSH: Sports—Vocational guidance | Sports—Psychological aspects |
Exercise—Psychological aspects | Career development
Classification: LCC GV734.3 .N38 2026 (print) |
LCC GV734.3 (ebook) | DDC 796.023—dc23/eng/20260408
LC record available at https://lccn.loc.gov/2026007614
LC ebook record available at https://lccn.loc.gov/2026007615

ISBN: 9781041319528 (hbk)
ISBN: 9781041319498 (pbk)
ISBN: 9781003781479 (ebk)

DOI: 10.4324/9781003781479

Typeset in Galliard
by codeMantra

Contents

About the Editors

Dr. Andrew P. Friesen (Canada)
Dr. Andrew Friesen is Associate Professor in the Department of Kinesiology at Penn State Berks, where he teaches sport, exercise, and performance psychology to the next generation of professionals. His research focuses on emotional intelligence and the applied practice of sport psychology. He has served on numerous integrated sport science teams supporting national sport programs across Canada, Great Britain, Australia, and the USA. His experience spans a wide range of sports, including hockey, baseball, softball, taekwondo, basketball, volleyball, synchronized swimming, swimming, lacrosse, golf, archery, racquetball, tennis, badminton, snowboarding, and figure skating. He is a Certified Mental Performance Consultant (CMPC) and a Fellow of the Association for Applied Sport Psychology (AASP). Originally from Manitoba, Canada, he completed his undergraduate studies under the tutelage of Drs. Cal Botterill and Tom Patrick at the University of Winnipeg. He then went on to earn a master's degree from the University of Ottawa under the supervision of Dr. Terry Orlick. Benefiting from a network of "global citizen" sport psychology professionals (e.g., Dr. Paul Davis), he was then awarded a PhD studentship with the Emotion Regulation of Others and Self (EROS) research group funded by a £2.1 million grant from the Economic and Social Research Council in England. Joining a network of British researchers studying emotion, he completed a PhD in interpersonal emotion regulation in sport under the guidance of Prof. Andy Lane at the University of Wolverhampton. He is an active member of AASP, having served as AASP Newsletter Editor and Chair of the Newsletter Committee, and served on the Dorothy V. Harris Memorial Award Review Committee and the Graduate Program Accreditation Committee. He held academic positions in Canada, the United Kingdom, and Miami, Florida, prior to relocating to Pennsylvania, where he currently resides.

Dr. Sebastian Brueckner (Germany)
Dr. Sebastian Brueckner is an internationally recognized expert in Applied Sport Psychology. Besides working in private practice in Münster, Germany, as a mental performance consultant and leadership coach, he provides consultancy to ongoing projects funded by the German Federal Institute of Sport Science (BISp) and the European Union, and acts as a reviewer for (inter)national sport psychology journals. His international career journey has included serving the AASP as Chair of the International Relations as well as Nominations and Leadership Development Committees, as AASP Newsletter Editor, member of the inaugural Advocacy Committee, and co-editor of the 13th edition of AASP's Graduate Program Directory. He is an AASP Fellow and certified as an expert in Sport Psychology Services by the German Association of Sport Psychology (asp). His applied work, specifically with the German National Badminton Team, has led to the facilitation of elite coaches' education and leadership training programs for German Gymnastics. Sebastian has established projects with colleagues at

Muenster University, Boston University, and Kingston University London, where he was appointed as Honorary Research Fellow. After transitioning from a 13-year career as a competitive swimmer that led him to participate in Olympic trials to studying sport science with a focus on Motor Behavior at Saarland University (Germany) and Texas A&M University, he earned his PhD from the University of Tennessee with a specialization in Applied Sport Psychology. For ten years, he worked at Saarbruecken Olympic Training Center, supporting (junior) national team and Olympic-caliber athletes on mental training and dual-career transitions from a holistic, humanistic performance-enhancement perspective. He has served as Executive Manager and Head of Applied/Certification Services for the German asp and shifting into private practice strategically broadened his clientele and service contexts. He now serves not high-performers in sport and business contexts across the globe, but also educators and coaches working with athletes with disabilities and exercisers.

Dr. Lauren S. Tashman (USA)
Dr. Lauren S. Tashman is the Senior Research Scientist at Mursion Inc., leading the Learning Strategy and Content team who develop immersive simulations and coaching solutions for workforce skill development. She is a Certified Mental Performance Consultant (CMPC) and a Fellow of the Association for Applied Sport Psychology. Residing in New York City, she also owns a part-time consulting business supporting athletes, performing artists, leaders, and teams in developing high-performance mindsets and cultures. Growing up in New Jersey, a 13-year professional equestrian showjumping career led her to study psychology. She completed her Bachelor of Arts degree at The College of New Jersey and then earned both her master's and PhD in Educational Psychology with a major in Sport Psychology from Florida State University. While completing her PhD, she also received certificates in Research Methods and Program Evaluation, and studied expert performance as a graduate assistant in the Human Performance Lab led by Dr. K. Anders Ericsson. After finishing her graduate studies, she worked as an Associate Professor and the Coordinator of Sport Psychology Services at Barry University, began her consulting business working with a wide variety of performers across performance levels and domains including spending six years consulting with the Canadian Women's National Softball team, mentored many diverse young professionals pursuing the CMPC credential, and then pursued coaching for the corporate and healthcare contexts as well as product research and development when she moved to New York, leading her to where she currently finds herself on her winding career journey.

Global Contributors

Our list of global contributors for volumes II and III is presented here by nation of current affiliation. Their country of origin appears in parentheses if different from their country of current affiliation. Contributors listed with an asterisk have contributed to *Navigating the Globally Evolving Field of Sport, Exercise, and Performance Psychology.*

Australia

Eugene Aidman* (Russia)
Renee N. Appaneal* (USA)
Jeffrey Bond*
John Crampton*
Kim Encel*
Gerry Fogarty*
Sandy Gordon (UK)
Stephanie J. Hanrahan* (USA)
Christopher Mesagno* (USA)
Donna O'Connor (UK)
Remco Polman (The Netherlands)
Véronique Richard* (Canada)
Michael Spittle*

Austria

Ulla Geifes*

Belgium

Paul Wylleman*

Botswana

Kapule David Mabuta*

Brazil

Claudio Godoi

Canada

Veronica Allan
Sommer Christie*
Diane M. Culver*
Natalie Durand-Bush*
Roger Friesen*
Stefanie Gazmin*
Cole E. Giffin*
Sydney Graper*
Aman Hussain
Chantale Lussier
Ashley-Raye Miles*
Ashwin J. Patel*
Siobhan Rourke*
Robert J. Schinke*
Elizabeth A. Steadman*
Penny Werthner*
Michael Whitehead

Croatia

Sanja Vrančić*

Denmark

Kristoffer Henriksen
Louise Kamuk Storm
Nikos Ntoumanis* (Greece)
Jacob Vinholt

Finland

Niilo Konttinen*
Aku Nikander*
Hannaleena Ronkainen*
Montse C. Ruiz* (Spain)
Tatiana V. Ryba*

Germany

Eric Biener (USA)
Sebastian Brueckner*
Caren D. P. Diehl*
Anne-Marie Elbe*
Barbara Halberschmidt*
Lena Henning*
Oliver Höner
Hannah Hüttemann*
Sascha Leisterer-Härtig*
Mathias Liebing*
Monika Liesenfeld*
Nicki Marquardt
Lisa Musculus
Ismael Pedraza-Ramirez (Columbia)
Nick Powell (USA)
Bernadette Ramaker* (The Netherlands)
Maximilian Richert*
Helena Schmitz*
Oliver Stoll*
Maike Tietjens*
Svenja Wachsmuth*
Christian Zepp*

Greece

Vassilis Barkoukis*
Anna Kavoura*

Hong Kong, China

Karen Lo*

Hungary

Lekgobo Masake* (Botswana)

India

Nimrod Mon Brokman (Israel)
Varadayini Gorhe*
Shruti Nair
Keerthana Swaminathan*

Indonesia

Rebecca Wong (Malaysia)

Ireland

Shannon Burke*
Cathal Sheridan*

Italy

Maurizio Bertollo*

Malaysia

Young-Eun Noh* (South Korea)

Mexico

Jimena González Menendez*

New Zealand

Craig Barretto*
Aramis Dennan*
Paula Dennan*
Daryl Gibson
Ken Hodge*
Ian Lambie*
Antoinette Minniti (USA)

Norway

Stiliani "Ani" Chroni* (Greece)

Poland

Natalia Pawelska*
Małgorzata Sławińska*
Grzegorz M. Więcław*

Singapore

Hansen Bay
Harry Lim*

Slovakia

Michala Bednáriková*

South Africa

Heinrich Grobbelaar*
Deborah Skinstad*

Sweden

Paul Davis* (Canada)
Göran Kenttä*
Sanna M. Nordin-Bates
Nicole Robertson (USA)

Switzerland

R. Zsanett Bondár* (Romania)
Violetta Oblinger-Peters* (Germany)
Roland Seiler*

Uganda

Edgar Kazibwe*

United Kingdom

Dawn-Marie Armstrong* (Barbados)
Lee Baldock*
Joanne Butt*
Isabella Cacciatore
Helen R Church
Brendan Cropley*
Jennifer Cumming (Canada)
Tracey J. Devonport*
Martin Eubank*
Sahen Gupta (India)
Sheldon Hanton*
Chris Harwood*
Karen Howells*
Heather Hunter*
Emma Huntley
Carrie Taylor Johnson
Anastasiya Khomutova* (Ukraine)
Aleksandra "Ola" Krukowska-Burke* (Poland)
Moira E Lafferty*
Andrew M. Lane*
Daniel R. F. Martin*
Kyle F. Paradis* (Canada)
David Price*
John Sandars
Lee-Ann Sharp*
Matt Slater*
Katy Steel*
Clara Swedlund* (France)
Richard Thelwell
James Tomlinson
Nick Wadsworth*
Christopher R. D. Wagstaff*

United States of America

Shelby Anderson*
Nicholas E. Anton
Paul Ashbrook
Alex Auerbach*
Timothy Baghurst (UK)
Jessica Bartley*
Eric Bean*
William Bean*
Matthew P. Bejar*
Robbi Beyer
Matthew D. Bird* (UK)
Lindsey C. Blom*
Robyn Braun-Trocchio
Angela Breitmeyer*
Kristin Brooks*
Charles H. Brown, Jr*
Angel Brutus*
Chelsea Butters Wooding
Carla Carter*
Greg Cartin
Elmer A. Castillo*
Sarah L. Castillo*
Hillary Cauthen*
Greg Chertok*
Dolores Christensen*

Tsz Lun (Alan) Chu* (Hong Kong, China)
Damien Clement* (Trinidad and Tobago)
Stephany C. Coakley* (The Bahamas)
Bruce Cohen*
Kaitlin Cohen-Maher*
Ashley Coker-Cranney*
John E. Coumbe-Lilley* (UK)
Frances Dallas*
Nicole DeFerrari*
Mitchell DeSimone
Jerry DeVore*
Alex Diaz* (Argentina)
Kristen Dieffenbach
Urska Dobersek (Slovenia)
Bradley Donohue*
David W. Eccles* (UK)
Frank O. Ely*
Anna Farello*
Adrian Ferrera*
Désarée Festa*
Cristina Fink* (Mexico)
Leslee A. Fisher*
Margaret M. Flores
Janaina L. Fogaça* (Brazil)
Joanna Foss*
Megan Fox*
Andrew P. Friesen (Canada)
Charlie Frost
Mary D. Fry*
Alexander Gamble*
Lori A. Gano-Overway*
Rich Gordin*
Thomas W. Gretton* (UK)
Marta Guivernau* (Spain)
Kensa K. Gunter*
Peter Haberl* (Austria)
Colleen M. Hacker
Lindsey Hamilton*
Jon Hammermeister*
Tracy Heller*
Tim Herzog*
Jerry Holt
Takehiro Iwatsuki* (Japan)
Riley Jensen*
Jackson Jin
Meighan Julbert*
Cindra Kamphoff*
Abby Keenan*
Mi-Sook Kim* (South Korea)
Grayson Kimball
E. Earlynn Lauer
Larry Lauer
Saemi Lee* (South Korea)
Eric LeNorgant
Bart Lerner*
Jack J. Lesyk*
Hannah Levy*
Marc Lochbaum*
Leilani Madrigal*
Charles A. Maher*
Phoebe Manalang-Monnier*
Jeffrey Martin* (Canada)
Sydney Masters*
Michelle M. McAlarnen*
Gily Meir* (Israel)
Tyler Miles*
Thomas O. Minkler*
Taryn K. Morgan*
Irene Muir* (Canada)
Adam Naylor*
Maria Newton*
Carl Ohlson*
Robert E. Owens
David Pargman
Amanda M. Perkins-Ball*
Artur Poczwardowski* (Poland)
Melanie Poudevigne* (France)
Alessandro Quartiroli* (Italy)
Johannes Raabe* (Germany)
Selen Razon
Nina Rios-Doria*
Seth Rose*
Michael L. Sachs*
Christine Sanchez*
Jen Schumacher*
Kimberly Shaffer*
Vanessa R. Shannon*
Sari Shepphird*
Amber M. Shipherd*
Elizabeth L. Shoenfelt*
Duncan Simpson* (Tanzania)
Leigh Skvarla
Christian Smith* (UK)
David J. C. Smith*

Christopher Stanley
Lauren S. Tashman*
Melissa Thompson
Tshepang Tshube* (Botswana)
Tiffanye M. Vargas
Amanda J. Visek*
Justine Vosloo* (South Africa)
Lennie Waite* (UK)
Jack C. Watson II*
Craig A. Wrisberg*
Danielle Wong Vickland*
Greg Young* (UK)
Shameema Yousuf* (Zimbabwe)
Leonard Zaichkowsky* (Canada)
Rebecca A. Zakrajsek
Derek M. Zike*

Preface

Our primary purpose with this book series is embedded within the series title, that is, to share *Global Perspectives on Sport, Exercise, and Performance Psychology* (SEPP). Under the original editorship of Drs. Gualberto Cremades and Lauren S. Tashman, SEPP authors from around the world, shared their stories in the first book of this series, published in 2010, about what it meant locally to become an SEPP professional. In 2026, we have added two additional books to this series, entitled *Navigating the Globally Evolving Field of Sport, Exercise, and Performance Psychology* and *Contextually Competent Applied Practice Across Sport, Exercise, and Performance Domains.* Our intent with these additions was, firstly, to provide updated content for our global SEPP community based on our field's evolution, and, secondly, to extend the invitation for additional global voices to provide such commentary.

To that end, we have solicited professionals from various corners of the world to share their perspectives and experiences in SEPP, providing readers with a diverse perspective on the field. In doing so, our goal is to continue advancing Dr. Gualberto Cremades's original vision for the first book of this series: to spark meaningful dialogue within our field and provide a valuable resource that fosters a truly global understanding of SEPP. Embracing that sometimes challenging yet rewarding journey, we aim to enhance the knowledge, training, continuing education, and overall quality of future professionals' career journeys. In honor of Gualberto's contribution back in 2010, we aimed to not only provide an up-to-date global perspective but also take his vision even further.

Much has changed in our field and in the world since *Becoming a Sport, Exercise, and Performance Psychology Professional: A Global Perspective* was published. Staying true to Gualberto's original idea and purpose, we aimed to provide not only an understanding of applied practice and mentorship/supervision but also a broader perspective that encompasses many other facets of what it means—or could mean—to be and develop as a professional in this field. And, we wanted to add our own spin on these two additions as well to try to increase the global reach and voices shared striving for breadth rather than depth. We can tell you now that we are wrapping up the project; this was quite the task we gave ourselves—one that ultimately led us to produce two volumes of global perspectives for readers! We felt that to do these new volumes justice, we needed to set out to find professionals we didn't personally know, research who is doing SEPP in underrepresented nations, and strive to include people who are outside of our own siloed networks. While we are happy with what we are offering you, we want to acknowledge that, if we are honest, we still didn't quite realize our vision. It was not an easy task to increase our global reach. As you can see in the list of global contributors, we have authors from 28 countries and many whose country of origin differs from where they currently reside; however, the vast majority are located in the USA (followed by the UK). While we hope that readers expand their perspectives while engaging with this book's content, we also want to encourage colleagues in the field around the world to join us in prioritizing a collective coming together. By learning with and from one another, we can continue to strengthen the future of the field. Such collaboration will benefit current and future professionals; enhance the research that advances our understanding of the psychology behind sport, exercise, and performance; and ultimately improve the quality of care and support our clients receive.

This second volume of this series is entitled *Navigating the Globally Evolving Field of Sport, Exercise, and Performance Psychology*. Section 1 of this book offers insights on the SEPP profession, providing readers with important reads on several topics, including a commentary on the question of what sport psychology actually is as well as discussions on the terminology we use; ethics in the profession; pursuing diversity, equity, and inclusion in SEPP; and the nuances of mental health, mental well-being, and mental performance. Section 2 focuses on career development in SEPP, including chapters on the entrepreneur mindset and business skills, careers and the global job market, and the experiences of being a "global citizen" professional in the field. Section 3 highlights the SEPP researcher, including discussions on the scientist-practitioner, basic research skills for the applied practitioner, engaging in collaborative research teams, conducting community-engaged research, and using knowledge mobilization to close the research-to-practice gap. Section 4 discusses practitioner development, with chapters on certification and continuing education, practicing what we preach, self-care for SEPP professionals, and building and maintaining communities of practice. Section 5 focuses on the SEPP practitioner, including the topics of philosophy of practice, technological advancements in the field, consulting versus coaching, doing applied work with individuals and groups, doing applied work in-person versus remotely, working as an independent versus integrated practitioner, and demonstrating return on investment in applied practice. Section 6 discusses the SEPP teacher, including chapters on navigating academia, teaching mental skills, and teaching for today's students. Lastly, Section 7 focuses on the SEPP mentor, with perspectives on mentoring future SEPP practitioners, developing oneself as a mentor, and peer mentoring and consultation. In the second new volume, focused on SEPP practitioners' Service Delivery Across Diverse Populations, readers can review diverse discussions on working with athletes, athletes with hidden disabilities, athletes with physical disabilities, youth sport, coaches, exercisers, esports, military and tactical populations, corporate clients, the performing arts, and healthcare.

Similar yet different from the first volume, we aimed to provide global perspectives; however, this time we wanted to incorporate more voices. To do so, across the two new volumes, you'll notice that each chapter is made up of several contributions from different authors or author groups. While our contributors had the challenging task of distilling their wisdom and experiences into a short amount of pages, our hope is that this multi-lens approach provides readers with an even broader perspective on each topic. We open each chapter with a brief introduction written by one of us editors to provide insight into why we included the topic in this book and frame the discussion on it provided by the various contributors. Then, following the individual contributions, we close out the chapter with some personal takeaways aimed to provoke further reflection. Each chapter culminates with a set of recommended exercises for readers to further engage with what they read and apply it to their unique contexts and situations.

Approaching the two new volumes of this series in this way, our aim was to provide a comprehensive read for individuals in SEPP around the globe. While we believe it will be a great resource for graduate courses and early-career professionals, we hope that professionals, regardless of their career stage and chosen path in the field, also find this book valuable for their continued professional development. True to Gualberto's original vision, our hope is that this book series promotes increased systemic globalization and further development of the SEPP field.

Acknowledgments

First, we would like to acknowledge Gualberto Cremades. Without his vision of promoting a global perspective in SEPP, we would not have had the opportunity to honor his legacy and continue the cause.

Second, we would like to acknowledge and thank Adél Stankovics, who offered her time, helping us to do the many tasks involved in making an edited book like this come together. Her tireless work in structuring, compiling, and aligning the huge amount of information in the two volumes was invaluable in bringing this project over the finish line. As a current graduate student and "global citizen" herself, we hope the deep-dive into the global perspective of SEPP has also inspired her to broaden her global perspective and professional career journey.

Section 1

The Sport, Exercise, and Performance Psychology Profession

1 What Is Sport Psychology?

At one point or another, everyone in our field has had to explain to someone else what exactly is sport psychology. Perhaps we have had to explain it to an aunt or uncle at a family gathering, or a stranger making polite conversation at the market, or even to a fellow colleague at the university during a faculty meeting. And over time, we likely have all learned to answer this question in our own way with certain descriptives, metaphors, and examples referencing the current local or national sports news stories of the day that featured a coach who lost control of their emotions, an athlete who faltered in a crucial moment, or a disgruntled teammate whose presence has perceptively now soured the locker room. But despite our own definitions, it is of course imperative that we—the practitioners, researchers, teachers, and students—in sport psychology have a shared definition and understanding of our profession. A shared understanding of what sport psychology is clarifies our professional identity to our clients—be they from sport, exercise, or other performance contexts. It guides curriculum and certification initiatives and supports research and theory development. Imperatively, it also helps with ethical boundaries and scope of practice. To help set the stage for our book, we have elicited three author groups to answer the question, "What is sport psychology?" from a global perspective.

WHAT IS SPORT PSYCHOLOGY: AN OVERVIEW

Kensa K. Gunter & Amanda M. Perkins-Ball

What Is Sport Psychology?

Sport psychology is an academic discipline and professional practice involving the use of psychological knowledge and skills to address optimal performance and well-being of athletes, developmental and social aspects of sports participation, and systemic issues associated with sports settings and organizations (American Psychological Association, 2008). Sport psychology is a global discipline and profession; thus, there are many organizations around the world committed to supporting professionals and advancing the field. For example, the International Society of Sport Psychology (ISSP) encourages and promotes the study of human behavior within sport, physical activity, and health settings, facilitates the sharing of knowledge, and strives to improve the quality of research and professional practice in sport psychology (International Society for Sport Psychology [ISSP], n.d.). The Association for Applied Sport Psychology (AASP) strives to "ensure every performer has the resources to strengthen their inner edge through the advancement and application of excellence in mental performance and mental

DOI: 10.4324/9781003781479-2

health" (AASP, n.d.). Division 47 of the American Psychological Association (APA) strives to support applied practice, research, and education, and works to promote specific competencies associated with "the delivery of psychological services within sport, exercise, and performance domains" (Society for Sport, Exercise & Performance Psychology [SSEPP], 2025). The mission of the Asian-South Pacific Association of Sport Psychology (ASPASP) (n.d.) is to "facilitate the development of sport and exercise psychology throughout the Asian South-Pacific region, which includes Asia, Australasia, and the South-Pacific Islands". The Chartered Association of Sport and Exercise Sciences (CASES) focuses on several areas of sport and exercise science including psychology and they have established a specific organizational division to support the academic and practical interests of those interested and passionate about the field of sport and exercise psychology (BASES, n.d.).

Sport psychology most often refers to work done with athletes and other sport personnel within traditional sport spaces. However, the term "sport psychology" is also used as a ubiquitous term to describe several distinct but related disciplines including performance psychology (the application of sport psychology principles to other performance domains such as the performing arts, military, etc.), exercise psychology (understanding the impact of physical activity on psychological development, health and well-being across the lifespan) (SSEPP, 2025), clinical mental health services (focus on well-being plus the assessment, diagnosis, and treatment of mental health conditions), and industrial-organizational psychology (examination of human behavior in organizations and the workplace) (APA, 2022; Portenga et al., 2016).

Historical Perspective

The origin of sport, exercise, and performance psychology is challenging to pinpoint due to its interdisciplinary roots in psychology and kinesiology, as well as its broad scope—and attempting to do so becomes even more tricky when looking at this from a global perspective. The field has evolved significantly over more than a century, with historical events that may be divided into five distinct periods. A few significant events for each period follow:

- Early beginnings (late 1800s–early 1900s): Norman Triplett is often credited with conducting one of the first experiments in the United States, examining how the presence of others affects cycling performance and highlighting the significance of spectators during sport performance (Triplett, 1898).
- Establishing the discipline (1920s–1940s): The 1920s saw the emergence of sport psychology as a formal discipline. Professor Wilhelm Wundt established the first sport psychology laboratory at the University of Leipzig in Germany and in the United States, Coleman Griffith, the "Father of American Sport Psychology," conducted research and published the first influential books in the field. Researchers began testing athletes in laboratories using experimental psychology methods during this period.
- Growth and development (1950s–1970s): The field gained momentum during this period. The ISSP was established in 1965. Across the globe, psychological skills training and mental preparation techniques were introduced to athletes, and increased interest in exercise and fitness catapulted interest in exercise psychology.
- Professionalization and recognition (1980s–1990s): CASES was established in 1984 (then as British Association of Sport and Exercise Sciences), AASP in 1985 (at that time it was the Association for the Advancement of Applied Sport Psychology), and the following year, the APA formed Division 47 specifically for exercise and sport psychology. The Sport

Psychology Council (SPC) was established in 1993 and currently exists as a collective of professionals representing sport psychology organizations around the world.

- Contemporary sport psychology (2000s–Present): The field continues to grow as more practitioners consult with athletes, teams, organizations, and performers in non-sport settings, and there is a greater focus on mental health and psychological support for athletes. As an example, the International Olympic Committee (IOC) has developed two online educational programs focused on mental health in elite sport.

Common Areas of Practice

Sport psychology professionals have three common areas of practice: teaching, conducting research, and engaging in applied work—or a combination of these activities.

Teaching

Sport psychology professionals working in academic settings teach undergraduate and graduate courses related to sport, exercise, and performance psychology, create course materials, deliver lectures, and facilitate discussions to help students understand theoretical knowledge and practical application in performance settings. Teachers in sport psychology regularly utilize interactive activities to facilitate learning, such as role-playing exercises, which allow students to practice delivering mental skills interventions like self-talk, imagery, and relaxation techniques. These hands-on activities help bridge the gap between theory and practice, allowing students to apply psychological concepts in real-world scenarios (Hutter et al., 2016). Furthermore, instructors often integrate evidence-based interventions, such as cognitive-behavioral strategies, mindfulness, and self-regulation techniques, to enhance students' classroom performances (Segool et al., 2014). Many sport psychology programs offer internships or practicum opportunities to support further skill development, where students engage in direct work with athletes, receiving valuable mentorship and guidance from experienced instructors (Fogaca et al., 2018; Hutter et al., 2016). Teaching professionals also provide academic and career advising, supervise research projects, and support students' professional development. Teaching professionals may also engage in research and professional service as part of their duties. The responsibilities outlined above elucidate the crucial role sport psychology professionals in educational settings play in training future practitioners; promoting psychological principles to enhance performance and well-being in sports, exercise, and performance contexts; and advancing research.

Research

Sport psychology professionals conduct empirical research in university, community, business, or other industry settings. Researchers prioritize ethical conduct and consider participants' well-being and rights during scientific investigations. Sport psychology researchers share findings and insights with the broader scientific community and sport, exercise, and performance professionals by writing and publishing their studies in peer-reviewed journals. This empirical support provides quantitative and qualitative approaches to understanding the psychology of sport, exercise, and performance as well as validation for methods and techniques used by sport psychology practitioners and clinicians. Research in sport, exercise, and performance psychology spans a wide range of topics, including mental skills interventions, injury management, personality, stress and coping, leadership, and exercise psychology

(Lindahl et al., 2015). Motivation is a particularly prominent area within the field, encompassing a significant portion of sport psychology research (Lindahl et al., 2015). In recent years, new and emerging topics have gained attention, such as cultural perspectives, sport transitions, the role of family and relationships in sport, sport technology, and the effectiveness of consulting practices (Goffena et al., 2021). Finally, researchers in educational settings may also contribute to teaching courses in psychology or kinesiology departments.

Applied Work

Applied sport psychology is educational in nature and primarily involves teaching and applying psychological principles, mental skills, strategies, and techniques to athletic or performance populations, in individual or team-based settings. Informed by theory and research, the strategies and skills can be used to develop and optimize performance at different times during the athletic process (e.g., training, competition, and recovery), across the span of one's athletic or performance career. Some of the more common psychological or mental skills utilized are focused on areas, including, but not limited to, goal-setting, motivation, imagery, self-regulation strategies, arousal control, emotion management, attention and focus, and others (AASP, n.d.; APA, 2008; Durand-Bush et al., 2022; Williams & Krane, 2021). In addition to direct service provision, applied work may also include assessment, observation, evaluation, organizational consultation (Schinke et al., 2021), and possibly the integration and utilization of technology to complement the work (Siekańska et al., 2021) or extend access to a larger service area (Price et al., 2022).

Consumers of Sport Psychology Services

Athletes are one of the primary consumer groups of sport psychology services, but depending on the services requested, sport psychology professionals can work with all stakeholders within a sport ecosystem. Depending on the structure of the organization, this may include athletes, coaches, administrators, parents, league organizers, umpires and officials, other health and performance professionals, or other athletic staff. Sport psychology professionals also work across different levels of competition (e.g., youth, collegiate, professional, Olympic, amateur, master's, recreational) and in different settings (e.g., independent practice, college campus, specific sport team, and governing sport league or organization).

Who Are Sport Psychology Professionals: Pathways to the Profession

While specific terminology will vary between countries, generally speaking sport psychology professionals include those who are trained as mental performance consultants (e.g., trained in the area of mental skills and (mental) optimization or enhancement), licensed mental health providers with specialized training in working with sport, exercise, and performance populations, and those who are dually trained in both the provision of mental health and mental performance services. In addition to taking applied sport psychology courses, sport psychology professionals typically take courses in sport sciences and psychology or counseling-related topics. Additionally, completing a supervised or mentored work experience is typically a component of the training process. In addition to formal education, several professional organizations offer certifications or credentials to denote competency in applied sport psychology. For example, the Certified Mental Performance Consultant credential, available through AASP, is designed to represent that someone has obtained minimum competency in the field of sport psychology and CASES offers the Sport and Exercise Psychology Accreditation Route designed to provide a pathway for practitioners to demonstrate competence in order to be able to use the term Sport and Exercise Psychologist.

Final Thoughts

Sport psychology is a dynamic and multifaceted field that plays a crucial role in enhancing the mental well-being and performance of athletes and individuals in performance-based settings. By integrating psychological principles with sports and exercise practices, professionals in this area work in various sectors, including teaching, research, and applied practice. The field has significantly evolved from its early beginnings, growing into a respected discipline with a global presence. This evolution is highlighted by the establishment of key professional organizations and a growing focus on mental health and well-being in competitive environments. The impact of sport psychology goes beyond just athletes; it also benefits a wide range of stakeholders, including coaches, administrators, and individuals in non-sport performance arenas.

As the field continues to advance, sport psychology professionals are dedicated to improving performance, fostering mental resilience, and addressing the psychological needs of individuals across various sporting contexts. Their commitment ensures the well-being of participants and contributes to overall success in performance outcomes. We hope this broad overview of the field, its history, and professionalization has provided useful context for the more in-depth information presented in the following chapters and sections of this book.

OKAY...BUT WHAT EXACTLY IS SPORT PSYCHOLOGY?

Christopher Wagstaff & Alessandro Quartiroli

How "What Is Sport Psychology?" Developed Over Time

Contemporary sport psychology is widely recognized as a multifaceted discipline, addressing psychological needs in both competitive and non-competitive environments (e.g., Portenga et al., 2017). The field has evolved significantly, shifting from individual-level interventions to systemic, organization-wide approaches. This transformation is marked by an increasing emphasis on environments, organizations, and systems (Wagstaff, 2019). Key milestones include integrating holistic psychological services into high-performance systems, adopting systems-led practices, and embedding mental health and well-being into organizational strategies. Emerging in the early 20th century as a niche academic discipline, sport psychology initially focused on understanding psychological processes like motivation and attention in athletes. By mid-century, its scope narrowed to performance enhancement, emphasizing psychological skills training (Kornspan & Quartiroli, 2019). Over time, the field expanded to include holistic models addressing diverse stakeholders, such as coaches, support staff, and senior leaders. Reflecting this broader practice landscape, professional societies, journals, and individuals have acknowledged the evolution of the field, now often referred to as "performance psychology" (Portenga et al., 2017), a shift that highlights the discipline's expanding relevance and application across diverse high-pressure domains. This broader approach aims to enhance not only performance but also mental health and well-being at individual, team, organizational, and system levels. Today, global professional credentialing processes (e.g., ISSP-R) drive the field's momentum, with applied practices supporting athletes, teams, and organizations in achieving peak performance while promoting well-being. Moreover, scholars have documented sport psychology's maturation into a multidisciplinary field embracing systemic and organizational change (Portenga et al., 2017; Wagstaff & Quartiroli, 2023).

What Are the Current Trends in Applied Sport Psychology Practice?

Contemporary sport psychology is characterized by several key trends:

Interdisciplinary Collaboration: While traditionally practitioners might have prepared for a practice context where they work individually with athletes, often practitioners will work within interdisciplinary teams to provide integrated support for athletes, coaches, and organizations (see Wagstaff & Quartiroli, 2023). Sport psychology practitioners play a vital role in multidisciplinary teams and adopting a collaborative approach ensures a holistic understanding of the athletic, team, and organizational issues, and an opportunity to integrate psychological support within day-to-day practices and system change. Practitioners typically contribute to these interdisciplinary teams by contributing to individual development planning, leading team formulation processes, and advising on culture and communication. Regular interdisciplinary meetings foster open communication and integrated planning, ensuring all specialists contribute to a unified athlete-centered approach. This collaboration promotes success by addressing complex needs holistically, enhancing performance, and supporting well-being.

Holistic Support Models: Mental health and well-being are increasingly recognized as critical to sustaining performance (Breslin & Leavey, 2019). Maher (2022) defined a systems-led approach as a philosophy and process informed by systems thinking, viewing sport organizations as complex adaptive systems where the organization itself becomes the primary focus of service delivery. This approach requires practitioners to consider system interrelationships, competing values, and unintended consequences, emphasizing that individual and team dynamics cannot be understood in isolation from the larger system. The value of a systems-led approach includes understanding interconnectedness across individual, team, and organizational levels, identifying risk and protective factors, involving diverse stakeholders, and fostering a mentally healthy organization (Maher, 2022). Daley et al. (2020) added that it democratizes psychology through mutual learning and shared practices. Additionally, this approach integrates consultative and supportive roles with proactive and reactive strategies, ultimately building shared ownership and collective responsibility for psychological well-being and performance. However, achieving these outcomes requires fostering self-organizing behavior, shared language, and awareness of cultural and systemic constraints when co-creating psychologically informed environments.

Mental Health: Depending on qualifications and competence, the role of practitioners might be as key providers of mental health support, addressing issues like anxiety, depression, and burnout in athletes (Schinke et al., 2024). Over the last decade, scientist-practitioners have repeatedly emphasized the importance of equipping sport psychology practitioners with counseling skills and knowledge of referral pathways. This shift reflects a broader understanding of mental health as a critical component of athlete well-being, moving beyond the traditional focus on performance optimization. Athletes face unique pressures, including the demand for consistent high-level performance, public scrutiny, injuries, and transitions between competitive and post-competitive careers. These stressors contribute to mental health challenges that can impact both personal well-being and athletic performance (Schinke et al., 2024). In response, sport psychology has expanded its focus, integrating mental health services into athletic settings (Van Slingerland et al., 2019).

Moreover, organizations increasingly employ mental health professionals to provide comprehensive care, addressing both performance and well-being, an approach that fosters a supportive environment where athletes can thrive (see Maher, 2022).

Organizational and Systems-Led Approaches: Practitioners in sport psychology are increasingly focusing on creating psychologically informed environments with work on cultural, systemic, and team-level dynamics. Organizational Sport Psychology has emerged as a vital subfield, emphasizing systemic factors such as culture, leadership, and organizational dynamics. This approach treats the organization itself as the client, highlighting the interconnectedness of individual, team, and systemic levels (Wagstaff, 2019; Wagstaff & Quartiroli, 2023). Practitioners adopt frameworks that promote shared ownership of psychological concepts across stakeholders, moving beyond individual-focused interventions. Over the past decade, the importance of advising on elite sport culture, climate, and organizational change has grown significantly. A systems-led perspective requires practitioners to develop sociocultural and political skills, as well as organizational psychology knowledge, to work flexibly across micro, meso, and macro levels of sport systems (McKenzie et al., 2023). This involves engaging with new stakeholders, applying new approaches, and using competencies beyond traditional training (Wagstaff & Quartiroli, 2023). Central to this approach is recognizing sport organizations as complex systems composed of interconnected stakeholder groups, each with its own unique dynamics, as well as distinct social, cultural, and historical contexts.

Broadening Scope: Practitioners' work has also expanded beyond the context of sport to include work with military (e.g., special forces), education (e.g., student well-being), performing arts (e.g., stage confidence), and corporate (e.g., executive coaching) settings, underscoring the transferability of psychological principles (Nordin-Bates, 2012). A growing body of literature highlights the versatility of psychological skills, performance under pressure, resilience building, and stress management and emotion regulation, which are relevant across various high-pressure domains. For example, the U.S. Army is the world's largest employer of sport psychology practitioners (Weir, 2018). In the military context, practitioners support soldiers by applying techniques like strategic communication, mental resilience training, and emotion regulation to enhance performance under duress and improve decision-making in mission critical situations (e.g., Taylor et al., 2011). They also contribute to well-being, lifestyle, and rehabilitation programs for veterans and families.

Conclusion

The field of sport psychology has evolved into a dynamic profession with diverse applications across individual, team, and organizational levels. By addressing the systemic gaps in training and embracing interdisciplinary and systems-led approaches, future practitioners can better meet the demands of contemporary practice. Graduate students and professionals should actively pursue opportunities to broaden their competencies and adapt to the evolving landscape of sport psychology. Moreover, we encourage trainees to see themselves as the performance psychologists of tomorrow and shape training and credentialing processes accordingly.

WHAT IS SPORT PSYCHOLOGY IN FINLAND?

Tatiana V. Ryba, Aku Nikander, Niilo Konttinen, & Hannaleena Ronkainen

We approach this chapter with the premise that "sport psychology is what sport psychology does" to emphasize that sport psychology is not only defined by theoretical frameworks but is intricately linked to its practical, context-specific applications. Grounded in the concept of situated knowledges (Haraway, 1988), we view sport psychology as a phenomenon co-constituted through practices, interventions, and the relational dynamics between practitioners, athletes, coaches, and institutional structures. This perspective rejects universalism and forefronts the dynamic, localized enactment of praxis. By focusing on the actions, interventions, and practices of the sport psychology practitioners, who contributed to this chapter, we offer a reflexive exploration of sport psychology in Finland.

The contributors to this chapter (AN, NK, and HLR), all affiliated with the Finnish Olympic Committee and providing psychological support to athletes and teams, engaged in a curated dialog, moderated by the lead author (TR). Each reflected on the question: "What does the practice of sport psychology mean to you? Please describe how you work." These reflections were shared and analyzed for discursive frames related to Finnish sport policy and elite sport governance. The subsequent dialog informs the multivocal account of sport psychology practice presented in this chapter, beginning with an overview of the Finnish sociocultural context.

Finnish Context

Finland, a Nordic country situated in Northern Europe, has a population of approximately 5.5 million people, the majority of whom are ethnic Finns; Swedish-speaking Finns and minority groups, such as Russians, Estonians, and the indigenous Sami people, have historically contributed to the country's cultural diversity. The country is a state democracy characterized by a parliamentary system and a commitment to human rights, equality, and social welfare. In Finland, the commitment to sport and physical activity is not only about elite competition but also about promoting health, well-being, and social inclusion for all citizens. As such, the Finnish Olympic Committee's (NOC) multifaceted approach to high-performance sports extends beyond elite athletes to include grassroots sports and mass participation, aligning with the country's ethos of accessible and inclusive sports opportunities for all (Finnish Olympic Committee, 2024). The NOC's High-Performance Unit plays a key role in overseeing and coordinating high-performance sports programs for elite athletes, working closely with multidisciplinary teams composed of experts in coaching, sports science, sports medicine, nutrition, psychology, and performance analysis. These experts collaborate to provide holistic support to athletes with the goal of optimizing their training, performance, and well-being through evidence-based practices and data-driven strategies.

Assembling Sport Psychology Practice in Finland

The work of a sport psychologist is a demanding, wide-ranging specialty that considers the psychological performance and psychological well-being of the athlete. It clearly separates the requirements for a psychologist to address mental health issues from athletic performance issues, which are more open to members of the athlete support network. Within the Finnish sport system, including Sport Academies and Olympic training centers that might employ sport psychologists, there are strict regulations regarding professional ethics and practices (e.g., patient records), which also contribute to the way sport psychology practice is constituted. The High-Performance Unit in the NOC strategically embraces holistic support and multidisciplinary collaboration. In this context, multidisciplinary teams function as dynamic assemblages, where sport psychology knowledge is co-constituted through the continuous intra-actions of different experts, athlete data, and practices that shape athlete development. This relational approach is explored in the curated dialogue to which we turn next.

TR: *Could you unpack how supporting the coaching process, and your embeddedness within multidisciplinary teams, plays out in practice?*

HLR: I'm currently involved in a multidisciplinary team working with an Olympic athlete. I have regular contact with both the athlete and the coaches, and we meet with the multidisciplinary team at least four times a year. The athlete chose not to participate in those team meetings but has given us full trust to share relevant information. This doesn't mean we disclose everything, but when it comes to important matters—like evaluating the season or identifying risks regarding mental health, physical condition, or technical aspects—we share information openly within the team.

I've found this openness and trust to be the most effective way to work. It makes sure we are all on the same page and can tackle issues together, while keeping some boundaries between the athlete, myself, and the coach. Although I don't need deep knowledge of areas like physiotherapy, it's important to understand enough—especially if injuries occur—so that I can integrate mental health support into the rehabilitation process. We have regular meetings so we can stay up to date on the athlete's progress.

NK: I think it really depends on the individual athlete. Some athletes are very active and want to be heavily involved in the coaching process, which is more than okay. That said, I believe the key figure in this setup is the coach. The coach is essentially the leader, the one who understands the entire process, and is responsible for talking with different experts and deciding what kind of expertise is needed for that specific athlete. Some athletes want to be really involved, while others prefer to take a more passive role. Ideally, the athlete would show some active participation, not just as an object of the process but also as a subject who contributes to it.

HLR: Ideally, the coach should assemble and lead the multidisciplinary team, but that's not always the case. Not all Finnish coaches have the necessary skills to lead such teams yet. Some coaches do possess strong leadership abilities, but there's still work to be done helping more coaches learn how to effectively manage a team around them. And it also depends on the context—whether it's an individual sport or a national team. In national teams especially, the coach should have the responsibility to choose the people they trust. Of course, athletes also have the right to choose their own support, but the NOC has built a system that concentrates experts in Olympic training centers and Sports Academies, so we aim to utilize those experts as well.

AN: Of course, there's education provided by the NOC for coaches, especially those hired for the academies. They offer training and guidance on how the system should function. It's effective, but when it comes to national teams, they mainly provide structure, expertise, and certain resources like doctors or psychologists who are directly involved with the teams. In addition, local teams can build their own systems and choose the experts they want to work with. This collaboration helps form the multidisciplinary teams, though there are recommendations about who should be involved.

HLR: The sport psychologist's role in a multidisciplinary team is more than just working with athletes or coaches. They can act as a key facilitator in creating a psychologically safe environment in the broader sports context. Especially when it comes to schedules and team dynamics, they play a crucial part in fostering this sense of safety and support.

AN: It's crucial to incorporate an educational approach because many Finnish coaches might claim to adopt a holistic perspective, yet their behavior often contradicts this. An educational perspective can help bridge this gap. Additionally, sports often come with rigid assumptions and especially young athletes face strict models about how they should train, perform, and live, which are tied to their athletic identity. A holistic approach involves not only working with experts but also encouraging athletes to learn about themselves, respect their learning process, and explore different roles and perspectives. Supporting this self-discovery and the clustering of their viewpoints is an essential part of the process.

NK: We are coaching an athlete, but we're also working with a human being.

Conclusion

In summary, the integrative work of a Finnish sport psychologist in multidisciplinary teams, with coaches often playing a central role, underscores the importance of holistic and collaborative approaches to athlete development. A truly holistic approach goes beyond performance, embracing the broader human dimensions of identity and lived experience to ensure that athletes can thrive in all areas of life. While trust and openness between athletes, coaches, and support teams are essential, there remains a need to further develop leadership and educational strategies that promote psychological safety and inclusivity, especially as the Finnish sporting community has been beset by cases of discrimination, sexual harassment, and inappropriate behavior at all levels of sport. While sport psychology practice in Finland is deeply rooted in the country's cultural and social values, it is also influenced by global trends toward evidence-based interventions and data-driven strategies. Multidisciplinary teams, endorsed by the NOC to optimize the athlete's well-being with performance excellence, highlight the contingent and emergent nature of sport psychology praxis, which despite regulatory frameworks and normalizing practices retains multiplicity and a transformative potential, as shown in the diverse narratives of Finnish practitioners.

EDITORS' TAKEAWAYS

What struck me (Andrew) across these three chapters is how they each invite us to pause and reflect on the bigger picture of sport psychology—where it comes from, where it's heading, and how it takes shape in different contexts. Gunter and Perkins-Ball's chapter nudges us beyond the familiar "what is sport psychology?" toward the deeper "why does sport (and exercise and performance) matter so much that it sparked an entire discipline?"—a question that connects us back to psychology's philosophical roots. Wagstaff and Quartiroli then turn our attention to the future, raising important questions about how graduate programs can keep pace with a rapidly changing field and whether specialization might reshape how we define ourselves as a profession. And Ryba and colleagues remind us that none of these conversations happen in a vacuum—that culture, institutions, and national contexts profoundly influence how sport psychology is practiced and understood. Taken together, these chapters encourage us to think not just about the nuts and bolts of training and practice, but about the deeper "why," the evolving "how," and the cultural "where" of our work—and they challenge each of us to carry these questions forward as we shape the next chapter of the field (and the chapters of this book!).

RECOMMENDED EXERCISES

1 Identify five to seven common myths about sport psychology (e.g., "only elite athletes need it," or "it only focuses on sport"). Label each as myth or truth and briefly explain why.
2 Discuss how cultural values shape athletes' views of sport psychology. Reflect on a cultural context meaningful to you (country, community, family, or sport) and explain how those norms influence acceptance of psychological support.
3 Define what sport psychology means to you. Create a 60-second elevator pitch introducing the profession. Look up quotes from performers or professionals and compare them to your definition. After finishing the book, return to your definition and note what changed or stayed the same.
4 Select one to two performance domains. Write three to four short scenarios per domain showing how sport psychology appears in daily performance.
5 Considering the history and current direction of the field, describe where you think it is heading. Write a short narrative imagining sport psychology 30–50 years from now, both in your context and globally.

REFERENCES

American Psychological Association. (2008). *Sport psychology.* https://www.apa.org/ed/graduate/specialize/sports

American Psychological Association. (2008). *Industrial and Organizational Psychology.* https://www.apa.org/ed/graduate/specialize/industrial

American Psychological Association. (n.d.). *Division history.* https://www.apadivisions.org/division-47/about/history

Asian-South Pacific Association of Sport Psychology. (n.d.). *About us.* https://aspasp.org/about/#mission

Association for Applied Sport Psychology. (n.d.-a). *About AASP: Where members and performers realize their potential.* https://appliedsportpsych.org/about-the-association-for-applied-sport-psychology/

Association for Applied Sport Psychology. (n.d.-b). *About sport and performance psychology.* https://www.appliedsportpsych.org/about/about-applied-sport-and-exercisepsychology/

Association for Applied Sport Psychology. (n.d.-c). *Our history.* https://appliedsportpsych.org/about-the-association-for-applied-sport-psychology/our-history/

Breslin, G., & Leavey, G. (2019). *Mental health and well-being interventions in sport.* Routledge.

British Association of Sport and Exercise Sciences. (n.d.). *Psychology division.* https://www.bases.org.uk/spage-divisions-psychology.html

Daley, C., Ong, C. W., & McGregor, P. (2020). Applied psychology in academy soccer settings: A systems-led approach. In J. G. Dixon, J. B. Barker, R. C. Thelwell, & I. Mitchell (Eds.), *The psychology of soccer* (pp. 153–172). Routledge.

Durand-Bush, N., Baker, J., van den Berg, F., Richard, V., & Bloom, G. A. (2022). The gold medal profile for sport psychology (GMP-SP). *Journal of Applied Sport Psychology, 35*(4), 547–570. https://doi.org/10.1080/10413200.2022.2055224

Finnish Olympic Committee. (2024, August 23). *What is the Finnish Olympic Committee?* https://www.olympiakomitea.fi/en/about-us/what-is-the-finnish-olympic-committee/

Fogaca, J., Koppang, R. M., & Zizzi, S. J. (2018). Three pathways to supervision in applied sport psychology: Challenges and strategies to deliver effective supervision in graduate programs. *Journal of Sport Psychology in Action, 9*(3), 172–181. https://doi.org/10.1080/21520704.2018.1451937

Goffena, J. D., Scheadler, T. R., & McCarver, Z. (2021). Contemporary hot topics in applied sport psychology: Past, present, and future. *Journal for Advancing Sport Psychology in Research, 1*(2), 7–22.

Haraway, D. (1988). Situated knowledges: The science question in feminism and the privilege of partial perspective. *Feminist Studies, 14*(3), 575–599. https://doi.org/10.2307/3178066

Hutter, R. I., Oldenhof-Veldman, T., Pijpers, J. R., & Oudejans, R. R. D. (2016). Professional development in sport psychology: Relating learning experiences to learning outcomes. *Journal of Applied Sport Psychology, 29*(1), 1–16. https://doi.org/10.1080/10413200.2016.1183152

International Society for Sport Psychology. (n.d.). *ISSP mission*. https://issponline.org/about/

Kornspan, A. S., & Quartiroli, A. (2019). A brief global history of sport psychology. In M. H. Anshel, T. A. Petrie, & J. A. Steinfeldt (Eds.), *APA handbook of sport and exercise psychology: Sport psychology* (pp. 3–16). APA.

Lindahl, J., Stenling, A., Lindwall, M., & Colliander, C. (2015). Trends and knowledge base in sport and exercise psychology research: A bibliometric review study. *International Review of Sport and Exercise Psychology, 8*(1), 71–94.

Maher, C. (2022). *Fostering the mental health of athletes, coaches, and staff*. Routledge.

McKenzie, G., Wagstaff, C. R. D., & McDougall, M. (2023). Walking the middle line: Organizational culture work in sport. *Journal of Sport Psychology in Action, 14*(3), 158–169. https://doi.org/10.1080/21520704.2022.2155740

Nordin-Bates, S. M. (2012). Performance psychology in the performing arts. In S. M. Murphy (Ed.), *The Oxford handbook of sport and performance psychology* (pp. 81–114). Oxford University Press.

Portenga, S. T., Aoyagi, M. W., & Cohen, A. B. (2016). Helping to build a profession: A working definition of sport and performance psychology. *Journal of Sport Psychology in Action, 8*(1), 47–59. https://doi.org/10.1080/21520704.2016.1227413

Portenga, S. T., Aoyagi, M. W., & Cohen, A. B. (2017). Helping to build a profession: A working definition of sport and performance psychology. *Journal of Sport Psychology in Action, 8*, 47–59. https://doi.org/10.1080/21520704.2016.1227413

Price, D., Wagstaff, C. R., & Thelwell, R. C. (2022). Opportunities and considerations of new media and technology in sport psychology service delivery. *Journal of Sport Psychology in Action, 13*(1), 4–15.

Schinke, R. J., Giffin, C., Cosh, S., Douglas, K., Rhind, D., Harwood, C., Si, G., & Papaiounnou, A. (2021). International society of sport psychology position stand: Mental health through occupational health and safety in high performance sport. *International Journal of Sport and Exercise Psychology, 20*(6), 1711–1733. https://doi.org/10.1080/1612197X.2021.1992857

Schinke, R. J., Henriksen, K., Moore, Z. E., Stambulova, N., Bartley, J., Cosh, S., … & Wong, R. (2024). International society of sport psychology position stand: Elite athlete mental health revisited. *International Journal of Sport and Exercise Psychology, 22*(4), 775–801.

Segool, N. K., von der Embse, N. P., Mata, A. D., & Gallant, J. (2014). Cognitive behavioral model of test anxiety in a high-stakes context: An exploratory study. *School Mental Health, 6*, 50–61.

Siekańska, M., Bondár, R. Z., di Fronso, S., Blecharz, J., & Bertollo, M. (2021). Integrating technology in psychological skills training for performance optimization in elite athletes: A systematic review. *Psychology of Sport and Exercise, 57*, 1–24. https://doi.org/10.1016/j.psychsport.2021.102008

Society for Sport, Exercise & Performance Psychology. (2025, February). *About Division 47*. https://www.apadivisions.org/division-47/about

Taylor, M. K., Stanfill, K. E., Padilla, G. A., Markham, A. E., Ward, M. D., Koehler, M. M., … & Adams, B. D. (2011). Effect of psychological skills training during military survival school: A randomized, controlled field study. *Military Medicine, 176*(12), 1362–1368.

Triplett, N. (1898). The dynamogenic factors in pacemaking and competition. *American Journal of Psychology, 9*, 507–533.

Van Slingerland, K. J., Durand-Bush, N., Bradley, L., Goldfield, G., Archambault, R., Smith, D., … & Kenttä, G. (2019). Canadian Centre for Mental Health and Sport (CCMHS) position statement: Principles of mental health in competitive and high-performance sport. *Clinical Journal of Sport Medicine, 29*(3), 173–180.

Wagstaff, C. R. D. (2019). A commentary and reflections on the field of organizational sport psychology: Epilogue to the special issue. *Journal of Applied Sport Psychology, 31*(1), 134–146. https://doi.org/10.1080/10413200.2018.1539885

Wagstaff, C. R. D., & Quartiroli, A. (2023). A systems-led approach to developing psychologically informed environments. *Journal of Sport Psychology in Action, 14*(4), 227–242. https://doi.org/10.1080/21520704.2023.2215715

Weir, K. (2018, November). A growing demand for sport psychologists. https://www.apa.org/monitor/2018/11/cover-sports-psychologists

Williams, J. M., & Krane, V. (Eds.). (2021). *Applied sport psychology: Personal growth to peak performance.* McGraw-Hill Education.

2 SEPP Terminology

Sport psychologist. Clinical sport psychologist. Mental performance consultant. Certified mental performance consultant. Professor of sport, exercise, and performance psychology. Accredited sport and exercise scientist. Mental skills coach. Resilience coach. Director of high performance. Head of player development. Cognitive skills specialist. Executive leadership development specialist. Performance strategist. Research scientist. Our list of titles feels endless as we try to balance training, accreditation requirements, and the titles preferred by employers. While this reflects an effort toward ethical accuracy, it also risks confusing those we serve about who we are and what we do. The same challenge appears in our terminology. For example, we cannot expect a coach to clearly distinguish among mental toughness, grit, hardiness, resilience, confidence, mental fortitude, inner strength, or a "warrior mindset." Collectively, we may be offering so many technical distinctions that we risk losing a shared professional identity. To address this, we invited three author groups to provide guidance on clarifying terminology in SEPP. Collectively, these chapters invite us to pause and consider not just the words we use but also the professional identity we project through them. By working toward greater clarity and alignment, we strengthen both our credibility as a field and the accessibility of our services to those we aim to support.

KEY SPORT PSYCHOLOGY TERMS USED IN NON-CLINICAL AND CLINICAL SETTINGS: A GLOBAL PERSPECTIVE

Natalie Durand-Bush, Göran Kenttä, & Véronique Richard

Sport psychology is a dynamic and evolving field that encompasses a wide range of concepts, theories, and applications relevant to both non-clinical and clinical contexts. As a discipline that integrates psychological and counseling principles with sport and exercise sciences, it plays a crucial role in enhancing performance and well-being at an individual, team, and organizational level in sport. The aim of this chapter is to briefly introduce key sport psychology terms that are used in non-clinical and clinical contexts, reflecting both the scientific and applied aspects of the field. We examined relevant content from the literature and leading sport psychology organizations including the International Society of Sport Psychology (ISSP), the European Federation of Sport Psychology (FEPSAC), the Association for Applied Sport Psychology (AASP), the Canadian Sport Psychology Association (CSPA), and the Chartered Association of Sport and Exercise Sciences (CASES).

To effectively conceptualize sport psychology terms across non-clinical and clinical domains, we opted to create a visual model. We first reviewed three existing evidence-informed frameworks targeting mental performance and mental health constructs, which underlie the scholarly and applied field of sport psychology: the Canadian Centre for Mental Health and Sport

DOI: 10.4324/9781003781479-3

(CCMHS) Continuum of Mental Health Zones (CCMHS, n.d.), AASP's Mental Health and Performance Services Continuum (AASP, n.d.), and Team Denmark's Applied Model of Athlete Mental Health (Henriksen, 2023). The CCMHS continuum offers a clear distinction between mental health states (i.e., Healthy, Reacting, Injured, Ill) and links them to specific indicators and practitioner roles. Similarly, the AASP model clarifies the types of professionals best suited for intervention at different levels of functioning and performance. The Team Denmark model takes a holistic, ecological approach, acknowledging that athlete well-being is shaped by different factors at different levels in the environment (e.g., individual, training, leadership, and everyday life). We integrated elements of each model to create a comprehensive framework comprising four zones of functioning (Healthy, Reacting, Injured, and Ill, summarized as HRI^2), across which key mental performance and mental health terms are mapped (bolded the first time they appear in the model).

In this framework (see Figure 2.1), we distinguish between the three interrelated constructs of mental performance, mental health, and mental illness, which influence the four zones we can experience (Durand-Bush et al., 2023; World Health Organization, 2022). We also included several mental performance and mental health constructs deemed important for success in high level sport, as summarized in the Gold Medal Profile for Sport Psychology (Durand-Bush et al., 2023).

Key Terms

We begin by defining the term sport psychology, which is at the crux of this chapter. According to Weinberg and Gould (2019), sport psychology is a research-driven discipline that seeks to understand and apply psychological principles to enhance athletic achievement and well-being. The ISSP defines it as the scientific study of people and their behaviors in sport and exercise contexts, while FEPSAC highlights its interdisciplinary nature, integrating psychology and sport sciences (e.g., skill acquisition) to enhance performance and experience. Collectively, these definitions demonstrate that sport psychology is a globally recognized applied science that combines empirical research, psychological theory, and practical application to support athletes, coaches, and organizations in achieving peak performance and well-being.

Within the discipline of sport psychology that we know today, understanding the dynamic relationship between mental performance, mental health, and mental illness is essential for optimizing well-being and success. These three constructs have been coined as the Mental Triad by Durand-Bush and colleagues (2022) and the CCMHS. Mental performance refers to a capability to use cognitive processes (e.g., perception, reasoning) and mental or self-regulation skills (e.g., confidence, emotion and arousal regulation) to perform in a dynamic environment (see GMP-SP for details; Durand-Bush et al., 2022). Mental health represents a state of well-being enabling us to realize our potential, cope with stress, learn and work productively, and contribute to society. Mental illness is a health condition ranging from short-term episodes to chronic disorders involving significant changes in thoughts, emotions, and behaviors, causing distress and impaired functioning (World Health Organization, 2022). These three interrelated constructs influence the zones we can experience, as depicted in Figure 1. Mental performance and mental health practitioners with different scopes of practice can provide support across the continuum, as indicated in the models proposed by the CCMHS (n.d.), AASP (n.d.), and Henriksen et al. (2023). It is important to note that professional titles, standards, education, and training vary across continent and countries.

The role of high performance environments is increasingly recognized as impacting mental performance, health, and well-being (Henriksen et al., 2023). The sport environment encompasses both physical elements (e.g., facilities, location, and logistics) and psychosocial

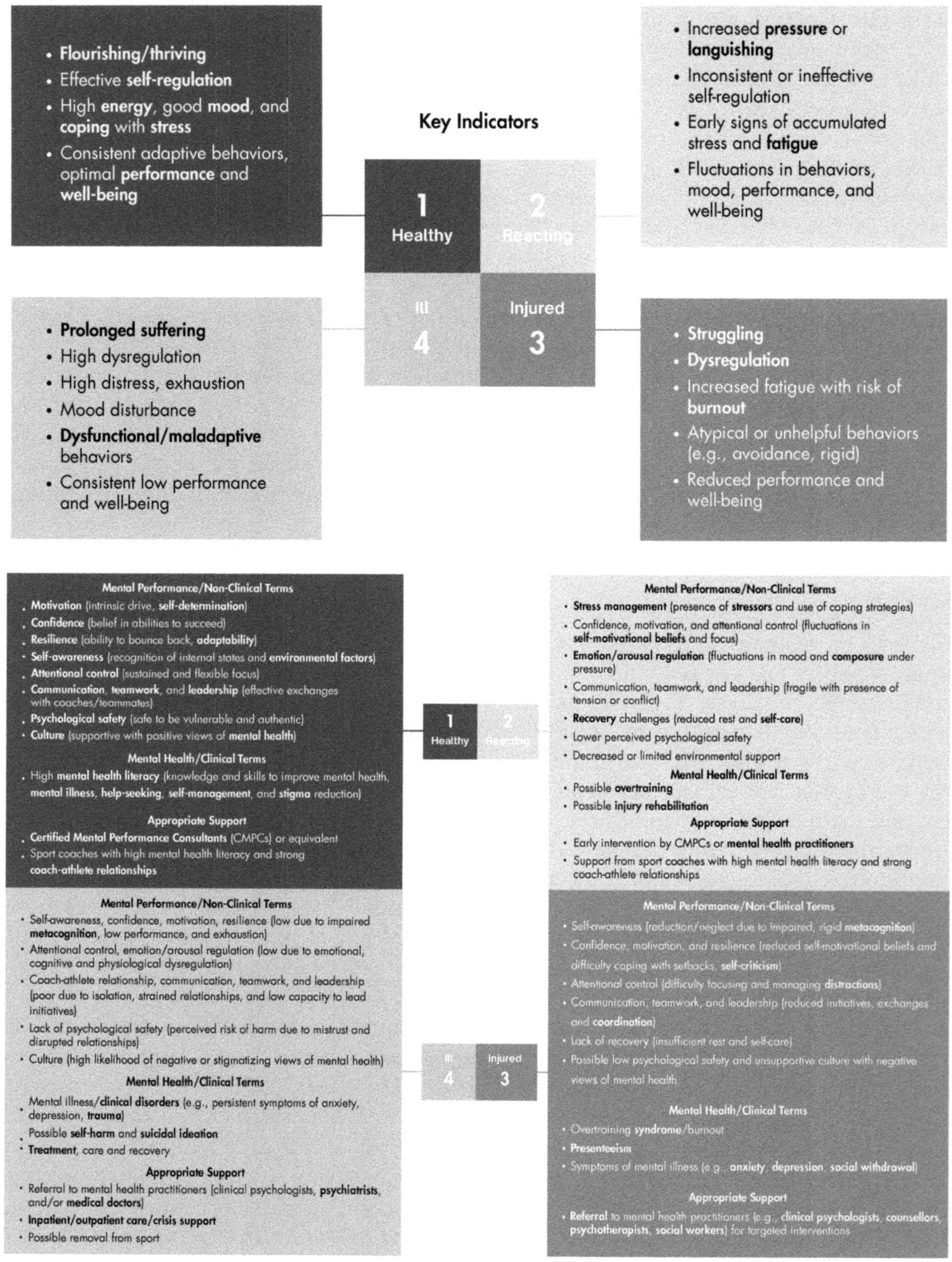

Figure 2.1 HRI2 sport psychology framework: Key terms used in non-clinical and clinical settings

aspects (e.g., cultural norms, expectations, respect for ethnic, religious, and sexual identities; (Schinke et al., 2024). Sport environments that support mental health are broadly characterized by trust, high-quality relationships, transparency, access to resources, healthy and sustainable athletic development (Henriksen et al., 2023), and psychological safety (e.g., freedom of expression without fear of negative consequences; Walton et al., 2024).

Summary

The terms introduced in this chapter set the stage for a nuanced understanding of sport psychology, emphasizing the need for an integrated view that bridges non-clinical (mental performance) and clinical (mental health, mental illness) considerations. While terminology may vary globally, the HRI^2 framework provides a structured way to identify and apply key terms across different contexts. This framework should be refined to enhance both support systems and practitioner effectiveness in the field of sport psychology.

WORDS MATTER: TERMS, TITLES, AND TERMINOLOGY OH MY!

Lauren S. Tashman

I grew up doing a pretty nontraditional sport, equestrian showjumping—well actually in one of my first graduate sport psychology classes, we debated the definition of sport and whether I was really an athlete because supposedly (as I was told) the horse does all the work. It was all in good fun and probably one of my favorite classes still to this day, but it did make me reflect that it seemed like I had a lot to learn about sport in comparison to most of my peers. I had watched other sports growing up (ice hockey was always my favorite likely to some extent a result of it being one of my high school's main sports), my parents were always into tennis and skiing, and my dad had me start playing golf with him at an early age; however, because riding was a full-time job, I had very little experience with, or exposure to, mainstream sport outside of that…and gym class. So, as I began my master's, I quickly realized that I wasn't familiar with all the terminology and other aspects of sport like many of my classmates. This was my first realization that terminology matters—I had a lot to learn not just about the psychology of sport, but also about the sports themselves so that I could speak their language, understand how to best apply what I was learning to their unique sports, and be seen as credible. Woolway and Harwood's (2020) exploration of the consultant characteristics that influence sport psychology consumer preferences, likelihood for seeking services, and perceptions of credibility supports this reflection, finding that athletic background and sport-specific knowledge are two of the top 12 characteristics.

My second realization about the importance of words and terminology came as a result of what was going on in the field (at least in the United States) when I was in graduate school. It was during this time that AAASP (i.e., the Association for the Advancement of Applied Sport Psychology) became AASP (i.e., the Association for Applied Sport Psychology), and there was conflict among people in the field about the use of titles like "sport psychologist" or "sport psychology consultant"—an important ethical and legal consideration. I remember my dad at the time being very confused about this—"How can you be going to school for sport psychology and you're not going to be able to call yourself a sport psychologist?" This is something I have continued to encounter throughout my career—I know I am not alone in this. Yet at that time, there was no ONE agreed upon title that those of us who were going the mental performance route in the United States were given to use (e.g., mental skills trainer, mental coach, cognitive performance specialist, the list goes on). How were we supposed to understand who we were and be able to help others understand that if we weren't given a clear title to use? While AASP has made efforts to correct this, the issue has not been completely resolved as we still see many titles used for the field and practitioners within it—just look at all the ones used throughout this book!

What Is Terminology and Why Do Words Matter?

Put simply, terminology is the words and phrases used within a particular subject, discipline, activity, or context (e.g., sports terminology, scientific terminology, finance terminology, military terminology, dance terminology, soccer terminology, dating terminology, generational terminology, New Yorker terminology). Unlike Humpty Dumpty's proclamation to Alice in Lewis Carroll's *Through The Looking Glass* that words mean what he wants them to, terminology is the lingo, jargon, and expressions that create a shared common language, means of communication, and understanding across people. According to Wittgenstein (1958), "Every word has a meaning. This meaning is correlated with the word. It is the object for which the word stands" (p. 3). Therefore, in the field of sport psychology (or is it sport, exercise, and performance psychology [SEPP] or sport and performance psychology or performance psychology?), terminology connects us to each other and is also, importantly, the means by which we "educate" those with whom we come in contact outside of our community.

However, just because we have terminology does not mean that we all agree on that terminology, use it consistently, or that all of our terminology is crystal clear in its meaning. For example, Johnston et al. (2023) wrote about the challenges associated with the lack of clarity about and differing perceptions of various terms used in athlete development, such as what it means to be "elite" or "talented," to have "grit" or "character," and what "training load" refers to (i.e., is it just the physiological demands of the sport or does the "load" also include other external and internal demands such as academic demands for student-athletes and the self-imposed demands athletes may place on themselves?). If, as noted above, words have meaning and "stand in" for the object they describe, it is at the very least unhelpful if not in some cases also dangerous to have terms take on their own or variable meanings.

Thus, inconsistent use of and clarity about terms and their associated definitions creates several challenges, two of which include the following: (1) our ability to accurately and effectively advance our field, and (2) our ability to disseminate knowledge to each other, the students who enter the field, and the consumers of our field's services. For example, Slisko and Dykstra (1997) wrote about the challenges of imprecise terminology and conceptualizations for research and teaching in physics—if a "hard science" grapples with this, it behooves us as a "soft science" to also pay greater attention to our use of terminology. As a professor and mentor, I remember many conversations with graduate students about terminology (e.g., what does "confidence" really mean and what is the difference between an "emotion" and a "feeling"?) as well as when and why we should use the jargon versus care less if clients know those terms and instead find memorable, resonating, and relevant ways to explain them. And, of course, we all navigate the challenges of correcting people in their use and (mis)understanding of various terms (e.g., "positive" and "negative" self-talk).

Terminology across Performance Domains

While our increasing scope of practice (i.e., application of our field into and across various non-sport domains) is in many ways of great benefit to us all, it also creates various challenges. As my career shifted into the corporate and healthcare contexts, again terminology became a prominent focus. For example, navigating the use of "Coach" and "Consultant" effectively (see the chapter focused on this topic) among others (e.g., "Facilitator" and "Speaker") to clearly distinguish the variety of services I could provide. Or, starting to use the title "Performance Coach"—in the business world this seemed to make sense to people but in sport they asked if I was a strength coach. It also quickly became apparent that there were many terms and concepts I needed to learn about that we don't focus on in our field (e.g., "imposter syndrome"). And, in addition to learning about the various sub-groups within these new performance contexts (e.g., sales, engineering, startups, global publicly traded corporations, physicians, nursing, academic medicine), I also had to learn their jargon (e.g., in business "straw man" refers to a brainstormed simple draft or first idea of something; healthcare often uses the term "provider" to be inclusive of the many disciplines and backgrounds of professionals who provide care to patients). Most recently, I've been given an entirely different title than I would have expected coming into the field (i.e., "Senior Research Scientist"); and with an expanding role I've been asked what I want my new title to be—a question I don't yet have the answer to.

Terms, and the varied meanings associated with them, have also at times led to a need to "defend" our field offering services in these performance domains (e.g., "Why am I matched with a coach who has worked with athletes instead of an 'operator'?", a term used for someone who has been in a corporate or senior corporate role previously). Yet, it has also led to great opportunity for showcasing and leveraging the value of our backgrounds and the SEPP field in these contexts (e.g., bringing a science-backed approach to helping people better understand, appreciate, and benefit from things like "psychological safety" and "mindfulness" among all the self-help noise and conversations about these hot topics).

Titles: In Search of Alignment

To conclude, let's circle back and hone in on one key focus of this chapter—titles. In their study of consultant characteristics, it is likely no surprise that Woolway and Harwood (2020) found that practitioner title was also a key characteristic; practitioners are using many different titles and the "sport psychologist" title may be a turnoff for some clients. More recently, in an interview study of 12 sport psychologists in the UK, Prior et al. (2025) found that there was a lack of consensus on the role (specifically, how mental health fits into it) and misaligned expectations between organization and practitioner. I think we'd all agree this is not just a UK experience, but a broader discussion about both title and role that needs to be had since a title is what defines a professional's identity and scope of work. As I've been working on this chapter, I've been reflecting on having "mental performance" in a title (and in the certification title AASP chose)—as someone who spent a large portion of her career working with coaches and teams on leadership and team culture, it seems limiting. But, this isn't just about alignment on our professional titles, it's also about alignment on the title for the field and associated organizations—as I somewhat flippantly alluded to a few pages above. If we can't align on a title for the field that captures its nuance—globally—how do we expect to all share an identity, common language, and understanding with each other, let alone ensure the potential consumers of our research, teaching, and services are aware of, understand, trust, and value our profession and the various professionals within it?

A ROSE BY ANY OTHER NAME ... EXPLORING COMPETENCIES WITHIN EXERCISE PSYCHOLOGY

Clara Swedlund, Nina Rios-Doria, Bruce Cohen, & Michael L. Sachs

One of the key questions that arises in working with exercise participants (see chapter on service delivery for exercise populations, specifically Sachs, Razon, & Holt) is what do we call the professionals who work with these individuals? There are many terms out there for such professionals, but does it really matter what term we use or are they all just a rose by any other name? (Ciaccio & Sachs, 2024).

The answer is, *it does matter*, at least from our perspective as professionals. Commercially, an exercise participant may only be concerned with your competence and effectiveness. Can you help them achieve their exercise/well-being goals and stick with exercise on a regular basis for the long term? But what you call yourself has both legal and ethical implications. While competence is a key issue, one which we will address shortly, an initial question arises about what terms are legal. For example, in Canada and the United States, only individuals who are licensed by a specific state/province/country can call themselves psychologists (e.g., exercise psychologist) or, in some places, counselors. Psychologists or counselors (such as Licensed Professional Counselors—LPCs, or Licensed Mental Health Counselors—LMHCs, or other related terms) must have certain coursework and internship hours and pass an exam to become licensed. There are also individuals who are Licensed Clinical Social Workers (LCWs) who are doing sport and performance psychology-based work, and some may even be doing exercise psychology work. While this provides an initial gatekeeping function, it doesn't ensure that this person is competent within the realm of exercise psychology.

It should also be noted that this is a U.S.-based perspective and other countries might do things differently. For example, in the United Kingdom (where the first author works), people who train through the British Psychological Society (BPS) become "Chartered Psychologists" whereas those who train through the Chartered Association of Sport and Exercise Sciences (CASES) become "Sport and Exercise Scientists," but both can work with the protected title of Sport and Exercise Psychologist. This is potentially confusing because it is not mandatory to do applied exercise psychology work on either pathway to obtain the title of Sport and Exercise Psychologist.

In the United States, within a broader allied health professions perspective, the physiologically related professions of physical therapist, athletic trainer, and registered dietitian require state licensure. However, most states generally do not require fitness trainers or personal trainers to be licensed. There are many other terms that do not require a license, such as individuals who are coaches (e.g., mental coach, life coach, etc.), or therapists, consultants, practitioners, or even exercise scientists, or fitness influencers. Anyone can use these terms and call themselves whatever they want. One does not need a degree to use such terms and, unfortunately, there are many deceptive marketing salespeople out there trying to sell you the secret to a healthy and happy life with non-scientific-based products and programs. But there are also many competent people with strong educational backgrounds who call themselves wellness coaches, exercise therapists, or use other terms and perhaps even have credentials in these areas. This may be a marketability consideration, or perhaps even a reflection of the potential negative connotations one still sometimes sees on calling oneself a psychologist: whether legally or not (Watson, 2023). Alas, it is buyer beware—when you see such terms used, you must consider the individual's credentials, experiential background, and especially their competence.

What credentials would, should, could one look for? For potential clients, this will depend on the level and type of support they are seeking from the professional. Ideally, a graduate degree would be a part of this person's educational background, at least a master's in Kinesiology, exercise and sport sciences, exercise psychology, or perhaps even a doctoral degree in one or more of these fields. A degree in clinical or counseling psychology or health behavior change, along with expertise/background in exercise, would be great as well. Experience across a variety of age groups, gender, ethnicity, and exercise interests would also be important.

Empowering our clients/exercise participants to ask the "right" questions—such as, "what is your training background?", "what organizations or certifying boards are you registered with?", and "who can I contact should I have any questions about your training, and/or conduct?"—and seek out this information is also part of our role as professionals. Indicating the relevant qualifications and educating the public on the difference between someone with graduate professional training qualifications versus someone with no certifications is important and is a joint responsibility for we the practitioners and for them, the consumers.

In terms of credentials, certifications, competence, having a basic knowledge of exercise physiology—what goes into regular exercise for your clients—is desirable. There are a multitude of personal trainer certifications available, nearly all which do not require you to have majored in the exercise sciences field. You do not need to become a personal trainer certified by any one specific entity but if a national/international certification is desired, one should consider obtaining one that has been accredited by The National Commission for Certifying Agencies (NCCA). Most personal training certifications have a sponsoring organization that, along with health behavior change, caters to a particular target population/group (athletics/sports, seniors, children, parents, musculoskeletal injury rehabilitation, cardiac health, etc.) For example, the American College of Sports Medicine (ACSM) certifications are more cardiovascular and general health fitness based, while the Certified Strength and Conditioning Specialist (CSCS) certification by the National Strength and Conditioning Association targets strength and athletic/sport fitness. Many of these same organizations also have separate certifications in health behavior change/coaching, but all of these certifications contain learning/testing modules on basic knowledge (such as information on sleep, physical activity/exercise, and nutrition, as well as on theories of behavior change, such as the transtheoretical model and self-efficacy theory), all of which contribute to being a well-rounded practitioner in exercise physiology and health behavior change.

Most importantly, however, you will need to be a competent practitioner. Hopefully you had a class (or at least part of a class) on exercise psychology. If you did not, we encourage starting with some excellent textbooks on exercise psychology and learning all about the field (e.g., Andersen & Hanrahan, 2015; Berger et al., 2015; Buckworth et al., 2013). Being a competent practitioner will extend to books within applied exercise psychology (e.g., Anshel, 2014; Cohen & Sachs, 2023; Razon & Sachs, 2024) and then texts specifically dealing with exercise as therapy (e.g., Hibbert, 2016) and other related topics. Competence then calls for gaining experience working with various exercise populations and being mentored or supervised by experienced professionals who will guide you in your journey as a practitioner.

It should be noted that navigating this is tricky; practitioners are faced with the reality and responsibility of both marketing their services in a way that is appealing to the consumer and doing so in a way that retains their integrity and reflects their ethically—and legally—sound knowledge base and qualifications. This often means simplifying technical knowledge to make it accessible to the client, while also honoring the nuances and complexities of health behavior change; it can also mean critically challenging misinformation and unsubstantiated claims made by unqualified or self-styled practitioners, and doing so in a way that promotes open dialogue with clients to maximize their understanding.

In summary, we are looking for a rose—a credentialed, competent, experienced, ethical professional who will be effective in working with exercise participants. As a profession, we must educate consumers in what to look for and help them select individuals who can be most effective in working with them to achieve their health and wellness goals.

EDITORS' TAKEAWAYS

Durand-Bush and colleagues write that the field is "dynamic and evolving." Does our terminology reflect this and has it kept up with the field's evolution? I (Lauren), as you might imagine after reading my contribution to this chapter, would argue that the answer is no. I'm not suggesting this is simple—however, I think we continue to do ourselves a disservice by not really addressing this and keeping up with the times. Or, after reading Swedlund et al.'s contribution, I find myself wondering if this is something we've just never really devoted time and attention to. No time like the present!

RECOMMENDED EXERCISES

1 If you could rename the field, what title would you choose and why? Also propose clear job titles that help newcomers and potential clients understand different roles and services.

2. Research laws and regulations in your country/context regarding professional titles. How do these rules influence whether your preferred titles could actually be used?
3. Choose three to four sport psychology concepts. Explain when you would use professional terminology and when you would use more accessible, audience-friendly language to describe them.
4. Identify one commonly used term in the field that lacks a clear or consistent definition. Offer your own definition and explain the sources or reasoning that support it.
5. If a participant asked why they should work with you (a sport and exercise psychology practitioner) instead of a personal trainer to boost motivation, how would you respond?

REFERENCES

Andersen, M. B., & Hanrahan, S. J. (2015). *Doing exercise psychology*. Human Kinetics.

Anshel, M. (2014). *Applied health fitness psychology*. Human Kinetics.

Association for Applied Sport Psychology. (n.d.). *Mental health and performance services continuum*. https://appliedsportpsych.org/site/assets/files/33107/aasp_mental_health_services_continuum.pdf

Berger, B. G., Weinberg, R. S., & Eklund, R. C. (2015). *Foundations of exercise psychology*. Fitness Information Technology.

Buckworth, J., Dishman, R. K., O'Connor, P. J., & Tomporowski, P. D. (2013). *Exercise psychology* (2nd ed.). Human Kinetics.

Canadian Centre for Mental Health and Sport. (n.d.). *Continuum of mental health zones*. https://static1.squarespace.com/static/62e2c0f6819a8b6d0668cf3f/t/673ba520219c96596dd02dc0/1731962145122/Aug+1-+Final+ENFR+Continuum+%281%29.png

Ciaccio, J., & Sachs, M. L. (2024). A rose by any other name … In S. Razon & M. L. Sachs (Eds.), *Applied exercise psychology: The challenging journey from motivation to adherence* (2nd ed., pp. 16–20). Routledge.

Cohen, B., & Sachs, M. L. (2023). *Excusercise: Inexcusable excuses for not exercising*. Excusercise.

Durand-Bush, N., Baker, J., van den Berg, F., Richard, V., & Bloom, G. (2023). The Gold Medal Profile for Sport Psychology (GMP-SP). *Journal of Applied Sport Psychology, 35*(4), 547–570. https://doi.org/10.1080/10413200.2022.2055224

Henriksen, K., Diment, G., & Kuettel, A. (2023). The team Denmark applied model of athlete mental health. *International Journal of Sport and Exercise Psychology, 22*(9), 2325–2341. https://doi.org/10.1080/1612197X.2023.2281525

Hibbert, C. (2016). *8 keys to mental health through exercise*. W. W. Norton & Company.

Johnston, K., McAuley, A. B. T., Kelly, A., & Baker, J. (2023). Language games and blurry terminology: Can clarity enhance athlete development? *Frontiers in Sports and Active Living, 5*, 1150047. https://doi.org/10.3389/fspor.2023.1150047

Prior, E., Papathomas, A., & Rhind, D. (2025). A balancing act: Sport psychologist insights into supporting athlete mental health in elite sport. *Journal of Applied Sport Psychology*, 1–21. https://doi.org/10.1080/10413200.2025.2462551

Razon, S., & Sachs, M. L. (Eds.). (2024). *Applied exercise psychology: The challenging journey from motivation to adherence* (2nd ed.). Routledge.

Slisko, J., & Dykstra, D. I. (1997). The role of scientific terminology in research and teaching: Is something important missing? *Journal of Research in Science Teaching, 34*(6), 655–660. https://doi.org/10.1002/(SICI)1098-2736(199708)34:6<655::AID-TEA7>3.0.CO;2–M

Watson, P. M. (2023). What it means to be an applied exercise psychologist: Reflections from 2003 to 2023. *Case Studies in Sport and Exercise Psychology, 7*(1), 122–134. https://doi.org/10.1123/cssep.2022-0035

Wittgenstein, L. (1958). *Philosophical investigations*. Wiley.

Woolway, T., & Harwood, C. G. (2020). Consultant characteristics in sport psychology service provision: A critical review and future research directions. *International Journal of Sport and Exercise Psychology, 18*(1), 46–63. https://doi.org/10.1080/1612197X.2018.1462230

World Health Organization. (2022). *Mental health: Strengthening our response*. https://www.who.int/news-room/fact-sheets/detail/mental-health-strengthening-our-response

3 Ethics in SEPP

In my (Andrew's) training, ethics always felt like the tack-on topic to the curriculum—something that only other practitioners had to be mindful of because I, of course, would always be able to identify and act on the ethical course of action. "Ethics follows logic," I thought, "and I'm a logical person." Fast forward to my first one-on-one with an athlete and suddenly my logic seemed to fail me. It is now a topic that I relish teaching because ethics is not about what we do to or for others; rather, it is the behavioral manifestation of our values and beliefs systems. It is the ultimate self-reflective journey. And as we are continually growing and developing, our ethical guidelines also must evolve and be refined (and sometimes, completely shatter). Our three author groups provide key conceptual insights—and also a case study example that reminds us of the messiness that is real-world ethical practice. Together, these contributions provide a sensitizing read, especially for student readers newer to the ethical world behind SEPP service delivery.

BALANCING THE ETHICAL AND LEGAL FRONTIERS IN PROVIDING ATHLETE WELL-BEING SUPPORT

Katy Steel, Lee Baldock, Sheldon Hanton, & Brendan Cropley

The Evolution of Applied Sport Psychology: Issues of Professional Competence

As the demand for sport psychology support services continues to grow, both within the context of sport and across an expanding number of performance populations (e.g., military; business), the profession of Applied Sport Psychology (ASP) has become characterized by continual change and evolution (Quartiroli et al., 2023). This has resulted in a significant diversification of the support services expected of, and provided by, practitioners working in ASP. This diversification has perhaps reduced clarity over how we, ASP Consultants (ASPCs), enact practice in a way that allows us to remain compliant with the ethical standards to which we are bound. To elaborate, there is a general agreement among governing bodies across different global regions (e.g., Australian Psychological Society [APS]; European Federation of Sport Psychology [FEPSAC]) that ASPCs must "only provide psychological services within the boundaries of their professional competence, described by their knowledge, skill, training, and experience" (Quartiroli et al., 2020, p. 4). For many ASPCs, the traditional role of supporting performers (e.g., athletes; coaches) to develop the cognitive, emotional, and behavioral strategies required to reach and maintain peak performance remains at the foundation of their training and practice. However, there is a clear movement toward a wider remit for ASPCs that includes (among others) organizational psychology, fostering positive youth

DOI: 10.4324/9781003781479-4

development, promotion of life skills, counseling, and lifestyle coaching and management (Neumann et al., 2024). Thus, there appears to be growing uncertainty regarding the ethical *scope of practice* within which ASPCs can operate, particularly as the recommendations from governing bodies are not universal (i.e., scope of practice differs across geographical regions and organizations [e.g., APA; AASP; and CASES]) or overly explicit (i.e., scope of practice is rarely defined, often being left to practitioner judgment, see HCPC, 2024).

One issue related to the scope of our practice that has perhaps become most prominent in recent years relates to the extent to which we are able to ethically support clients presenting symptoms related to *mental well-/ill-being*, and *mental health/illness*. This has perhaps emerged because of two main factors. First, the increased visibility of mental health challenges experienced by sport performers has resulted in a higher prevalence of individuals seeking support for such issues from ASPCs (Sly et al., 2020). However, given the lack of conceptual clarity over mental well-/ill-being and mental health/illness, it can be difficult for ASPCs to accurately label a client's presenting symptoms as clinical, subclinical, or non-clinical, and thus establish whether they are ethically competent and positioned to offer support. Second, while governing bodies explicitly refer to the need for ASPCs to "make client well-being their paramount concern" (see BASES, 2021), when working in sporting contexts, there is often conflict between a focus on performance and the moral responsibility of ASPCs to consider athletes as human beings. This often results in the subduing of mental well-being promotion (performance and well-being are often not seen as conceptually linked).

To address these issues, we aim to offer some clarity over the concepts of mental health and illness, and well- and ill-being, linking these to the ethical standards by which ASPCs must abide. Our goal is to support more informed decision-making regarding scope of practice as ASPCs seek to maintain the integrity of the profession.

Framing Ethical Scope of Practice through the Clarification of Concepts

A fundamental obligation of those working in ASP is the need to exercise a duty of care to those with whom they work. To do this, we (ASPCs) must operate "within the limits of our competence and know and understand the legal, professional, ethical and, where applicable, organizational rules that regulate the psychological services we provide" (APS, 2007, p. 18). We must, therefore, make ethical and informed decisions about whether the training we have received adequately equips us to provide a service safely and effectively (HCPC, 2024). There are several situational factors that can make such decisions more complex (e.g., the context in which the issue presents [non-sport versus sport]; the extent of the working alliance; pressure from the organization employing the ASPC) and perhaps orientate ASPCs to begin or continue working with a client presenting with issues beyond the "norm." However, if the required service is thought to fall outside of our scope of practice (i.e., our training is inadequate for the presenting condition), then we are ethically obligated to refer that individual to an appropriately qualified professional, offering support until the referral process is complete (AASP, 2024).

Understanding the scope of our practice regarding mental health and illness has arguably been constrained as considerations of performers' mental health have typically been framed in the language of mental illness (Baldock et al., 2020). Nevertheless, it is posited that mental health should be considered more than the mere *absence* of mental illness, and that instead of health and illness being at opposite ends of the same continuum, they should be conceptualized as distinct but related dimensions existing on two separate continua (Keyes, 2002). For ASPCs, this means that we should consider the scope of our practice for mental health and mental illness separately. Specifically, mental illness refers to the experience of a "clinically significant disturbance in an individual's cognition, emotional regulation, or behavior … usually associated with distress or impairment in important areas of functioning" and often manifests as a specific disorder (World Health Organization [WHO], 2022). Mental illness is, therefore, clinical in nature and affects all aspects of an individual's life, not just their ability to perform in an isolated context, for example, sport. Accordingly, ASPCs who are trained in performance enhancement might not be equipped to diagnose or treat clinical disorders unless they have the appropriate clinical qualifications and must consequently exercise their duty of care by referring the client to a qualified mental health professional (AASP, 2024). Conversely, mental health is considered "a state of well-being in which the individual realizes his or her own abilities, can cope with the normal stresses of life, can work productively and fruitfully, and is able to make a contribution to his or her community" (WHO, 2005, p. 2).

Mental health cannot, therefore, be separated practically from the concept of mental well-being, given that the WHO's definition implies that augmenting an individual's mental well-being results in the outcome of a more complete state of mental health (Baldock et al., 2022). Thus, given its focus on functioning and flourishing (Keyes, 2002), practitioners should be ethically duty-bound to seek to promote mental health, through augmenting mental well-being whenever possible. To achieve this, ASPCs should view mental well-being as a multidimensional construct that encompasses both *hedonic* and *eudaimonic* perspectives (Baldock et al., 2022). Eudaimonia refers to the *process* element of mental well-being and encompasses individuals living a meaningful life in accord with their values, fulfilling their potential, engaging in purposeful action, and experiencing environmental mastery and personal growth (Baldock et al., 2020). It is proposed that the more an individual experiences eudaimonia, the more likely it is that they experience hedonic *outcomes*, represented as happiness, increased positive affect, and life/job satisfaction. Finally, like mental health and mental illness, mental well-being should be distinguished from mental ill-being (e.g., a state of negative affect, lack of control, exhaustion, and reduced sense of accomplishment) because they are thought to represent distinct, but potentially related, dimensions of psychological health (Baldock et al., 2022).

Considering mental well- and ill-being in this way provides ASPCs with a clear understanding of how the provision of *well-being support* fits ethically within their scope of practice. Intuitively, these conceptualizations of mental health and mental well-being align closely to typical constructions of *performance* and thus the normative training program content for ASPCs (e.g., coping; self-actualization; goal setting; emotional control; pursuit of mastery). Further, researchers have argued that eudaimonia and hedonia are experienced when individuals achieve a balance between personal and situational resources and the demands they experience (cf. Baldock et al., 2020), which also associates with underpinning principles of performance enhancement. Consequently, it is proposed that mental well-being and athletic performance are not entirely distinct concepts, but fundamentally connected (e.g., mental well-being is likely to augment performance). APCs should be mindful, therefore, of how focusing on the promotion of mental well-being and the reduction of mental ill-being could elicit meaningful and holistic client outcomes, which fits directly within their scope of practice.

Summary: Applied Practice Ethical Principles and Standards

We argue that the promotion of service-user mental health through the augmentation of mental well-being falls within the ethical and legal remit of ASPCs, particularly given how these states are aligned with performance. However, we appreciate that not all practitioners will have the qualifications or competence to ethically and legally offer support services to clients presenting with symptoms associated with mental illness, and thus ASPCs must be mindful of their obligation to a duty of care. Thus, as ASPCs, we must remember our duty to maintain the highest standards of competence in our work to protect the safety and well-being of service users, the integrity of the field, and our own professional status. In accord with the International Society of Sport Psychology's (ISSP) Ethics Code (Quartiroli et al., 2020), to do this, we must:

1 Only provide psychological services within the boundaries of our professional competence based on our education, training, supervised experience, state and national professional credentials, and appropriate professional experience.
2 Not misrepresent our qualifications or expertise in any way that deceives service users. Additionally, we should be aware of the limitations of our service delivery and must not make claims or take actions that exceed these limitations.
3 Make ongoing efforts to maintain competence in the skills we use within their service delivery and recognize the importance of ongoing training and supervision where necessary and appropriate to facilitate the development of service delivery competence.
4 Uphold the obligation to refer a service user to a more appropriately qualified and/or competent practitioner if the care, treatment, or other services required by the service user(s) are beyond the scope of our competence.
5 Monitor ourselves for signs of impairment from our own physical, mental, or emotional problems and refrain from offering or providing professional services when impaired.

ETHICAL ISSUES FOR DUALLY TRAINED SPORT AND PERFORMANCE PSYCHOLOGY PROFESSIONALS

Ashley Coker-Cranney & Sarah L. Castillo

Dual training in clinical mental health and mental performance consulting has long been suggested as the most appropriate model to ensure the competence and employability of graduate students and aspiring professionals in the field of sport and performance psychology (Aoyagi et al., 2012; Martin, 2020; Silva, 2010). As a long-time advocate of dual training, Silva's 2010 conference address highlighted the prevalence of United States Olympic & Paralympic Committee (USOPC) and National Collegiate Athletic Association (NCAA) sport psychology positions requiring applicants to hold clinical licensure. He argued that those wishing to build their sport psychology careers within a collegiate athletic department would be effectively "shut out" without clinical training, regardless of their mental performance credentials. Aoyagi and colleagues (2012) reached the same conclusions about dual training, although their rationale centered on issues of client protection, professional title, clear training standards, and the accountability and legal protections that occur with clinical licensure. Finally, Martin (2020) argued that careers in mental performance are largely unavailable, and that newcomers to the field would be better served to consider mental performance an adjunct to a more viable career path such as clinical mental health. Although the literature seems to support dual training, McHenry et al. (2022) observed that there is an absence of discussion regarding the ethical challenges inherent in the careers of dually trained professionals. We address some of these challenges here.

Establishment of Professional Identity

Relevant professional ethics codes require consultants to accurately represent themselves and their work, specifying for clients and the public practitioners' relevant training, competence, certification and licensure (see Association for Applied Sport Psychology [AASP] Code of Ethics Definition of Public Statements; Consultation, Mentorship, or Supervision, 2024; American Counseling Association [ACA] C.3.a, C.4.a, C.4.d, 2014; American Psychology Association [APA] 5.01.b, 2017). Ethical practitioners also "make reasonable efforts" to remedy cases in which the nature of their work has been misrepresented. However, clients might not always understand nuanced differences between practitioner training, expertise, and subsequent competence. For instance, dually trained mental performance consultants who act in the role of a master's-level counselor in some settings and a doctoral-level mental performance consultant in others might find clients can have difficulty distinguishing roles and titles.

Protection of Client Welfare

The primary purpose of ethics codes is to protect clients and the public, then professionals and the profession. Whether in the context of multiple roles, boundaries, assessment, advocacy, fees and bartering, reporting, or documentation, the dually trained practitioner avoids situations wherein clients might be exposed to harm; when harm occurs, dually trained practitioners take immediate and appropriate action. For dually trained practitioners, protecting client welfare may include mandated reporting and involuntary in-patient admission, which is less common for practitioners singularly trained in kinesiology.

Competence

Dually trained practitioners might face unique challenges regarding actual and perceived competency. For example, a dually trained sport and performance psychology professional might have earned mental health licensure and a performance consultant certification. However, the practitioner who has worked solely in mental health settings with non-athletes for a decade might no longer be competent to accept a contract as a mental performance consultant. On the other hand, a dually trained practitioner who has not treated a client with a mental health disorder since their graduate internship might no longer be competent to treat a veteran with PTSD. Whereas both could re-tool their competencies, it would be unethical to switch foci without consultation, continuing education, and self-study prior to accepting such contracts/clients.

Multiple Relationships

Multiple relationships tend to be common within applied sport and performance psychology, in that a dually trained practitioner might work with a coach of a team to enhance their performance as a coach, the collective team to enhance their performance, the captains to enhance their leadership, as well as individual athletes to enhance their personal performance. Even so, the AASP code of ethics states that practitioners should enter multiple relationships carefully, mitigating risks for coercion, exploitation, or harm to the greatest extent possible (AASP, Multiple Relationships, 2024). However, clinical codes of ethics indicate role changes should be precipitated by extensive documentation and informed consent (ACA, A.6.d.,

2014; APA 3.05.a, 3.05.b, 3.11.a, 3.11.b; 2017) or that when multiple relationships are unavoidable, informed consent and clear expectations are clearly established prior to initiation and whenever changes occur (APA, 3.05, 2017).

Primacy of Clinical Ethical Codes over SEPP Ethical Codes

Given the nature of the work conducted by dually trained practitioners, allegiance to codes of ethics should flow to the most stringent and conservative codes. Clinical ethical codes (e.g., ACA, 2014; APA, 2017) tend to be more detailed and explicit in their guidance and prohibitions. Therefore, dually trained SEPP practitioners are ***strongly encouraged*** to first adhere to clinical codes of ethics, with deference to legal considerations applicable in the practitioner's geographic area of practice.

Defining the Dual Practitioner Role

The role of a sport psychology practitioner is predicated on time, culture, structural employment systems, training, expertise, credentials, and effective communication. For dually trained practitioners, the issue of professional identity might also be prominently demonstrated in considerations for "who" to treat first: the person or the athlete (Winter & Collins, 2024), reflecting a perspective that dually trained practitioners must choose between treating mental health or performance issues. Where presenting concerns are in the "gray area" of mental health and performance, dually trained practitioners tend to experience the greatest discomfort in how to proceed (Winter & Collins, 2024). Moreover, research indicates that whereas clinically trained practitioners endorse treatment models that prioritize the social environments that influence client concerns, kinesiology-trained practitioners tend to gravitate toward cognitive behavioral models of treatment (Collins & Winter, 2020), creating potential conceptual and treatment challenges for dually trained practitioners.

Communicating the Dual Practitioner Role to Employers

Given the practitioner's ethical responsibility to accurately represent, and take reasonable efforts to correct misrepresentations, in combination with recent moves by hiring agencies toward dually trained practitioners (Winter & Collins, 2024), practitioners must delineate their role at the outset of employment. The dually trained practitioner needs to clarify duties/responsibilities early and often. It is then up to the practitioner to educate the potential employer about potential benefits, as well as legal and ethical issues that might arise from the employer's expectations of scope of work. To that end, dually trained practitioners might highlight research delineating additional mental health considerations for athletes compared to non-athlete peers and research outlining the benefits of different sport-specific mental health practice models (e.g., Albert et al., 2024). Further, the dually trained practitioner might outline specific ethical codes and applicable laws that impact their work within the position, and present case studies whereby they could explore potential outcomes and identify necessary resources (e.g., access to legal support services) to successfully navigate similar cases. Rarely, it may be the practitioner who must terminate an interview in instances where the employer and practitioner cannot align their expectations for the position (e.g., the employer expects the practitioner to serve as counselor and consultant to the same athlete, at the same time). Moreover, the practitioner should work with their employer to accurately communicate their role, expertise, and limitations, projecting a unified message to their future clientele. Should clients present with concerns that extend beyond the agreed-upon role of the dually trained practitioner, appropriate referral is the practitioner's responsibility.

Conclusion

Dual training is not a license to be a jack-of-all trades. Although it may present advantages to both practitioners and clients, it also presents ethical, legal, and practical drawbacks. For the practitioner interested in working with a range of clients on a range of issues in clinical and performance domains, dual training can provide the necessary education, training, and credentials. However, the exact path and ongoing methods to develop dual *expertise* are dependent upon the practitioner's individual engagement with opportunities, as well as efforts to remediate oversteps as necessary. Ultimately, despite building consensus that performance excellence is significantly influenced by performer mental health (e.g., Henriksen et al., 2020), the answer to whether/when dually trained practitioners provide both mental health and mental performance services to the same clients remains fraught with ethical and legal challenges. Notwithstanding the ongoing debate about dual training in the mental performance space, the nuances of exploring dual training and scope of work, as well as adherence to both legal and ethical requirements, remain the full responsibility of the practitioner.

SPORT PSYCH ETHICS OUTSIDE THE CLASSROOM

Tim Herzog, Tracy Heller, & Angel Brutus

Sport psychology, often portrayed through textbook case studies and theoretical models, might appear as a field where theory and practice align seamlessly. However, real-world practice frequently presents a more complex and "messy" reality. In this chapter, we explore the nuanced challenges faced by practitioners in the field culminating in a vignette to highlight the importance of virtue ethics, reflective growth, multiple roles, evolving relationships, boundaries multiple relationships, subcultures, and conflicts of interest informed by a systems perspective. Through this discussion and example, we aim to illustrate how sport psychologists and mental performance consultants can manage these complexities artfully and ethically.

Virtue Ethics and Reflective Growth

Graduate classes in sport psychology ethics commonly discuss "virtue ethics," efforts to do good rather than a constant rigid effort to do no harm—which could prevent some doing good (Aoyagi & Portenga, 2010). This shift in paradigm contrasts from a more typical framework associated with clinical psychology, that centers more on the principle of nonmaleficence (do no harm), and has some practical appeal for a consultant who carefully weighs risk/reward and sees strong benefit for the client, in pursuing an unconventional route. It is important, however, to avoid using virtue ethics to simply rationalize ethically questionable behavior and to recognize that one can still be held accountable by their state board or by their professional organization's ethics committee (Herzog & Zito, 2023). While it might be difficult in an applied/embedded context to document every single interaction because they are frequent and informal, the ethics adage "document, document, document," holds true particularly for behaviors that stray outside of professional norms that might require later justification. Frequency and pace of decision-making in ASP contexts can feel unwieldy, hence the need for regular peer consultation, self-care, and self-compassion when, not if, mistakes are made. Practitioners are advised to accept small mistakes (avoiding big, cumulative "gambles"), be truly reflective, and do better with subsequent opportunities (Cropley et al., 2010).

Multiple Roles and Evolving Relationships

Further complicating the provision of services for sport psychology professionals is that applied work frequently comes with multiple roles (e.g., professor and psychologist or consultant), particularly when a practitioner is embedded (e.g., full-time or frequently traveling with the team). To be more concrete, a professor who also does applied work for their university athletics program may notice that an athlete on the basketball team they work with is also taking their class. The professor may engage in efforts to pre-emptively avoid this scenario (e.g., encouraging the athlete to take the class in a subsequent semester or having a different professor teach the course), but sometimes these scenarios may prove unavoidable (e.g., university politics or the athlete needs the class this semester to graduate on time). It can be useful to conceptualize a continuum of emotional vulnerability from psychotherapy to mental performance coaching (Herzog & Hays, 2012), or a wider continuum of psychotherapy to professor or coach (Herzog et al., 2015). The more vulnerable a client has been with a psychotherapist or consultant, the more efforts should be engaged to mitigate potential negative impacts (e.g., communicating directly with the athlete and collaborating on solutions that diffuse power differentials).

Boundaries and Multiple Relationships

An inherent piece of ASP, particularly in embedded settings, is the existence of multiple relationships and boundary blurring. Counseling psychology literature refers to this inevitability within rural communities, but sport psychology also frequently presents these scenarios. With embedded work, there can be a blurring of professional and personal life. Some examples could include time together with team members or their supporters during downtime, meals, with lodging, or in celebration. Boundary decisions should be deliberate and mindfully made based on some form of rationale, even if imperfect, and even if seemingly inconsequential in the short run. A practitioner should ask themselves, "Why do I (or don't I) want to do this? What are the pros and cons?" Considerations might include rapport building, contextual awareness development, practicality, the client's bigger picture needs, your needs as a human-being (secondary to their needs), interacting authentically, modeling vulnerability, and more. These decisions are often not formulaic, frequently need to be arrived at quickly, and could be (*but should not be*) rationalized to completely suit the desires of the consultant. Authenticity and vulnerability could stand in the face of objectivity; however, an adept consultant cannot function like a robot. While the practitioner might rationally know that focus ought to be centered on process not outcomes, a consultant might be heavily invested in a client's performance success or well-being. Along the same vein, there may be moments when it is important to model the appropriateness of having one's own needs, even in the face of clients' discomfort, for the sake of self-respect and/or mutual learning (Cogan et al., 2022). Again, it is paramount to consult with others, make small mistakes, and engage in reflective practice.

Embedded roles, where practitioners integrate directly into their clients' settings, frequently present these kinds of conundrums (Johnson et al., 2005). Benefits, including rapport building, and the contextual understanding gained whereby the structure of the group, the patterns of their behavior, the attitudes that manifest, and the means through which members influence each other, are all better understood (Peterson et al., 2012). Embedded roles can come with practical and ethical challenges, however. Direct access to observe or interact with athletes may be dependent on coach buy-in, rapport, and endorsement, and yet management of boundaries is paramount. Practitioners must engage in solid communication skills, providing adequate informed consent with stakeholders, while being experienced as trustworthy by all.

Subcultures, Conflicts of Interest, and a Systems Perspective

Subcultures may have aspects of it that are driven by the personalities of leaders and other stakeholders in the ecosystem. Prior to intervention, understanding stakeholder factors such as family background (Shitama, n.d.), age/maturity (Stura & Johnston, 2018), and individualistic versus collectivistic cultural origin (Boroş et al., 2010) can contribute to conceptualization, building rapport, and informed interventions. Commonly, a norm of indirect communication or "triangulation" may need to be addressed by a team or organization, whereby one person (e.g., Player) could feel like a "victim" in a dynamic with another (e.g., Coach) who is made out to be the "villain," and so someone else (e.g., Consultant) is drawn into the mix as the "rescuer" (McMahon, 2005). Anyone can be pulled into each of the three roles; in this manner, well-meaning rescuers aiming to solve problems might actually perpetuate issues as people that need to speak directly with each other, do not. Triangles tend to be toxic and can permeate entire organizations until better norms are established. Working to shape team or organization norms, consultants may face challenging scenarios, whereby a balance is struck between providing stakeholders with ongoing confidentiality reminders and exercising appropriate flexibility with boundaries, aimed at facilitating an ongoing growth and learning for everyone in the system.

Vignette: Messy Enough?

You're a consultant working with the Women's Lacrosse High Performance Director (HPD) for over ten years; the work morphed from mental performance into psychotherapy to address depressed mood, then services ended about five years ago. The HPD brought you on to work with the National Team because of your pre-existing trusted relationship. Team dynamics need to be sorted in the next six months before the Olympics. Given difficulties with the Head Coach, the HPD unilaterally decided to hire you (a fact you only learned after your hire), and now she regularly complains about Coach. Coach does not want your involvement; he joked with the athletes before you arrived, "What do we need a sport psych for? You ladies aren't broken!" When athletes (rarely) seek you out, they complain about Coach, HPD, or each other. Nobody talks directly with each other. It seems your only opportunities to build rapport are when people are trying to persuade you to somehow intervene with other people on their behalf. To make matters worse, Coach prevents you from attending meetings and from delivering team workshops. Individuals are permitted to seek you out, "if it doesn't interfere." Additionally, support staff (e.g., marketing director, facilities manager, etc.) like to ask you questions such as, "How are they doing? Will they rise to the occasion with the pressure of our next tournament?"

Conclusion

Effective consultation outside the classroom hinges on adaptability and embracing the inherent messiness within high performance systems. Practitioners must nimbly strike a balance of virtue ethics, reflective growth, and professional accountability, all while negotiating multiple relationships, cultural nuances, and conflicts of interest. The vignette presented calls into consideration a number of factors: (1) Point of entry; (2) Gatekeeper buy-in; (3) Role clarification; (4) Triangulation; (5) Practitioner performance within *their* role. The delicate interplay between trust, power dynamics, and systemic influences, reinforces the importance of consultants' deliberate engagement of ongoing reflection, artful boundary setting, frequent peer consultation, and all-around adaptability.

EDITORS' TAKEAWAYS

This chapter builds nicely upon the first two in that it is important to view ethics more broadly as a field, rather than simply being about the challenges and decisions one may face in applied practice, research, or teaching. As I (Lauren) read Steele et al.'s contribution, I couldn't help but think about the ethical implications of the expansion and diversification of the field. Are our ethics and ethical codes following suit or are we stuck looking more in the rearview mirror at the field rather than through the front windshield catching up to where it has gotten to today and preparing for where it is, or will be, heading in the future? Reading Coker-Cranney and Castillo's contribution, this question echoed louder for me—while there is a need for a set of ethical guidelines for the field that is irrespective to the particular path one takes within it, it strikes me that there are then unique ethical dilemmas and responsibilities for the nuanced pathways in this field that speak to the unique nature of work. And, from Herzog et al.'s use of "outside the classroom" and "messy enough," I hope readers get a sense of ethics in the real world. As a professor, ethics was one of my favorite classes to teach because it truly, as Andrew wrote about in the introduction, is much more complicated than it may at first seem. Ethics isn't just about big, complex, stressful dilemmas (e.g., determining how to navigate a potential threat of suicide made by a client) that one is likely to encounter several times throughout their career, it's also about the day-to-day responsibility to make "good" decisions (e.g., whether to text back a client when you are out on a Friday evening with friends, knowing how to hold space for an athlete who is venting about a coach or teammate) that has both everything and nothing to do with your core values and who you are as a person and professional.

RECOMMENDED EXERCISES

1 How would you respond to the challenges in the "Messy Enough?" case? Consider cultural dynamics, role boundaries, multiple relationships, virtue ethics and reflective practice, conflicts of interest, and any systems-level factors you feel are relevant.
2 Based on Aoyagi and Portenga (2010), identify one core character virtue (e.g., fairness, honesty, courage) you will rely on when facing ethical dilemmas. Also identify one personal motivator (e.g., desire to be liked, financial pressure) that might challenge your ability to remain aligned with that virtue.
3 If you are a student, identify the career role you hope to pursue, the competencies you must develop, and what credentials (licensure, certification) you will need. If you are professional, how has your role evolved, how might it continue to change, and what new competencies or credentials will support ongoing ethical and effective practice?
4 Imagine a client discloses potential imminent harm. Describe the role you would like to play in this situation. Then describe the role your current training, credentials, and scope of practice require you to play.

REFERENCES

Albert, E., Joshua, M., & Machin, A. S. (2024). Sport psychology in collegiate athletics: A review of mental health service models. *Journal of College Student Mental Health, 38*(1), 21–35. https://doi.org/10.1080/87458225.2022.2117114

American Counseling Association. (2014). *2014 ACA code of ethics.* https://www.counseling.org/docs/default-source/default-document-library/ethics/2014-aca-code-of-ethics.pdf?sfvrsn=55ab73d0_1

American Psychological Association. (2017). *Ethical principles of psychologists and code of conduct.* https://www.apa.org/ethics/code/ethics-code-2017.pdf

Aoyagi, M. W., & Portenga, S. T. (2010). The role of positive ethics and virtues in the context of sport and performance psychology service delivery. *Professional Psychology: Research and Practice, 41*(3), 253–259. https://doi.org/10.1037/a0019483

Aoyagi, M. W., Portenga, S. T., Poczwardowski, A., Cohen, A. B., & Statler, T. (2012). Reflections and directions: The profession of sport psychology past, present, and future. *Professional Psychology: Research and Practice, 43*(1), 32–38. https://doi.org/10.1037/a0025676

Association for Applied Sport Psychology. (2024). *Association for applied sport psychology ethical principles and standards.* Zito, M., Carter, C., Herzog, T., Kerulis, M., Muscat, A., Shigeno, T., Skvarla, L., Chu, T. L., Rose, S., Wahl, C., & Watson, J., (Eds.). https://appliedsportpsych.org/about-the-association-for-applied-sport-psychology/ethics/

Association for Applied Sport Psychology [AASP]. (2024, January 9). *Ethics code: AASP ethical principles and standards.* https://appliedsportpsych.org/about-the-association-for-applied-sport-psychology/ethics/ethics-code/

Australian Psychological Society [APS]. (2007, December 10). *APS code of ethics.* https://psychology.org.au/getmedia/d873e0db-7490-46de-bb57-c31bb1553025/18aps-code-of-ethics.pdf

Baldock, L., Cropley, B., Mellalieu, S. D., & Neil, R. (2020). The stress and well-being of those operating in groups. In R. J. Schinke & D. Hackfort (Eds.), *The Routledge international encyclopedia of sport and exercise psychology: Vol. 1: Theoretical and methodological concepts* (pp. 620–634). Routledge.

Baldock, L., Cropley, B., Mellalieu, S. D., & Neil, R. (2022). A longitudinal examination of stress and mental ill-/well-being in elite football coaches. *The Sport Psychologist, 36*(3), 171–182. https://doi.org/10.1123/tsp.2021-0184

Boroş, S., Meslec, N., Curşeu, P., & Emons, W. (2010). Struggles for cooperation: Conflict resolution strategies in multicultural groups. *Journal of Managerial Psychology, 25*(5), 539–554. https://doi.org/10.1108/02683941011056903

British Association of Sport & Exercise Science [BASES]. (2021, November 15). *Code of conduct.* https://www.bases.org.uk/imgs/code_of_conduct202.pdf

Cogan, K., Conviser, J., Gunter, K., & Bader, C. (2022, October 26). Navigating risks and responsibilities: Case studies in sport psychology [Conference presentation]. *Annual Conference of the Association for Applied Sport Psychology*, Fort Worth, TX.

Collins, D., & Winter, S. (2020). Psychological models in sport psychology: A preliminary investigation. *European Journal of Sport Science, 20*(9), 1235–1244. https://doi.org/10.1080/17461391.2019.1694588

Cropley, B., Hanton, S., Miles, A., & Niven, A. (2010). Exploring the relationship between effective and reflective practice in applied sport psychology. *The Sport Psychologist, 24*(4), 521–541. https://doi.org/10.1123/tsp.24.4.521

Health & Care Professions Council. (2024, August 31). *Identifying your current scope of practice.* https://www.hcpc-uk.org/standards/meeting-our-standards/scope-of-practice/what-is-your-scope-of-practice/identifying-your-current-scope-of-practice/

Henriksen, K., Schinke, R., Moesch, K., McCann, S., Parham, W. D., Larsen, C. H., & Terry, P. (2020). Consensus statement on improving the mental health of high-performance athletes. *International Journal of Sport and Exercise Psychology, 18*(5), 553–560. https://doi.org/10.1080/1612197X.2019.1570473

Herzog, T., Hays, K., Eiring, K., Hiatt, M., & Trennery, M. (2015, October). Boundaries of therapy, mental training, and coaching: Who, what, where, when, and how? [Panel presentation]. *Annual Association for Applied Sport Psychology Conference*, Indianapolis.

Herzog, T., & Hays, K. F. (2012). Therapist or mental skills coach? How to decide. *The Sport Psychologist, 26*(4), 486–499. https://doi.org/10.1123/tsp.26.4.486
Herzog, T., & Zito, M. (2023). Chapter 7: Ethics in sport and performance psychology: Realities of practice in a multi-disciplinary field. In D. Tod, V. Krane, & K. Hodge (Eds.), *Routledge handbook of applied sport psychology* (2nd ed.). (pp. 51–60). Routledge.
Johnson, W. B., Ralph, J., & Johnson, S. J. (2005). Managing multiple roles in embedded environments: The case of aircraft carrier psychology. *Professional Psychology: Research and Practice, 36*(1), 73–81. https://doi.org/10.1037/0735-7028.36.1.73
Keyes, C. (2002). The mental health continuum: From languishing to flourishing in life. *Journal of Health and Social Behavior, 43*, 207–222. https://doi.org/10.2307/3090197
Martin, J. (2020). Is the profession of sport psychology an illusion? *Kinesiology Review, 9*, 92–103. https://doi.org/10.1123/kr.2019-0021
McHenry, L. K., Beasley, L., Zakrajsek, R. A., & Hardin, R. (2022). Mental performance and mental health services in sport: A call for interprofessional competence and collaboration. *Journal of Interprofessional Care, 36*(4), 520–528. https://doi.org/10.1080/13561820.2021.1963218
McMahon, M. (2005). Chapter 53: The drama triangle: A unilateral control program for helping others. In R. M. Schwarz, A. S. Davidson, M. S. Carlson, & S. C. McKinney (Eds.), *The skilled facilitator workbook* (pp. 421–432). Jossey-Bass.
Neumann, D., Piatkowski, T., Moffitt, R., & Minahan, C. (2024). Perceived benefits and receptivity to sport psychology consulting services of elite athletes in developing nations of the Oceania region. *International Journal of Sport Science & Coaching, 19*(3), 1175–1185. https://doi.org/10.1177/17479541231188455
Peterson, K., Brown, C., McCann, S., & Murphy, S. M. (2012). Sport and performance psychology: A look ahead. In S. M. Murphy (Ed.), *The Oxford handbook of sport and performance psychology* (pp. 741–753). Oxford University Press.
Quartiroli, A., Fogaça, J., & Wagstaff, C. R. D. (2023). Professional training and development: The bedrock of ethical, competent, and sustainable sport psychology. *Journal of Applied Sport Psychology, 35*(3), 349–371. https://doi.org/10.1080/10413200.2022.2043485
Quartiroli, A., Harris, B. S., Brückner, S., ... & Zito, M. (2020). *The International Society of Sport Psychology (ISSP) ethical code for sport psychology practice.* https://issponline.org/wp-content/uploads/ISSP-R_Ethics_Code.pdf
Shitama, J. (Executive Producer). (n.d.). Podcast Episode 288: An interview with Dr. Kathleen Smith [Audio podcast]. *The non-anxious leader blog: Resources for the personal and professional non-anxious presence.* https://thenonanxiousleader.com/podcast-episode-288-an-interview-with-dr-kathleen-smith-part-1-of-4/
Silva, J. (2010). No one told you when to run: The past and present is not the future of sport psychology [Keynote presentation]. *25th Annual Association for Applied Sport Psychology Conference*, Providence, RI.
Sly, D., Mellalieu, S. D., & Wagstaff, C. R. D. (2020). "It's psychology Jim, but not as we know it!" The changing face of applied sport psychology. *Sport, Exercise, and Performance Psychology, 9*(1), 87–101. https://doi.org/10.1037/spy0000163
Stura, C., & Johnston, L. M. (2018). Cross-cultural conflicts within sports teams. *Journal of Peace Education, 15*(1), 97–114. https://doi.org/10.1080/17400201.2017.1409199
Winter, S., & Collins, D. (2024). Mental health matters: Evaluating the preparedness of sport psychologists to incorporate within their role. *European Journal of Sport Science, 24*, 1664–1670. https://doi.org/10.1002/ejsc.12205
World Health Organisation [WHO]. (2005). *Promoting mental health: Concepts, emerging evidence, practice.* WHO Press.
World Health Organisation [WHO]. (2022, June 8). *Mental disorders.* https://www.who.int/newsroom/fact-sheets/detail/mental-disorders

4 Pursuing Diversity, Equity, and Inclusion in SEPP

It was our explicit goal as editors of this book to pursue a truly global perspective on the field, with diversity and inclusion at the forefront. To achieve this, we looked beyond our immediate networks, reaching out to professionals around the world—sometimes through "cold calls." I, Andrew, even scrolled through the entire AASP membership directory, country by country, seeking voices that were new to me. We regularly sought recommendations from the International Society of Sport Psychology (thank you, Ale!) and, when invited contributors declined, we asked whether they might suggest colleagues from their own regional communities. While pursuing this global perspective came with its challenges, we are proud to share contributions from authors across the world who describe what it means to be a sport, exercise, and performance psychology professional from their own vantage points. At the same time, we acknowledge that not every country is represented. This reality underscores that diversity is not a final destination but an ongoing pursuit that we as editors, practitioners, and organizations need to embrace individually and collectively.

A CALL TO ACTION: EMBRACING DIVERSITY, EQUITY, INCLUSION, BELONGING, AND JUSTICE IN SPORT, EXERCISE, AND PERFORMANCE PROFESSIONAL PRACTICE

Amanda M. Perkins-Ball, Stephany C. Coakley, & Derek M. Zike

Diversity, equity, inclusion, belonging, and justice (DEIBJ) is a framework that communities and organizations adopt to cultivate an environment where all individuals feel valued and included. *Diversity* refers to differences such as race, ethnicity, ability, age, sex, sexual orientation, gender, religion, national origin, and socioeconomic status. *Equity* involves ensuring fair treatment and actively working to identify and eliminate barriers that have contributed to disparities over time. *Inclusion* means creating an environment where people feel welcomed, respected, valued, and safe. *Belonging* refers to fostering connection and acceptance within a community, and *justice* calls for systemic change to address inequities and injustices within that community (UC Berkley, n.d.). In recent years, there has been a growing recognition of the importance of DEIBJ within the field of sport, exercise, and performance psychology (SEPP). This chapter presents key considerations to enhance DEIBJ in SEPP education, research, and applied work. We also encourage readers to browse the DEIBJ resources available on the AASP website (Association for Applied Sport Psychology, n.d.).

DOI: 10.4324/9781003781479-5

Table 4.1 Key DEIBJ Competencies to Be Integrated into SEPP Education

Competency	*Description*
Cultural awareness and sensitivity	Recognizing your own cultural identities and biases, as well as the cultural backgrounds of those with whom you work, including how culture shapes behavior, attitudes, and experiences in sport and performance.
Knowledge of social justice issues	Identifying and addressing social justice issues relevant to sport, including systemic inequalities related to race, gender, sexual orientation, and socioeconomic status. This also involves understanding how these issues impact athletes' mental health and performance.
Advocacy skill development	Teaching students the importance of advocating for equitable practices within sports organizations and communities, and equipping them with the necessary advocacy skills.
Collaboration and communication	Skill in communicating and collaborating with individuals from various backgrounds, ensuring that differing perspectives are heard and valued.
Ongoing education and self-reflection	A commitment to continuous learning about DEIBJ issues and engaging in self-reflection to assess one's own practices and beliefs.

Integrating DEIBJ into SEPP Education

As the sociopolitical landscape evolves, there has been an increasing demand to integrate and enhance multicultural competence within education and training programs. For instance, the AASP (2024a) Ethics Code's Principle on Respect for People's Rights and Dignity highlights the importance of education concerning diversity and inclusion, emphasizing the understanding of individual and cultural differences across a range of identities. The code also underscores that AASP members and Certified Mental Performance Consultants (CMPCs) must be mindful of how their biases in relation to these identities might influence their work. In addition, certification requirements and program accreditation standards have begun to incorporate greater knowledge of diversity. For instance, the knowledge area K8: Diversity and Culture, which necessitates graduate-level coursework focused on the "understanding of diversity, multiculturalism, and cultural awareness," was implemented in 2018 (AASP, 2024b). However, there is still a need for more comprehensive guidelines and competencies concerning DEIBJ. See Table 4.1 for key DEIBJ competencies to integrate into SEPP education.

Integrating DEIBJ into SEPP Research

Research is often shaped by power imbalances and biases associated with factors such as race, ethnicity, gender, socioeconomic status, age, and ability. These factors can affect various aspects of the research process, including the composition of research teams, the formulation of research questions, the diversity of samples, the availability of funding, and the publication process. To address these issues, researchers can integrate DEIBJ principles into their research practices (see Table 4.2). By doing so, they strive to identify and challenge power imbalances and biases. This commitment helps ensure that research practices do not disproportionately impact marginalized communities. Researchers who adopt DEIBJ practices actively include a diverse range of perspectives, identities, and experiences, which helps mitigate bias, enhances research integrity, and enriches both research outputs and the overall research environment.

Table 4.2 Research Practices That Implement DEIBJ Principles

Research Practice	*Description*
Inclusive research teams	Lead researchers commit to recruiting research team members who represent different identities and perspectives that reflect the study population's diversity, and have diverse training backgrounds.
Creating an equitable research environment	Lead researchers actively work toward creating a more just and welcoming research environment by addressing historical and ongoing inequities. When all voices have equal weight, the voices of the historically excluded are centered, and those with dominant identities actively engage in re-education about their social privileges, the research team will truly embody DEIBJ principles.
Engaging in reflexivity	Engaging in a reflexive process to understand the distribution of power among the members of the research team. This involves recognizing who holds power, who doesn't, and how power influences relationships. To do this, researchers must look beyond self-reflection and consider how marginalized and privileged identities intersect, taking personal responsibility for their role in these dynamics (Jones, 2010).
Community engagement	Collaborating with community members throughout the research process to ensure that the research goals and activities align with community needs and values. This includes co-designing research questions, interpreting findings, and tailoring the dissemination of these findings to communicate effectively with communities.
Culturally sensitive methods	Considering the accessibility and relevance of research methods for different populations. This includes developing culturally appropriate research instruments and methodologies that are accessible to diverse populations, as well as adapting existing research tools to make them relevant to specific cultural contexts.

Ultimately, these practices promote fair treatment and equitable access for all participants, while addressing systemic inequalities and fostering justice throughout the research lifecycle.

Integrating DEIBJ into SEPP Professional Practice

Sport participation is one of the most diverse and unifying human pursuits. Mega sporting events and the globalization of sports make culturally competent SEPP practitioners an ethical and moral obligation (Quartiroli et al., 2022). Athletes from diverse, marginalized, and unique intersecting identities who work with SEPP practitioners should expect their practitioners to be culturally competent and employ a DEIBJ lens when providing services to individuals and teams, focusing on the mental and emotional aspects of consistently performing to their full potential (see Table 4.3). Failure to address the unique identities and lived experiences of clients limits practitioners' ability to be effective, therefore doing the client a disservice.

Conclusion

Integrating DEIBJ into SEPP is both a professional responsibility and a moral obligation. Incorporating these principles into education, research, and practice helps develop culturally responsive professionals, promotes inclusive and impactful scholarship, and ensures equitable and affirming services to all clients. As SEPP continues to evolve, its educators, researchers,

Table 4.3 Key Applied DEIBJ Competencies

Competency	*Description*
Identity exploration	Engaging in self-exploration of your own identity for effective practice, recognizing that social identities and role identities influence your interactions with clients, which can lead to psychological distress and negatively impact the consulting relationship.
Cultural knowledge, awareness, and skills	Developing cultural knowledge, awareness, and skills about yourself and your clients, and using this knowledge to integrate it into relevant techniques to provide culturally competent services (Sue et al., 2019). This also includes considering the potential lack of client privilege and power.
Reflective self-review	Engaging in regular self-reflection on your cultural positioning and worldviews (Schinke et al., 2018), recognizing that a consistent praxis to increase self-awareness of your cultural background and views (Sue et al., 2019) influences service provision.
Cultural humility	Developing authentic relationships with peers, mentors, and clients from other backgrounds to learn from their experiences, understanding they are not the expert of all things related to their culture. Recognizing that you cannot become fully culturally competent due to the multiple layers of DEIBJ categories, which are ever-evolving. You can, however, develop a willingness to have difficult conversations about racism, heterosexism, gender bias, and many other topics, accepting that you will make mistakes and not being afraid to have these crucial conversations for fear of making a mistake.

and practitioners must adopt DEIBJ as a foundational perspective, supported by ongoing learning, reflection, and advocacy.

A SCIENTIST-PRACTITIONER'S VANTAGE OF CULTURAL SPORT PSYCHOLOGY: POSSIBLE IMPLICATIONS FOR DIVERSITY, EQUITY, AND INCLUSION

Robert J. Schinke, Cole E. Giffin, & Elizabeth A. Steadman

Positioning Cultural Sport Psychology

Cultural Sport Psychology (CSP) has gained considerable attention since its formal reference in 2009 (see Schinke & Hanrahan, 2009). Earlier writings did integrate elements of identity, such as a special issue devoted to gender-based approaches found in *The Sport Psychologist* as early as 2001 (see Gill, 2001), and solitary commentary papers from people who are regarded as diversity, equity, and inclusion (DEI) scholars (see Anderson, 2002). With a deeper awareness of CSP, and the associated advocacy of DEI, the sport and exercise psychology field has mandated cultural modules found within three international accreditations: the Association for Applied Sport Psychology's CMPC, the International Society of Sport Psychology's Registry status (ISSP-R(S)), and the European Federation of Sport Psychology's Certification (FEPSAC-C). These societies and the international professionals who undertake their courses are now being asked to gain a rudimentary education in DEI.

Though a growing number of professionals endorse cultural inclusion and the foundational term of CSP, there remains confusion of the parameters of these terms. As contentious as it might be to say, a few remaining oversights will be resolved in due time. One element pertains to the terms "diversity" and "inclusion." Where diversity reveals parts of a given identity and how these might be combined, it can sometimes be misused and misunderstood given its inherent value when seeking to reveal and uncover differences, power inequities, and the necessary remedial actions that must happen in a socially just world, via the medium of sport and physical activity. Diversity is needed to make space for people whose identities were either disregarded or simplified resulting in misunderstanding within this profession and beyond. Inclusion is often conflated with diversity. Inclusion pertains equally to advocacy, though with the intent of ensuring that all people, of all identities, are encouraged forth, be they from the margins or not. CSP must endorse clarity relating to both terms.

Contextualizing CSP Practice with Indigenous Athletes

The catalyst to change one's approach to knowledge comes from recognition that oneself or another person is not being understood. I (Robert) initially began my career with a cross-cultural approach to sport psychology service. Sport psychology has always been infused with cultural values, such as a preference for the self in mainstream English language scientific outlets, evidenced through using interventions built to augment self-efficacy, self-determination, self-regulation, self-esteem, self-empowerment, self-concept, and self-actualization (Ryba & Wright, 2005). These terms and their interventional approaches were a large part of my interventional satchel, along with mental skills exercises. Traditionally taught sport psychology skills, though often useful when an aspiring athlete seeks to advance in athletic career, sometimes misalign with a performer's worldview. Whilst initially working with Canadian Indigenous athletes, I found that the very provider of these services could become the first step in harmful sport psychology service (Schinke, Ryba et al., 2007). Traditional Canadian Indigenous athletes, in this case referring to athletes from geographic cultural lands relatively unharmed and untouched by European religion and education, have historically resourced medicine men and elders when seeking guidance in all aspects of their lives, including their athletic pursuits. I recall learning that my services were not always relevant with members from Indigenous Canadian boxers' communities. My skills could be supplemental when deemed useful by traditional non-western athletes, and at best, a secondary resource to those provided by relevant cultural providers. Drummers also hold a place as motivators of these aspiring performers, particularly during their walk from the warm-up area to the field of play. Sacred medicines, such as tobacco, sweetgrass, and sage, provided by community elders and medicine men, are also used when seeking to gain calmness and mindfulness within daily training regimes (Schinke, Hanrahan et al., 2007). Finally, the motivational value for such athletes displaces individualized ambitions and centralizes the value that the athletes bring to their community.

Within the Canadian Sport System, including boxing, when Indigenous athletes chose to return to their communities, they were regarded by their mainstream coaches as self-deselecting from their sport, suggesting a lack of self-interest and motivation. Misunderstandings cause grave harm to people who originate from cultural communities where marginalization has been systemic and longstanding. What the coaches and support staff failed to understand when supporting aspiring Indigenous athletes is that when one is of a collective mindset, they take what they learn and gift it to others in their community, indicating reciprocity as opposed to lack of commitment. Simply, the commitment extends beyond oneself to one's community of origin.

Culturally Informed Science to Inform Safe and Inclusive Practice

Just as there are practical skills that each scientist-practitioner must understand, there are important methodological skills needed to inform evidence-based practice, via systematic research. The commonly used approaches to research with diverse populations reveal a vastness of quantitative and qualitative strategies. Ten years ago, I (Robert) co-edited a special issue of *Qualitative Research in Sport, Exercise, and Health*, devoted to community-based methods. The analytic approaches were undertaken within North America, Europe, Australia, and the African continent (Schinke et al., 2013). Though these projects were well funded and highly successful at the time, they reflected early days in terms of the integration of DEI. The methodologies and underpinning philosophical tenets were European in origin. Five years earlier, a colleague and I undertook a special issue focused on decolonizing methodologies, which refer to research approaches that align with the ontological worldviews of local participants, found in the *International Journal of Sport and Exercise Psychology* (Ryba & Schinke, 2009). Though these and a few subsequent attempts have been made to centralize inclusion through science in sport psychology, which then informs practice, there is often a tendency for scholars to approach their research contexts, questions, data collection, analysis, and subsequent writing from a preferred, and likely, a comfortable lens. The importance of developing ecologically relevant science to develop matching ecologically suited interventions cannot be understated, though it often is.

What might be an ecologically relevant research project? In relation to CSP approaches, communities are contextually enriched and idiosyncratic. The approaches my colleagues and doctoral students have attempted include arts-based methods, such as mandalas, rivers, trees, and temporal representations when working with elite newcomers and Indigenous athletes (Blodgett et al., 2013). These approaches encourage openness for participants and researchers. The intention is to centralize participants as the experts in terms of their own stories and experiences. Mobility strategies are equally effective to understand cultural and sub-cultural contexts. The reason is that the participant athletes and coaches can share the most relevant parts of their training and living environments with the researcher. Throughout these moving interviews, important details such as artifacts hanging on walls, training equipment, broader training environments, travel to and from training from one's home, and one's living conditions become clearer, augmenting holistic understanding of a human condition. Our researchers have gone fishing with sport participants, sat at family meals, traveled in buses to and from training, traveled to competitions, and sat in ceremonial sweat lodges. The conditions varied, but an openness to contexts often led to better questions than would have been developed outside of the contexts where performances take place (see Middleton et al., 2022). This openness to understanding augmented relationships contributed to friendships rather than objective and de-contextualized representations of participants' stories and experiences, which tend to provide, at best, limited knowledge and understanding, and at worst, colonization, silencing, and harm.

Evidence Back to Practice

There has always been a reciprocity among our authors when examining practical support, informed knowledge acquisition, and deepened knowledge translation. In place of siloed approaches from the vantage of knowledge and the vantage of intervention, scientist-practitioners straddle both elements in a holistic interventional world. The stimulant and subsequent accelerant of CSP among our authors has been practical commitments in high-performance amateur and professional sport contexts comprising an international complement of diverse athletes, coaches, and managers. These people have sometimes struggled to understand one another, which, in turn, led to conflict, silencing, and alienation in place of thriving performance environments. Understanding creates openness, trust, belonging, and only then, sustained excellence and human potential. Professionals in this field are best positioned to succeed when they are receptive to the ecological data in their work environments; for only this information permits ecologically relevant decisions, actions, and performance, furthering human potential.

FOSTERING AN INCLUSIVE TEAM CULTURE THAT RESPECTS ATHLETES' RELIGIOUS IDENTITIES

Young-Eun Noh

Faith can serve as a source of strength and a guiding principle in sports. Many athletes with strong religious identities incorporate faith into their performance mindset, using prayer, scripture, or meditation as tools for mental preparation (Noh & Shahdan, 2022). While religious beliefs can provide motivation and resilience, they might also present unique challenges. Athletes sometimes face conflicts between faith-based commitments and sport participation, such as disruptions to training schedules and energy depletion due to fasting or heightened pressure to succeed due to religious expectations (Amjad et al., 2024). Given the profound influence of religion on an athlete's psychological framework, SEPP professionals should understand its implications. This chapter examines the intersection of religion and sport, offering practical strategies to support athletes with diverse religious commitments.

The Role of Religion in Sport Psychology Practice

Religion has long played a significant role in sports, not only enhancing performance but also providing psychological benefits, particularly in coping with stress and anxiety (Noh & Shahdan, 2022). Religion encompasses beliefs and rituals centered on a higher power or God, often practiced within organized institutions. We know performers often face unexpected challenges, including career-ending injuries, losing seasons, academic pressures, rigorous training, illness, competition for playing time, and struggles with identity development. In such situations, religious beliefs can serve as a source of inner strength, helping athletes manage emotional stress and anxiety more effectively (Noh & Shahdan, 2022). Additionally, religion can foster resilience by encouraging athletes to find deeper meaning in both success and failure throughout their careers (Noh & Shahdan, 2022). However, for some, religious beliefs may also create distress, such as feelings of punishment, doubts about faith, or frustration with their relationship with God, particularly when facing serious injuries (Wiese-Bjornstal et al., 2018).

Understanding Athletes with Strong Religious Identities

For many religious athletes, faith serves as a foundation for identity formation and finding meaning in both their lives and athletic achievements. Elite athletes with strong religious beliefs often perceive their physical abilities as God-given athletic gifts (Parker et al., 2023). Their participation in sports is seen as an act of worship, reinforcing a sense of religious responsibility to dedicate their talents to glorifying God (Shirvani et al., 2024).

Recognizing the integral role of faith in sport, Noh and Shahdan (2022) introduced the Religion and Sport Performance (RSP) model to explain how religious beliefs influence athletic performance. The model identifies three fundamental factors shaping the experiences of religious athletes: religious practices, the strength of religious beliefs, and religious culture.

Beyond these core elements, the RSP model highlights six additional factors that contribute to sport performance: coping strategies, religious support, psychological effects, performance outcomes, religious dietary practices, and mental health and healing. These interconnected factors collectively influence how athletes navigate their sporting careers. By integrating these dimensions, the RSP model provides a comprehensive framework for understanding the complex relationship between religious beliefs, psychological mechanisms, and athletic performance.

Challenges Faced by Religious Athletes

While strong religious identities can offer psychological and performance benefits, they may also present practical and emotional challenges in sports. Athletes who observe religious holidays, fasting periods (e.g., Ramadan), or specific prayer times often face difficulties in maintaining energy levels, hydration, total caloric intake, and training intensity. These challenges can also lead to sleep disturbances, mood fluctuations, and overall mental and emotional strain (Amjad et al., 2024).

Beyond physical and emotional concerns, differences in religious beliefs between athletes, teammates, or coaches can create social tension or feelings of isolation. For example, Parker et al. (2023) explored how high school athletes navigate their religious identities within team settings, including interactions with coaches, highlighting that conflicting beliefs might lead to internal struggles and strained relationships.

Practical Strategies for SEPP Professionals

How can sport psychology professionals effectively support religiously committed athletes? Do we possess the cultural competence needed to navigate faith-related challenges in sports? The following strategies offer practical ways to foster a supportive environment for religious athletes.

Culturally Competent Communication

Effective support begins with open and respectful communication. Rather than assuming that religion plays a significant role in an athlete's performance, professionals should ask, "How does your faith influence your approach to sports?" A study by Ronkainen et al. (2020) found that some Christian athletes did not view their athletic careers as connected to their religious beliefs. They did not perceive their talent as a gift from God or see injuries as part of a divine plan, instead maintaining a clear separation between faith and sport. These findings highlight the diversity of religious perspectives among athletes and underscore the importance of individualized meaning and values of sport.

Moreover, athletes should feel comfortable expressing their religious beliefs without fear of judgment or bias. For example, Muslim student-athletes have emphasized the need for open communication among coaches, athletic trainers, and teammates of different faiths. They suggest that fostering religious awareness, particularly around practices such as Ramadan, can lead to greater understanding and support from those around them (Amjad et al., 2024).

Integrating Religion into Mental Skills Training

Faith-based approaches can be effectively incorporated into psychological skills training to enhance confidence, resilience, and focus. While research on religious self-talk and imagery remains limited, findings from studies on general self-talk and mental imagery offer valuable insights into faith-based applications.

Athletes can use short prayers or scripture-based affirmations to reinforce mental preparation, maintain composure, and build confidence before competition. For example, a Christian soccer player experiencing pre-game nerves might use self-talk by reminding themselves to be strong, courageous, and confident, knowing they are not alone. A Buddhist martial artist could repeat. *Do not dwell in the past, do not dream of the future, concentrate the mind on the present moment* to cultivate mindfulness during competition. Similarly, a Muslim weightlifter might enhance their focus by visualizing a successful lift while mentally repeating a reassuring phrase about perseverance and ease. These examples illustrate how religious athletes can integrate faith-based practices into their mental training to enhance focus and performance.

Addressing Ethical and Practical Challenges

Supporting religious athletes requires a careful balance between faith and professional ethics. Coaches and sport psychology professionals should maintain neutrality and inclusivity, ensuring that religious beliefs do not create division within teams. Practical accommodation, such as adjusting training schedules during fasting periods or religious observances, can help athletes perform at their best. For example, Muslim student-athletes have expressed a need for more flexible training sessions, modified prayer times, and access to *iftar* (the meal eaten after sunset to break the fast) during Ramadan (Amjad et al., 2024).

While it is essential to acknowledge and respect an athlete's faith, sport psychologists and coaches should avoid promoting specific religious practices. Instead, they should ensure that faith-based elements are incorporated only when initiated by the athlete (Sarkar et al., 2019). By fostering an inclusive environment, professionals can support religious athletes in a way that respects both their beliefs and the integrity of the sport.

Conclusion

Religion significantly influences an athlete's psychological resilience, focus, and overall performance, offering confidence and meaning through faith-based practices such as prayer, scripture, and religious self-talk. Fostering an inclusive team culture that respects athletes' religious identities while maintaining professional neutrality not only enhances individual performance but also strengthens team cohesion. By balancing faith and ethical considerations, sport professionals can support religiously committed athletes in a way that aligns with best practices, promoting both personal well-being and success in sports.

EDITORS' TAKEAWAYS

One question that arises when organizations emphasize DEI is: what does meaningful competence actually look like? As Perkins-Ball and colleagues note, "You cannot become fully culturally competent due to the multiple layers of DEIBJ categories, which are ever-evolving." This reminds us that growth in both DEIBJ and SEPP domains is an ongoing journey rather than an endpoint—sustained by viewing competence as continuous practice.

Schinke and colleagues' narratives on CSP were especially thought-provoking, particularly in considering how institutional realities might complicate culturally grounded practices. Could funding structures support activities like fishing with participants to build rapport?

How might an ethics board respond to requests to observe or join a ceremonial sweat lodge? Such questions highlight the tension between meaningful cultural engagement and the procedural limits of academic research.

We also valued Young-Eun Noh's contribution on religion in sport, especially the practical strategies for supporting athletes of diverse faiths. A natural next step may be examining how practitioners navigate their own religious or spiritual identities alongside their professional roles, offering further insight into the ethical and relational dimensions of applied practice.

RECOMMENDED EXERCISES

1 Write down three aspects of your identity (e.g., race, gender, socioeconomic status) and reflect on how they influence your interactions with others. What biases might you carry into those interactions? How can this awareness help you create a more inclusive environment?
2 Identify a community or group you belong to. Consider the level of diversity present and any barriers to inclusion. What steps could you take to begin DEIBJ-focused conversations? Outline a brief plan to encourage belonging for all members.
3 Recall an academic or applied experience working with someone from a different cultural background. What values did you bring into the relationship? How did these values interact with theirs? Identify one strategy you will use in future work to better support DEI.
4 Reflect on your own beliefs and biases regarding religion in sport. How might these shape your work with religiously committed athletes?
5 Consider a situation where an athlete's religious practices (e.g., fasting, prayer times) conflict with performance demands. How would you approach this scenario as a sport psychology professional?

REFERENCES

American Psychological Association. (2017). *Multicultural guidelines: An ecological approach to context, identity, and intersectionality*. https://www.apa.org/about/policy/multicultural-guidelines.pdf

Amjad, M., Cavallario, J. M., Harris, N. A., & Welch Bacon, C. E. (2024). Muslim collegiate student-athletes' experience with fasting during Ramadan while participating in sport. *Journal of Athletic Training*, *59*(5), 474–486. https://doi.org/10.4085/1062-6050-0363.23

Anderson, E. (2002). Openly gay athletes: Contesting hegemonic masculinity in a homophobic environment. *Gender & Society*, *16*(6), 860–877. https://doi.org/10.1177/089124302237892

Association for Applied Sport Psychology. (2024a). *Association for applied sport psychology ethical principles and standards*. Zito, M., Carter, C., Herzog, T., Kerulis, M., Muscat, A., Shigeno, T., Skvarla, L., Chu., T, L., Rose, S., Wahl, C., & Watson, J. (Eds.). https://appliedsportpsych.org/about-the-association-for-applied-sport-psychology/ethics/

Association for Applied Sport Psychology. (2024b). *Certified Mental Performance Consultant (CMPC) Certification Program Candidate Handbook*. AASP. https://appliedsportpsych.org/site/assets/files/30025/11_24_cmpccandidatehandbook_web_final.pdf

Association for Applied Sport Psychology. (n.d.). *Resources and references*. https://appliedsportpsych.org/diversity-and-inclusion/resources-and-references/

Baum, F., MacDougall, C., & Smith, D. (2006). Participatory action research. *Journal of Epidemiology and Community Health*, *60*(10), 854–857. https://doi.org/10.1136/jech.2004.028662

Blodgett, A. T., Coholic, D. A., Schinke, R. J., McGannon, K. R., Peltier, D., & Pheasant, C. (2013). Moving beyond words: Exploring the use of an arts-based method in Aboriginal community sport research. *Qualitative Research in Sport, Exercise and Health*, *5*(3), 312–331. https://doi.org/10.1080/2159676X.2013.796490

Gill, D. (2001). Feminist sport psychology: A guide for our journey. *The Sport Psychologist, 15*(4), 363–372. https://doi.org/10.1123/tsp.15.4.363
Jones, R. G. (2010). Putting privilege into practice through "intersectional reflexivity": Ruminations, interventions, and possibilities. *Reflections: Narratives of Professional Helping, 16*(1), 122–125. https://reflectionsnarrativesofprofessionalhelping.org/index.php/Reflections/article/view/800
Middleton, T. R. F., Schinke, R. J., Habra, B., Coholic, D., Lefebvre, D., McGannon, K. R., & Giffin, C. E. (2022). Centralizing forced immigrant male youths' stories in the development of socially just and inclusive community sport programs. *Sport, Exercise, and Performance Psychology, 11*(2), 156–173. https://doi.org/10.1037/spy0000289
Noh, Y., & Shahdan, S. (2022). A model for formulating the relationship between religion and sport performance: A grounded theory approach. *International Journal of Sport and Exercise Psychology, 20*(3), 661–676. https://doi.org/10.1080/1612197X.2021.1891123
Parker, A., White, J. B., & Meyer, A. R. (2023). Youth, sport, and faith: Identity formation in high school athletes. *Religions, 14*(10), 1293. https://doi.org/10.3390/rel14101293
Quartiroli, A., Schinke, R. J., Giffin, C., Vosloo, J., & Fisher, L. A. (2022). Cultural competence in a multinational group of sport psychology professionals. *Journal of Applied Sport Psychology, 35*(6), 919–940. https://doi.org/10.1080/10413200.2022.2140224
Ronkainen, N. J., Ryba, T. V., & Tod, D. (2020). 'Don't ever mix God with sports': Christian religion in athletes' stories of life transitions. *Sport in Society, 23*(4), 613–628. https://doi.org/10.1080/17430437.2019.1599199
Ryba, T. V., & Schinke, R. J. (2009). Methodology as a ritualized Eurocentrism: Introduction to the special issue [Special issue]. *International Journal of Sport and Exercise Psychology, 7*(3), 263–274. https://doi.org/10.1080/1612197X.2009.9671909
Ryba, T. V., & Wright, H. K. (2005). From mental game to cultural praxis: A cultural studies model's implications for the future of sport psychology. *Quest, 57*(2), 192–212. https://doi.org/10.1080/00336297.2005.10491853
Sarkar, M., Hill, D. M., & Parker, A. (2019). Working with religious and spiritual athletes: Ethical considerations for sport psychologists. In B. Hemmings, N. J. Watson, & A. Parker (Eds.), *Sport, psychology and Christianity* (pp. 158–170). Routledge. https://doi.org/10.4324/9781351165488
Schinke, R., Blodgett, A., Ryba, T., Kao, S., & Middleton, T. (2018). Cultural sport psychology as a pathway to advances in identity and settlement research to practice. *Psychology of Sport and Exercise, 42*, 58–65. https://doi.org/10.1016/j.psychsport.2018.09.004
Schinke, R. J., & Hanrahan, S. J. (2009). *Cultural sport psychology*. Human Kinetics.
Schinke, R. J., Hanrahan, S., Peltier, D., Michel, G., Danielson, R., Pickard, P., Pheasant, C., Enosse, L., & Peltier, M. (2007). The pre-competition and competition practices of Canadian Aboriginal elite athletes. *Journal of Clinical Sport Psychology, 1*(2), 147–165. https://doi.org/10.1123/jcsp.1.2.147
Schinke, R. J., McGannon, K. R., & Smith, B. (2013). Expanding the sport and physical activity research landscape through community scholarship: introduction [Special issue]. *Qualitative Research in Sport, Exercise and Health, 5*(3), 287–290. https://doi.org/10.1080/2159676X.2013.847477
Schinke, R. J., Ryba, T. V., Danielson, R., Michel, G., Pickard, P., Peltier, D., Enosse, L., Pheasant, C., & Peltier, M. (2007). Canadian Aboriginal elite Athletes: The experiences of being coached in mainstream cultures. *International Journal of Sport and Exercise Psychology, 5*(2), 123–141. https://doi.org/10.1080/1612197X.2007.9671815
Shirvani, H., Asadzandi, M., & Amini, A. (2024). The relationship between spirituality and sports from the point of view of sports psychology researchers: A systematic review of research over two decades. *Journal of Religion and Health, 64*(5), 3613–3645. https://doi.org/10.1007/s10943-024-02204-3
Sue, D. W., Sue, D., Neville, H. A., & Smith, L. (2019). *Counseling the culturally diverse: Theory and practice* (8th ed.). Wiley.
University of California, Berkeley. (n.d.). *DEIBJ mission, vision, and values*. University of California. https://udar.berkeley.edu/deibj/deibj-mission-vision-and-values
Wiese-Bjornstal, D. M., Wood, K. N., White, A. C., Wambach, A. J., & Rubio, V. J. (2018). Exploring religiosity and spirituality in coping with sport injuries. *Journal of Clinical Sport Psychology, 14*(1), 68–87. https://doi.org/10.1123/jcsp.2018-0009

5 Mental Health, Mental Well-Being, and Mental Performance

Most of us will agree that the recent increase in societal attention to and prioritization of mental health is a positive shift in tone. Athletes' and performers' mental health needs—long neglected—are now receiving overdue attention, though much work remains. However, for the sport, exercise, and performance psychology community, the growing emphasis on mental health and well-being can muddy the lexical waters, prompting a need to revisit definitions, theories, and categorical distinctions (if any). Do these constructs exist along a continuum? If so, is it the same continuum? Are they categorically different? Or perhaps they are merely variations of the same construct, rebranded using the latest generational lingo. Clarifying these distinctions is more than semantics—it has implications for training, service delivery, and professional identity. To help explore these and other related questions, we have invited three author groups to offer commentary and experiential reflection. Collectively, our global author groups present different ways that sport, exercise, and performance psychology professionals can practically attend to the mental health, mental well-being, and mental performance needs of our clients.

THE COEXISTENCE OF MENTAL HEALTH AND MENTAL PERFORMANCE IN SPORT

Désarée Festa & Jimena González Menendez

Over the past decade, athlete mental health awareness has substantially increased for various reasons. First, broader societal understanding and acceptance of mental health has improved, and stigmas have decreased. Similarly, there has been a greater awareness in the sports world of mental health's impact on athletes' well-being and its influence on performance. This chapter will demonstrate that mental health and mental performance are intricately connected, and in many cases, cannot be effectively addressed in isolation. It will also explore mental health policies, best practices, and standards established by major sports organizations, including the National Collegiate Athletic Association (NCAA), the National Football League (NFL), and the International Society of Sport Psychology (ISSP). Additionally, it will examine medical versus societal perspectives on mental health while incorporating diverse cultural and professional perspectives. Finally, the chapter will also discuss how mental health interventions extend beyond the individual to encompass a broader, team-based approach. It is worth highlighting that this chapter offers a global perspective by drawing on the expertise of two professionals from different cultural and national contexts—the United States and Mexico.

DOI: 10.4324/9781003781479-6

Medical vs. Social Perspective

There are several mental health frameworks and perspectives, each with various points of emphasis and contributing factors. Within a medical framework, mental health is viewed on a similar continuum as physical health, from optimal to injury/illness. A medical perspective usually focuses on clinical issues or diagnosable mental disorders according to the Diagnostic and Statistical Manual of Mental Disorders (DSM-5; American Psychiatric Association, 2013). Common clinical issues in sport include anxiety, depression, substance issues, eating disorders, trauma, and attention deficit hyperactivity disorder. These clinical issues are best treated with therapy and sometimes psychotropic medication. In severe cases, mental health crises can occur (e.g. harm to self/others, psychosis), which require intensive intervention (e.g. inpatient hospitalization). Thus, it is important to have licensed mental health providers to properly assess, treat, and refer for clinical mental health issues. Many athletes do not meet the criteria for clinical issues but have mental health concerns that are subclinical, such as family/relationship issues, identity exploration, life decision-making, and life/sport transition.

From a social perspective, people who seek mental health services are not necessarily looking for a diagnosis or do not have a clinical issue. Rather, they seek mental health services and therapy to be heard by a professional who is unbiased, empathetic, and knowledgeable. These licensed professionals might have different theoretical approaches toward therapy, such as humanistic, cognitive behavioral, and third-wave among others. The aim is to work collaboratively toward personal or performance improvement while preserving psychological well-being, which encompasses six core dimensions: positive relationships, a sense of purpose, autonomy, environmental mastery, personal growth, and self-acceptance (Ryff, 2014). Athletes do not need to be experiencing a mental health or performance issue to benefit from counseling. For example, many athletes use therapy for leadership development and to work on areas such as communication and relationship skills. Many mental health professionals work with athletes (collectively or individually) throughout the season and support mental health and wellness in various ways (such as psycho-education, prevention, mental skills training, and player development).

Mental Health and Performance

Mental health and mental performance are not mutually exclusive domains. Mental health can significantly influence athletic performance, and conversely, athletic performance can affect an athlete's mental health. For example, an athlete sustains a career ending injury during the Olympic Games and, as a result, experiences grief and depression. Or, a professional athlete has a performance decline resulting in the loss of his starting position, which triggers a subsequent substance use issue. There is substantial overlap between mental health and mental performance concerns, and distinguishing between the two can often be challenging. Also, performance issues can be early indicators or the only sign of an underlying mental health concern. Therefore, integrating a mental health perspective when addressing performance concerns can be extremely valuable.

Team Approach to Mental Health and Wellness

In high-performance sports, the "team around the team" is just as critical as the athletes themselves. Coaches and other staff members play an important role in optimizing mental health for their athletes. First, sport psychology professionals can utilize an interdisciplinary approach to mental health and collaborate with other relevant staff members (e.g. athletic trainers, dietitians, strength coaches, etc.). For instance, in the treatment of eating disorders and disordered eating, it is essential for licensed mental health professionals to collaborate with the team dietitian and the team physician to ensure comprehensive care for the athlete. In addition to athlete mental health, coaches and other staff members may struggle with mental health concerns. For example, coaches can experience anxiety symptoms and insomnia due to job instability, long work hours, and lack of feedback within results-driven sport leagues. Finally, the overall mental well-being of a team or organization can be affected by a critical incident, such as a death of a teammate, in-game cardiac arrest, or community traumatic events. Thus, in addition to the mental health of individuals, it is important for sport psychology professionals to consider the mental wellness of their organizations and provide systemic approaches, such as creating psychological safety within the team culture by collaborating with team leaders/coaches.

Sports Organizations Recognition of Mental Health

Given the recent recognition that psychological well-being plays a pivotal role in performance and development, many sports-governing bodies have emphasized the importance of mental health in the sports population. For example, in 2014, the NCAA published *Mind, Body, and Sport* (Brown, 2014), which includes student-athlete mental health best practices for universities and athletic departments. In 2019, the NFL-NFLPA Collective Bargaining Agreement required every NFL club to have a licensed mental health provider integrated into their organizations. And, in 2017, the ISSP Position Stand on "Athletes' Mental Health, Performance, and Development" highlighted a diverse range of mental health experiences among athletes from around the world. Schinke et al. (2017) emphasized that mental health and sport performance exist on a continuum, with athletes fluctuating between states of mental well-being, the presence of subclinical symptoms, and diagnosable clinical disorders. These fluctuations can be a result of multiple factors, including overtraining and injury, culture and training environments, and career development stressors. The ISSP model provides a comprehensive framework that enables practitioners to assess and align interventions with an athlete's current psychological and performance states, while also understanding the athlete from a holistic ecological perspective. These best practices and standards reinforce the critical need for qualified mental health professionals who are culturally competent in sport and understand the life/demands of a performer.

Mental Health Education and Licensure

Given the requirements for licensed mental health in sport and the need to effectively support athletes navigating mental health challenges, sport psychology professionals ideally possess both counseling and mental performance training. Training and education in both mental health and mental performance provide a holistic approach which supports both the individual and the performer. Counseling training provides critical skills when working with an athlete in a one-on-one setting, such as rapport-building, active listening, egalitarian approach, multicultural competence, ethical knowledge, and assessment (especially risk assessment). Additionally, mental health education supports accurate differentiation between clinical disorders, subclinical symptoms, and performance-related concerns, thereby enhancing the professional's ability to provide appropriate care.

Mental health training and educational requirements may differ based upon your country, state, or province. For example, in order to work in the mental health field in the United States, sport psychology professionals must be licensed as a mental health provider at a master's or doctoral level. A sport psychologist is a professional who has a doctoral-level mental health license and is trained or certified in mental performance. In Mexico, a licensed psychologist has completed a four-year degree entirely in psychology along with approximately 980 hours of social work and 420 hours of professional field work, both supervised. Then, the licensed psychologist pursues a sport psychology specialization through his or her graduate studies.

Summary

Overall, mental performance and mental health undeniably coexist and cannot be treated independently when it comes to youth or elite sport. Mental performance and mental health are evolving together in the world of sport. Both have been decreasing the stigma of their presence in the lives of those involved in the competitive sports realm.

MENTAL HEALTH AND PERFORMANCE OPTIMIZATION IN SPORT PSYCHOLOGY

Bradley Donohue & Kristin Brooks

Mental Health and Sport Performance Optimization Theory

The strong positive relationship between mental health and sport performance is now widely recognized (Donohue & Phrathep, 2021), and athletes are increasingly being educated in these processes through many sport-specific mental awareness programs (Breslin et al., 2017). In treating athletes who have been formally assessed for mental health disorders, clinical trials funded by the U.S. National Institutes of Health show The Optimum Performance Program in Sports (TOPPS) consistently improves sport performance and decreases psychiatric symptom severity (see toppscience.com for a review of these studies). While there are a number of theories linking mental performance to health, according to Performance Optimization Theory (Donohue et al., 2018), positive outcomes associated with mental health and sport performance are influenced by optimal thoughts, perceptions, behaviors, and feelings, which, in turn, permit stressors to be effectively managed. Although impactful, feelings are visceral and thus relatively uncontrollable. Therefore, efforts to optimize mental health and sport performance are focused on helping athletes improve their cognitive (i.e., thoughts, perceptions) and behavioral skills along a continuum from nonoptimal to optimal. In this regard, optimal performance is theorized to occur when athletes think, do and perceive the best they can with their available skills and resources given environmental demands.

Therapeutic Style of Mental Health and Sport Performance Providers

Consistent with performance optimization theory, providers working to optimize mental health and sport performance in athletes should emphasize positive feedback and encouragement, ignore undesired behaviors, empathize with expressed concerns, and passionately and descriptively praise thoughts, perceptions and actions of athletes reported to occur during performance situations. Whenever possible, optimum thoughts, actions, and perceptions (TAPS) should be attributed to their character and personal values. Humor, modeling, behavioral rehearsal, and imagery can be used to teach skill acquisition, and providers can use non-stigmatizing nomenclature (e.g., "performance programming" instead of "treatment plan").

Mental Health and Sport Performance Interventions

TOPPS (Donohue et al., 2018) involves 12 performance meetings of 60–90 minutes duration, with meeting frequency and duration fading out across time. The program is relevant to athletes in all sports. Protocol checklists are used to guide intervention implementation, and these guides include intervention rationales, implementation procedures, handouts, and worksheets (Donohue & Perry, 2022).

TOPPS interventions focus on the optimization of TAPS that occur in performance situations, both in sport and life outside of sport, which helps athletes balance sport and mental health goals. Athletes determine personal goals and practice scenarios. Role-playing is used to assist skill acquisition, and assignments are prescribed. The participation of supportive others is encouraged to help athletes attend meetings, share insights, develop goals, model skills, and assist with therapeutic assignments. Athletes choose which supportive others to involve in each performance meeting (e.g., family, coaches, teammates, partners). Meetings usually occur in outpatient centers or sport facilities, and are customarily decorated in motivational posters, team paraphernalia, game schedules, and pictures of athletes. The following intervention components of TOPPS are prioritized by the athlete/performer, and implemented sequentially and cumulatively.

Performance Optimization Exercise

Providers initiate each TOPPS meeting with an exercise to assist optimum mindset in a past or upcoming performance scenario, alternating between sport and life outside of sports to effectively address both sport performance and mental health. Optimum TAPS for the respective scenario are generated, and providers model and instruct athletes to practice these statements sequentially and aloud in the simulated scenario while the provider assists athletes with their timing, intensity/passion, and content.

Dynamic Goals

Athletes are encouraged to optimize their TAPS in performance situations that occur across five domains (i.e., relationships, mental strength and stability, sports and physical health, creativity, work and/or school). They disclose their perceived optimal TAPS, and are descriptively praised for their efforts and gently challenged to retrospectively indicate how their TAPS could have been optimized further if desired. In this way, important life domains are balanced in the extent to which they are reviewed.

Cultural Interview

The validated Semi-Structured Interview for Consideration of Sport Culture Scale (see Donohue et al., 2020) is recommended to assess positive and negative experiences with sport culture. Participants are prompted to choose if it would be helpful to discuss sport culture, and if so, semi-structured interviews are utilized to prompt questions about the participants' experiences with sport culture, disclose cultural commonalities, and provide opportunities to empathize with difficult experiences.

Goal Inspiration

To enhance motivation for goal achievement, athletes are prompted to review positive consequences for goal achievement with providers. Athletes are also asked to rank word categories that are generally perceived to be motivating when athletes say these words to themselves, or others say these words to them. For instance, one category is spiritual (e.g., "God's shining on me") and another category is aggressive (e.g., "I'm going to dominate"). Once determined, athletes and their supportive others are taught to use these words in performance situations.

Communication Skills Training

Athletes and their supportive others exchange statements of appreciation with one another, and when disagreements are experienced, they are instructed to assertively and respectfully initiate positive requests following specified guidelines (i.e., request a specific action, report why the action would be appreciated, offer to return the favor). When upset is encountered, athletes are taught to use HEARD (i.e., Hear what the person is saying, Empathize with the person's concerns, Ask what could be done to solve the problem, Review the pros and cons for each of the generated solutions, ask the person what Decision will be made).

Career Development

Athletes brainstorm career options to determine a "dream job." Supportive others assist athletes in generating positive consequences that would occur if their dream job was accomplished, achieving their dream job, and reviewing potential dream job experiences to build excitement.

Job-Getting Skills Training

Athletes are taught interviewing skills and methods of obtaining job interviews using networking skills. Supportive others assist skill development specific to networking and interviewing.

Financial Management

Athletes determine their current and anticipated income and desired lifestyle. Standardized prompts from worksheets and advice from supportive others assist athletes in the improvement of income and decreasing expenses.

Environmental Control

People, places, activities, and emotions compatible and incompatible with goal attainment are solicited and recorded on a list. During future meetings athletes and their supportive others learn to optimize athletes' thoughts, perceptions, and actions during their time with these stimuli.

Self-Control

Athletes learn to perform a series of mental skills when problems are encountered, including focus statements, diaphragmatic breathing, problem-solving, imagining successful performance of generated solution(s), and imagining reinforcement for solution performance.

Meeting Reviews

At the end of each meeting, athletes review positive aspects of skills practiced during the meeting and which supportive others will be involved in the next meeting.

Concluding Remarks

TOPPS is a theoretically grounded, family-based intervention that comprehensively targets the optimization of thoughts, actions, and perceptions in both sport performance situations, and life outside of sport, through skill development (Donohue et al., 2020). Studies have shown mental health and sport performance are both positively influenced by similar underlying constructs (e.g., relationships, social skills, motivation, creativity, occupational functioning, objective thinking, nutrition, physical activity), which is probably why TOPPS has been successful.

THE PSYCHOLOGIST AS WELFARE OFFICER AT THE OLYMPIC GAMES

Paul Wylleman & Jessica Bartley

Sport psychologists' involvement in preparing athletes and coaches for, and providing on-site support at, the Olympic Games has surged in the past 20 years (e.g., Birrer et al., 2012; Elsborg et al., 2015). The growth of this *in situ* role exponentially increased when more Olympic teams began integrating one or more psychologists in a structural way (e.g., full accreditation, housing in the Olympic village; Wylleman, 2019). The second factor of influence was the impact of the COVID-19 pandemic on athletes' mental and social well-being before the 2020 Tokyo Olympic Games (e.g., social distancing, travel restrictions to competitions, social isolation), rescheduling the Olympic Games to 2021, and the strict health and safety regulations during the Olympic Games itself. The third factor was the International Olympic Committee (IOC) reprioritizing health and safety for athletes (IOC, n.d.), providing support with, among others, the possibility for Olympic delegations to add a "Welfare Officer" (WFO) to their Olympic staff (IOC, 2023, 2024). As the IOC required WFOs to be a nationally licensed/registered mental health practitioner, or an internationally certified safeguarding practitioner, and to adhere to the different requirements it had set (e.g., a focal point of contact for athletes' mental and physical well-being, reporting to the IOC Safeguarding Officers, being present in the Olympic Village opening to closing), the IOC established an accreditation specifically for WFOs. This new accreditation was transformative for psychologists as it fully recognized their function as mental health professionals (rather than previously as medical providers or coaching staff), with full rights to reside in the Olympic village, use Olympic transport, and be present at Olympic training and competition venues.

This chapter illustrates how the team psychologists of Team Belgium (first author) and of Team USA (second author) took up the role of their respective country's Lead WFO at the 2024 Paris Olympic Games and will conclude with recommendations for psychologists who pursue or take on the WFO role.

Team Belgium

Before the Olympic Games

Team Belgium set up an intradisciplinary Welfare Team, led by the WFO. With two more sport psychologists and one Safeguarding Office, we provided on-site performance enhancement as well as (sub-)clinical psychological support to all delegation members (i.e. athletes, coaches, staff members). Three lines of mental health support were set up: first line was the Welfare Team providing on-site support, second line was the 16 sport psychologists at home who worked with athletes and teams in the run up to the Games, and third line was a specialized group of psychologists, therapists, and safeguarding experts on stand-by on the home front. The WFO communicated closely with the Chief Medical Officer and Chef de Mission via weekly meetings headed the special "P5" program (Psychological Preparation and Performance for Paris and Post-Olympic Games) and prepared the Welfare Team to function on-site at Olympic Games. From three weeks before the start of the Olympic Games, the Welfare Team was available at Team Belgium final training camps.

At the Olympic Games

The WFO discussed and prepared with his colleagues daily the provision of on-site specific support services, attended the medical team meetings, and met with the Chef de Mission and Chief Medical Officer to reflect on and formulate recommendations for specific mental health and safeguarding situations. When specifically asked by the Chef de Mission, the WFO also worked directly with athletes and coaches on performance issues. As some athletes (e.g., sailing) resided in Olympic accommodation outside of Paris, we needed to provide support in a decentralized way (live or mostly online). Following up on an earlier international webinar, the WFO organized an informal meeting with fellow sport psychologists from some 30 countries, discussing experiences and practical issues to function as WFO after the first week of the Olympic Games.

After the Olympic Games

The welfare team remained available to all athletes, coaches, and staff for (continued) support during one month after the end of the Games. However, as for most athletes and teams, "after the Olympic Games" was generally 48 hours after their final competition, the welfare team needed to provide the initial steps of post-Olympic support for some athletes already during the first days of the Olympic Games. In view of this post-Games transition, athletes could, after leaving the Olympic Village, reside in Team Belgium accommodation in Paris for a couple of days and, later on, return from home to Paris to participate in the closing ceremony. This provided the welfare team with further possibilities for (brief) consultations. After a debrief with the welfare team, the WFO provided the Chef de Mission with a (self-)evaluation report including recommendations for the functioning of the WFO and the welfare team before, during, and after the next Olympic Games. Finally, the WFO also developed further the concepts of performance behavior, performance health, and performance well-being in view of support provision toward Los Angeles 2028.

Team USA

Before the Olympic Games

Team USA selected three WFOs who were licensed in mental health and credentialed in mental performance. We had another team member who completed the IOC safeguarding course and secured the Safeguarding Officer credential, who was a mental health provider and credentialed in mental performance. All these providers had long-standing relationships with many Team USA athletes, teams, and coaches as well as sports medicine and sports performance providers. Leading into the Games, our providers capitalized on relationships built with Team USA and attended Olympic Trials and other events. We worked closely with our Chief Medical Officer and the lead medical providers of each national governing body to deploy the Sport Mental Health Assessment Tool-1 (SMHAT-1) as a part of our health history in-person when possible or virtually when necessary. We collaborated with our team of 15 providers employed by the United States Olympic & Paralympic Committee (USOPC) and 12 contracted providers in mental health and mental performance. For the entire Team USA delegation, we completed several virtual trainings on how to prepare mentally for the Olympic Games and were educated on mental health resources that would be available to athletes and staff in-country and back home in the United States. We also designed and trained around our Mental Health Emergency Action Plans.

During the Olympic Games

During the Games, we staggered arrivals to greet Team USA athletes and staff. Each morning, our lead WFO attended Games Operations overviews with the Chef de Mission, all WFOs attended sports medicine and sports performance meetings led by the Chief Medical Officer, and we met briefly to discuss our schedules for the day. We rotated in shifts that covered hours between 0600 and midnight. We had a private office space in our Athlete Resource Center in Team USA housing within the Olympic Village—a common space with couches and televisions streaming Olympic competitions and hosting American cuisine. We also spent time at our High-Performance Center—an offsite training facility reserved for Team USA athletes—or various competitions venues. We had one WFO housed in the Olympic Village while other providers were housed at a hotel outside of it. In total, we had eight USOPC providers in Paris and one in Tahiti with surfing as well as nearly 12 contracted providers. These providers documented more than 900 sessions, and we utilized our mental health emergency action plan three times. Our providers also spent time supporting trainings and competitions. We also enjoyed connecting with WFOs from other countries, the IOC, and attending trainings hosted by the IOC.

After the Olympic Games

As the primary mental healthcare providers for Team USA athletes, our services continued after the Games. We also attempted additional outreaches to unengaged Team USA athletes through multiple platforms in individual and groups services. We made other efforts to connect with Team USA athletes as they celebrated their Olympic accomplishments at our nation's capital approximately two months after the conclusion of the Games. We sent our WFOs to this event to provide support and skills sessions around unpacking emotions related to the Olympic experience and decision-making around the next steps in their athletic journeys. WFO were also involved in "PIVOT" programming that was offered to Team USA athletes who were transitioning out of sport.

Conclusion and Recommendations

For sport psychologists to broaden or strengthen their role in mental health and welfare in elite sport, it is recommended that they are nationally licensed mental health practitioners, have long-term applied experience in providing support to athletes, teams, coaches, and staff, as well as have completed specialized training in topics directly related to mental health and well-being. These sport psychologists will find more success when working in interdisciplinary ways with other experts (e.g., coaches, medical personnel, safeguarding officers) and intradisciplinary ways with other mental health experts (e.g., [other] clinical psychologists, neuropsychologists, psychiatrists). Finally, the sport psychologists need to not only focus on providing performance enhancement, but understand and detect subclinical aspects of mental health and welfare.

EDITORS' TAKEAWAYS

We have three very diverse contributions on this topic. I (Lauren) thought it was interesting and helpful to open the chapter with an explanation written by two professionals in different countries at the pro/NGB sport levels and then close the chapter with case studies from two professionals from two different countries. Sandwiched in the middle, Donohue and Brooks provide a great example of an evidence-backed intervention—we need more of these in the field, and we need to continue to share our interventions and their outcomes with each other. I also like that the last contribution makes readers aware of a career path and role that is rarely discussed. As someone who has taken a winding journey into a role I could never have imagined, we all benefit from seeing the varied career paths potentially available to us in addition to the more "traditional" ones. As the field continues to evolve, knowing how to competently and ethically support mental health, mental well-being, and mental performance is key to ensuring we provide the most impactful support to our clients. While these three aspects of being a human are inevitably interrelated, our various career pathways require that we all have a fundamental knowledge about each but then mindfully choose to specialize in supporting people with one or more of these aims.

RECOMMENDED EXERCISES

1. Reflect on the following: Why do you want to become a Sport Psychologist? Do you understand the licensure requirements in your country/state/province? Are you passionate about the training process involved? How do you see your future work contributing to sport and society?
2. Dynamic Goals supports athletes across five life domains (relationships, mental stability, sport/physical health, creativity, and work/school). What benefits might athletes gain by improving performance in multiple domains?
3. TOPPS involves supportive others (coaches, teammates, family) in performance discussions. Why is including these key people important for the athlete's performance and well-being?
4. Even straightforward cases at the Olympic Games tend to be multidimensional. What factors might influence an athlete's emotional state differently at the Olympics compared to other competitions?
5. What knowledge, skills, attitudes, and experience would a Sport Psychologist need to serve effectively as a Welfare Officer in a major club or sport governing body?

REFERENCES

American Psychiatric Association. (2013). *Diagnostic and statistical manual of mental disorders* (5th ed.). https://doi.org/10.1176/appi.books.9780890425596

Birrer, D., Wetzel, J., Schmid, J., & Morgan, G. (2012). Analysis of sport psychology consultancy at three Olympic Games: Facts and figures. *Psychology of Sport and Exercise, 13*(6), 702–710. https://doi.org/10.1016/j.psychsport.2012.04.008

Breslin, G., Shannon, S., Haughey, T., Donnelly, P., & Leavey, G. (2017). A systematic review of interventions to increase awareness of mental health and well-being in athletes, coaches, and officials. *Mental Health and Physical Activity, 13*, 93–101.

Brown, G. T. (Ed). (2014). *Mind, body and sport: Understanding and supporting student-athlete mental wellness.* National Collegiate Athletic Association.

Donohue, B., Gavrilova, E., Danlag, A., Perry, J., Phillips, C., Allen, D. A., & Benning, S. (2020). A comprehensive examination of collegiate athletes' utilization of psychological assessment and intervention services. *Psychology in the Schools, 58*(3), 458–474. https://doi.org/10.1002/pits.22458

Donohue, B., Gavrilova, Y., Galante, M., Gavrilova, E., Loughrana, T., Scott, J., Chow, G., Plant, C., & Allen, D. A. (2018). Controlled evaluation of an optimization approach to mental health and sport performance. *Journal of Clinical Sport Psychology, 12*(2), 234–267. https://doi.org/10.1123/jcsp.2017-0054

Donohue, B., & Perry, J. (2022). *Athlete mental health and performance optimization: The Optimum Performance Program for Sports (TOPPS).* Elsevier.

Donohue, B., & Phrethap, D. (2021). Mental health in sport. In M. Lang (Ed.), *The Routledge handbook of athlete welfare* (pp. 141–152). Routledge.

Elsborg, P., Diment, G. M., & Elbe, A.-M. (2015). Sport psychology consultants' perceptions of their challenges at the London 2012 Olympic Games. *The Sport Psychologist, 29*(2), 183–195. https://doi.org/10.1123/tsp.2013-0105

International Olympic Committee. (n.d.). *Athletes' declaration.* Athlete365. https://www.olympics.com/athlete365/topics/athletes-declaration

International Olympic Committee. (2023, November 3). *Provision of welfare officers and a safe sport hub at the Olympic Games.* https://olympics.com/ioc/safe-sport/provision-welfare-officers-safe-sport-hub-olympic-games

International Olympic Committee. (2024, October 31). *Championing mental health: IOC's blueprint for major sports events.* https://olympics.com/ioc/news/championing-mental-health-ioc-s-blueprint-for-major-sports-events

National Collegiate Athletic Association. (2014). *Mind, body and sport: Understanding and supporting student-athlete mental wellness.* NCAA. https://www.ncaapublications.com

NFL–NFLPA. (2019). *Collective bargaining agreement.* https://nflpaweb.blob.core.windows.net/website/PDFs/CBA/March-15-2020-NFL-NFLPA-Collective-Bargaining-Agreement-Final-Executed-Copy.pdf

Ryff, C. D. (2014). Psychological well-being revisited: Advances in the science and practice of eudaimonia. *Psychotherapy and Psychosomatics, 83*(1), 10–28. https://doi.org/10.1159/000353263

Schinke, R. J., Stambulova, N. B., Si, G., & Moore, Z. (2017). International society of sport psychology position stand: Athletes' mental health, performance, and development. *International Journal of Sport and Exercise Psychology, 16*(6), 622–639. https://doi.org/10.1080/1612197X.2017.1295557

Wylleman, P. (2019). An organizational perspective on applied sport psychology in elite sport. *Psychology of Sport and Exercise, 42*, 89–99. https://doi.org/10.1016/j.psychsport.2019.01.008

Section 2

Career Development in SEPP

6 The Entrepreneur Mindset and Business Skills

What does it mean for an SEPPP to be a business owner? Is that even the mindset people come into the field with? It seems more common or traditional that people use the term "private practice" given the field's origins—part sport science and part psychology. But is private practice an accurate framing for professionals as they delve into the world of, whether part-time or full-time, providing services to clients? By and large our preparation for a career in the field is focused on the "what" and "how" of doing sport psychology, not the bigger picture of making a living from it. As Richard Branson stated, "The entrepreneurial journey is a bit like going into the unknown with no GPS." The aim of this chapter is to provide readers with some tangible insights into navigating the rollercoaster, that is, owning and operating a business through an American, European, and Indian lens.

BUILDING A BUSINESS IN SEPP: THINKING AND ACTING LIKE AN ENTREPRENEUR

Carla Carter, Abby Keenan, & Riley Jensen

Over the past two decades, the field of sport psychology has shifted significantly, creating more diverse career opportunities. In their comprehensive review, Vosloo and colleagues (2020) found that while universities once provided the most viable and widely available career path, academic appointments in North America now represent less than a third of all employment settings in the field. In contrast, applied practice has expanded significantly, particularly within military and private practice sectors, reflecting the growing demand for mental performance expertise in diverse, real-world settings. This underscores the need for developing an entrepreneurial mindset and skill set in addition to their applied sport psychology knowledge and skills in order to successfully navigate and capitalize on the evolving job market.

What is Entrepreneurship?

Entrepreneurship involves recognizing opportunities to evaluate, commit to, and create new value for the benefit of your defined stakeholders, and includes (Hindle, 2015):

- **Entrepreneurial opportunities:** Recognizing where new knowledge and innovative processes can be brought together to create new value.
- **New knowledge:** Innovative ideas, insights, or information that allows you to differentiate yourself and your offerings from others in the field.

DOI: 10.4324/9781003781479-8

- **Innovative process:** A systematic approach used to define, refine, and implement new ideas, products, services, and business models involving creativity, experimentation, and problem solving to meet the needs of your stakeholder in novel ways.
- **New value:** Benefits or improvements that are created by taking new knowledge and applying an innovative process.
- **Defined stakeholders:** Anyone who is involved in or has a stake or interest in your business or is affected by the course of action being taken. This may include customers, employees, investors, or the broader community.

As you might imagine, becoming an entrepreneur in the sport psychology field appeals to some, but not all. While there is a lot to gain from starting your own practice, there is inherently risk and uncertainty involved, which require certain mindsets and skills to endure and excel.

Embracing Fundamental Mindsets

The mindsets, beliefs, and attitudes that you embrace as a mental performance entrepreneur will have a direct impact on your success, or lack thereof. Friedrich Nietzsche (1878, p. 105) once said, "Our vanity, our self-love, promotes the cult of the genius... To call someone 'divine' means: Here there is no need to compete." The idea of "genius" often holds us back from our potential. To be a successful entrepreneur, you don't need genius, but you do need effort, work ethic, and to embrace fundamental entrepreneurial mindsets, including:

- **Kaizen,** which is Japanese for "change for the better." This emphasizes the belief in ongoing learning, incremental progress, and commitment to quality, which can be facilitated through a growth mindset.
- **Being purpose-driven,** or knowing and utilizing your why, your values, and your mission as your unique compass within your business, whether you're setting the direction or bouncing back from setbacks.
- **Openness to opportunity,** or the optimism and energy to create new offerings that add value, which may include flexibility and healthy risks.
- **Centering your customer,** or deeply understanding your stakeholders and ideal client so that you keep them in mind as you make decisions, develop services and products, and continue to learn, helping them to benefit in the end.
- **Collaboration over competition,** or the idea that we are better when we build relationships and work together; we don't have to do business alone.
- **The significance of self-care,** or prioritizing and personalizing health and wellness activities in order to practice what we preach, prevent burnout, and create sustainability.

The mindsets you hold impact what you do, and those actions can affect you and your business. By embracing and practicing these mindsets, you'll better position yourself to act in ways that facilitate growth and success throughout your journey as an entrepreneur.

Building Consulting and Entrepreneurial Skills

To embody kaizen as an entrepreneur, you can prioritize building skills to support yourself and your business, namely, consulting skills and entrepreneurial skills. While it might seem like common sense, it is not always common practice for mental performance consultants to work to continuously improve their craft. Following our initial education and training, when we choose to engage in ongoing professional development, consult with colleagues and mentors, and practice and apply what we learn, not only do we get better professionally (and personally), but so do our clients or stakeholders (Tashman & Keenan, 2022). Continually upskilling in these ways allows us to do good work based on what we know right now, knowing that there is always space to learn more. In turn, when we are able to provide high-quality support to our clients and execute with excellence on service delivery or products, that's when we make a positive impact on people, and that is when people start talking. These are called "word of mouth" referrals, where your current and former clients market your services for you by telling others about how much you have helped them. These referrals significantly impact your ability to grow your business and make it sustainable. Entrepreneurs in our field often improve consulting skills by:

- Enhancing their knowledge and skills related to the Job Task Analysis for Certified Mental Performance Consultants (Association for Applied Sport Psychology, 2025),
- Developing a niche (Blann et al., 2011), or specialized expertise where they become known for a particular problem they solve, and
- Determining or refining their model of performance excellence (Aoyagi et al., 2018), and/or innovating their process to support clients from assessment to evaluation.

Each of us come into entrepreneurship with a different level and set of skills that we can apply to our business, all of which with opportunities for continued growth. As such, Pennetta and colleagues (2023) proposed the Entrepreneurial Skill Map, which includes four main categories of skills. We've adapted this map below for the purposes of an entrepreneur in sport, exercise, and performance psychology (SEPP) (Figure 6.1):

What's Next?

As you continue to learn more about entrepreneurship in our field, we invite you to reflect on whether or not this career pathway is right for you. Here are a few suggestions, resources, and ideas that might help you to actively engage in growth and learning in the entrepreneurial space:

- Join the *Business Ownership Special Interest Group* if you are a member of the Association for Applied Sport Psychology (AASP). Contact the coordinator, attend virtual meetings, and engage with other aspiring and current entrepreneurs.
- Download *the Explore guide* from Project E, which is a free resource and reflection guide to help you consider the entrepreneurial path within the field.
- Research mental performance entrepreneurs in your area and note what helps them to stand out or makes them unique.
- Seek out various workshops and training opportunities that are business-focused.

Much like how we support athletes and other performers, building entrepreneurial mindsets and skills is a marathon, not a sprint, and it's important to remember that if you choose this pathway, you're not alone on the journey.

Core Entrepreneurial *Skills that distinguish entrepreneurship from other managerial roles*	**Managerial** *Skills for management and administration of a business*
Innovativeness Risk-taking Developing Executing Inner discipline Change-orientation Perseverance Resilience	Planning & Organizing Decision Making Problem Solving Motivation Leadership Collaborating Marketing Sales Bookkeeping Time Management
SEPP Service Delivery Product Design Client & Stakeholder Communication Ethical & Legal Considerations Cultural Competence & Multicultural Humility Technology	Self-Awareness Accountability Emotional Agility Creativity Empathy Integrity Communication Reflective Practice Self-Care
Technical *Industry-specific skills that are essential for service delivery and product development*	**Personal** *Individual skills that allow for sensitivity within environments where the business operates*

Figure 6.1 The entrepreneurial skill map

Source: Adapted from Pennetta et al. (2023)

SEPP PRACTITIONER DEVELOPMENT OF ENTREPRENEUR MINDSET AND BUSINESS SKILLS

Michala Bednáriková, Sanja Vrančić, & Maximilian Richert

Securing positions in SEPP often means creating them. Herein lies the challenge for emerging SEPP practitioners, as such pursuits demand skills, which were either not cultivated during our academic training or were cultivated for entirely different purposes. In the following chapter, we will discuss what those skills are and how to use them for building our dream jobs.

Transferability of Skills to Build a Business/Private Practice

Initially, one might assume that as psychology or sport psychology graduates, we lack business skills. Nonetheless, we contend that while we might indeed be deficient in certain areas, many of the skills essential for becoming proficient practitioners are transferable and applicable to establishing our private practices. Among such skills we can count communication, networking, teamwork, and organizational skills, which as graduates of SEPP, we could expect to have developed well. When building a business, we need communication for creating good first impressions, effectively analyzing needs, negotiating finances, delivering our services, as well as maintaining long-term relationships with our clients. Networking is something that comes naturally with communication. Our first professional contacts will be the ones we have from our academic training and university studies. We add on to them by creating new ones via attending conferences, workshops, and many other events in the world of sport psychology. Good international opportunities in Europe include the annual conferences of the European Network of Young Specialists in Sport Psychology (www.enyssp.com) and bi-annual Congress of the European Federation of Sport Psychology (www.fepsac.com).

Another quality we surely possess from our college years is teamwork. There we had to do a lot of group work, which aligns well with the demands of practicing sport psychology, as we regularly find ourselves collaborating with coaches, parents and other members of our athlete's teams. The practical aspect of building and running a business entails organizing our time, setting up pricing structures, and managing business costs, yet having a colleague or supervisor willing to share their best practices can significantly ease this process. Project management might not look like a skill that we have developed; however, we are experienced with running research and that is kind of a project too. Using a calendar app or a physical planner can be highly beneficial for planning and managing time effectively.

New and Challenging Skills

Maybe the most challenging part of building a business is financial management. When starting a business, the income fluctuates, and we cannot foresee how much money we will earn each month. It would be beneficial to keep track of our financial balance, so we can see how much money we are spending, what exactly we are spending it on, and how we can cut unnecessary costs. In the beginning, it is normal to spend more than you earn, but with a steady influx of clients, it will be balanced out after some time.

As SEPP professionals, we might be missing some basic economic education, which these days is easily accessible online. It is important to note that we should consider if we need to develop certain skills to run our private practice or outsource to a professional. For example, we need to create our website, but it might be more efficient to pay for its development rather than learning to develop it ourselves.

Marketing Your Own Business

Building a practice entails acquiring clients, who, if satisfied with our services, will refer others over time. However, before this occurs, self-promotion is necessary. This may not come naturally to many, and ethical boundaries must be maintained, hence a preferable alternative for some practitioners could be brand-building through networking. If you are just starting your business, gathering clients is your number one priority. In today's world, social media and online presence is very important. Scott (2020) highlights that your internet identity is defined by the content you create and share. Marketing is not something everyone is cut out for and comfortable with, but in today's world it is becoming a vital skill.

The most common way to build your brand is via social media; but there is a lot of work and time needed. You will need to remain consistently engaged, ready to showcase both your work and yourself, while being highly creative with your content. Your clients can be a valuable resource too, if they are comfortable with it and give their consent to talk about your work with them. However, this approach can be incredibly time-consuming, as social media evolves rapidly; what works today might fail completely tomorrow. That is why it is essential to stay up to date with current trends when using this type of marketing, while also managing the time spent on social media, as excessive use can be an unhealthy habit with its drawbacks (e.g. Ulvi et al., 2022). Additionally, you must be cautious about the risks associated with sharing your personal life and business openly on the internet.

Social-Emotional Skills for the Entrepreneur Mindset

Emotional intelligence plays a critical role in personal and professional development. Goleman et al. (2013) offered a framework for cultivating skills; these can be particularly valuable for SEPP practitioners navigating their dual roles as professionals and business owners. They have defined four domains that include 12 competencies in their model of leadership competencies (see Table 6.1). According to this model, everything begins with strong self-awareness, as it is only through this foundation that we can regulate our emotions and build social awareness. From there, we can develop the competencies in the final domain—relationship management. Relationship management as one can see is both the ultimate goal of our applied practice, as well as a useful tool for building up our business.

Although developing so many competencies might seem overwhelming, we are confident that both novice and experienced practitioners already possess many of these skills, which have been cultivated through their education and further enhanced by their experiences. However, recent graduates often feel not ready for the job (Tod, 2007). From our experience, novice practitioners frequently feel as though they haven't learned enough, leading to low self-confidence and an underestimation of their own knowledge and competencies. While it is natural to wish we were more prepared than we feel at the start, the truth is that this feeling can only be overcome by simply taking action. Is that not what we encourage our clients to do? Moreover, it is often an inaccurate self-assessment rather than reality. For this reason, we should engage in (peer) supervision to help align our perceptions with a secondary reflection.

Finally, it is important to develop adaptability and stay persistent in one's own professional journey. Working in the sport psychology field can be challenging, due to unusual working hours, variable income, complicated organizational structures, or short-term contracts. Engaging in self-care, reflecting about our "why", speaking to a therapist, or seeking peer supervision can be useful techniques to navigate the professional challenges that come with carving your niche and creating your career path in the field of SEPP.

Closing

You likely already possess many of the skills and competencies needed to develop your business, even if you were not aware of them before. We hope that by now, you feel at least a bit

Table 6.1 Leadership Competencies

	Self	*Social*
Recognition	Self-awareness	Social awareness
	Emotional self-awareness	Empathy
	Accurate self-assessment	Organizational awareness
	Self-confidence	Service orientation
Regulation	Self-management	Relationship management
	Self-control	Inspirational leadership
	Transparency	Developing others
	Adaptability	Influence
	Achievement drive	Change catalyst
	Initiative	Conflict management
		Building bonds
		Team & collaboration

Source: Goleman et al. (2013).

more confident, which means you have begun to develop an entrepreneurial mindset. We are convinced that in navigating the limited and time-consuming opportunities in the field, it is also crucial for graduates in SEPP to remain flexible and maintain a broad perspective on the job market. Considering alternative job fields can be an effective step to gain relevant applied experience and strengthen your ability to provide holistic support. A diverse employment history can also create more network opportunities and allow SEPP practitioners to develop a professional philosophy that is driven from multiple helping professions.

NAVIGATING ETHICS, VALUES, AND PRINCIPLES: THE BALANCING ACT FOR SPORT PSYCHOLOGIST ENTREPRENEURS IN INDIA

Keerthana Swaminathan & Varadayini Gorhe

In India's early days of sport psychology, public awareness and understanding of the field were minimal. The concept of the mind playing a crucial role in sporting performance was a relatively new and largely unrecognized idea. As entrepreneurs and sport psychologists, our journey began about 12 years ago with the challenge of bridging this significant gap. Our goal was to elevate sport psychology to a recognized and valued component of sporting success across India. From the outset, the business models we envisioned were deeply rooted in the realms of building the right awareness; it was not merely about providing services. There was an urgent need to differentiate between the different factors of sports psychology (e.g., mental well-being, performance psychology) and clinical psychology. Many of our initial efforts were focused on launching educational initiatives, organizing workshops, and creating referral networks. Establishing this educational foundation was essential to cultivating a culture that valued mental well-being as much as physical well-being in sports.

The COVID-19 pandemic marked a crucial turning point in our endeavor. The sudden and widespread emphasis on mental health led to an unprecedented increase in the number of athletes seeking psychological support across all age groups. However, this surge in demand sharply contrasted with the limited availability of qualified sport psychologists. Navigating this demand-supply imbalance required a careful balance between seizing new opportunities and maintaining professional integrity. This period necessitated intense reflection, where our values as sport psychologists were continually weighed against the entrepreneurial urge to expand the business.

Reflecting on this journey, it becomes evident that being an entrepreneur in sports psychology in India involves more than just business acumen. It requires a deep commitment to education, ethical practice, understanding culture, and collaboration. It is about navigating the delicate balance between upholding professional values and responding to market opportunities while continually advocating for the crucial role of mental well-being in sports. This chapter delves into two experiential case studies, offering insights into the multifaceted role of a sport psychologist entrepreneur in a rapidly evolving Indian sport landscape.

The Performance Doctor: A Collaborative Approach to Athlete Well-Being

Collaboration with other sports science specialists became a vital component of my (Keerthana) entrepreneurial journey. In India, there was notable skepticism among sport science professionals regarding the effectiveness of sports psychology. To address this, Dr. Harini Muralidharan, a sports medical doctor, and I focused on building bridges and fostering collaboration, leading to the establishment of the multidisciplinary sport science clinic, "The Performance Doctor."

It's crucial to have like-minded professionals who bring different perspectives but work toward the same vision and mission (Seville, 2016). In our case, Dr. Harini and I shared a common goal: ensuring that athletes have a comprehensive sports science team and support system. This shared vision was not just about offering isolated services, it was about creating a holistic environment where experts could contribute their unique insights to the athlete's overall well-being (Wylleman et al., 2013). Incorporating a multidisciplinary approach in Indian sport psychology presents unique challenges, particularly when introducing the concept to athletes, families, and coaches who may have little to no awareness of what sport psychology entails.

When guiding an athlete and their family through the informed consent process, the first step is education. Many families initially see sport psychology as either unnecessary or something meant only for "problem-solving." I often use relatable examples from their sport to illustrate how mental skills affect performance. For instance, in cricket, I highlight how mental preparation can help a bowler manage pressure in the final over. This practical framing often shifts their perception from skepticism to curiosity. The consent process itself requires patience and clarity. I explain what type of information might be shared with other professionals in the support team and how it benefits the athlete's overall care. Parents often ask, "What exactly will you tell the coach?" or "Will my child's fears or struggles be shared with others?" I address these concerns by emphasizing that only relevant, performance-related information will be communicated—and only with their explicit approval. This conversation is essential in building trust, especially in cultures where mental health discussions are still stigmatized.

Building a multidisciplinary team that understands sport psychology in the Indian context is equally complex. Many professionals in sports medicine, physiotherapy, and nutrition may not have worked with a sport psychologist before or might hold outdated ideas about the field. To address this, I actively seek practitioners who are open to collaboration and willing to understand the role of mental skills in performance. This often means initiating conversations about how psychological strategies can complement their work. For example, I might explain to a physiotherapist how anxiety during rehab can affect muscle tension and recovery, emphasizing the value of integrated care. Facilitating open communication within the team is another critical step. Once consent is obtained, I encourage regular case discussions where each professional contributes insights while aligning on common goals for the athlete. These meetings help minimize conflicts of interest and ensure the athlete's best interests remain central to all decisions. In both educating families and collaborating with professionals, patience, clear communication, and relationship-building are key to ensuring sport psychology is integrated effectively into an athlete's support system.

Reflecting on these experiences, it's clear that ethical dilemmas are an inherent part of the practice, especially in a multidisciplinary setting. However, by adhering to ethical principles, fostering open communication, and always prioritizing the athlete's well-being, these challenges can be effectively managed, allowing for a collaborative approach that truly benefits the athlete.

Mindfirst Perform: Collaborating with Sport Psychologists

When I (Varadayini) started visualizing the concept of setting up MindFirst Performance, I had a simple tagline that was the base of my business: "Mind first, then perform." As soon as I entered the post-education space, I felt the requirement of being supervised and guided. Although I was very lucky to have interned with a sports mental trainer, the depth of supervised practice was, and is still, lacking in India. While I was interning, I realized that my passion was to help sport psychology training be available on the grassroots level, not just for elite athletes.

Starting a business meant that I would have to proactively go visit coaches and academies to develop networks and clients. Signing an informed consent was a challenge. Taking advance payment was also seen as very unusual. It was, and is, still difficult for athletes to travel to a particular "office" for sessions. Storage of confidential documents and protection of intellectual property was, and is, still a debate while collaborating with others—be it academies, associations, support staff, or sometimes even sport psychologists. Navigating through these challenges made me think about the "ethical-entrepreneurial slippery slopes."

When I actively started collaborating with sport psychologists, I met and worked with some very like-minded professionals who had the same passion for sports development. The benefits of collaborating with other sport psychologists ensure we get a better reach, have different approaches toward the same goals and also do meaningful work. Within this collaborative approach, it is also very important to be mindful of the paperwork. Recently, while collaborating with a sport psychology consulting organization, I consulted a legal team to check whether the goals and conditions in the Memorandum of Understanding were in line with my ethical considerations and philosophical assumptions. This was a very helpful experience in my decision-making process even in collaborating with sport psychologists. On the other hand, while hiring neophyte sport psychologists for projects, it was obvious that generational and cultural gaps were emerging. I realized that their expectations, including salaries, are driven by the materialistic world. Bridging the gap between expectations and company goals can be mended by some training before their on-field work starts.

Having experienced challenges directly from the athletes to the systems and organizations as well as working with fellow sport psychologists, I just feel there are so many ways to get entrepreneurship engaged and growing. While financial growth may be a critical factor for a business, I recommend prioritizing the right collaborations to the projects that match your goals.

So How Can We Navigate and Build an Ethical and Value-Based Business?

With our experience in the field for the last 13 years, it is critical to reflect upon the challenges (see Figure 6.2) as well as the way ahead (see Figure 6.3) for young sport psychologists who want to begin their journey as entrepreneurs.

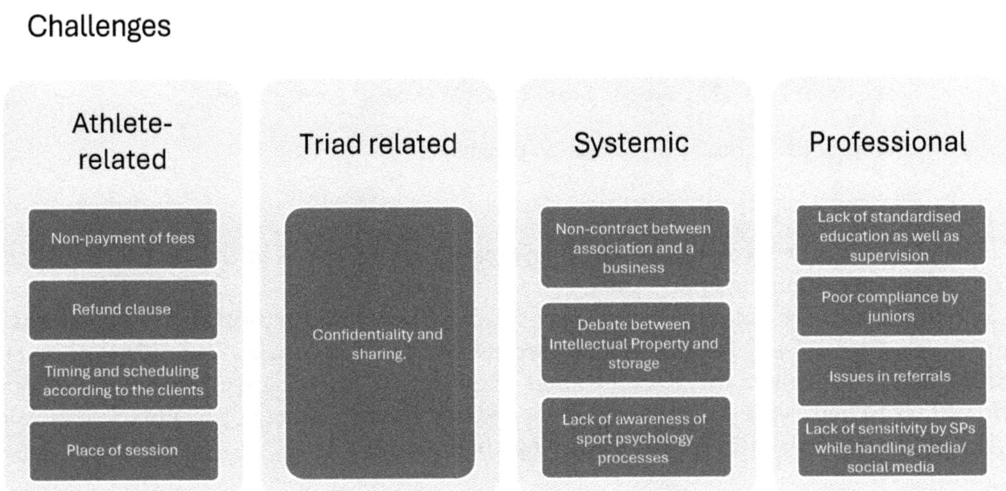

Figure 6.2 Challenges of an SEPP-E

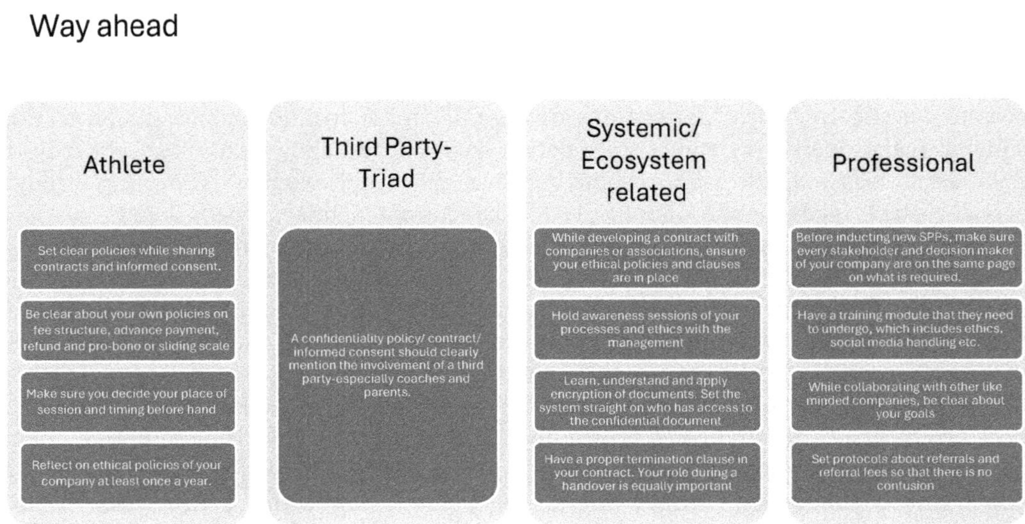

Figure 6.3 Navigating through challenges

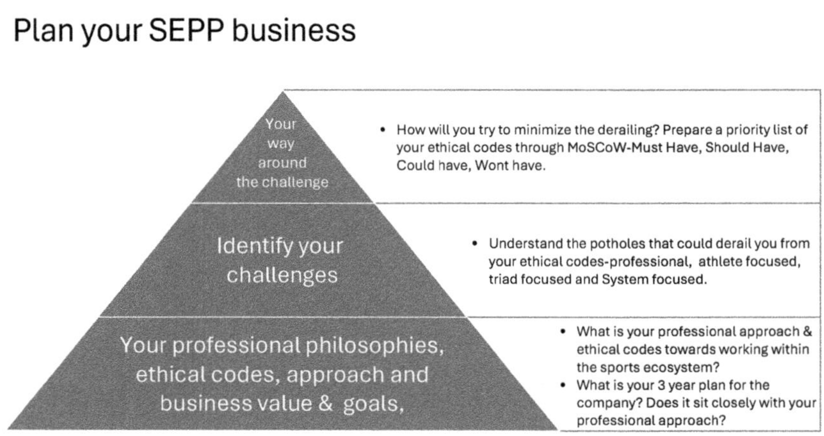

Figure 6.4 Plan your SEPP Business—Reflection pyramid

Apart from this, we would also advise answering the questions in the proposed diagram for SEPP-Es (see Figure 6.4).

In conclusion, we find the term "Sports, Exercise and Performance Psychologist - Entrepreneur (SEPP-E)" relevant because we are not just academicians, scientists, or practitioners. Most of the time, we are everything! The reason is that we are entrepreneurs, people who will try to make sport psychology a business and yet help athletes, sport psychologists as well as students on their journey to becoming champions.

EDITORS' TAKEAWAYS

In just a short amount of pages, this chapter is full of useful and practical material for entrepreneurs or those interested in pursuing entrepreneurship in the field. Across the three contributions, most notable to me (Lauren) are: (a) the discussion of mindsets—thinking about the mindsets needed to be a business owner and entrepreneur has been key for me when I've presented on this topic as well as in my own journey and experiences of owning and operating a business both part-time and full-time in SEPP; (b) the need for developing skills—that have nothing to do with the field!; (c) the idea of personalization—finding your voice, approach, unique value proposition, etc. as an entrepreneur rather than copying or imitating what others are doing or what you find in your textbooks; (d) some of the key challenges you might—or will most certainly—face; and (e) the reflection pyramid—an essential tool for planning your business. Starting a business is the easy part—creating a thriving one and maintaining it over time is the real challenge. Mindset, business skills, and resources are key!

RECOMMENDED EXERCISES

1 Which entrepreneurial mindsets resonated most with you? Which might be more difficult for you to adopt, and why? How could you challenge yourself to strengthen the mindsets that feel less natural?
2 Consider the four categories of entrepreneurial skills in Figure 6.1. Which skills do you already possess, and which do you need to develop? Identify resources that could help you build these new skills. What barriers might you encounter, and how might you work around or overcome them?
3 Choose five values that you live by and create a short company motto that reflects those values. Then, develop a business name and a basic idea for a logo that communicates your message to future clients.
4 Conduct a SWOT analysis (strengths, weaknesses, opportunities, threats) of yourself as an SEPP entrepreneur in your region. Describe two ways you can maximize strengths and opportunities, and two ways you can reduce or work around weaknesses and threats over the next year.
5 Create a checklist to ensure your marketing is ethical—for example, accurate representation of title and services, clear explanation of qualifications, and realistic claims about outcomes. Use the checklist to refine your current or future marketing materials.
6 Identify a sports science professional with whom you could collaborate. Plan a joint session or workshop that combines your areas of expertise and consider how this collaboration could improve athlete development. Consult a legal professional to formalize your business and draft a Memorandum of Understanding to structure the partnership.

REFERENCES

Association for Applied Sport Psychology (AASP). (2025, March 25). *Certification program candidate handbook* (pp. 17–25). https://appliedsportpsych.org/certification/certification-program-candidate-handbook/

Aoyagi, M. W., Cohen, A. B., Poczwardowski, A., Metzler, J. N., & Statler, T. (2018). Models of performance excellence: Four approaches to sport psychology consulting. *Journal of Sport Psychology in Action, 9*(2), 94–110. https://doi.org/10.1080/21520704.2017.1355861

Blann, F. W., Shelley, G., & Gates, S. C. (2011). Marketing sport psychology consulting services. *Journal of Sport Psychology in Action, 2*(1), 33–52. https://doi.org/10.1080/21520704.2011.564719

Goleman, D., Boyatzis, R. E., & McKee, A. (2013). *Primal leadership: Learning to lead with emotional intelligence*. Harvard Business School Press.

Hindle, K. (2015). Entrepreneurship: If you can't define it, you can't do it. *Australasian Biotechnology, 25*(3), 15–16.

Nietzsche, F. (1878). *Human, all too human: A book for free spirits* (R. J. Hollingdale, Trans.). Cambridge University Press. (Original work published 1878)

Pennetta, S., Anglani, F., & Mathews, S. (2023). Navigating through entrepreneurial skills, competencies, and capabilities: A systematic literature review and the development of the entrepreneurial ability model. *Journal of Entrepreneurship in Emerging Economies, 16*(4), 1144–1182. https://doi.org/10.1108/JEEE-09-2022-0257

Scott, M. D. (2020). *The new rules of marketing & PR: How to use content marketing, podcasting, social media, AI, live video, and newsjacking to reach buyers directly*. John Wiley & Sons Inc.

Seville, E. (2016). *Resilient organizations: How to survive, thrive and create opportunities through crisis and change*. Kogan Page Publishers.

Tashman, L. S., & Keenan, A. (2022). The beauty and challenge of the mental performance pathway. In S. Brueckner, A. Chu, & D. Christensen (Eds.), *Directory of graduate programs in applied sport psychology* (13th ed., pp. 22–37). AASP. https://appliedsportpsych.org/publications/graduate-program-directory/

Tod, D. (2007). The long and winding road: Professional development in sport psychology. *The Sport Psychologist, 21*(1), 94–108. https://doi.org/10.1123/tsp.21.1.94

Ulvi, O., Karamehic-Muratovic, A., Baghbanzadeh, M., Bashir, A., Smith, J., & Haque, U. (2022). Social media use and mental health: A global analysis. *Epidemiologia, 3*(1), 11–25. https://doi.org/10.3390/epidemiologia3010002

Vosloo, J., Harenberg, S., Quartiroli, A., Wagstaff, C., & Durand-Bush, N. (2020). Job opportunities and compensation for mental performance work: A comprehensive review (2014–2019) [Conference session]. *AASP 35th Annual Conference, Presented Virtually*.

Wylleman, P., Reints, A., & De Knop, P. (2013). A developmental and holistic perspective on athletic career development. In P. Sotiaradou, V. De Bosscher (Eds.), *Managing high performance sport* (pp. 191–214). Routledge.

7 Careers and the Global Job Market

Circa 2002, Winnipeg, Canada. A spry young Andrew Friesen exclaims to his undergraduate mentor, "I want to be a sport psychologist!" The mentor replies, "That's great...what else do you want to do? Because it'll be a decade before you actually have a sustaining job in sport psychology." This was my introduction to the challenging job market for sport, exercise, and performance psychology professionals. Our jobs did not come advertised in the newspaper classifieds, and nearly every practitioner had the dual role of an academic position to provide the job security needed to work, often for free, with athletes and sport federations. But with the evolution of our field comes the evolution of what our careers and job markets look like. Although the information in this chapter might be the most subject to rapid change, we, as editors, felt it was important to provide a critical, up-to-date snapshot of SEPP careers for early-career professionals.

SPORT, EXERCISE, AND PERFORMANCE PSYCHOLOGY CAREERS AND THE JOB MARKET

Jeffrey Martin

Five years ago, I (Martin, 2019) speculated on whether the profession of sport psychology was an illusion because there were very few full-time jobs available. The purpose of the current chapter section is to revisit the topic of careers in applied sport psychology. I do this by providing an update to my 2019 paper by reviewing the limited research from the last five years.

First, in one study sponsored by the Association of Applied Sport Psychology (AASP), the results from American sport psychology practitioners (SPPs) were summarized in an infographic that was publicly disseminated and a published companion paper (Vosloo et al., 2023). A striking feature were the low sample sizes (i.e., $N = 626$ for the infographic; $N = 333$ for the Vosloo et al.), which while large for a research study, are low in absolute terms for a profession, suggesting that the overall pool of applied SPPs from which research participants were recruited is small. Only 169 respondents (27%) in the infographic data reported that they exclusively engaged in mental performance consulting. For context, that is about 3–4 SPPs per U.S. state and the average state has about 30 college athletic programs across all National Collegiate Athletics Association (NCAA) levels and (National Association of Intercollegiate Athletics (NAIA). Another interesting feature was the reported three median years' experience. This finding suggests that SPPs are leaving the field after a brief career and one potential reason is that it is because they cannot find full-time work. In contrast to the above data, a 2021 survey of athletic trainers had a response rate of 7,593 (NATA salary survey).

DOI: 10.4324/9781003781479-9

While both 169 and 7,593 only reflect those who participated in the research, it is another objective measure showing both the low absolute and relative numbers of applied SPPs compared to athletic training.

A second study involved interviews with 13 American sport psychology graduates and their early work experiences (Wooding et al., 2022). Participants were recruited from a pool of 110 participants from a previous study when participants were graduate students (Fitzpatrick et al., 2016). Participants indicated several challenges including the scarcity of non-academic positions, a lack of applied work job security, the challenge of establishing a private practice, and a sense of aloneness if not in an academic position. In general, for the 13 participants working in the field their views of the job market ranged from pessimistic to optimistic. Optimism was grounded in the perception that there is a recent increase in jobs, particularly in the military and high-level intercollegiate sport. Pessimism was found in an overall lack of positions.

In a third study (Fitzpatrick et al., 2021), 21 recent American Ph.D. graduates reported their work experiences. Thirteen of 21 were working full-time for an organization, 2 were working part-time, and 2 were full-time self-employed. Of the working Ph.D. graduates, 15 of 21 reported that SPP was a primary focus, 4 reported a secondary emphasis, and 1 had no SPP focus. At the masters' level, nine graduates were working full-time, but only three reported that SPP was their primary focus. These findings, while limited to a small sample, suggest that a career involving SPP work is more likely to happen if graduates obtain a Ph.D. It is important to note that 16 of the 19 Ph.D. graduates were employed in universities with 12 of those 16 working in Kinesiology departments, suggesting some (or most) of their work revolved around the triumvirate of research, teaching, and service; not consulting. Four were working in university psychology or consulting positions. Five of the 19 had "applied sport psychology" positions.

A fourth study by Menaker et al. (2023) involved surveying 1,109 athletic department staff directories, based in the USA, for evidence of mental health practitioners (MHP). Less than 12% of the schools employed MHPs and most were in Division I programs as only 19 of 759 Division II and III athletic programs had MHPs. AASP certified mental performance consultants (CMPC) were also noted—across all divisions 48 CMPCs were employed in 1,109 schools. For a comparison, 22 social workers and 20 chaplains/ministers were noted.

In a fifth study, Jones et al. (2022) analyzed 253 staff directories of American Division I university athletic department websites for evidence of mental performance consultants, licensed mental health professionals, and licensed sport psychology professionals. Jones et al. found about a quarter (N = 65) employed 99 professionals who provided mental performance and mental health services. The most frequent terminal degree (n = 71) was a Ph.D., suggesting a master's degree is likely not adequate preparation for careers in these settings. Furthermore, over half (56/99) of the professionals provided both mental health and mental performance services, indicating athletic directors see the most value in professionals who can do both. Jones et al. concluded by noting that 75% of the schools did not have either mental health or mental performance services. Given the value of a Ph.D. and mental health expertise, it would appear that a master's degree (as a terminal degree) studying sport psychology in a Kinesiology department is not the best educational path for a full-time sport psychology position.

Finally in a unique sixth study, a team of researchers analyzed 170 CMPC (2020–2024) graduates from the Midwest, with a particular focus on their websites (Coumbe-Lilley, 2024). The sample was obtained from the AASP "Find a certified mental performance consultant (CMPC)", link on the AASP website. The websites received a grade of C, based on the HubSpot Web grader, with the following results: Only 31% of CMPCs had a website, 26% of

CMPCs had a social media account and 26% had a LinkedIn account. The authors concluded that there was room for significant improvement in the marketing and sales skills of CMPCs. When discussions about the challenging job market in sport psychology arise, aspiring SPPs are often told they will need an entrepreneurial spirit as well as marketing and business skills (see Chapter 6 on *The Entrepreneur Mindset & Business Skills*). Preliminary evidence based on the Coumbe-Lilley (2024) study suggests that most CMPC's are lacking in this regard. Finally, the authors also concluded that "program directors might be wary of pursuing program accreditation because there is no obvious career pathway" (Coumbe-Lilley, 2024, p. 7).

Optimism about the future of full-time applied sport psychology careers is often rooted in anecdotal observations of the increasing number of positions advertised for university athletic departments in the USA. In light of the above sentiment, I next share some relevant news from the NCAA. The NCAA board of governors recently approved the newest Mental Health Best Practices manual. All NCAA schools are required to adhere to it as of August 1st, 2024, with evidence that the best practices are being followed by November 2025 (NCAA, 2024). The Mental Health Best Practices note that licensed providers should evaluate and treat student-athletes. However, such providers can be outside the athletic department (e.g., university counseling) and the university (e.g., local psychologist). In brief, the NCAA doesn't require athletic departments to hire in house mental health or mental performance providers. This means that even athletes at the few schools with SPPs are unlikely to be able to walk down the hall and see them or make an appointment. This contrasts with the many student-athletes who can access athletic trainers or strength and conditioning coaches who are in house and frequently attend practices and games.

In summary, four conclusions warrant emphasis. First, and foremost, research in the last five years is limited and none of it contradicts my 2019 conclusions about limited full-time applied opportunities or suggests significant growth in the last five years. Second, mental health-focused positions in university athletic departments have likely increased and the NCAA mandate is a promising development. However, the job increase is minimal and limited to Division I schools. Third, it appears full-time jobs in college settings are mostly going to licensed Ph.D.s who can provide mental health services and performance enhancement. Fourth, given the above conclusions and in support of Coumbe-Lilley's (2024) assertion, the AASP move to program accreditation appears premature. Prior to AASP's program certification initiative, individuals could become certified. Program accreditation will require department chairs to commit significant, yet scarce, resources to a profession with limited career opportunities. It will be fascinating to see if Kinesiology department chairs and college deans take this route given the financial challenges in higher education (Ambrose & Nietzel, 2023).

THINGS ARE NOT ALWAYS WHAT THEY SEEM: CHALLENGING WHAT A CAREER IN SEPP "SHOULD" LOOK LIKE

Frances Dallas & Danielle Wong Vickland

Sport, exercise, and performance psychology (SEPP) is a dynamic field. Thus, when crafting your career, it may require creativity, experimentation, and discomfort given that pathways to becoming a professional may not always be streamlined or obvious. Starting a career in SEPP will also require you to practice and test your own psychological flexibility. Within this section, we aim to address the assumptions of what a job in SEPP "should" look like. Like any good performance plan, we will also discuss some challenges and considerations for the job application process, and encourage a new way to frame a flexible, yet fulfilling, career.

Taking a Look Back: Traditional Jobs in SEPP

During the mid 2010s, when we, the authors, started our journeys in SEPP in the United States, the assumption was that if one achieved a master's degree, they were either going into applied work via private practice, university athletics, or the military in hopes of ending up in professional or Olympic sport. Another common assumption was that it was up to the individual to find their niche in the applied world because the number of existing positions (e.g., consulting) were so limited. At the time, an interview opportunity for these positions was a rarity out of graduate school, and the establishment of a stable private practice was just as difficult. In summary, the assumption was that you had to be willing to do a lot of work *for free* to build experience, and your resumé, before acquiring a full-time (paid) job.

The most common career choice for those getting a doctorate was a university tenure-track position. In the United States, the emphasis on research during graduate education has been traditionally understood to prepare individuals to be competent in the three pillars of academia: research, education, and service (i.e. research mentorship, supervision, or university committees) (Muthama & Mckenna, 2024). The push was that publishing was the pathway to being a competitive candidate. Other options were to seek a post-doctorate or to piece-meal a string of adjunct faculty positions that cumulatively make full-time work. Although, the latter was not what we thought a career "should" look like during our academic years. However, what if one has a passion for academia but does not gravitate toward tenure life?

Thinking Outside the Box

In today's everchanging culture, climate, and economy, the norm is multiple streams of income. If we can first be open to accepting this possibility, then we can be more expansive in our exploration of all the possibilities this field *now* has to offer regardless of your degree or title(s). Thanks to the professionals in this field who have blazed trails, broken glass ceilings, questioned established assumptions, and found spaces where performance psychology had not previously existed- there are more formal positions than ever. While still competitive, the current U.S. job market allows early career professionals positions in academia, professional sport, collegiate sport, performing arts, extreme sports, government entities, tactical populations, youth sports, community fitness, medicine, and even in corporate businesses (AASP, 2020, 2021; Quartiroli et al., 2022).

The job market in American academia looks drastically different and the landscape continues to evolve. With the expansion and creation of several SEPP graduate programs, teaching-faculty positions and remote positions are alternate routes to consider when it comes to employment. However, it is important to keep in mind that there may be years where several faculty positions are open and other years where there are very few options. Individuals with a master's degree, who have become Association for Applied Sport Psychology Certified Mental Performance Consultants (CMPC), can work in a sport, performance, or exercise settings *or* teach at the undergraduate level and continue involvement in research and mentorship. In other words, there is a need for more applied expertise in the world of academia to adequately prepare the next generation of graduate students.

Individuals with CMPC certifications can obtain positions that are both in the public and private sectors. In the USA, the military is still one of the largest structured employers of consultants (AASP, 2020). Where there once were only a few contracts hiring for the Army, there are now several employers across multiple branches of the military with positions all over the world. In addition to applied positions, the U.S. military also has research contracts for those with a passion for applied research. Major League Baseball and other professional sport organizations have now expanded their sport science departments to employ multi-consultant/clinician teams specializing in developmental programs, minor leagues, injury rehab, and scouting. Some teams are now also offering paid internships to cater toward neophyte consultants. Finally, collegiate athletic departments are now creating positions for consultants and sport psychologists to provide on-site services for universities rather than relying solely on faculty and navigating external contracts (although those do still exist for performance work). Within private practice, individuals may still create their own businesses. Established practices now offer remote employment opportunities for consultants and recent graduates, especially since the COVID-19 pandemic. The ratio of jobs to people seeking employment may always be out of balance, and the application process will always be competitive. However, we now have more pathways in the job market that are constantly growing and evolving than there were a decade ago.

Pitfalls of Limiting Yourself and Considerations When Applying for Jobs

As you continue to create the career you want, be mindful of what it is that you are genuinely interested in and passionate about. The stress of getting a job within the SEPP field can feel discouraging. Half the battle is being the right candidate, at the right time, for the right job, for you. One major pitfall that can be detrimental to your job search can be limiting what you are willing to apply for based on perceptions you have about the job you "think" you want at the start of your SEPP journey. Continue to keep an open mind so as not to limit or inadvertently cancel potential options that may be available in the future. One final pitfall to consider is the belief that the jobs you see now are the *only* opportunities out there. Patience can be difficult; especially when you feel the pressure to have a job right out of school.

When applying for jobs do not sell yourself short! Illustrate how your unique experiences in the field, internship with certain domains, or research you published will directly facilitate your success in the position you are applying for. Selling yourself short also applies to the types of jobs by which you limit yourself. Although many of us dive into this field to work with athletes and performers, consider expanding on your definition of performer. Many positions within human resources or talent development departments in the corporate world are seeking applicants with our knowledge and skill bases (i.e. group cohesion, culture, stress management, leadership, coaching skills, etc.). In addition, many positions require tracking progress to demonstrate return on investment which can then evolve into research opportunities. When applying to these types of positions, your cover letter or interview could create a unique opportunity to educate search committees about how the principles of performance enhancement carry over to corporate team settings. For example, sharing experiences in assisting with the development of a team's culture can highlight your impact on high task cohesion and overall contribution to their success that season. Employers could see that as an engaging opportunity to increase productivity and minimize workplace conflict.

Second, create boundaries. Knowing your mental and physical *willingness* helps you to communicate what is realistic to ensure longevity and prevent burnout. Will the position continue to build your career? Can this be a unique opportunity to expand your repertoire of clientele? Will you get a professional development budget to help you maintain your credentials? If not, are you able to fund necessary requirements to maintain credentials? Can you meaningfully live in the location? Can you do great work remotely? Find the balance between being picky and being open to unexpected learning opportunities. Be willing to expand your horizons but be honest with your practical limitations. What's the quote from the Disney movie "Up"? ... "Adventure is out there!"

Final Thoughts

Your ideal career may evolve over time. We exist in a dynamic field that is rapidly growing and so is the global job market. The job you take now does not have to be your forever job, but it might just be where you need to be for now. In addition, be open to ask for feedback from the jobs that do not offer you a position. It can be discouraging, but there is something to take away from each interview to prepare you for the next. Also, be open to redirecting your focus, changing your plan, or even turning down opportunities you "thought" you wanted (e.g., shifting career goals from academia to applied work or vice versa). It is all a part of building a foundation for a fruitful and fulfilling career. Our careers never stop, and each step is a new opportunity to keep building upon our passions and interests which we might find in roles we never expected or planned for.

PURSUING A PROFESSIONAL PASSION

Thomas W. Gretton, Anna Farello, & Thomas O. Minkler

Passion is a felt experience. It cannot always be orchestrated or planned for, but it can be pursued once it is felt. In this chapter, we share with you what pursuing passion has been like for us and how we have arrived at passion in our early SEPP careers. We aim to portray passion as an achievable and transformative experience that lies ahead of each of us by sharing key stories from our own careers to date, and reflections on central themes from across these stories.

Tommy M's Story: Demystifying Uncertainty Through Connection

I vividly remember laying on a treatment table during my sophomore year of college, recovering from a nearly career-ending knee injury, and questioning everything about myself, from my future as an athlete to my worth as a person. My anguish was palpable to anyone who paid attention, which fortunately included a supportive network of family, friends, and mentors. My first introduction to the sport psychology and counseling spaces was, as it is for many, in the role of the client. I needed help to resolve how deeply dissatisfied I was with my situation and the lack of clarity I had about life. I learned that there were more adaptive and compassionate ways of relating to myself, and the ways in which I learned (and continue to learn) to engage with the world guided me toward the path of serving others, first as a coach and now as a SEPP professional. Uncertainty has characterized much of my professional journey to date, and I used to fear that lack of clarity because I felt insecure and alone in it. The impact that key people have had on my growth is evident in my development in the SEPP space. Finding passion in SEPP, for me, has been more about finding people. The excitement I feel toward my work is largely due to the excitement I feel engaging with people with whom I feel valued. The opportunity to reciprocate those feelings in the pursuit of learning, growing, and understanding is intrinsically motivating. Demystifying and disarming the effect that uncertainty can have has been a key element in my search for professional passion and has presented numerous opportunities which I would have otherwise been unable to recognize.

Anna's Story: Small Moments Lead to Big Passions

An overwhelming but half-expected aroma of curry filled my body with anticipation as we disembarked the plane and walked through the terminal to baggage claim. The Delhi airport seemed a lot like others I had visited, but never had I been in a different country—let alone across the globe—with my master's supervisor and four of her most brilliant colleagues. I tried to mimic the team's confidence and resourcefulness as we endured long customs lines and hailed a taxi, but my wary thoughts belied my actions. Seven days of warm, humid, sunny weather were filled with workshop after workshop with Indian sports coaches. Teaching conflict resolution skills to adults is no small task, not to mention managing group dynamics of both the coaches and our research team. Nonetheless, I observed every workshop, collected data, and led sports activities with stars in my eyes, thinking maybe, just maybe, I am making a small difference in coaches' lives. During that week, it felt like a faceless figure took my hand and led me to the edge of sport psychology, opening another door into the field of sport for development. My growing passion was confirmed when, in a small moment on a bus, one of our team members told me to leave, "If you want to study sport for development, you'll want to go overseas, because the field is stronger in other parts of the world." A year later I found myself in London, earning a terminal degree in sport for development. Advisors and mentors alike offered me incredible opportunities over the years, and saying "yes" to being part of those research teams ultimately confirmed that I was exactly where I needed—and wanted—to be, which was pursuing my passion.

Tom G's Story: Passion through Failure

I was out of ideas. No matter what I did, recruitment for my first PhD study was failing. It was troubling and, after speaking with my advisor, I knew I needed to change something. My PhD depended on resolving this. A week after admitting the need to alter the population being studied, I was in Gainesville, Florida at a Rugby Union referee course. I was missing the sport I once played and thought picking up the whistle may soothe the ongoing absence of identity I felt. This course, however, became a hugely significant moment in my career and not because I became a referee; thankfully. Rather, I had found the perfect population for my PhD research: Rugby Union referees. Under-researched, under-supported, and misunderstood.

Following this referee course, I connected with many referee managers across the globe, one of whom was Alhambra. Alhambra is a high-performance referee manager at World Rugby and, after forming a relationship, she allowed me the chance to interview some of the international Rugby Union referees she worked with for my first PhD study. Not only that, but Alhambra sensed possibility in the research and subsequently invited me to do some work with these referees as a CMPC. My relationship with them blossomed and not long after, I began my PhD dissertation with the same group, collecting data during the 2022 Rugby World Cup in New Zealand. Approximately three years after failing in my first PhD study recruitment, I concluded the data collection phase of my dissertation by sitting with Alhambra on the podium after one of the most dramatic Rugby World Cup finals. We sat silently, overcome with pride in the group and immense gratitude for one another. What started off as a failed recruitment of jiu-jitsu referees resulted in one of the most transformative moments of my life; living the experience of a Rugby World Cup with people I had learned about through research, supported as a CMPC, and come to care deeply for. I found passion through failure.

Nonlinear Path

One salient commonality among our three professional journeys is that each contained its own set of unanticipated and/or fortuitous events that ultimately brought us to SEPP. Our unique, nonlinear trajectories resulted in transformational experiences guided by trusted mentors and experts in the field. A different way to conceptualize our journeys is to analogize it to amateur sculpting. Each of us had a rough plan or foundation for our individual sculptures: helping others through our work. This foundation is akin to choosing marble as our material. The journey thereon consisted of chipping away at our blocks to create work that represented us as individuals and professionals. For Tommy, a career-ending sport injury transformed into a career-starting opportunity in SEPP. Anna's research trip to India led her away from SEPP, only to be brought back into the field by trusted mentors and colleagues. Finally, Tom unexpectedly had to shift his Ph.D. research to a different population, which blossomed into the current thriving relationship he has with World Rugby. Our journeys contained an element of risk in that we were unsure where our decisions combined with happenstance would take us. Perhaps the most intriguing aspect of our nonlinear journeys, however, is that our paths intersected in meaningful ways. In pursuing our own individual passions, we all said "yes" to opportunities where our paths crossed; from these instances, we have found ways to follow our passions, and even generate new, collective ones investigating things such as referee psychological preparation (Gretton et al., 2024), emotionally demanding research experiences (Gretton & Farello, 2024), and person-centered consulting.

Growth-Fostering Relationships

Ryan and Deci (e.g., 2022) have frequently reminded us that satisfaction of the basic psychological need for relatedness with others has a critical impact on human motivation and well-being. In many ways, our collective experiences serve as a case study in support of the essential role of human connection, which has served as the catalyst in our pursuit of finding passion. Just as each of us have journeyed on relatively nonlinear professional paths, another notable commonality in our experiences is that we have been aided by the impact of several important relationships that have been foundational in our trajectory. The exciting aspect of a career that involves graduate education is the fact that, on some level, people have the opportunity to choose with whom they surround themselves. In reflecting on our experiences, we have all felt pulled energetically in certain directions based on how we felt when we were in the presence of specific people. This pull—which is how the three of us came together as work colleagues and friends—has shaped our paths.

Transformational experiences with key people in our professional lives have left us all with a sense of wonder, empowerment, and the belief that engaging with these people may be mutually growth-fostering, using the language of Relational Cultural Theory (RCT; Miller, 1976). In RCT, it is theorized that growth and well-being are supported through meaningful and empathetic relationships that emphasize mutual empowerment and human connection (Miller, 1976). The effect of such empowering and human connections with mentors, colleagues, and friends has been central to our search for passion as SEPP professionals.

Closing

As shown in our stories, we felt, and subsequently now believe, that passion can be found in the pursuit of unique experiences with people who support your journey. Looking back, our paths crossed unexpectedly and while we each hold different areas of focus in our careers, our passion for helping others connects us and guides us toward unexpected, growth-fostering opportunities. Our passion binds us and is our home among ever evolving career trajectories.

FITTING IN AND STANDING OUT: NAVIGATING THE FIELD OF SPORT PSYCHOLOGY IN EUROPE AS A YOUNG PRACTITIONER

Anastasiya Khomutova, Svenja Wachsmuth, & R. Zsanett Bondár

The field of applied sport psychology is popular and fast developing across Europe, yet the standards and expectations of sport psychology services seem to differ from one European country to another, including the legal protection of the "sport psychologist" title, educational opportunities, and the general public's knowledge of what sport psychology may offer. Based on a research project (Khomutova et al., 2022) initiated by FEPSAC (European Federation of Sport Psychology) and ENYSSP (European Network of Young Specialists in Sport Psychology), this chapter discusses the careers of specialists in sport and exercise psychology and recent developments of the European job market. FEPSAC, established in 1969, and ENYSSP, established in 2004, are two key organizations in the field of Sport Psychology in Europe. FEPSAC brings together academics, researchers, and practitioners, with a particular focus on representing national sport psychology federations, while also welcoming individual members at all career stages. ENYSSP is geared especially toward early-career professionals and students, providing support in research, education, and applied practice. Both organizations play an important role in fostering connection, collaboration, and professional development within the sport psychology community (Araújo et al., 2006; Bednárikova et al., 2016; Elbe et al., 2019).

Over the last few years, former and current members of the FEPSAC and ENYSSP management councils have joined forces in a large-scale research project investigating the development pathways and career journeys of European specialists in sport psychology. The project aimed to understand common steppingstones toward becoming a specialist in sport and exercise psychology, strengths and weaknesses of different development pathways, and the perspectives on the future of Sport Psychology in Europe and beyond. The study included specialists in sport and exercise psychology from several European countries, (e.g., Belgium, Estonia, Hungary, Italy, Romania, Slovakia, and others). In this sample, we tried to represent our diverse membership based on geography and gender. We particularly focused on experienced practitioners (i.e., five to ten years; Tod, 2017), who could reflect on their early career with the added perspective of time, yet whose experience was still recent enough considering the many changes our field had been going through over the last decades.

Not surprisingly, we found many aspects that connect the community within Europe (and probably beyond). While the boundary conditions (e.g., study programs, regulations for certification/accreditation, structures of national sport systems and professional bodies) seem vast across European countries, participants in this study shared a substantial number of developmental experiences. The main topic for debate pertained to opportunities of formal education (or a lack of such) in sport psychology. Universities in many European countries did not provide a degree in sport and exercise psychology when our interviewees started their educational journeys, which is still the case in some countries. Instead, many specialists in sport and exercise psychology typically studied psychology or sport science, although some have entered the field with backgrounds in business or teaching. Overall, most participants agreed that their academic studies were worthwhile and covered interesting topics yet rarely delivered immediately relevant and applicable content to their work after graduation. While it was recognized that to "fit into the profession" a basic understanding of theory and research was essential, they emphasized the need for more business-related knowledge (e.g., starting a business, ethical marketing) and an improved development of professional competencies (e.g., psychological coaching skills, self-care). Though it can be argued that the development of such competencies should form part of a postgraduate program, such sport psychology training or certification routes were not accessible everywhere in Europe. However, even where such training and formal education was available, its content and quality differed substantially across countries (e.g., differences in practice and supervision hours, submissions), and did not always fit the requirements of international certifications, for instance, the European certification for Specialists in Applied Sport Psychology offered by FEPSAC.

Several participants went through the EMSEP program (European Masters in Sport and Exercise Psychology) which was delivered between 2009 and 2016. This is a prominent international master's program within the European context (Papaioannou et al., 2017), which followed in the footsteps of the European Master in Exercise and Sport Psychology facilitated by FEPSAC and starting in 1996 (Araújo et al., 2006). All of the EMSEP-graduate respondents praised its academic foundation and emphasized the significance of the intercultural experiences that the program allowed them to gain. These results confirm the previous study of the EMSEP graduates (Lintunen et al., 2009; Papaioannou et al., 2017).

Turning to the informal development experiences and related career journeys, the study's participants occupied a variety of roles and jobs during their career, often simultaneously. Only a few of the interviewed practitioners worked as full-time employees within sports or could cover their living expenses by "only doing sport psychology," many of them held one or several positions in, for example, other performance areas, academia, psychotherapy, or business consultancy. While this was perceived as challenging and required sound self-regulation strategies, the different experiences also complemented each other and contributed to individual's professional development. These experiences helped practitioners to define their working philosophies, value systems, and boundaries, and also exposed them to different types of roles and/or organizations which they considered useful to have in their network. It was especially the more difficult experiences (e.g., severe conflict, power abuse, ignorance toward practitioners) that shaped their willingness to "fit into a system" (e.g., adhere to cultural norms) or readiness to "stand out", for example, by challenging common practices (e.g., leadership styles, performance expectations) or leaving an organization. Significant throughout this process was individuals' commitment to lifelong learning and regular engagement in reflective practice, aspects which were often criticized for not having been addressed sufficiently in professional training. Unsurprisingly, all participants in this project emphasized the importance of gaining sound supervision and/or intravision (peer consultations). What stood out from the interviews though was the role of mentorship and career guidance including and continuing from early career stages—often based on a relationship that provided a "safe space to fail." However, especially the most experienced specialists in sport and exercise psychology in this study spoke about the difficulties related to finding high-quality supervision, peer consultations, or mentorship. They criticized that especially in group sessions, the discussions were based around an attitude of "showing off" (i.e., emphasizing success; "standing out") rather than "showing up" (i.e., reflecting difficulties). Thus, advanced practitioners created exclusive groups for intravision or sought supervision from outside sport to avoid such situations and receive high-quality support from other perspectives (e.g., clinical or organizational psychologists).

Finally, another topic discussed pertained to the market development and future perspectives of the sport and exercise psychology profession. There was a general perception among the study's participants that the market had grown substantially in recent years, meaning there was increased competition and some rivalry among novice and early-career specialists in sport and exercise psychology within a relatively small profession. Consequently, participants felt that the pressure to stand out had intensified, particularly for younger practitioners, sometimes leading to perceptions of unethical marketing and practice (e.g., overpromising and underdelivering; too many clients to handle all of them to highest standards; working "for the coach", etc.). Sport federations and clubs were able to negotiate lower salaries and replace practitioners that "did not fit into their system" (e.g., those who challenged existing attitudes and practices). At the same time, it was also acknowledged that organizations increasingly struggled to identify well-trained specialists in sport and exercise psychology, partly due to varied training routes and qualifications.

Considering the insights gained into European practitioners' career pathways and challenges along the way, ENYSSP and FEPSAC are in a position to help address some of the concerns raised, particularly those linked to creating more equal educational and training opportunities across the continent. Some steps have already been taken on that journey such as the increased provision of online educational and developmental opportunities (e.g., webinars, peer consultations), the SASP-FEPSAC qualification, or stipends for international internships to increase mobility. Outstanding are also those practitioners who took on the challenge of not having resources and formal education readily available. As pioneers in their countries, they created their own way toward a career in sport and exercise psychology—relying on resources in other languages or temporarily moving abroad for their training (and then often translated textbooks or developed educational opportunities to pave the way for the next generation of practitioners). Instead of relying on those individual initiatives though, international organizations could form task groups targeting countries where the basic learning opportunities one needs to embark on a career in sport and exercise psychology are lacking. There is still much scope to grow as a profession, but to do so effectively and ethically, the members of the national and international sport and exercise psychology community must join forces—working toward standing out as an impactful profession.

EDITORS' TAKEAWAYS

I (Andrew) found Martin's overview of the SEPPP job market sobering, but necessary. One limitation I noticed, though, is the heavy emphasis on applied roles, with less focus on teaching and research. In my experience, most of us end up building careers that stretch across all three—practice, teaching, and scholarship. Developing that balance has been both practical and essential, and I think early-career professionals need to hear that more often. Future conversations on career prep should take this "triadic" model more seriously so trainees aren't blindsided by the broader scope of demands and opportunities.

Dallas and Vickland's line really resonated with me: "We exist in a dynamic field that is rapidly growing, and so is the global job market." This field moves so quickly that even a chapter like this may feel outdated within a few years. Early on, I assumed there'd be a neat, clearly advertised role that fit my training—an assumption that led to frustration. What I've since realized, and what Dallas and Vickland highlight, is that creativity and openness to nontraditional paths are critical. Some of the most meaningful opportunities I've had weren't "found", I had to create them.

I often think about this through the metaphor of the journeyman athlete. Unlike the rare star with a multimillion-dollar contract, most athletes grind through semi-pro leagues and short-term deals. When I've asked these athletes what sustains them, the answer is almost always the same: passion. Gretton et al. touch on this, and I think they're right—we don't talk enough about passion in SEPPP graduate training. For me, passion isn't just motivation; it's been a lifeline for career sustainability.

And then there's Khomutova et al.'s point about "showing off." I laughed when I read that—maybe even winced—because it rings true. In a field with limited full-time jobs, competition is inevitable, and sometimes that spills into showboating. I've seen it, and I've felt the pressure myself. It makes me wonder how much the structure of our job market shapes not just the paths we take, but the culture we create.

RECOMMENDED EXERCISES

1. When you picture your ideal career in SEPP, what does it look like and why? What path do you imagine taking to get there? What assumptions have you held about SEPP careers, and how have those perceptions changed over time? What challenges have you faced so far, or do you expect to face?
2. Use the "play the tape forward" exercise, a CBT-based technique commonly used in decision-making. Imagine the short- and long-term consequences of key professional choices—selecting a graduate program, choosing a mentor, accepting a job, or shifting career directions. What might life look like if you make one choice versus another? What would you gain or give up? Does the future you imagine feel meaningful and energizing?
3. As a teacher, supervisor, or mentor, consider what you want students or mentees to take from this chapter. What core message do you want to communicate about pursuing a career in SEPP, and why?
4. Reflect on how you—as either an experienced or early-career practitioner—can help advance the field in ethical and sustainable ways.
5. Identify three qualities that have supported your professional growth so far. Are there qualities that have held you back or ones you want to strengthen to pursue the career you want now and in the future?

REFERENCES

Ambrose, C. M., & Nietzel, N. T. (2023). *Colleges on the brink.* Rowman and Littlefield.

Araújo, D., de Oliveira, R. F., Jannes, C., Carlsson, B., Snauwaert, E., & Sanchez, X. (2006). The origins, current activities and future challenges of the European Network of Young Specialists in Sport Psychology (ENYSSP). In F. Boen, B. de Cuyper, & J. Opdenacker (Eds.), *Current research topics in exercise and sport psychology in Europe* (pp. 115–121). LannooCampus.

Association for Applied Sport Psychology. (2020, May 27). *Compensation report for mental performance work.* https://appliedsportpsych.org/site/assets/files/33107/association_for_applied_sport_psychology_compensation_report_for_mental_performance_work.pdf

Bednáriková, M., Schneider, P., & Więcław, G. (2016). Looking for guidance and support among colleagues: Peer supervision and mentoring in ENYSSP. In J. G. Cremades & L. S. Tashman (Eds.), *Global practices and training in applied sport, exercise, and performance psychology* (pp. 298–306). Routledge.

Elbe, A.-M., Bertollo, M., Debois, N., de Oliveira, R. F., Fritsch, J., Hatzigeorgiadis, A., Moesch, K., Raab, M., Sanchez, X., & Vaisetaite, L. (2019). Preface to the special issue: 50 years of FEPSAC. *Psychology of Sport and Exercise, 42*, 5–7. https://doi.org/10.1016/j.psychsport.2018.09.009.

Fitzpatrick, S. J., Monda, S. J., & Wooding, C. B. (2016). Great expectations: Career planning and training experiences of graduate students in sport and exercise psychology. *Journal of Applied Sport Psychology, 28*(1), 14–27.

Fitzpatrick, S. J., Monda, S. J., & Wooding, C. B. (2021). Career planning and training experiences of early career professionals in sport and performance psychology: A five-year follow-up. *Journal of*

Performance Psychology, 13, 1–18. https://www.nu.edu/wp-content/uploads/2021/02/Journal_of_Performance_Psychology_Issue_13_Final.pdf
Gretton, T. W., & Farello, A. (2024). Emotionally demanding research: A wartime quest or a journey of connection. *Qualitative Report, 29*(9), 2407–2429.
Gretton, T. W., Farello, A., Minkler, T. O., Caya, J., & Eccles, D. W. (2024). Impossible perfection: A storytelling reflection. *Qualitative Inquiry, 30*(7), 607–617.
John-Coumbe-Lilley. (2024, July 25). *Summary report Great Lakes CMPC Web presence analysis 2020–2024* [LinkedIn post]. LinkedIn. https://www.linkedin.com/posts/jec-l_great-lakes-cmpc-2020-2024-web-presence-report-activity-7204436873920860160-Q3XU
Jones, M., Zakrajsek, R., & Eckenrod, M. (2022). Mental performance and mental health services in NCAA DI athletic departments. *Journal for Advancing Sport Psychology in Research, 2*(1), 4–18.
Khomutova, A., Bondár, R. Z., & Wachsmuth, S. (2022, July 11–16). 'I don't feel like I am a sport psychologist yet': Reflections on career trajectories by applied practitioners in Europe [Conference presentation]. 16th FEPSAC Congress, Padova, Italy.
Lintunen, T., Elbe, A.-M., Apitzsch, E., Strengell, A.-M., Alfermann, D., Bakker, F., Boen, F., Cruz, J., Gernigon, C., Johnson, U., Papaioannou, A., Roberts, G., Serpa, S., Stambulova, N., & Stelter, R. (2009). Career and employment survey for the former students of the European Master's Programme in Sport and Exercise Psychology. *Abstract Volume* [Electronic version] to the 12th World Congress of the International Society of Sport Psychology (ISSP), Marrakesch, Marokko.
Martin, J. (2019). Is the profession of sport psychology an illusion? *Kinesiology Review, 9*(2), 92–103.
Menaker, B. E., North, E. H., & Curtis, A. K. (2023). Examining the likelihood of employing mental health, mental performance, and ministry professionals in intercollegiate athletic department staffs. *Journal of Issues in Intercollegiate Athletics, 16*(1), 23–39.
Miller, J. B. (1976). *Toward a new psychology of women.* Beacon Press.
Muthama, E., & McKenna, S. (2024). The whole is greater than the sum of its parts: A case study of the nexuses between teaching, research and service. *Higher Education Research & Development, 43*(1), 211–226. https://doi.org/10.1080/07294360.2023.2215182
National Collegiate Athletic Association (NCAA). (2024). *New NCAA mental health best practices approved for all schools to follow.* https://www.ncaa.org/news/2024/1/10/media-center-new-ncaa-mental-health-best-practices-approved-for-all-schools-to-follow.aspx
NATA. (2021). *NATA salary survey.* https://www.nata.org/sites/default/files/nata_2021_salary_survey_executive_summary.pdf
Papaioannou, A., Krommidas, C., Elbe, A. M., Lintunen, T., Apitzsch, E., Alfermann, D., ... & Serpa, S. (2017). Careers and employability of graduates of the European Master in Sport & Exercise Psychology from 2009 to 2016 [Conference presentation]. 12th World Congress of the International Society of Sport Psychology (ISSP), Marrakesch, Marokko.
Quartiroli, A., Wagstaff, C. R., Hunter, H., & Martin, D. R. (2022). The identity of the sport psychology profession: A multinational perspective. *Psychology of Sport and Exercise, 60*, 102140. https://doi.org/10.1016/j.psychsport.2021.102140
Ryan, R. M., & Deci, E. L. (2022). Self-determination theory. In F. Maggino (Ed.), *Encyclopedia of quality of life and well-being research* (pp. 6229–6235). Springer. https://doi.org/10.1007/978-3-319-69909-7_2630-2
Tod, D., Hutter, R. V., & Eubank, M. (2017). Professional development for sport psychology practice. *Current Opinion in Psychology, 16*, 134–137. https://doi.org/10.1016/j.copsyc.2017.05.014
Vosloo, J., Harenberg, S., Yarnell, A., Blakeslee, V., & Gorden, L. (2023). Sport psychology employment and income data: An update. *Journal of Sport Behavior, 46*(2), 48–54.
Wooding, C. B., Fitzpatrick, S. J., Monda, S. J., & Statler, T. (2022). Transitioning from student to professional: Experiences of recent US graduates in sport and performance psychology. *Journal of Ethnographic & Qualitative Research, 16*(4), 324–343.

8 The "Global Citizen" Professional

Sport, exercise, and performance psychology (SEPP) is a small world yet spans the entire globe. While it is a popular discipline, there are only a few universities throughout the world that offer targeted programs to students interested in SEPP from undergraduate degree to Ph.D. Furthermore, sport at the highest levels (i.e., professional, amateur elite, and Olympic) is extremely competitive, and organizations do not see distance or nationality as a hindrance to hiring exceptional SEPP talent. Consequently, many of us become "global citizens"—professionals who relocate self and family to follow education and employment opportunities. I (Andrew) myself often introduce myself as being "born in Canada, schooled in England, working in the USA." This professional globetrotting is so common we thought it warranted a chapter in our book to sensitize SEPP students to the realities of our profession and provide insight for others in the profession to the experience of being a global citizen in the field—both the opportunities and the challenges. Collectively, our three diverse author groups share their lived experiences of what life is like as a "global citizen" in our discipline.

OVER THE HILLS AND FAR AWAY: NAVIGATING GLOBAL PATHWAYS IN SPORT PSYCHOLOGY RESEARCH, TEACHING, AND APPLIED PRACTICE

Paul Davis, Shameema Yousuf, Nikos Ntoumanis, & Małgorzata Sławińska

Increasing internationalization and integration amplify important issues such as diversity and inclusion that are relevant to sport, exercise, and performance psychology professionals (SEPPPs) both in research and practice as well as personal and professional development. Therefore, we outline a variety of challenges and opportunities for transnational or global citizens, considering international education, professional accreditation, applied consulting, research, and teaching, as well as implications for personal life and well-being. This chapter reflects the lived experiences of the authors and aims to offer diverse perspectives on navigating life as an international SEPPP.

Challenges of Being a "Global Citizen" Sport, Exercise, and Performance Psychology Professional

As a relatively young multidisciplinary subject, sport, exercise, and performance psychology (SEPP) education was historically offered at a limited number of universities; aspiring SEPPPs were often required to search out and travel to established programs in other countries due to a lack of locally available courses. Currently, there is a wider spread of programs and multiple pathways to gain education, yet for many SEPPPs in training the choice to study abroad

DOI: 10.4324/9781003781479-10

continues to raise many issues that warrant consideration. For example, international (i.e., "overseas") tuition fees, changes in government administration that may restrict and withdraw funding, studying in another language, navigating relocation (e.g., visas, travel, living costs), restrictive laws that impede working while a student, gaining recognition of previous experience and transferring credits, as well as integrating into different student-cultures can all present challenges that impact career development.

On completion of education and training, attempts to transfer credentials across borders and gain accreditation with local governing bodies can be an arduous and costly process. Gaining recognition of education by professional associations can be complicated by a variety of factors including the use of protected titles (e.g., "psychologist"). For instance, in Australia to work as a psychologist is a straightforward process for psychologists registered in New Zealand, but quite a lengthy process for those registered in other countries (see Psychology Board of Australia, n.d.). Additionally, dominant superior attitudes that suggest international accreditations do not match the "gold standard" of the host nation is often a narrative. Differing requisites, for example, completion of supervised experience or nomination/sponsorship by an existing member, can demand additional time and social capital to attain certification (see for example AASP, n.d.). Moreover, if an SEPPP maintains accreditation with multiple professional associations, this will incur additional financial costs associated with membership fees, continuing education, and professional development.

The "start-up" of professional practice/applied consulting in a different country can be inhibited by the absence of an established network of clients (e.g., athletes and coaches). Referrals for work with governing bodies and/or sports clubs are likely to be slow in coming as potential clients tend to work with professionals they already know or those recommended by trusted sources. In addition, gatekeeping by established professionals prevents widening the pool of diverse professionals in the field. As such, integrating into a professional network and/or gaining mentorship from established practitioners can help to build social capital and entry into referral pathways. Building a profile in the wider sport community and media can be difficult without a track record or a high level of proficiency to communicate in the local language with cultural humility and support not forthcoming.

Gaining acceptance in the local sport community can be subject to dynamics of discrimination and privilege as well as marginalization that can arise when working across countries and cultures with a meshed cultural identity. Issues relating to intersectionality, racial injustice, Islamophobia, identity politics, and hegemonic patriarchal systems and policies that target and empower non-dominant female transnational SEPPPs and students can be present when working internationally. Although professional organizations within sport are making efforts through the decolonization of professional career development to address issues of gender and the fallacy of meritocracy, rates of progress are inconsistent across countries.

Codes of conduct and ethics for professional practice (e.g., British Psychological Society, n.d.) as well as research activity vary across countries with many not fully considering anti-discrimination and advocacy ethics. Indeed, many policies reify and underpin marginalization. Moreover, data management regulations (e.g., the European Union's General Data Protection Regulation; European Commission, n.d.) differ across regions; identifying locally available research infrastructure and expertise can support the undertaking of ethical research. Without local knowledge or previous experience, the targeting of appropriate research funding bodies can be difficult. A limited track record with related domestic funders and relevant stakeholders can influence assessments of feasibility ascribed by reviewers of grant applications. Developing collaborations with local researchers possessing a history of successful grant capture and completion with local stakeholders can support research activity and impact. Relatedly, the evaluation of research quality differs across countries (e.g., the UK's Research Excellence Framework.) and relies on a variety of bibliometrics and criterion wherein grant capture can be weighted most significantly by some institutions.

Teaching quality has recently also received greater scrutiny with implications for international SEPPPs teaching within education systems they might not have studied within themselves. Understanding local variations in program structure (e.g., assessments, course delivery), the relative value of teaching versus research, teaching in another language, and navigating cultural differences relating to interpersonal relationships and hierarchy can all impact opportunities for promotion, appointment to leadership roles, and broader career development. Further, postgraduate recruitment and supervision as well as wider roles within academia, such as acting as an external examiner in PhD defences, are inherently influenced by cultural norms and regional regulations that can be challenging for transnationals or global citizens to navigate.

It is important to also reflect on life beyond professional practice. SEPPPs are people too, and there are lifespan considerations for transnationals or global citizens (e.g., retirement pensions). For example, SEPPPs might consider having a family and this can be difficult when social support is limited due to distance from family and friends. Establishing a local support network is key, yet it is difficult when local cultural norms differ. Moreover, navigating social systems (e.g., taxation, children's schooling) requires additional effort in new countries and when operating in another language. Work eligibility, access to healthcare, and other factors relating to citizenship are vulnerable to changes in government and policy (e.g., "Brexit", US executive orders) with implications for work and well-being. Marginalized intersectional individuals are often most at risk of impaired well-being as they navigate structures and systems that impede their ability to thrive, with an extra load to contend with.

International Opportunities and Benefits for SEPPPs

Despite the numerous challenges for global SEPPPs, there are many opportunities for personal and professional development. Collaborative research with international partners can promote diversity in approaches and perspectives. Multinational partnerships on collaborative projects can facilitate eligibility for wider funding opportunities (e.g., Canada, New Zealand, and Korea recently became eligible for European Union Horizon 2020 funding). International SEPPPs are more likely to accrue a broader professional network, as such they can facilitate introductions and serve as global "matchmakers" in coordinating collaborative projects. Moreover, international collaborations can increase the likelihood of research having broader implications and impact on policy if the findings are generalizable and/or the efficacy of interventions are demonstrated across multiple countries and cultures.

Global citizen SEPPPs can also possess teaching experience on topics that are not traditionally taught by locals and can introduce novel pedagogical approaches that may resonate with an increasingly diverse student body. A lived immigrant experience can also support recruitment and retention of international students. Further, with increasing diversity and internationalization in elite level sport, SEPPPs possessing a wider appreciation of the challenges of being a global citizen can form a stronger working alliance with international athletes and coaches as they endeavor to navigate foreign sport organization and systems. Although cliché, the notion that "travel broadens the mind" can facilitate personal and professional development, which, in turn, benefits the SEPPP as well as their clients with potential implications both locally and globally.

CROSSING BORDERS AND CONTINENTS AS SEPP PROFESSIONAL WOMEN

Stiliani "Ani" Chroni, Cristina Fink, & Renee N. Appaneal

As described in the previous section by Davis and colleagues, building a transnational career might require you to follow a long and winding road. In this section, you will be introduced to the lived experiences of three women transnational SEPP professionals for whose career development and advancement entailed moving from their home countries. You will read about the values that informed (and continue to inform) their decision making, some of the lessons they learned, their willingness (and skills) to cope with challenges, and how they came to view the realities of migrating as women aiming to develop and sustain their careers over time.

Who are Ani, Cristina, and Renee

Ani's journey took her from her native country Greece to the USA, back to Greece, and eventually to Norway. Early on she moved alone and later with her son as a single mom. During her journey, she consulted with European, Asian, and North and South American athletes, teams and coaches, with children and their parents, developing youth, and elite performers both professionals and amateurs. As an academic, she has educated future SEPPP and coaches from many different countries. Today, she feels fortunate to "feel at home" in some very diverse environments, like the Mediterranean, Scandinavia, and the USA.

Cristina's journey exposed her to some extraordinary experiences as she got to be an athlete and a sport psychologist at the same time. She was working as the Head of Psychology for the CONADE (Mexican Sports Ministry) while competing at the Olympic level in Barcelona in 1992. Later, she attended three more Olympics as a sport psychologist (2000, 2004, 2008), each time working with different athletes and teams representing Mexico. In 2009, she moved from Mexico to the USA with her two children.

Renee's journey involved migrating from the USA to Australia with her family. Simultaneously, she transitioned from a faculty member in an SEPP graduate program to an embedded sport psychologist position working across several national sport organizations. She worked across the sporting ecosystem providing direct support to individual performers, both able-bodied and para-athletes, and their coaches as part of multidisciplinary performance health teams as well as to management. One of the greatest outcomes of her family's migration has been that with her partner, they realized one of their values—to raise global citizens.

Ani: Learning That "Fitting In" Means Being True to Me

Work in some academic and sport domains proved to be challenging as a woman. When my research on sexual harassment experiences of Greek female athletes was published, colleagues greeted me in hallways with, "Good morning, Ms. Sexual Harassment." Words like these made me feel alone and unwelcome, were hurtful, harmful, and had a role in my decision to move to Norway. As a female consultant my work has been contested even halted by the significant others of my clients (men and women). As an SEPPP, I have been sexually harassed by high level sport officials via unsolicited flirting and unwanted comments and jokes of sexual content. At the age of 52, as an international Technical Delegate for alpine ski racing, following a jury meeting where I summarized discussion points on a procedural matter in presence of a "Big Alpine Boss," I was shocked and infuriated when told that "I take too much space." Incidents like these, signified that I can't cross all roads, made me feel uncomfortable as a person, and unequal as a woman. Looking back, my preparation as a professional by some of the best (e.g., Mimi Murray, Carole Oglesby, and Bob Rotella) and the support of people by my side proved to be solid resources grounding me and giving me the courage to find ways to cope with incidents, keep loving me as a woman and moving forward.

To keep walking through work and life, I revisited the concept and realities of relating and fitting in both as a woman and a non-native because satisfying self-determination theory's need for relatedness (see Standage & Ryan, 2020) by meeting others where they stand, felt oppressive at times. Honesty has been a core value of mine, yet I learned that you won't find it in all places and people. One of the most difficult lessons to learn was to let go of circumstances and walk away from seemingly attractive spaces that challenge freedoms. Ongoing negotiations with self and others (see Gerson & Peiss, 1985) and redirecting one's narratives (Wilson, 2011) became essential skills for all my professional and personal roles, and for safeguarding my self-care and well-being (see Chroni, 2025; Chroni et al., 2021). Today, I invest time and effort to fit in with people, settings, and purposes that align with my value system.

Cristina: Learning to Set Boundaries and Enjoy the Process

My work inside football for more than 30 years showed me the way to adapt and work with diversity. I found my way by observing and experiencing yet without judging others' thoughts and actions (see Fink, 2021). While peers from other countries, backgrounds, and disciplines influenced me and my work, I also learned to stand by my values and beliefs. Traveling with a group of 42 men and one woman (me) meant that I had to adjust to work in all-male environments. Traveling with a large men's team, I found support in one of the coaches when someone else joined the group and asked if I was a "soccer mom" and the coach responded, "she is a doctor, be smarter." I also had to deal with stupid assumptions about the role I play in a team. I had a coach who said to me that he would prefer to work with a male sport psychologist because as a woman I would be too soft and would cuddle the players. Experiences like these shaped the way I work. While experiencing work in so many diverse settings, looking back I feel fortunate to have encountered more support than boundaries.

Today, I know it matters to meet my clients where they are, and to not be afraid to extend and expand myself for meeting them at their comfort zones. I make sure to understand the clients' ways of being. Nonetheless, the most important lesson to learn is that to help others take care of themselves, you need to set your boundaries and take care of yourself first. It was the professional footballers who taught me to ask questions and evaluate the choices in front of me; and if it comes down to not being the right fit for me and/or them, then I don't need to be there.

Renee: Learning to Navigate Boundary Crossings with Courage

The language differences between Australia and home involve only a few noticeable differences in spelling (i.e., behaviour vs behavior) and pronunciation (i.e., blu-BERRY vs BLU-berry). However, the differences in people's understanding (and related expectations) of sport psychology were far more challenging to discern. Navigating the Australian high-performance (HP) sport system as a sport psychologist required quickly learning the structure and history of HP sport, but it also exposed the ways in which psychological services in sport are viewed differently by both those working in the profession as well as those working alongside us. Interpersonally, the Australians' preference for conflict avoidance was rather challenging to recognize and respond to, especially as an outspoken (and if I'm honest, sometimes opinionated) woman within a predominantly male-led and misogynistic culture. For me, my values of integrity, humor, and courage guided me through uncomfortable waters and unknown terrains.

I found the slightly vulgar sense of British-style humor in Australia natural and familiar. As the youngest of five and the only girl in my family, I connected quite easily at first among the predominantly male staff. However, because it was familiar to me, my responses to inappropriate sexist or patronizing comments made by male colleagues were delayed, or if I did it was in a sarcastic manner using humor, which meant it often wasn't taken seriously. When I did confront situations, even with careful preparation and in a respectful manner, it was received as confrontational. After forming relationships and realizing how much effort people put toward avoiding conflict (and discomfort), I was better able to call attention to comments that seemed patronizing or controlling. This didn't always go well for me. It was often difficult to tease out whether my lack of agency in discussions and decision making within these teams was due to being a psychologist or a woman—it was likely both. Furthermore, while courage enabled me to acknowledge and accept mistakes to learn and improve, colleagues rarely were willing to put their hands up and share some responsibility for when things weren't working well. Instead, I sought feedback and support from both informal and formal support networks. Going forward, I now check for partners and allies before I raise concerns or attempt to address what might be considered difficult truths. At this later stage of my career, I have greater confidence in my competence and won't waste my time in roles that seem set up to fail. I am privileged where I can decline roles that aren't a fit with my values. I ask a lot of specific questions around the team/organization's direction, alignment, and commitment to sport psychology to determine whether or not I can be effective in a role being offered but also whether the role provides an opportunity to "do good work, with good people"—another value of mine.

Women on the Move: Paving Our Way Forward

In closing, this section was about three ambitious cisgender women from three countries and continents who migrated and walked their paths by staying true to their multiple, intersecting identities. As transnational women SEPPs they stood on the corner values of integrity, courage, honesty, frankness, and humor. While moving and settling abroad is not the easiest thing to do, the most beautiful thing is becoming a global citizen and feeling fortunate to have the best parts of multiple worlds at the tips of your hands.

JOURNEYING THE WORLD TO DISCOVER OURSELVES IN SHAPING OUR PROFESSIONAL PHILOSOPHY

Caren D.P. Diehl & David J.C. Smith

This chapter will explore how we've navigated the challenges and opportunities of life in a new culture as sport psychology professionals by sharing personal experiences that reflect our journey and how it has shaped our personal and professional identities. First, Caren will discuss her journey growing up, living, and studying in various countries, sharing cultural insights she learned along the way. Then, David will discuss his experiences as an openly gay, cisgender male, stepping outside of his cultural bubble and entering a performance context known to be hostile to LGBTQ+ people.

Caren's Journey: A Third Culture Kid Diving into the Sport Psychology World

I grew up as a "third culture kid," born in Germany and at the age of two moving to Ghana where we lived for 5 years followed by Tanzania for 12 years. Growing up surrounded and immersed in various ethnic groups, cultures, religious beliefs, and socioeconomic backgrounds was my normal that shaped who I am today. In college, I decided to pursue my BSc in sport psychology in Wales, an M.Ed. kinesiology (sport psychology) in Philadelphia at Temple University, and my PhD back in the UK in Wolverhampton. After completing my PhD I moved to and lived in the UAE for 4 years, then moved to Malaysia for 2.5 years, and currently live in Germany. Both my lived experiences growing up and education made me more curious and open-minded. I learned that one's background and upbringing shapes their sense of self and worldview, and also influences motivation and drive.

After I finished my M.Ed. in the USA, but before starting my Ph.D. in the UK, I worked in Ghana as a sport psychology consultant for a soccer team. Having lived in Africa for most of my childhood and adolescence, I understood the culture quite well, which helped me build relationships with the coaches and players. While I may have been a bit naive at the start of this journey thinking it would be similar to my experience in the USA, I soon realized that the Ghanaians had a different understanding of sport psychology that needed to be addressed promptly. I was challenged to find solutions to some of our cultural differences and recognized that some sport psychology theories and interventions were not transferable and needed to be adapted. For example, Parker et al. (2005) suggested that emotion intelligence (EI) could be a culturally bound construct. Recognizing emotions from facial expressions is part of various EI models, yet there are cultural variabilities in this ability. Bringing the two worlds of cultural applied work and theory together was something I enjoyed. It was key to the development of my professional philosophy of taking a person-centered approach (i.e., getting to know the person, how they view the world, and what motivates them) and creating a space for them without judgment on their background, physical ability, socioeconomic background, ethnicity, sexual orientation, or religious beliefs.

Sport Psychology, Culture, and Diversity

I have learned several key insights from working in different countries, including: what being on time means, an understanding of religion and spirituality, that it is better to ask a few too many questions than not enough, the factors driving participation in sport can be different among athletes from the different cultures and will impact the way you work with them, and that motivation is not always intrinsic. For example, in Ghana as well as some of the ethnic groups in Malaysia, a lot of the athletes didn't start their sport because they loved it, they wanted a better life for themselves and their family. Working in Ghana I also learned about juju (black magic) and needed to consider how it impacted my work with the team because if they felt they were cursed they wouldn't play (Diehl et al., 2009). And, I also learned about GMT (i.e., Ghana Maybe Time) after meeting the team for the first time, when it was agreed I should be there the next day for their morning training session at 6:00 am. Being German, I was there at 5:50 and by 6:30 still no one had shown up. I called the team manager, and he said 6:00 am means 7:00 am.

A Woman Working in the Sports World and in Different Cultures

As a woman working in sport, traditionally a male dominated field, and across various cultures that have diverse views regarding gender equality and gender roles, I have had many important experiences and lessons learned. For example, being a white European woman working in Ghana meant I had a few coaches and players show romantic/sexual interest in me. In the UAE having a Ph.D. made working there easier as that held more weight than if I just introduced myself without my Dr. title where I would have been ignored. In some countries, I often faced situations where being a woman meant I wasn't always listened to, respected or treated fairly. I've sat in discussion groups where I was the only woman present, I was talked over, ignored and not even given a chance to speak. While I can't "prove" it, I feel that being a woman has prevented me from getting some jobs, especially in the more male dominated sports. These experiences have helped me develop resilience and grit to where, despite the discrimination, I am continuing this journey.

David's Journey: Gays in Sport—A Psychological Journey to Better Understand My Own Experiences in Sport and Life

As an openly gay, cisgender male, my journey toward becoming a sport psychology practitioner traces its roots long back to my adolescent years when I was just a kid in the USA, exploring feelings and identity that I knew were not consistent with that of my peers. While the other kids in my school were all dating each other, I lacked interest in pursuing anything other than platonic friendship. However, I did find myself crushing on several guys within my social circle, daydreaming about holding hands and being together, but the reality of such was simply too scary to face. During this time, I was a member of a club swim team, and as I slowly and cautiously revealed my homosexuality to some of my friends, I found myself facing acceptance from some but bullying from others. I learned that being a young gay teenager was rife with struggles of bullying and harassment from my teammates, peers, even coaches and teachers. So, I quit the team and pursued other interests that lent themselves to be more open, safe, and diverse for "outcasts" like me.

LGBTQ+ Sport and Community

A few years after high school, I returned to competitive swimming when I joined my local LGBTQ+ swim team and attended the 2010 Gay Games in Cologne where I found myself in a worldwide LGBTQ+ sport community and movement, one that celebrated who I was and offered a safe and empowering place to do sport. The experience was so profound for me, that it helped me truly discover the physical, mental, and social benefits of sport and exercise, so much so that I chose to make a career out of it. Finishing my BSc in sport and exercise science, I endeavored on a career working in community fitness, personal training, and sport. After a few years, I found myself stagnate and frustrated in that I knew I could do more and offer more. I was also eager to move away from my hometown and experience life elsewhere, realizing that if I wanted to fulfill a lifelong dream of living abroad, this was the time to do it. I applied for English language graduate programs all over Europe and Australia, with my first choice being the German Sports University in Cologne, the host of the 2010 Gay Games. A few seemingly long weeks later, I found an acceptance letter waiting for me and within six weeks had sold most of my belongings, packed up what was left to carry with me on the plane, and took a leap of faith to start a new life across the world.

As I was getting settled in Germany and grad school, I knew the most important thing I could do to expand my social and cultural development was to be involved with things outside of school. I also wanted to avoid other Americans since I came to Germany to experience German culture. So, my first step was to seek out and join the local LGBTQ+ swim team, SC Janus. While I initially joined as an athlete, my time and work with them soon transformed into something much greater throughout my career, such as advocating for LGBTQ+ inclusion, workshops on allyship and best DEI practices with Compete Sports Diversity, Leap

Sports Scotland, and You Can Play, and doing coaching and applied sport psychology work for numerous LGBTQ+ specific clubs.

Persistence of Prejudice

Unfortunately, the prejudices that haunted me during my youth are still present in sport. According to Denison (2020) and Menze et al. (2019), up to 82% of LGBTQ+ people in sport have directly witnessed homophobic and transphobic language use in sport settings, while a further 90% of people believe homophobia and transphobia continue to be a problem. This is further highlighted by the aggressive discriminatory actions taken by US politicians to ban LGBTQ+ and especially trans people from sport. Throughout my career, I made it no secret that I am gay, and I refuse to hide who I am for nothing more than a job. However, several incidences while working for various non-LGBTQ+ sport jobs with people who hold anti-gay prejudices led to drama about me being gay, even when I had done nothing inappropriate or unprofessional. I found myself out of a job and unable to even defend myself, subject solely to the whims of ignorance and fear. While I can't "prove" anything, I also believe my openness has inhibited my opportunities for employment and has created considerable obstacles and challenges I and my fellow LGBTQ+ sport peers have faced that many of my heterosexual counterparts have not.

Stepping out of my American bubble and becoming a "foreigner" myself, I have had the opportunity to connect with so many people from a wide array of cultural backgrounds and diversity. As a result of my lived experiences, my professional philosophy is built around empowering confidence and authenticity for all athletes, students, peers, and colleagues I work with. It comes down to building psychological safety and an empowering motivational climate, setting a standard of expectation to respect one another and ourselves. The experiences I have developed while abroad, working with athletes representing a vast diversity of cultural backgrounds, languages, races, religions, ethnicities, sexual orientations, and gender identities, has helped me better reinforce and appreciate the strength and resilience of diversity as it pertains to athletic and team development. I aspire, above all else, to be the kind of sport practitioner that younger me needed when push came to shove.

Conclusion

The diversity of our experiences represents only a brief insight into the diversity and complexity of navigating life in a new culture. From adjusting to new languages, navigating bureaucracies to even simply figuring out where to buy everyday items. Despite all the challenges we have faced, we would not trade our experiences for anything in the world. Those challenges helped us build resilience and a more nuanced perspective that has helped shape our identities and capabilities to navigate life.

EDITORS' TAKEAWAYS

Sport is global by nature, and our field offers chances to live and work across borders, though, as Davis and colleagues remind us, it comes with real challenges too. Their chapter made me (Andrew) about how important it is to stay adaptable and open when navigating different systems and opportunities abroad. Chroni, Fink, and Appaneal also made me realize how much our values matter when moving into new cultures—those anchors guide us when we're unsure what to do, and there's a lot of that when starting fresh in another country. I was especially struck by how they wrote from a woman's perspective, which added a layer of insight I hadn't considered before. Diehl and Smith took this reflection further, showing how global citizenship isn't just about where we go, but about discovering which values we hold onto and which shift as new experiences shape who we are. In that way, being a global citizen isn't only about mobility; it's also about growth, self-discovery, and learning how to navigate both professional opportunities and personal transformation.

RECOMMENDED EXERCISES

1 Reflect on a time when you entered a new group or community. How does that experience relate to entering a new cultural or professional environment? What strategies helped you integrate—or maintain your identity without fully assimilating? How might these approaches support you when working internationally or transnationally in SEPP?
2 Research and compare the codes of ethics from two sport psychology organizations in different countries. Identify key differences and consider how these may shape decisions when working across borders (e.g., title protection, working with minors, and confidentiality).
3 Reflect on your views about making a transnational move, personally or professionally. What factors would motivate such a move, and what barriers might prevent it? Which environments or regions would you seek out or avoid, and why (e.g., language, distance from family, and lifestyle needs)? Who would be part of your support system to help you stay grounded and accountable?
4 Choose a current controversial topic. Even if you already have a clear opinion, research the opposing viewpoints. Imagine debating with yourself: How would you respond to the other side's arguments? How might they respond to yours? Gaining perspective from multiple angles can strengthen your understanding and nuance your position.
5 Consider the emotional, physical, financial, and social demands of working as a transnational or global SEPPP. Create a personal sustainability plan. Identify boundaries to protect well-being, strategies to maintain motivation and long-term supports (e.g., financial planning, mentorship, continuing education, community). Revisit and adjust this plan as your context evolves.

REFERENCES

Association for Applied Sport Psychology (AASP). (n.d.). *Become certified.* https://appliedsportpsych.org/certification/become-certified/

British Psychological Society. (n.d.). *Code of ethics and conduct.* https://www.bps.org.uk/guideline/code-ethics-and-conduct

Chroni, S. (2025). My journey against sexual misconduct in sport. In L. A. Fisher (Ed.), *Social justice through sport and exercise psychology: Expert approaches and intergenerational voices* (pp. 94–107). Routledge.

Chroni, S. A., Raikonen, N., Elbe, A.-M., & Ryba, T. (2021). Negotiating transnational migration: Women's stories in boundaryless academia. *Psychology of Sport and Exercise, 56*, Article 101990. https://doi.org/10.1016/j.psychsport.2021.101990

Denison, E., Bevan, N., & Jeanes, R. (2020). Reviewing evidence of LGBTQ+ discrimination and exclusion in sport. *Sport Management Review, 24*(3), 389–409. https://doi.org/10.1016/j.smr.2020.09.003

Diehl, C. D. P., Hegley, A., & Lane, A. M. (2009). Working with Ghanaian athletes. In S. J. Hanrahan & R. J. Schinke (Eds.), *Cultural sport psychology: From research to practice.* (pp. 173–184). Human Kinetics.

European Commission. (n.d.). *Rules for business and organisations on data protection reform.* https://commission.europa.eu/law/law-topic/data-protection/reform/rules-business-and-organisations_en

Fink, C. (2021). Cristina Fink. In A. Poczwardowski & M. Aoyagi (Eds.), *Expert approaches to sport psychology: Applied theories of performance excellence* (2nd ed., pp. 65–84). FIT Publishing.

Gerson, J. M., & Peiss, K. (1985). Boundaries, negotiation, consciousness: Reconceptualizing gender relations. *Social Problems, 32*(4), 317–331. https://doi.org/10.2307/800755

Menzel, T., Braumüller, B., & Hartmann-Tews, I. (2019). The relevance of sexual orientation and gender identity in sport in Europe: Findings from the outsport survey. Cologne: German Sport University Cologne, Insitute of Sociology and Gender Studies.

Parker, J. D. A., Saklofske, D. H., Shaughnessy, P. A., Huang, S. H. S., Wood, L. M., & Eastabrook, J. M. (2005). Generalizability of the emotional intelligence construct: A cross-cultural study of North American aboriginal youth. *Personality and Individual Differences, 39*, 215–227.

Psychology Board of Australia. (n.d.). *Overseas applicants.* https://www.psychologyboard.gov.au/Registration/Overseas-Applicants.aspx

Research Excellence Framework. (n.d.). *Home.* https://www.ref.ac.uk/

Standage, M., & Ryan, R. M. (2020). Self-determination theory in sport and exercise. In G. Tenenbaum & R. C. Eklund (Eds.), *Handbook of sport psychology* (Vol. I, pp. 37–56). Taylor & Francis.

Wilson, T. D. (2011). *Redirect: Changing the stories we live by.* Little, Brown and Company.

Section 3

The SEPP Researcher

9 The Scientist-Practitioner

The scientist-practitioner model is grounded in the idea that high-quality practice must be informed by a solid research base. In discussing the structure of this book, we editors debated whether this chapter on the scientist-practitioner should be included in the Applied Practice or Research section. We concluded that positioning this chapter in the research section emphasizes that the scientist-practitioner is, first and foremost, fundamentally engaged in the process of knowledge generation and translation. It highlights that effective applied work does not emerge in isolation but is grounded by the rigor, validity, and cultural relevance of its research foundation. By locating this chapter in the research section, we offer that practitioners are not just consumers of research but also contributors to the advancement of knowledge. This placement reinforces the importance of methodological awareness, critical appraisal skills, and sensitivity to context—all of which ensure that scientific findings can meaningfully guide service delivery as described by our chapter authors.

A GLOBAL PERSPECTIVE ON THE DEVELOPMENT OF SCIENTIST-PRACTITIONERS IN SPORT AND EXERCISE PSYCHOLOGY

Tshepang Tshube, Kapule David Mabuta, & Lekgobo Masake

This chapter aims to give sport, exercise, and performance psychology professionals (SEPPPs) a global perspective on the training and professional development of sport and exercise psychologists from a scientist-practitioner perspective. With that lens, this chapter begins with a discussion of the qualities of a scientist-practitioner, followed by the training and development of sport and exercise psychologists, and concludes with a global example providing a discussion on sport and exercise psychology in Africa.

Qualities and Characteristics of Scientist-Practitioners

The International Society of Sport Psychology's (ISSP) position stand on the scientist-practitioner notes that despite significant growth in sport psychology research, few and isolated publications exist on the characteristics of scientist-practitioners (Schinke et al., 2024). Sport psychologists often contend with what constitutes legitimate scientific knowledge. Who is qualified to engage in sport psychology practice? What evidence meets the scientific threshold to guide a sport psychology intervention? Michael Polanyi likened scientist-practitioners to crime investigators who study a crime scene with the curiosity to look for clues and meaningful patterns in a rather disorganized crime scene (Martens, 1987). Scientists-practitioners

DOI: 10.4324/9781003781479-12

must have critical thinking and imagination to work with clues that seem random and can have multiple interpretations (Moore, 2007). In addition, they:

- have a disciplined inquiry and scientific questioning character that guides their research and applied sport psychology practice. Scientist-practitioners must demonstrate critical thinking in both practice and research, employ empirical methods, and integrate scientific research and practice to effectively serve clients (Paulik et al., 2020).
- understand that integrating science and practice requires that they use knowledge that helps them understand clients and advance knowledge, rather than relying solely on lab-based experiments (Martens, 1987). Utilizing case studies, introspection, observation, and clinical experience are equally useful scientific methods that contribute to knowledge advancement, including in low and middle-income countries.
- must be critical consumers and evaluators of knowledge while consistently seeking up-to-date, empirically supported, and culturally competent practices.
- demonstrate cultural humility and embrace self-exploration in relation to their clients, organizational framework, and societal structures (Ryba et al., 2024). The overreliance on applying the orthodox rules of science to behavior may be accepted; however, the complexity and diversity of sport and exercise psychology clientele may necessitate non-conventional approaches to sport psychology practice.

Sport and Exercise Psychologist Training and Development

Historically, the scientist-practitioner model in psychology was one of the early attempts to develop a framework that guides the training and professional development of graduate students, postdoctoral fellows, and early career professionals. The model is traced back to the 1949 Boulder Conference on Graduate Education in Clinical Psychology. The model emerged when clinical psychologists were on a quest to define the nature of clinical psychology and develop standards, a code of ethics, certification, and accreditation (Strickland, 2015). It was, and still is, important to reflect on the values, skills, and competencies espoused by students of psychology. Martens (1987) cautioned the sport psychology community about the two divergent sport psychologists, one who focuses primarily on research, while another focuses on practice. Thus, the quality of graduate programs and postdoctoral fellows is central to any discipline.

The mission of graduate programs largely states that critical thinking skills, innovation, cultural competence, and the use of empirical methods are core to the quality of graduate programs in sport and exercise psychology. Graduate programs need to provide courses that equip students with the historical knowledge of the scientist-practitioner model and the integration of science and practice. The dual emphasis on science and practice continually ensures that they are not divergent but inform each other. One of the challenges in graduate programs is to ensure that students are provided with opportunities for graduate practice. Graduate programs that offer practicums, external projects, and consultation experiences expose students to on-the-field experiences. However, students need to be ready and have mentorship that shares knowledge, provides advice, and offers counsel. In an effective environment, various supervision models, including group supervision, individual supervision, tele-supervision, and direct/indirect supervision, are used to support a well-designed and effective supervision program. The faculty equally needs to demonstrate competencies in the scientist-practitioner model in their teaching and research. A faculty member with an overemphasis on practice and who does not inspire confidence in research undermines the scientific-practitioner model and vice versa. Faculty members need to be well-trained and actively involved in both research and practice to mentor and supervise sport psychology students.

A Global Example: Sport and Exercise Psychology in Africa

The first laboratory with a focus on psychology programs in sub-Saharan Africa was established in 1965 (Oppong, 2022). The program was first established in Zambia and subsequently in other countries, including Ghana, Kenya, and Botswana, primarily incorporating psychology into the service training of teachers, health care providers, and social and missionary work. It was not a standalone and independent discipline until the 1970s and 1980s. Today, the Department of Psychology at the University of Botswana is housed in the Faculty of Social Sciences, offering double majors in psychology and other disciplines, including economics, sociology, public administration, and political science. Single majors in psychology are offered to a small number of students. Consistent with the scientist-practitioner model, undergraduate and graduate students are required to complete a practicum at a psychology clinic. The University of Botswana is one of the few universities in Africa that offer an undergraduate major in sport psychology. It is offered in the Department of Sport Science, housed in the Faculty of Education. Similar to other psychology-related programs in Africa, the program offers a minimum of 12 weeks of internship and a research project. Over 90% of the students are attached to the national sports association and work with national athletes at all levels.

Eurocentric views and dominance are ingrained across several disciplines, including sport and exercise psychology. For example, even though Africa is one of the most diverse continents, it is common and easy for scholars and students outside Africa to have a monolithic view of Africa and think it is a homogeneous community. Botswana, Chad, Ghana, and Kenya, like many sub-Saharan countries, are diverse in ecology, ethnic and linguistic composition, and other important cultural traits. Despite this diversity in ecology and language, textbooks used in graduate programs across Africa are largely authored and published in Western Europe, North America, and Australia.

The Indigenous form of education and knowledge systems was barred and replaced by Western-developed constructs in the colonial era. Psychology programs, including behavior change interventions and other psychological constructs that were directly imported from Western countries, largely France and Great Britain, were implemented across Africa (Appiah, 2022). In some cases, European scholars dehumanized Africans and decoupled ancient Egypt, which had undisputed evidence of psychology even before 2700 BC (Oppong, 2022). Consequently, educational programs in Africa, including in psychology, are major recipients of imposed external influences. African dependence on neocolonial cultures undermined psychological autonomy and promoted cultural bondage (Mawere, 2015). For example, even though the University of Botswana offers sport psychology, exercise physiology, and sport management, the program does not offer any Indigenous sport.

In conclusion, scientist-practitioners in Africa navigate working in less-studied communities. Unlike in high-income countries with decades of research and written guidelines and models on several areas (e.g., mental health, or talent development), scientist-practitioners in Africa must develop tests, guidelines, and models as they implement and largely test models and guidelines developed in industrialized countries. Scientist-practitioners in Africa function in unique settings that include a shortage of professionals in sport science, kinesiology, and related disciplines. Consequently, a sports psychologist might be often asked to advise on areas outside their standard scope of work. For example, it is common for coaches to ask sports psychologists about nutrition, physical injuries, or any issues they may be dealing with. It is therefore important for scientists-practitioners in Africa to develop basic knowledge outside their scope to support their teams. Africa is the second-largest continent and the second most populous continent in the world, with numerous cultures. Scientists-practitioners in Africa constantly weigh the uncertain risks versus the benefits of the use of various cultural beliefs across the continent. These beliefs relating to health, wellness, and performance might be nonconventional, culturally acceptable, and unregulated approaches, including in treating mental health symptoms and disorders.

THE SCIENTIST-ARTIST-PRACTITIONER PHILOSOPHY: PERSPECTIVES FROM HONG KONG AND SINGAPORE

Karen Lo & Harry Lim

Employing science and evidence-based practices should be considered one of the foundational pillars that anchor the work of sport, exercise, and performance psychology practitioners who subscribe to the scientist-practitioner model; though in reality, science and practice oftentimes are still separated (Quartiroli et al., 2022). According to the position stand (Schinke et al., 2024) by the ISSP, one of six roles/characteristics that define a scientist-practitioner is the ability to take in, synthesize, and apply the latest theories and empirical research to current best practices. Nonetheless, this can be challenging for practitioners who operate in cultures that are not Western, Educated, Industrialized, Rich, and Democratic (WEIRD; de Oliveiras & Baggs, 2023). Thus, we aim to provide practitioners operating in non-WEIRD contexts a roadmap to successfully navigate cultural minefields.

Cultural Research Gap

A key hallmark of the scientist-practitioner model is the integration of science and practice, leading to mutual sharing and synthesis which culminates in holistic understanding and application (Schinke et al., 2024). Yet psychology research in general, and by extension, sport psychology research as well has been largely dominated by WEIRD societies, resulting in a research base that is highly skewed and likely scientifically applicable only to certain demographics (de Oliveira & Baggs, 2023). In more recent times, there has been an increase in research studies from Asian countries such as China, Japan, and India as the call for more culturally situated work gets heeded. Nonetheless, for regions or countries such as Hong Kong and Singapore whose societies have a mix of Eastern and Western cultures, the current research landscape makes the direct application of evidence-based practice problematic.

Multiple sport psychology studies that emphasize cultural competence illustrate the importance of exercising cultural awareness in our provision of services to athletes, such as familiarizing the self on aboriginal culture when working with aboriginals (Schinke & Hanrahan, 2009), Taoism and Confucianism when working with Chinese athletes (Si et al., 2011), or Samurai ideals when working with Japanese athletes (Kozuma, 2009). Therefore, a practitioner needs to understand the local cultural context to be effective.

Hong Kong and Singapore Culture

Although Hong Kong and Singapore are Asian cities/countries with close ethnic (Hong Kong, Singapore) and geopolitical (Hong Kong) ties to China, it would be remiss to assume that their values, beliefs, and cultures would reflect that of China. Ironically, Hong Kong and Singapore have a lot more in common with each other, particularly from a historical, financial, and economic policy point of view. Both areas have a predominantly Chinese population whose forefathers were immigrants from Mainland China. Generational changes have led to distinct identities that are separate from China itself. Nonetheless, certain Chinese cultural characteristics, including keeping face, social hierarchy, and harmony of social relationships (Si et al., 2015), are deep-rooted and continue to be prevalent.

As part of the four Asian Tigers together with South Korea and Taiwan, Hong Kong and Singapore experienced accelerated economic and social development in a relatively short span of time, resulting in a well-trained and highly educated workforce (Chang et al., 2019). Part of the economic strategies that drove growth was the willingness to welcome foreign international investment and consequently an influx of foreign workers. As a result of these factors, both Hong Kong and Singapore have strong Western influence despite deep East Asian roots. This also includes the influx of foreign coaches and other support staff to fill up opportunities within sport environments at different levels of play.

The Nature of High-Performance Sport

Both Hong Kong and Singapore are renowned for their academic rigorous education systems, and sport is mostly considered a favored pastime for students. Yet, in the past decade, both regions have produced Olympic champions. While the primary focus has been mostly on academic excellence, pockets of high-performance sport have emerged, demonstrating that athletic achievement can coexist alongside educational pursuits.

High-performance sports operate in a highly dynamic, ruthless, and fast-paced environment where constant evaluation of one's input on performance is the norm (Eubank et al., 2014; Sotiriadou & De Bosscher, 2018). This demands innovation and speed of application to possibly gain minute but significant competitive advantages. At first glance, such contexts can appear diametrically opposed to a scientist-practitioner approach, especially if we hold firm to the principles of science-informed, evidence-based practices. Nonetheless, this should not deter practitioners who operate in the high-performance sport context to explore opportunities to push the boundaries of what sport psychology can offer (Schinke et al., 2024). Leveraging robust concepts and theories from other disciplines or domains coupled with a nuanced understanding of the culturally situated needs of the athletes and coaches we work with may provide some indirect yet equally suitable and robust interventions and strategies to enhance performance in time-critical periods.

The Scientist-Artist-Practitioner

The sport psychology practitioner acts, in many ways, as an artist, and we propose that working with athletes in the psychology space, particularly those from non-WEIRD countries, is a craft. Practitioners need to have fundamental knowledge and scientifically validated techniques. Yet, they also need fluidity and tacit knowledge, most of which is considered abstract and unarticulated, and not merely a transference of scientific knowledge to the applied setting. The gap, however, between the ***knowing*** and the ***doing*** will continue to exist unless the practitioner has the craftsmanship to close it, which includes the development and maintenance of the therapeutic alliance, when to use a certain evidence-based method, and the timing to best use it (Lazarus, 2019). Hence, we postulate that the effectiveness of a sport psychology practitioner working in different cultural contexts hinges on this delicate balance between

$$E = Q \times A$$

(Effectiveness) (Quality) (Acceptance)

The overall Effectiveness (E) of any approach is a product of both quality and acceptance. Quality (Q) refers to the robustness of the solution, while Acceptance (A) measures the level of buy-in from those impacted by the change.

Figure 9.1 Level of effectiveness in change management (Polk, 2011)

science and artistry. Their role as the *cultural artist* becomes essential. This in-between role allows for the seamless translation of theoretical insights into actionable strategies, ensuring that athletes receive tailored support within a certain cultural context. This can be succinctly brought across via an equation that is borrowed from change management literature (Polk, 2011) and captured in Figure 9.1:

From this equation, it is evident that no matter how extensive your knowledge, experience, and skill sets may be, without gaining acceptance (A) from the coaches and athletes you work with, your support will never reach its full potential. In this context, (A) can also symbolize the *artist*, highlighting the importance of creativity and rapport in the therapeutic process.

The Role of the Artist in the Hong Kong and Singapore Contexts

Applying culturally relevant science is paramount. Due to the absence of such frameworks within the literature, practitioners must skillfully integrate cultural understanding into their methodologies, adapting existing scientific principles to fit specific contexts. Yet, how they might work effectively will be influenced by factors such as their centralization, location, national culture, and prevailing zeitgeist (Schinke & Hanrahan, 2009). Thus, the timing and context of interventions are as critical as the individuals involved.

In Hong Kong and Singapore, practitioners often encounter challenges athletes face in pursuing dual careers in sport and academics. While this is often promoted in Western research discourse, it can create significant stress for student-athletes in these regions, particularly in environments where high academic expectations complicate the equilibrium between sports and studies. Thus, reframing sport psychology to emphasize support for academic achievement can enhance greater buy-in from stakeholders. Additionally, the coach-athlete relationship is a pivotal factor that determines successful performance (McCarthy, 2021; Phillips et al., 2023), and hence, should be one of the main focus areas of our work. Yet, we find that local coaches often harbor a skeptical view of sport psychologists, questioning the value we can contribute. Therefore, establishing strong relationships with coaches are crucial in order to work effectively with athletes. For instance, maintaining face is a significant cultural characteristic that must be considered when providing feedback and observations to coaches. Moreover, it is crucial to update coaches on our plans and keep them informed of progress whenever possible. This fosters a sense of control and helps prevent any feelings of undermined authority. One key challenge, however, lies in balancing the sharing of information while maintaining confidentiality—particularly when coaches believe they must be privy to everything discussed in sessions to retain control.

Conclusion

Endorsing and developing culturally sensitive professionals is vital for advancing the field and addressing the unique challenges athletes face across various cultural landscapes.

Consequently, discourse, education, training, and research investigations of these approaches must be contextualized rather than treated as universal truths (Ryba et al., 2013). There is no one-size-fits-all approach dictated by a single region. Instead, each context demands tailored strategies that reflect local nuances, and this chapter illustrates how these tailored strategies can be effectively implemented by taking up the role of a scientist-artist-practitioner.

HOW NEUROSCIENCE INFORMS MENTAL HEALTH AND SPORT PERFORMANCE

Alex Diaz & Hillary Cauthen

Athletes strive to win. When we watch them compete, they are often identified by the color of their uniforms or the names on their jerseys. However, what remains unseen by spectators is the person beneath the uniform, whose physiological and psychological foundation enables these performances. A basketball player facing a crucial free throw, a tennis player concerned about a family member's health, a football player coping with a mild concussion, or a rower receiving criticism from a coach are all dealing with external stressors that elicit internal stressful responses. Observers (e.g., coaches, parents, or teammates) who are primarily focusing on performance might be overlooking the athlete's stress levels, which can be the direct or indirect factor leading to underperformance.

Lacking the tools to manage stress might be manifested in racing thoughts, loss of focus, impulsive behaviors, or wanting to give up (Tossici et al., 2024), which often lowers athletes' self-confidence (Rice et al., 2016). Furthermore, these stressors can affect mental health, including anxiety, depression, or obsessive thoughts that manifest in sleep disturbances, eating issues, or substance use (Ogden et al., 2006). While performance pressure is a common experience, high-intensity and unaddressed chronic stress can lead to physiological changes that reinforce unhealthy behavioral patterns (Tossici et al., 2024). Building emotional regulation skills to manage stress is essential for both mental health and sports performance. Thus, we offer a scientist-practitioner approach for working with athletes on those skills.

From Science to Practice: The Autonomic Nervous System and Brain Interaction

The human nervous system continuously transmits external stimuli from the spinal cord up to the brain in a bidirectional process to engage survival responses, social connections, and emotional regulation (Ogden et al., 2006). Humans are biologically organized to regulate emotions in social contexts (Siegel, 2012). When a coach and an athlete engage in conversation, the interaction is more than the exchanged words. It's a connection between two nervous systems, each affecting the other's physiological state. During a calm exchange, their nervous systems enhance listening, reduce heart rate, improve focus, and boost immunity. These responses promote emotional regulation, social engagement, and a sense of safety (Porges, 2008). A composed coach is more likely to have attentive players who can internalize feedback constructively.

As a practitioner, I (Diaz) find that educating coaches about bidirectional communication often leads to enhancing athletes' emotional regulation and performances. Coaches approach me wanting to understand why talented players avoid taking risks, such as a soccer player choosing to pass the ball even when they have an open shot opportunity. I teach coaches that their frustration raises the players' autonomic survival responses at the expense of feeling calm. Athletes feel their heart rate increase, pupils dilate, and stress hormones like cortisol and epinephrine surge. Most importantly, their brains memorize this unpleasant experience and, subconsciously, start to "play safe" to avoid re-experiencing the incriminating situation. As coaches become more self-aware of their communication style, they are more likely to address athletes in a constructive and encouraging tone of voice. Their emotionally regulated response will lead to enhancing the athletes' mental health, raise confidence, and improve performance.

A calm nervous system will trigger calmness in another person's nervous system (Siegel, 2012). I (Cauthen) work with individual athletes on building awareness in their feelings to assist in managing their emotions in order to perform at their best. I tell athletes to "feel their feels" and encourage them to identify the feeling and explore it by asking themselves, "is this feeling helping or hurting my performance right now?" Once the athlete recognizes the impact of the emotion, they can hit the "reset mindset" button, which is a cue to utilize a grounding technique, such as breathing, visual focal cue, or mindfulness to get their mind and emotions back in their ideal performance state.

Practical Strategies to Enhance Emotional Regulation

Grounded in neuroscience, our practice takes the form of many different interventions. We present here three common strategies directly informed by science.

Breathing Techniques

Breathing patterns can influence different branches of the nervous system, hence influencing emotional regulation (Nestor, 2020). I (Diaz) teach athletes about the autonomic difference between inhalation, which stimulates arousal, and exhalation, which induces calm. By shortening the inhale and lengthening the exhale (e.g., a 4-count inhale and 8-count exhale), a calming effect is achieved; extending the exhale to a larger number (4–12) may lead to a deeper relaxation experience (Nestor, 2020). Alternatively, longer inhales with shorter exhales (e.g., 6-count inhale, 3-count exhale) can increase heart rate. When working with athletes who are performing under pressure, I coach them to effectively distinguish between these two breathing patterns by having them repeat the breathing patterns about five times, rather than advising athletes to "just breathe." Consequently, an athlete who is experiencing performance pressure will know which breathing pattern will be more effective to meet the emotional needs of competition.

Imagery

Through mental rehearsal, athletes strengthen these neural pathways, promoting more efficient and effective simple and complex motor skills as well as cognitive skills without physical exertion. At its core, imagery leverages the brain's predictive coding system, the process by which the brain generates internal models to anticipate sensory experiences and outcomes (Friston, 2010). Rather than reacting only to external stimuli, the brain constantly predicts what will happen next based on previous experiences and current goals. When athletes intentionally imagine successful performances, they refine these internal mental models, increasing the likelihood of adaptive, automatic responses under pressure. I (Cauthen) utilize imagery and mental rehearsal as a core component of pre-performance routines, encouraging athletes to identify a specific skill or play they intend to execute in their performance. Utilizing their imagery script and breathing techniques allow them to be in a regulated emotional state as they mentally rehearse their performance. This predictive sharpening technique reduces cognitive load during competition, allowing them to execute with greater fluidity and confidence.

Studies also demonstrate that vivid, emotionally congruent imagery can modulate physiological arousal, not just motor preparation: lowering heart rate, decreasing muscle tension, and promoting parasympathetic activation associated with calm and recovery states (Decety, 1996). I (Cauthen) inform athletes that when utilized intentionally, imagery becomes a method not only for skill refinement but also for emotional regulation, stress management, and recovery. I also integrate imagery protocols for athletes pre- and post-surgery to help bridge the gap between psychological readiness and physical return to play and compete.

Athletes facing injury often experience a loss of agency and a loss of motor pathways due to inactivity. Neuroscientific findings suggest that maintaining mental rehearsal of sport-specific movements during injury can help preserve neuromuscular patterns, reduce fear of re-injury, and facilitate smoother reentry into sport once physically cleared (Jackson et al., 2001).

Mindfulness Practices

I (Diaz) teach mindfulness practices to individuals and teams as it offers numerous mental health benefits, including emotional regulation, greater focus, improved sleep, enhanced immune response, and reduced negativity (Kaufman et al., 2018). One particular mindfulness exercise is sitting meditation (Ogden et al., 2006). Clients are invited to either sit on the ground or a seat for about 5–20 minutes, paying full attention to the inhaling and exhaling. One way to enhance this experience is by noticing the difference between the inhale and exhale air temperature. When clients notice their minds wandering, I first help them to normalize this experience and then invite them to gently return their focus back to the breath. I explain that the brain is bound to get distracted as the average human attention span is relatively short (Siegel, 2012). Athletes that practice mindfulness by incorporating a meditating routine are therefore training their brains to enhance refocusing.

Conclusion: A Neuroscience-Intervention Approach to Mental Performance

Neuroscience provides us with a deeper understanding of the profound connection between what is happening in our brain and sports performance. A trained scientist-practitioner is better equipped to recognize the impact stress has in competition and how mind-body strategies improve emotional regulation, hence helping athletes to perform at their best while enhancing their mental well-being. As sports psychology continues to evolve, a scientist-practitioner that integrates neuroscience-based approaches can holistically support athletes to achieve both mental health and peak performance.

EDITORS' TAKEAWAYS

My (Andrew) takeaway from the first two contributions is that the scientist-practitioner perspective remains murky, in part because of the sterile nature of our empirical research foundation. Both Tshube and colleagues (Africa) and Lo and Lim (Hong Kong & Singapore) argue that good science must account for cultural context if it is to inform practice and service delivery meaningfully. Reading Diaz and Cauthen's contribution, I found myself asking: What is the right balance between explaining the science behind a skill and simply introducing it to an athlete or coach? This highlights the need not only to understand the science but also to communicate it clearly and concisely—a tricky skill for the scientist-practitioner to master.

RECOMMENDED EXERCISES

1 How can you, as a scientist-practitioner, help ensure emerging theories in sport and performance psychology stay informed by and relevant to applied practice?
2 To what extent should non-Western scientist-practitioners adopt Western-developed theories and models, and how might they adapt or challenge them?
3 Choose an underrepresented population in research. Design a study that is both scientifically rigorous and meaningful for that group.
4 Reflect on a time (real or hypothetical) when you balanced scientific evidence with a client's unique needs. How did you decide on an approach? What challenges arose, and what would you do differently now? How would you proceed if little or no empirical evidence existed for interventions with a specific population, while maintaining ethical and effective practice?
5 Consider your "scientist," "practitioner," and "artist" selves. How does each approach work in your applied role? Estimate the proportion each contributes in your client interactions (e.g., scientist 20%, practitioner 50%, and artist 30%). Write a dialogue between these selves about a recent or potential ethical or applied dilemma, allowing them to question, challenge, and debate one another.

REFERENCES

Appiah, R. (2022). Context matters: Sociocultural considerations in the design and implementation of community-based positive psychology interventions in sub-Saharan Africa. *Culture & Psychology, 28*(4), 613–639. https://doi.org/10.1177/1354067X221118916

Chang, C. C., Batmunkh, M. U., Wong, W. K., & Jargalsaikhan, M. (2019). Relationship between capital structure and profitability: Evidence from Four Asian Tigers. *Journal of Management Information and Decision Sciences, 22*(2), 54–66.

Decety, J. (1996). The neurophysiological basis of motor imagery. *Behavioural Brain Research, 77*(1–2), 45–52. https://doi.org/10.1016/0166-4328(95)00225-1

De Oliveira, G. S., & Baggs, E. (2023). *Psychology's WEIRD problems.* Cambridge University Press.

Eubank, M., Nesti, M., & Cruickshank, A. (2014). Understanding high performance sport environments: Impact for the professional training and supervision of sport psychologists. *Sport and Exercise Psychology Review, 10*(2), 30–37.

Friston, K. (2010). The free-energy principle: A unified brain theory? *Nature Reviews Neuroscience, 11*(2), 127–138. https://doi.org/10.1038/nrn2787

Jackson, P. L., Lafleur, M. F., Malouin, F., Richards, C. L., & Doyon, J. (2001). Potential role of mental practice using motor imagery in neurologic rehabilitation. *Archives of Physical Medicine and Rehabilitation, 82*(8), 1133–1141. https://doi.org/10.1053/apmr.2001.24286

Kaufman, K. A., Glass, C. R., & Pineau, T. R. (2018). *Mindful sport performance enhancement.* American Psychological Association.

Kozuma, Y. (2009). Samurai and science: Sport psychology in Japan. In R. J. Schinke & S. J. Hanrahan (Eds.), *Cultural sport psychology* (pp. 205–216). Human Kinetics.

Lazarus, C. N. (2019, August 30). Weaving together the art and science of therapy: Why therapy is an art that should rest on a solid scientific foundation. *Psychology Today.* https://www.psychologytoday.com/us/blog/think-well/201908/weaving-together-the-art-and-science-of-therapy

Martens, R. (1987). Science, knowledge, and sport psychology. *The Sport Psychologist, 1*(1), 29–55. https://doi.org/10.1123/tsp.1.1.29

Mawere, M. (2015). Indigenous knowledge and public education in sub-Saharan Africa. *Africa Spectrum, 50*(2), 57–71. https://doi.org/10.1177/000203971505000203

McCarthy, E. (2021). The role of the coach-athlete relationship in world class coaching success. *Journal of Swimming Research, 28*(1), 22–31.

Moore, Z. E. (2007). Critical thinking and the evidence-based practice of sport psychology. *Journal of Clinical Sport Psychology, 1*(1), 9–22.

Nestor, J. (2020). *Breath.* Penguin Random House.

Ogden, P., Minton, K., & Pain, C. (2006). *Trauma and the body: A sensorimotor approach to psychotherapy.* W. W. Norton & Co.

Oppong, S. (2022). Indigenous psychology in Africa: Centrality of culture, misunderstandings, and global positioning. *Theory and Psychology, 32*(6), 953–973. https://doi.org/10.1177/09593543221097 33

Paulik, G., Thomas, N., Glasshouse, E., & Hayward, M. (2020). Chapter 26 – Being a scientist–practitioner in the field of psychosis: Experiences from voices clinics. In J. C. Badcock & G. Paulik (Eds.), *A clinical introduction to psychosis* (pp. 615–635). Academic Press. https://doi.org/10.1016/B978-0-12-815012-2.00026-2

Phillips, K., Rhind, D., Krukowska, O., & Jowett, S. (2023). The quality of the coach-athlete relationship predicts objective performance in elite cricket. *International Journal of Sport Psychology, 54*, 32–47.

Polk, J. D. (2011). Lean Six Sigma, innovation, and the change acceleration process can work together. *Physician executive, 37*(1), 38.

Porges, S. W. (2008). The polyvagal theory: New insights into adaptive reactions of the autonomic nervous system. *Cleveland Clinic Journal of Medicine, 75*, 81–85.

Quartiroli, A., Wagstaff, C. R. D., Hunter, H., & Martin, D. R. F. (2022). The identity of the sport psychology profession: A multinational perspective. *Psychology of Sport & Exercise, 60*, 102140. https://doi.org/10.1016/j.psychsport.2022.102140

Rice, S. M., Purcell, R., De Silva, S., Mawren, D., McGorry, P. D., & Parker, A. G. (2016). The mental health of elite athletes: A narrative systematic. *Sports Medicine, 46*, 1333–1353. https://www.ncbi.nlm.nih.gov/pmc/articles/PMC4996886/pdf/40279_2016_Article_492.pdf

Ryba, T. V., Schinke, R. J., Quartiroli, A., Wong, R., & Gill, D. L. (2024). ISSP position stand on cultural praxis in sport psychology: Reaffirming our commitments to the ethics of difference, cultural inclusion, and social justice. *International Journal of Sport and Exercise Psychology, 22*(3), 533–552. https://doi.org/10.1080/1612197X.2024.2310988

Ryba, T. V., Stambulova, N. B., Si, G., & Schinke, R. J. (2013). ISSP position stand: Culturally competent research and practice in sport and exercise psychology. *International Journal of Sport and Exercise Psychology, 11*(2), 123–142.

Schinke, R. J., Blodgett, A., Ritchie, S., Pickard, P., Michel, G., Peltier, D., Pheasant, C., Wabano, M. J., George, C. W., & Enosse, L. (2009). Entering the community of Canadian Indigenous athletes. In R. J. Schinke & S. J. Hanrahan (Eds.), *Cultural sport psychology* (pp. 91–102). Human Kinetics.

Schinke, R., Wylleman, P., Henriksen, K., Si, G., Wagstaff, C. R. D., Zhang, L., Tshepang, T., Noce, F., & Li, Y. (2024). International Society of Sport Psychology position stand: Scientist practitioners. *International Journal of Sport and Exercise Psychology, 22*(1), 1–23. https://doi.org/10.1080/1612197X.2023.2174681

Siegel, D. J. (2012). *The developing mind: How relationships and the brain interact to shape who we are.* The Guilford Press.

Si, G., Duan, Y., Li, H. Y., & Jiang, X. (2011). An exploration into socio-cultural meridians of Chinese athletes' psychological training. *Journal of Clinical Sport Psychology, 5*(4), 325–338.

Si, G., Duan, Y., Li, H.-Y., Zhang, C.-Q., & Su, N. (2015). The influence of the Chinese sport system and Chinese cultural characteristics on Olympic sport psychology services. *Psychology of Sport and Exercise, 17*, 56–67. https://doi.org/10.1016/j.psychsport.2014.08.008

Sotiriadou, P., & De Bosscher, V. (2018). Managing high-performance sport: Introduction to past, present and future considerations. *European Sport Management Quarterly, 18*(1), 1–7.

Strickland, B. R. (2015). Training in clinical psychology in the United States: Scientist–practitioner model. In J. D. Wright (Ed.), *International encyclopedia of the social & behavioral sciences* (2nd ed., pp. 524–527). Elsevier. https://doi.org/10.1016/B978-0-08-097086-8.21087-8

Tossici, G., Zurloni, V., & Nitri, A. (2024, February 29). Stress and sport performance: A PNEI multi-disciplinary approach. *Frontiers in Psychology, 15.* https://www.frontiersin.org/journals/psychology/articles/10.3389/fpsyg.2024.1358771/full

10 Basic Research Skills for the Applied Practitioner

I (Andrew) visibly cringe when students tell me, "I want to do applied work because research isn't my thing." I try to remind the students that part of being a good practitioner is being able to access and digest the latest empirical research because it both ensures that we remain science-practitioners as discussed in the previous chapter (emphasis on the science!) and helps to differentiate us from the motivational speakers and former athletes who rely solely on their own lived experiences as a source of knowledge for others. Furthermore, being able to understand research with all its statistical methods and ontological perspectives allows the practitioner to critically appraise the science from which they operate. Was the sample appropriate for the proposed research question? Is there evidence of variable measure validity and reliability? Are the researchers overselling their results? Practitioners must maintain a baseline research skill set otherwise they risk their knowledge becoming outdated and stagnated. To provide our readers with a brief refresher course, we have solicited several researchers to tell us how practitioners might keep their research skills sharp. Collectively, we hope these contributions inspire our readers, especially those with the most adverse reactions to SPSS or NVivo, to recommit themselves to developing their basic research skills.

THE APPLIED SPORT PSYCHOLOGY PRACTITIONER AND RESEARCH: RATIONALE AND STRATEGIES

Roland Seiler & Monika Liesenfeld

To make a distinction from self-made mental trainers or gurus, applied sport psychology practitioners are requested to use evidence-based interventions. In this chapter, we will show why this is not as easy as it seems to be, outline the rationale behind research strategies that are needed, and make some suggestions for applied sport psychology practitioners and researchers for reducing the gap in evidence.

The Need for Scientific Evidence

To protect athletes from unqualified or even harmful practices, but also to protect the profession of sport psychology, it is important to be able to show the efficacy of interventions. For many years, however, researchers lamented the lack of empirically sound intervention studies. Reinebo et al. (2024) highlighted this in their series of meta-analyses that included 111 studies on varsity team or regional level athletes that utilized a quantitative performance outcome measure. Separate meta-analyses were conducted for multimodal psychological skills training, mindfulness acceptance approaches, imagery, internal versus external attentional focus,

DOI: 10.4324/9781003781479-13

and promotion versus prevention of regulatory focus. The authors concluded that, when non-randomized studies were removed, effects were non-significant and confidence intervals were wide. In addition, randomized controlled trials are difficult to conduct, particularly with elite sport populations, for at least three reasons: (1) the number of athletes competing at a comparable level is rather small, so the statistical power of studies is too low; (2) it is not possible to conduct control group designs with a sample of elite athletes for ethical reasons; and (3) research does not take sufficient account of the complexity of sport psychology practice and tends to focus on individual aspects and linear-causal relationships, the results of which are then difficult to put into practice (Liesenfeld, 2023).

Thus, the lack of scientific evidence supporting sport psychology applied practice may be attributed to a low number of experimental field studies or missing guidelines and standardized procedures for the evaluation of sport psychology interventions (Brown & Fletcher, 2017). Moreover, applied sport psychology practitioners are in most cases self-employed. This results in prioritizing paid intervention over unpaid publication work, for pure economic reasons. Against this background, the question arises as to which other methods and research approaches are needed to increase evidence in sport psychology practice and what applied practitioners can implement to evaluate their daily work and foster evidence-based practices.

Specificity of Sport Psychology Interventions

The field of sport is characterized by numerous aspects such as the specificity of the different sports with their unique physical, technical or mental demands, the organizational framework, communication and group dynamic processes, as well as individual factors and their development over time (Gardner & Moore, 2005). For example, team athletes and individual athletes differ in the degree of freedom they have. Individual athletes generally have more opportunities to exert influence than team athletes. This has an impact on the topics of sports psychology counseling. And the topics and approach to counseling young people often differ from those of adult athletes. Especially in top performance sport, successful interventions as an applied sport psychology practitioner need to be individualized and adapted to the complexity of the situation and the specific context. In most cases, a systemic approach needs to be taken that views the athlete as embedded in a system necessitating work with the athlete's inner and outer system accordingly. The athlete's behavior is meaningful and explainable when considering the functions of specific patterns in their subjectively perceived system. One of the goals of systemic sports psychologists is therefore to ask athletes about their subjective theories and explanatory models in as much detail as possible, as this helps to make distinctions and initiate changes in structures, relationship patterns, or ways of thinking (Weidig & Liesenfeld, 2020). To conclude, we assume that sport psychology interventions, especially in high performance sport, are individualized and systemic in nature. Therefore research strategies need to focus on the individual and its systemic context.

The Single-Case Methodology

Considering our line of arguing that sport psychology interventions are highly individualized, it is surprising that the number of single-case studies in sport psychology is still low, as has been stated already 30 years ago by Hrycaiko and Martin (1996). Single-case research designs show the effects of a specific intervention to one individual and are appropriate to test an intervention in top performance sport where the number of subjects is small. The designs may be integrated into the daily routine of top-level athletes. And because repeated measures show individual variation and development, and there is no control or waiting-list-group, the willingness to participate is high (Hrycaiko & Martin, 1996). The most important types of single-subject designs are: (1) AB or ABA-designs, where a period B with intervention alternates with a period A without intervention; (2) multiple baseline designs, for example across situations such as home or away matches; (3) changing criterion designs, where for example, mental readiness, emotional state or attentional focus are assessed; and (4) alternating or multi-treatment designs, where, for example, relaxation, goal setting, and self-talk are used as methods (Eldar, 2005; Hrycaiko & Martin, 1996).

Single-case studies are important to generate knowledge of change and conditions. This creates enormous potential for the transfer from research to application. In psychotherapy research, there has been a trend toward more personalized research aimed at identifying relevant subgroups of patients (Gloster et al., 2024). Gloster and colleagues made a plea for idiographic approaches which allow for individualized psychotherapy. Similarly, sport psychology practitioners trying to support the individual development of athletes are encouraged to systematically document and analyze their cases and thus contribute to the development of evidence. To this end, it is recommended to stick to the Single-Case Reporting Guideline In BEhavioural Interventions (SCRIBE) (Tate et al., 2016). These 26 items that should be reported when publishing single-case studies allow interventions to be reproduced and thus demonstrate their internal validity.

The Systemic Research Approach

Based on our systemic understanding of sport psychology consultancy, not only an individualized but also a context-oriented research approach is needed. Both approaches can complement each other, especially when it comes to understanding individual phenomena in the context of broader systems. A central question is whether the research methods allow practitioners to assess the system's qualities, such as interactions, networks, synchronizations, and dynamical changes over time (Ochs & Schweitzer, 2012). For example, the effects of individual coping strategies on competition anxiety in the sense of a linear-causal analysis model are of less interest; rather the focus is on connections between the phenomenon of competition anxiety and variables such as the coach-athlete relationship, team and environment dynamics, or cultural expectations. Taken together, systemic research is a multi-perspective, multi-methods, and multi-level approach that is based on four different basic orientations: (1) relationship and interaction, (2) intra- and inter-individual reflective processes, (3) changes in complex dynamics of the biopsychosocial system over time, and (4) context sensibility for the side-effects of interventions and the role of the researcher.

Methods of data collection and data analysis need to be applicable in the sport psychology practitioner's work and provide added value. This means replacing linear-causal analysis models with models that do justice to the complexity of the sport system, for example through case-reconstructive qualitative approaches. The decisive factor is to capture the specificity and individuality of the individual case in conjunction with the structural framework conditions. Because this type of data is easier to apply in practice, it is more readily accepted by practitioners and helps bridge the gap between sport psychology research and applied practice (Liesenfeld, 2023).

Conclusion and Recommendations

Self-employed applied sport psychology practitioners are in most cases not trained in scientific work and publication procedures. Nevertheless, it is important for them to evaluate the effectiveness of their work. Understanding what is required for a valid single-case design and how relational and systemic factors of the sport system may be integrated is important. Sport psychology practitioners could discuss and coordinate their methods and designs in intervision groups, which would enable comparability without neglecting the individual needs of the athletes. In cooperation with a university, the documented counseling cases could be evaluated and published as part of their scientific mandate, thereby increasing the credibility of sport psychology as a profession. Further, scientists must refine and further develop methodological tools in order to adequately capture the complexity of systems in an advisory context. This will contribute to ensuring the quality of sport psychology work.

HOW CAN MASTERING STATISTICS ENHANCE EVIDENCE-BASED PRACTICE?

Andrew M. Lane

In my work as a sport psychologist, I've had the privilege of supporting athletes during some of the most critical moments of their careers. One such moment came when I worked with a professional boxer, standing on the edge of a career-defining fight. His emotions were palpable—anticipation, determination, and, above all, the drive to perform at his absolute best. He came to me to ensure his mind was in peak shape for this high-stakes event. He wanted every possible edge, and he turned to me for help (Lane, 2001). Working from a scientist-practitioner perspective, my responsibility is clear: I must guide athletes to use the best tools available, grounded in science. But this raises an essential question—how do I know that the science I'm turning to is sound? When I do a literature search, I see one study claiming a particular intervention will work, while another promotes a specific mindset as the key to success. The challenge is knowing whether this research is good science—whether it is reliable, valid, and will genuinely help the athletes I work with.

This is where statistical knowledge becomes one of my most valuable tools. It's the foundation that allows me to critically interpret research findings and decide which evidence will best support my practice. Just as the professional boxer needed to prepare his body for the fight, I must prepare my mind to evaluate the data. Understanding statistics helps me separate the studies that truly matter from those that might mislead, ensuring that the interventions I choose give athletes the best chance of success.

It's not uncommon for many practitioners to feel uneasy about statistics. For some, statistics can seem confusing, even intimidating, throwing a veil of mystery over the interpretation of results. It is not limited to sport; in the field of psychology across all areas of application, evidence-based practice is fundamental. A wealth of evidence indicates that practitioners must rely on empirical data to inform their decisions and interventions (Turner & Barker, 2021; Van Raalte & Vincent, 2022). This reliance on data is rooted in the scientific process, where theories are rigorously tested using statistical methods (Popper, 2005). Hypotheses, which are specific and testable predictions derived from theories, are examined against established criteria, often involving statistical measures such as p-values or confidence intervals (Kazdin, 2011). These criteria help determine whether observed effects are statistically significant or merely due to chance (Cumming, 2014). To be able to read studies and gather knowledge from science, trainees and practitioners need to be competent statisticians (Harris, 2020).

Lies, Lies, and Statistics: The Dark Arts of Data Manipulation

The phrase "Lies, lies, and statistics" underscores how statistical data can be manipulated or misinterpreted, emphasizing the need for sport psychologists to be skilled in understanding and interpreting statistics. Researchers can influence statistical outcomes through their choice of analyses, and without a critical eye, one can be misled by misleading conclusions. For example, it is possible to alter the interpretation of a correlation test result by using a one or two-tailed hypothesis. A correlation test is used to measure the strength and direction of the relationship between two variables. It helps determine whether changes in one variable are associated with changes in another—whether positively or negatively. In a one-tailed correlation test, the hypothesis is directional, meaning you expect the relationship to go in only one specific direction (e.g., one variable increases as the other increases). This type of test is more sensitive, meaning it can detect a significant result more easily. A two-tailed test, on the other hand, is non-directional. It tests for the possibility of a relationship in either direction (e.g., one variable could either increase or decrease as the other increases). This test is more conservative, requiring stronger evidence to reach significance since it looks for any relationship, not just a specific one. For instance, with a sample size of 30, a correlation between anger and performance (e.g., $r = 0.35$) might be significant in a one-tailed test, suggesting that anger negatively impacts performance. However, this significance may disappear with a two-tailed test. This is a simple explanation for a well-known technique.

If the statistical tests are more complex, it is possible to throw a veil over the meaning of the results. For example, in structural equation modeling (SEM), the goal is to examine complex relationships between multiple variables, both observed and latent (unmeasured). SEM allows researchers to test theoretical models that describe how different variables are interconnected, helping to understand cause-and-effect relationships. It combines factor analysis and multiple regression, providing a comprehensive way to analyze data. Fit indices in SEM assess how well the proposed model fits the data. They help determine whether the model adequately represents the relationships in the data. Common fit indices include the Comparative Fit Index (CFI) and Root Mean Square Error of Approximation (RMSEA), which guide researchers in evaluating the model's overall accuracy and reliability. Researchers may selectively report indices that present their model in the best light, leading to biased conclusions. CFI values above 0.90 are typically acceptable, but RMSEA values can vary depending on sample size or model complexity, illustrating how subjective thresholds can affect results.

The examples above illustrate how a practitioner can become distrustful of statistics. Interpreting statistics often involves making several relatively arbitrary decisions—decisions that are not always transparent in the final presentation of the results. Hidden biases and subjective choices are a fundamental part of the research process, and practitioners should scrutinize these decisions. Therefore, I argue that acquiring statistical skills is essential—not only to understand the data itself but also to unravel the relative influence of these underlying decisions and evaluate the strength of the conclusions drawn.

Overcoming the "I'm Not Good at Stats" Mindset: Applying Self-Efficacy Theory

Many trainee practitioners develop a kind of phobia about their statistical skills, often telling themselves, "I'm just not good at stats." This belief can create a mental block that prevents further development. However, I argue that statistical skills, like any other, can be learned. A cognitive-behavioral approach can be especially helpful here—trainees must engage with the material, take the initiative to try, reflect on their performance, and through this process of active reflection, gradually build both knowledge and skills.

One useful theoretical framework to utilize is self-efficacy, an individual's belief in their ability to succeed in specific tasks or domains (Bandura, 1997). This belief influences effort exerted, persistence in the face of challenges, and emotional responses. By fostering efficacy expectations through repeated practice and reflection, trainee practitioners can overcome their fear and develop competence in statistics. In my own journey as a practitioner, I've continually worked to develop my competence in research and statistical analysis, recognizing how critical this is to supporting evidence-based practice. Over time, I've changed how I access and process information. Back in 1994, I relied heavily on a single book about how to use SPSS—this was my go-to guide. Now, however, my approach is more dynamic. I turn to YouTube for tutorials and explanations, and more recently, I've discovered how artificial intelligence (AI) can assist me in interpreting results—for example, I simply copy and paste the statistical outputs into tools like ChatGPT and ask what the results mean. This has made it easier to understand complex concepts and integrate them into my practice. I've found that integrating AI into my work has boosted my confidence, especially when I'm unsure about certain aspects of data analysis. It provides immediate, understandable feedback that helps me take the next step, without the fear of misinterpreting complex statistical outputs. This makes the learning process more enjoyable and less intimidating, as I now have a tool to assist in making data-driven decisions more confidently. Through this ongoing practice with AI and by applying self-efficacy principles, I'm able to continually improve my statistical skills and build greater confidence in my ability to interpret and act on research data effectively.

Balancing my professional commitments and busy schedule can be challenging, but I've found that consistently integrating small, manageable learning sessions into my day makes a significant difference. For example, I allocate time each week to read recent research, gradually building up my knowledge base. I also rely on the principle of self-reflection to monitor my progress. After reading a study or engaging with a new statistical concept, I reflect on what I've learned and how I can apply it in my practice. This process reinforces my belief in my ability to improve and helps maintain motivation. I also seek out mentorship and feedback from colleagues and experts, which boosts my confidence and provides vicarious experiences of success. By taking these steps, I continue to grow as a professional and ensure that my research interpretations and interventions are grounded in solid, reliable evidence. As I continue to apply the principles of self-efficacy, I'm steadily becoming more proficient, not only in my statistical capabilities but also in my ability to apply this knowledge to support athletes in achieving their highest potential.

Mastering statistics is essential. It is a crucial part of ensuring evidence-based practice and making informed decisions that will have a tangible impact on athletes' performance and well-being. By embracing Bandura's self-efficacy theory, we can break down the barriers that often make statistics seem intimidating. Through mastery experiences, learning from others, receiving constructive feedback, and managing stress, we can build the confidence required to improve our statistical skills over time. Additionally, the integration of AI tools has proven to be a valuable asset in this process. AI provides immediate, understandable feedback, guiding me through statistical interpretations and helping me refine my approach to data analysis.

AN SEPP PRACTITIONER'S PLAYBOOK FOR QUALITATIVE RESEARCH

Deborah Skinstad & Heinrich Grobbelaar

The initial psychological assessment, through an intake interview, is fundamental to the work of sport, exercise, and performance psychology (SEPP) practitioners. The aim during the initial consultation phase is to explore and gain a better understanding of the often complex and multifaceted presenting problem, as well as to build trust and rapport with the athlete client. A key question during the initial consultation(s) is, "What is the larger story here?" In this chapter, we aim to highlight the parallel between the approaches, methodologies, and techniques used by applied SEPP practitioners and qualitative researchers. The analogy of the practitioner's playbook denotes a parallel between qualitative research and applied practice, and the overlap between these roles stands central to the scientist-practitioner's methodological enquiry.

Qualitative research is a broad term that represents several approaches and sub-approaches within its methodological scope (e.g., basic qualitative research, grounded theory, narrative, phenomenology, thematic analysis, action research; Babchuk, 2019; Creswell & Guetterman, 2019; Merriam & Tisdell, 2016). Focusing on the human experience in naturalistic settings, the methodological appeal of qualitative research is arguably well suited to the SEPP disciplines (Babchuk, 2019; McGannon et al., 2021). For the SEPP scientist-practitioner, the challenge of qualitative approaches lies in their practical application given they are tethered to the subjective nature of the procedures they employ (Babchuk, 2019; Creswell & Guetterman, 2019; Merriam & Tisdell, 2016). These procedures are, in turn, anchored in a rich philosophical history and milieu (McGannon et al., 2021; Smith & Caddick, 2012).

To understand the methodological procedures and the complexity of their interpretations, the scientist-practitioner must navigate the, sometimes, less familiar terrain of philosophy (Babchuk, 2019; McGannon et al., 2021; Smith & Caddick, 2012). Table 10.1 provides a comparison of qualitative and quantitative research characteristics. The starting point is selecting the appropriate philosophical lens to evaluate and understand the complexity of the presenting problem. Once the research process (or process of enquiry) is identified and understood conceptually, the procedures associated with a specific qualitative approach can

Table 10.1 Comparing Qualitative and Quantitative Research Characteristics

Characteristics	*Qualitative Research*	*Quantitative Research*
Ontology (what is true or real)	The world and reality are partially understood	The world and reality are systematically observed and understood
Epistemology (the theory of knowledge)	Ongoing search to understand the world through interpretation; non-positivist	Positivist and/or postpositivist
Purpose	Emphasis on meaning	Emphasis on explanation; hypothesis testing
Researcher role	Subjective narrator	Objective reporter
Theoretical framework (literature)	Minor role	Major role
Data collection methods	Interviews and observations; smaller sample sizes	Numeric data collection; standardized and validated instruments; large sample sizes
Data analysis methods	Meanings in the text; interpreting and describing; themes used to answer the research question	Numeric explanation; statistical analysis (e.g., differences, relationships, and cause and effect)
Reporting the findings	Narrative reporting; presenting experiences and meaning of participants	Standardized procedures; objective criteria

be articulated and systematically applied through what is known as methodological congruency and coherency, that is, best fit from start to finish (Babchuk, 2019; Creswell & Guetterman, 2019; Merriam & Tisdell, 2016; Smith & Caddick, 2012).

Navigating the Methodological Terrain and Application for the Applied Practitioner

Quantitative research, the proverbial lab coat approach to conducting research, can be considered somewhat distant from the nuances of human experience. Statistical analysis allows comparisons, determines the relationships between variables, and establishes cause-and-effects. In contrast, qualitative research seeks to understand the nuances of unique human experiences (Babchuk, 2019; Merriam & Tisdell, 2016). Understanding the complexity of the athlete and/or person beyond the sports field and their underlying motivation(s) for performance are key to informing best practice for the applied SEPP practitioner (Friesen & Orlick, 2010).

The appeal for adopting a holistic position suggests that qualitative inquiry may be suitable for improved consultation and practice, with an emphasis on "growth and improvement of the athlete as a human being" (Friesen & Orlick, 2010, p. 227). When considering the subjective nature of individual athlete experiences, trusted pragmatic guidelines, that is, play by plays will inform best practice for the applied practitioner. From a holistic perspective, the athlete is recognized as the protagonist and expert of their life story within the microcosm of sport and beyond it. The practitioner playbook concept recognizes the athlete's (subjective) voice in their life story while employing guidelines that are pragmatic, flexible to the athlete-client's needs, and overlap with a qualitative research framework. These play by plays are aligned with the holistic endeavor of both the qualitative researcher and SEPP practitioner. Table 10.2 presents an overview of qualitative principles, and the parallels between the qualitative researcher's endeavors and the work of applied SEPP practitioners.

The Qualitative Research Process: A Marathon of Reflexivity, Congruency, and Coherency

The qualitative research process is not a sprint but rather a marathon of inclines, declines, twists, and turns. Starting with the end in mind (i.e., the larger story), both as a qualitative researcher and as an applied SEPP practitioner, is a useful position when tracking and assessing the trustworthiness and integrity of one's endeavors (Creswell & Guetterman, 2019). Utilizing procedural checklists, known as strategies of validation, are integral to the research process from the start, helping guide the research process in its pursuit of congruency and coherency to create a total methodology from beginning to end (Creswell & Guetterman, 2019).

When I (Debbie) embarked on my PhD in Sport Science, entitled *Transitioning out of the professional player pathway: A grounded theory on the process in South African Men's tennis*, I wrestled with the concept of total methodology and questions around congruency and coherency. I inevitably made a few rookie mistakes along the way that turned into valuable stepping stones, such as: (1) My own position and lens; (2) Finding the best methodological fit, and (3) Trustworthiness; the cornerstone of rigorous qualitative research. Looking back, these mistakes helped me forge a framework for conducting systematic qualitative research in future studies.

A parallel can be drawn with the applied SEPP practitioners' endeavors and their pursuit of congruency and coherency in their professional philosophy and methodology. The methods implemented by scientist-practitioners should align with their personal worldviews, core

Table 10.2 Principles and Pragmatic Play by Plays for the SEPP Practitioner Playbook

Principles	*Qualitative Researcher*	*Applied Practitioner*	*Play by Plays (Practical Examples)*
Position Babchuk (2019)	Subjective; curious; explorer	Expert consultant; curious	Exploring the complexity of the presenting problem (e.g., asking open-ended questions on the presenting problem during the initial assessment).
Holistic approach Friesen and Orlick (2010)	Seek to understand deeper meaning; exploring larger story of human experience	Seeking to understand the complexity of the athlete within and beyond sport	Active listening and probing questions related to the duality of the athlete-self (e.g., seeking to understand the purpose, motivations, and challenges both on and off the field).
Contextual dynamic Thrower et al. (2024)	Exploring central phenomenon and processes; stories of participants	Exploring complex systems; behavior, performance and well-being	Open-ended, semi-structured questions that elevate the athlete as an expert in their life story, refraining from a conclusive assessment until the complexity of the presenting problem has been explored fully.
Data collection methods Creswell and Guetterman (2019)	Interviews to gain depth of understanding	Interviews to gain insight; inform best practice	Follow-up questions and active engagement (e.g., asking the athlete to capture their reflections in a journal) and encouraging athletes to self-reflect on their experiences and use these as ongoing threads (insights) for discussion.
Iterative process Friesen and Orlick (2011)	Following emerging leads through feedback from data; adapting in the process of inquiry (flexible)	Informing care and treatment through feedback; adapting approach and procedures	Continuous exploration through open-ended discussion/feedback (e.g., recurring questions and self-reflection on specific goals and development areas).
Application Friesen and Orlick (2011)	Informing practice and policies through understanding the complexity of the human experience	Improving best practice interventions or treatment by understanding the complexity of the athlete and their environment(s)	Ongoing assessment of (holistic) interventions that are tailored to the individual athlete's needs (e.g., a flexible outlook/ timeline with a recognition of their present, future and ongoing development and growth both on and off the field).

beliefs and values, and will take time to develop fully. We trust that this chapter will spark an interest in developing and refining your qualitative enquiry skillset as an applied SEPP practitioner to benefit your athlete client as person, and performer.

EDITORS' TAKEAWAYS

I (Lauren) will be honest—I was one of those students starting out in graduate school that Andrew mentioned in the introduction. I didn't want to do research, I wanted to work with athletes! And it certainly didn't help the cause when my master's thesis involved doing SEM when at that point all I had learned about was basic stats and research methods. It wasn't until later that I realized the types of research I found most interesting and even thrilling, and developed an appreciation for how important understanding research findings is for quality applied practice. Now, I love reading research and thinking about how to apply it. I may never want to be a "researcher" but no matter where my career has taken me in this field, an understanding of research has been essential and, in many cases, given me a competitive advantage. My sincere hope is that people reading this book, particularly those new to the field or in graduate school, don't skip past this essential section of the book because their mindset is as it was for many of us. "I don't want to be a researcher."

RECOMMENDED EXERCISES

1 Think of a statistical concept or test you find confusing. Spend 30 minutes exploring it—use statistical software, watch tutorials, and try performing the test yourself. Reflect on how hands-on practice changed your understanding and what you learned from mistakes or challenges.
2 Conduct an intake interview with an athlete to gather rich information about contextual and situational factors affecting performance. Be aware of and bracket your preconceptions, then analyze the data systematically using appropriate qualitative methods.
3 Find a recent sport or exercise science study. Evaluate its design strengths and weaknesses, and assess your confidence in its conclusions.
4 When two studies report differing findings on the same topic, how should a practitioner decide what to trust or apply?
5 Use an AI tool (e.g., ChatGPT) to summarize two studies on the same topic. Compare these summaries to the original abstracts: what was accurate, what was missing? Then ask the AI to explain a statistical concept from one study (e.g., effect size, p-value, and confidence interval) and cross-check with a textbook or other reputable source. What did the AI explain correctly, and what would you revise or clarify?

REFERENCES

Babchuk, W. A. (2019). Fundamentals of qualitative analysis in family medicine. *Family Medicine and Community Health, 7*(2). https://doi.org/10.1136/fmch-2018-000040
Bandura, A. (1997). *Self-efficacy: The exercise of control* (Vol. 11). Freeman.

Brown, D. J., & Fletcher, D. (2017). Effects of psychological and psychosocial interventions on sport performance: A meta-analysis. *Sports Medicine, 47*, 77–99. https://doi.org/10.1007/s40279-016-0552-7

Creswell, J. W., & Guetterman, T. C. (2019). *Educational research: Planning, conducting, and evaluating quantitative and qualitative research* (6th ed.). Pearson Education.

Cumming, G. (2014). The new statistics: Why and how. *Psychological Science, 25*(1), 7–29. https://doi.org/10.1177/0956797613504966

Eldar, E. (2005). Single subject research: Roots, rationale and methodology. In G. Tenenbaum & M. P. Driscoll (Eds.), *Methods of research in sport science: Quantitative and qualitative approaches* (pp. 543–573). Meyer & Meyer.

Friesen, A., & Orlick, T. (2010). A qualitative analysis of holistic sport psychology consultants' professional philosophies. *The Sport Psychologist, 24*(2), 227–244.

Friesen, A., & Orlick, T. (2011). Holistic sport psychology: Investigating the roles, operating standards, and intervention goals and strategies of holistic consultants. *Journal of Excellence, 14*(1), 18–42.

Gardner, F. L., & Moore, Z. E. (2005). Using a case formulation approach in sport psychology consulting. *The Sport Psychologist, 19*(4), 430–445. https://doi.org/10.1123/tsp.19.4.430

Gloster, A. T., Nadler, M., Block, V., Haller, E., Rubel, J., Benoy, C., Villanueva, J., Bader, K., Walter, M., Lang, U., Hofmann, S. G., Ciarrochi, J., & Hayes, S. C. (2024). When average isn't good enough: Identifying meaningful subgroups in clinical data. *Cognitive Therapy and Research*. https://doi.org/10.1007/s10608-023-10453-x

Harris, R. (2020). *Statistics for research: A practical guide* (3rd ed.). Routledge.

Hrycaiko, D., & Martin, G. L. (1996). Applied research studies with single-subject designs: Why so few? *Journal of Applied Sport Psychology, 8*, 183–199.

Kazdin, A. E. (2011). Evidence-based treatment and practice: New opportunities to bridge clinical research and practice, enhance the knowledge base, and improve patient care. *American Psychologist, 66*(7), 685–698. https://doi.org/10.1037/a0024561

Lane, A. M. (2001). Reflections on the psychology of boxing. *Athletic Insight: The Online Journal of Sport Psychology, 3*(1), 85–90.

Liesenfeld, M. (2023). Passung von Beratungsansatz und Forschungsansatz – welche Bedeutung hat das für die Praxis? [Fitting consulting approach and research approach - what does this mean in practice?]. In N. Schott, H. Krobus, & T. Klotzbier (Eds.), *Human performance: Assessment, Intervention & Analysen* (pp. 99–100). Universität Stuttgart, Institut für Sport- und Bewegungswissenschaft.

McGannon, K. R., Smith, B., Kendellen, K., & Gonsalves, C. A. (2021). Qualitative research in six sport and exercise psychology journals between 2010 and 2017: An updated and expanded review of trends and interpretations. *International Journal of Sport and Exercise Psychology, 19*(3), 359–379. https://doi.org/10.1080/1612197X.2019.1655779

Merriam, S. B., & Tisdell, E. J. (2016). *Qualitative research: A guide to design and implementation* (4th ed.). Jossey-Bass.

Ochs, M., & Schweitzer, J. (2012). *Handbuch Forschung für Systemiker* [Handbook research for systemics]. Vandenhoeck & Ruprecht.

Popper, K. R. (2005). *The logic of scientific discovery*. Routledge.

Reinebo, G., Alfonsson, S., Jansson-Fröjmark, M., Rozental, A., & Lundgren, T. (2024). Effects of psychological interventions to enhance athletic performance: A systematic review and meta-analysis. *Sports Medicine, 54*, 347–373. https://doi.org/10.1007/s40279-023-01931-z

Smith, B., & Caddick, N. (2012). Qualitative methods in sport: A concise overview for guiding social scientific sport research. *Asia Pacific Journal of Sport and Social Science, 1*(1), 60–73. https://doi.org/10.1080/21640599.2012.701373

Tate, R. L., Perdices, M., Rosenkoetter, U., McDonald, S., Togher, L., Shadish, W., Horner, R., Kratochwill, T., Barlow, D. H., Kazdin, A., Sampson, M., Shamseer, L., & Vohra, S. (2016). The

Single-Case Reporting guideline In BEhavioural interventions (SCRIBE) 2016: Explanation and elaboration. *Archives of Scientific Psychology, 4*, 10–31. https://doi.org/10.1037/arc0000027

Thrower, S. N., Barker, J. B., Bruton, A. M., Coffee, P., Cumming, J., Harwood, C. G., Howells, K., Knight, C. J., McCarthy, P. J., & Mellalieu, S. D. (2024). Enhancing wellbeing, long-term development, and performance in youth sport: Insights from experienced applied sport psychologists working with young athletes in the United Kingdom. *Journal of Applied Sport Psychology, 36*(3), 519–541. https://doi.org/10.1080/10413200.2023.2274464

Turner, M. J., & Barker, J. B. (2021). The use of Rational Emotive Behavior Therapy (REBT) in sport and performance: A systematic review. *Journal of Applied Sport Psychology, 33*(3), 260–283. https://doi.org/10.1080/10413200.2020.1720049

Van Raalte, J. L., & Vincent, A. (2022). Psychological skills training in sport: A systematic review of meta-analyses from 2011 to 2021. *International Review of Sport and Exercise Psychology, 15*(2), 375–393. https://doi.org/10.1080/1750984X.2021.1930569

Weidig, T., & Liesenfeld, M. (2020). Professionelles Selbstverständnis [Professional self-image]. In K. Staufenbiel, M. Liesenfeld, & B. Lobinger (Eds.), *Angewandte Sportpsychologie für den Leistungssport* [Applied sport psychology for the performance sport] (pp. 46–58). Hogrefe.

11 Collaborative Research Teams

Many of us SEPPPs who are employed by academic institutions are familiar with the "publish or perish" mentality that implicitly runs through academia. Even our colleagues who primarily focus on applied work can feel pressure to contribute periodically to peer-reviewed publications to maintain credibility, signal expertise, and align with the scientist-practitioner model discussed in Chapter 9. But conducting research as a soloist can be slow, inefficient, stagnating, and prone to old ideas simply being rebranded. This is where collaborative research groups become vital. They foster innovation, accountability, and momentum. However, for those of us in the field just getting started, and especially for those of us whose master's education followed an applied stream, it is beneficial to hear about the advantages and disadvantages of collaborative research groups. It helps demystify the process, sets realistic expectations, and empowers newcomers to find their place within scholarly communities that can fuel both their academic and applied development. We hope this chapter will inspire increased networking among our professionals resulting in fruitful research productivity.

RESEARCH TEAMS AS LIVED COLLABORATIVE COSMOPOLITANISM

Anne-Marie Elbe & Vassilis Barkoukis

Maybe one of the most fascinating aspects of conducting research in sport psychology is that it does not need to be a "one person show" but can be a collaborative project. Collaboration can take the form of, for example, the supervision of a Ph.D. project, sitting on the committee of other graduate students in different programs or at different universities, or with researchers at the same or other universities both nationally and internationally. And if a researcher is successful in acquiring funds for their research project, collaborators might be partners from a wide variety of fields, for example, academics from other disciplines (e.g., medicine, psychology, or informatics) or even private institutions like sport federations and associations, political stakeholders, or insurance and health companies. With modern technology, collaboration is not limited by geography and can occur across universities, countries, and disciplines. This multifaceted partnership is often called "collaboration cosmopolitanism" (Bozeman & Youtie, 2017). The increase in the number of co-authors on scientific publications (Huang, 2015; Turner & Baker, 2020) not only in sport psychology but in almost all research disciplines is an indication of the increase in research collaborations and makes it worthwhile to take a closer look at the topic of collaborative research teams.

DOI: 10.4324/9781003781479-14

Defining Collaborative Research Teams

Collaborative research teams involve multiple individuals or groups that work together to achieve a common research goal. This research goal could be, for example, a joint publication or the completion of an externally funded research project with multiple research questions to answer. Collaborative research involves the sharing of information, ideas, and resources. It is understood that collaborative research teams are composed of diverse members and all team members contribute with unique perspectives, skills, and expertise that is vital for completing the research. Research collaborations have several advantages but also come with certain challenges.

Advantages of Research Collaborations

There are four main advantages of research collaborations: (a) larger resources, (b) more innovation and diligence, (c) stronger results, and (d) its capacity building potential. Research collaborators jointly have greater access to research infrastructure than individual researchers. This can pertain to specific software, equipment, laboratories as well as access to specific populations, cultures, and languages. At the same time, pooling resources can reduce research costs. A second advantage is that research conducted in a team is likely to be more innovative and comprehensive because multiple people bring different ideas that provoke creativity. When researchers come from diverse backgrounds, cultures, and disciplines, chances are high that this might lead to new discoveries and insights and consequently could lead to the development of new theories, models, and solutions that are relevant to a wider range of end-users. A third advantage is that research conducted in a team has the potential to increase accuracy and validity of results because facts can be more thoroughly cross-checked. Results can be compared more critically because more people are engaged in the research process and provide feedback. This can ensure that the data is more reliable and that results are stronger and deliver a deeper understanding of the research question. Lastly, collaborations contribute to researchers' capacity building. They provide unique opportunities for skill development (e.g., cross-cultural, interpersonal, and language skills) and knowledge exchange among researchers thereby further enhancing the researcher's portfolio and competencies (Dusdal & Powell, 2021). In addition, subsequent professional opportunities may arise as a result of fruitful collaboration.

Challenges in Research Collaborations

Despite the advantages to engaging in research collaborations, it is important to keep in mind the potential challenges: (a) conflict, (b) increased length of time, (c) issues with consistency, and (d) increased costs. Collaborative efforts might not always be a bed of roses. For example, collaboration can lead to conflict. Conflicts are a normal and necessary part of becoming a high-performing team (Mallett, 2013). However, if they are not resolved, this can ultimately lead to dissolution of the research team and consequently the research goals not being achieved. Another challenge is that collaborative research can take longer to complete. Correspondence takes longer, more schedules need to be accommodated, and larger teams are also more susceptible to miscommunication resulting in delays. Also, due to the number of parties involved and diversity of their expertise, it can be difficult to ensure that research protocols that are carried out by multiple partners are consistent across people or sites. This can lead to inconsistencies in results, and makes it difficult to draw reliable conclusions from the research. Lastly, even though larger resources were outlined as an advantage, research collaborations may actually be more expensive (e.g., travel costs and expenses related to larger group meetings).

Best Practices

In order to ensure that advantages prevail over challenges, we suggest the following best practices. First and foremost, leaders of collaborative research teams should receive training in teamwork and how to collaborate effectively (Turner & Baker, 2020). During this training, leaders should learn how to pay attention to team functioning and essential interpersonal skills (e.g., social sensitivity, emotional engagement, and communication patterns; Slater et al., 2021). They should also learn how to conduct team-building activities (Parker & Hackett, 2012) in order to ensure an effective start to each research collaboration. In addition, they should be educated in communication and conflict resolution (Martono et al., 2020).

Another key practice is developing a project plan that includes a delivery strategy, time frames, budget information as well as monitoring, performance indicators, and evaluation procedures. Such a plan should also define the roles and responsibilities of each partner. A clear division of tasks makes each team member's role in the project clear and can assist in accountability. In this respect, it is important to allocate the project tasks according to partners' expertise and capabilities. Furthermore, this plan should provide the timeframe of the project activities, where a clear description of tasks' deadlines defines the workload and sets the basis for control. The use of relevant platforms and tools (e.g., Gantt charts for scheduling) which provide a visual representation of the project tasks and timeline helps to ensure that all tasks are completed on time. In addition, information about the budget allocation and financial monitoring should be included in the project management plan. A clear description of the budget allocated to each task and each partner is important to estimate the effort required to complete the planned tasks and can assist in monitoring expenses and task completion.

It is also important to discuss intellectual property rights at the start. An agreement on the intellectual property rights and authorship at the beginning of the project can help avoid confusion and disagreements during the project phase. Additional best practices are to implement democratic decision-making procedures and share all documents. Online platforms can be used for document sharing, allowing all partners access to the latest information thus ensuring full transparency.

Conclusion

Collaborative research is a valuable tool for researchers in many different fields. It allows for the sharing of resources and ideas, and can lead to new discoveries and advancements. It is important to keep in mind, however, that this type of research entails specific challenges and does require dedication and coordination among the participants in order to be successful. Following our suggested best practices might assist in achieving collaborative research goals and desired outcomes.

EMBODYING AN ETHICS OF CARE IN COLLABORATIVE RESEARCH TEAMS

Saemi Lee, Anna Kavoura, & Janaina Fogaça

Collaborative research teams are not only common but based on our shared experience is also necessary for conducting good research. Collaborations can offer rich and meaningful knowledge production and dissemination through the integration of multiple perspectives and resources. A collaborative approach also reflects how problem-solving actually occurs in the real world. For example, real-life problems such as health disparities cannot be solved by a single person or by a single discipline and require a collaborative and interdisciplinary approach with multiple stakeholders.

Despite being important, collaboration is easier said than done. Beyond practical concerns of who does what tasks, there are ethical nuances to consider when engaging in collaborative research. In this chapter, we introduce a feminist ethics of care perspective and explain why it is needed in collaborative research teams in sport, exercise, and performance psychology (SEPP). Specifically, we will describe how and why collaborative research teams can embody an ethics of care throughout the entire research process. Adopting such a perspective requires the centralization of care when approaching, cultivating, and maintaining (ongoing) relationships with the "researched" and when collaborating and interacting among research team members.

Feminist Ethics of Care in Research

Despite several institutional practices regarding research ethics and care such as the development of professional ethics codes or institutional ethics review boards, feminist scholars have argued that such practices tend to focus on avoiding litigation rather than truly interrogating power relations within, and as a result of, research practices. In contrast, feminist ethics of care frameworks tend to challenge dominant research practices based on hierarchical notions of power (Sevenhuijsen, 1998). In particular, feminist scholars aim to center ethical care as the priority of research and to facilitate empathetic, reflexive, and "care-full" (Miele et al., 2024, p. 134) research processes and products. According to Sevenhuijsen, the ethics of care focuses on responsibilities and relationships rather than rules and rights, concrete situations rather than formality and abstraction, and can be described as an "activity of caring" rather than a set of principles to be followed. In the following sections, we discuss how the feminist ethics of care framework can be applied to care for the research process, and care for the research team.

Care for the Research Process

Incorporating feminist ethics of care into collaborative research teams demands a fundamental shift from traditional approaches that often prioritize objectivity, neutrality, and distance between researchers and the "researched." Instead, researchers are called to recognize that the research process and the knowledge produced is co-constructed through deep engagement between the researchers and the community. At its core, feminist ethics of care calls on researchers to reflect on how the research processes and selected frameworks, as well as their own positionality and the power dynamics inherent in the processes of knowledge production impact the communities that are being researched. Equally important is reflecting on how we as researchers are affected by the relationships we develop with our communities. Inspired by efforts to decolonize the ways we approach and construct "scientific knowledge," research approaches that center on care do not just study inequalities but make active efforts to challenge them (Miele et al., 2024). This entails moving beyond research practices that merely fulfill academic requirements to producing knowledge that is socially just and transformative, prioritizing the well-being, integrity, and the local knowledge of the communities involved.

Critical SEPP scholars have also engaged in rich discussions regarding how to conduct participant- and community-centered research that moves away from exploitative ways of knowledge extraction, especially when our research involves communities that have been historically marginalized in sport (e.g., Muriwai et al., 2023). Though engaging the community is central in the feminist ethics of care, it is not enough if the researcher approaches this endeavor from a paternalistic stance in which researchers are the "custodians of care" (Toombs et al., 2017, p. 3). It is crucial to acknowledge the important contributions that participants bring to the research process and outcome. This requires ensuring that participants' voices are central to the research narrative and that the research is conducted with and for the communities rather than on them. Other concrete practices of caring include sharing decision-making power and involving the communities in research design and knowledge production, reflecting on ethics and on our own biases in every step of the research process, being transparent about the goals and potential outcomes of the research, and being attentive to the concerns and the actual needs of the community (that often might differ from our initial research goals). This care should be maintained throughout the research process (and even after the end of the research) with reciprocity, ongoing communication, and continued investment in the well-being of the community. Finally, when it comes to disseminating research findings, feminist ethics of care urges researchers to reflect on how they are "giving back" to the community and whether the research outcomes are accessible, useful, and support community-driven goals.

Care for the Research Team

Research teams are often composed of researchers with different backgrounds, identities, and career levels. It is an invaluable experience when senior researchers provide the time and effort to mentor younger researchers and involve them in more complex studies than what they are currently capable of leading to help them acquire the necessary knowledge and skills to conduct these projects. It is also positive to have researchers with diverse backgrounds and identities, as it has the potential to increase diversity of thought and ideas, and even boost productivity. These differences, however, can be difficult to navigate. Different ideas are not always accepted, cultural differences can affect expectations about behaviors and communication, and all these factors can contribute to an imbalance of power within the research team (Chao et al., 2022).

Because of this power differential, practical problems can occur, such as abusive co-authorship where senior researchers distort authorship credit to their benefit. To solve this specific issue, many journals instruct authors to follow the International Committee of Medical Journal Editors' (ICMJE, 2024) guidelines for authorship, and the Contributor Role Taxonomy (CRediT) was developed to highlight the contributions that are not considered authorship-worthy (National Information Standards Organization, 2022). Although these solutions are helpful in providing structure to increase the likelihood of fair authorship, they are not enough to maintain an ethics of care.

To develop an ethics of care in the research team, it is necessary to develop relationships that contribute to an empowering space that allows research members to speak freely, discuss with respect, and care about each other. For example, Miele et al. (2024) suggested the strategy of opening and closing research meetings by sharing personal and professional activities, which brought researchers closer and improved their relationships. In addition, the authors attempted to increase their ability to listen to each other by using reflexive turn-taking during research meetings, which allowed all researchers to contribute with their perspectives, ask questions, and participate in the decisions.

Beyond the structure that provides opportunities for everyone in the research team to participate and the intra-team relationships that need to be developed, Miele et al. (2024) argued that it is necessary to centralize power and oppression to engage in feminist ethics of care. Considerations of power may help researchers note, for example, that junior researchers need to trust senior members to feel comfortable talking freely and honestly during their turn (Chao et al., 2022). Power differences may also affect cultural differences in how punctuality, seniority, workload, communication, deadlines, and rest are seen. We suggest that the research team explicitly discuss expectations regarding these issues in the beginning stages of their collaboration and consider the multiple points of view while doing so. This discussion should help the research team develop their own functioning structure and minimize defaulting into dominant cultural values such as having junior members take most of the workload.

Conclusion

Although the ethics of care does not include a set of principles to be followed (Sevenhuijsen, 1998), we suggest that research teams develop relationships and structures that support an ethics of care and invest in the relationships within the research team and with surrounding communities to increase trust and vulnerability. The combination of centralizing relationships and structure can help research teams navigate the research process without being too formal or abstract.

THE PURDUE POSSE: OUR EXPERIENCE OF BUILDING A CLUTCH COLLABORATIVE RESEARCH TEAM

Mary D. Fry, Maria Newton, Lori A. Gano-Overway, Marta Guivernau, & Mi-Sook Kim

Sustaining effort and motivation to conduct and publish high quality research can be a challenge for scholars across their professional careers. We are fortunate that we have been able to do this, and part of our good fortune lies in establishing a collaborative research group early in our careers that has lasted for 25 years. In this chapter, we share how we came to form a research group, how it has been structured over time, and how it has served to strengthen us as sport and exercise psychology professionals and human beings.

Our story began at Purdue University where we are all alumnae of the graduate program and were mentored by a leader in our field, Dr. Joan Duda. We all overlapped during our years at Purdue with some of us together for only one year and others for two or more years. After we graduated, we looked forward to meeting up each year at the Annual Meeting of the Association for Applied Sport Psychology. In fact, one year when the conference was held over Halloween and there was a costume banquet, we came as the "Purdue Posse," dressed in jeans, vests, western hats, and deputy badges. While it was great to catch up and spend time with one another at conferences, we felt there wasn't enough time for in-depth interaction and discussion about our research activities, challenges, and breakthroughs.

Mary had the idea of having our own mini conference that would give us a chance to gather for a few days, share our research, brainstorm ideas to advance motivation research, and support one another. We held this first meeting in Memphis, Tennessee and Mary served as the host. We were all energized after that meeting and decided that we were committed to meeting the following year, which became a recurring event year after year. To keep costs down we stayed in each other's homes. In retrospect, this was a very important and impactful characteristic of the Posse. Our personal connections grew because we shared our families (including companion animals), homes, recipes, neighborhoods, and lives with each other. Our understanding of each other became multidimensional as opposed to unidimensional. The bonds we share today are due, in large part, to the intimacy of those gatherings.

We had in common a shared approach to our research efforts, as we all employed achievement goal perspective theory (AGPT; Nicholls, 1989) as the lens to our scholarship. In particular, we utilized this framework to examine the motivational climate established within physical activity settings such as sport. According to Nicholls, there are four features of a task-involving climate, and these unlock the key to creating an optimal motivational environment that is most likely to maximize each person's potential. Briefly, Nicholls purported that in achievement settings, the leaders should strive to help each member: (a) gauge their success based on their effort and improvement, (b) view mistakes as an inevitable part of striving and see them as opportunities for growth and development, (c) see how they are each important to the group, and (d) develop relationships so that cooperation can be fostered. While Nicholls' focus was on educational settings, Duda and many others (including the Purdue Posse) have examined the benefits of a task-involving climate in sport.

As we began our collaborative research group, Maria introduced Nel Noddings' (2003) work at one of our early annual meetings. She had been reading the educational philosopher's compelling body of work and wanted us to discuss it. Noddings argued that when working with young people, if we succeed in anything it should be to help youngsters feel genuinely cared for. We all dove into this literature and decided that the notion of a "caring climate" complimented Nicholls' features of a task-involving climate and added a more explicit focus on kindness and respect. We defined a caring climate as "the extent to which individuals perceive a particular setting to be interpersonally inviting, safe, supportive, and capable of providing the experience of being valued and respected" (Newton et al., 2007, p. 70). We created a caring climate measure to use in physical activity settings, went about investigating the positive outcomes associated with it, and have explored how to help coaches create a caring climate. We have had projects where our entire group collaborated and then, over time, we found that breaking off into smaller work groups for projects has been extremely fruitful and rewarding. In 2020, our work culminated in a book titled, *A Coaches' Guide to Maximizing the Youth Sport Experience: Work Hard and Be Kind*. We have come to believe a caring and task-involving climate is the key to maximizing individuals' experiences and potential in sport settings, and we also firmly believe these climate features are a model for living life, including developing a collaborative research group. We briefly describe each of the features of a caring and task-involving climate (see Figure 11.1) in the following sections and their effect on our group.

Each Member's Effort and Improvement is Recognized and Valued

Across our years together, our personal effort and growth has been consistently recognized by each member of the team. It has been interesting to see both in the moment and over time how leaning into effort and improvement has fostered our progression. We have collectively progressed in our ability to: (a) formulate interesting research questions; (b) develop methods to address these questions; (c) apply appropriate rigorous and advanced statistical analyses; (d) build studies onto one another; and (e) manage the publication review process. These are invaluable skills for any research group to develop and streamline. By focusing on and recognizing the unique skillset and effort of each Posse member, we were able to facilitate personal growth in relation to the research process.

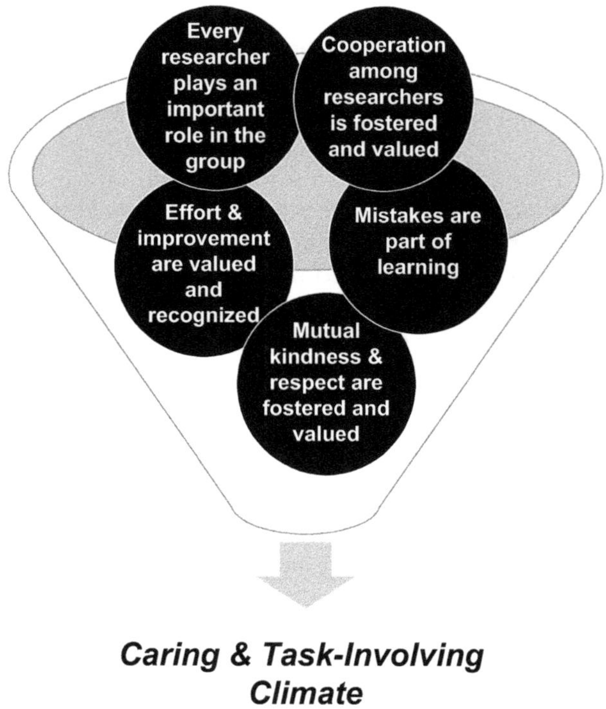

Figure 11.1 Features of a caring and task-involving climate
Source: Adapted from Fry et al. (2020)

Mistakes are Considered Avenues for Growth and Development

In a research collaboration such as ours, it's not so much that members are making mistakes but there have definitely been times when situations arose that we could have handled better. For example, we weren't able to contribute to a project as fully as we had hoped, or we feel we let the group down in some way. Our approach has always been to cut one another slack, pick up the load and help carry it, and fully understand that life will be challenging for each of us at different times and for many different reasons. Our philosophy has always centered around being team players and supporting one another; we've never been in the business of pointing fingers, placing blame, or expressing disappointment in one another.

Each Person Plays an Important Role in the Group

Each of us has a gift for recognizing all the amazing qualities each person brings to the Posse. For example, Mi-Sook has strong organizational and leadership skills. We've watched her serve as a faculty member, then the Chair of a department, and now as a Dean. She would have our vote if she ran for President of the United States. Marta is kind and nurturing and has beautiful writing skills. While each of us has played a variety of important roles within the group, what is most remarkable is that we have helped one another see that they play these important roles. It is easy, at times, to see positive qualities in others but not ourselves, and it has been powerful to have colleagues who help us recognize these attributes in ourselves. Being able to recognize the attributes each member brings to the Posse has allowed members to lean into what they are good at and learn from others. Additionally, as our group continued to develop, we came to appreciate the varied perspectives each person brought to the table. Therefore, we sought to make sure all voices were heard and to understand another's perspective when it differed from ours. This process, while sometimes difficult, along with leaning into and learning from others' strengths, improved the quality of our work.

Cooperation Is Fostered Among All Members

Nicholls (1989) believed that teachers could build relationships with their students, but the more challenging aspect was helping build relationships among students. In the Purdue Posse, there is a ten-year-age gap between the youngest to the oldest members. Some of us knew each other well in the beginning and had already formed strong friendships. Over these years, our friendships have grown as we worked to develop our caring relations (Noddings, 2003) by engaging in engrossment (i.e., getting to know another's interests, needs, and goals), motivational displacement (i.e., supporting each other in meeting our goals), and reciprocating care. Now, we would be hard pressed to indicate who we are the closest to within the group. Nicholls would be proud, we think, because he recognized that a group, like a chain, is only as strong as each relationship or link.

Everyone Is Treated with Kindness and Respect

Over the years, our collaborative research group has evolved far beyond the research focus that brought us together in the beginning. We have become the best of friends and been there for one another through the challenges of life (e.g., raising children; deaths of parents; health issues; a home destroyed by fire) and the challenges of living in an academic world (e.g., tenure and promotion; toxic work environments; gender bias). We've been a sounding board; we've had each other's backs and been a constant source of support and encouragement. Life and navigating academia is hard. Being surrounded by a group of individuals who are able to understand and empathize with each other allows each burden to weigh a bit less. The feeling of being treated with kindness and respect allows for personal resilience to germinate.

EDITORS' TAKEAWAYS

Reading this chapter it struck me (Lauren) that it is common to hear applied practitioners talk about how isolating their work can be; yet, less often do we talk about that this may also be the case for research. I wonder how much of our pursuit of solo vs. group ventures, when in our control, is based on our personalities and experiences working in groups during our education. I have had many opportunities over the years to work alone and work in groups of various makeups—both have been both positive and negative experiences. While the members of the group certainly make a difference, I have always thought that diversity (of thought, background, etc.) leads to better outcomes, something I know is supported by the research. The contributors of this chapter make a strong case for the value of collaboration as well as considerations to be mindful of to make them most successful—whether in research, or applied practice or any endeavor.

RECOMMENDED EXERCISES

1 Brainstorm a list of people you respect and would like to collaborate with. What qualities do they have that you admire, want to model, or motivate you to work with them?
2 Outline the steps you would take at the start of a collaborative research project to ensure success. How would you respond if a partner fails to meet agreed tasks or deadlines?
3 To structure a research team, proactively discuss the following with your team, and add any other questions you find important:

   a Primary communication methods and response expectations during weekdays and weekends
   b Division of tasks and responsibilities
   c Expectations for independent work, and when junior members should seek guidance
   d Punctuality for meetings and how to handle schedule changes
   e Handling deadlines and accommodating changes

4 List the strengths and gifts you bring to a collaborative team. How would these benefit others? How might your demographic or cultural background influence your thinking and actions, aligning or conflicting with others' expectations?
5 Reflect on whether your worldview aligns more with a caring/task-focused or ego-driven approach. Which aspects of each climate appeal to you, and where would you thrive? What current behaviors help foster your preferred climate in a collaborative setting?

REFERENCES

Bozeman, B., & Youtie, J. (2017). *The strength in numbers: The new science of team science*. Princeton University Press.

Chao, D., Badwan, M., & Briceno, E. M. (2022). Addressing diversity, equity, inclusion and belonging (DEIB) in mentorship relationships. *Journal of Clinical and Experimental Neuropsychology, 44*, 420–440. https://doi.org/10.1080/13803395.2022.2112151

Dusdal, J., & Powell, J. J. (2021). Benefits, motivations, and challenges of international collaborative research: A sociology of science case study. *Science and Public Policy, 48*(2), 235–245.

Fry, M. D., Gano-Overway, L. A., Guivernau, M., Kim, M., & Newton, M. (2020). *A coaches' guide to maximizing the youth sport experience: Work hard, Be kind*. Routledge.

Huang, D. (2015). Temporal evolution of multi-author papers in basic sciences from 1960 to 2010. *Scientometrics, 105*(3), 2137–2147. https://doi.org/10.1007/s11192-015-1760-x

International Committee of Medical Journal Editors (January, 2024). *Recommendations for the conduct, reporting, editing, and publication of scholarly work in medical journals*. https://www.icmje.org/icmje-recommendations.pdf

Mallett, C. J. (2013). Conflict management. In S. J. Hanrahan & M. Anderson (Eds.), *Routledge handbook of applied sport psychology: A comprehensive guide for students and practitioners* (pp. 335–344). Routledge.

Martono, S., Khoiruddin, M., Wijayanto, A., Ridloah, S., Wulansari, N. A., & Udin, U. (2020). Increasing teamwork, organizational commitment and effectiveness through the implementation of collaborative resolution. *The Journal of Asian Finance, Economics and Business, 7*(6), 427–437.

Miele, R., Root, J., Godderis, R., & Meerai, S. (2024). Towards a feminist research ethics of care: Reflections, lessons, and methodological considerations for doing research during a pandemic. *Studies in Social Justice, 18*(1), 125–142.

Muriwai, E., Manuela, S., Cartwright, C., & Rowe, L. (2023). Māori exercise professionals: Using Indigenous knowledge to connect the space between performance and wellbeing. *Journal of Applied Sport Psychology, 35*(1), 83–109.

National Information Standards Organization (2022). *CRediT, contributor roles taxonomy.* https://groups.niso.org/higherlogic/ws/public/download/26466/ANSI-NISO-Z39.104-2022.pdf

Newton, M., Fry, M., Watson, D., Gano-Overway, L., Kim, M., Magyar, M., & Guivernau, M. (2007). Psychometric properties of the caring climate scale in a physical activity setting. *Revista de Psicología Del Deporte, 16*(1), 67–84. https://www.redalyc.org/pdf/2351/235119232005.pdf

Nicholls, J. G. (1989). *The competitive ethos and democratic education.* Harvard University Press.

Noddings, N. (2003). *Caring: A feminine approach to ethics and moral education* (2nd ed.). University of California Press.

Parker, J. N., & Hackett, E. J. (2012). Hot spots and hot moments in scientific collaborations and social movements. *American Sociological Review, 77*(1), 21–44. https://doi.org/10.1177/0003122411433763

Sevenhuijsen, S. (1998). *Citizenship and the ethics of care: Feminist considerations on justice, morality and politics.* Routledge.

Slater, M. J., Thomas, W., & Evans, A.l. (2021). Teamwork and group performance. In S. A. Haslam, K. Fransen & F. Boen (Eds.), *The new psychology of sport & exercise: The social identity approach* (pp. 75–94). Sage.

Toombs, A., Gross, S., Bardzell, S., & Bardzell, J. (2017). From empathy to care: A feminist care ethics perspective on long-term researcher–participant relations. *Interacting with Computers, 29*(1), 45–57. https://doi.org/10.1093/iwc/iww010

Turner, J. R., & Baker, R. (2020). Collaborative research: Techniques for conducting collaborative research from the science of team science (SciTS). *Advances in Developing Human Resources, 22*(1), 72–86. https://doi.org/10.1177/1523422319886293

12 Community-Engaged Research

Community-engaged research (CEnR) is increasingly recognized as vital in SEPP because it bridges the gap between scientific inquiry and real-world application. Rather than treating participants as passive subjects, this approach involves performers, coaches, organizations, and communities as active partners in the research process. It is also a perspective now frequently mandated by funding agencies and higher education leadership. While undeniably messy—adding steps to the process, requiring cooperation across diverse groups, and stretching the workload for researchers—its potential impact is significant. We are fortunate, then, to spotlight four research groups who share their experiences to help make CEnR more effective and sustainable. Our global author groups bring a rich blend of expertise and lived experience, offering valuable insights into the practice and promise of CEnR.

THE IMPORTANCE OF COMMUNITY INVOLVEMENT IN RESEARCH WHEN SEEKING TO ATTAIN GLOBAL PERSPECTIVES

Tracey J. Devonport & Montse C. Ruiz

Community participation, engagement, and involvement in research reflect varying degrees of community input, decision-making power, and collaboration throughout the research process. Sport and exercise psychology research has typically been carried out on, about, or for people, implying they have no say or influence in the generation of the research question, methods, and interpretation and dissemination of findings. This is known as research participation (see Figure 12.1). Community engagement also denies influence on the research

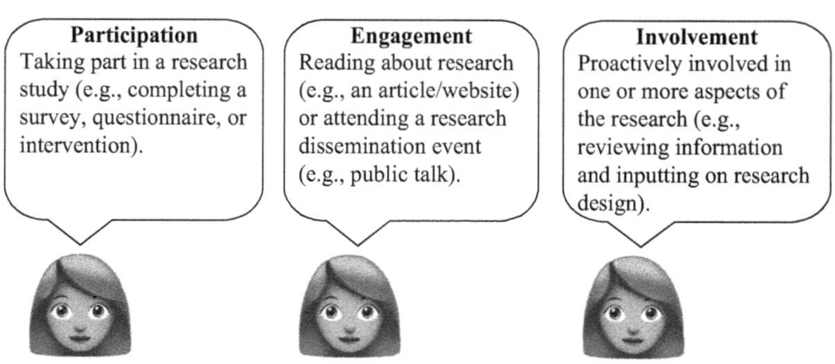

Figure 12.1 Levels of interaction between researcher(s) and the public

DOI: 10.4324/9781003781479-15

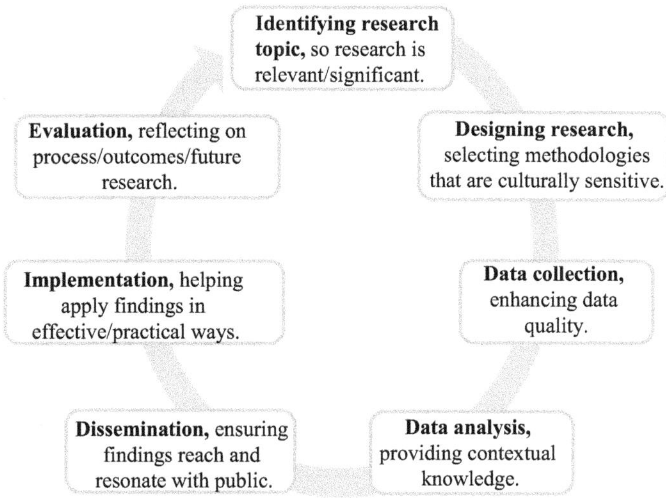

Figure 12.2 Stages of research and benefits of community involvement

process as members of the community are delimited to engaging with research outcomes in some way. Community involvement or co-creation means different things to different people and is used differently in different disciplinary contexts (Evers & Ewert, 2021). However, the common thread running across community involvement wherever and however it is applied is the proactive involvement of community stakeholders in one or more aspects of the research process.

Developing or delivering research with community stakeholders (e.g., end users, organizations, and influencers) is a growing, indeed required, practice in some areas of health research (e.g., when applying for public funding), and is a process known as co-production (Mockford et al., 2012). Community involvement can take place at all stage(s) of research and strengthens the process and global impact of the outcomes (see Figure 12.2).

Involving community stakeholders in research as co-producers may result in the following benefits:

Research Relevance and Rigor. Ensures research questions, methods, and outcomes are relevant and meaningful to all community stakeholders involved (Boaz et al., 2016). Illustrative examples of ways in which research relevance and rigor can be enhanced include: developing user-friendly participant materials, establishing appropriate recruitment strategies, increasing adherence to experimental protocols, supporting the interpretation of findings, and generating recommendations that are actionable and applicable in real-world settings, leading to greater impact on policy and practice.

Empowerment. Empowerment is defined as giving voice to community stakeholders and valuing their knowledge, expertise, and lived experiences. This empowers community stakeholders by fostering a sense of ownership and agency in the research process. This contributes to capacity building among community stakeholders by providing opportunities for skill development, knowledge exchange, and mutual learning (Mockford et al., 2012).

Improved Health or Societal Outcomes. Incorporating community stakeholders' perspectives in research helps identify areas for improvement (Brett et al., 2014). This ensures services are tailored to meet the needs and preferences of end users, leading to better experiences and outcomes (Mockford et al., 2012).

Dissemination and Uptake. Supporting the co-production of knowledge, where both professional and experiential knowledge are valued and integrated into decision-making processes (Grindell et al., 2022). This helps to ensure that research findings are accessible, understandable, and applicable to diverse audiences (Brett et al., 2014) improving dissemination, utilization, and implementation (Pinto et al., 2021).

Trust and Collaboration. Building trust and strengthening relationships between researchers and community stakeholders fosters a culture of collaboration and reciprocity (Cargo & Mercer, 2008). This can help bridge divides between academia and practice facilitating meaningful engagement and dialogue between different sectors (O'Mara-Eves et al., 2014). It can also help reduce skepticism and distrust among the community toward research institutions (Entwistle et al., 2008).

Cost-Effectiveness. Involving community stakeholders in research from the outset can prevent costly mistakes and enhance the efficiency of research activities (Brett et al., 2014). For example, community involvement can lead to more efficient use of resources by aligning service provisions with actual needs and priorities.

Community Involvement to Support Equality, Diversity, and Inclusion

The benefits outlined *can* offer contributions in challenging ethnocentric biases and enhancing our understanding of the human experience of sport and exercise from a global context. *Can* is emphasized because in order to ensure this is the case, it is important to recognize the underpinning principles of equity. Equality means each individual or group of people is given the same resources or opportunities. However, equity recognizes that each person has different circumstances and allocates the exact resources and opportunities needed to reach an equal outcome.

To ensure that community involvement supports equality, diversity, and inclusion, it is important to establish representations from different community groups (e.g., cultural and religious groups). This is because different groups may have different needs or different responses regarding the phenomenon or concept of interest. The type of lived experience required will vary depending on the focus of the research, and diverse community representation will generate a wider range of opinions, ideas, and solutions. Community involvement in research should be purposive, seeking the involvement of marginalized or underrepresented communities to ensure that their needs and interests are met by the research priorities and outcomes addressed (Pratt, 2020). Such an approach may challenge traditional power dynamics and promote inclusivity in research processes (Cornwall & Jewkes, 1995), thereby increasing the likelihood of meeting the needs of different groups and enhancing global understandings, ultimately leading to greater impact on policy and practice (Boaz et al., 2016).

In supporting the participation of marginalized or underrepresented communities, it is important to consider the barriers to engagement in research, and work with representatives of these communities to minimize barriers so that everyone can be involved. For example, potential barriers might include language (scientific/cultural), preconceptions (age/experience/cultural), accessibility (physical/cultural), power sharing, confidence, and interest/motivation. Initial and ongoing support and encouragement for community involvement from these groups is important also, as there may be greater suspicion and less confidence in taking part among these groups. Encouragement and support may be fostered by establishing psychological safety in respect of freedom of speech and equity of voices thereby avoiding generalizations and stereotypes. In view of these benefits, we advocate careful planning for the use of community involvement and co-production in the sport, physical activity, and exercise science domains.

COMMUNICATION AND CULTURAL AWARENESS: BUILDING-BLOCKS FOR COMMUNITY-ENGAGED RESEARCH

Stephanie J. Hanrahan

Participating in community-engaged research (CEnR) can be meaningful and beneficial for both community members and academics, but it is not as easy as simply going to a community to do research. As much effort needs to be given to the relationship between partners as to the research itself. Who will play what role? Is there a power imbalance? CEnR rarely involves randomized controlled trials so coveted by many universities and journals. It can be messy and fluid, but so is real life!

What Is Community?

We all live in communities of some sort, but communities may be more than just suburbs or neighborhoods. In addition to communities of place (e.g., tribe, neighborhood, state/province), there are communities of identity (e.g., ethnicity, race, disability) and communities of affiliation (e.g., religious group, sporting club).

What Is Community Engagement?

Conventional research in communities has not really involved community participation (even if the American Psychological Association did change nomenclature from "subjects" to "participants"). Some researchers believe they have had community participation because community organizations were used to recruit study participants. At most, this level of community involvement is tokenism because no real power is vested in community partners (London et al., 2020). For a community to be engaged in a research project, they should be involved in multiple steps of the research project (e.g., problem definition, research design, participant selection, data collection, data analysis, consideration of implications, application, and dissemination).

CEnR increases the opportunity for community knowledge and experiences to be understood. It gives community members the power to shape what happens within their community. Instead of being pawns subjected to the whims of external researchers, they actively are involved in identifying and addressing issues affecting the community. The process can also strengthen trust between researchers and community members.

It's a Balancing Act

Nevertheless, community members might not need to be involved in every step of the research project. The needs, capacities, and resources of both community members and researchers need to be considered. The researchers may have greater experience with quantitative statistics and have access to statistical computer packages, but community members may have a clearer understanding of how themes present in qualitative data might link together.

The project partners need shared goals. These goals do not need to be identical. For example, community members might not care about publishing in a high impact journal, and researchers might not be invested in the community having improved recognition at the government level, but these non-identical goals can be complimentary. In a project I was involved with in Papua New Guinea, a local organization gained respect and clout with the government when they were able to provide academic publications that demonstrated the effectiveness of one of their programs. The government officials seemed to place greater value on the results when they were printed in an academic journal than when they were provided in local annual reports.

During the research process, consider how to build capacities (knowledge, skills, abilities) of both academic and non-academic partners. Academics might be accustomed to being teachers, but when it comes to CEnR, they also need to be prepared to be learners—researchers are not the experts about the community with whom they are working.

Potential Issues That May Arise

What follows are issues I have encountered while participating in CEnR. These issues are not intended to be a complete list nor a representation of what typically occurs, but rather a glimpse into situations that have occurred when trying to meet the needs and requirements of my university as well as those of the community.

Traditional University Structure and Expectations May Not Align with Community-Engaged Research

Many universities want their academics to publish in high impact journals. Impact is assessed by the number of citations received by the journal's articles. Journals with high impact factors are not always accessible in low economic countries. I was literally yelled at by a higher-up in my university for publishing in an African journal (a journal published in the country where the research project took place). I (and others involved in the research) strongly believed the research should be published somewhere it would be accessible by locals, and not just journals with high impact factors. Some people in my university strongly disagreed. By publishing in this small African journal, I was bringing down the average impact factor for the department/faculty. If I had been a new academic trying to get tenure, our publication decision might have negatively affected my progression within the university.

A second example revolves around informed consent requirements of a university's ethical review committee. Ethics committees generally require signed parental consent for youth participating in a research project, particularly when participation is more than just completing an anonymous questionnaire. Ethics applications become complicated when working in communities with low literacy rates or with young people who might be orphaned or otherwise find themselves living on the streets. A solution found for a project in one Pacific Island nation was to make regular broadcasts on the local community radio about what would traditionally be in an information sheet, asking parents to speak to a teacher or principal if they had any questions or concerns. In a project with gang members in a Latin American country, the ethics committee eventually agreed any risks potentially present in the project were significantly less than the risks of everyday life for these individuals, and the participants could provide their own informed consent even if under the age of 18. If they were fending for themselves on the streets without parents, they could speak for themselves in the project.

Does the Community Agree with the Project taking Place?

Having an "in" with a particular person or organization does not necessarily mean the individual members of the community are being represented, considered, or involved. It is not unheard of for a research study to be used for political clout or personal gain. Investigate the actual level of community involvement, or better yet, arrange a community meeting to discuss the project.

Possible Power Imbalances

The most common power imbalance favors universities. Academic researchers represent centers of power, status, and privilege. The communities with which they engage may have been shaped by a history of socio-economic, structural, and racial/ethnic inequities. (Andress et al., 2020). It is less likely for the community to have greater power, but I have known an early-career researcher who was so intent on doing what the community wanted, the resultant project had no academic rigor and was unpublishable. An intervention that involved a two-month exercise program and group workshops exploring values and behavior change was originally going to have four groups of participants (exercise only, workshops only, both exercise and workshops, neither exercise nor workshops). The community wanted all participants to do both the exercise program and the workshops. In addition, pre- and post-questionnaire measures of values and motivation turned into only post-intervention evaluation of their experiences. The resultant findings that participants did not like having sessions on Tuesday evenings because they wanted to watch Dancing with the Stars on television, and that they preferred one of the gym instructors over the other one, were academically meaningless.

Locally Relevant or Generalizable?

Researchers usually want to use measures that allow research outcomes to be compared to past (and future) research. Nevertheless, existing measures may not be culturally relevant and meaningful. For example, physical activity questionnaires may include activities that do not exist in the community and omit activities that do. If you tailor-make the questionnaire to the community, results may not be able to be compared to previous studies. Similarly, when planning a cross-cultural study involving Africa and the Pacific Islands, the World Anti-Doping Agency wanted us to use pre-established questions. Betel nut was the drug of most concern to some in Oceanic countries, but did not exist in the African countries or the pre-existing questionnaires. A balance was struck—the majority of the pre-established questions were used, but questions about Betel nut were added.

Communication Is Key

Effective CEnR requires early and consistent communication between partners. The program structure may need to be flexible over time (the real world is much less controllable than a lab), so both parties need to be able to work together to adapt to changes. In addition to the actual research project, relationship building (between and within academic and community partner groups) needs to be an on-going consideration.

DOING RESEARCH WITH YOUTH SPORT PARTICIPANTS AND ORGANIZATIONS AROUND THE WORLD: CULTURAL PERSPECTIVES AND KEY CONSIDERATIONS

Lindsey C. Blom & Amanda J. Visek

Engaging youth sport participants in community-based participatory research provides opportunities to gain insight into their ideas and experiences, which are essential for reimagining and structuring sport experiences designed for them. Furthermore, viewing them as experts in their lived experiences for the purposes of research has broad implications for advancing a strong evidence base on which youth-based organizations can turn for data-driven guidance that ultimately shapes these experiences (Visek et al., 2023). In this chapter, we share athlete-centered research approaches from our work with sport participants from youth-based organizations across different community-based settings from around the world—specifically the United States, Liberia, Sweden, Jordan, and Saudi Arabia. Herein we describe athlete-centered study designs that use innovative methods to engage youth in research and share approaches for conducting scientific rigor with cultural competence.

Athlete-Centered Study Designs Using Innovative Methods

Our work has been underpinned by translational science study designs that center athletes' voices in creative, engaging, and developmentally appropriate methods. Some of our most exemplary positive youth development work has included mixed-method study designs including group concept mapping (see Visek et al., 2015, 2025), in addition to study designs that have incorporated guiding principles of appreciative inquiry (see Bronk et al., 2024) and photovoice (see Blom et al., 2020).

In Liberia, photovoice, a participatory method of data collection whereby participants use photography and narrative components to share their lived experiences, allowed youth participants with limited language exposure to take pictures to illustrate their stories. Likewise, appreciative inquiry, a strength-based approach, has been particularly helpful for ensuring cultural sensitivity and relevance when understanding and promoting youth development in diverse contexts. More specifically, within our cross-cultural research teams, appreciative inquiry has been foundational to building collaborative relationships with community partners and engaging in shared ownership of the research studies being undertaken and the co-creation of new knowledge. Finally, concept mapping, which combines participant-driven brainstorming, sorting, and rating activities with sophisticated multivariate analyses that result in rich, illustrative, easy-to-understand conceptual frameworks, have been particularly useful for leveraging youth sport participants' ideas and insights in unique and actionable ways. In the United States and Sweden, group concept mapping has successfully facilitated national sport governing bodies uptake of key study results because of the easily understood research findings.

Indeed, the aforementioned approaches are especially helpful toward building trust with youth sport participants and the important adult gatekeepers to recruiting youth in research. This is because the study designs purposefully emphasize youth's capacity, assets, and expertise when engaging them as research participants, while establishing strong research alliances with their parents/caregivers, and the sport organizations and community programs from which they are recruited.

Conducting Culturally Competent Research with Youth

Cultural competence, alongside knowledge of the country-specific research standards and sport norms, are important for informing the conceptualization of study designs and facilitating feasibility and ease of carrying out research around the world. We encourage interested researchers to establish in-country partnerships with other research scientists as part of the cross-cultural investigative team, spend time immersed in the community/country, and have community or organizational partners as investigative consultants or advisors. In-country partners often serve as important stewards in championing research projects to gain stakeholder buy-in at national, regional, and local levels and assist in navigating critical aspects of conducting research when youth are involved. Such stewards are often integral to connecting researchers with important stakeholders who are gatekeepers to youth.

Some countries will require research approval through a national research board (see Office for Human Research Protections International Compilation of Human Research Standards) in accordance with that country's law. For example, in Saudi Arabia, ethical research regulations are also influenced by Islamic law. Before research can commence, multiple other approvals may also be required. For instance, countries and their institutions may require Institutional Review Board (IRB)-approved documents from the principal investigator's (PI's) institution, proof of ethics training, and paid review or filing fees. The PI's own institution may also require cross-cultural review of the research protocol by a researcher in the country in which the research is proposed to take place. Moreover, all research approvals typically come with additional protections and permissions to safeguard young people as minors. Engaging youth in studies might require access granted by a sport ministry, followed by the sport organization and coaches, or education ministry, school principals, and teachers if recruited through classrooms. Following these approvals and access granted, subsequently parental/caregiver informed consent, atop youth's voluntary informed assent is required. Of note, countries may also operationally define important ethical terms, like "youth," "guardian," "consent," and "adult," differently. For example, "youth" in Liberia typically refers to individuals between the ages of 15 and 35 years. In Jordan, some families may only allow the father or male relative to offer legal authority. These nuances may not only vary by country, but also by community and/or partnering organizations. In the United States, engaging youth as young as five years old with waiver of documented consent has been possible. However, in Sweden, engaging youth in research earlier than 11 years old is unusual and doing so requires higher IRB review. Racial ethnic identity is also not commonly measured in Sweden, whereas it is often compulsory in the United States and expected by many research sponsors. In Liberia, ethnic identity is often based on tribal heritage, although participants may not be comfortable sharing that information for fear of discrimination.

Understanding cultural norms also assists with study design and research protocol considerations. In some cultures, girls might not have the same access to sport as boys and asking girls about their sport interests or ideas might be forbidden by a parent/caregiver based on normative gender restrictions. This could make conducting research with girls all the more challenging or less acceptable. In addition to sex and gender norms, we recommend researchers are informed of country-specific research norms as these can shape study designs in important ways. For example, in Saudi Arabia, only female researchers could enter girls' schools to conduct data collection and only male researchers could enter boys' schools. Inability for cross-sex/gender interactions necessitates study teams are sufficiently staffed, depending on the complexity of the study design. In other cases, like in Jordan, gender matching research participants with a same gender interpreter, can enhance a youth's comfort when answering research questions.

Alongside cultural norms, the language in which evaluation measures are administered to research participants must be culturally relevant and thoughtfully considered. Information sheets, informed consent forms, demographic forms, and other measures are often easier received when in participants' native language and local dialect. The Liberian youth who participated in Blom and colleagues research spoke Liberian English with regional dialects. Thus, it was crucial to have local adults offer suggestions on terms, examples, and concepts. When conducting cross-cultural research, having a bilingual native speaker who can translate research materials and back-translate data collected is essential. Visek and colleagues have used Marin and Marin's (1991) translation-back-translation method for studies conducted in Swedish and Arabic. Also, measures that utilize cultural/context-specific visual scales can be incredibly helpful in making research questions and measurement items more accessible for youth of differing abilities, in turn reducing response error and increasing the accuracy of measurement. In Liberia, Blom and colleagues used a visual scale with images to represent Likert-type scale choices—and similarly in the United States, Visek and colleagues used varying numbers of tennis balls in a pressurized can/sleeve that corresponded with gradient response choices for a measured construct when collecting data with neurodiverse tennis players.

Finally, when research designs involve community-engaged partners who will assist in aspects of conducting the research, like interpreters, school administrators, program staff, and religious leaders who are crucial to the completion of community-engaged participatory research, they often must also become certified research investigators. Under the requirements of an IRB, this may necessitate the completion of human subjects research training and health information privacy and security training. In Liberia, Blom and colleagues involved local Liberians to help co-facilitate the youth focus groups to help increase the participants' comfort and trust and demonstrate collaboration. In the United States, Visek and colleagues involved organizational leadership and program staff to assist in collection of data with neurodiverse tennis players, which required a larger research team to successfully collect data under constrained time limits around sport programming. In both instances, our partners were required to complete human subjects research trainings, which was a novel experience for them.

Conducting culturally competent research with youth sport participants and the sport or school-based organizations in which they play requires considerable thought, creativity, and importantly, planning. The additional oversights, approvals, and trainings required add considerable time demands that must be accounted for in project timelines. Alongside thoughtful planning, the cross-cultural research we have conducted around the world has been successful because of strong, trusted relationships with sport organizations and communities, that has been accelerated by partaking in their cultural norms (e.g., attending a religious community event in Libera, gathering for coffee with Jordanian and American colleagues before the research day commences, accepting tea and dates from Saudi Arabian school and sport administrators upon arrival for data collection, and breaking for fika midafternoon with Swedish sport administrators and coaches). Such customs can be integral to building social capital that makes possible important sport science research being undertaken around the world.

RELATIONSHIP-ORIENTATED PERSONAL DISCLOSURE AND MUTUAL SHARING: A COMMUNITY-ENGAGED APPROACH TO MENTAL PERFORMANCE IN UGANDAN CRICKET

Edgar Kazibwe & Matt Slater

Relationship-Orientated Personal-Disclosure Mutual-Sharing

The purpose of Relationship-Orientated Personal-Disclosure Mutual-Sharing (ROPDMS) is to foster understanding and relationships among athletes through sharing unique personal stories (Dunn & Holt, 2004). The purpose of this chapter is to exemplify a collaboration with community partners, the Uganda Cricket male and female national representative teams, to deliver, and reflect on, ROPDMS.

ROPDMS and CEnR

ROPDMS is potentially an important intervention that embodies the core principles of CEnR as it promotes deeper connections, trust, and shared understanding among researchers and community members. We set up a project to involve female and male elite adult cricketers representing the Uganda National teams at Lugogo Cricket Oval located in Kampala, Uganda. We used a one group pretest-posttest design to examine the effect of ROPDMS intervention on groupness and perceived interdependence. We involved 29 elite adult Ugandan cricketers (male = 20, female = 9) of Ugandan origin with an age range from 18 to 42. The national representative teams had been training together from the beginning of the year ahead of several competitions. While a one-group study is exposed to threats of internal validity, a combination of qualitative and quantitative methods to determine intervention effectiveness was used. Informed consent was obtained for all participants before the cricketers took part in the ROPDMS intervention sessions with quantitative data collected at three time-points (i.e., Baseline—one week before the personal-disclosure mutual-sharing (PDMS) session for the female participants and two weeks before the PDMS session for the male participants, post-PDMS, and follow up after four weeks for both female and male participant groups).

Based on qualitative data, ROPDMS bridged the divide between researchers and community members as a connection-building exercise targeting the team functioning needs of both the male and female Ugandan cricket team. In other words, ROPDMS was seen to serve a community need. Further, unlike traditional methods of research where researchers may be viewed as external authorities or in positions of differential power, the fabric of ROPDMS is vulnerability and transparency through dissolving hierarchical boundaries between the individuals involved. From a background of kinship systems and traditional leaders, such as clan heads, elders, and chiefs, who are seen as custodians of culture and community well-being, Ugandans have considerable respect for authority, and this transcends to sports spheres such as in cricket. The respect for authority also affects how individuals interact with researchers, seeing them as authority figures. This has often led to a tendency to answer questions in ways they believe the researcher wants, rather than expressing their honest opinions. This social desirability is not unique to Uganda, but such an "authority bias" requires researchers to work carefully to build rapport, establish trust, and encourage open communication.

Case Study

The case study examined the effect of ROPDMS intervention on groupness and perceived interdependence among female and male elite adult Ugandan cricketers. We preferred the choice of ROPDMS to challenge the changing dynamics of communication and interaction in Uganda between the younger population in which social transformation, and the societal changes of its systemic characteristics, has tilted the tides toward use of social media and online platforms rather than previously known physical facetime for building bonds and relationships (Mukasa & Kaddu, 2016). In addition, the team needs were enhancing understanding, relationships, and team cohesion between the cricketers following consultative meetings between the coaching staff and players of both the male and female national representative teams.

Trust and Authentic Relationships

ROPDMS mirrored CEnR through augmenting trust as a key construct resulting from sharing personally meaningful stories (Dunn & Holt, 2004). Inductive thematic analysis carried out with all social validation data produced two higher order themes: Improved togetherness and enhanced assertiveness, alongside the lower order themes of: Enhanced motivation and apprehension. With respect to several Ugandan cultural backgrounds, story-telling—synonymous with ROPDMS norms—has been the core of local traditions using the mechanism to educate values, beliefs, and acceptable behavior, with common tales permeating through to the current education system (Ssentanda & Andema, 2019). Therefore, ROPDMS was easily welcomed to foster togetherness and trust (a higher order theme) as reported by one of the male Ugandan cricketers; "I believe the mutual sharing was important to build trust and oneness for the team."

Trust has been a slowly growing concept in African societies despite low scores in regions with various tribes and ethnic backgrounds in countries such as Uganda. Afrobarometer further reports that there has been effort in East African countries to accept diversity especially with projects like Uganda's Vision 2040, and Tanzania's Vision 2025; however, Africans continue to trust cautiously; relatives are the only people whom a majority (58%) of Africans say they trust "a lot" (Malephane & Owusu, 2024). In sport, trust may influence performance because it can reduce anxiety, increase confidence and, on the other hand, the absence of trust may lead to fear of failure, avoidance of difficult tasks and collapse in team dynamics (Cresswell & Eklund, 2007). On reflection, a relationship of trust was fostered in the Ugandan cricket teams despite some of the participants initially having feelings of apprehension to share due to the different levels of trust emanating from that fact the teams boast a variety of ethnic backgrounds. Athletes' apprehension to share is typically in ROPDMS research (e.g., Windsor et al., 2011). The practitioner opened with their own story, with the first author sharing to foster trust and set a strong emotional tone for the female ROPDMS session. The premise of diversity in ethnic backgrounds informed the practitioner's involvement to bridge the gap that exists based on Afrobarometer's report on trust ranking at 45% in the Uganda/African context (Malephane & Owusu, 2024).

Power Redistribution

CEnR seeks to offer an equal status to the participating community so that they are recognized as co-contributors to knowledge rather than being mere subjects (Cook, 2019). The aforementioned core principle of CEnR was brought to the fore through the ROPDMS study, with the practitioner sharing their story first in the study with the female cricketers, a close replica to Windsor et al. (2011) whose PDMS study had the practitioner equally tell her own story after the 21 male professional soccer players from a top division club within the UK had finished sharing. The purpose of the practitioner's involvement also fostered a renewed sense of belief among the female cricketers, as evidenced in Windsor et al. (2011). This, however, was not the case for the male Ugandan cricketers' ROPDMS session. The practitioner purposely intended to start with a core national team player and end with the team captain during the male cricketer's ROPDMS session to create a better understanding of the activity but also inspire confidence of expression.

Co-learning and Capacity Building

We examined whether groupness and perceived interdependence were influenced by the ROPDMS team building intervention. The joint research with (rather than on) the two groups of male and female cricketers emphasized co-learning that led to later unmasking a previously unknown qualitative knowledge gap that ROPDMS enhances motivation, assertiveness and togetherness. This aligned with CEnR's purpose of ensuring co-learning opportunities were created between the cricketers and the practitioner; as the duo were educated on the need for applicability of ROPDMS with respect to the teams' requirements in a bid to enhance performance (Hacker et al., 2012). Re-engagement with the cricket teams' coaches to break down the results of the study, and discuss when best the team building intervention can be applied even in absence of the practitioner, also brought to the fore how ROPDMS ensured another principle of CenR, capacity building. Capacity building was explained as a practitioner working themselves out of the job, and the cricketers and technical staff being empowered to continue to optimize team functioning (Hacker et al., 2012). To further underscore the impact of ROPDMS, the practitioner also observed changes in the way the female cricketers related with him (unlike the men's session where he did not share a story) after directly taking part in their ROPDMS session; with more assumed closeness and a feeling of oneness as also reported by one of the female participants; "I felt a sense of belonging. Everyone was expressing themselves and I am sure some stories were emotional but they managed to share them and that is something to appreciate."

Conclusion

Grounded in the principles of CEnR, ROPDMS is a transformational culturally aligned intervention that bridges hierarchical divides, enhances trust, and cultivates meaningful connections among participants. With respect to the Ugandan cultural settings, storytelling facilitates openness and relatability, reinforcing the intervention's cultural validity. Furthermore, the practitioner's role in redistributing power, fostering co-learning, and building capacity is worth consideration when implementing the intervention. Overall, while ROPDMS requires careful navigation of cultural nuances and individual apprehensions, it holds potential for enhancing team dynamics and promoting inclusivity in sports settings.

EDITORS' TAKEAWAYS

My (Lauren) resounding reflection after reading this chapter is that it seems far more common to say, hear, and see "research on..."—research on self-talk, research on elite athletes, research on the key factors that lead to resilience, research on leadership. What if we shifted to more frequently using "research with..."? The authors in this chapter share powerful examples of the impact that taking a community-engaged approach to research can have for those communities as well as on the outcomes that we (practitioners, teachers, mentors, and researchers) leverage every day in our work. Even if this is just a mindset shift (though I strongly recommend taking the recommendations from the authors in this chapter to actually engage communities in research), it seems like a powerful one we should all embrace!

RECOMMENDED EXERCISES

1 Identify three key challenges in community research and how they might be addressed. What challenges could arise when co-creating psychological support for minority or marginalized groups in sport or exercise contexts? When co-constructing research on team culture, success, and challenges, how can stakeholders be involved at different stages? How can community involvement increase trust, enhance research outcomes, and amplify impact?
2 Reflect on a specific community-research project or community you are not a member of:

   a What knowledge, skills, or abilities do you bring, and what can you learn from the community?
   b How is power balanced between you and the community?
   c What assumptions might you hold about the community, and what assumptions might they have about you?
   d How can communication between all parties be strengthened and maintained?

3 Consider a situation with a power imbalance between researcher and community. How could PDMS help address this? Reflect on potential challenges and solutions.
4 If organizing a PDMS session where participants feel apprehensive about sharing personal stories, how would you manage the situation to ensure the session is successful?

REFERENCES

Andress, L., Hall, T., Davis, S., Levine, J., Cripps, K., & Guinn, D. (2020). Addressing power dynamics in community-engaged research partnerships. *Journal of Patient-Reported Outcomes, 4*(24). https://doi.org/10.1186/s41687-020-00191-z

Blom, L. C., Bronk, K. C., Sullivan, M., McConchie, J., Ballesteros, J., & Farello, A. (2020). Peace and development indicators in Liberia youth through Sport for Development. *Peace and Conflict: Journal of Peace Psychology.* https://doi.org/10.1037/pac0000463

Boaz, A., Biri, D., & McKevitt, C. (2016). Rethinking the relationship between science and society: Has there been a shift in attitudes to patient and public involvement and public engagement in science in the United Kingdom? *Health Expectations, 19*(3), 592–601. https://doi.org/10.1111/hex.12295

Brett, J., Staniszewska, S., Mockford, C., Herron-Marx, S., Hughes, J., Tysall, C., & Suleman, R. (2014). Mapping the impact of patient and public involvement on health and social care research: A systematic review. *Health Expectations, 17*(5), 637–650. https://doi.org/10.1136/bmjopen-2022-060861

Bronk, K. C., Blom, L. C., Fryatt, S., Miawo, F. M., & Appleton, Y. (2024). Appreciative inquiry: Guiding principles for majority and minority world teams conducting research in majority world countries. *Journal of Youth Development, 19*(4), 119–131. https://open.clemson.edu/jyd/vol19/iss4/1

Cargo, M., & Mercer, S. L. (2008). The value and challenges of participatory research: Strengthening its practice. *Annual Review of Public Health, 29*(1), 325–350. https://doi.org/10.1146/annurev.publhealth.29.091307.083824

Cook, T. (2019). Community-based participatory research for health: Advancing social and health equity. *Educational Action Research, 27*(1), 144–145. https://doi.org/10.1080/09650792.2018.1520135

Cornwall, A., & Jewkes, R. (1995). What is participatory research? *Social Science & Medicine, 41*(12), 1667–1676. https://doi.org/10.1016/0277-9536(95)00127-S

Cresswell, S. L., & Eklund, R. C. (2007). Athlete burnout: A longitudinal qualitative study. *Sport Psychologist, 21*(1), 1–20. https://doi.org/10.1123/tsp.21.1.1

Dunn, J. G. H., & Holt, N. L. (2004). A qualitative investigation of a personal-disclosure mutual-sharing team building activity. *Sport Psychologist, 18*(4), 363–380. https://doi.org/10.1123/tsp.18.4.363

Entwistle, V. A., Renfrew, M. J., Yearley, S., Forrester, J., Lamont, T., & Laybourne, A. (2008). Lay perspectives: Advantages for health research. *BMJ, 316*(7129), 463–466. https://doi.org/10.1136/bmj.316.7129.463

Evers, A., & Ewert, B. (2021). Understanding co-production as a social innovation. In E. Loeffler & T. Bovaird (Eds.), *The Palgrave handbook of co-production of public services and outcomes* (pp. 133–153). Palgrave Macmillan.

Grindell, C., Coates, E., Croot, L., & O'Cathain, A. (2022). The use of co-production, co-design and co-creation to mobilise knowledge in the management of health conditions: A systematic review. *BMC Health Services Research, 22*(1), 877. https://doi.org/10.1186/s12913-022-08079-y

Hacker, K., Tendulkar, S. A., Rideout, C., Bhuiya, N., Trinh-Shevrin, C., Savage, C. P., Grullon, M., Strelnick, H., Leung, C., & DiGirolamo, A. (2012). Community capacity building and sustainability: Outcomes of community-based participatory research. *Progress in Community Health Partnerships: Research, Education, and Action, 6*(3), 349–360. https://doi.org/10.1353/cpr.2012.0048

London, J. K., Haapanen, K. A., Backus, A., Mcak, S. M., Lindsey, M., & Andrade, K. (2020). Aligning community-engaged research to context. *International Journal of Environmental Research and Public Health, 17*(4), 1187. https://doi.org/10.3390/ijerph17041187

Malephane, L., & Owusu, F. S. (2024). Social cohesion: An African collage of imperfect tolerance and cautious trust. *Afrobarometer Dispatch, 871,* 1–23.

Marin, G., & Marin, B. V. (1991). *Research with Hispanic populations.* Sage Publications. https://doi.org/10.4135/9781412985734

Mockford, C., Staniszewska, S., Griffiths, F., & Herron-Marx, S. (2012). The impact of patient and public involvement on UK NHS health care: A systematic review. *International Journal for Quality in Health Care, 24*(1), 28–38. https://doi.org/10.1093/intqhc/mzr066

Mukasa, G., & Kaddu, S. (2016). Social media and social transformation in Uganda's families. 1–11.

O'Mara-Eves, A., Brunton, G., McDaid, D., Oliver, S., Kavanagh, J., Jamal, F., & Thomas, J. (2014). Community engagement to reduce inequalities in health: A systematic review, meta-analysis and economic analysis. *Public Health Research, 2*(4), 1–526. https://doi.org/10.3310/phr01040

Pinto, R. M., Park, S., Miles, R., & Ong, P. N. (2021). Community engagement in dissemination and implementation models: A narrative review. *Implementation Research and Practice, 2,* 2633489520985305. https://doi.org/10.1177/2633489520985305

Pratt, B. (2020). Developing a toolkit for engagement practice: Sharing power with communities in priority-setting for global health research projects. *BMC Medical Ethics, 21,* 1–14. https://doi.org/10.1186/s12910-020-0462-y

Ssentanda, M. E., & Andema, S. (2019). Reclaiming the space for storytelling in Ugandan primary schools. *Per Linguam, 35*(3). https://doi.org/10.5785/35-3-873

Visek, A. J., Achrati, S. M., Manning, H., McDonnell, K., Harris, B. S., & DiPietro, L. (2015). The fun integration theory: Toward sustaining children and adolescents sport participation. *Journal of Physical Activity & Health, 12*(3), 424–433. https://doi.org/10.1123/jpah.2013-0180

Visek, A. J., Albenze, R., Stranieri, A., Jin, Y., Vile, S., & Fordham, N. (2025). Group concept mapping fun determinants among junior tennis players in the United States: An ecological systems perspective. *International Journal of Sport Science & Coaching*, 1–19. https://doi.org/10.1177/17479541251345942

Visek, A. J., Ivarsson, A., Putt, G., & Learner, J. (2023). To have fun: What it means and its significance in sport. In M. Toms & R. Jeanes (Eds.), *Routledge handbook of coaching children in sport* (pp. 51–61). Routledge.

Windsor, P. M., Barker, J., & McCarthy, P. (2011). Doing sport psychology: Personal-disclosure mutual-sharing in professional soccer. *Sport Psychologist, 25*(1), 94–114. https://doi.org/10.1123/tsp.25.1.94

13 Knowledge Mobilization

Closing the Research-to-Practice Gap

What good is knowledge if people don't know about it and it is never applied? Every year, numerous scholarly journals publish the newly empirically validated findings that our research colleagues have worked on so tirelessly. So many athletes, coaches, performers, and community members would greatly benefit from the knowledge these researchers have generated and refined, but how can they access it and learn about it—yet understand it? This is why sport, exercise, and performance psychology professionals need to consider knowledge mobilization—the process of translating, sharing, and applying research-based knowledge in ways that make it accessible, meaningful, and useful to non-academic audiences—such as practitioners, policymakers, athletes, coaches, performers, or the public. While some university professors are incorporating more assignments into their courses that focus on knowledge mobilization, e.g., creating infographics rather than written research article summaries, the digital world has opened up a whole world of possibilities for all of us in the field to share knowledge. This chapter addresses the possibilities for knowledge mobilization and key considerations to keep in mind in our quest to make practical use of our evidence-based knowledge.

KNOWLEDGE MOBILIZATION: CHALLENGES AND SUGGESTIONS

Frank O. Ely & Irene Muir

What would you say if you were asked to list the main phases of scientific research? You might say conceptualization, ethics approval, participant recruitment, data collection, and analysis, as well as manuscript preparation, all in hopes of publication. While these are critical steps in developing empirical knowledge, scholars often stop at publication, thereby missing a critical step of the research process. This step is knowledge mobilization, which involves disseminating research findings to those who will apply it in practice (i.e., knowledge users)—thus narrowing or potentially even eliminating a research-to-practice gap. Knowledge users could include mental performance consultants (MPCs), coaches, or even the performer themselves. Unfortunately, for reasons no fault of their own, many knowledge users are drawn to user-friendly resources (e.g., websites, podcasts, and social media) or anecdotal experiences that often lack empirical evidence (Gould, 2016). Thus, our field is often faced with a disconnect, or gap, between research and practice (Ely et al., 2021). Therefore, knowledge mobilization is vital to eliciting relationships between the academic and applied communities to inform evidence-based practice (Eklund & Crocker, 2019). This chapter discusses knowledge mobilization and its role in narrowing the research-to-practice gap in sport, exercise,

DOI: 10.4324/9781003781479-16

and performance psychology. Additionally, the challenges of knowledge mobilization are discussed, and suggestions are offered for how researchers and MPCs can routinely integrate knowledge mobilization into their work.

What Is Knowledge Mobilization?

In the health sciences, research findings can take 17 years to be integrated into practice (Morris et al., 2011). This significant time gap prevents patients from receiving the most effective care based on recent scientific evidence (Graham et al., 2006). The field of sport, exercise, and performance psychology is no exception, as the psychological techniques and approaches used in performance settings might not always be grounded in empirical evidence. Consequently, knowledge mobilization has evolved as a viable approach to narrowing the research-to-practice gap through the "synthesis, dissemination, exchange, and application of knowledge" (Eklund & Crocker, 2019, p. 12). In other words, knowledge mobilization is the bridge between knowledge and action. To effectively guide knowledge mobilization, Graham and colleagues (2006) developed a conceptual framework (i.e., the Knowledge-to-Action Process) consisting of two primary concepts: ***knowledge creation*** and the ***action cycle***. Knowledge creation is described as a funnel, where literature is initially gathered on a broader scale, becoming more refined as it is synthesized (e.g., meta-analyses and systematic reviews) and then re-produced into knowledge products (e.g., infographics, workshops, and training modules). These products aim to present knowledge in a clear and concise manner, while tailoring content for potential knowledge users. The action cycle pertains to the activities necessary for knowledge application. This involves adapting content to the needs of knowledge users, while considering their barriers to knowledge uptake (e.g., time, access, and attitude). Next, knowledge is implemented, monitored, and evaluated, with the intention of long-term sustainability by knowledge users (Graham et al., 2006).

Despite guidance from the work of Graham et al. (2006), empirical evidence on the effectiveness of knowledge mobilization in sport, exercise, and performance psychology are infrequent. In fact, practical articles have been published voicing the need for and importance of knowledge mobilization in coaching (Gould et al., 2016) and in the design of sport psychology interventions (Ely et al., 2021). Although few in quantity, some knowledge mobilization initiatives have been conducted. For instance, PYDSportNet used the Knowledge-to-Action Process to promote positive youth development in sport through infographics, media engagement, conference presentations, and magazines (Holt et al., 2018). Similarly, Muir and Munroe-Chandler (2020) put forth visual and content recommendations for MPCs on creating infographics to promote mental health among elite and student-athletes. However, further investigation of the effectiveness of the knowledge mobilization initiatives above has yet to occur.

Challenges and Suggestions to Improve Knowledge Mobilization

Several challenges to knowledge mobilization should be noted. Firstly, researchers tend to focus their efforts on the output of research data rather than its dissemination. This is often motivated by an academic culture wherein success is measured by the number of publications and amount of external funding. Such publications are often inaccessible to knowledge users, unless they are willing to purchase the article for viewing. Furthermore, the use of scientific jargon can make it difficult for knowledge users to interpret and in turn apply key findings. Under-reporting is also common, as page restrictions enforced by peer-reviewed

Table 13.1 Suggestions to Improve Knowledge Mobilization

Strategy	*Researcher*	*Mental Performance Consultant*
Practical need	Explore research questions that address a practical need of knowledge users and/or practitioners.	Identify areas where new or updated research is needed and relay such areas to researchers.
Feasibility	Design applied interventions that balance effectiveness and feasibility in real-world contexts.	Share real-world contextual factors that impact their ability to use applied interventions with researchers.
Knowledge products	Consider the development and evaluation of knowledge products a key aspect of the research process.	Create and disseminate knowledge products to enhance awareness of the field to the broader community.

journals leave minimal space to offer practical implications (Ely et al., 2021). Thus, replicating research in the real-world is often not feasible. For effective knowledge mobilization to occur, we believe it takes researchers and MPCs working in collaboration; each doing their part to advance the field and impact the lives of knowledge users (Gould, 2016). As such, the following suggestions highlight the varied, yet coupled, roles of both the researcher and MPC (see Table 13.1).

To facilitate the interests of knowledge users, effort should be placed on addressing their needs. Since ***practical needs*** might be apparent to MPCs, who often work alongside athletes and coaches, they are uniquely situated to identify areas where research is needed. In some cases, it might be that research needs "updating" to account for various societal changes (e.g., social media) that question the relevancy of older research studies. If these practical needs are shared with researchers, they can be integrated into current research programs. Similarly, MPCs might also be aware of contextual barriers that limit their capacity to implement evidence-based interventions in applied settings. If researchers could consider how various personal, logistical, organizational, or cultural factors might impact their intervention design, perhaps findings would be more ***feasible*** for real-world application (e.g., Ely et al., 2021). Lastly, the development and evaluation of ***knowledge products*** should be considered part of most (if not all) research programs in our field. MPCs may also look to develop knowledge products to share with their (prospective) clients.

Additionally, we would like to forward three more suggestions for knowledge mobilization that impact the field more broadly. First, conferences attended by both researchers and MPCs are an ideal venue to discuss and promote knowledge mobilization (Eklund & Crocker, 2019). In addition to holding specific sessions for knowledge mobilization, working groups could be developed that allow space for researchers and MPCs to come together and discuss current issues and topics. Second, a working repository of knowledge products and tools could be developed, with the goal of disseminating and sharing these knowledge products. For instance, *Sport Psychology for Coaches* is a website developed by researchers to help disseminate knowledge products to sport coaches (www.sportpsychologyforcoaches.ca). A similar tool could be developed where researchers and MPCs populate their knowledge products and discuss their effectiveness across a variety of settings. Third, developing and writing content for applied audiences (e.g., athletes, parents, exercisers) is a ***skill***; one that is not often fostered in graduate programs (Gould, 2016). As such, education on writing for applied audiences and the fundamentals of knowledge mobilization (e.g., frameworks, research) would seemingly serve both the research- or applied-focused graduate student and enable them to further promote knowledge mobilization as a professional.

Conclusion

This chapter discussed the importance of knowledge mobilization in sport, exercise, and performance psychology. The Knowledge-to-Action Process (Graham et al., 2006) was introduced as a conceptual framework to guide knowledge mobilization initiatives. Challenges associated with knowledge mobilization were also discussed, along with suggestions for how researchers and MPCs can, collaboratively, work to narrow the gap between research and practice in our field.

KNOWLEDGE MOBILIZATION: COMMUNICATING RESEARCH TO THE BROADER COMMUNITY

Alex Auerbach, Stefanie Gazmin, & Ashley-Raye Miles

In the previous chapter, Ely and Muir discussed what it means to mobilize knowledge and its role in narrowing the research-to-practice gap in sport, exercise, and performance psychology. With that foundation in mind, we can explore how to effectively make scientific knowledge more accessible to the non-scientific and broader community.

Understanding the Audience

All effective writing starts with the audience in the writer's mind. The main recipient of your message determines your tone, choice of words, and the way that you synthesize information. If you are not clear who you are writing to and who you are writing for, it will be hard to clearly pass along your knowledge.

A useful framework for thinking about understanding your audience is the concept of the "ideal customer profile," a term taken from marketing that refers to the demographics, psychographics, and behavioral data of the profile of the audience you are trying to reach (Jefferson & Tanton, 2015). Creating a profile of your audience allows you to more clearly articulate information in a tone and with language that's useful to them. For example, it is common for practitioners to want to share information with coaches. To improve your communication with coaches, you could complete an ideal customer profile. Identify their key demographics (e.g., average age, gender, education) and needs (e.g., job security, get the most out of their players, their own well-being). Then, highlight their fears or aspirations. These data points will provide you with insights about what information would be most valuable to share and how to best communicate that information to reach your desired audience.

The profile of your audience sets the foundation for better understanding their needs, interests, and knowledge level about the information you are planning to share. For example, if your ideal audience member is a 17-year-old male high-school athlete (demographics), you might identify needs around belonging, inclusion, and managing peer relationships (psychographics). You might also identify that they are interested in sports, motivated to go to college, socially active, and concerned with their status (behavioral data). Finally, your profile would suggest that they lack scientific knowledge of the field, and thus your communication may need to first establish a shared set of facts before explaining the impact of a particular study.

Research Dissemination Methods

Your audience will also determine the best way for you to disseminate research. Each audience will have a different and best way to reach them with the information.

Scholarly Methods

The traditional methods of disseminating research include poster presentations, academic journals, and conference presentations. These methods are effective for sharing research with the scientific community but are unlikely to make a broader impact with performers and coaches. However, these methods are the gold standard for sharing information among fellow practitioners and are valuable for knowledge sharing in the scientific community.

Digital Methods

Websites, blogs, and social media are the most readily accessible way for non-scientists to access the most up-to-date science. Websites can serve as a repository for information designed to be more accessible to the public. Websites will often be designed with an ideal customer in mind and thus the shared information should be written with that same audience in mind. Websites are ideal for sharing large volumes of data on a range of topics but lack the ability to consistently and readily be put in front of consumers. The most effective way to consistently reach a new audience is via social media. These platforms allow for a quick and wide reach, though the ever-evolving nature of how the platform algorithms surface content is something to be considered. These mediums work well for short-form content that clearly communicates just one core idea.

Direct Communication Methods

Practitioners and scholars alike can engage end users in direct communication methods (e.g., workshops, seminars, and community engagement). These methods allow for a richer experience and for a greater volume of information to be shared, often with an audience that has opted in to hearing the message. These formats are very effective for reaching a smaller number of people, but with more depth, appreciation for nuance, and customization.

The advantage of these methodologies is that they are designed to reach a more lay audience at a higher volume of participants than the "traditional" and scholarly methods. We have a responsibility to try and leverage the science we know to improve the communities we are in and the lives of the people around us. These direct communication methods provide an effective forum for doing so.

Accurately Disseminating Research

When sharing research, in any of the previously mentioned formats, a premium must be placed on accuracy and transparency. In this case, accuracy refers to:

- Verifying the accuracy of your statements before sharing them;
- Establishing the credibility of the sources you are using to make your point;
- Representing the science in an unbiased and professional manner;
- Citing your sources as applicable;
- Making an earnest attempt to honestly represent the most up-to-date research.

Transparency refers to:

- Addressing limitations or remaining open questions about the information;
- Sharing the message in clear, accessible messages;
- Offering the audience an avenue for learning more about the work you are referencing;
- Using multimedia methods for sharing the information (e.g., visuals and infographics).

We have a responsibility to ensure that the knowledge we share can be easily understood and verified by an examination of the research. Holding ourselves to these standards allows us to more effectively engage in dialogue about misunderstandings or misinterpretations of the research and to represent the field of sport psychology professionally.

Ethical Considerations and Challenges

Disseminating research to the public is not without its ethical considerations and challenges. The main challenges facing the practitioner or scholar aiming to disseminate research include ensuring accuracy to avoid misinterpretation or misuse of the data, navigating conflict publicly with other providers and practitioners, and addressing bias.

In today's media (popular and social), there is an unfortunate propensity toward misrepresentation of facts and information in service of sensationalization. For that reason, it has become even more important for scientists and practitioners to ensure that the information they share is supported by the best available research. Where possible, attempts should be made to address limitations or unknowns in what is being shared and to proactively provide an explanation for why those limitations or unknowns exist. To the extent that our community can accurately represent the state of our field, we can be a beacon of good dialogue and information exchange for the broader community, while maintaining the integrity of our field. Failing to accurately represent the science risks jeopardizing the credibility of not just the sharing practitioner or scholar, but the broader community.

This also requires acknowledging and addressing biases–both in our own minds and in the data we are sharing. Most psychological research is conducted on WEIRD populations (Western, Educated, Industrialized, Rich, and Democratic), and as a result, it cannot be so easily generalized to people across the world. Yet, some of the platforms where this information is shared, like social media platforms, serve a global audience. Acknowledging these limitations allows the audience to accurately incorporate the data into their existing knowledge.

Finally, practitioners and scholars who share information regularly are likely to be subject to scrutiny, public attempts to discredit them, and combative responses from people who do not agree with the science being shared. In these instances, take the proverbial high road. Each of these interactions puts the disagreements and disconnects of the field on public display and undermines our credibility as professionals. However, these interactions can be frustrating and discourage further sharing. Rather than choosing to withdraw, it is best to return to the facts that you are representing, continue to emphasize accuracy and transparency, and to disengage from any public disputes. Dialogue and building mutual understanding is encouraged; disparaging other practitioners should be avoided altogether.

In today's era of social media, knowledge is a commodity. What helps practitioners stand apart is their ability to communicate complex ideas clearly, with guidance on application and implementation. Doing that with credibility requires effectively translating research to practice and understanding how to best reach the audience. The principles outlined in this chapter can help you to clarify your message, vary your methodology for how it's delivered, and provide high-value, actionable information to the broader scientific and lay communities.

"WWW.DIE-SPORTPSYCHOLOGEN.DE": TRANSFER OF KNOWLEDGE, TRANSPARENCY, NETWORKING: A PLATFORM FOR SPORTPSYCHOLOGISTS

Oliver Stoll & Mathias Liebing

In Germany, every football enthusiast still remembers the legendary match at the World Cup in Brazil in June 2014, when Germany defeated Brazil 7–1 in the semi-final round. This was the first time, at least in Germany, that experts provided sport psychology commentary on the big TV-channels for this never-expected phenomenon.

Just one month prior, the internet-based network platform and blogging webpage: Die Sportpsychologen (the sportpsychologists) was launched with the aim to present and discuss the science behind phenomena like the above mentioned victory of the German soccer national team. However, this event in June 2014 is linked to a coincidence: Parallel to the launch of the website www.die-sportpsychologen.de, Axel Springer founded the blog 1530, where a small editorial team curated the content of the then popular soccer blogs such as Spielverlagerung.de and Colinas Erben helping these niche publications to achieve mass distribution in the media world. A few days after the launch of Die Sportpsychologen, the platform was also added to the supplier list and even received Gold status, which is only granted to publications whose content is deemed to be of exceptional value by the editorial team. This is rewarded with a prominent position for the content in the 1530 blog and direct republication of the specialist information via the media of Axel Springer Editor, that is in particular *Welt*, *Bild-Zeitung* and *Sport-Bild*, the most influential print journals in Germany. As a result, the content of Die Sportpsychologen reached an audience of millions within just a few days during the 2014 World Cup. Well-founded sport psychology content was therefore available virtually overnight to people who were interested in or looking for this type of knowledge.

For us, it was unbelievable because what I usually was only discussing with some colleagues or telling my students at that time was suddenly in the mass media. Sport psychology was suddenly a topic in German media and so also recognized in the German sport psychology community as well as in the academic field. With a few exceptions, the statements on the website were also reproduced in such a way that the core content remained correct, even if the complexity was adapted to the respective readers or users by the editorial offices. Sport psychology seemed to be on everyone's lips for the first time—a fact that really surprised us. I would never have thought such a thing possible, even though I was the first supporter and key pioneer of the platform as the director of the Institute of Sports Science at Martin Luther University Halle-Wittenberg.

About six months earlier, in November 2013, I asked Mathias Liebing, a former student who was now working as a journalist, to hold a workshop for my master's graduates in applied sport psychology. The idea was to prepare my students for their own press and media work, showing them ways in which young sport psychologists can become more effective in the public eye without a large network and contacts. Despite our two-year training program, which is very practice and applied-oriented, it was a real challenge for many graduates to be seen with their qualities on the sport psychology job market. The workshop went really well, but the feedback from Mathias Liebing was sobering; he said that a person without a network behind them cannot generate a profitable reach. In principle, that was exactly the moment when Die Sportpsychologen was born, our new internet platform for blogs about sport psychology topics with accompanying author profiles. There were links that connected these blogs to the authors and the sport psychology services they offered.

The Beginning of a New Platform in the Field of Sport Psychology

Six months later, we launched the final version of the portal, which initially only featured students from my master's degree program and a few graduates. But it only took a few days for the first colleagues who had not graduated from Halle-University to get in touch with this platform. Among them was Dr. Hanspeter Gubelmann from Switzerland; the isolated solution for my degree course very quickly became an international project for sport psychologists from Germany, Austria, and Switzerland. What is exciting is that now, ten years later, the basic assumptions are still the same—the platform provides recommendations for sport psychologists, offers quality content for visitors to learn about various sport psychology topics, is a searchable library of years of publications on various topics, provides multiple ways of contacting the authors of the publications, and is available free of charge.

Practitioner Recommendation

In the analog age, a recommendation from a teammate or from the coaching and support staff was enough to seek direct contact with a sport psychologist. Today, after this recommendation, which is still incredibly important and has a quasi initial effect, an intermediate step has been added; before the potential client seeks contact with a sport psychologist, the recommended professional is "researched" with the help of search engines or social networks. The quality of the content that can be found online about professionals determines whether the contact is sought or not. Thus, the platform provides an opportunity for professionals to not only be found but also make an impression on visitors that entices them to initiate contact.

Quality of the Content

The content that visitors find online about a sport psychologist's work is their digital business card. More than a piece of paper, however, the texts, videos, graphics and audios can enable clients to understand the respective style of the practitioner, making the type of approach clear or even revealing favored methods of working with clients. Athletes and coaches thus have the opportunity to get an idea in advance of whether they find the professional likeable and inspiring.

Topicality as a Relative Value

Customers decide when the content is read and noticed. In this respect, the vast majority of content on the platform has had no expiration date. Even if content relates to specific events, the information, background, and context it contains is not time-bound. This means that even years after publication, readers can still connect with the sport psychologists, as the vast majority of them do not consume the platform like a daily newspaper or magazine, but are guided by their interests via search terms such as "sport psychology + topic or type of sport."

Barrier-Free Contact

All content has been personalized since day one. The blog posts therefore lead directly to the sport psychologist's profile page. There you will find the contact information that the author has published in their profile. This can be the mobile number, various social media channels, or the email or postal address. A personalized contact form is now also available for inquiries. Athletes and coaches can therefore choose the method that is most convenient to them.

Free of Charge Beats Paywall

Since the start of the platform, the content has been available free of charge. We are aware that the knowledge on the site is also perceived and used by competitors on the market. We accept this and even regard it as a transfer of knowledge to the sport psychology and mental training community. Much more important is the fact that athletes and coaches, our core target audience, can access the content free of charge. A paywall would significantly reduce traffic and be counter to the fundamental aim of the platform which is to share sport psychology knowledge, to fill gaps in knowledge, dispel prejudices, and create interest in the scientific discipline and its practical applications.

An Evolving Platform

Since 2014, we have counted 1,083,960 users, 4,573,429 page views, and 4.2 as an average number of pages visited per user. And, we have had 1,048 inquiries via the contact form since 2021 (when we first started offering this feature). When the platform was launched as a blog in summer 2014, this form of communication was modern, fresh, and innovative. Social media platforms were still in their early stages or were not even on the market yet. Thus, as the internet changes, the website continues to change. Changes in search algorithms, a fundamental shift in online search behavior, and, of course, artificial intelligence have long since ushered in major upheavals.

The platform has also adapted to become a network adding features, such as online supervision and other continuing education opportunities to mobilize knowledge among the sport psychologist community. In addition, the network has also developed its own products, such as an online coaching tool, combining video and text content with online coaching face-to-face. We also edit and sell sport psychology books and develop new coaching approaches for working with sport teams.

A good ten years since Die Sportpsychologen was founded, the discipline of sports psychology has so much more standing than it once did that TV commentators like Béla Réthy (a famous German sports journalist) no longer have to grope in the dark when describing certain phenomena. But the network's mission is far from over.

EDITORS' TAKEAWAYS

When I (Lauren) am asked about why I decided to enter this field, my answer has always been because I find the science underlying human behavior and performance fascinating and important. I could talk about it all day long, yet know that many people just want to hear the bottom line (i.e., what to do, quick fix) whose eyes glaze over when research is discussed. While it can be challenging and frustrating that research isn't always made accessible (in availability, understanding, and engaging format), including for practitioners who have raised the issue of limited access to journals when not affiliated with an academic institution, it is still our responsibility regardless of our role in the field (teacher, researcher, practitioner, speaker, presenter) to learn how to accurately and effectively share and explain our knowledge. The contributors in this chapter share a wealth of practical strategies for doing so, and I hope that readers take away several ideas they can begin to implement in order to be stewards of knowledge mobilization—along with a consideration of how to best "tell the story" of theory and research so that it resonates, sticks, and creates impact with the audience.

RECOMMENDED EXERCISES

1 What prevents you from sharing your ideas publicly? How could the dissemination methods in this chapter help you communicate more clearly?
2 Recall a time you explained a research finding to someone outside academia (e.g., athlete, coach, or family). What worked well, what didn't, and what does this reveal about your communication style?
3 What knowledge mobilization tools could you incorporate into your research, teaching/mentoring, or professional practice?
4 Select a recent research finding in sport or exercise psychology. Identify three to five audiences (e.g., athletes, parents, policymakers, coaches, students) and describe how you would present the finding to each to match their background and needs.
5 Which audience do you most enjoy engaging with, and why? What approach do you take, and what impact does it have? Now consider an audience you struggle to connect with—what strategies could help you better engage and enjoy interactions with them?

REFERENCES

Eklund, R. C., & Crocker, P. R. E. (2019). The nature of sport, exercise, and physical activity psychology. In T. S. Horn & A. L. Smith (Eds.), *Advances in sport and exercise psychology* (4th ed., pp. 3–16). Human Kinetics.

Ely, F. O., O, J., & Munroe-Chandler, K. J. (2021). How intervention research designs may broaden the research-to-practice gap in sport psychology. *Journal of Sport Psychology in Action, 12*(2), 101–113. https://doi.org/10.1080/21520704.2020.1798573

Gould, D. (2016). Conducting impactful coaching science research: The forgotten role of knowledge integration and dissemination. *International Sport Coaching Journal, 3*(2), 197–203. https://doi.org/10.1123/iscj.2015-0113

Graham, I. D., Logan, J., Harrison, M. B., Straus, S. E., Tetroe, J., Caswell, W., & Robinson, N. (2006). Lost in knowledge translation: Time for a map? *The Journal of Continuing Education in the Health Profession, 26*, 13–24. https://doi.org/https://doi.org/10.1002/chp.47

Holt, N. L., Camiré, M., Tamminen, K. A., Pankow, K., Pynn, S. R., Strachan, L., MacDonald, D. J., & Fraser-Thomas, J. (2018). PYDSportNET: A knowledge translation project bridging gaps between research and practice in youth sport. *Journal of Sport Psychology in Action, 9*(2), 132–146. https://doi.org/10.1080/21520704.2017.1388893

Jefferson, S., & Tanton, S. (2015). *Valuable content marketing: How to make quality content your key to success*. Kogan Page Publishers.

Morris, Z. S., Wooding, S., & Grant, J. (2011). The answer is 17 years, what is the question: Understanding time lags in translational research. *Journal of the Royal Society of Medicine, 104*(12), 510–520. https://doi.org/10.1258%2Fjrsm.2011.110180

Muir, I. L., & Munroe-Chandler, K. J. (2020). Using infographics to promote athletes' mental health: Recommendations for sport psychology consultants. *Journal of Sport Psychology in Action, 11*(3), 143–164. https://doi.org/10.1080/21520704.2020.1738607

Section 4

Practitioner Development as SEPP Professionals

14 Certification and Continuing Education for the SEPP Professional

While clinically trained and licensed professionals meet specific legal requirements to work as respective psychologists, across the globe, the laws governing their work differ. Thus, respective certification programs to adequately train professionals doing applied work in sport, exercise, and performance domains have been established by national and international sport psychology organizations. Navigating the options and choices one has as a graduate student or early career professional regarding clinical/non-clinical training pathways as well as a multitude of available certification options certainly has become increasingly complex and difficult. This chapter aims to provide some guidance and examples how professionals can carve out their own path to lifelong learning and professional growth. Besides graduate training pathways and relevant certification credentials, continuing education also plays a pivotal role in this process—as highlighted by these diverse author groups.

THE JOURNEY OF CONTINUING EDUCATION IN SPORT, EXERCISE, AND PERFORMANCE PSYCHOLOGY

Christine Sanchez

Working in applied sport, exercise, and performance psychology (SEPP) is a dynamic, lifelong journey—not a destination. Think of your professional path as an outward spiral: each turn brings you back to familiar places, but you return wiser, more refined, and better equipped than before (Allison, 2024). Continuing education (CE) is one of the many important tools that fuel this cyclical journey resembling an outward spiral. Sometimes, CE comes in formal packages—like earning a Certified Mental Performance Consultant (CMPC) credential or becoming Board Certified in Biofeedback (BCB). Other times, it's more informal—like joining webinars from the Association for Applied Sport Psychology (AASP) or reading up on emerging trends. No matter the format, the goal is the same: to grow, refine your skills, and stay relevant in the ever-evolving world of performance. This section will provide a framework and tools to assist in navigating CE's through connecting with purpose, creating a CE plan, and self-reflecting on integration.

Connect with Purpose and Values

In a fast-paced profession, taking time to pause and reconnect with your purpose and values is one of the most important things you can do (Duffy et al., 2018). When you set personal and professional goals that align with your purpose, you're more likely to experience satisfaction, energy, and a greater sense of well-being. Think of your purpose as your anchor—a steady

DOI: 10.4324/9781003781479-18

point from which your journey spirals outward. Your values are like your internal compass. They represent the principles and priorities that matter most to you. Self-reflection on your values can help you decide where to focus your time and energy (Iqbal et al., 2022). Here are a few self-reflection questions to guide your process:

- What would your life look like if your day-to-day decisions were guided by your values?
- Are your values consistent across your personal and professional life? Or do they differ?
- If they differ, is that intentional—and are both sets serving you well?

Once you've explored these foundational questions, begin tying those insights into your professional development. Aligning your CE efforts with your purpose and values brings clarity, intrinsic motivation, and a greater sense of alignment in both work and life.

Create a Continuing Education Plan

Every meaningful journey has a starting point—even if the destination is still unfolding. Creating a CE plan can help you take purposeful steps forward, rather than passively waiting for opportunities to appear. Think of your plan as a map for the next rotation around your professional spiral. Here are some key tools to guide you as you design your CE journey: (1) needs analysis, (2) personal interests and growth opportunities, (3) available funding, (4) networking and collaboration, and (5) required CEUs for certifications.

Start with a Needs Analysis

Begin by conducting an informal or formal needs analysis of the environment where you're currently working, whether that's with individual clients, teams, organizations, or other performance contexts. Meet with a coach or leader regarding the team's goals, strengths, opportunities for growth, culture, or even upcoming competition schedules. Ask yourself (and your collaborators) questions such as:

- What are the key performance demands?
- What are the current strengths?
- Where are the gaps or opportunities for growth?
- What is your client/team interested in learning or receiving help with?
- What obstacles are standing in the way of success?
- How does the client or team define success?

These insights will help you identify where *you* need to grow in order to meet those demands. Compare the knowledge, skills, and values required with your current competencies. This needs analysis will point you toward your next CE priorities.

Consider Your Own Interests and Growth Areas

In addition to what's needed in your current role, reflect on what you're *curious* about. What areas of the field light you up? Are there emerging trends or hot topics that inspire you to learn more? If you're drawn to areas outside of standard certification pathways (i.e., CMPC or APA routes), that's okay! You might be discovering your unique niche. For example, my journey included specialized training in clinical biofeedback and capnography—because that aligned with client needs

Table 14.1 Continuing Education Examples

Performance Need	*Course or Certification*	*Rationale*
Mental skills training and program development	Certified mental performance consultant	Ethically demonstrate core competencies in sport and performance psychology.
Restorative practices for performance recovery and managing allostatic load/overload	Registered yoga teacher 200 hr; Yin Yoga, Restorative Yoga, Yoga Nidra	Provide chronically stressed, elite performers with practical exercises and space for self-regulation and Autonomic Nervous System balance.
Mindfulness based self-regulation skills for managing physical mental, and emotional stress	Board Certified in Biofeedback (BCB)	Provide objective biofeedback data that facilitates self-awareness and self-regulation of psychophysiology.
Dysfunctional breathing habits in various performance domains	Certified Breathing Behavior Analyst (CBBA)	Advanced training in respiratory chemistry and capnography biofeedback to facilitate discussions with clients on dysfunctional breathing habit triggers, as well as, how to unlearn and relearn more effective breathing behaviors.
Coaching certification	International Coaching Federation (ICF) Associate Accredited Coach	Clients working through career transitions (progressing to senior leadership roles or switching to a new job/career) at times benefit more from a thought partner/ally lens vs. a performance consultant lens.

and personal interest. Table 14.1 provides some real-life examples from my own CE journey, showing how specific learning experiences were chosen to meet various performance needs.

Fund Your Education

Let's face it—CE can get expensive. But before you dip into your own pocket, explore these options:

- Employer Assistance: Does your workplace offer professional development stipends, tuition reimbursement, or conference funding?
- Work-Related Education Tax Deductions/Credits: In many countries, CE related to your work may be tax-deductible if it helps to maintain or improve your job-related skills. If you're self-employed, this is especially relevant. Speak with a tax advisor to understand how these apply in your region.
- Scholarships or Grants: Some professional associations or foundations offer CE funding. Explore what's available through AASP or similar organizations.

Networking and Conferences

Another rich source of CE? People. Conferences, workshops, and webinars are not simply for gathering information, they're for building connections. Attending regional or national events helps you stay current on research, discover practical tools, and meet colleagues who share your interests. You may even meet mentors or collaborators. Reach out to professionals whose work inspires you—formally (through courses) or informally (over coffee or Zoom).

The Power of Self-Reflection

Let's circle back to where we started: Self-reflection. It's easy to consume information. What's harder—but much more powerful—is taking time to absorb and *integrate* what you've learned. Self-reflection helps you connect new knowledge to your existing practice and make sense of successes, missteps, and insights along the way (Cropley et al., 2020). Here are a few ways regular self-reflection can support your development: (1) deepen your understanding of your beliefs, biases, and coaching style, (2) improve your emotional regulation under pressure, and (3) strengthen ethical awareness and help you stay within your scope of practice. Whether you journal, record voice notes, or debrief with a mentor—just make space for it.

Conclusion

Success in applied sport and performance psychology goes beyond textbooks and theory. It calls for creativity, resilience, and the willingness to explore new approaches that meet your clients where they are (Ryba et al., 2024). Your CE journey is not just about keeping up, it's about leaning in. Lean into your values, your curiosity, and your call to service. That's how you stay ahead of the curve—and how you grow into the professional you're meant to become.

COMPLEXITIES OF NAVIGATING TRAINING AND CERTIFICATION OPTIONS IN SPORT, EXERCISE, AND PERFORMANCE PSYCHOLOGY

Kyle F. Paradis & Shannon Burke

Navigating Career Entry Transitions

The career entry stage often involves a juggling act between completing training and certification and trying to navigate stable paid employment, whether in academic, applied, or hybrid roles. Career entry professionals in academia face a very competitive landscape, which may include applying and securing funding for postdoctoral positions and applying for limited term, part-time contracts, or full-time lectureships or assistant professorships. Career entry stage professionals are often juggling many tasks, such as building their research portfolios and teaching dossiers, writing and publishing academic articles, networking and presenting at conferences, and applying for grant funding in attempts to become established in their field. Career entry professionals in applied practice face similar challenges, whereby they are navigating a competitive market with limited opportunities to gain entry for applied work (Martin, 2020). As such, career entry professionals are often faced with a juggling act between professional responsibilities, and their personal priorities. It is a period of rapid professional development and growth but can also be an overwhelming period of great stress and even burnout (Hollywood et al., 2020). CE and professional certification play a pivotal role during this transition, not only by ensuring compliance with professional standards and regulatory requirements but also by increasing global employability and supporting the continued professional development of core competencies. This chapter explores the complexities of navigating training and certification options, alongside the practical realities of building a career in both academic and applied settings.

Applied Practice: Pathways to Certification

The field of sport and exercise psychology possesses roots in both psychology and sport science (Moran, 2004). As a result, there are a few options for pathways to certification in the discipline through both psychology and sport science streams. In the United Kingdom for example, the Health and Care Professions Council (HCPC) regulates the profession of practitioner psychologists. That is, "practitioner psychologist" is a title protected by law, and therefore it is a legal requirement that individuals adopting this protected title are registered with the HCPC. In line with this, in 2009, the HCPC introduced regulation which also protected the title "Sport and Exercise Psychologists." As a result, only individuals who meet HCPC standards in education, training, and practice are legally entitled to use the title.

At present, there are two professional organizations which provide training and accreditation routes for aspiring sport and exercise psychologists in the United Kingdom, and subsequent HCPC registration eligibility: (1) The British Psychological Society (BPS) and (2) The Chartered Association of Sport & Exercise Sciences (CASES).

In North America, the main governing body for certification is through the AASP based in the United States. However, AASP does partner with the Canadian Sport Psychology Association (CSPA) in the administration of the certification program. The certification designation is Certified Mental Performance Consultant (CMPC).

The European Federation of Sport Psychology (FEPSAC) has developed a European certification designation as "Specialists in Applied Sport Psychology" (SASP-FEPSAC) with guidelines on applied practice and certification. The International Society of Sport Psychology (ISSP) also has generated a registry (ISSP-R) for Emerging Practitioners and Established Practitioners (8+ years of consulting experience post-graduation from degree) which aims to provide a worldwide database of internationally recognized practitioners to increase visibility and credibility that represents a minimum standard of sport psychology practice and acknowledges the international mobility of both clients and practitioners.

From Certification to Applied Practice

Certification is designed not only to ensure that practitioners meet professional and ethical standards but also to help prepare individuals for the complex realities of applied work. When working as an applied sport and exercise psychologist, practitioners may operate or provide psychological support in a variety of settings. For example, practitioners might work in community, development, performance pathways, or professional-level sport, across a diverse range of sports. Additionally, practitioners might provide support to an individual athlete or coach, a group of athletes or coaches, a sport organization, or a national governing body (Keegan, 2016). As elucidated by McCarthy et al. (2024), each sport type and level present their own unique demands. It is important to highlight that for trainee practitioners, gaining access to high performing athletes or teams at the beginning of certification can be difficult. Therefore, gaining entry to local clubs, youth sport teams, or with varsity teams, are common placement settings during the first year of practice. This work may include providing psychological skills education and support to youth athletes, in addition to coach and parent-education. While garnering experience, trainee practitioners begin to develop their professional competencies and experiment with delivery methods, (McEwan et al., 2019; Tod, 2010) and become exposed to more diverse settings in their training period.

From an applied perspective, Martin's (2020) commentary on the profession of applied sport psychology highlights many of the barriers that the field continues to face since its inception including: a competitive market with low demand and few opportunities to gain entry for applied work, as well as limited paid opportunities across the field. Thus, the main pertinent barrier to entry for aspiring sport and exercise psychologists includes the financial cost associated with the training and certification process in addition to graduate school (Martin et al., 2021). In addition, trainee practitioners incur supervision fees in addition to training and accreditation fees. Thus, it can take practitioners several years of applied work in order to recoup all of these fees. As a result, it is commonplace for trainees to take on additional roles outside of sport, to augment their income (Martin et al., 2021).

The cost associated with training is further exacerbated by the limited paid roles available for career entry practitioners, let alone established practitioners (Martin, 2020). That is, in the early stages of training, as previously stated, much of practitioners' work might include providing pro bono services to local sports organizations and clubs in order to meet the applied practice hours requirement. In such settings, clients may often be limited by the financial resources available to support sport psychology services or opt to allocate their budgets elsewhere, and as such might not be able to employ a chartered practitioner. Therefore, trainee practitioners in the early stages of certification may end up providing a significant portion of their services for free or in kind or with expenses covered to meet their training hours requirement. Although the lack of paid work is an ongoing issue in the field, it should be noted these settings can provide critical development opportunities for neophyte practitioners in a lower stakes environment. That is, as individuals garner service delivery experience, they develop their professional competencies, explore methods of operating, and develop consulting styles, reflecting their philosophies and theoretical orientations (McEwan et al., 2019; Tod, 2010). As practitioners gain this experience, they can become better equipped to secure paid roles.

For career entry practitioners that do secure employment within a professional organization, the challenge can then relate to managing work-life balance. Previous research has indicated that early career practitioners are often expected by employers to be both emotionally and physically available, contributing to challenges in balancing personal and professional roles and practitioner burnout (Martin et al., 2021). Furthermore, the isolated environment in which practitioners operate can also present challenges (Martin et al., 2021). For career entry sport and exercise psychologists, the journey toward becoming a qualified independent practitioner comprises many demands and challenges (Martin et al., 2021). Given the absence of professional resources that trainee practitioners can draw on to manage such demands, it is here that the effective use of supervision, peer support, and communities of practice become important to provide neophyte practitioners with opportunities to gain feedback, share experiences, while also providing opportunity for self-reflection (McEwan et al., 2019; Tod, 2010).

Conclusion

Whether pursuing certification through the BPS, CASES, AASP, FEPSAC, ISSP, or other international bodies, each pathway presents unique opportunities and challenges. However, what remains consistent across all routes is the commitment to developing core competencies, maintaining professional standards, and engaging in evidence-based practice. The certification process provides career entry professionals with the opportunity to develop essential competencies across multiple domains. Furthermore, whether in academic or applied settings, certification can provide access to employment opportunities and professional networks that support career development. That is, many positions in both academic and applied settings now require evidence of certification. Moreover, certification provides career flexibility by attaining credentials that are increasingly recognized across different contexts and geographical locations. That is, career entry professionals with certification can more easily transition between academic and applied roles, work across different sports and populations, and may even have options to relocate to new countries if desired where their qualifications are recognized. While the career entry stage can present challenges, CE and professional certification can play a pivotal role during this transition, enhancing professional competencies, developing peer networks, and increasing employment opportunities in both academic and applied settings.

BEYOND BORDERS: CONTINUING EDUCATION IN APPLIED SPORT PSYCHOLOGY

Christian Zepp

Continuing education is a cornerstone of professional development in applied sport psychology (e.g., Quartiroli & Wagstaff, 2025). As the field continues to evolve rapidly, practitioners are expected to stay up-to-date with the latest research, techniques, and interventions that optimize athletic performance, mental health, and well-being. However, despite the increasing importance of ongoing professional development, sport psychologists often face significant challenges in accessing continued education. Many of these challenges stem from barriers such as the high cost and geographical limitations associated with attending major conferences, where much of the most current knowledge is disseminated. For practitioners working in underfunded environments or remote regions, this inaccessibility can hinder their ability to stay informed about new research and best practices (McEwan et al., 2020).

Knowledge sharing and collaboration among sport psychology professionals play a crucial role in overcoming these barriers. Engaging in collaborative networks allows practitioners to gain insights from peers, share case studies, and develop evidence-based strategies that enhance their skills and improve their service delivery (Andersen, 2021). However, the existing models for CE often emphasize attending large-scale conferences or subscribing to expensive journals, leaving out many sport psychologists who cannot afford these resources. As a result, the field risks creating a divide between those with access to the latest developments and those who are left behind due to systemic barriers (Stambulova & Schinke, 2020).

Understanding the significance of making CE more accessible and inclusive is critical for the global growth of applied sport psychology. This chapter addresses these issues by highlighting the importance of alternative learning opportunities, such as online platforms, regional workshops, and professional networks. These initiatives not only reduce barriers to knowledge acquisition but also foster a global exchange of ideas, making the field more equitable and innovative.

In today's interconnected world, simplifying access to applied sport psychology knowledge has become more feasible through the use of digital resources. Online platforms and e-learning tools offer cost-effective and geographically inclusive ways for professionals to continue their education without the need for physical attendance at conferences or workshops. Initiatives such as webinars, online courses, and virtual conferences make it possible for practitioners to gain exposure to the latest developments in the field. Additionally, leading organizations like the AASP, the ISSP, and the FEPSAC are increasingly providing resources that are accessible remotely, including certification programs and databases with research publications (Henriksen et al., 2020). These innovations help bridge the gap for those in remote areas or working with limited budgets, ensuring that CE is an achievable goal for all sport psychologists.

Beyond the convenience of online learning, fostering personal connections among sport psychologists from diverse backgrounds is crucial for the profession's growth and the cultivation of a global perspective. Collaborative networks that bring together practitioners from different countries and cultural contexts enable the sharing of unique experiences and insights, promoting innovation and cultural sensitivity in practice. Programs that pair professionals in mentorship relationships or establish peer support groups can help build these connections, regardless of location (Schinke et al., 2019). These professional relationships are vital for knowledge exchange and personal development, as they allow practitioners to discuss challenges, share solutions, and grow through collective learning. In this way, the field of applied sport psychology can expand its reach while also embracing inclusivity and diversity.

In addition to established sport psychology organizations such as AASP and ISSP, platforms like VirtualSportPsych (VSP) have embraced online formats to provide webinars, workshops, and group supervision for CE purposes. The offerings at VSP cover a broad range of topics, including professional development areas such as cultural competence and diversity, digital and remote coaching, ethical and legal issues, and the development of one's professional philosophy. Furthermore, specialized workshops addressed applied work with athletes, teams, and coaches, focusing on topics like motivation, neuroscience, cognitive training, mindfulness, resilience, leadership, and team dynamics. Importantly, VSP also addressed emerging fields like esports, helping practitioners to be knowledgeable to work in these new domains. By integrating evidence-based practices and learning from applied research, VSP strived to meet diverse needs of sport psychologists globally. The platform offered at least one workshop or webinar per month, each focused on one of these critical areas of CE.

VSP's offerings were officially recognized for continuing education credits, for example by the Arbeitsgemeinschaft für Sportpsychologie (ASP) in Germany and other national associations. Furthermore, attendees of live online workshops and group supervisions often expressed relief in discovering that many of the issues they faced were shared across different cultural contexts, highlighting the universal nature of certain professional challenges. This collective learning, combined with expert guidance and feedback, helped practitioners refine their approach and feel supported in their work. Nonetheless, VSP also experienced what Quartiroli and colleagues (2021) had highlighted: while sport psychology professionals generally consider continuing education and lifelong learning important, actual engagement and financial investment often remain limited. Ultimately, this contributed to the discontinuation of the project. This experience suggests that improving access alone may not be sufficient, and that future initiatives may need to address additional motivational, structural, and contextual barriers to ongoing professional development.

Looking ahead, the future of CE in applied sport psychology will rely on the development of diverse and accessible learning opportunities for professionals at every stage of their careers. As the field continues to evolve, it will be essential for practitioners to engage with a variety of educational platforms and resources to stay current with new developments and techniques (Quartiroli et al., 2021). Cross-organizational collaboration, both nationally and internationally, will play a critical role in maintaining and improving the quality of sport psychology practice. Partnerships between organizations, such as AASP, ISSP, and other virtual platforms like VirtualSportPsych, will ensure that CE remains innovative, inclusive, and aligned with the practical demands of the field (Henriksen et al., 2020).

Elevating the practice of sport psychology through continued learning not only enhances the expertise of practitioners but also directly contributes to the well-being and performance of athletes. By fostering holistic athlete development—encompassing mental, emotional, and social growth—well-informed sport psychologists will be better equipped to support athletes in achieving their full potential. The ongoing advancement of professional development opportunities will be key to driving the field forward and ensuring that both practitioners and athletes benefit from the latest evidence-based practices and insights.

EDITORS' TAKEAWAYS

This chapter holds a special place for me (Lauren) as a former professor and current Chair of AASP's CE Committee—and relates to the key topic of competency development we (me, Gualberto Cremades, Ale Quartiroli) spent some time on in the first edition of the book. Sanchez's concept of the *journey and spiral* reflects the varied paths a career in this field can take. Learning doesn't end with formal education—ongoing growth is essential as the field and science evolve. A recurring theme throughout the chapter—and the book—is shared responsibility: each of us must uphold ethics, self-care, effective practice, and lifelong learning, while the field and its organizations must create systems that make this growth possible and feasible. Ideally, in another decade, the collective advancement of our global field will make such reminders almost redundant.

RECOMMENDED EXERCISES

1 Reflect on your personal interests and growth opportunities.
   a What topics excite you and could become a specialty? What knowledge gaps currently limit your effectiveness as a consultant or practitioner? Which performance needs from your needs analysis can be addressed short-term (quick wins) versus long-term (require more effort)?
   b Are your professional skills preparing you for future success, or do you need to strengthen certain areas to stay competitive? What CMPC or APA CE opportunities could help expand your expertise or close performance gaps?
2 Create a one-year Personal Continuing Education Plan. Prioritize key topics (e.g., cultural competence, digital coaching, and trauma-informed care) and identify how you will access these learning opportunities.
3 Recall working with a client from a different cultural background. How did this understanding shape your approach, and what steps could further develop your competence?
4 Choose a country you might consider moving to and explore the feasibility of relocating there for a job opportunity.
5 Identify barriers you face in accessing CE. How can digital platforms—webinars, virtual conferences, or online courses—help you overcome these barriers?

REFERENCES

Allison, S. T. (2024). Circles, spiral dynamics, and heroism. In S. T. Allison, J. K. Beggan, & G. R. Goethals (Eds.), *Encyclopedia of heroism studies*. Springer.

Andersen, M. B. (2021). *Doing sport psychology*. Human Kinetics.

Cropley, B., Hanton, S., Miles, A., & Niven, A. (2020). Developing the effectiveness of applied sport psychology service delivery: A reflective practice intervention. *Sport & Exercise Psychology Review, 16*(1), 38–60.

Duffy, R. D., Dik, B. J., Douglass, R. P., England, J. W., & Velez, B. L. (2018). Work as a calling: A theoretical model. *Journal of Counseling Psychology, 65*(4), 423–439. https://doi.org/10.1037/cou0000276

Henriksen, K., Larsen, C. H., & Diment, G. M. (2020). Online learning in sport psychology: Opportunities and challenges. *Journal of Applied Sport Psychology, 32*(4), 355–371. https://doi.org/10.1080/10413200.2019.1657250

Hollywood, A., McCarthy, D., Spencely, C., & Winstone, N. (2020). "Overwhelmed at first": The experience of career development in early career academics. *Journal of Further and Higher Education, 44*(7), 998–1012. https://doi.org/10.1080/0309877X.2019.1636213

Iqbal, M. B., Li, J., Yang, S., & Sindhu, P. (2022). Value-driven career attitude and job performance: An intermediary role of organizational citizenship behavior. *Frontiers in Psychology, 13,* 917350. https://doi.org/10.3389/fpsyg.2022.917350

Keegan, R. (2016). *Being a sport psychologist.* Bloomsbury Publishing.

Martin, D. R., Quartiroli, A., & Wagstaff, C. R. (2021). An exploration of sport psychology professional quality of life in British neophyte practitioners. *The Sport Psychologist, 35*(4), 329–339. https://doi.org/10.1123/tsp.2020-0145

Martin, J. (2020). Is the profession of sport psychology an illusion? *Kinesiology Review, 9*(2), 92–103. https://doi.org/10.1123/kr.2019-0026

McCarthy, P., Burns, L., McCann, B., & Gupta, S. (2024). *Training and supervision in sport and exercise psychology.* Routledge.

McEwan, D., Tod, D., & Eubank, M. (2020). The effectiveness of online learning in applied sport psychology: A systematic review. *Journal of Applied Sport Psychology, 32*(4), 409–428. https://doi.org/10.1080/10413200.2019.1657252

McEwan, H. E., Tod, D., & Eubank, M. (2019). The rocky road to individuation: Sport psychologists' perspectives on professional development. *Psychology of Sport and Exercise, 45,* 101542. https://doi.org/10.1016/j.psychsport.2019.101542

Moran, A. (2004). Introducing sport and exercise psychology: Discipline and profession. In A. Moran (Ed.), *Sport and exercise psychology: A critical introduction* (pp. 3–33). Routledge.

Quartiroli, A., & Wagstaff, C. (2025). Continuing education in sport psychology: A survey of where we are and where we need to go. *International Journal of Sport and Exercise Psychology, 23*(7), 1287–1307. https://doi.org/10.1080/1612197X.2024.2371496

Quartiroli, A., Wagstaff, C. R., Herms, M., & Kemmel, C. (2021). The future of continuing education and lifelong learning in sport psychology professionals: A Delphi study. *Professional Psychology: Research and Practice, 52*(2), 173–182. https://doi.org/10.1037/pro0000319

Ryba, T. V., Schinke, R. J., Stambulova, N. B., & Elbe, A. M. (2024). ISSP position stand on cultural praxis in sport psychology. *International Journal of Sport and Exercise Psychology, 22*(1), 10–18. https://doi.org/10.1080/1612197X.2022.2107787

Schinke, R. J., Stambulova, N., & Barker, D. M. (2019). Cultural sport psychology: A decade of theory, research, and practice. *Psychology of Sport and Exercise, 42,* 100–109. https://doi.org/10.1016/j.psychsport.2018.11.014

Stambulova, N., & Schinke, R. J. (2020). Enhancing global knowledge exchange in applied sport psychology: Reflections on trends, challenges, and opportunities. *International Journal of Sport and Exercise Psychology, 18*(6), 669–683. https://doi.org/10.1080/1612197X.2020.1749974

Tod, D. (2010). Training and professional development in applied sport psychology. In D. Tod, K. Hodge, & V. Krane (Eds.), *Routledge handbook of applied sport psychology* (pp. 21–29). Routledge.

15 Practicing What We Preach

The Consultant as Performer

Work as a sport, exercise, and performance psychology (SEPP) professional is inherently guided by client needs, and as such we need to engage with a helping and caring mindset. However, it is also imperative we embrace the fact that not only our clients are performers: we are (high-)performers too. Personally, it took me (Sebastian) quite some time to realize this when I started working with coaches and athletes at one of the German Olympic-training centers. Initially, I always put athletes' and coaches' needs first—they were the performers, I was serving them in the background. But ultimately, I realized that to be able to care, serve, and perform for your clients, you need to embrace, utilize, and embody the same tools, strategies, and mindsets you are asking your clients to work on. We as editors are thrilled that an outstanding, truly global group of SEPP experts will share their insights about what it means to "practice what we preach" with you in this chapter.

PRACTITIONER SELF-DEVELOPMENT: FINDING "YOUR WAY" BY PRACTICING WHAT "YOU" PREACH

Roger Friesen

As a practitioner in performance psychology, it is imperative that significant personal work has been done to understand oneself in order to be effective with the people or teams we work with. Anyone who pursues work in this profession must accept the responsibility that comes with a "service" profession. We need to accept that words are not enough, we hone all the concepts, strategies, tools, and skills in our own lives both as individuals and practitioners. We must "find our way"—our unique methods of working in this profession that reflect our personality.

Accept That We also Are on Stage and as Such Must Learn to Lead by Example

Any athlete, competing at any level essentially is "on stage" when they step into competition. On stage simply means their performance is on public display. And as such, being "on stage" implies that their actions are visible to anyone watching. This also implies that the individual's actions will be assessed and examined by anyone watching the event.

Throughout my time working in the field of sport psychology consulting, I encountered an unspoken understanding or assumption that the athletes or performers whom we worked with were on stage and as such they needed to embody the components of excellence. It was the athletes who needed to sign "code of conduct" agreements, which spelled out how they needed to conduct and carry themselves as they represented their team or their country. As

DOI: 10.4324/9781003781479-19

national team members, for example, they needed to conduct themselves in ways that would reflect being good ambassadors of their sport as well as good ambassadors for their country.

In recent years, the concept and conversations around "culture" became more common, specifically the idea of a "culture of excellence," which implied that the organization cared about the health and dynamic nature of an organization and that codes of conduct were adopted which would ensure behaviors associated with excellence both in terms of performance and also as it related to interpersonal behavior. This is deemed to be important within the team and also with respect to the image portrayed to the public.

Over the years of being involved with national teams, and observing organizations in action, I came to appreciate that if we truly cared about a culture of excellence, then it followed that everyone within the organization should hold themselves to the same standards of excellence. It made no sense that one group of individuals (athletes) within an organization should be the sole contributors to this culture. In fact, what I came to appreciate was that administrative staff and coaching staff needed to lead the charge in upholding the elements laid out to ensure a culture of excellence.

The role of mental performance consultants (MPC) has always been unique in that the role is most often a support role to coaches and athletes and most often practitioners in this role are in the "background" and as such backstage. And yet, I came to appreciate that anyone in this role should not only help in the design and implementation of this culture of excellence, but should also accept the responsibility of modeling the characteristics associated with this culture of excellence. As consultants, we too are on stage and need to go through our own preparation to ensure that we remain highly functional in contexts of stress and pressure. We must accept that we who function in these roles with teams or organizations are also scrutinized and as such need to ensure that we demonstrate and model what we want others to do in these contexts.

Accept That in Order for Us to Gain Respect, We Must Practice What We Preach

Anyone working in the capacity of MPC needs to accept being a role model for all with whom they work. I had the great fortune of functioning in two capacities throughout my professional life—a professor of sport psychology as well as a practitioner in the field of sport psychology. In the early years of my career, I had to work hard to learn how to function in both of these contexts. The process I chose for this personal growth and development was to observe others and also be reflective on the practice in both domains. I wanted to learn what was important both as an educator as well as a practitioner.

Two concepts that revealed themselves quickly were authenticity and integrity. These values resonated on a deep and profound level and remain so to this day. What did this mean? Authentic meant I had to find my voice—my way of interacting with others, relaying information, and functioning on stage. As such, I needed to do my own work to discover who I was as an individual and what I had to offer to anyone who came into my care. I made a commitment early on to be authentic to my personality, my way of interacting with the world around me, and my way of presenting information.

One of the things I was committed to throughout my career was to ensure that I incorporated each and every concept, strategy and tool available in the world of performance psychology into my own personal functioning. I made a commitment to every person I have ever worked with that there would not be a single concept that I would suggest to someone unless I had personally incorporated this into my own life and practice. This was important to me as through observation, I witnessed many occasions where someone would present one thing however, there was a disconnect between words and actions. It seemed imperative that in order to gain the respect of the people whom we work with, that our words and personal actions fully lined up. I accepted this as non-negotiable.

Required of anyone in this field is to accept a growth mindset, a continual examination of what we do and how we function. To do this, we must hone reflection skills to understand on a deep level how we do anything and the impact our actions and way of being have on others. We need to learn about ourselves, our gifts and abilities, and our unique personality traits. We also have to learn alternative behaviors that allow us to remain highly functional in a wide range of contexts. We must also understand that there is no "one way" of being that is associated with success in this profession. Yes, there are common behaviors required in this profession, however, when it comes to interaction and delivery of services there is not one way of success; rather, there is the way that is unique to each practitioner based on their unique personality and their creativity in the delivery of services.

Develop an Accountability Circle

How does one learn about authenticity and integrity? The first step is to educate ourselves on the concept of authenticity. Second, there must be a desire to adhere to this concept. This then leads into the practice of functioning in an authentic manner. Next comes the question of how we are perceived by others in our work. It is normal to have our own perception and perspective of how we operate. For example, we could ask questions like, "is our view consistent with how others view our work and way of behaving?" It is normal for us to not necessarily have a fully accurate view of ourselves and as such we need to have a structure whereby we can be held accountable for the values and beliefs and accompanying behaviors we desire—enter accountability strategies.

Another way of working toward authenticity is to develop accountability partnerships. This requires us to nurture relationships with trusted colleagues or other individuals who are able to observe our work. We need people in this circle who know us well, and also have an appreciation of what behaviors are effective in any context. In other words, people whom we desire feedback from must know something of what our context looks and feels like. Trust is also required in order for true and accurate feedback to be given. We are not looking for cheerleaders, we are looking for individuals who will be able to speak truthfully into our lives. At times, feedback may not be easily accepted especially if it is critical in nature and we may face feedback that is hard in nature and as such not easily accepted. In this event, we need people whom we trust, value, and respect so that the feedback will naturally be more palatable.

Understand "Ego": What It Means and Ways in Which It Can Compromise Our Work

Ego, by definition, refers to "self" in relation to ourself or others in our context. It is an integral part of each person's unique personality and encompasses aspects such as self worth, self identity, self esteem, or in simple language "our personal identity." Ego can be a positive phenomena when an individual has an accurate view of themselves in relation to the context they function in. It will present positively when an individual has a healthy level of self esteem, and understands their gifts and abilities relative to the context they function in.

On the other hand, ego can be viewed as negative when an individual has an inflated sense of themselves or when they have a distorted or misguided view of their value and importance relative to the environment in which they function. It is a term which presents itself often in conversations around team and team culture. For example, we often hear or make statements like, "there is no place for ego in this culture," or "we must leave our ego at the door." These statements generally refer to the negative aspect of ego.

What I have observed to be most effective in a profession such as MPC is that of genuine humility. Our role is that of support, education, guidance, at times being mentors, and so on. Our job is to make others successful in their respective performance context and as such, we need to be comfortable with a "behind the scenes" role providing this support. The "show" is not about us, rather, we work persistently and consistently to help others thrive and function at their full potential. Anyone who does not understand ego and functions from an inflated sense of ego, or in other words "does not get their ego out of the way," will often do more harm than good. In short, true and genuine humility are integral to effective work with teams or individuals.

PRACTICING WHAT YOU PREACH: WEARING THE CONSULTANT AS PERFORMER HAT

Artur Poczwardowski, Stiliani "Ani" Chroni, Alessandro Quartiroli, & Aleksandra "Ola" Krukowska-Burke

Clearly, the challenges and opportunities for your ongoing growth (e.g., as a graduate student, early professional, or seasoned professional who is looking to continue their education and develop more of a global perspective) are ever-present and multiple. Here, we will link them to becoming and being a sport, exercise, and performance psychology (SEPP) professional while managing different "hats" you are wearing or viewpoints you're assuming as a consultant (Poczwardowski, 2019). Our assertion is that when you compartmentalize your "hats" (i.e., viewpoints), your pressures, and your resources as consultant-as-expert, consultant-as-person, consultant-as-performer, and as-a-self-regulator, you will be more deliberate in using them as mirrors for both self-reflecting and processing with professional colleagues. As a result, you will gain greater clarity in knowing what aspects of your work and what viewpoints of yourself you need to self-manage and grow. As active consultants ourselves, we will join you in this chapter in sharing a composite and quite personal on occasion account in applying self-managing skills. First, we briefly elaborate on these four mirrors (i.e., hats) for reflection purposes. Second, we invite you to consider three spaces of practicing what we preach: (1) aiming at sustainability and fulfillment; (2) building on the benefits of reflection through collegial consultation and support groups; and (3) engaging in deliberate learning and practicing.

Four Mirrors: You as an Expert, Person, Performer, and Self-Regulator

Socrates is commonly credited with saying, "The unexamined life is not worth living." Metaphorically, the four viewpoints on becoming and being an SEPP professional (Poczwardowski, 2019) could be compared to four mirrors, in which a practitioner examines themselves and their practices. Briefly, your *expert* mirror reflection gives you feedback on where you are in your journey with developing, mastering, and applying the requisite knowledge, skills, abilities, and attitudes (KSAAs) that align with current professional and ethical standards. As a human being, your *personal* content vividly and continually populates the mirror with your deep personhood with all its virtues, shortcomings, incentives, pressures, and resources. Examining yourself as a *performer* allows you to grow in execution of the KSAAs in the presence of a multiplicity of pressures and positive and negative distractions that come from both you as an expert and person (Brown, 2009). Lastly, you can meta-cognitively examine your *self-regulator*'s efforts, mistakes, and successes in self-leading and in the consulting process itself. In doing so, I (Artur) am considering the dynamics and outcomes of each client session (e.g., prematurely assigning a homework resulting in my client's complaints about their busy schedule), entire consulting projects (e.g., client's parents referring a family they know for my services), and turning points in my career (e.g., attracting an organization as a client).

Sustainability and Fulfillment

Let's reflect on the "why" and the usefulness of the "practice what you preach" maxim with the perspective of one's entire professional career. The sentiment behind practicing what one is preaching may encourage you to inspect your values and how they guide you; this could help you understand your professional identity (Quartiroli et al., 2024). A practitioner's comprehension of their professional philosophy and implementation style is typically a part of one's educational or training journey (Poczwardowski & Sherman, 2011). However, it is equally important to reflect on your professional identity and philosophy as you progress through various phases of career development as values can change (e.g., Vilar et al., 2020). For example, thanks to various personal and professional experiences, my (Ola's) understanding of *professionalism* has changed significantly over the years. In the past, it meant perfection and seriousness, which didn't allow much space for authenticity (e.g., dry sense of humor). Nowadays, it's more about healthy boundaries that allow me to balance professional standards with authentic self-representation. Rediscovering your sense of purpose, guiding principles, and other factors (e.g., social or financial) influencing practice might help you appreciate the learning journey thus far, and recognize your authentic self.

Viewing yourself as a performer and practicing the same techniques you teach your clients (e.g., breathing techniques; goal setting), can help you increase the effectiveness of your applied work as well as reflect on and engage in self-care practices. As every practitioner will face work-related challenges (e.g., distress, emotional exhaustion; Quartiroli et al., 2019), it is of utmost importance to engage in appropriate self-care and prevent resource depletion (e.g., motivation, passion, or curiosity) as well as maintain a healthy, flourishing life outside the job. For example, almost daily I go for a walk and switch my phone off. Even if it is brief, my mind can rest, my body experiences the joy of movement, and I am in contact with nature, which tends to be invigorating.

Self- and Shared-, Strength- and Deficiency-Based Reflective Practice: Choose as Needed

While self-reflection can be a valuable tool for your development as a person and a professional, shared reflection can provide added value (Knowles et al., 2023). Shared reflection with colleagues, supervisors, mentors, and coaches facilitated the interchange of experiences, views, knowledge, values, theoretical frameworks, and became part of my (Ani's) practical tools for achieving greater understanding than reflecting alone. Early on, I also learned to not underestimate the fresh eye of persons unrelated to the job and sport altogether, particularly when reflecting as a person and self-regulator. Throughout my career, entrepreneurs, managers, politicians, physicians, and opera directors offered some eye-opening "aha" moments for me.

Whether reflecting solo or with others, you need to "go beyond superficial layers of thought" (Dr. Ryall in Knowles et al., 2023, p. 30). It is easy for reflective practice to stop at the "what happened" level and avoid the harder step(s) that touch on values, philosophy, purpose (and ambitions), and creation of meaning—all of which lie behind each matter you encounter. To find your true meanings through reflection, you should also consider its direction, the reasons and objectives for reflecting, and then the content of it. Proactive self-reflection is not fed by a problem, a gap, a weakness, a failure or any deficiency on you or others. On the contrary, it entails forward thinking based on your strengths (see Dixon et al., 2013). At turning points in my career, like experiencing burnout or engaging with a country's policy development, strength-based reflective practice became both a self-care tool and a tactical tool, respectively, helping me to both sustain hardships and move forward.

Engaged Practitioner: Deliberate Learning, Preparing, and Delivering

The journey of SEPP practitioners does not conclude with the completion of formal education and attainment of professional qualifications; rather, it is a continuous, mindful process of professional (and personal) growth that evolves throughout your career (Fogaça et al., 2023). As an engaged practitioner, you must rely on professionalism and maintain a dynamic, ongoing commitment to both personal and professional growth (Quartiroli et al., 2023). I (Ale) have consistently upheld these principles in my own development, purposefully engaging in reflective practice and meaningful self-improvement. This professionalism encompasses a value system guiding your SEPP practitioner's behaviors, which ethically compels you to strive to be the best version of yourself in every client interaction, ensuring you provide the highest quality of care (Grus et al., 2018). In my own practice, this commitment is grounded in a set of core values. While love is my main guiding principle, other values, such as kindness, integrity, inclusion, growth, service, courage, and authenticity, are pivotal in guiding me through my journey. As the field evolves, professionalism must adapt alongside the practitioner, incorporating new knowledge, adapting to diverse contexts, and addressing the changing needs of clients and the field (Quartiroli et al., 2023).

To remain effective, ethical, and responsive in a field where the half-life of professional knowledge is about eight years (Quartiroli et al., 2022) and where practice and research evolves rapidly, SEPP professionals must continuously update their skills, as initial training soon becomes insufficient to meet current standards (Quartiroli & Wagstaff, 2024). Therefore, ongoing professional development through both formal continuing education and self-driven lifelong learning is therefore essential to stay current and deliver competent services. Together, these processes are crucial for maintaining competence, adaptability, and ethical standards. By embracing both continuing education and lifelong learning, you will be in a good place toward your ethical obligation to provide the highest standard of care, ensuring that you meet clients' evolving needs (Quartiroli & Wagstaff, 2024). For example, I stay up to date by reading new material (e.g., articles, books, and blogs), listening to and learning from colleagues, supervisors, and supervisees, and engaging in ongoing continued professional development opportunities.

Conclusion

Becoming and being an SEPP professional is a dynamic, lifelong endeavor that demands conscious engagement with the roles of expert, person, performer, and self-regulator. As the professional landscape continues to evolve, so too must our practices and perspectives. Embracing this journey with intentionality and openness, anchored in both personal values and professional commitments, can foster not only competence and adaptability but also authenticity, ethical integrity, and long-term impact. We invite you to consider how professional excellence in SEPP is not a destination but an ongoing, reflective and relational journey of becoming.

THE CONSULTANT AS PERFORMER: PRACTICING WHAT YOU PREACH

Renee N. Appaneal & Charles H. Brown, Jr

An effective consultant needs skills to engage rapidly with individual athletes, teams, and coaches, and to communicate effectively while delivering information, designing interventions and implementing programs—always in a manner that is culturally sensitive and contextually intelligent (Brown et al., 2005). To do this consistently well, it is paramount that Sport/Performance Psychology Consultants (S/PPC) develop, refine, and review their own set of performance skills and strategies, taking a view of the "consultant-as-performer" (Poczwardowski, 2019; Brown, 2009). There is no roadmap or standardized approach for how consultants cultivate their own regulation of attention, emotions and thoughts, energy/activation, as well as social interactions. Rather, the process toward self-improvement is developed through behavior change and informed by self-awareness, reflection, and feedback. In this chapter, the first author (RNA) shares her own performance skills and strategies (see Table 15.1), including a brief explanation of how they were developed and examples of how they were implemented at home (i.e., in the daily training environment) and while traveling with teams.

Development of Optimal Performance Strategies

My optimal consulting performance strategies were originally developed in consultation with the co-author (CHB), whom initially I engaged as my own professional coach and who quickly became a cherished colleague and eventually a beloved friend. I have always considered

Table 15.1 Optimal Performance Strategies for Sport Psychology Consultants

Self-Care	*Description*
Self-awareness	Recognizing personal emotions, triggers, and needs. Understanding your mental and physical state.
Self-regulation	Managing emotions, attention, and reactions to maintain balance and calmness.
Managing boundaries	Setting and maintaining healthy personal and professional boundaries to protect time and energy.
Personal support system	Building and leaning on relationships with family and close friends for emotional and moral support.
Professional/peer support network	Engaging with colleagues and mentors to share experiences, challenges, and solutions.
Performance plan (while away and when "on")	Creating a focused plan for peak performance while actively engaged in work or specific tasks.
Re-entry and recovery time (back at home)	Allocating time to unwind, recover, and recharge to maintain long-term well-being.

myself a *performer* and valued performance excellence, learning, and self-improvement. While I value and take pride in being independent and autonomous, I sought the support of CHB to provide objectivity and accountability toward my goals.

Our first objective together was to identify both role and contextual demands to determine what I needed to do my job and cope with both the expected and unexpected. We identified that prioritizing my health was paramount to performing well, which aligns with my personal values and reflects my professional philosophy that health underpins everything, including optimal performance. Just as elite athletes must have and maintain adequate energy availability (Melin et al., 2024), S/PPCs also require sufficient energy availability to perform well, albeit substantially lower levels than what athletes themselves need.

Attentional and energy requirements are always important considerations. When traveling domestically or overseas, the availability of resources often varies greatly from one's home environment. While traveling internationally with a team, you're often expected to be "on" 24/7 for long days across several weeks during staging camp and throughout competition, as well as once the competition is finished. These demands occur without access to one's usual support network and daily routines. To maintain self-care and optimal performance, consultants must proactively plan stress-recovery balance (coping strategies, social support, etc.) and then routinely refine these plans while in the "bubble" of a tour or major competition. To accomplish this, good self-awareness via self-reflection, flexible and appropriate self-care, and performance strategies via self-regulation are critical for the consultant—just as they are for our clients.

Strategies in Action: Self-Awareness and Self-Regulation

With the aim of staying healthy and performing well, we developed a process for checking-in with myself via reflective practice and assessment. First, I would schedule (and protect) time to reflect on how I was feeling overall (health and well-being), my energy levels, and how well I had allocated my attention to my priorities (i.e., what was important in work and life). To evaluate and monitor my status, I rated these three areas on a 5-point Likert-type scale. Any ratings below 3 would prompt further reflection, and sometimes feedback or input from others on where and how to adjust.

Maintaining holistic stress-recovery balance was critical to support my health, and this involved strategies for several areas. For quality sleep, I sought out various techniques to quiet my mind and allow thoughts to come and go loosely, which was important when I'd ruminate on a problem or situation that I was dealing with (also quite frequent while on tour with a team). When I was unable to do this well, again I leaned into acceptance and would aim to adjust as soon as possible to minimize further sleep disruption and reduce accumulative sleep deficit. Regular physical activity at home involved my usual activities (i.e., weekly yoga classes, group strength training, hiking and cycling with friends), and when on tour with teams it depended largely on the location and daily schedule for that sport. I also prioritized nutrition, which involved adequate fuel and hydration (protecting mealtimes in the dining hall or packing snacks and water bottles when at training all day) and monitoring my caffeine and alcohol intake. Alcohol and caffeine negatively impact sleep, but these are also integral to Australian culture—regular invitations to "grab a coffee" and catch up or drinking to manage stress as well as to bond with other staff on tour. In terms of energy and attention, this meant being clear about what is essential and then maintaining attention to what matters. Specifically, my ability to listen/observe, think clearly, and be present without mood and thoughts interfering.

Strategies in Action: Social Support

My professional philosophy and consulting approach is anchored in the belief that behavior change does not occur in a vacuum nor is it solely an individual's responsibility. Rather, it involves both individual strategies for self-management and strategic and intentional utilization of social support. As such, my coach and I put strategies in place for how to best stay connected to those who matter most to me—family (i.e., two young kids at home, husband/partner acting in my absence as a single-parent) and those professional supports who could support my optimal consulting performance while away from home. Our approach reflected the Optimal Matching Theory of Social Support (Cutrona, 1990) where the type of support and connections I needed to stay healthy and perform optimally was matched with the appropriate strategies and accessible resources.

In contrast to being at home with regular and easy access to family and friends, being on tour required navigating boundaries and negotiating availability when I may be "in role" all day, every day. Honest and supportive communication with significant others regarding availability and expectations helped to mitigate (though not prevent) feeling guilty about being an absent mom and leaving my partner a single parent. While I valued staying connected to family and friends, it is quite difficult when you are in a different time-zone and fully immersed in the "bubble" with a team in preparation for benchmark events. Managing boundaries while on tour is a constant balance, determining when to be available versus when, where, and how to "switch off." When taking time for myself, I had to choose the best way to spend it and regardless of the choice I made, there was a cost.

These challenges further underscore the importance of a professional support network. Prior to my departure, I arranged who was available for various types of support I anticipated needing while away. Sometimes I would message or email a colleague (informal consultation, peer supervision), and other times I would reach out more formally to someone contracted to provide supervision/mentoring during the tour. My professional support network provided objectivity and reality checks, offering a safe outlet for brain-dumps, case conceptualization, and working through challenging situations. Using my support also facilitated effective mental and emotional recovery, where after those conversations, I was better able to be present and enjoy catching up w/family, take a walk outside, or quiet the mind at night to fall asleep.

Reflections: Strengths and Challenges

All the strategies listed in Table 15.1 facilitate my optimal consulting performance; though, the first two—*self-awareness* and *self-regulation*—provide a foundation for maintaining and protecting my health, as well as to inform how and when I utilize the remaining strategies. Mostly these strategies worked well with a few refinements over time. Acceptance and self-compassion were paramount to enable greater flexibility and acknowledge areas for growth, improvement, and behavior change. Yet, despite my efforts, I encountered barriers to implementation that prompted further reflection about my performance strategies.

While I prioritized my well-being to perform well, at times this seemed at odds with the priorities of others. In pressure situations, the interest of "the athlete/team" becomes paramount—no matter the cost. For example, while overseas with a team on tour, the Chief Medical Officer said in earshot of other staff and athletes that they could "sleep when they were dead." While this was said quite casually in conversation, it contradicted my own approach to working effectively on tour. I would sometimes sleep-in or return to my room early as a means of protecting my health and safeguarding optimal attention and energy, depending on the next day's schedule and priorities. The trade-off with my solo recovery time meant I was not often socializing with team staff and taking time for myself was sometimes perceived as counter to team norms. After the tour ended, I was taken back by anonymous feedback that I was "not a team player." I thought I performed well as a consultant on tour, as evidenced by athletes trusting me with the psychological difficulties they were experiencing just prior to and during a world championship. In response to this revelation, I needed to (1) develop a quick "solution" and appropriate support to continue performing in this role, and (2) to understand what had happened and why. Both were achieved through several months of self-reflection and many sessions of formal and peer supervision—and uncomfortable honest dialogue with my direct manager and team staff from the previous tour. My lessons learned involved ensuring role clarity and priorities with key leadership (i.e., high performance managers) and seeking input from and alignment with team staff. To improve and perform well as a consultant, I recognized that I prefer and need feedback in a timely manner and need to let my colleagues know that it is safe to give critical feedback.

EDITORS' TAKEAWAYS

Reading Friesen's (no relation) commentary on an "accountability circle," where trusted colleagues help one refine an authentic service delivery, put a smile on my face—I (Andrew) am the benefactor of Roger's circle. Before moving to British Columbia, Roger helped establish SportPsychMB, an informal community of practice for sport psychology professionals in Manitoba. This group was instrumental in my development as an SEPP practitioner; not only did I learn from respected colleagues like Roger, but I was also encouraged to "find my own voice" in a supportive and nonjudgmental environment. As an undergraduate student at the time, having access to this informal professional network allowed me to observe experienced practitioners, debrief their service delivery and decision-making, and see firsthand how the top professionals in our field truly practice what they preach.

Continuing on this train of thought from Poczwardowski and colleagues' contribution, I find myself dwelling on Ani's commentary that strengths-based self-reflection can be viewed as a form of self-care. Indeed authenticity is a running theme throughout this chapter on practicing what you preach—capped by Appaneal and Brown sharing how they co-created and put into action a practice-what-you-preach program to sustain Renee's optimal health and performance when supporting her clients domestically and when traveling internationally.

RECOMMEND EXERCISES

1 How do you commit to being a mindful and engaged practitioner throughout your career? When, where, and how do you incorporate mindfulness and recovery exercises into your daily, weekly, and monthly schedule? If gaps exist, what specific daily, weekly, and monthly actions can you take to practice what you teach your clients? Set achievable goals to stay accountable.
2 List the performance strategies you usually teach clients. How much did you experiment with these strategies before using them with clients? What makes them valuable for clients? If you don't use them yourself, why don't they resonate for you?
3 At least once a year, reflect with trusted peers on your strengths and how they contribute to sustainable personal and professional fulfillment.
4 Develop your own performance plan. Consider your needs to perform well in consulting roles, as well as broader life domains where self-care and optimal performance are

important. Reflect on different environments and demands, and identify what is required for optimal performance (e.g., health, preparation, and recovery, performing when it matters). You can adapt strategies from Table 15.1 or use those you already employ.

REFERENCES

Brown, C. (2009). The consultant as performer. In K. F. Hays (Ed.), *Performance psychology in action* (pp. 309–328). American Psychological Association. https://doi.org/10.1037/11876-015

Brown, C. H., Gould, D., & Foster, S. (2005). A framework for developing contextual intelligence (CI). *The Sport Psychologist, 19*(1), 51–62. https://doi.org/10.1123/tsp.19.1.51

Cutrona, C. E. (1990). Stress and social support: In search of optimal matching. *Journal of Social and Clinical Psychology, 9*(1), 3–14. https://doi.org/10.1521/jscp.1990.9.1.3

Dixon, M., Lee, S., & Ghaye, T. (2013). Reflective practices for better sports coaches and coach education: Shifting from a pedagogy of scarcity to abundance in the run-up to Rio 2016. *Reflective Practice, 14*(5), 585–599. https://doi.org/10.1080/14623943.2013.840573

Fogaça, J. L., Quartiroli, A., & Wagstaff, C. (2023). Professional development of sport psychology practitioners: From systematic review to a model of development. *Psychology of Sport and Exercise, 70*, 102550. https://doi.org/10.1016/j.psychsport.2023.102550

Grus, C. L., Shen-Miller, D., Lease, S. H., Jacobs, S. C., Bodner, K. E., Van Sickle, K. S., Veilleux, J., & Kaslow, N. J. (2018). Professionalism: A competency cluster whose time has come. *Ethics & Behavior, 28*(6), 450–464. https://doi.org/10.1080/10508422.2017.1419133

Knowles, Z., Miles, A., Huntley, E., Picknell, G., Mellalieu, S. D., Hanton, S., & Cropley, B. (2023). The reflective sport and exercise science practitioner. In B. Cropley, Z. Knowles, A. Miles, & E. Huntley (Eds.), *Reflective practice in the sport and exercise sciences* (pp. 27–37). Routledge. https://doi.org/10.4324/9781003202911-4

Melin, A. K., Areta, J. L., Heikura, I. A., Stellingwerff, T., Torstveit, M. K., & Hackney, A. C. (2024). Direct and indirect impact of low energy availability on sports performance. *Scandinavian Journal of Medicine & Science in Sports, 34*(1), e14327. https://doi.org/10.1111/sms.14327

Poczwardowski, A. (2019). Deconstructing sport and performance psychology consultant: Expert, person, performer, and self-regulator. *International Journal of Sport and Exercise Psychology, 17*(5), 427–444. https://doi.org/10.1080/1612197X.2017.1390484

Poczwardowski, A., & Sherman, C. P. (2011). Revisions to the sport psychology service delivery (SPSD) heuristic: Explorations with experienced consultants. *The Sport Psychologist, 25*(4), 511–531. https://doi.org/10.1123/tsp.25.4.511

Quartiroli, A., Etzel, E. F., Knight, S. M., & Zakrajsek, R. A. (2019). Self-care as key to others' care: The perspectives of globally situated experienced senior-level sport psychology practitioners. *Journal of Applied Sport Psychology, 31*(2), 147–167. https://doi.org/10.1080/10413200.2018.1460420

Quartiroli, A., Fogaça, J. L., & Wagstaff, C. R. D. (2023). Professional training and development: The bedrock of ethical, competent, and sustainable sport psychology. *Journal of Applied Sport Psychology, 35*(3), 349–371. https://doi.org/10.1080/10413200.2022.2043485

Quartiroli, A., Wagstaff, C. R. D., Martin, D. R. F., & Tod, D. (2024). A systematic review of professional identity in sport psychology. *International Review of Sport and Exercise Psychology, 17*(1), 264–290. https://doi.org/10.1080/1750984X.2021.1998577

Quartiroli, A., Wagstaff, C. R. D., Zakrajsek, R. A., Knight, S. M., & Etzel, E. F. (2022). The role of self-care and professional quality of life in sustaining a long-lasting career in sport psychology: A qualitative exploration. *Journal of Applied Sport Psychology, 34*(6), 1334–1351. https://doi.org/10.1080/10413200.2021.1907483

Vilar, R., Liu, J. H.-f., & Gouveia, V. V. (2020). Age and gender differences in human values: A 20-nation study. *Psychology and Aging, 35*(5), 345–356. https://doi.org/10.1037/pag0000448

16 Self-Care for SEPP Professionals

As SEPP professionals, we often are called upon to assist coaches and athletes in coping effectively with stress. As such, SEPP can inherently be considered a caring and helping profession. Ironically, we sometimes tend to overlook the self-care that is essential to maintain our own mental health, clear mind, and stamina needed to live a balanced life while successfully helping and caring for our clients in various high-performance domains. In fact, our specialized knowledge, skills, and competence in this area may create a false illusion of immunity to mental health challenges and the need for self-care. Yet, we also are vulnerable to stressors of high-performance, high-pressure environments that we help our clients deal with. I (Sebastian) can certainly attest how easy it is to fall into this "immunity trap"—having neglected the need for self-care too long while working in high-performance Olympic and academic contexts. Several burnout episodes later I have found ways to better integrate personal self-care practices into my daily life—which my clients also benefit from. Collectively, our three global author groups share research as well as lived-experience perspectives we hope you will find helpful for setting up your own self-care practice.

CHARTING THE ETHICAL PATH TO SUSTAINABLE WELL-BEING FOR PROFESSIONALS IN SPORT AND PERFORMANCE PSYCHOLOGY: A CASE FOR SELF-CARE

Alessandro Quartiroli, Daniel R. F. Martin, Christopher R. D. Wagstaff, David Price, & Heather Hunter

Self-Care as the Bedrock of Ethical Professional Practice

In recent decades, the construct of self-care has evolved from an anecdotally discussed personal wellness strategy to an empirically investigated professional necessity for psychology professionals (Quartiroli et al., 2019). Sport, exercise, and performance psychology practitioners (SEPPPs) must navigate the complex and ever-changing demands of providing psychological support in sport, exercise, and performance settings. Indeed, these demands are plentiful, and include, among others, the emotional labor of client relationships (Hings et al., 2020), navigating nontraditional and high-pressure environments (Champ et al., 2021), and delivering services in hybrid environments (Price et al., 2022). Therefore, for SEPPPs, self-care not only supports personal health and career longevity but also forms a critical foundation for maintaining professional competence and safeguarding clients' well-being (Quartiroli, Wagstaff et al., 2022). To date, the only definition of self-care for SEPPPs is the one presented by Quartiroli et al. (2022), co-constructed by international panelists; foundation for our chapter.

DOI: 10.4324/9781003781479-20

> Sport [and Performance] Psychology Self-Care (SPSC) is the purposeful engagement in activities grounded in one's values. It involves prioritizing, developing, preserving, protecting, monitoring and restoring holistic (i.e., physical, psychological, social, spiritual, and emotional) health, wellbeing and satisfaction with work and life.
>
> (p. 1359)

By adopting self-care as a core professional value, SEPPPs can create a sustainable and ethical foundation for long-term well-being and effectiveness. As such, this chapter advocates for an embedded, proactive approach to self-care, positioning it as the ethical cornerstone of sustainable professional well-being.

Self-Care as an Ethical Imperative: Beyond Prevention, Toward Flourishing

Self-care has historically been viewed as a preventive measure, primarily aimed at buffering against detrimental outcomes such as burnout and emotional exhaustion (Dorociak et al., 2017). Nevertheless, this rather narrow view elides a plethora of wider potential impacts of self-care, which has been found to lead to personal and professional flourishing among psychology professionals (Quartiroli et al., 2019). For practitioners, ethical practice involves maintaining high levels of competence and fitness to practice, as outlined in the codes of conduct and professional standards of various regulatory bodies, including the Health Care Professions Council (UK), the American Psychological Association (USA), and the Australian Psychological Society (Australia). The ethical dimension of self-care becomes even more evident when considering the potential harm that can result from neglecting oneself. Given the emotionally demanding nature of the field, neglecting self-care can result in professional impairment and compromise the quality of services provided to clients (Barnett et al., 2007).

The risk associated with professional impairment makes self-care a non-negotiable component of ethical practice. SEPPPs may experience burnout or emotional exhaustion because of ineffective coping (Quartiroli, Wagstaff et al., 2022) and in such instances are more likely to make poor ethical decisions, experience diminished empathy for clients, and encounter reduced job satisfaction (Norcross & VandenBos, 2018). Arguably, these consequences do not only affect the practitioner but also pose risks to clients, and the reputation of the profession, making it imperative that self-care be seen as an ethical responsibility that transcends personal well-being and extends to the quality of professional service delivery. In its most effective form, self-care is more than a reactive strategy; it is a proactive commitment to personal and professional growth (Quartiroli et al., 2022). For example, self-care not only acts as a buffer against burnout and compassion fatigue but also enables SEPPPs to achieve higher levels of job satisfaction, life satisfaction, and career fulfillment (Quartiroli, Wagstaff et al., 2022). Positioning self-care proactively encourages SEPPPs to develop reflective professional sensibilities, ensuring they are continually monitoring and adjusting their well-being practices as needed, using reflective practices (Quartiroli et al., 2023).

Early-Career Professionals: Laying the Foundation for Sustainable Self-Care

For early-career professionals, the transition from graduate training to professional practice marks a critical period of growth and potential vulnerability. New SEPPPs often enter the field with a strong focus on technical skills and a rigid application of their theoretical knowledge, but might lack the practical experience necessary to balance personal well-being with professional demands (Martin et al., 2023). Early-career SEPPPs are particularly vulnerable to burnout, job dissatisfaction, and compromised ethical practice if they neglect self-care from the outset (Martin et al., 2023). To address these risks, self-care should be integrated as a central theme during training, with supervisors modeling it as an essential component of ethical practice (Fogaça et al., 2024). Mentorship plays a critical role in guiding early-career professionals toward sustainable self-care practices during the formative periods of their careers. Mentors should emphasize the importance of self-care as a long-term strategy, encouraging mentees to develop personalized self-care plans tailored to their individual preferences and professional contexts (Martin et al., 2023). These plans should integrate practices that support physical and psychological well-being, as well as emotional, social, and spiritual well-being contributing to professional resilience and competence (Quartiroli et al., 2022).

The formative stages of a career are often characterized by an eagerness to prove oneself, which can lead to overwork and neglect of personal well-being. Yet, by prioritizing self-care from the beginning, early-career SEPPPs can cultivate habits that sustain them throughout their careers. These practices might include engaging in mindfulness exercises, seeking peer support, and regularly reflecting on one's emotional state (Norcross & VandenBos, 2018).

Evolving Self-Care Strategies Across the Professional Lifespan

As practitioners progress in their careers, their self-care needs evolve. Strategies that were effective in the early stages might require adaptation to address the demands of more senior roles. With increased autonomy and professional responsibility, experienced SEPPPs often encounter additional stressors, including greater demands on their time and energy. Thus, they must frequently reassess and refine their strategies to navigate these evolving challenges while safeguarding their personal and professional well-being (Quartiroli et al., 2019).

From the available literature, several key insights for more experienced SEPPPs are evident. For instance, autonomy is a key feature of professional maturity and requires a self-directed approach to self-care. Whilst early-career professionals often rely on external support, such as that of their supervisor, more experienced SEPPPs must develop internal resources to monitor and maintain their well-being. Here, we place emphasis on self-care not necessarily being an individual endeavor. Paradoxically, there is evidence to suggest that self-care practices can be enhanced when supported by others and carried out through other people (Quartiroli et al., 2025). Reflective practices, such as journaling, mindfulness, or peer supervision can help seasoned professionals stay attuned to their evolving self-care needs (Quartiroli et al., 2023). By embedding self-care into their professional routines and sharing such experiences through and with other practitioners and performance professionals, experienced SEPPPs can ensure their continued effectiveness, uphold their ethical obligations, and maintain long-term career satisfaction.

Embedding Self-Care into Professional Identity: A Call for Systemic Change

Self-care must not be regarded as an add-on *to* professional practice, but rather as an integral component *of* professional practice. By embedding self-care into their routines, SEPPPs can cultivate resilience, maintain ethical standards, and sustain their ability to provide effective, compassionate care throughout their careers. Nevertheless, this shift requires a systemic change in how the profession views, promotes, and supports self-care (Wise & Barnett, 2016).

Supervisors, educators, and institutions all play a fundamental role in fostering a collective culture that values self-care as an essential cornerstone of professional development and ethical practice (Quartiroli et al., 2025). This systemic approach to self-care should begin in graduate training and continue through ongoing professional development programs and reinforcement from professional bodies. Embedding self-care into training curricula and supervision can normalize it as a core professional competency, rather than an optional or secondary concern. In doing so, the profession may help protect individual well-being and potentially improve the quality of care provided to clients (Quartiroli, Wagstaff et al., 2022).

Conclusion: A Sustainable Future through Ethical Self-Care

Self-care is essential for sustaining SEPPPs' careers, helping them remain effective, ethical, and resilient in a demanding field. By framing it as an ethical obligation rather than a personal choice, we propose a shift in how it is understood and practiced, globally. The aim should not be to solely prevent burnout and other negative outcomes, but to cultivate flourishing professionals who thrive personally and professionally. We envisage that a proactive, embedded approach to self-care will empower SEPPPs to advocate for their well-being in fast-paced, emotionally demanding environments, while also equipping them to support the self-care and well-being of performance staff and coaches, who face similar challenges (Quartiroli et al., 2019; 2025).

SELF-COMPASSION AS A SUPERPOWER FOR SELF-CARE

Tsz Lun (Alan) Chu

Showing care and concern for others is an essential quality of helping professionals, including sport psychology professionals (SPPs) ranging from psychologists and mental performance consultants to mentors. Meanwhile, turning that care and concern toward oneself (i.e., self-care) is necessary for having a sustainable career. If SPPs do not practice self-care, they may experience an imbalance in their personal and professional lives, leading to burnout and health problems that do not allow them to serve the best interests of their clients, students, and professional communities.

While there are various conceptualizations and forms of self-care in general and in the field of sport psychology (see Quartiroli et al., 2022), self-compassion practice is a simple and effective way to model and practice self-care. Self-compassion consists of three foundational elements—mindfulness, common humanity, and self-kindness (Neff, 2003), offering a way of holding the distress experienced in helping professions with presence, connection, and kindness. In addition to engaging in healthy self-care activities outside of work, self-compassionate people also care for themselves during stressful moments at work while professionally caring for others (Ferrari et al., 2017).

Although self-compassion has been heavily studied in Western contexts based on Neff's work, it stems from a Buddhist worldview where suffering, failure, and imperfection are seen as a natural part of life (Neff et al., 2008). A recent meta-analysis of studies across 27 cultures showed similar effect sizes in the associations between self-compassion and well-being (e.g., life satisfaction, professional quality of life), as well as between self-compassion and psychological distress (depression, anxiety, and stress), independent of levels of collectivism versus individualism (Chio et al., 2021). Therefore, SPPs across the globe can expect to benefit from incorporating self-compassion practices into their self-care.

Diversity and Flexibility of Self-Compassion Practices

There are various ways to practice self-compassion for self-care. Comforting, soothing, and validating oneself is known as *yin* or *tender* self-compassion, which focuses on being with and accepting oneself (Neff & Germer, 2018). This is what people typically think is self-compassion. On the other hand, protecting, providing, and motivating oneself is known as *yang* or *fierce* self-compassion, which focuses on acting in the world (Neff & Germer, 2018). As Quartiroli et al. (2022) suggested, "Self-care activities must be grounded in one's own personal values and cannot be blindly prescribed" (p. 1364). Self-compassion practice provides the flexibility for anyone to explore and engage in activities that align with their core values by asking themselves, "What do I need right now?"—thus enhancing intentionality and locus of control in difficult situations. For example, when an SPP is overwhelmed by their work, they may incorporate yin self-compassion by taking a nature walk or doing guided meditations (e.g., aligned with values of tranquility and spirituality). Meanwhile, they can engage in yang self-compassion to ask for changes in their work tasks or schedules to maintain a more manageable workload (e.g., aligned with values of honesty and courage). In addition to promoting better self-care and well-being, self-compassion also enhances people's authenticity to act on their values (Zhang et al., 2019).

Informal Self-Compassion in Action

Self-compassion practices can be implemented informally anywhere, at any time, when people experience emotional distress. Such practices, unlike other structured self-care activities, require no specific supplies or prescribed rituals. For instance, an SPP who just had an emotionally difficult client session might not have the time to take a walk and do formal meditation; thus, their self-compassion practice can be as simple as (1) acknowledging the emotional pain (e.g., "this is hard for me right now")—mindfulness, (2) reminding oneself that it is part of human nature to suffer (e.g., "everyone struggles")—common humanity, and (3) offering kindness to oneself in that moment through a supportive statement/phrase (e.g., "you've done the best that you can") or gesture (e.g., placing a hand on the heart)—self-kindness.

It is also not uncommon for SPPs to work with teams during challenging situations (e.g., a losing streak). Consider having a heated team meeting where athletes direct their frustration at the coaching staff and question the value of the mental skills they have learned, which could shake an SPP's confidence. The inner critic might begin its familiar attack, "Maybe they're right. Maybe you're not helping them." Instead of getting caught in this spiral, the SPP can pause and apply the three elements of self-compassion in less than two minutes to gain clarity and approach the situation with resilience (e.g., "This is stressful (mindfulness). Everyone working in high-pressure environments faces criticism and setbacks. This is part of the territory, not a personal failing (common humanity). I've been working hard to support this team, and sometimes progress isn't linear (self-kindness)."

Formal Self-Compassion Practices

Although informal practices are helpful and easy to implement, engaging in more formal self-compassion practices, which take only five to ten minutes each day, can further enhance SPPs' capacities and habits for mental, physical, and spiritual self-care (i.e., mind, body, and spirit). Beyond guided meditations such as affectionate breathing and self-compassion breaks, writing exercises like finding compassionate voices through journaling or writing a letter to oneself can be effective, offering both yin and yang self-compassion according to individual needs and preferences. For example, SPPs could write a letter using the prompt, "What would you say to a friend struggling with a similar situation?" to ground themselves when feeling distressed and dealing with difficult emotions (yin self-compassion). Alternatively, they could use the prompt, "How would your wise coach or mentor advise you about this difficult situation?" to motivate themselves with kindness to take value-based actions (yang self-compassion). Reading the letter immediately and revisiting it periodically is recommended, especially during moments of struggle, as part of a self-care routine.

SPPs may also draft an email or letter with encouraging words, scheduled for delayed delivery at a particular time. For example, during my second year in a new faculty position, I was juggling multiple research projects, new courses, and service commitments while also maintaining my mentorship and consulting work in addition to having a newborn in my family. I drafted a letter on www.futureme.org and scheduled it to arrive in my inbox during the first week of having the newborn.

> *Dear Me,*
>
> *I know you're probably feeling overwhelmed right now with seeing clients and deadlines looming. Please remember that you're exactly where you need to be. You chose this career because you're passionate about helping others and contributing to the field. Remember that you don't have to be perfect. Your research doesn't have to revolutionize the field overnight. Your teaching doesn't have to inspire every single student. Your service doesn't have to solve every issue in the field. Just show up authentically and do your best work. Take a deep breath! Look at your calendar and identify two to three meaningful and manageable tasks you can complete today. Celebrate those wins, however small they may seem. And remember to believe in yourself!*
>
> *With kindness, Wise Me*

Reading these words from a calmer, more mindful self is like receiving a hug from a dear friend. It reminds you that emotional states are temporary and that you have resources, skills, and support that you sometimes forget about in difficult moments.

A Culture of Compassion and Care for All

It takes time for people to buy into the value of practicing self-care due to cultural norms and perceived obstacles, which both individuals and systems need to tackle. Two common internal obstacles to self-care that SPPs have are lack of awareness and lack of self-compassion (Quartiroli et al., 2022). These obstacles may stem from the guilt about and fear of self-compassion due to SPPs' ambitious standards for excellence and serving others in a high-performance culture. Understanding that self-compassion indeed contributes to compassion and care for others and the community can help mitigate potential guilt and fear, creating a culture of excellence rooted in compassion and care for all (Neff et al., 2020). This cascading effect promotes self-care behaviors and work performance in high-performance cultures (Neff et al., 2020). For example, in healthcare, helping professionals who are self-compassionate are more likely to feel compassion satisfaction rather than compassion fatigue, take responsibility for mistakes, and improve patient care and outcomes (Kemper et al., 2019; Smart et al., 2014).

Imagine a sport psychology graduate program where faculty and mentors prioritize and model self-compassion as a foundation for self-care that creates a ripple effect as students and mentees start openly discussing their needs rather than hiding mistakes and exhaustion or feeling guilty about them. Mentors start checking in on mentees' needs and offering practical support, such as sharing resources for managing challenging cases or schedules. The entire program culture shifts from viewing self-compassion and self-care as weakness or selfishness to recognizing them as professional competence. Students graduating from these programs enter the field with established self-care routines and realistic expectations about professional sustainability. Clients report greater satisfaction with sport psychology services because professionals who practice self-compassion and self-care are more consistent, emotionally regulated, and present in their work. Therefore, self-compassion could truly be a superpower for SPPs to engage in self-care practice aligned with their values and contribute to a culture of excellence grounded in compassion and care.

SELF-CARE AS A TRANSNATIONAL BLACK FEMALE SPORT PSYCHOLOGIST

Dawn-Marie Armstrong

Race and Representation in Sport Psychology

To shed some light on my professional journey, it is important to note that I was born on the small Caribbean Island of Barbados and through my postgraduate studies as an international student, I was able to qualify and position myself as a transnational British Psychological Society (BPS) Chartered and Health and Care Professions Council (HCPC) Registered Sport and Exercise Psychologist via the Professional Doctorate (Prof. Doc.) route. In becoming the first professional from my region to complete the qualification in 2022 as well as being the first Black woman from that program, I must highlight that only 1% of sport and exercise psychologist professionals (SEPPs) in the UK identify as Black (HCPC, 2023). In outlining steps toward greater representation, Carter and Davila (2017) suggested centering racism and discrimination in sport psychology research, education and training to validate the experiences of Black SEPPs with considerations for self-care since difference and discrimination in sport psychology have not received much literary attention (Ryba et al., 2020). In this respect, my engagement with self-care over the course of my career has been far from traditional.

Racism-Related Coping as an Antecedent to Self-Care

My experiences as a student, trainee, and practitioner in the UK have always been racialized due to being classed as an "ethnic minority." Presently, within England and Wales, persons identifying as Black African, Black Caribbean, or Black (other) constitute for 4.0% of the population (this figure excludes persons who identify as "mixed race"; Population of England and Wales, 2022). Additionally, in Scotland, Black Caribbean people in 2022 accounted for 0.12% of the population (Scotland's Census, 2024), which is important to note since most of my time during training was spent there on placement with a national organization.

Placement and Work Opportunities

In 2018, I left the Caribbean as a well-paid professional (part-time physical education teacher and sport psychology consultant) and had grown accustomed to receiving a salary commensurate with my qualifications. Equally, during the period between 2016 and 2017 (leading up to my UK return), I was contracted with an international team as a mental skills coach which saw me traveling with a sports team in preparation for a 2018 World Cup. After this work was completed, I left the Caribbean believing that the rate of pay in the UK was higher and due to the advancement of the field, thought that more exciting opportunities would be forthcoming. Unfortunately, what occurred was quite the opposite and as a result, in March 2018, I negotiated a two-year unpaid placement with an organization that was willing to only offer GBP 100 per month as a salary with tax deductions. Knowing that I would have never accepted that figure as payment, I requested that the total of GBP 2,400 be placed in a continuing professional development (CPD) fund for me to access over the duration of the placement. I also wish to add now that I had tremendous difficulty accessing those funds and was even denied utilizing the full amount that was due to me; a decision that was made by a manager at the time. It was interesting that I sought out to work with this organization because I had finished a previous cycle with another team in that same sport, but the two experiences were like night and day. Culturally, there was a lot to learn in Scotland, but racially, it left a bitter taste of what I was to eventually savor over the duration of my time in the UK. Indeed, I must mention that the highlight of my disappointment came with the promise of accompanying that team to the 2020 World Cup, but a last-minute decision saw that unfulfilled since psychology was not deemed to be an important factor in the team's performance. I had undertaken all the free work in preparing them for the World Cup but still was not found deserving to see the work to completion. This resulted in a conversation that would spark my first attempt at self-advocacy. A social media post in November 2019 and one which saw me unfollowed by some of my colleagues in the field. There was no peer group for me to have discussions on these experiences, no one that looked like me who I felt I could relate to, and most importantly, no one that I thought would understand. As such, I began leaning on my family and friends in Barbados for support because for the first time in my life, I came to realize that the color of my skin was an impediment to my practitioner development. Undoubtedly, I knew that they truly cared about what I was going through, but my entire perspective of the world and profession had shifted. Following this experience, paid work opportunities that followed would continue seeing me as the only Black woman in the room and below is a list of some of the microaggressions I encountered:

- A coach from an opposing team approaching to fist bump me after offering my white, male colleagues a handshake;
- Repeatedly being asked if I was the one in the office smelling like coconut;
- Repeatedly being asked about the food I was eating;
- Being mistaken for a maid;
- Being mistaken for a parent of an athlete;
- Repeatedly being asked to speak more clearly;
- Repeatedly being asked about when I was going to go home [to my country];
- Being asked if I smoked marijuana;
- Icebreakers around rum (which I never drank);
- Being asked about whether Universities in the Caribbean were on the beach;
- A manager once said to me in front of my colleagues that when he was on holiday in the Caribbean, hotel workers kept asking him for money;
- On another occasion that same Manager came into the staff office and told me I was "mean" in front of colleagues while I was sitting and working quietly at my desk.

There are other experiences to recall but these are the few that have stuck out over the years. Over time, there was a repeated cycle of holding my tongue, calling my family, sharing the stories, venting, and ultimately, pressing on.

Supervision, the COVID-19 Pandemic and Program Completion

There were also many challenges throughout the course of my supervisory relationship, which I shared via social media in some instances, but for the purposes of anonymity, I will not here. However, the COVID-19 pandemic saw international students disproportionately affected, with some (like me) having to return to our home countries due to the lack of support in addition to strict government policies with respect to visas and immigration. As a result, I subsequently left the UK in August 2020 and returned when travel restrictions were lifted in September 2021. I then completed the Prof. Doc. in May 2022 and the period leading up to my portfolio submission was marred by what I believed to be racial challenges. As such, my first act of self-care came in seeking mental support, particularly in the last two months of my studies. It is something that I have shared here for the first time. A crisis call—that was my self-care.

Self-Care and Race in Applied Practice

There has been little exploration of self-care and race within applied practice even though the intersection of race and gender is seen to be of critical importance with respect to the lived experiences of Black female SPPs (Hyman et al., 2022). Equally, within this space, because of Eurocentric, male-centric dominant ideologies and perspectives, Black women must navigate an unequal requirement for emotional labor because of everyday microaggressions (Champ et al., 2021), some of which I outlined earlier. As such, in an attempt to be proactive with respect to my self-care in my second full-time role after completing the Prof. Doc. I finally enrolled in counseling psychotherapy in April 2024. At this stage in my career, I was focused on reducing the professional threats and challenges (Porter, 1995) that I repeatedly encountered since I was finally in an academic role that I really wanted to remain in. I was aware of my personal needs and the strategy that was necessary to meet those needs (Knapp & Vande-Creek, 2006) and I needed a safe space to share my experiences with a qualified professional who understood them. In selecting my therapist, I sought out another Black woman who had extensive experience consulting within occupational settings and she allowed me to share everything that I had endured. When reflecting on my reason for engaging in this form of self-care, I realized that in every work environment where I had found myself "othered," I was constantly under attack for just existing. It always seemed as if people within the work environment were constantly at war with me and there was no peace. As a result of this, my focus while engaging in therapy was and always will be personal safety and I find it unfortunate that self-care and its personal implications have not been explored widely in professional practice (Quartiroli et al., 2019), especially considering race. I believe that if I had greater knowledge of self-care prior to experiencing my adversity, I may have been better able to cope.

EDITORS' TAKEAWAYS

We find it fitting that the self-care chapter comes right after the "practice what you preach" chapter. It made us reflect on how much grad school culture normalizes the grind—perhaps one reason self-care often feels so elusive. The intensity becomes expected, even celebrated, and it can make caring for ourselves feel like a luxury rather than a necessity. That said, we actually don't think self-care should be treated as another grad school training requirement. Just as athletes often build up experiential knowledge of which mental skills work for them, so too graduate students should have a space where they can experiment with their own strategies as an exercise in self-awareness before having formalized training or outside perspectives. As the text points out, mentorship seems a more appropriate space for those conversations. That said, we really appreciated Alan's framing of self-care through self-compassion. It's a reminder that self-care doesn't have to be complicated or indulgent—it's about giving ourselves grace, as long as it doesn't slip into avoidance.

Dawn-Marie's chapter stood out to us as well, especially her willingness to name therapy as a self-care strategy. Within SEPP, this deserves far more open discussion—whether in classrooms, professional meetings, or even in the research itself. Talking about therapy as self-care not only reduces stigma but also models the kind of honesty our field often asks of clients, but struggles to extend to ourselves.

RECOMMENDED EXERCISES

1 Reflect on a recent professional experience where you felt emotionally taxed or overwhelmed. What emotions did you experience, and how did they affect your ability to act ethically and effectively? How might regular self-care have helped, and what actions could you take in the future to prevent burnout in similar situations?
2 Consider your practice, service delivery, and workplace demands. How does self-care support a positive daily professional experience (see Quartiroli et al., 2022)?
3 First, ask yourself: What do I need right now? Then reflect on self-compassion strategies:
    a Yin self-compassion
        i Comforting: How can I care for my emotional needs?
        ii Soothing: How can I feel physically calmer?
        iii Validating: What can I tell myself to validate my feelings?
    b Yang self-compassion
        i Protecting: How can I stop harm from others or myself?
        ii Providing: How can I give myself what I need to achieve goals?
        iii Motivating: How can I encourage myself with kindness and support rather than harsh criticism?
4 How does your background or identity influence your access to or need for certain self-care? What barriers exist? Which practices help you feel grounded and empowered, and how can you make space for them regularly? Who in your support network understands your challenges, and where could you build new connections for mutual support?
5 What cultural norms in your education program, workplace, or field feel unsupportive of well-being? What small actions could you take to advocate for change or create more supportive environments, particularly for marginalized groups? If a colleague shared that their well-being was negatively impacted, how would you respond? How would you discuss self-care and self-compassion with them?

REFERENCES

Barnett, J. E., Baker, E. K., Elman, N. S., & Schoener, G. R. (2007). In pursuit of wellness: The self-care imperative. *Professional Psychology: Research and Practice, 38*(6), 603–612. https://doi.org/10.1037/0735-7028.38.6.603

Carter, L., & Davila, C. (2017). Is it because I'm Black? Microaggressive experiences against Black professionals in sport and exercise psychology. *Professional Psychology: Research and Practice, 48*(5), 287–293. https://doi.org/10.1037/pro0000145

Champ, F., Ronkainen, N., Tod, D., Eubank, A., & Littlewood, M. (2021). A tale of three seasons: A cultural sport psychology and gender performativity approach to practitioner identity and development in professional football. *Qualitative Research in Sport, Exercise and Health, 13*(5), 847–863. https://doi.org/10.1080/2159676X.2020.1833967

Chio, F. H. N., Mak, W. W. S., & Yu, B. C. L. (2021). Meta-analytic review on the differential effects of self-compassion components on well-being and psychological distress: The moderating role of dialecticism on self-compassion. *Clinical Psychology Review, 85,* 101986. https://doi.org/10.1016/j.cpr.2021.101986

Dorociak, K. E., Rupert, P. A., & Zahniser, E. (2017). Work life, well-being, and selfcare across the professional lifespan of psychologists. *Professional Psychology: Research and Practice, 48*(6), 429–437. https://doi.org/10.1037/pro0000160

Ferrari, M., Dal Cin, M., & Steele, M. (2017). Self-compassion is associated with optimum self-care behaviour, medical outcomes and psychological well-being in a cross-sectional sample of adults with diabetes. *Diabetic Medicine, 34*(11), 1546–1553. https://doi.org/10.1111/dme.13451

Fogaça, J. L., Quartiroli, A., & Wagstaff, C. (2024). Professional development of sport psychology practitioners: From systematic review to a model of development. *Psychology of Sport and Exercise, 68,* 102550. https://doi.org/10.1016/j.psychsport.2023.102550

Hings, R. F., Wagstaff, C. R. D., Anderson, V., Gilmore, S., & Thelwell, R. C. (2020). Better preparing sports psychologists for the demands of applied practice: The emotional labor training gap. *Journal of Applied Sport Psychology, 32*(4), 335–356. https://doi.org/10.1080/10413200.2018.1560373

Hyman, J. E., White, D. A., & David, J. L. (2022). The sisters of sport psychology: An examination of the professional Black female experience. *Journal of Applied Sport Psychology, 34*(3), 624–645. https://doi.org/10.1080/10413200.2021.1872733

Kemper, K. J., McClafferty, H., Wilson, P. M., Serwint, J. R., Batra, M., Mahan, J. D., Schubert, C. J., Staples, B. B., & Schwartz, A. (2019). Do mindfulness and self-compassion predict burnout in pediatric residents? *Academic Medicine, 94*(6), 876–884. https://doi.org/10.1097/ACM.0000000000002546

Knapp, S. J., & VandeCreek, L. D. (2006). *Practical ethics for psychologists: A positive approach.* American Psychological Association. https://doi.org/10.1037/11377-000

Martin, D. R. F., Quartiroli, A., & Wagstaff, C. R. D. (2023). A qualitative exploration of neophyte sport psychology practitioners' self-care experiences and perceptions. *Journal of Applied Sport Psychology, 35*(5), 874–896. https://doi.org/10.1080/10413200.2022.2046659

Neff, K. D. (2003). Self-compassion: An alternative conceptualization of a healthy attitude toward oneself. *Self and Identity, 2*(2), 85–101. https://doi.org/10.1080/15298860309032

Neff, K. D., & Germer, C. K. (2018). *The mindful self-compassion workbook: A proven way to accept yourself, build inner strength, and thrive.* Guilford Press.

Neff, K. D., Knox, M. C., Long, P., & Gregory, K. (2020). Caring for others without losing yourself: An adaptation of the mindful self-compassion program for healthcare communities. *Journal of Clinical Psychology, 76*(9), 1543–1562. https://doi.org/10.1002/jclp.23007

Neff, K. D., Pisitsungkagarn, K., & Hsieh, Y. P. (2008). Self-compassion and self-construal in the United States, Thailand, and Taiwan. *Journal of Cross-Cultural Psychology, 39*(3), 267–285. https://doi.org/10.1177/0022022108314544

Norcross, J. C., & VandenBos, G. R. (2018). *Leaving it at the office: A guide to psychotherapist self-care.* Guilford Press.

Population of England and Wales. (2022, December). *Main facts and figures.* UK Government. https://www.ethnicity-facts-figures.service.gov.uk/uk-population-by-ethnicity/national-and-regional-populations/population-of-england-and-wales/latest/

Porter, N. (1995). Therapist self-care: A proactive ethical approach. In H. Lerman & N. Porter (Eds.), *Feminist ethics in psychotherapy* (pp. 247–266). Springer.

Price, D., Wagstaff, C. R. D., & Thelwell, R. C. (2022). Opportunities and considerations of new media and technology in sport psychology service delivery. *Journal of Sport Psychology in Action, 13*(1), 4–15. https://doi.org/10.1080/21520704.2020.1846648

Quartiroli, A., Etzel, E. F., Knight, S. M., & Zakrajsek, R. A. (2019). Self-care as key to others' care: The perspectives of globally situated experienced senior-level sport psychology practitioners. *Journal of Applied Sport Psychology, 31*(2), 147–167. https://doi.org/10.1080/10413200.2018.1460420

Quartiroli, A., Hunter, H., & Martin, D. R. (2023). Self-care as the bedrock of ethical and competent service delivery: The practitioner's journey. *Journal of Sport Psychology in Action, 14*(3), 145–157. https://doi.org/10.1080/21520704.2022.2154876

Quartiroli, A., Wagstaff, C. R. D., & Thelwell, R. (2022). The what and the how of self-care for sport psychology practitioners: A Delphi study. *Journal of Applied Sport Psychology, 34*(6), 1352–1371. https://doi.org/10.1080/10413200.2021.1964107

Quartiroli, A., Wagstaff, C. R. D., Zakrajsek, R. A., Knight, S. M., & Etzel, E. F. (2022). The role of self-care and professional quality of life in sustaining a long-lasting career in sport psychology: A qualitative exploration. *Journal of Applied Sport Psychology, 34*(6), 1334–1351. https://doi.org/10.1080/10413200.2021.1907483

Quartiroli, A., Martin, D. R., Hunter, H., & Wagstaff, C. R. (2025). A thematic-synthesis of self-care in sport psychology practitioners. *International Journal of Sport and Exercise Psychology, 23*(1), 1–25. https://doi.org/10.1080/1612197X.2023.2291102

Ryba, T., Ronkainen, N., & Lee, S. M. (2020). Historicising cultural sport psychology: Dare we de-centre methodological eurocentrism? *Quaderns de Psicologia, 22*(3), e1566. https://doi.org/10.5565/rev/qpsicologia.1566

Scotland's Census 2022. (2024, August). *Ethnic group, national identity, language and religion.* https://www.scotlandscensus.gov.uk/2022-results/scotland-s-census-2022-ethnic-group-national-identity-language-and-religion/#section3

Smart, D., English, A., James, J., Wilson, M., Daratha, K. B., Childers, B., & Magera, C. (2014). Compassion fatigue and satisfaction: A cross-sectional survey among US healthcare workers. *Nursing & Health Sciences, 16*(1), 3–10. https://doi.org/10.1111/nhs.12068

The Health and Care Professions Council. (2023, July 4). *Diversity data.* https://www.hcpc-uk.org/about-us/insights-and-data/diversity/

Wise, E. H., & Barnett, J. E. (2016). Self-care for psychologists. In J. C. Norcross, G. R. VandenBos, D. K. Freedheim, & L. F. Campbell (Eds.), *APA handbook of clinical psychology: Education and profession* (pp. 209–222). American Psychological Association. https://doi.org/10.1037/14774-014

Zhang, J. W., Chen, S., Tomova Shakur, T. K., Bilgin, B., Chai, W. J., Ramis, T., Shaban-Azad, H., Razavi, P., Nutankumar, T., & Manukyan, A. (2019). A compassionate self is a true self? Self-compassion promotes subjective authenticity. *Personality and Social Psychology Bulletin, 45*(9), 1323–1337. https://doi.org/10.1177/0146167218820914

17 Building and Maintaining Communities of Practice

Somehow networking has always been something that I, Sebastian, have felt drawn to as part of my professional journey. Connecting with others, building networks and collaborations has certainly played a pivotal role in shaping and advancing my professional growth and journey. From connecting with mentors who would end up becoming my advisors during my Ph.D. studies and enable me to attend graduate school in the United States, to joining committees or special interest groups specifically within the Association for Applied Sport Psychology (AASP), personal interactions with other professionals have helped shape who I am and what I have done professionally throughout my career. This chapter introduces key insights regarding a strategic approach to networking—building and maintaining communities of practice (CoPs).

COMMUNITIES OF PRACTICE IN SPORT, EXERCISE, AND PERFORMANCE PSYCHOLOGY: SHAPING OURSELVES AND SHAPING THE FIELD... TOGETHER

Adam Naylor

Communities of colleagues that challenge one another and learn together lead to excellent professional practice. It has regularly been stated that CoPs have existed since humans began taking pride in any sort of profession and were social together. From gatherings as informal as cafes in Paris where writers and artists regularly met to ponder ideas together, through in recent times, corporations trying to formally harness the transformational potential of knowledgeable professionals sitting and talking together, building them into corporate activities and behaviors. Somewhere in between these two examples seem to lie special interest groups of academic and professional organizations. In one form or another, all of these groups can be considered CoPs. In recent decades, these peer-to-peer learning opportunities have been formally conceptualized and evolved in their range of implicit and explicit goals (Cox, 2005).

Put simply, the purpose of a CoP is to both elevate the professional practice of individual group members as well as raise the bar for service delivery and interventions in the field as a whole. In sport, exercise, and performance psychology (SEPP), CoPs are purpose-driven and passionate groups that gather regularly to improve how they serve athletes, exercisers, and performers. The concept of CoPs has received a good amount of scholarly attention since the turn of the century. In 2011, Wenger identified three characteristics at the core of design and delivery of a CoP—shared domain expertise, robust community engagement, and sustained participation over time. Although casual conversations among professionals and organizational encouraged conversations among subject matter experts might appear to be a CoP,

DOI: 10.4324/9781003781479-21

upon inspection not all CoPs are created equal in achieving the goals for elevated professional practice. When considering closely, the nature of group member experience and motivation shape the cohesion, member development, and ultimately, CoP success. Considering all of this, if you were to join or start a CoP how would you know it is on a track for success?

First, reasonable "domain expertise" ought to be expected of all group members—a shared commitment to and competence in a specialty. In SEPP, this could be as specific as professionals that work in a particular sport to as broad as a group of performance psychology professionals with a base level of applied experience and training. Group members' depth of knowledge and range of experience impact a CoP's potential (Carron & Hausenblas, 1998). A reasonable variability in both is acceptable as it can provide fresh perspectives and energy. Wenger and colleagues' (as cited in Li et al., 2009) view CoPs as somewhat similar to apprenticeship relationships which allow for this variability. However, where the knowledge gap is significant between members, it can be a threat to both knowledge sharing and growth, unbalancing the power in group relationships making some members teachers and other members students. The negative potential of knowledge gaps can be minimized by good faith efforts of less knowledgeable members to deepen knowledge outside of CoP meetings and more knowledgeable members having a stance of positive regard to encourage reasonable motivation from everyone.

Next, a CoP is an "engaged and active community" driven by sharing ideas and activities which lead to learning together. This engagement can range from regular attendance and participation in meetings through ongoing sharing of articles and insights outside of formal time together. Inequitable participation in conversations and knowledge sharing by group members is a second threat to CoP success. Members without a voice whether it be due to passivity or not feeling invited to actively participate can both rob the group of diverse and deep insights as well as create ill will in those making a regular effort. Whether it be through formalized rules and regulations or a group of informal norms that are developed, behaviors that invite and organize equal contribution from group members benefit all. At a formal level, a CoP may have explicit expectations given to select members each gathering to be prepared to share insights and seed discussion. Informally, trusting relationships are necessary. Trust that belittling and bullying ideas will not occur, as well as trust that insights shared will be held in appropriate confidence and with professional care. In high-performance sport settings as well as the competitive corporate industry, use of insights and information to create competitive advantages over fellow group members can be costly to group cohesion. CoPs that bring together those who may be opponents in one form or the other outside of conversations can only succeed if there is a care for one another and a culture of creating a rising tide for all. A divisive, competitive spirit leaves CoPs mere performative gatherings rather than ones that achieve the clear goal of improving performance of all group members.

Lastly, CoP groups are practice-driven, both in that they are made up of professional practitioners and also in that they require deliberate efforts to develop "muscles" around practitioners' service delivery. CoP success is only achieved through competent professionals devoting "time and sustained interaction" together on topics and practices that shape the work they do and the fields in which they exist. Successful execution of these three factors shape the ability of a CoP to reach the learning goals and satisfaction of all members of the group. Lastly, consistency over time of CoPs gathering and members showing up is at the core to their success. Conversation topics among professional peers are not held to a single moment in time, but rather, are ongoing stories and ever evolving understanding. In robust CoPs, times between meetings lead to marinating and testing of the ideas discussed, which leads to iterative and connected conversations. If engagements do not regularly occur for a sustained period of time, or if members are not regularly active in conversations, CoPs cannot thrive.

With these foundations for success understood, it likely comes as no surprise that CoPs are truly living and breathing organisms. Much like how a group becomes a functioning team, potential members initially come together around an interest of elevating an area of professional practice, but need to find leadership, norms for group behavior, and structures for engaging and growing together to achieve their telos. Tuckman's psychological stages of a team's lifecycle should be considered here: forming, storming, norming, performing, and adjourning (Tuckman & Jensen, 1977). Energy around ideas can fairly easily be found (forming). Group leadership and structure is critical for a CoP to be more than a social group, so effort and time spent to determine rules of the road and member roles is worth the effort (storming and norming). On this path, it is valuable to appreciate that leading a group of knowledgeable professionals can be a daunting task and one requiring shared values toward learning to appreciate one another. These initial stages allow for sustained quality participation from CoP participants to thrive (performing). While it is likely that members of a CoP value lifelong professional growth it is reasonable to appreciate that in time, all members will waver in their energy and engagement. It is at these times that bringing the CoP to a close might make sense (adjourning).

There is great power in a quality CoP for individual practitioners and SEPP as a whole. The cooperative learning aspect among qualified peers leads to growth promoting challenge, curiosity, and insight. When practicing professionals regularly engage, it truly creates a rising tide for all. This said, being thoughtful about the creation, structure, and maintenance of a CoP is critical for all the potential benefits to be reached. CoPs thrive when they are made up of caring and credible professionals that show up together and engage consistently.

COMMUNITY OF PRACTICE

Carl Ohlson, Nicole DeFerrari, Meighan Julbert, & Jon Hammermeister

We hope to bring you knowledge and share anecdotal experiences that we as an author group have found invaluable in our own CoPs. In different capacities, we've all worked together, some for years, with the shared mission of elevating an athlete's mentality and helping them thrive both on and off their field of play. The majority of this author group has spent the bulk of their professional careers working with Power Five Division I athletes and athletic organizations. One of the wonderful things about sport psychology is how translatable the skill set is across professions, so please know that our varied experiences are also coming from backgrounds with the United States military, professional athletes and organizations, and Olympic athletes as well. While our backgrounds are assorted and multifaceted, we all bear graduate specializations under the umbrella of SEPP with a mix of kinesiology, education, and counseling psychology degrees. Additionally, we all have either obtained, or are in pursuit thereof, Certified Mental Performance Consultant (CMPC) status through the Association for Applied Sport Psychology (AASP). At the end of the day, it takes a village to help athletes thrive. As such, we are so grateful to introduce you to what it means to foster and experience what that can look like through a CommUNITY of Practice.

Athletes at the Center

As we embark on reviewing types, characteristics, and demonstrated values of CoPs, with examples woven throughout, we must underscore the importance of athlete agency—placing the athlete at the center of the CoP. Athlete agency acts as the hub from which culture, decisions, and goals arise within the CoP. By empowering athletes to take ownership of their growth and learning, CoPs can foster authentic and lasting change.

Member Characteristics

Successful CoP members share critical traits that make them effective contributors to the community itself. While there are many valuable traits, we have anecdotally found the following to be the most effective in fostering a strong and healthy CoP: (a) having a secure and quiet ego, (b) leading with curiosity, and (c) engaging as a compassionate, direct, and clear communicator. These character traits provide a combination in which collective success is truly the primary outcome when problem-solving for an athlete or benchmarking is taking place. It's not to say that mistakes aren't made or summits are constantly successfully reached—no. Some of the most admirable components of a CoP is their humanity and humility which both allow for growth, pivoting, and learning no matter what the task at hand might be.

Ego Check

Being a part of a CoP requires sustaining a secure, quiet ego; and keeping the athletes' needs centralized before one's own. As practitioners, it's crucial to recognize that we are not the center of the process—the athlete is. Further, secure and quiet ego is a major part of what drives the "iron sharpens iron" mentality that we greatly emphasize, and which is a component of the growth mindset that benefits the practitioner as well as others around them (Chew & Ang, 2023). Below are examples of characteristics that might provide for a community built on humility and a growth mindset.

- Willingness to be curious and build relationships, knowing that no one person has all the answers.
- Allowing the athlete to be in the helm space with you, recognizing their expertise in their own lived experiences joining together with your content matter expertise.
- Engaging in self-reflection, a vital part of learning and growth in order to identify where improvements can be made; and values can be maintained.

Communication and a Shared Value System

Relationships are the bedrock of a successful CoP. The connections you establish with other practitioners create a network of trust and collaboration, ensuring that the necessary communication will allow for a collective path forward when challenges arise. Identifying a shared value system with the athlete centered in the process allows engagement with colleagues in a way that fosters mutual support and a seamless collaboration.

Types of Communities of Practice

CoPs can exist in both intradisciplinary and interdisciplinary formats. Intradisciplinary CoPs consist of members from the same or similar competencies while interdisciplinary CoPs consist of members from differing expertise. For example, an intradisciplinary CoP at Team Work University is the Performance Psychology Team which consists of CMPCs, sport psychologists, and interns. With some nuance, all have either experience and/or expertise in providing mental intervention for athlete populations, which offers a familiar foundation for their work and engagement with each other. However, each member's continuing education, connections with other networks, and potentially differing areas of emphasis within the shared field allow for unique lenses on a particular topic, issue, or theoretical underpinning. No single practitioner is likely to know everything that could be helpful when facing an athlete challenge, so a CoP with members who have a secure quiet ego, who want to sharpen each other, can advance the individual and collective knowledge for the benefit of all athletes receiving support from said CoP. The above example at Team Work University is a structure we have all worked within, and we found incredible value in these "iron sharpens iron" conversations. However, you need not limit CoP membership to your current institution. Indeed, expanding membership to include peers at other institutions and at different levels of athletics can enrich the learning opportunities in virtually limitless ways. We found incredible value in such inclusion especially during the COVID-19 pandemic lockdown. We shared knowledge with our networks about staying connected to coaches and athletes in a virtual environment, ideas for team bonding and mutual support, leadership challenges and solutions, and even the concept of shifting the emphasis from surviving to thriving during unprecedented complexities, ambiguities, and persistent shifts in guidance and requirements.

An example of an interdisciplinary CoP at Team Work University is the Sport Wellness and Performance Team. The CoP consists of one or more representatives from several intra-CoPs, such as personnel from the following departments: Athlete Development, Sport Medicine, Sport Nutrition, Performance Psychology, Strength & Conditioning, Athlete Academics, etc. Again, this author team has operated within such a CoP and found great value in doing so. A cautionary note here is this CoP cannot just be a standing meeting where each member reports out what they have been working on. Such meetings have their place, yet fall short of the developmental and solution-oriented nature of a CoP. We've worked in CoPs that met regularly where individual athletes, positions, or entire teams are put at the center of the conversation and the CoP members partner with each other to help the coaching staff determine a plan for growth or response to adversity. This could include, for example, individual performance challenges; leadership/followership shortcomings; team culture issues; return to sport after injury; and periodization of physical, mental, and emotional preparation for different parts of a season.

Demonstrated Value

The value of a CoP lies in its ability to generate authentic, athlete-centered outcomes by fostering relationships, collective learning, and open communication. CoPs provide an ecosystem in which shared growth and problem-solving take place. There are benefits and drawbacks to maintaining both types of CoPs within an organization, yet maintaining both is necessary for optimal athlete-centered service provision. Intra-CoPs allow for concentrated expertise and ethical service delivery; however, ideas, schools of thought, and resources are at risk of getting stale if not intentionally assessed. Inter-CoPs allow for a variety of experts to come together for multifaceted projects and initiatives, but they might have to mitigate inter-system differences and/or differing governing or organizational regulations. Still, the strength of a CoP lies in the diversity of those within the community. In our experience, coaches welcome the different voices and integrate that knowledge into everything they plan. We've even invited interested coaches to join us in some of these discipline-specific discussions, resulting in new and lasting relationships. Approaching the planning process with lenses from staff such as medical, strength, nutrition, and psychology-related, and academic support has paid dividends in sustaining competitiveness while mitigating fatigue, injury, and stress; along with providing overall collective growth. The overarching value of both types of CoPs lies in the relationships and the ability to embrace athlete-centered care. Ultimately, CoPs serve as more than just standing meetings or routine collaborations. They are spaces where genuine learning, relationship building, and mutual support occur, while maintaining the athlete at the center. Then functioning optimally, the community can unlock athlete agency and foster an environment where athletes are active participants in their own growth.

BECOMING A SOCIAL LEARNING LEADER: A NEW DIMENSION TO YOUR PRACTICE

Diane M. Culver, Siobhan Rourke, & Sydney Graper

CoPs are groups of individuals who share a common interest, practice, or goal who engage in collective learning to improve their skills and/or understanding (Wenger, 1998). Rather than focusing on CoPs for SEPP professional development, this chapter shifts direction toward the leadership of these communities, which is often shared, dynamic, and organic. Indeed, a key question arises when considering those who are best suited to lead CoPs, with the evidence noting the importance of this function (e.g., Culver et al., 2021). Wenger-Trayner introduced the role of the Social Learning Leader (SLL) to their Social Learning Theory (SLT), as the person or persons who facilitate the cycles of individual and collective reflection and action that create value for the participants in a CoP. Here, we argue there is potential for a specialized Mental Performance Consultant (MPC) to thrive in this leadership position in the context of sport. MPCs are well versed in a variety of knowledge areas, such as mental performance (for a wide variety of performers), group and team dynamics, and organizational structure. As a result, these individuals are well positioned, especially in the high-performance sport landscape to utilize their various skills and experiences to lead CoPs.

Opportunities for Mental Performance Consultants in Social Learning Leadership

A CoP thrives on mutual engagement, joint enterprise, and engaging uncertainty (Wenger, 1998). The leader within such a group must create an environment that facilitates interactions that enable members to engage in shared reflections on practice, learn from one another, and co-create new knowledge. For example, CoPs have been used in a variety of sport contexts to advance understanding on topics such as gender equity (Kraft et al., 2021), concussion support (Seguin et al., 2021), and most recently MPC leadership (Culver et al., 2024). From the SLL perspective, benefits include an increased ability to collaborate with key stakeholders, and an approach to learning and development that is new and insightful. For newer MPCs, training in both mental performance foundations and social learning strategies will be needed to build confidence and credibility in group settings. In contrast, more senior practitioners may find their existing experience with team dynamics and system-level thinking offers a strong base to expand into social learning leadership, enhancing the depth and scope of their practice. Demonstrating expertise in social learning leadership can strengthen an MPC's professional portfolio, showcasing their ability to impact not just individual athletes, but entire sport systems. This broader influence may position MPCs for opportunities in interdisciplinary collaborations, corporate wellness, and other emerging areas where human performance and group dynamics intersect (Henriksen et al., 2019).

While we believe MPCs are uniquely positioned to excel in an SLL role, we contend that previous experience engaging in CoPs as a participant and perceived leadership capabilities, alone, do not constitute adequate training to effectively lead CoPs. The role of the SLL within a CoP differs from traditional leadership roles in more hierarchical settings (Kraft et al., 2021). A prerequisite for leading a CoP is a good understanding of SLT (for a quick introduction see https://www.wenger-trayner.com/resources-overview/). To lead a CoP, an individual must first engage with the community, gaining the experience necessary to understand the dynamics at play. This "backchanneling" work is critical for SLLs in providing the insights and knowledge required to lead effectively, through understanding the community's needs, strengths, and challenges. As such, significant training in SLT is necessary for one to thrive in the role of SLL.

Key Characteristics of Mental Performance Consultants and Social Learning Leaders

Both MPCs and SLLs share a fundamental role in setting the cultural tone in groups, a foundation upon which learning, trust, and collaboration are built. SLLs create these conditions by managing group dynamics, promoting openness and vulnerability, and encouraging sharing even of uncertainty. MPCs also excel at fostering such environments, particularly through their understanding of human behavior and mental performance, which allows them to support members in reaching their optimal potential in a collaborative setting (Durand-Bush et al., 2022). Additionally, both MPCs and SLLs possess strong interpersonal and intrapersonal communication skills, essential for facilitating group interactions, managing conflicts, and ensuring inclusivity (Durand-Bush et al., 2022; Wenger-Trayner & Wenger-Trayner, 2020). Both MPCs and SLLs are focused on their clients/participants, using their active listening and observation skills to guide their leadership. These communication and facilitation skills are vital for leaders who seek to keep their communities engaged, aligned with their broader contexts, and focused on the goals and objectives of the CoP. Moreover, both SLLs and MPCs prioritize continuous learning and self-improvement, a necessary mindset for those leading a CoP where growth and evolution are constant (Wenger-Trayner & Wenger-Trayner, 2020).

There are some differences between the traditional roles of MPCs and SLLs, especially regarding ethics, theoretical approaches, and comfort with nonlinear learning processes. SLLs often work within ambiguous settings, relying heavily on established theories of social learning to guide their practice (Wenger-Trayner et al., 2023). In contrast, MPCs are more likely to work within well-defined ethical frameworks, draw from a range of psychological and performance-based theories, applying them in a context where the goal is not just knowledge transfer, but also the mental and emotional development of the participants. However, MPCs are skilled at navigating complex, unpredictable situations and can use this skill to help individuals in the community maintain focus and perform at their best. Both SLLs and MPCs may focus on surfacing tacit knowledge; SLLs to advance practical knowledge and MPCs to bring awareness to the factors that influence performance.

Qualities to Lead a CoP

Leading a CoP is a more complex and nuanced task than simply participating in one. To lead a CoP effectively, an MPC must possess a deep understanding of SLT concepts, mental performance principles, and the application of these theories in practice (Culver et al., 2024). SLT emphasizes the role of interaction in the learning process, and an MPC must understand how to facilitate these interactions to promote effective learning outcomes, many of which are undefined a priori. For example, knowledge of the Value Creation Framework (VCF; Wenger-Trayner & Wenger-Trayner, 2020) is a helpful tool for planning, assessing, and measuring the impact of the CoP, ensuring that value is realized in different ways across the community and able to be reported to outside stakeholders in order to sustain its long-term success. In addition to theoretical knowledge, an SLL must be comfortable with nonlinear learning pedagogies since the learning process in a CoP is rarely straightforward. Leaders must be able to navigate uncertainty, adapt to changing circumstances, and embrace new challenges; which requires flexibility, resilience, and the ability to stay focused on the things the community cares to impact. It is not uncommon for people to ask about the end goal or topics that will be discussed in the CoP. Transparently, the frequent response to questions of this nature is "it depends" which can cause frustration, resistance, and tension for some. SLLs must be empathetic and patient in the process of others navigating uncertainty, leaning into the discomfort of confrontation thus empowering others and challenging current ways of thinking without dominating conversations (Wenger-Trayner, 2013).

Leaders must also balance structure with the freedom to explore new ideas, approaches, and strategies all while encouraging and surfacing the learning value that can flow from the CoP activities. Non-judgmental attitudes are thus crucial for engagement. An MPC must be able to create a brave space (Arao & Clemens, 2013) for the expressing of different viewpoints without fear of criticism so that all voices are heard and valued (Wenger-Trayner & Wenger-Trayner, 2020), and to ensure CoPs are not simply centers of knowledge reproduction (Culver et al., 2021). MPCs must then also be adept at managing and responding to differing opinions, since these nurture the advancement of practical knowledge. An SLL must possess the mental resilience to lead through these challenges, supporting the community while maintaining focus on the broader objectives.

The use of social learning and CoPs across multiple domains such as education, health, business, and yes, sport has led to the misappropriation of the term, with many users not adequately understanding the key concepts. Indeed, we often hear people say "We do CoPs" and when we ask what that entails, they mention activities like attending conferences and webinars. It is for this reason that we are advocating for MPCs interested in expanding their horizons to explore the theory and seek to develop their abilities for leading CoPs. Paradoxically, one of the most important elements of leading social learning is the capacity to let go of control and allow the proximal, practical needs of the participants in the CoP to shape the conversations and activities. Your role as an SLL is to pay attention to the learning that is happening (or not) and to help articulate that learning value or figure out how better to enable this.

EDITORS' TAKEAWAYS

For many of us, our first CoP in the field is our graduate group of peers. I (Lauren) don't think I truly appreciated how beneficial this community of colleagues was until I left graduate school and was out in the world on my own. I have had the opportunity over the years to be part of many CoPs (including one facilitated by Adam!) and really agree with Adam's notion that engaging in CoPs is an opportunity to raise the bar for ourselves, each other, and the field. Practically, this chapter offers many valuable insights and takeaways about how to make this not just a great idea, but more importantly an effective one. As Ohlson and colleagues mentioned, it takes a village to help people thrive—including ourselves.

It also resonated with me the many different purposes and focuses that CoPs can have, including those we can develop and facilitate for others. When I was working at Barry University during the early part of my career, for example, I facilitated monthly coach sessions—my favorite memory of this was a session where I had the coaches in pairs pretend they had a 3D printer they could use to create athletes for their teams that resulted in a powerful discussion about perceptions and expectations and the role they play on how they lead and coach their teams. As Ohlson and colleagues mentioned, they are valuable ecosystems if we design and facilitate them to live up to the value they could create for the people who participate in them. Building on that notion, Culver and colleagues highlight the potential MPCs have to become invaluable Social Learning Leaders, carving out a unique niche for themselves professionally and also helping to address misunderstandings and organizational challenges that so far thwart the potential for learning and change within CoPs settings.

RECOMMENDED EXERCISES

1 Imagine planning a CoP. What would its purpose be, and how would you develop and facilitate it based on this chapter? What would ideal member participation look and sound like? Identify three signs that consistent commitment has been achieved and three signs that the CoP may be flagging.
2 What are the pros and cons of a virtual CoP? Could you envision a hybrid model?
3 Reflect on your current role in a CoP, as a participant or leader. Evaluate yourself on comfort with ambiguity, vulnerability, adaptability, and communication (including active listening) on a scale of 1–5. How can you develop these qualities further? What specific actions could improve areas where you rated yourself lowest?
4 Describe a recent situation where learning was nonlinear. What challenges, emotions, and strategies were involved? How did this affect your learning or performance? As an MPC or future CoP leader, how comfortable are you navigating uncertainty, and how could you use these experiences to guide others? How will you keep the learning imperative central in your CoP?
5 Reflect on a time you participated in a CoP or group activity. How was vulnerability present or absent? Describe one instance where being vulnerable helped or hindered the group's learning. What are the risks and benefits of vulnerability, and how could you create a safe space for others to embrace it without judgment?

REFERENCES

Arao, B., & Clemens, K. (2013). From safe spaces to brave spaces: A new way to frame dialogue around diversity and social justice. In L. M. Landreman (Ed.) *The art of effective facilitation* (1st ed., pp. 135–150). Routledge. https://doi.org/10.4324/9781003447580-11

Carron, A. V., & Hausenblas, H. A. (1998). *Group dynamics in sport* (2nd ed.). Fitness Information Technology.

Chew, L. C., & Ang, C. S. (2023). The relationship among quiet ego, authenticity, self-compassion and life satisfaction in adults. *Current Psychology, 42*(7), 5254–5264. https://doi.org/10.1007/s12144-021-01915-y

Cox, A. (2005). What are communities of practice? A comparative review of four seminal works. *Journal of Information Science, 31*(6), 527–540. https://doi.org/10.1177/0165551505057016

Culver, D. M., Duarte, T., & Rourke, S. (2024). Leading a safe sport community of practice for high performance coaches: A role for mental performance consultants. *Journal of Applied Sport Psychology, 15*(4), 193–206. Advance online publication. https://doi.org/10.1080/21520704.2024.2332737

Culver, D. M., Duarte, T., & Vinson, D. (2021). Communities of practice: Common misconceptions. In A. Whitehead & J. Coady (Eds.), *Myths of sports coaching* (pp. 24–35). Sequoia. https://www.sequoia-books.com/catalog/whiteheadcoe/

Durand-Bush, N., Baker, J., van den Berg, F., Richard, V., & Bloom, G. A. (2022). The gold medal profile for sport psychology (GMP-SP). *Journal of Applied Sport Psychology, 35*(4), 547–570. https://doi.org/10.1080/10413200.2022.2055224

Henriksen, K., Storm, L. K., & Larsen, C. H. (2019). Organizational culture and environment in high performance sport. In R. Schinke, K. McGannon, & B. Smith (Eds.), *Routledge international handbook of sport psychology* (pp. 347–357). Routledge.

Kraft, E., Culver, D. M., Din, C., & Cayer, I. (2021). Navigating the labyrinth of leadership in sport: A community of practice of femininity. *Advancing Women in Leadership Journal, 40*(1), 1–31. https://doi.org/10.21423/awlj-v40.a370

Li, L. C., Grimshaw, J. M., Nielsen, C., Judd, M., Coyte, P. C., & Graham, I. D. (2009). Evolution of Wenger's concept of community of practice. *Implementation Science, 4*, 11. https://doi.org/10.1186/1748-5908-4-11

Seguin, C. M., Culver, D. M., Mellalieu, S. D., Christie, S., Goss, J., & Roorda, S. (2021). What's our role? Mental performance consultants' perspectives on supporting concussed athletes. *Journal of Sport Psychology in Action, 13*(3), 168–179. https://doi.org/10.1080/21520704.2021.1971811

Tuckman, B. W., & Jensen, M. A. (1977). Stages of small-group development revisited. *Group & Organization Studies, 2*(4), 419–427. https://doi.org/10.1177/105960117700200404

Wenger, E. (1998). *Communities of practice: Learning, meaning and identity.* Cambridge University Press.

Wenger, E. (2011). *Communities of practice: A brief introduction.* National Science Foundation. https://hdl.handle.net/1794/11736

Wenger-Trayner, E. (2013). The practice of theory: Confessions of a social learning theorist. In V. Farnsworth & Y. Solomon (Eds.), *Reframing educational research: Resisting the "what works" agenda* (pp 105–118). Routledge.

Wenger-Trayner, E., & Wenger-Trayner, B. (2020). *Learning to make a difference: Value creation in social learning spaces.* Cambridge University Press.

Wenger-Trayner, E., Wenger-Trayner, B., Reid, P., & Bruderlein, C. (2023). *Communities of practice within and across organizations: A guidebook.* The Social Learning Lab. Creative Commons license, attribution - Non-Commercial 4.0 International (CC BY-NC 4.0).

Section 5

The SEPP Practitioner

18 Philosophy of Practice

Philosophy—kind of an intimidating word and concept. What does philosophy of practice actually mean, what does it look like for you, and how can you shape, revisit, and align it with your continued professional growth and journey? This chapter is aimed at providing you, the reader, at any career stage with tangible insights into what a practice philosophy is (and isn't), some key questions and prompts to get you started developing or evolving one, and how this process is entwined with your core values and beliefs as well as your contextual influence. My (Sebastian's) philosophy of practice has certainly been shaped by several factors and continued to evolve as my career has taken numerous turns and led me to new places. What does yours look like, how will it take shape? Let our diverse author groups inspire you to (re-)drafting your personal philosophy of practice.

PHILOSOPHY OF (AND IN) PRACTICE

Nick Wadsworth & Martin Eubank

Demystifying Practice Philosophy

The development of a clear and congruent practice philosophy is foundational to successful service delivery (Poczwardowski et al., 2004). However, the process of developing an authentic philosophy is often surrounded by uncertainty, doubt, fear, and anxiety, particularly for early career practitioners taking their first steps into the applied space (McEwan & Tod, 2023). To avoid the anxiety associated with practice philosophy development, practitioners often choose to simplify the concept, which can provide some much-needed short-term comfort as they navigate the applied world. For example, we might choose to define our practice in line with one dominant theoretical orientation and approach, for example, "I am a holistic person-centred practitioner who aligns to the principles of Humanism." This form of alignment provides structure when engaging with clients, which can increase role clarity, enhance perceptions of competence, and reduce anxiety. However, articulating a theoretical orientation or model of practice is *different* to articulating the philosophy that underpins it. This limited view of philosophy is a common misconception among many practitioners and lacks an explicit focus on core beliefs and values as the foundation of understanding one's own practice philosophy (Poczwardowski et al., 2004).

Knowing and being able to articulate our beliefs and values is important to practice philosophy development, given they guide our behavior (e.g., the value of honesty might encourage us to communicate openly with our clients to develop trusting relationships). However,

DOI: 10.4324/9781003781479-23

practitioners that do differentiate between philosophy and theory can still fall into the trap of oversimplification by only referring to values in the absence of philosophical beliefs, for example, "I am a practitioner who values honesty, transparency, and trustworthiness and the importance of giving clients autonomy to change." Given time, oversimplification of practice philosophy will lead to a surface-level understanding of ourselves, preventing growth, and undermining our applied capability. However, we must be careful not to overcompensate by moving too quickly from oversimplification to overcomplication. For example, we have noticed an increasing commonality for practice philosophy to be discussed through the lens of ontology and epistemology. Whilst understanding our beliefs about the nature of reality (ontology) and how reality can be known (epistemology) are important (especially for practitioners combining applied practice and academic research), we have found these concepts, and the language required to discuss philosophy in this way, to be too far removed from the applied context and in some cases detrimental to an early career practitioner's understanding of philosophy. Instead, we believe it is important to find the optimal balance between embracing the complexity of philosophy and simplifying these concepts enough to allow for meaningful dialogue and reflection. To achieve this balance, and make practice philosophy more accessible, it is important to articulate the separation *and* interconnection between philosophy and theory. Philosophy is best understood as *our beliefs and values about the world and human nature and behavior* and theories are *the models we choose to use to guide our interactions with that reality.*

Discovering Our Philosophical Beliefs

When asked to articulate practice philosophy it can be useful to start our response with the words "I believe..." Starting our response in this way makes it more likely that what follows is a philosophical belief (and not a discussion of theory, values, or characteristics). For example:

- I believe that people view the world subjectively.
- I believe that short-term discomfort can lead to long-term growth.
- I believe an individual's current behavior can be shaped by past events.

Starting with these "I believe..." statements can make the discussion of our practice philosophy more accessible and encourage deeper reflections on our philosophy and identity (Wadsworth, 2024). For example, we might then start asking ourselves questions, such as:

- How do people experience change?
- Why do some people not change?
- To what extent am I responsible for the change my clients make?
- What do I believe to be the connection between performance and well-being (if any)?
- Is objective measurement of performance possible? How can I evaluate my practice?
- To what extent do I believe the consultancy process is collaborative?

Life experiences can also be a catalyst for deeper reflections about our philosophical beliefs, given they are so often shaped by our experiences of the world and our work within it. Critical moments (i.e., moments of anxiety associated with a change in our identity; Nesti et al., 2012) in our personal (e.g., loss of a loved one) and professional (e.g., leaving an applied role) lives can provide us with an opportune moment to reflect on important questions (Wadsworth et al., 2021) to help us (re)define our beliefs, such as:

- Who am I? Who do I want to be? Am I living an authentic life?
- What is it to live a meaningful life?
- What is my purpose? How do I want to define success?

This means we must acknowledge that the evolution of our practice philosophy is a life-long process (Ronnestad & Skovholt, 2013) that involves individuation (McEwan et al., 2019), where over time, we become aware of the personal beliefs, values, and qualities that govern an authentic practitioner identity and allows us to act *with* rather than *on* the client.

Understanding our philosophical beliefs ensures we possess higher levels of self-knowledge and provides us with a platform to start embracing complexity in an applied context. By understanding that our beliefs are distinct from theory, we create the space to align our beliefs to multiple theoretical approaches and provide more holistic support to our clients. For example, one of our philosophical beliefs might be "I believe people are influenced by their social context." This belief can be aligned to multiple theories, such as the concept of Functional Contextualism within Acceptance Commitment Therapy (ACT) or the Existential principle of Situated Freedom (as both theoretical concepts align to the notion that we cannot understand a person in isolation). Being able to confidently articulate our philosophical beliefs means we can now attend more closely to our clients and draw from multiple theoretical approaches to support them with their unique needs. This also helps us navigate the ever-changing landscape of applied practice and bring nuance and balance to our approach. For example, with a stronger awareness of our philosophical assumptions, we might be better placed to both recognize, and navigate, the trade-offs (or paradoxes) that so often occur in applied contexts. For example:

- What is my role in supporting coaches to find the optimal balance between structure (establishing and maintaining high standards, creating rules, encouraging conformity, enhancing clarity, etc.) and freedom (developing independent decision-makers, providing choice and autonomy)?
- How can I support individuals in becoming the person they want to be (supporting future goals, ambition, growth, development, and excellence), whilst also helping them accept (with love and compassion) who they are right now?

Our philosophy of practice can act as a guide to navigate these complex questions and ensure we are well positioned to offer meaningful support to our clients. Furthermore, a deep awareness of our philosophical beliefs and values can allow us to find the optimal balance between adopting an authentic approach to practice and demonstrating adaptability to meet our client's unique and diverse needs. Authenticity requires us to be grounded in our philosophical roots, whilst understanding the extent to which we can flex these beliefs to adapt to the cultures and context in which we work. To find the balance between authenticity and adaptability, it is important not to view authenticity as something that is fixed. Our authentic self cannot be understood separately from the context in which we are situated, and so it is more useful to think of authenticity as a negotiation between us and our context. Similarly, it might also be useful to differentiate between our philosophy *of* practice (our beliefs about the world) and our philosophy *in* practice (the application of our beliefs within the context in which we are situated). Sometimes, this negotiation is gentle and calm as our values and beliefs align with the culture we exist within (e.g., believing that the role of a sport psychology practitioner is to provide holistic support and being afforded opportunities to engage in support for both the person and performer), but we might also experience times when it can feel more like a fight or battle (e.g., believing in and advocating for diversity and equity whilst feeling pressure to conform to a male-dominated sexist environment).

When negotiating our authentic self with the context, the goal is not to achieve complete authenticity (as this is very rare), but instead, to be less inauthentic. This negotiation then involves the acceptance that we must adapt, with the understanding that too much adaptation might take us too far from our philosophical beliefs. To help us navigate this negotiation, it might be useful for us to ask ourselves: "how *willing* and *capable* am I to flex to meet the needs of the client within their context?".

EMBODIED PRACTICE: AN INTEGRATION OF SPORT PSYCHOLOGY, MOTOR BEHAVIOR, AND CULTURAL STUDIES OF SPORT

Leslee A. Fisher & Craig A. Wrisberg

Context: Our Story (Les and Craig)

Our story is somewhat unique! It began like this...Craig was hired by the University of Tennessee's (UT) Department of Physical Education in 1977 to develop a concentration in motor behavior, mentor graduate students, and teach and conduct research in that discipline. His only connection to sport psychology was a graduate course that he taught each fall semester. In 1981, the women's volleyball coach took the class, saw the potential of sport psychology for his student-athletes, and asked Craig to work with his team. Soon after that, word got around and other coaches expressed interest in Craig's services; this led the athletic director to put him on retainer as a resource for any coaches and/or athletes interested in improving their mental game. In 2001, Craig passed along the oversight of mental training services to a former PhD of his—Dr. Joe Whitney—after convincing the athletic director to create a full-time position for a Director of Mental Training. Today, Dr. Whitney is still serving in that position. Until his retirement in 2011, Craig personally assisted 42 NCAA champions and 23 individuals who participated or are currently participating in professional sports.

In 1991, Dr. Richard Wisniewski, former Dean of UT's College of Education, Health, and Human Sciences, helped engineer a restructuring of the entire college (Wisniewski, 1996). At that time, faculty were given the option: Instead of aligning with their disciplinary departments or "homes" (e.g., Exercise Science or Sport Management for Craig), they were encouraged to form a "unit" with those they had the most research and practice affinity with. Thus, the birth of UT's Cultural Studies in Education (CSE) unit, where faculty like Craig (a sport psychology/motor behavior scholar) chose to work alongside Dr. Handel Wright (a cultural studies scholar), Dr. Bill Morgan (a sport philosopher), Dr. Joy DeSensi (a sport sociologist), Dr. Barb Thayer-Bacon (a philosophy of education scholar), Dr. Steven Pope (a sport historian), and, eventually, Dr. Diana Moyer (a history of education scholar). Les was hired by Dr. Joy DeSensi, head of the CSE unit, in 2000 to work alongside Craig in sport psychology and motor behavior, to bring in a feminist sport psychology lens, and as a bridge between sport psychology, motor behavior, and cultural studies. The overall goal of Les' research and applied practice was to increase athlete empowerment and coach/sport psychology professional awareness through the development of culturally sensitive and socially just projects.

Philosophical Underpinnings of UT SPMB

In our Sport Psychology and Motor Behavior Graduate Program (UT SPMB), Craig and I tried to create a "family" environment where all students felt welcomed and were encouraged to reach their full potential. Our program was unique. We integrated three areas of study—equally—into faculty and student research and practice: Sport psychology, motor behavior, and cultural studies.

Sport Psychology and Motor Behavior Beliefs and Values

We have grounded our practice in seven core ethical values and beliefs in line with both our professional ethics and commitments (Fisher & Anders, 2010, 2020) and to the scientist-practitioner model (Jones & Mehr, 2007): (a) we practice *applied sport psychology and motor behavior* with athletes/performers who want to perform at their best; (b) we *do not do clinical psychology work* with athletes/performers and refer athletes/performers who would like help with clinical issues to qualified professionals whom we know and have worked with before; (c) we engage in *performance-enhancing consulting*; (d) we use a *psycho-educational approach* (e.g., equip athletes/performers with the tools necessary to undertake their change process outside of sessions essentially trying to work ourselves out of a job); (e) we use *evidenced-based practice, which* means that we stay up on the latest research, use it in our practice, and then feed back what we learn in practice into better research; (f) we focus on *enhancing athletes/performers' own strengths*; and (g) we help build athletes/performers' *composure, consistency, and confidence* when performing under pressure.

Helpful Sport Psychology and Motor Behavior Mantras in Our Work

Related to our core values and beliefs, we also find three sport psychology and motor behavior mantras very helpful in our work: (a) *It is what it is. Control the controllables.* While most athletes/performers realize that the final outcome of a competition can sometimes be due to things *beyond their control* (e.g., bad bounce, superior opponent, poor officiating, and bad weather), we encourage them to resolve to accept those things rather than wasting mental energy by worrying about them; (b) *The focus is on a full focus.* We work with athletes/performers to help them identify the *thoughts, feelings, focus, and emotions* associated with their more effective performances and then develop mental strategies for strengthening those features during practice and in competition; and (c) *Make practices more like competition.* We help athletes identify strategies to practice like they compete, such as scenarios that simulate competitive conditions as closely as possible and incorporate the technical, tactical, and mental skills necessary for achieving productive outcomes. When athletes/performers' practices are virtually identical to competition conditions, they are able to develop the skills and mental toughness necessary for achieving the outcomes they desire in competition (Wrisberg, 2007, 2010).

Cultural Studies Beliefs and Underpinnings

Part of the uniqueness of working with Dr. Handel Wright (a cultural studies scholar) and our other faculty colleagues in the CSE unit was that we all attended a seminar entitled, *Cultural Studies in Education* together with our graduate students once a week. In this seminar, we read and then discussed foundational articles related to *critical cultural scholarship* and the role of education, consulting, and scholarship in a democratic society. This included Freire's (1970) and hooks' (1994) notions that education is a process whereby learners *actively* (versus passively) engage with information presented by the teacher and co-construct knowledge together. Thus, our cultural studies beliefs informed our philosophy of practice and how we prepared students for applied work. For example, Les began including social justice concepts into both her classes and her supervision/mentoring sessions (Fisher, 2024, 2025). In graduate classes like *CSE 543: Women, Sport, and Culture*, she included concepts such as learning is the practice of freedom, self-emancipation, and critical literacy (e.g., how do I know what I know about sport? How do bodies move and train the best? What power relationships exist between me and those I work with?). She also created learning conditions for graduate students to talk about ideologies and the potential conditions responsible for the oppression and domination of athletes/performers in society looked like; most importantly, self-reflection moving to *praxis*—the incorporation of knowledge/theory into real-life action in one's communities (Fisher, 2024, 2025).

Further, Les and two of our former Ph.D. students (Dr. Ted Butryn and Dr. Emily Roper) developed some of the first scholarship around what was originally called *cultural sport psychology* (e.g., Fisher et al., 2003, 2005). They suggested at least six ways to integrate cultural studies: (a) interrogating the institution of sport and how and when it has influenced athlete and consultant identities; (b) choosing academic methods and theories based on intellectual sensibilities (e.g., theoretical orientation or critical stance) versus disciplinary boundaries; (c) seeing athletes and consultants in their webs of power dynamics and relationships; (d) focusing on athlete and consultant identities as multiple, fragmented, and dependent upon location; (e) critically exploring the politics of race and class (and sexual orientation, able-bodiedness, etc.) and how they affect athletes and consultants; and (f) addressing embedded politics and potentially exploitative relationships and damaging long-term health consequences in sport (e.g., Fisher et al., 2009). They also began to explore developing athletes as citizens of the world (e.g., "athletes-as-citizens"); in other words, one of their goals was to help athletes see themselves as more than just athletes, but as people capable of understanding how politics occur in everyday life, including in their own lives.

Taking a Relational Approach

Finally, our approach to performance psychology is *relational* and has evolved because of our relationships with friends and colleagues. Les' friendship and work with former UT qualitative and cultural studies of education scholar Dr. Allison Anders has greatly influenced her commitment to integrating what she would now call *cultural studies of sport* into sport psychology (see also Fisher & Anders, 2010, 2020; Fisher, 2025). In addition, Craig's current approach to performance consulting with athletes/non-sport performers incorporates the method and methodology of phenomenology (Hector et al., 2018; Wrisberg & Raabe, 2019), a decision that was the direct result of a close friendship with the late UT Professor of Counseling Psychology, Mark Hector.

We have come to believe that the theory and processes of critical reflection—as we have learned through our work both together and apart—is crucial to expanding our understandings of ourselves as agents of change in a changing world.

PHILOSOPHY OF PRACTICE: AN INDUSTRIAL-ORGANIZATIONAL PSYCHOLOGY PERSPECTIVE

Elizabeth L. Shoenfelt, Alexander Gamble, & Lennie Waite

Industrial-Organizational (I-O) Psychology is an empirical science with more than a century of research and theory building that, when applied, helps to ensure optimal performance by individuals, teams, and organizations. Many of the principles and practices in I-O psychology are applicable to performance in other applied contexts such as sports, military, and performing arts. Both the "I" focus and the "O" focus of I-O psychology comprise evidence-based practices relevant to athletes/coaches/teams/organizations. Industrial psychology practices such as selection, training, and performance management ensure the individual has the knowledge, skills, and abilities (KSAs) that enable them to do the job. Operating at the micro (individual), group/team, and macro (organizational) level, organizational psychology practices addressing motivation, commitment, satisfaction, group and team dynamics, leadership, and organization development, ensure individuals will do the job. For more detail on the content of I-O psychology, see Shoenfelt et al. (2020). In this brief chapter, three applied performance consultants with backgrounds in both I-O and sport psychology share their philosophy of practice grounded in I-O.

I-O psychology is replete with theories and models of organizational dynamics and human interaction in the workplace. There are, however, far fewer models and theories of organizational consulting. Three, in particular, have influenced our philosophies of practice. Edgar Schein is equally well known for his groundbreaking work on organizational culture and his theories of organizational change. It is the latter, Schein's (1988) model of Process Consultation, emphasizing the importance of joint diagnosis and the development of skill in the client, that is impactful in guiding applied practice. Chris Argyris, who first coined the term "psychological safety" in organizations, proposed Intervention Theory (1970) that identifies the conditions faced by a consultant, qualities needed to be a consultant, and consultant behaviors that lead to effective interventions. Schneider's (1987) Attraction, Selection, Attrition (ASA) model focuses on the importance of the individual and the utility of personality and interest measures as predictors of important individual work behaviors. Below, each author describes how one or more of these theories has impacted their philosophy of practice across their career stages.

Gamble: Early Career

Although my philosophy of practice is still developing and evolving as a recent graduate and early career practitioner, it is grounded in a collaborative, person-centered approach built on the foundational principles of intersectionality and cultural humility. I recently completed my doctorate in organizational psychology with a concentration in sport psychology. My previous training and background are in counseling psychology, working as a behavioral health clinician in athletics. It is my belief that relationships are at the core of any domain in life; the quality of relationships will determine the consultant's effectiveness as well as the growth and performance of the individual, group/team, or organizational client. My philosophy of practice, born out of and remaining inspired by my clinical training, is heavily informed by Schein's (1988) model of Process Consultation. This model in many ways is an extension of my clinical practice as it emphasizes empowerment, collaboration, self-awareness, and the client as the "expert" on their own organizational circumstances. Furthermore, it empowers the client and organization to become self-sufficient, thus replacing the consultant's skills with their own.

Early on in my training I felt consumed with learning theoretical models, modalities, and evidence-based practices, which at times led me to overlook the importance of relationship building and consequently undermined my effectiveness. Schein's Process Consultation model has significantly influenced my development as a student and early career applied sport psychology practitioner because it provides an operational framework rather than a strict prescription to be followed step by step. Thus, when I begin working with a team/organization, my initial focus always is on building trust and rapport with both athletes and staff through informal conversations and observations (e.g., going to practices, games, events). Having a consistent presence and prioritizing authenticity and relationship building across the individual, team, and organizational levels early in the process sets the foundation to later be able to facilitate a change and co-develop strategies in alignment with shared goals. Although tools and strategies certainly offer value, it's the establishment of trust and collaborative relationships that ultimately serve as the catalyst for growth and improvement, related to both well-being and performance.

Waite: Mid-Career

I started my I-O Psychology doctoral program the same year that I commenced my pursuit to become an Olympian in track and field. My dual roles as an I-O psychologist and professional athlete formed the basis of my philosophy of practice and guide the work I do with individuals, teams, and organizations today. First, the organization is vital in supporting the performance of the people and teams embedded in the organization. Second, the characteristics of the people in the organization impact their *individual* success and the *overall* success of the organization. For example, a high performing athlete will struggle to find success in an organization that doesn't promote the health, well-being, and performance goals of the athlete. Additionally, an athlete will struggle to find long-term success if they lack the individual characteristics needed to consistently perform on an elite stage and their underperformance will impact the overall success of the organization. I work from the lens that both the individual (micro-level) and the organization (macro-level) must be healthy and have a mutualistic relationship to optimize performance.

As an I-O psychologist, I rely on needs assessments to help leaders understand the organizational-level and individual-level factors that are potentially preventing optimal outcomes and to help uncover what is needed for success. This foundational process provides an evidence-based framework to instigate targeted change and adapt to rapidly evolving work environments. Ultimately, the organization is made up of people, and according to Schneider's ASA model, "the people make the place." You need great people, and you need to listen to your people to make a great place. Implementing rigorous tools around selection and assessment, prioritizing person-organization fit, and understanding personality psychology are core pieces of my philosophy to help tackle organizational challenges and promote individual well-being. Thus, when working with a professional sporting organization, I like to begin by conducting a comprehensive needs assessment through interviews and surveys with leadership, staff, and athletes. This 360-degree approach uncovers consistent themes and discrepancies between perspectives at different levels of the organization. For example, if leadership emphasizes the holistic development of an athlete's well-being but athletes report feeling unsupported in that area, the inconsistency becomes a focal point for intervention. Using these insights, I help drive alignment between individual and organizational-level goals to support a healthier workplace.

Shoenfelt: Late Career

As a consultant with more than four decades of experience and a strong belief in continuous learning, it is hard to separate the influence of a myriad of theories and experiences on my philosophy of practice. However, that I taught Schein's (1988) evergreen Process Consultation model to my I-O graduate students throughout my career indicates my implicit belief in its importance. Schein's model emphasizes the importance of helping the organization define the problem through a process of joint problem solving, and then jointly determining an appropriate intervention. A consultant rarely is able to learn enough about the client to independently identify successful interventions. Schein's data-based process is foundational for a successful consultation because it helps to ensure an accurate diagnosis, and client understanding and ownership of the intervention. Schein noted this process helps the client be more effective in learning to diagnose and manage their own problems. An effective consultant must be an expert in facilitating this process based on a broad knowledge of the science of group/team and organizational functioning. Argyris's (1970) wisdom about the characteristics required for a successful consultation likewise are top of mind with every consulting opportunity and prove a source of confidence in particularly challenging situations.

Following Schein's model, when working with individual athletes or teams, information (from a variety of sources—e.g., athlete, coach, teammates) is shared about the perceived "problem" until we agree we have identified the source/root of the issue and not just symptoms. Only then will I suggest and explain alternative interventions, which are discussed until we decide on a course of action. Commitment to the intervention, often requiring substantial time and effort from the coaches, players, and consultant, is achieved through joint diagnosis and problem solving. For example, a coach contacted me to do leader development for his team captains. Because it was not readily apparent which skills needed to be developed, we decided to begin with multi-source feedback for these team leaders. All players and coaches evaluated each captain on an inventory of leader skills and traits to identify strengths and gaps. The captains were receptive to this feedback because it captured perceptions from all teammates and coaches and the data provided the basis for individualized leader development.

Conclusion

Three applied performance consultants, ranging from early-to-mid-to-late career and each with backgrounds in both I-O and sport psychology, shared the theoretical and experiential bases for their philosophy of practice. These different perspectives indicate the important roles of relationships, individual and organizational factors, and data-based decision-making when working with clients. The I-O perspective provides complementary theories and practices to those traditionally utilized in sport psychology. Developing a philosophy of practice can help sport and exercise psychology professionals bridge the gap between theory and real-world application by clarifying values, assumptions, and decision-making processes to support contextually relevant interventions.

EDITORS' TAKEAWAYS

Wadsworth and Eubank's point about the difference between articulating your theoretical orientation and philosophy that underpins your model of practice is a key takeaway in my (Lauren) opinion for readers, particularly those beginning their education or careers. A philosophy of practice is about much more than which theory grounds your approach—it encompasses other essential ingredients, such as your values as a practitioner, your beliefs and the factors that have influenced it, your perception of the purpose of your work and the roles you and your clients take in the process, and the methods you use to provide services to clients. Therefore, it plays a key role in every decision you make as a practitioner. Thus, as Wadsworth and Eubank point out, there is a real danger in oversimplifying it. Another point that stood out to me from their contribution was the idea of balancing authenticity and adaptability, and the goal of being less inauthentic. Given the nature of this work that seems like a valuable perspective shift, particularly when you encounter ethical dilemmas. What stood out to me most from the other two contributions is the key influence that one's graduate program(s) have on a professional philosophy—at least while you are a student and in your early career if not longer. Additionally, Fisher and Wrisberg's mantras are a great takeaway for readers to think about their own that can be useful reminders of one's philosophy. Last, I really loved the portrayal of stages of career—my philosophy has changed and evolved so much, as it should, throughout my career likely as the result of many factors, such as my growing understanding of the field, emerging research and interventions, the winding journey of my career, and changes in my worldview as I get older and further into my life and career.

RECOMMENDED EXERCISES

1 Undertake a Core Beliefs and Values Exercise to generate "I believe" statements and a list of personal values that define your philosophical foundations. Start by reflecting on your views of human nature and behavior change—for example, you may believe individuals have equal self-worth and an innate capacity to adapt. Then consider your role in helping clients grow and reach their goals. Use a values worksheet to identify your most important values and how they manifest in your actions as a practitioner.
2 Next, undertake a Consultancy Style Exercise to explore the alignment between your beliefs, values, and the approaches you use in practice. Using Keegan's (2015) ten continuums, consider:

   a Practitioner style: practitioner-led or client-led
   b Practice aims: performance enhancement/education vs. client welfare, growth, and empowerment
   c Approach: educate/recommend/persuade vs. explore/delve/develop mutual understanding
   d Guiding principles: expert-led vs. client-led collaborative exploration
   e Questioning style: focused/specific vs. open/flexible
   f Role: analyze/assess/educate vs. curious facilitator/critical friend
   g Importance of scientific theory: evidence-based vs. formal theories less relevant
   h Relationship priority: formal vs. actively pursued warm relationships
   i Use of questionnaires: highly useful and validated vs. potentially misleading

3 Consider your career stage and milestones that influenced your consultancy philosophy. How did these experiences shape your beliefs and approach?
4 Reflect on effective consultation through listening and data gathering. How have you gathered information to form solutions in your work?
5 Consider your identity. Which identities are most salient, why, and how do they shape your philosophy of practice? How might they influence your work with individuals, groups, or organizations?

REFERENCES

Argyris, C. (1970). *Intervention theory and method: A behavioral science view.* Addison-Wesley.
Fisher, L. A. (2026, April 6). *Faculty bio.* The University of Tennessee, Knoxville. https://cehhs.utk.edu/krss/leslee-a-fisher-ph-d/
Fisher, L. A. (2025). *Social justice through sport and exercise psychology: Intergenerational voices and an embodied approach.* Routledge.

Fisher, L. A., & Anders, A. D. (2010). Critically engaging with sport psychology ethics through cultural studies. In T. Ryba, R. Schinke, & G. Tenenbaum (Eds.), *The cultural turn in sport and exercise psychology* (pp. 101–126). Fitness Information Technology.
Fisher, L. A., & Anders, A. D. (2020). Engaging with cultural sport psychology to explore systemic sexual exploitation in USA Gymnastics: A call to commitments. *Journal of Applied Sport Psychology*, *32*(2), 129–145. https://doi.org/10.1080/10413200.2018.1564944
Fisher, L. A., Butryn, T. M., & Roper, E. A. (2003). Diversifying (and politicizing) sport psychology through cultural studies: A promising perspective. *The Sport Psychologist*, *17*(3), 391–406.
Fisher, L. A., Butryn, T. M., & Roper, E. A. (2005). Diversifying (and politicizing) sport psychology through cultural studies: A promising perspective revisited. *Athletic Insight*, *7*(3). 23–35 https://www.athleticinsight.com
Fisher, L. A., Roper, E. A., & Butryn, T. M. (2009). Engaging cultural studies and "traditional" sport psychology. In R. Schinke & S. J. Hanrahan (Eds.), *Cultural sport psychology* (pp. 23–34). Human Kinetics.
Freire, P. (1970). *Pedagogy of the oppressed* (M. B. Ramos, Trans.). Continuum.
Hector, M. A., Raabe, J., & Wrisberg, C. A. (2018). Phenomenological consulting: A viable alternative for sport psychology practitioners. *Journal of Sport Psychology in Action*, *9*(2), 111–120. https://doi.org/10.1080/21520704.2017.1355862
hooks, b. (1994). *Teaching to transgress: Education as the practice of freedom*. Routledge.
Jones, J. L., & Mehr, S. L. (2007). Foundations and assumptions of the scientist-practitioner model. *American Behavioral Scientist*, *50*(6), 766–771.
Keegan, R. (2015). *Being a sport psychologist*. Palgrave Macmillan.
McEwan, H. E., Tod, D., & Eubank, M. (2019). The rocky road to individuation: Sport psychologists' perspectives on professional development. *Psychology of Sport and Exercise*, *45*, 101542. https://doi.org/10.1016/j.psychsport.2019.101542
McEwan, H. E., & Tod, D. (2023). Trainee clinical, and sport and exercise psychologists' experiences of professional development: A longitudinal study. *Psychology of Sport and Exercise*, *64*, 102343. https://doi.org/10.1016/j.psychsport.2022.102343
Nesti, M., Littlewood, M., O'Halloran, L., Eubank, M., & Richardson, D. (2012). Critical moments in elite premiership football: Who do you think you are? *Physical Culture and Sport. Studies and Research*, *56*(1), 23–32.
Poczwardowski, A., Sherman, C. P., & Ravizza, K. (2004). Professional philosophy in the sport psychology service delivery: Building on theory and practice. *The Sport Psychologist*, *18*(4), 445–463.
Ronnestad, M. H., & Skovholt, T. M. (2013). *The developing practitioner: Growth and stagnation of therapists and counselors*. Routledge.
Schein, E. H. (1988). *Process consultation: Its role in organization development* (Vol. 1). Addison-Wesley.
Schneider, B. (1987). The people make the place. *Personnel Psychology*, *40*(3), 437–453. https://doi.org/10.1111/j.1744-6570.1987.tb00609.x
Shoenfelt, E. L., Hays-Thomas, R., & Bryan, L. K. (2020). An introduction to industrial-organizational psychology. In E. L. Shoenfelt (Ed.), *Mastering industrial-organizational psychology: Training issues for master's level I-O psychologists* (pp. 1–16). Oxford University Press. (Available upon request from the first author.)
Wadsworth, N. (2024). Reflective practice as an intrapersonal process. In B. Hemmings, T. Holder, & S. Winter (Eds.) *Professional skills in sport psychology consultancy* (pp. 19–31). Routledge.
Wadsworth, N., McEwan, H., Lafferty, M., Eubank, M., & Tod, D. (2021). Stories of critical moments contributing to the development of applied sport psychology practitioners. *The Sport Psychologist*, *35*(1), 11–21.
Wisniewski, R. (1996). The transformation of a college. *Teacher Education Quarterly*, *23*(1), 9–17. https://www.jstor.org/stable/23477707
Wrisberg, C. A. (2007). *Sport skill instruction for coaches*. Human Kinetics.
Wrisberg, C. A. (2010). *Answers to questions athletes typically have about sport psychology consultants*. Unpublished manuscript.
Wrisberg, C. A., & Raabe, J. (2019). Phenomenological consulting: Long-term mental training with an elite college football place kicker. *Case Studies in Sport and Exercise Psychology*, *3*(1), 20–25. https://doi.org/10.1123/cssep.2018-0011

19 Technological Advancements in SEPP Practice

We keep exploring essential concepts, trends, and considerations for working with clients in SEPP settings. Reflecting on and crafting your personal philosophy of practice as highlighted in the last chapter is certainly a must. However, in today's day and age of rapid technological advances, fueled by social media, digitalization, and AI, taking stock of your personal stance on what technology has to offer and the training and competency needed to incorporate it into practice is also essential. While technology certainly isn't a "one-size-fits-all" solution that will suit every clients' needs, you might very well have some clients that will benefit from being able to engage in some kind of psychophysiological, biofeedback or neurofeedback training. Our author groups share some key insights regarding use of technology and cutting-edge work on a conceptual and organizational level—a must-read for any SEPPP.

INTEGRATING PSYCHOPHYSIOLOGY TECHNOLOGY INTO PRACTICE

Seth Rose, Jerry DeVore, Phoebe Manalang-Monnier, William Bean, & Megan Fox

In sport, exercise, and performance psychology (SEPP), technology has become commonly embedded in both client experiences and professional practice that allow for efficient collection, dissemination, and utilization of information. While many clients are familiar with digital platforms, user comfort and efficacy can vary based on factors such as demographics, generational differences, and personal experience. Practitioners in SEPP use technology for multiple purposes, including scheduling, record-keeping, communication, and the delivery of interventions. This chapter provides an overview of technological advances in SEPP from a psychophysiological perspective. It highlights key characteristics and examples of these tools, discusses associated ethical and legal considerations, and offers practical guidance for integrating them into performance interventions to optimize client outcomes.

Wearable technologies have become widely adopted tools for performance enhancement, especially when integrated into an applied psychophysiology framework. By providing objective data on internal functioning, they extend biofeedback principles beyond clinical settings and promote real-world self-regulation skills such as breath control, heart rate variability (HRV) awareness, and recovery monitoring. Devices, including GPS trackers, smartwatches, and rings offer insights into physiological, cognitive, and behavioral states. They can track sleep quality, recovery, movement patterns, and autonomic activity (e.g., HRV), making them valuable for both self-monitoring and professional consultation. However, accuracy, reliability, and applicability vary, and practitioners should encourage clients to use these tools

DOI: 10.4324/9781003781479-24

for awareness rather than as definitive measures of performance or well-being. Over-reliance can cause issues such as reduced autonomy, misinterpretation of performance readiness, or orthosomnia (i.e., disruption from obsessive sleep tracking; Baron et al., 2017). Similarly, data-driven stress may occur, where constant monitoring increases performance pressure or dependence on external feedback (Peters et al., 2018). When used intentionally and interpreted within the broader context of psychological and physical needs, wearables can reinforce self-regulation, support recovery strategies, and enhance performance routines. Their real-time and retrospective data can bridge the gap between subjective experience and objective measures, fostering informed decision-making, meaningful discussion, and individualized performance enhancement.

Other technologies such as biofeedback, neurofeedback, and wearables have specifically transformed SEPP by equipping practitioners with tools for real-time assessment and targeted intervention (Schack et al., 2020). These systems allow for the measurement and analysis of psychophysiological data (e.g., HRV, muscle tension, brain activity), supporting a mind-body approach that can be used to measure, monitor, train skills, and optimize functioning. Applied psychophysiology, grounded in psychophysiological theory, and the utilized tools and technologies help athletes and performers deepen self-awareness, strengthen self-regulation, manage stress more effectively, and enhance performance through intentional use of both live feedback and retrospective insights (Grady, 2023; Watson & Coker-Cranney, 2018).

Psychophysiological Approach to Technology in Applied Practice

Adopting a psychophysiological approach to understanding performance emphasizes the reciprocal relationship between physiological and mental-emotional states, where changes in one are inherently linked to changes in the other (Quadt et al., 2022). Training includes two different psychophysiological learning processes: operant conditioning of physiology (biofeedback and neurofeedback) and neurostimulation. Operant conditioning uses learning theory applied to learning to control different physiological processes (Weerdmeester et al., 2019). These might include autonomic variables (e.g., respiration, heart rate, skin temperature, electrodermal activity), neuromuscular (e.g., muscle tension), and brainwave activity (e.g., EEG). There are a variety of other advanced technologies supporting the mental and physical performance of athletes and performers beyond the scope of this chapter, such as transcranial direct current stimulation (tDCS), transcutaneous vagal nerve stimulators (tVNS), pulsed electromagnetic field stimulation (PEMF), audio-visual stimulation (AVS), photobiomodulation, vibration platforms, and sensory deprivation floatation tanks.

Biofeedback works by training physiological behavior through operant conditioning, reinforcing and shaping desired responses based on real-time data (Edmonds & Tenenbaum, 2012). For instance, information displays are ineffective if they are not reinforcing or do not prompt adaptive responses. As individuals learn to recognize and regulate physiological signals, such as lowering heart rate during stress or decreasing muscle tension, they may gain greater control over their mental and physical states. These physiological adjustments can lead to meaningful behavioral changes, such as improved reaction time, reduced anxiety, or enhanced movement efficiency, which ultimately translate into better performance outcomes (Khazan et al., 2023). Table 19.1 provides examples of how various psychophysiological assessments and technologies are applied in performance contexts, along with associated learning mechanisms.

Table 19.1 Psychophysiological Assessment and Learning Applications in Performance Contexts

Assessment	*Physiology*	*Technology*	*Applications*	*Learning*
Skilled control of movement	Muscle contraction/ relaxation	Surface Electromyography (sEMG)	Muscle at rest/ motion Muscle efficiency Injury risk assessment Muscle fatigue Muscle bracing	Operant
Arousal and activation	Respiration rate Heart rate or heart rate variability Skin temperature Activation of sympathetic nervous system	Strain gauge Photoplethysmograph or HR monitor Thermal finger sensor Galvanic skin response sensor	Insufficient or over arousal	Operant
Focus	Frontal cortex Pre-frontal cortex Default mode network Attention network Executive network	Electroencephalography (EEG) and Event Related Potentials (ERP)	Ability to focus Sustain focus Ability to deeply relax Let go of distractions Reaction timing	Operant and neurostimulation

Evidence for Biofeedback Effectiveness

Biofeedback training has been shown to support the development of skills critical to performance across professional fields, military, music, and athletics (Khazan et al., 2023). Specifically, biofeedback can be used to enhance the following qualities (for reviews, see Da Silva & De Souza, 2021; Goessl et al., 2017; Kennedy et al., 2019; Lehrer et al., 2020):

- self-regulation ability and stress management;
- athletic performance, endurance, and reaction time;
- ability to sustain attention and focus;
- executive functioning: decision-making, emotion regulation, goal-directed behavior, memory recall, situational awareness;
- physical and mental health: recovery from physical training and enhanced overall well-being outcomes.

However, transferring these improvements to competitions or performances requires intentional practice. Success depends not just on regulating physiological parameters during training, but also on learning to apply these skills under realistic, stressful conditions. Effective transfer involves practicing biofeedback-informed techniques in environments that mimic cognitive, emotional, and physical demands of actual performance.

For example, practitioners may use EEG-based biofeedback (also known as neurofeedback) to train performers to shift into a focused, calm mental state by reinforcing optimal brainwave activity. These focus states can then be paired with goal setting or attentional cueing strategies and practiced under pressure in simulated competition environments. When integrated with mental skills training, neurofeedback has been shown to improve sustained attention and decision-making accuracy in high-performance domains such as sport and music (Gruzelier et al., 2014; Mirifar et al., 2017). Similarly, respiratory biofeedback can be used to help athletes gain awareness and control of breathing through diaphragmatic breathing and self-regulatory practices. This breathing control can then be incorporated into centering or pre-performance routines and applied during sport-specific practices that replicate competitive demands. When used this way, respiratory biofeedback has been linked to improved outcomes in precision-based sports such as rifle shooting (Ortega & Wang, 2018).

Getting Started in Psychophysiology and Biofeedback

The prospect of pursuing education and training in applied psychophysiology and/or certification in biofeedback can seem daunting. Biofeedback and applied psychophysiology are niche areas of expertise in SEPP. It is not uncommon if you receive little to no training in these areas in your graduate education (performance or clinical). Access to reliable technology can also be a major barrier to entry. Table 19.2 provides some key considerations if you're interested in adding applied psychophysiology/biofeedback to your SEPP repertoire.

Table 19.2 Key Considerations for Adding Applied Psychophysiology/Biofeedback[a]

Education and Training	*Device Selection*	*Professional Integrity*	*Ethical Considerations*
Pursue higher education, specialized certification or training through a BCIA-accredited program or university. Connect with mentors or peer groups for support.	Choose devices aligned with your training, certification, or license. Know the difference between clinical vs. consumer-grade devices and marketing claims.	Understand physiology to optimize outcomes. Gain proficiency with your device; practice on yourself first.	Align with ethical standards of relevant governing bodies (e.g., AASP, AAPB, and APA). Biofeedback use varies by licensure status—know your scope of practice.

[a] BCIA (Biofeedback Certification Intenational Alliance), AASP (Association for Applied Sport Psychology, AAPB (Association for Applied Psychophysiology and Biofeedback), APA (American Psychological Association).

INCORPORATING TECHNOLOGY INTO THE PRACTICE OF SPORT PSYCHOLOGY

Penny Werthner, Sommer Christie, & Maurizio Bertollo

As researchers and practitioners in the field of sport psychology, we are always looking for ways to enhance human performance in sport while ensuring a healthy and optimal high-performance environment for athletes, coaches, and staff. Over the last 10–15 years, technology-based interventions have been utilized to enhance the learning of many psychological skills and to improve the practice of self-regulation, both physiologically and psychologically, using multimodal and multidimensional frameworks and ecologically valid protocols (Bertollo et al., 2020). The purpose of this chapter is to discuss the use of biofeedback and neurofeedback training as a complement to psychological preparation. Indeed, integrating technology into psychological skills training facilitates the identification and tracking of optimal performance and supports the development of more effective, personalized interventions (Siekańska et al., 2021).

We know competitive sport is very demanding and inherently stressful, with high expectations and pressure for all involved. We also know optimal performance in sport requires a number of specific skills: for example, the development of a deep level of self-awareness; the ability to shift one's focus of attention and inhibit irrelevant stimuli; the skill to be flexible and adapt to the changing environment; an understanding and ability to relax and recover on a regular basis, physiologically and psychologically, and quiet one's mind and body; and an ability to effectively manage one's emotions and arousal and activation levels, again depending on the individual athlete's needs and the sport demands. Importantly, self-awareness allows an athlete to step back and reflect on their thoughts, feelings, and behaviors and is a critical component to developing the ability to self-regulate (Anderson et al., 2014). Self-regulation is comprised of both a psychological and physiological component (Blumenstein et al., 2002) and one evidence-based technique for facilitating the learning of effective self-regulation and managing the activation levels of one's nervous system is biofeedback and neurofeedback (e.g., Bar-Eli & Blumenstein, 2004; Di Fronso et al., 2021; Werthner et al., 2013).

Biofeedback and Neurofeedback

There is considerable research in biofeedback/neurofeedback training and a developing body of research in relation to its applicability in competitive sport (e.g., Blumenstein et al., 2014; Christie et al., 2020; Di Fronso et al., 2021). Learning to achieve one's own ideal internal psychological state consistently is not a simple task and biofeedback and neurofeedback training, when used as a complementary tool to the well-established skills of sport psychology, can provide enhanced awareness of the connection between the mind and body (Bertollo et al., 2021), significant control over physiological and neurological mechanisms, and an ability to develop strategies to effectively self-regulate.

Biofeedback and neurofeedback training entails attaching sensors to the body that acquire biological and neurological signals measuring muscle tension, sweat, body thermoregulation, respiration rate, and heart rate (i.e. biofeedback modalities) and brainwave activity (i.e. neurofeedback modality). Those signals are then fed back to the individual with the purpose of enabling a deep understanding of how they respond physiologically and neurologically to a variety of situations. Specific training is designed to help individuals learn to regulate aspects of their central and autonomic nervous systems (Schwartz & Andrasik, 2003; Thompson & Thompson, 2003). To illustrate this, we present a case study intervention utilized with two Olympic athletes and provide a summary of key learnings when utilizing biofeedback and neurofeedback.

Case Study

The two cases presented here are two elite male Olympic athletes (both in their late 20s) preparing for a world championship and a second Olympic Games. The training, conducted by a sport psychology practitioner trained in biofeedback and neurofeedback, took place in a lab setting over the course of two years leading up to the Games and consisted of approximately 25 sessions for each athlete, organized around training and competition schedules. ProComp Infinity equipment from Thought Technology Ltd. was used to gather measures in seven areas: electroencephalography (i.e., EEG—the active electrode was placed on the scalp at Cz, for training a narrow focus, in accordance with the 10–20 system; Jasper, 1957);

surface electromyography (sEMG); respiration rate; heart rate; HRV; skin conductance; and peripheral body temperature. Each of the 25 training sessions included three components:

a **Biofeedback Training** to help the athletes learn to quiet their autonomic nervous system by developing self-awareness and self-regulation of muscle tension, respiration rate, heart rate, skin conductance activity, and peripheral body temperature,
b **Neurofeedback Training** included the measurement and feedback of EEG signals to facilitate (a) the learning of brief mental recovery/wide focus, (b) narrow focus, and (c) the switching of states between narrow focus and brief recovery (Thompson & Thompson, 2003), and
c **Simultaneous Biofeedback and Neurofeedback Training** to facilitate relaxation and deep recovery by decreasing activation in both the autonomic nervous system and the central nervous system. Paced breathing was used in both the biofeedback and neurofeedback training to help the athletes decrease activation in both systems (Lehrer et al., 2000).

Importantly, within each session, discussions occurred between the sport psychology practitioner and each of the athletes on how the learning in the lab could be transferred to the training and competition setting. For example, when working on the physiological skills using the biofeedback modalities, a conversation would take place about how relaxing the shoulders (measured through EMG modality) could help prior to the start of a race or a hard workout. Similarly, the work of breathing, practiced at the rate of approximately six breaths per minute, measured by respiration rate and heart rate, was discussed so the athlete could think about how to use breathing for both brief mental recovery and managing nervousness and anxiety prior to competing. The athletes were also encouraged to practice this paced breathing at home between sessions.

Each athlete had different sport demands (one competed in a 30 second sprint event, and the other competed in a longer distance four minute event) as well as quite different ways of reacting to stressful situations, neither particularly effective (one athlete reacted by slowing down his thoughts and closing down, the other athlete reacted with a very busy, "ruminating" mind). As a result, the training was individualized for each athlete. While the space limitations of this chapter do not allow for an in-depth discussion of the interventions and results, each athlete, over the course of the two years of biofeedback and neurofeedback training, along with regular integration of the skills into training and competitions, developed an ability to be narrowly focused for the requirements of their event and an understanding and ability to effectively activate and deactivate their mind and body, at will. As one of the athletes said,

> It was a really helpful tool to understand what it means to be in different states, and I can now feel when I am getting out of a relaxed state and when I am getting anxious…and I am able to do something about it.

What this quote emphasizes is an ability to shift one's internal states at will—the athlete developed the ability to recognize when he is becoming anxious and by slowing his own breathing, for example, he was able to shift to a calmer state, both physiologically and neurologically, which, in turn, allowed for an appropriate and effective "paying attention to" the right cues for a training session or race.

In summary, biofeedback and neurofeedback is a tool that can effectively enable an athlete to develop self-awareness of how they react to stress and the ability to put themselves in an optimal state, physiologically and neurologically, to perform well in the stressful environment of competitive sport. It is also important to note that biofeedback and neurofeedback are best used in conjunction with a comprehensive psychological skills intervention (Vealey, 2023), including skills such as planning, effective communication, debriefing, and analysis.

COGNITIVE FITNESS FRAMEWORK: A NEW PARADIGM FOR NEUROSCIENCE-INFORMED PERFORMANCE ENHANCEMENT TECHNOLOGIES

Leonard Zaichkowsky, Eugene Aidman, John Crampton, Gerry Fogarty, & Jeffrey Bond

What it takes from a psychological perspective to consistently produce and sustain high-performance under pressure is remarkably common across many occupations. The factors contributing to such performance go beyond mere "wellness" (i.e., the absence of pathology) and include, apart from knowledge and skills, a range of "capacity" factors, such as strength, endurance and flexibility, that are best summarized by the concept of "fitness." The concept of "mental fitness" emerged in the mental health and positive psychology literature (Seligman, 2008) aimed at promoting a positive and proactive notion of mental health (Robinsons et al., 2015). The mental fitness literature is focused on protective factors, such as cognitive flexibility, implicated both in the prevention of mental illness and promotion of flourishing. On the other hand, the concept of military cognitive readiness (Grier, 2012) emerged to reflect a broad set of performance predictors, from trainable skills to dynamic functional states and trait-like characteristics ranging from cognitive ability to attentional styles. The Cognitive Fitness Framework (CF2; Aidman, 2020) was developed by sport psychologists and neuroscientists to integrate the growing evidence from brain sciences, map out the key drivers of cognitive functioning under pressure, and bring together the mental health professions focused on psychological deficit/dysfunction and the human performance field aimed at improving psychological functioning of healthy individuals.

By integrating cognitive readiness and mental fitness with the growing consensus on key domains of cognitive functioning (Morris & Cuthbert, 2012), the CF2 enables neuroscience evidence to inform high-performance applications. The CF2 has evolved into a transdisciplinary consensus (Albertella et al., 2023) and now offers a unifying conceptual toolkit for practitioners working in performance-focused applications such as sport and exercise, performing arts, military, law enforcement, acute medicine, paramedic and emergency-response domains. The meaning of "Cognitive" in the CF2 is deliberately broader than is strictly defined in the specialist cognitive literature. This logic reflects our growing knowledge about information processing behind all behavior and mental operations—for example, the neuro-cognitive mechanisms of emotional regulation (or dysregulation) that manifest when our fear degrades our decisions, as well as when cognitive reframing helps shape affective responses.

Similar to physical conditioning, cognitive fitness can be improved with deliberate and structured practice (Zaichkowsky & Peterson, 2018) using well-known and tested practices, such as inexpensive apps to assess and teach controlled breathing, (e.g. Calm), imagery, and high-tech applications such as bio/neuro-feedback (e.g. Thought Technology). Currently, systematic assessment and training protocols are being developed (Aidman et al., 2022; Franks et al., 2024; Taylor et al., 2023). In addition to integrating the health and performance perspectives, the cognitive fitness approach offers an important advantage of reducing the "mental health" stigma, which is known to undermine help-seeking treatment compliance.

So, reframing "mental health service" into "mental/cognitive fitness training" would go a long way toward making it more attractive to a performance psychologist's target audiences.

The three pillars of the performance mindset—staying calm, focused, and flexible when faced with challenges and adversity—correspond to three distinct skill sets that sport and performance psychologists have worked with for decades: (1) Stress Management skills to cultivate Calm, (2) Attention Control skills to stay Focused, and (3) Mental Agility to be Flexible and adapt to change. The CF2 offers a new paradigm to help demystify the key psychological aspects of high-performance preparation and execution (Aidman et al., 2022; Fogarty et al., 2023). The preliminary requirements are an understanding of the key components of cognitive fitness and an evidence-based framework upon which to develop relevant knowledge and training drills for high-performance individuals and teams.

The CF2 has received considerably more traction than previous work on Mental Fitness and Cognitive Readiness. Importantly, it was followed up by an international Delphi study (Albertella et al., 2023) that established a transdisciplinary, world-wide expert consensus on key elements of cognitive fitness (see Figure 19.1).

While this important international academic work was being conducted, Zaichkowsky and Peterson (2018) published "The Playmaker's Advantage: How to Raise Your Mental Game to the Next Level," to expose the dearth of our understanding of elite athlete thoughts and emotions, and introduce three key pillars of Cognitive Fitness and the *Cognitive Gym*:

- Self-regulation skills to cultivate composure and calmness.
- Attention control knowledge and skills to stay focused on the right thing at the right time.
- Mental agility to be flexible and adapt to dynamic and variable performance demands.

These essential psychological skills are supported by core cognitive capacities (cognitive primaries) such as self-awareness, working memory, task switching, impulse control, and

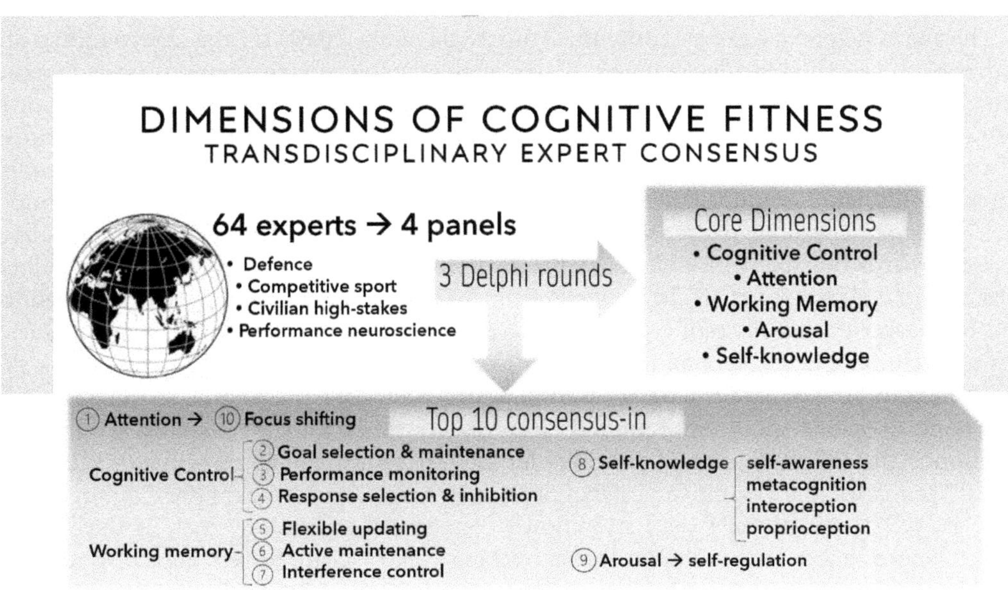

Figure 19.1 Summary of the CF2 expert consensus

Source: CF2 Delphi—details in Albertella et al. (2023)

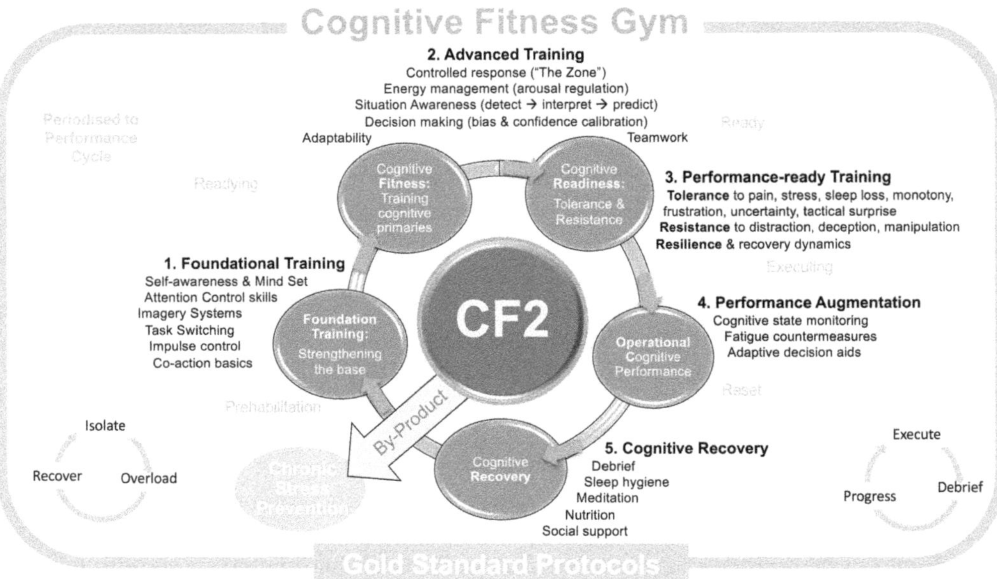

Figure 19.2 The cognitive fitness cycle

Source: Adapted with permission from Aidman et al. (2022)

cognitive flexibility. Similar to the power, speed, flexibility, and endurance elements of general (physical) fitness, these cognitive primaries support the development of all skills, from reading, remembering, and problem-solving to job-specific technical skills, as well as more complex cognitive fitness attributes, such as frustration tolerance and resistance to distraction. Figure 19.2 explains the cognitive fitness cycle.

The transdisciplinary expert consensus (Albertella et al., 2023) on the key cognitive primaries has accelerated the development of new standards for cognitive testing and systematic, and evidence-based approaches to cognitive training. Traditional cognitive tests are a poor fit for practical applications, such as establishing cognitive baselines and tracking developmental or training progress, primarily because they are either notoriously unreliable or require unrealistically large amounts of testing time to produce reliable assessment. In addition, their measurement range is almost always limited to dysfunction. Recent developments have pushed what is possible with reliable and realistically timed cognitive fitness testing (Albertella et al., 2024; Kucina et al., 2023; Wells et al., 2021). New generation scenario-embedded and biomarker-enhanced testing protocols have been developed. These advanced cognitive testing technologies are becoming increasingly practical, which is critical to optimizing this investment by employing fieldable tools to objectively track the progress of its outcomes and informing decisions about any required changes/adjustments to the training program. In addition to the earlier mentioned technologies used for assessment and training of "cognitive fitness" primaries, the Cognitive Fitness Foundation relies extensively on the Cognitive Gym App, as well as scientifically valid and known commercial technology such as the "Stroop Task," Neurotracker (for multiple object tracking), and "GameSense" currently used for baseball, softball, and tennis. Overall, we are witnessing a ground swell of new applications that make measurable improvement in cognitive fitness a realistic proposition. Performance psychology practitioners are well-positioned to both benefit from, and contribute to, this growing field.

EDITORS' TAKEAWAYS

My (Lauren) first introduction to biofeedback was in graduate school as my program had a lab full of the complex and expensive technology on the market at that time. However, it wasn't until later that I began using it in applied practice, in particular using the emWave solution (a cheaper, simpler option). While it made it seem like it was extremely easy to integrate it into applied practice with its game-like approach, a discerning practitioner would quickly realize that there is a need for additional education and competency development in order to integrate such tools into practice. I'll be honest, it took me some time to understand HRV—in particular, the idea that higher HRV indicating more variability in heart rate is more desirable than lower HRV, which sounded counterintuitive to me. I was fortunate in graduate school that my advisor, Gershon Tenenbaum, had many colleagues around the world, some of whom he would bring in to supplement our learning—including Boris Blumenstein who shared with us a five-step mental training approach that incorporated biofeedback (Blumenstein et al., 1997). This was my first exposure to not only understanding the value that technology such as this could have in applied practice, but also the need to really understand the science underpinning it and have a framework for bringing it into one's practice. As my career progressed, I incorporated various other types of technology and was grateful for this foundation in order to effectively and ethically incorporate it into my practice. I strongly encourage anyone interested in bringing technology into their approach to read this chapter and pursue other resources and credentials in order to ensure you safely and effectively use it with clients.

RECOMMENDED EXERCISES

1 What are the benefits and limitations of using biofeedback and neurofeedback in your practice? How can you ensure ethical and legal compliance when integrating new technologies?
2 How would you introduce athletes to discussions about decision-making and other cognitive skills? How would you engage coaches in supporting their athletes' decision-making development?
3 Being fully focused—narrow in individual sports, slightly broader in game sports—combined with recovery skills, is critical. How will you train these skills with athletes?
4 Coaches and practitioners can help athletes develop self-awareness by asking questions and listening before offering solutions. What questions would you ask after a strong versus weak performance? Reflect on your own coaching or practitioner performance—how could you improve your self-awareness?
5 How can athletes regulate themselves physiologically and psychologically in relation to different performance experiences? What action- and emotion-based strategies could they use, considering the MAP model (Kellermann et al., 2022)?

REFERENCES

Aidman, E. (2020). Cognitive fitness framework: Towards assessing, training and augmenting individual-difference factors underpinning high-performance cognition. *Frontiers in Human Neuroscience, 13,* 466. https://doi.org/10.3389/fnhum.2019.00466

Aidman, E., Fogarty, G. J., Crampton, J., Bond, J., Taylor, P., Heathcote, A., & Zaichkowsky, L. (2022). An app-enhanced cognitive fitness training program for athletes: The rationale and validation protocol. *Frontiers in Psychology, 13,* 957551. https://doi.org/10.3389/fpsyg.2022.957551

Albertella, L., Kirkham, R., Adler, A. B., Crampton, J., Drummond, S. P., Fogarty, G. J., ... & Yücel, M. (2023). Building a transdisciplinary expert consensus on the cognitive drivers of performance under pressure: An international multi-panel Delphi study. *Frontiers in Psychology, 13,* 1017675. https://doi.org/10.3389/fpsyg.2022.1017675

Albertella, L., Kirkham, R., Rotaru, K., Aidman, E., & Yücel, M. (2024, December). Cognitive fitness: Reliable measurement with implications for high-pressure job performance and resilience. Paper presented at the Defence Human Sciences Symposium, Melbourne, Australia.

Anderson, R., Hanrahan, S. J., & Mallett, C. J. (2014). Investigating the optimal psychological state for peak performance in Australian elite athletes. *Journal of Applied Sport Psychology, 26*(3), 318–333. https://doi.org/10.1080/10413200.2013.856396

Bar-Eli, M., & Blumenstein, B. (2004). Performance enhancement in swimming: The effect of mental training with biofeedback. *Journal of Science and Medicine in Sport, 7*(4), 454–464. https://doi.org/10.1016/S1440-2440(04)80263-0

Baron, K. G., Abbott, S., Jao, N., Manalo, N., & Mullen, R. (2017). Orthosomnia: Are some patients taking the quantified self too far? *Journal of Clinical Sleep Medicine, 13*(2), 351–354. https://doi.org/10.5664/jcsm.6472

Bertollo, M., Berchicci, M., & di Fronso, S. (2021). Mind-body interaction in sport psychophysiology. In E. Filho & I. Basevitch (Eds.), *Sport, exercise and performance psychology* (pp. 169–184). Oxford University Press. https://doi.org/10.1093/oso/9780197512494.003.0009

Bertollo, M., Doppelmayr, M., & Robazza, C. (2020). Using brain technologies in practice. In G. Tenenbaum & R. C. Eklund (Eds.), *Handbook of sport psychology* (4th ed., pp. 666–693). Wiley-Blackwell. https://doi.org/10.1002/9781119568124.ch32

Blumenstein, B., Bar-Eli, M., & Tenenbaum, G. (1997). A five-step approach to mental training incorporating biofeedback. *The Sport Psychologist, 11,* 440–453.

Blumenstein, B., Bar-Eli, M., & Tenenbaum, G. (Eds.). (2002). *Biofeedback applications in performance enhancement: Brain and body in sport and exercise.* John Wiley & Sons.

Blumenstein, B., Hung, E., & Orbach, I. (2014). Self-regulation and biofeedback. In P. Papaioannou & D. Hackfort (Eds.), *Routledge companion to sport and exercise psychology* (pp. 402–416). Routledge. https://doi.org/10.4324/9781315880198

Christie, S., Bertollo, M., & Werthner, P. (2020). The effect of an integrated neurofeedback and biofeedback training intervention on ice hockey shooting performance. *Journal of Sport and Exercise Psychology, 42*(1), 34–47. Advance online publication. https://doi.org/10.1123/jsep.2018-0278

Da Silva, J. C., & De Souza, M. L. (2021). Neurofeedback training for cognitive performance improvement in healthy subjects: A systematic review. *Psychology & Neuroscience, 14*(3), 262–272. https://doi.org/10.1037/pne0000237

di Fronso, S., Werthner, P., Christie, S., & Bertollo, M. (2021). Using technology for self-regulation in sport. In M. C. Ruiz & C. Robazza (Eds.), *Feelings in sport: Theory, research, and practical implications for performance and well-being* (pp. 178–186). Routledge. https://doi.org/10.4324/9781003052012-19

Edmonds, W. A., & Tenenbaum, G. (2012). *Case studies in applied psychophysiology: Neurofeedback and biofeedback treatments for advances in human performance.* Wiley-Blackwell.

Fogarty, G., Crampton, J., Bond, J., Zaichkowsky, L., Taylor, P., & Aidman, E. (2023). Neurobiological foundations of cognitive fitness in high-performance applications. In B. Boyle, G. Northoff, A. Burbey, F. Fregni, M. Jahanshahi, A. Pascual-Leone, & B. Sahakian (Eds.), *The Sage handbook of cognitive and systems neuroscience: Cognitive systems, development and applications* (pp. 574–590). Sage.

Franks, K., Albertella, L., Rousseau, J., & Yücel, M. (2024, December). Dynamic cognitive fitness testing for NZDF cognitive conditioning program: A Cognitive Gym application. Paper presented at the Defence Human Sciences Symposium, Melbourne, Australia.

Goessl, V. C., Curtiss, J. E., & Hofmann, S. G. (2017). The effect of heart rate variability biofeedback training on stress and anxiety: A meta-analysis. *Psychological Medicine, 47*(15), 2578–2586. https://doi.org/10.1017/S0033291717001003

Grady, B. (2023). The role of information technology in enhancing sport psychology interventions for athlete development and performance optimization. *Revista de Psicología del Deporte, 32*(4), 41–50.

Grier, R. A. (2012). Military cognitive readiness at the operational and strategic level: A theoretical model for measurement development. *Journal of Cognitive Engineering and Decision Making, 6*(4), 358–392. https://doi.org/10.1177/1555343412456062

Gruzelier, J. H. (2014). EEG-neurofeedback for optimising performance. I: A review of cognitive and affective outcome in healthy participants. *Neuroscience & Behavioral Reviews, 44*, 124–141. https://doi.org/10.1016/j.neubiorev.2013.09.015

Jasper, H. H. (1957). The ten-twenty electrode system of the International Federation. *Electroencephalography and Clinical Neurophysiology, 10*(2), 371–375. https://doi.org/10.1016/0013-4694(58)90053-1

Kellermann, B., MacPherson, A., Collins, D., & Bertollo, M. (2022). Reading the MAP: A pracademic perspective on the current state of play of the multi-action plan model with regard to transitions between mental states. *International Journal of Environmental Research and Public Health, 19*(23), 15520. https://doi.org/10.3390/ijerph192315520

Kennedy, L., & Parker, S. H. (2019). Biofeedback as a stress management tool: A systematic review. *Cognition, Technology & Work, 21*(2), 161–190. https://doi.org/10.1007/s10111-018-0503-5

Khazan, I., Shaffer, F., Moss, D., Lyne, R., & Rosenthal, S. (2023). *Evidence-based practice in biofeedback and neurofeedback.* Association for Applied Psychophysiology & Biofeedback.

Kucina, T., Wells, L., Lewis, I., de Salas, K., Kohl, A., Palmer, M., Sauer, J. D., Matzke, D., Aidman, E., & Heathcote, A. (2023). Calibration of cognitive tests to address the reliability paradox for decision-conflict tasks. *Nature Communications, 14*(1), 2234. https://doi.org/10.1038/s41467-023-37860-9

Lehrer, P., Kaur, K., Sharma, A., Shah, K., Huseby, R., Bhavsar, J., & Zhang, Y. (2020). Heart rate variability biofeedback improves emotional and physical health and performance: A systematic review and meta-analysis. *Applied Psychophysiology and Biofeedback, 45*(3), 109–129. https://doi.org/10.1007/s10484-020-09466-z

Lehrer, P. M., Vaschillo, E., & Vaschillo, B. (2000). Resonant frequency biofeedback training to increase cardiac variability: Rationale and manual for training. *Applied Psychophysiology and Biofeedback, 25*(3), 177–191. https://doi.org/10.1023/A:1009554825745

Mirifar, A., Beckman, J., & Ehrlenspiel, F. (2017). Neurofeedback as supplementary training for optimizing athletes' performance: A systematic review with implications for future research. *Neuroscience & Behavioral Reviews, 75*, 419–432. https://doi.org/10.1016/j.neubiorev.2017.02.005

Morris, S. E., & Cuthbert, B. N. (2012). Research domain criteria: Cognitive systems, neural circuits, and dimensions of behavior. *Dialogues in Clinical Neuroscience, 14*(1), 29–37. https://doi.org/10.31887/DCNS.2012.14.1/smorris

Ortega, E., & Wang, C. J. K. (2018). Pre-performance physiological state: Heart rate variability as a predictor of shooting performance. *Applied Psychophysiological Biofeedback, 43(1)*, 75–85. https://doi.org/10.1007/s10484-017-9386-9

Peters, D., Calvo, R. A., & Ryan, R. M. (2018). Designing for motivation, engagement and wellbeing in digital experience. *Frontiers in Psychology, 9*, 797. https://doi.org/10.3389/fpsyg.2018.00797

Quadt, L., Critchley, H., & Nagai, Y. (2022). Cognition, emotion, and the central autonomic network. *Autonomic Neuroscience, 238*, 102948. https://doi.org/10.1016/j.autneu.2022.102948

Robinsons, P., Oades, L., & Caputi, P. (2015). Conceptualising and measuring mental fitness: A Delphi study. *International Journal of Wellbeing, 5(1)*, 53–73.

Schack, T., Hagan, J. E., Jr., & Essig, K. (2020). New technologies in sport psychology practice. In D. Hackfort & R. J. Schinke (Eds.) *The Routledge international encyclopedia of sport and exercise psychology. Volume 2: Applied and practical measures.* (pp. 458–471). Routledge.

Schwartz, M. S., & Andrasik, F. (Eds.). (2003). *Biofeedback: A practitioner's guide* (3rd ed.). Guilford Press.

Seligman, M. E. P. (2008). Positive health. *Applied Psychology: An International Review, 57*, 3–18.

Siekańska, M., Bondár, R. Z., di Fronso, S., Blecharz, J., & Bertollo, M. (2021). Integrating technology in psychological skills training for performance optimization in elite athletes: A systematic review. *Psychology of Sport and Exercise, 57,* 102008. https://doi.org/10.1016/j.psychsport.2021.102008

Taylor, P., Walker, F. R., Heathcote, A., & Aidman, E. (2023). Effects of multimodal physical and cognitive fitness training on sustaining mental health and job readiness in a military cohort. *Sustainability, 15*(11), 9016. https://doi.org/10.3390/su15119016

Thompson, M., & Thompson, L. (2003). *The neurofeedback book: An introduction to basic concepts in applied psychophysiology.* Association for Applied Psychophysiology & Biofeedback.

Vealey, R. S. (2023). A framework for mental training in sport: Enhancing mental skills, wellbeing, and performance. *Journal of Applied Sport Psychology, 36*(2), 365–384. https://doi.org/10.1080/10413200.2023.2274459

Watson, J. C., II, & Coker-Cranney, A. M. (2018). Introduction to the special issue: Using technology in applied sport psychology. *Journal of Sport Psychology in Action, 9*(4), 213–215. https://doi.org/10.1080/21520704.2018.1552446

Weerdmeester, J., van Rooij, M. M., Engels, R. C., & Granic, I. (2019). An integrative model for the effectiveness of biofeedback interventions for anxiety regulation: Viewpoint. *Journal of Medical Internet Research, 22*(7), e14958. https://doi.org/10.2196/14958

Wells, L., Kucina, T., Kohl, A., Lewis, I., de Salas, K., Aidman, E., & Heathcote, A. (2021). A flexible gaming environment for reliably measuring cognitive control. In *Proceedings of the NATO STO-HFM Symposium "Applying Neuroscience to Performance: From Rehabilitation to Human Cognitive Augmentation*, Rome (Italy)." NATO.

Werthner, P., Christie, S., & Dupee, M. (2013). Neurofeedback and biofeedback training with Olympic athletes. *NeuroConnections Summer 2013 Newsletter,* 32–37.

Zaichkowsky, L., & Peterson, D. (2018). *The playmaker's advantage: How to raise your mental game to the next level.* Simon & Schuster.

20 Consulting and Coaching in SEPP Practice

When working within organizations or with individual clients, it is imperative that SEPP professionals (SEPPPs) intentionally engage with their clients aligned with what they are contracted for. Broadly speaking, SEPPPs might wear a coaching hat—engaging more openly and client-centered with the client setting the agenda—or engage wearing a consulting hat. As a consultant they share their expert knowledge and provide more structure and guidance for clients, setting the agenda for the consulting work. Depending on the context and specific client needs, we might be able to embrace coaching as well as consultant roles. Thus, we also need to consider engaging in respective training and certification programs, to be able to do our work ethically aligned with our competencies. To be successful when working with our clients, it is important to understand and embrace the differences between wearing a consultant or a coaching hat—as often SEPPPs use coaching and consulting interchangeably.

MASTERING THE BLEND: HOW COACHING CAN ELEVATE YOUR CONSULTING WORK

Cindra Kamphoff & Eric Bean

At the heart of being an effective applied sport psychology practitioner is your ability to build trust, establish a meaningful connection, and build rapport with the clients you serve. Without a connection, there is no relationship. And without a strong relationship, clients are unlikely to embrace or implement the insights, skills, and mental skills essential for performance excellence. As such, it is quite difficult to build a career in the field without effective coaching and consulting skills.

In this chapter, we will be discussing the difference between coaching and consulting and demonstrate why professionals in sport and performance psychology (SPP) should have both competencies. As both Certified Mental Performance Consultants (CMPCs) with the Association for Applied Sport Psychology (AASP) and Professional Certified Coaches (PCC) with the International Coach Federation (ICF), we have seen the substantial value of having both competencies and certifications allowing us to serve our clients more effectively and powerfully. We will then share the top three coaching skills that have made the most impact for our clients as well as considerations for graduate education directors and graduate students.

The Difference between Coaching and Consulting

Coaching and consulting are used interchangeably in SPP yet the approaches are very different. We believe both are necessary to do incredible, life-changing work. Both coaching

DOI: 10.4324/9781003781479-25

Table 20.1 Key Differences between Coaching and Consulting Skills

Aspect	*Coaching*	*Consulting*
Expertise	The client is the expert	The consultant is the expert
Role of practitioner	Acts as a guide or partner	Acts as an expert or advisor
Approach	Facilitative: Empowers the client to find solutions	Directive: Provides expert advice and solutions
Client involvement	Encourages the client to be in the "driver's seat" of the session and take ownership of outcomes	Typically, less participative; the consultant provides the answers, frameworks, and tools
Key skills	Active listening, empathy, acknowledging, and using empowering questions	Analytical thinking, client planning, use of assessment to determine areas of growth
Methodology	Uses tools like empowering questions, reflection, and accountability frameworks	Uses performance psychology frameworks, knowledge, and research-backed strategies
Measure of success	Growth in the client's confidence, clarity, and skills	Growth in mental skills and implementation of mental tools

and consulting require excellent communication and interpersonal skills but differ in methodology and nature of implementation. The ICF, globally recognized as the gold standard in coaching, promotes a client-centered approach where the client sets the agenda and is viewed as the expert (see ICF, 2021 for insight into specific competencies). The coach serves as a partner, asking powerful questions, facilitating insights, and only offering advice when invited. This facilitative model fosters trust, empowerment, and ownership in the client. In contrast, a consulting approach positions the consultant as the expert who often sets the agenda, provides assessments, and delivers directive guidance using psychological frameworks and performance tools. Consulting is particularly valuable for addressing specific challenges, improving team dynamics, and enhancing performance through tailored, research-based strategies. Table 20.1 outlines the key differences between coaching and consulting skills.

Top Three Coaching Skills

While a consultant will likely use the aforementioned "coaching skills" when consulting, the coach approach is different because the client is the expert in the relationship and the coach follows the client. The focus remains on the client's agenda, not the coach's interpretation or assumptions. When implementing the coach approach, there are three fundamental skills to master to provide your clients with a powerful experience:

- *Intuitive Listening:* When using intuitive listening, you are using *all* your senses to listen for the *real* message. You would consider the client's shift in voice, energy level, feelings, non-verbal communication, and what the client is saying and not saying. The coach would be listening for the client's values, beliefs, and challenges while suspending their own agenda.
- *Acknowledging:* This is one of the most powerful tools when coaching because it lets the client know you are *really* listening. Acknowledging is a deep way of mirroring back what you are hearing the client say to help them gain insights in themselves. When acknowledging, the coach could focus on the client's unique abilities, talents, positive qualities and what matters most to them. Some prompts to use when acknowledging include, for

example, *Let me see if I get this…; What I hear you saying is…; So when you________, ________happens; Let me give this back to you to make sure I got it….*

- *Empowering Questions:* Empowering questions are open-ended, powerful, thought-provoking, challenging, and future-directed. Empowering questions invite the client to reflect and explore possibilities rather than offering a yes/no answer. Effective questions challenge the client's assumptions or thinking patterns in a supportive way, encouraging them to stretch their thinking. Focus on questions that start with "How…" "What…" "When…" "Where…" and "Who…" and avoid questions that start with "Why…" because they might be perceived as judgmental to the client (i.e., "Why did you decide to do that?"). Some examples of empowering questions include: *What's most important to you about this decision? How will you define success in this situation? What's standing in your way?*

The Value of the ICF Certification + CMPC Certification

Many SPP professionals have the CMPC certification which tends to be based on a consulting perspective, is more sport-focused, and does not explicitly embrace a coaching perspective. Adding the ICF coaching credential will add professional coaching skills, provide an added credential, help professionals stand out in a crowded market, and enable them with a broader skill set during sessions. While the field grows, many people remain unaware of SPP outside of athletics and the military. As a result, business leaders seek executive or life coaches to meet their coaching needs. Therefore, adding the ICF credential allows SPPs to attract a broader range of clients including business professionals and executives. In addition, many organizations prefer certified professional coaches, making the ICF credential a valuable addition to the CMPC.

Adding coaching competencies enhances versatility during sessions. Sometimes, a performer may require a coach-like partner to help with clarity, motivation, or decision-making. For example, the second author leveraged the coach approach recently to help a senior leader navigate an issue he was having with an underperforming employee. Other times, they may need a consultant to analyze issues, provide solutions, and implement research-based interventions. For example, the first author leveraged her consulting approach working with an athlete who needed strategies and tools on how to handle pressure for an upcoming event. Possessing both skill sets allows seamless transitions between roles to meet client needs. To find out more about how to earn an ICF Certification, you can visit their website (www.coachingfederation.org).

Considerations for Graduate Educators and Students

To conclude, we like to share takeaways for graduate education directors and graduate students to effectively combine coaching and consulting.

For Graduate Educators and Coordinators

- *Adding Courses on Coaching Frameworks:* Include ICF-aligned coaching courses in the graduate curriculum including the Top Three Coaching Skills.
- *Consider Offering Dual Certification Opportunities:* You could partner with the ICF or other coaching organizations to provide pathways to earn a coaching certification alongside their SPP degree.
- *Add Role-Playing Exercises to Courses:* Use simulations to let students practice scenarios that require both coaching (e.g., the client is the expert) and consulting (e.g., delivering expert advice).

- *Facilitate Professional Development:* You could invite dually certified ICF and CMPC practitioners to speak in courses. You could also provide resources like coaching books and coaching webinars to your students.

For Graduate Students

- *Seek Dual Training:* Enroll in coaching courses or a certification program that leads to the ICF credential, alongside pursuing your CMPC credential.
- *Develop Key Coaching Skills:* Keep mastering the Top Three Coaching Skills and focus on building rapport and trust with peers, supervisors, and clients.
- *Hone Consulting Expertise:* Keep learning to assess clients' needs and growing your SPP knowledge to effectively deliver actionable, research-backed tools and strategies.

By implementing these suggestions, graduate educators and students can ensure a well-rounded education that prepares future professionals to meet the growing demands of SPP, blending coaching and consulting for maximum impact.

COACHING AND CONSULTING AS A SPORT, EXERCISE, AND PERFORMANCE PSYCHOLOGY PROFESSIONAL FROM A LEADERSHIP PERSPECTIVE

Sebastian Brueckner

Professionals working across diverse sport, exercise, and performance contexts will benefit from embracing multiple skillsets and mindsets when engaging with diverse clients. Kamphoff and Bean (see previous section) have argued that professionals will benefit from acquiring dual credentials, e.g., ICF coach certification and a respective certification as Mental Performance Consultant. Building on this notion, this chapter aims to help readers at various career stages as sport, exercise, and performance psychology practitioners (SEPPPs) reflect on their interaction with clients across a coaching-consulting continuum from a leadership perspective. While scholars have recently proposed developmental models for SEPP growth (Fogaça et al., 2024), the literature thus far does not include discussion of relevant leadership models and frameworks. However, the leadership model proposed here as well as the implications for SEPPPs in their respective professional contexts have been implemented successfully in a high-performance context with German Gymnastics national-team athlete coaches (see details about the "CULTurn project" on the project website; Tietjens & Brueckner, 2025). The central theme of this chapter is to discuss coaching and consulting through a leadership lens. When engaging in coaching and consulting with clients, SEPPPs will benefit from intentionally embracing different leadership roles and respective behaviors. However, service delivery will not be an either/or of coaching and consulting. Most often working with clients will involve switching and adjusting to multiple leadership roles across a coaching-consulting continuum. Aside from formal training and certifications as previously discussed, having a clear understanding of oneself as a professional leader will help SEPPPs to be more successful when engaging with clients.

Leadership Roles and Mindsets

To bring the complex, dynamic environment in which SEPPPs operate to life, let's look at what kind of leadership roles, respective mindsets, and leadership behaviors help navigate real-life challenges one might encounter. While you, as an SEPPP, might have your personal style, strengths, and mindsets that you prefer to act from, being successful in complex environments requires you to be flexible, adjust your approach to each situation, and resolve conflicting systemic and client needs. These conflicting needs are reflected in the Competing Values Framework (CVF; Lawrence et al., 2009). The CVF can conceptually be combined with the construct of visionary-charismatic leadership (Antonakis et al., 2016) to form a 5C-model of leadership. The CVF nicely captures "the polar nature of organizational dynamics" (Lawrence et al., 2009, p. 88) and contrasting behavioral leadership demands SEPPPs face when working with clients.

SEPPPs need to be able to identify and use the "appropriate" leadership role and mindset depending on the situational context—as well as be able to switch between various roles and behaviors when encountering different situational demands (Brueckner & Tietjens, 2025). Leadership roles within the CVF are structured within four distinct fields of action: Collaboration—Competition and Creativity—Control, complemented by Charisma. As demonstrated in the CULTurn project, leadership behavior across these five fields of action can be used to illustrate the complex everyday life of coaches and the difficult task of adapting their role and behavior as leaders. Certainly, performance plays a role in Olympic elite sports, results matter, and fighting opponents can increase motivation (Competition)—but at the same time, athletes' sustainable, holistic performance development and mental health require them to be empowered and make personal decisions. Thus, coaches and athletes need to learn to work together as a team, and training groups need to function as teams, even if individual athletes compete for medals, starting positions, or sponsorship when on stage (Cooperation). Additionally, in addition to embracing new ideas, openness to ideas of others, the creative search for new solutions, and adaptation to constant change (Creativity), rules, agreements, and structure are of course also important for developing reliable and sustainable high-performance contexts (Control). Finally, Charisma fosters the ability to adapt and communicate one's actions along the Cooperation—Competition and Creativity—Control continuums, which are characterized by contradictory values and respective behavioral actions.

While specific leadership roles within the Collaboration, Competition, Creativity, and Control fields of action might vary depending on the specific performance context and culture you are working in, here are some examples for you as an SEPPP, to bring the concept to life:

- In line with the idea of "doing things together," aligned leadership roles with Collaboration include personality or team developer, and mentor. Collaborative SEPPPs promote a cooperative way of working with individual clients or teams, working toward common goals and cultivating interpersonal relationships. They support team members and bolster individual strengths in the group context.
- For Competition, the motto is "Doing things decisively," with an emphasis on acting quickly, setting ambitious goals and promoting personal responsibility. The focus is on driving results and performance as well as return on investment. Respective leadership roles for SEPPPs might be challenger or driver.
- Creativity might encompass leadership roles such as innovator or stimulator: The motto of creative leadership is "do things first." Creative SEPPPs are characterized by openness to change and a willingness to innovate. They are always up to date with the latest developments in their professional context and are willing to push existing boundaries.
- Controller and regulator are key leadership roles for Control. A controlling leader is focused on "doing things right." The focus for SEPPPs might be on monitoring or process optimization, relying on clear rules and guidelines.

As stated before, Charisma helps leaders engage in respective leadership behaviors aligned with situational demands, and to adapt to contextual changes appropriately. In that sense, charismatic leadership consists of behavioral traits, which can be learned and improved—a concept that the CULTurn coaches were surprised and intrigued by at the same time. Specific areas of charismatic leadership (Antonakis et al., 2016) are: substance (e.g., values, empathy), delivery (expression, body language, humor), and framing (use of metaphors, comparisons, storytelling).

Coaching vs. Consulting Through a 5C Model Lens

While it is beyond the scope of this short discussion to dive deeper into the theoretical underpinnings of the 5C leadership model and the respective implications for SEPPP applied practice, let's explore some practical considerations and potential benefits of reflecting on your SEPPP work through a 5C leadership lens. As illustrated above, acting from a Collaboration or Creativity angle aligns more with an intentional coaching approach. Subsequently, engaging with clients with a Competition or Control mindset means being in more of a consultant role. As such, the 5C model can provide a helpful reference point when assessing how you are engaging with clients—and if you are not only aligned with your intended role as coach or consultant, but meeting their needs in complex and dynamic situational contexts. Thus, reflecting on how the respective components of the 5C model resonate with you, your training, identity, personality, and context will help SEPPPs at any career stage in identifying strengths and gaps you might currently have. Consider the following specific action items:

- Identify which of the 5Cs you are most comfortable using when working with clients. Where do you fall on the Cooperation—Competition and Creativity—Control continuums? How much of a charismatic leader are you in your work? Where do you have strengths in Substance, Delivery, Framing, and which strategies do you already use?
- Identify where you have gaps related to the 5Cs and how you could address those gaps.
- Shift your perspective and try identifying the needs of individual clients or organizations you serve. What leadership roles might they benefit most from? Are you meeting those needs? Or can you identify any specific gaps that you need to address by building your 5C leadership repertoire and competencies?

This intentional self-reflection holds a unique opportunity to learn and grow as an SEPP leader who successfully works with clients across multiple domains. Building self-awareness and self-regulation skills are key to learning and growing at any stage of your professional career, as is intentional self-reflection. Doing so aligned with the 5C model might help you to use your coaching and consulting training and techniques to their fullest potential. To conclude, some tips for putting the 5C model into practice as a successful SEPP leader for your clients, include: (1) prepare and plan for each client interaction intentionally, (2) be open, perceptive, flexible, and ready to adjust, and (3) be transparent in what leadership role you might be embracing and ask your client for feedback if this meets his needs, or you need to pivot and adjust.

UNLOCKING POTENTIAL: INTEGRATING COACHING TECHNIQUES INTO SPORT AND EXERCISE PSYCHOLOGY EDUCATION

Maike Tietjens, Lena Henning, & Hannah Hüttemann

"Coaching" and "teaching" are two professions with distinct aims and methods, though they share certain similarities. In the traditional sense, teachers—much like consultants—are seen as experts in their subject matter, possessing a deeper body of knowledge than the individuals they teach. Their primary goal is to transmit this knowledge and ensure that students master specific skills and concepts in a structured and systematic process.

In contrast, a "coach," in an educational or professional setting, is not necessarily an expert in the subject at hand. Rather, a coach's strength lies in facilitating the development of others by asking insightful questions to improve their performance and achieve specific goals, often focusing on process and mindset rather than content mastery. Coaching is inherently relational and dialogic, emphasizing an interactive partnership between coach and coachee (Hawkins & Turner, 2019). Despite these differences, both roles share certain commonalities. Both teaching and coaching involve the instruction of skills, techniques, and strategies (Drewe, 2000), and both require the establishment of a trust-based relationship to foster learning and growth.

In this chapter, we will base our approach to apply coaching techniques in teaching on a systemic understanding of coaching. "Systemic thinking" in coaching means adopting a holistic perspective, being solution- and problem-oriented, always considering the coachee's or student's issue in relation to the systems around them, rather than focusing solely on isolated issues, and asking "systemic questions" to encourage reflection and offer new perspectives on the coachee's or student's situation (Lawrence, 2021).

Integrating coaching techniques into sport and exercise psychology education offers a dynamic approach to teaching, with a strong emphasis on skill development and practical application. This chapter explores the benefits and strategies of incorporating coaching methods into sport and exercise psychology curricula, serving three primary objectives. First, readers will gain an understanding of coaching techniques. Second, they will learn how these techniques can be applied within the context of sport and exercise psychology education, enhancing both student's theoretical knowledge and practical competence. Third, examples of how techniques can be transferred to student's future professions (e.g., coaching) will be outlined.

Coaching Techniques and Their Applicability: The Basics

Applying coaching techniques in classroom settings requires a safe space, clear boundaries, and voluntary participation. Trigger warnings, withdrawal options, and support outside class should be available. University settings may challenge this approach due to mandatory participation, which needs careful reflection.

To pursue systemic thinking, student-centered teaching considers the students' perspectives and interests in shaping the course, including their different backgrounds, experiences, contexts, and relationships—this is referred to as their "systemic backpack." Personalization involves adapting instruction to meet individual needs, preferences, challenges, and students' learning styles, as well as contextual factors such as family and peer support or learning and living environments. For example, if a student is more of a visual type, you can use visualization techniques to help him or her learn. If the student is more of a kinesthetic learner, learning through tactile, hands-on experiences might be a more effective way. Finally, coaching methods should engage students both cognitively and emotionally to deepen learning in university classrooms. Building on students' experiences often helps to facilitate learning processes.

Coaching Techniques and Their Application: Examples

Below, we present two selected examples of commonly used coaching techniques and how they can be applied in classroom settings, connected to different phases of a seminar lesson. For two tools, we briefly illustrate rationales of use and transfer ideas to students' future teaching or professional contexts. While we decided to choose two examples (e.g., in the beginning and during the seminar), further coaching techniques such as circular questions or scaling questions can also be applied in teaching settings especially for deeper understanding.

Beginning the Seminar: Coaching Cards

At the beginning of the lesson, without diving too deeply into the topic of the session, tools like "coaching or mood cards" (e.g., landscapes, weather maps), symbols (e.g., smileys), or objects (e.g., animals) can be used. Coaching cards are a valuable tool for activating students both cognitively and emotionally. Using these cards might help students and teachers to open the seminar in a meaningful way. If they wish, students can reflect on past experiences that influence their current mood. The cards might help to express feelings that are not easy to articulate (e.g., abstract representations of situations, objects, symbols, colors, etc.). By sharing these reflections, students can either lighten their emotional burden or celebrate positive past experiences with others (similar to diary entries). This process helps students to clear their minds and focus fully on the subsequent session instead of being distracted by past thoughts. Moreover, these shared experiences might also be helpful for the student's classmates. They might adapt the way they interact with each other (e.g., by avoiding jokes if someone is feeling sensitive). This fosters a more respectful and supportive classroom climate. Finally, teachers might tailor their subsequent methods more precisely to students' needs by adjusting activities—such as switching from group work to individual tasks. Additionally, teachers can build on the students' shared experiences to deepen engagement and relevance throughout the lesson.

The simplicity of coaching cards also makes them transferable to various professional contexts. As students recognize how mood cards help verbalize emotional states, they may add this tool to their personal toolbox and apply it in future situations. For example, in coaching sessions, mood cards can assist athletes to express feelings they find difficult to put into words (e.g. prior to or after an important competition feeling anxious, uncomfortable, or under pressure). This, in turn, enables coaches to identify the most appropriate strategies to help manage those emotions effectively.

Sparking Students' Interest in the Seminar, Understanding Relationships: Constellations

Using "systematic constellations" in the classroom can be a powerful tool to engage students on a deeper level with a specific topic. This technique can make relationships and group dynamics visible, allowing hidden patterns and underlying issues to emerge. For students, this embodied approach provides an opportunity to better understand different perspectives, roles, and influences within the group. Constellations also encourage active participation and engagement. By physically representing their perspective or emotions—whether in the classroom, gym, or outdoors—students become more invested in the learning process. The method can be applied in various contexts. First, when students are asked to position themselves along a line, constellations can quickly reveal the range of experiences or prior knowledge present in the group. Students can be encouraged to share experiences related to the positioning, which the teacher can then build upon later in the session. Second, positioning can help students grasp different theoretical or empirical associations (similar to drawing). What relation do they have? How are they positioned in relation to one another? Constellations are also effective for visualizing complex systems such as ecosystems, organizational structures, or social dynamics. Third, constellations offer a unique way to explore and experience relationships and changes in relationships. By physically adjusting their positions (e.g.

moving closer or further apart until someone indicates to stop) students can, for example, reflect on and respect personal boundaries. This can be different between people and can also change depending on who students are facing. This embodied experience fosters new insights, greater empathy, and a deeper understanding of interpersonal dynamics.

Students might transfer this method to, for example, future coaching situations. Athletes might reflect on relationships within a training group or to different trainers. They also might change position if roles change (e.g., a peer becoming a trainer). This method might help the athletes to reflect on different relationships. By incorporating movement, athletes can gain a more tangible sense of how their relationships shift in response to changes in roles or group dynamics. This physical experience not only deepens their self-awareness and understanding of team structures but also equips them with strategies to navigate interpersonal challenges more effectively in both sports and other collaborative settings.

Conclusion

We have only provided a brief glimpse into how techniques commonly used in coaching can be applied to teaching by using two methods as examples. When applying coaching techniques in teaching, it is important that teachers adopt a systemic mindset (i.e., they should be aware of student's experiences, preferences, interests etc. as well as their different environments). This systemic mindset can be understood as a foundational attitude for teaching. Building on this, a range of tools can be applied in different phases of the lesson (e.g., visualization techniques, body-centered tools, questioning techniques). We encourage teachers to get creative and experiment with these techniques in the classroom, as they offer students new perspectives.

EDITORS' TAKEAWAYS

My (Lauren) initial awareness of the difference between coaching and consulting began when I was in graduate school during a time when these titles were used interchangeably and people were calling attention to the idea that they are not in fact synonymous. Yet, I don't think I really understood their true difference until I began working in the corporate world and I could more clearly see not only the nuance of what it means for the role you play as a practitioner (e.g., a consultant brought in to provide expertise versus a coach helping someone train their mental game) but also, importantly, for the approach you take in sessions with clients. In one of my corporate roles, one of my responsibilities was to support the advancement of the company's executive coaches. My observation and experience of supporting colleagues who came from our field mirrored what I had experienced myself—it takes time, effort, and intention to seamlessly combine an approach of consultation (i.e., psychoeducation on mental skills) and coaching (i.e., utilizing coaching skills such as open-ended questions and active listening skills). Doing so, or as I refer to it "being the rudder on the ship not the captain of the boat, enables you to coach" while incorporating your expertise and guidance. As Kamphoff and Bean explained, there are key differences between these two approaches that can be intentionally and effectively combined—as demonstrated by Brueckner and Tietjens et al. useful examples. This chapter provides essential insights not only for those interested in pursuing applied practice outside of the sport domain, but really for any of us in the field to ensure we have the greatest impact with the many tools and approaches available to us. And, I strongly encourage program coordinators and professors to more strategically incorporate this into their courses. Having one or a few counseling skills courses may not appropriately prepare future professionals for navigating the real-world demands of consulting and coaching in SEPP practice.

RECOMMENDED EXERCISES

1 Define in your own words what it means to coach versus to consult. Give one example (real or hypothetical) for each role. Are there gray areas where the roles overlap, and how would you navigate them?
2 Consider how you might use both coaching and consulting skills in practice. Identify a current client:

 a As a coach, what would your approach look like?
 b As a consultant, how would your methods or goals differ?
 c How could shifting your approach benefit the client?

3 Using the 5C Model of Leadership, reflect on your engagement with the client:

 a Coaching hat: How much does your approach emphasize Collaboration and Creativity versus Competition or Control?
 b Consulting hat: How much of your consulting work emphasizes Competition and Control, and how much still leans toward Collaboration and Creativity?

4 How could you use Charisma techniques—values-based action, empathy, body language, humor, metaphors, storytelling—to adjust between coaching and consulting mindsets?
5 What should you be mindful of when using coaching techniques as a teacher? What benefits or added value do these techniques bring to sport and exercise psychology education? Reflect on a past seminar and how you could integrate coaching techniques into it.

REFERENCES

Antonakis, J., Bastardoz, N., Jacquart, P., & Shamir, B. (2016). Charisma: An ill-defined and ill-measured gift. *Annual Review of Organizational Psychology and Organizational Behavior, 3*(1), 293–319. https://doi.org/10.1146/annurev-orgpsych-041015-062305

Brueckner, S., & Tietjens, M. (2025). *Erfolgreich führen im Sport: Ressourcen nutzen, Kompetenzen stärken, mit Führung gestalten – Ein CULTurn-Arbeitsbuch zur Selbstreflexion und Weiterentwicklung für Trainer:innen im Sport* [Successful leadership in sports: Using resources, strengthening competencies, and developing through leadership – A CULTurn workbook for self-reflection and professional development for sports coaches]. https://doi.org/10.5281/zenodo.15963611

Drewe, S. B. (2000). An examination of the relationship between coaching and teaching. *Quest, 52*(1), 79–88. https://doi.org/10.1080/00336297.2000.10491700

Fogaça, J. L., Quartiroli, A., & Wagstaff, C. R. (2024). Professional development of sport psychology practitioners: From systematic review to a model of development. *Psychology of Sport and Exercise, 70*, 102550. https://doi.org/10.1016/j.psychsport.2023.102550

Hawkins, P., & Turner, E. (2019). *Systemic coaching: Delivering value beyond the individual.* Routledge.

International Coaching Federation. (2021). *ICF core competencies.* https://coachingfederation.org/app/uploads/2021/07/Updated-ICF-Core-Competencies_English_Brand-Updated.pdf

Lawrence, K. A., Lenk, P., & Quinn, R. E. (2009). Behavioral complexity in leadership: The psychometric properties of a new instrument to measure behavioral repertoire. *The Leadership Quarterly, 20*(2), 87–102. https://doi.org/10.1016/j.leaqua.2009.01.014

Lawrence, P. (2021). Team coaching: Systemic perspectives and their limitations. *Philosophy of Coaching, 6*(1), 52–82. https://doi.org/10.22316/poc/06.1.05

Tietjens, M., & Brueckner, S. (2025). *The CULTurn project.* University of Muenster. https://www.uni-muenster.de/Sportwissenschaft/en/Sportpsychologie/ueber-uns/CULTurn.html

21 Doing Applied Work with Individuals and Groups

Context matters when working as an SEPP professional. One key contextual factor to consider when engaging with clients is whether you are working with an individual client, an individual that is part of a group you are working with, a whole team, or even an entire organization. For example, building trust and establishing boundaries might be more difficult and complex if you are actually being paid by an organization. Engaging with high-performance staff, coaches, as well as athletes could make building trust with the athlete much more challenging should they worry about you maintaining confidentiality of anything shared with you. Navigating these contexts, then, requires not only awareness but also key competencies and skills. Our global author groups reflect about their experiences and share key lessons learned when engaging with high-performers in respective settings they have navigated.

FOR ONE AND FOR ALL: PERFORMANCE PSYCHOLOGY SERVICE DELIVERY CONSIDERATIONS BETWEEN INDIVIDUAL AND TEAM CONTEXTS

Jen Schumacher & Cathal Sheridan

In this contribution, we will explore performance psychology consulting with individual athletes, teams, and an individual within the team. We explore contextual differences, strategies for effective and ethical service delivery, special considerations, and practical approaches. Additionally, we explain that regardless of consultation context there remains the need to conduct a needs assessment, develop a mental skills training program, and engage in program evaluations.

Working with an Individual Performer

One of the most common forms of service in this field is one-on-one consulting with an individual performer. One-on-one sessions can allow time and space to develop a strong working relationship and a deep connection. This type of consulting affords the opportunity to do thorough, individualized, and meaningful mental skills training that addresses the performer's unique needs (Thelwell et al., 2006). Establishing systems that allow for a holistic understanding of the athlete's performance and well-being is crucial. One effective approach is to triangulate the one-sided perspective of the athlete with additional sources of information, such as practice observation and feedback from coach and support staff. This method helps to balance the athlete's subjective experience with objective insights from others who are closely involved in the athlete's development, and can lead to a more accurate and comprehensive

DOI: 10.4324/9781003781479-26

understanding of the athlete's needs, strengths, and areas of improvement (McCullagh & Weiss, 2002). By collecting feedback from various stakeholders, including coaches, strength and conditioning professionals, and medical staff, mental performance consultants can better tailor their interventions, ensuring that they align with both the athlete's self-reported challenges and the observations of those who work with the athlete regularly. This triangulated approach ultimately fosters more effective and targeted mental skills interventions, allows for greater accountability in the athlete-consultant relationship, enhances the athlete's overall performance, and promotes a more supportive environment for their growth. Similarly, close collaboration with any additional service providers, such as therapists or counselors if applicable, is essential for providing expert service (Herzog & Hays, 2012).

Having an evidence-based framework to work from is key, not only to develop a connection with the individual but also to guide the work in a direction that is going to provide value (Poczwardowski et al., 1998). Examples of this might include foundational work on the person's belief systems, understanding the overarching goal and vision that they have for themselves, developing an action plan that will hold both parties accountable to the work done, or other strategies that can lead to a holistic framework (Friesen & Orlick, 2010).

Finally, the environment in which one-on-one consulting occurs can vary greatly and differ significantly from that of working with individuals within a team context. Often, this type of working relationship occurs in the context of the professional's office space or remotely via phone or video call. This can often lead to a more structured and scheduled approach, which inherently imparts a more formal dynamic to the working relationship.

Working with a Team

Consulting in a team setting is a common format in the field of performance psychology. This work typically involves high levels of group interaction. Service delivery in team settings could look like presenting to large groups, commanding attention in boisterous environments, consulting with smaller groups within the team, facilitating group conversations, or providing broader education around mental performance to coaches and leaders thereby extending influence throughout the organization. Defining the role and setting expectations are paramount to success. The professional should collaborate with leadership to clearly define the aims of the service, lines of reporting, evaluation, expectations around practice and game involvement, approaches to communication and coach consultation, and confidentiality practices. One critical consideration is understanding *who is the client*—a question that often becomes blurred in team environments where multiple stakeholders are involved. Identifying the primary client is essential for maintaining clarity around confidentiality, dual relationships, and the scope of practice (McCullagh & Weiss, 2002).

Effective work in these spaces is often predicated upon one's ability to gain entry, forging meaningful and trusted relationships with key members of the organization (e.g., coaches, sports medicine staff, strength and conditioning, administrators, etc., Ravizza, 1988). Further, integration of a mental skills training program is dependent on support from leadership and other critical stakeholders (Walsh & du Plooy, 2023). In the world of high-performance, a professional's ability to understand the unique demands of the context of the environment and adapt to a team's dynamic needs is essential. Practically speaking, this means everything from knowing where to stand and how to engage in practice settings to social norms around hallway communication and staff meetings to being prepared to conduct a group session with the full 20 minutes scheduled while also being willing to shift to just seven minutes (and do so effectively!). Efficiency with time and delivery is crucial, as most elite sporting teams operate in high-paced environments. Focusing on practical application of the research in language utilized by the team is valued and often better received than overly technical and theoretical communication (Wrisberg & Dzikus, 2016). Putting in time and presence in many high-performance environments not only engenders trust but also allows the professional to more thoroughly understand subtleties of normative behavior.

Working with an Individual Within a Team Environment

A third context for performance psychology service delivery is with individuals on a team that the professional is already providing team services to. This may be an individual athlete, a coach, or a support member of the team that has access to services per the professional's contract. Additional considerations are essential to ensure proper ethical practices around confidentiality and service utilization, especially when considering the multidimensional relationships between individuals competing for roster spots on a team and the inherently unique group dynamic needs of team sports (Evans et al., 2012). When executed thoughtfully, delivering such services can provide great value to the team by way of enhancing individual mental performance at key positions in targeted ways.

When individuals seeking services are leaders within the organization (i.e., captain, coach, and impact player), such engagement can increase buy-in and decrease stigma of help-seeking behaviors within other members of the team. However, in such cases, it is imperative that the professional clearly communicates confidentiality practices with all parties involved and upholds boundaries as they are naturally challenged. It can also be helpful to discuss motive with athletes to build trust in cases where they feel uncomfortable, e.g.,

> When I am able to support your coaches with their own mental performance needs, and discuss ways in which coaches can utilize best practices from our field to improve communication and feedback delivery, it ultimately enhances performance of individual athletes and the team as a whole.

Individual service provision within a team environment may also occur when an athlete on a team with a performance psychology professional already has, or begins to, contract with an external service provider. In such cases, the athlete may prefer that these services are kept separate, which should be respected. In others, the athlete may allow or even encourage both professionals to connect to discuss the athlete's progress; however, this should be driven by the athlete and be followed up with ongoing conversations about what information should be shared. In cases where this is not possible due to an unknown entity or contract restrictions, one can always ask the performer what mental skills they have exposure to or are working on building, which has the benefit of providing insight as well as keeping the client in full control of what gets shared with whom.

In all cases, effectively delivering a high-quality service requires the performance psychology professional to have a clear understanding of who they work for, and moreover, what success looks like. Discussions regarding the nature of reporting and confidentiality should occur before service delivery begins and be regularly communicated clearly to all members of the team. When working with individuals within a team environment, one must ask themselves who they serve—is it the individual client, the team as a whole, the coach, or owner of the organization? Clarity around these questions can allow for proper communication of information and allow for ethical record keeping and service delivery (Fifer et al., 2008).

Additional Considerations

Regardless of the context of consultation, each of these three scenarios requires a thorough needs assessment to determine the scope of services that is ideally conducted with a variety of perspectives in mind, although this can be challenging in isolated individual consultations. Once the service needs are identified, a holistic, evidence-based mental skills training program can be developed. Lastly, program evaluation throughout and upon the conclusion of services provided is crucial for continued consultant development and improvements for future services if applicable, and helps to engender trust and accountability with program stakeholders (Anderson et al., 2002).

APPROACHING SPORT PERFORMANCE INTERVENTIONS: A COMPARATIVE ANALYSIS OF INDIVIDUAL, TEAM, AND INDIVIDUAL-WITHIN-TEAM CONTEXTS

Tyler Miles, Hannah Levy, & Dolores Christensen

Sport psychology practitioners (SPPs) work with athletes in diverse settings—one-on-one with individual clients in the office, in practice spaces with teams, and with individual clients in team contexts, which will be referred to as the individual-within-team context. Consultation might include attending team events (e.g., team meals) or attending practices and competitions to observe complexities that might be missed in a typical clinical setting. This varied access gives SPPs a deeper understanding of the athlete's experience and corresponding team dynamics. An SPP might see an individual client for services, deliver a team intervention, and observe practice in which their client is participating, all in one day. Building on the contextual considerations shared in the previous contribution, this chapter provides guidance on approaches to sport performance interventions tailored for individuals, teams, and individuals-within-teams, emphasizing commonalities and unique considerations across contexts.

Similarities in Delivering Sport Performance Interventions

Despite the varied settings in which sport psychology interventions occur, several foundational similarities exist across individual, team, and individual-within-team contexts:

- Foundation: Sport psychology interventions are rooted in psychological well-being and performance enhancement, tailored to the unique needs of the athlete(s).
- Consulting Relationship: Building trust and rapport is essential. The SPP may employ a "trial and error" approach to identify what works best for the athlete(s), centering on the client's needs and wishes (Zhang et al., 2024).
- Sport-Specific Interventions: Interventions must be tailored, considering the demands, culture, and challenges inherent to that sport. This tailored approach ensures that the psychological support provided is relevant and effective (Lochbaum et al., 2022).
- Goals: Establishing process and outcome goals is critical to sport performance interventions (Chow et al., 2024). Individual goals may focus on personal growth, while team goals could aim at collective success and upholding team values.
- Psychoeducation: Educating athletes on psychological concepts helps them manage performance and advocate for their needs.

- Reflection: Guiding athletes to reflect on their experiences, behaviors, and outcomes fosters self-awareness, growth, and an understanding of their optimal performance state. The potent combination of psychoeducation and reflection supports athletes in truly integrating what they are learning for long-term change and application.

Differences in Delivering Sport Performance Interventions

While there are broad similarities across different individual, team, and individual-within-team settings, critical differences also exist across them. These differences are particularly evident in how content is determined, the physical and contextual space of sessions, and the delivery of the content. Each section below contrasts the individual and team settings and then explores the intersection at the individual-within-team level.

Content

In individual sport performance sessions, the athlete determines the goals and focuses with guidance from the SPP. This individualized approach allows for personalized interventions tailored to the athlete's needs, experiences, and goals (Lochbaum et al., 2022). The collaborative nature of these sessions fosters self-reflection, personal growth, and the development of skills relevant to the athlete's unique psychological and performance profile.

In contrast, team sessions involve input from multiple stakeholders, including coaches, captains, and athletic trainers. These sources influence the direction and content of sessions, sometimes introducing competing priorities. A coach might request a focus on enhancing team cohesion, while team members might prefer addressing conflict management. Additionally, the SPP might identify different needs based on their observations and assessments, leading to nuanced balancing of perspectives to optimize team dynamics and performance outcomes.

The individual-within-team context offers a unique blend of both approaches. Here, the SPP can simultaneously address personal development and team-related dynamics. This dual focus is informed by direct observations of the athlete's interactions within the team environment, such as during practices or competitions. Understanding these interpersonal dynamics allows the SPP to tailor individual consultations effectively, respond thoughtfully to coach referrals, and bridge the gap between personal and collective performance goals. This context highlights the complexity of aligning individual growth with team objectives while maintaining the athlete's autonomy and well-being.

Physical and Contextual Space

Sport performance varies depending on the physical space and other contextual factors. Individual consulting can typically be conducted in a controlled office setting that offers a consistent environment conducive to deep, personal exploration. However, contextual considerations offer logistical challenges that must be considered, such as the athlete's ability to travel to the office, time constraints, and confidentiality concerns in "public" spaces, like being seen in the waiting room or coming in and out of the office.

Team sessions often physically occur in less controlled environments, such as training facilities, where factors like noise, space availability, weather, and the presence of other teams can influence the session. Logistical considerations can also include the availability of, for example, a screen, table and chairs, and writing utensils. SPPs must navigate these challenges to create a productive atmosphere. Additional contextual considerations for team interventions include navigating different personalities (e.g., contributive, quiet, or disruptive) and managing both individual and collective energy levels (Low et al., 2023). It is also essential to consider whether coaches, athletic trainers, or other teams can overhear sessions or are present during the sessions. For example, a team session on helpful versus unhelpful self-talk might produce less authentic and honest answers from athletes if their coach is in the room with them. At the same time, SPPs must weigh the use of coaches in sessions as they may be in a better position to regularly help implement the sport psychology tools discussed.

When working with individuals-within-team, office and practice space intersect, requiring attention to physical and contextual factors, including team dynamics and confidentiality. For instance, an SPP's response to a dismissive comment about suicide during a team session could impact their individual work with an athlete on that team who has previously expressed passive suicidal ideation. Similarly, observing how certain players respond to high-stakes drills, such as a teammate shutting down after a mistake or how a coach's feedback style influences the team's overall confidence, can inform individualized interventions.

Content Delivery

The content in individual sessions is tailored to the athlete's needs. These sessions are often more conversational than didactic allowing for a focus on past sport experiences, self-reflection, and personal growth (Low et al., 2023). Content can include how the individual relates to self, supports self, and relates the past to the present (Chow et al., 2024).

The content is generally broader in team settings, focusing on shared learning and collective goals. These sessions may be more didactic and interactive, addressing themes such as teamwork, communication, and group dynamics. For example, an SPP could lead a session on body image for a team of distance runners, guiding them to define the locker room culture they want around food and body-related discussions. The focus is typically on the "here and now" or near future, such as a team session on developing pre-performance routines before the season's first competition (Low et al., 2023).

Content in the individual-within-team context blends individual and team-focused material, addressing how the athlete's personal goals and behaviors align with and impact the team's objectives. This context also requires attention to the individual's adaptation to the team environment, including how the self relates to the team, coaches, trainers, and other athletic staff (Low et al., 2023). A basketball player working on taking more offensive risks might have to adjust their approach if the team prioritizes patient ball movement and defensive stability. The SPP must also consider external factors, such as how an athlete's relationships with key stakeholders (e.g., a coach's leadership style or a teammate's dominating presence) shape their sense of belonging, confidence, and motivation. By integrating personal and team-level perspectives, SPPs can help athletes develop strategies to optimize individual growth while strengthening team dynamics.

Conclusion

In sport psychology, intervention approaches must adapt to the context—whether working with an individual athlete, a team, or an individual within a team. While foundational principles remain consistent, content, setting, and delivery variations require flexibility. By tailoring interventions to these dynamics, SPPs can effectively enhance performance and well-being, benefiting both individuals and teams.

WORKING RELATIONALLY: THE COLLECTIVE WISDOM OF APPLIED PRACTICE IN AOTEAROA NEW ZEALAND

Craig Barretto, Aramis Dennan, Paula Dennan, & Ian Lambie

The New Zealand Sporting Environment

Aotearoa New Zealand has a strong sports culture, which is deeply embedded within our national identity. In many ways, our sporting performance is a major cultural export, a high-profile activity that therefore impacts athletes' individual expectations and identity. The haka, for example, has become synonymous with our teams whilst being a meaningful indigenous cultural practice. The metaphor of "punching above our weight" is a common one when describing the collective aspirations of our sportspeople—partially due to the success we tend to achieve despite our relatively small population, but also due to the budget constraints that our sporting organizations work within. Inevitably, we are often working with athletes who are performing against international peers with far more financial and practical resources. The availability of performance psychology resources for both individual athletes and teams can vary, largely due to significant funding differences between sports and between urban and rural regions. There is a shortage of suitably qualified and experienced sports psychologists nationally; and not being a specialist "scope" of psychology within the New Zealand psychologists' registration system also contributes to this lack of availability. Many New Zealand athletes rely on personal funding or support from organizations like High Performance Sport New Zealand (HPSNZ) to access psychological input. In this chapter, we discuss how New Zealand's culturally embedded relational approach manifests in different examples of service delivery between individual athletes and teams.

The Importance of a Relational Approach

New Zealand is a culturally diverse country with a significant indigenous Māori population (17.8%), Asian (17.3%), and non-Māori Pacific peoples (8.9%), alongside various other ethnic groups and the majority European/Pākehā (NZ-born European) population (67%; Stats NZ, 2023). Performance psychologists need to be culturally aware and sensitive to the values and beliefs of Māori and other cultures, especially in how these values influence performance and mental health. New Zealand has the largest "Pasifika" population in the world (those from islands in the Pacific, such as Samoa and Tonga, who have moved here or were born here). These collectivist cultural origins inevitably produce a highly relational context where diversity is embedded across many levels beyond the individual athlete, whether across family, tribal/community groupings, cultural heritage, school, sporting organization, or professional team.

Tikanga—a Māori term for the right way of doing things—thus becomes an important facet of working with athletes, teams, and organizations in New Zealand. Incorporating relevant cultural processes, including transitioning from a position of noa (unrestricted, common) to tapu (sacred, protected, important) via Karakia (Māori prayer), Lotu (Pasifika prayer), or Whakataukī (proverbs), aids clinicians in fostering working alliances with clients, and can be incorporated into athletes' own performance plans. It is also important to have a knowledge of Māori and Pasifika models (e.g. Durie's Te Whare Tapa Whā, 1994; and Pulotu-Endemann's Fonofale model, 2009) which conceptualize well-being as the collective function of multiple domains, including physical, relational, spiritual, environmental, and mental health.

Wisdom from Clinical Work Within These Relational Interfaces

Working with Individual Athletes

Understandably, individual athletes are at the heart of the work we do and are most directly affected by the therapeutic alliance, both as a mechanism for building trust but also to facilitate effective interventions and change behavior. Athletes have tended to demonstrate positive expectations toward psychologists; we have witnessed a belief in the therapeutic process where athletes often present to initial appointments with an expectation that psychological interventions will contain something of value. At times, expectations need to be managed in terms of the timelines within which athletes can expect change, and indeed the amount of change possible. Athletes can sometimes see psychological therapy as a form of coaching or physical therapy, whereby something is to be diagnosed and "fixed"; they may be driven by perfectionism or a fear of reprisal in the form of self-criticism. It can be difficult to convey that psychological change may be slow, subtle, and difficult to measure, as well as something that is difficult to perfect.

The process of fostering effective intervention through therapeutic relationships is not new to the practice of psychology but is of particular importance in New Zealand. Working with clients of diverse cultural backgrounds requires practitioners to embrace the concept of whakawhanaungatanga (which can be translated as about actively making good relationships, like building a family or "whānau"), through which clinician and client take time to find common ground and collective interests, before "business" is discussed. This has implications for psychologists not only in individual work, but when working with teams that are seeking to build cohesion and chemistry.

The involvement of parents in the therapeutic work of younger athletes (under the age of 18) is an integral part of the work due to the proximity and investment of families in individuals. We find that it is important to maintain a level of curiosity about referrals that come from parents—whether they are heavily involved or not at all. There might be certain cultural norms and parental expectations at play, and parents provide important background information about the athlete's context within their family. Sometimes this extends to the wider family system, particularly in Māori and Pasifika communities. Whakapapa, connecting to one's ancestral lines, is a significant part of Te Ao Māori (Māori worldviews). Stories of those who have come before often permeate through sports organizations, clubs, and teams, being used as calling cards to unity, approach, and values. Working individually with clients can involve supporting them to connect into their own lineage, to identify important people in their own history through which they can derive pride, inspiration, or drive. It is common rhetoric among athletes in New Zealand to talk about what it means to "wear the fern" (the national symbol based on the silver fern plant), which embodies this concept of whakapapa—the legacy of the collective (i.e., the fern) is greater than any individual or team.

For Pasifika cultures, family relationships are considered central to one's identity. Although from diverse island communities, several common cultural values connect Pasifika: reciprocity, collectivism, humility, respect, and love (Ministry for Pacific Peoples, 2022). Relationality is a key notion within the Pasifika worldview and is central to one's sense of self (Mamea et al., 2018). The relational self is the foundation of the theoretical construct of Va, which can be used to understand how Pasifika communities interact and identify with one another. Va is recognized among Samoan, Tongan, and Fijian communities as the space that relates to and governs the relationships between people, community, land, and cosmos (Ioane, 2023). Va also acknowledges the relationship between Pasifika well-being, members of a sporting team, and the community.

Working with Teams

Working with teams includes the dynamics of getting "buy-in" and earning trust; not all members of the team will hold the same views about the involvement of a psychologist or will have different goals for their role and purpose with the team. Psychologists may draw on the concepts of manaakitanga (care for others) and kotahitanga (unity) when supporting a collective unity and orientation toward goals. For example, the New Zealand All Blacks' haka is a Māori enactment of challenge toward incoming opponents. However, not only is the challenge of competition laid down to opponents but also the process of laying down that challenge together, as one, is intentional in fostering closeness between teammates.

We have also found that in-group/out-group effects need to be effectively managed to work harmoniously as a sports psychologist with a team. In some ways, working with a team requires us to align with a group of individuals as well as the collective whole, which requires both clinical skill as well as clear communication with players and coaches, often across diverse cultural backgrounds and wide-ranging personal needs. Generally, it is important to establish presence and trust, and to clarify where we sit in relation to existing boundaries; for example, whether to join the system as an "outsider" or peripheral team member; and how to find a balance between expectations to provide sports psychology for performance enhancement against a more clinical role focusing on pathology resolution. Athletes from ethnic minority and indigenous communities may also have faced challenges such as racism and social deprivation in both life and sport that are different from challenges faced by those from ethnic majority or more privileged backgrounds.

Conclusion

Aotearoa New Zealand is a unique country, and our work must be nuanced as a result, whether it be with individual athletes or with teams. We face many challenges that accompany our size and remoteness relative to our international peers and competitors but also take great pride in rising to great heights in our sporting performance and achievement. As clinical psychologists working in sport, we believe that we have a unique contribution to offer to athletes and sporting teams, with a focus on athletes' overall psychological well-being in the context of their high-performance roles and expectations, as well as attending to the cultural relationships within which they are embedded. We welcome opportunities to connect with and contribute to international sports psychology networks and forums and share what we have learned and are learning in our small piece of paradise in the South Pacific.

EDITORS' TAKEAWAYS

Personally (Sebastian), what I take away from this chapter is a deep gratitude for being exposed to the intriguing contribution by our New Zealand group of contributors. They truly shared their collective wisdom—current clinical psychology-based and, thankfully, also their ancient cultural Māori-based heritage. Being able to engage and reflect on what this highly relational context and deeply collectivist cultural origins mean for individual as well as groups of clients one might work with really brings the "global perspective" idea to life! Interestingly, as our New Zealand group, Miles, Levy, and Christensen are also clinically trained professionals. I really appreciate the structured approach they take to describing shared foundations, and distinct differences between individual athlete, team, or individual within a team service delivery. They also highlight many contextual factors to consider in order to build trusting relationships and gain buy-in, complementing the deep cultural roots described by Barretto and colleagues. Lastly, I really appreciate how Schumacher and Sheridan highlight the importance of transparent needs assessment, targeted, evidence-based interventions, role clarity, ethical practice, and program evaluation across the various contextual settings as they provide a good reference point to assess, reflect, or plan one's own programs.

RECOMMENDED EXERCISES

1. How would you define your role when working with an individual client, a team, or an individual within a team? What steps would you take to prevent dual-role conflicts with individuals in a team?
2. What benefits, opportunities, limitations, and challenges have you experienced—or anticipate—in each consultation context? How can you remain mindful of these limitations and mitigate risks to ensure ethical, high-quality service?
3. Case Example: Jenny, a junior volleyball player, performs well in practice but "draws a blank under pressure" in games. Her teammates can become negative during high-pressure moments. Coach Kendra has asked for a team session on "handling pressure."
    a. Assuming Jenny is your individual client:
        i. What contextual factors must you consider for the team session?
        ii. How could individual interventions for negative self-talk (e.g., reframing) be applied at the team level?
        iii. How would your approach differ if coaches/staff are present versus absent?
        iv. How would you navigate collaboration or questions from the athletic trainer or coach while maintaining Jenny's confidentiality? How would you handle pressure to share information Jenny expects you to keep private?
4. What is meant by "cultural identity," and how can understanding it enhance relationships with athletes and teams? Why is culture important, and how can it improve service delivery?
5. How would you navigate situations where an individual client's goals conflict with team values or a coach's philosophy?

REFERENCES

Anderson, A. G., Mahoney, C., Miles, A., & Robinson, P. (2002). Evaluating the effectiveness of applied sport psychology practice: Making the case for a case study approach. *The Sport Psychologist, 16*(4), 432–453.

Chow, G. M., Garinger, L. M., Freeman, J., Ward, S. K., & Bird, M. D. (2024). "It's about going from good to great": Expert approaches to conducting a first sport psychology session. *Journal of Clinical Sport Psychology, 18*(1), 14–36.

Durie, M. (1994). *Whaiaora—Māori health development*. Oxford University Press.

Evans, M. B., Eys, M. A., & Bruner, M. W. (2012). Seeing the "we" in "me" sports: The need to consider individual sport team environments. *Canadian Psychology, 53*(4), 301.

Fifer, A., Henschen, K., Gould, D., & Ravizza, K. (2008). What works when working with athletes. *The Sport Psychologist, 22*(3), 356–377.

Friesen, A., & Orlick, T. (2010). A qualitative analysis of holistic sport psychology consultants' professional philosophies. *The Sport Psychologist, 24*, 227–244.
Herzog, T., & Hays, K. F. (2012). Therapist or mental skills coach? How to decide. *The Sport Psychologist, 26*(4), 486–499.
Ioane, J. (2023). *You've just got to think about your family and what type of person you want to be. Listening to young Pasifika people in the youth justice system and their families. Research and recommendations.* Health Research Council of NZ & Massey University School of Psychology. https://mro.massey.ac.nz/server/api/core/bitstreams/77615d2f-0192-46dc-8fdf-bc047469aeb5/content
Lochbaum, M., Stoner, E., Hefner, T., Cooper, S., Lane, A. M., & Terry, P. C. (2022). Sport psychology and performance meta-analyses: A systematic review of the literature. *Plos One, 17*(2), e0263408.
Low, W. R., Stoker, M., Butt, J., & Maynard, I. (2023). Pressure training: From research to applied practice. *Journal of Sport Psychology in Action, 15*(1), 3–18.
Mamea, K., Ioane, J., & Slater, P. (2018). A Samoan sense of self: An exploration. *Ata: Journal of Psychotherapy Aotearoa New Zealand, 22*(1), 103–113. https://doi.org/10.9791/ajpanz.2018.08
McCullagh, P., & Weiss, M. R. (2002). Observational learning: The forgotten psychological method in sport psychology. In J. L. Van Raalte & B. W. Brewer (Eds.), *Exploring sport and exercise psychology* (2nd ed., pp. 131–149). American Psychological Association.
Ministry for Pacific Peoples. (2022). *Yavu: Foundations of Pacific engagement.* Ministry for Pacific Peoples. https://www.mpp.govt.nz/assets/Resources/Yavu-Booklet.pdf
Poczwardowski, A., Sherman, P., & Henschen, K. (1998). A sport psychology service delivery heuristic: Building on theory and practice. *The Sport Psychologist, 12*, 191–207.
Pulotu-Endemann, F. K., & Tu'itahi, S. (2009). Fonofale: Model of health. Workshop for Pacific models of health promotion, Wellington, Sept 2009. https://www.openpolytechnic.ac.nz/current-students/wellbeing/the-fonofale-model/
Ravizza, K. (1988). Gaining entry with athletic personnel for season-long consulting. *The Sport Psychologist, 2*(3), 243–254.
Stats NZ–Aotearoa. (2023). https://www.stats.govt.nz/2023-census/
Thelwell, R. C., Greenlees, I. A., & Weston, N. J. (2006). Using psychological skills training to develop soccer performance. *Journal of Applied Sport Psychology, 18*(3), 254–270.
Walsh, A., & du Plooy, K. (2023). Mental skills training in elite sports environments: Current status of integration. *The Journal of Sport and Exercise Science, 7*(2), 1–8.
Wrisberg, C., & Dzikus, L. (2016). *Routledge international handbook of sport psychology* (R. J. Schinke, K. R. McGannon, & B. Smith, Eds.). Routledge.
Zhang, X., Rogers, M., & Werthner, P. (2024). Exploring a practitioner-athlete relationship and facilitated learning throughout a psychological skills training program. *Frontiers in Psychology, 15*, Article 1354129. https://doi.org/10.3389/fpsyg.2024.1354129

22 Doing Applied Work In-Person and Remotely

Certainly one of the lasting changes brought about by the COVID-19 pandemics' restrictions on in-person interaction was the rise of virtual interactions in its various forms and settings. Using online communication and interaction has impacted SEPP research, teaching, and most certainly also applied work. I (Sebastian) remember having to argue with an organization that I contracted with a few years before COVID-19 hit: They told me I had to consult in-person with athletes I was working with, otherwise they wouldn't pay me for my services. That certainly has changed! In fact, now most interactions with my global client-base happen online, often fully remote. While this has taken some skill building, adapting, and adjusting, embracing new challenges and skills, it definitely also comes with its advantages. Our three highly experienced global author groups share "best practices" regarding in-person and virtual/remote work, and argue for a way forward that doesn't focus on an "either/or," but rather skillfully integrates and combines both approaches in context-dependent and client-centered ways.

CONSULTING IN THE DIGITAL AGE: PRACTICAL CONSIDERATIONS FOR VIRTUAL CONSULTING

Matthew D. Bird & Jack C. Watson II

Grounded in both sport science and psychology, one may assume a sport, exercise, and performance psychology (SEPP) consultation would take place face-to-face in a sophisticated laboratory or confidential office setting. The characteristics of SEPP environments, however, can make it difficult for individual consultations to take place in typical settings and have the appearance of traditional sessions. Practitioners have recognized how SEPP consultations may occur at practice sites, competition venues, weight rooms, or hotel lobbies and may appear less formal and brief compared to the office setting where counseling sessions take place.

Although the non-traditional situations in which SEPP practitioners work can be difficult to define, the advancement of communication technologies has created opportunities for SEPP consultations to occur in virtual environments. Telepsychology (referred to as virtual consulting in this chapter) is known as the provision of psychological services using telecommunication technologies (APA, 2013). Once considered to be largely text-based, the advancement of smartphones and videoconferencing platforms has provided plentiful opportunities for virtual SEPP consulting to replicate services offered in face-to-face settings (Hanley, 2021). Historically, virtual consulting was viewed with skepticism as many practitioners were critical of the ability to build a therapeutic alliance in an online setting (Rees &

DOI: 10.4324/9781003781479-27

Table 22.1 The Benefits of Common Technologies Used in Virtual Consulting

Technology Type	*Benefits*
Videoconferencing	Accessible due to a variety of platforms and software. Can be used on many different devices including personal computers, laptop computers, tablets, and smartphones. Allows face-to-face contact to be maintained when consulting from different locations.
Text messaging and email	Allows for an asynchronous (i.e., not in real time) exchange of messages. Provides practitioner and client time to carefully consider the content of messages. Presents opportunities to maintain contact between sessions.
Mobile applications	Clients can experience SEPP programs and interventions without the need for a practitioner present. Can compliment face-to-face interactions by conducting a needs analysis (e.g., performance profiling) or promoting behavior change (e.g., goal setting). Applications are available to facilitate relaxation or mindfulness.

Stone, 2005). However, as virtual consulting has become more frequently used, researchers have identified similarities in the strength of the client-consultant relationship between online and face-to-face environments (Sucala et al., 2012). Today, the use of technology to facilitate SEPP consultation is more common than ever (see Table 22.1 for the benefits of common technologies).

Important Considerations in Virtual Consulting

There are some important factors to consider before beginning virtual consultations. For example, most practitioners have not received formal education preparing them to provide services to clients in a virtual setting. As virtual consulting is not the same as in-person consulting, practitioners should engage in continuing education, supervision, or mentoring to help them become more knowledgeable and effective in these settings.

Virtual consultations vary a great deal within and between the method of delivery. For instance, most forms of asynchronous communication (e.g., texting and email) do not allow the practitioner to visibly see the client and limit gathering important information such as facial expressions, presentation, dress, timeliness, initial reactions, and other factors. Even synchronous communication through videoconferencing has its drawbacks in being able to see body language. Further, with virtual consulting, the practitioner has less ability to establish a space that is most conducive to learning. Careful consideration therefore needs to be given to the potential loss of information when engaging in virtual consulting.

Conducting virtual assessments and interventions should also be carefully considered. Most SEPP assessments have been developed and validated using paper-and-pencil delivery methods. With virtual consulting, current assessments are often converted to online versions and may not be re-validated. Further, most research evaluating the efficacy of specific interventions was done with clients in-person yet practitioners probably use these same interventions with their clients in virtual sessions. While there is reason to believe these interventions would be effective in a virtual environment, their efficacy should be considered more closely.

Relevant Ethical Considerations When Consulting Virtually

Several ethical issues related to competency, confidentiality, and intake information and informed consent should be considered before consulting virtually.

Competency

Practitioners should only provide services for which they have developed a high level of competency via education, training, supervised experiences, mentoring, consultation, and/or self-study (AASP, 2024; Principle A). While this ethical standard is extremely important to both in-person and virtual consulting, it applies slightly differently in telepsychology. Within virtual consulting, practitioners need not only to be competent with the topics and skills with which they are working but also to possess the technical and practical competencies necessary to effectively use and troubleshoot issues with the technology and how to communicate effectively when using the technology (ISSP-R, 2019; Standard 10 (a)).

Confidentiality

Confidentiality is one of the biggest and most cited concerns identified with virtual consulting. Practitioners should take reasonable steps to maintain a client's confidentiality. However, when working with clients virtually, such precautions must also entail preventing unintended individuals from accessing emails, chats, videos, and other information stored from sessions. For virtual consultations, these processes, along with the potential limits to confidentiality, should be discussed with clients at the outset of consultation (AASP Standard 23(c); ISSP-R; Standard 10(h)). Even further, clients may decide to attend their consultation session in a public location where others might hear what they are saying. In such situations, it is important that consultants talk with clients about the potential impacts of their location.

Intake Information and Informed Consent

It is essential that practitioners collect basic intake information including name, address, telephone number, physician, and emergency contacts during a first session. However, when working virtually, it is also appropriate to identify contact information for a backup practitioner in the area, and specific hotline numbers in case of emergency (Watson et al., 2020). Practitioners should also take steps to ensure the identity of their clients (AASP, Standard 23(d); ISSP Standard 10(i)). It is much easier for a client to pretend to be someone else or for the client to be impacted by the presence of another in a virtual environment.

Informed consent processes for virtual consulting may go beyond the normal information discussed with in-person clients. For instance, clients should be informed about the technology used, the parameters for its use, the benefits, potential drawbacks, and ethical issues associated with its use (AASP Standard 23(b)(e); ISSP Standard 10 (d)). Practitioners should also discuss issues such as the frequency of checking and replying to messages, and methods for alternative communication (Watson et al., 2020).

In closing, virtual consulting with SEPP clients can promote flexibility and accessibility for clients and practitioners, but it also brings with it unique challenges that require thoughtful introspection and ethical vigilance. As technological advancements continue to reshape consulting processes, practitioners must maintain their competency through continuing education, and consuming research and best practices articles to ensure effective, competent, and ethically sound virtual practice.

"IT DEPENDS": BEST PRACTICES FOR VIRTUAL DELIVERY IN MENTAL PERFORMANCE

Greg Young, Lindsey Hamilton, Duncan Simpson, & Christian Smith

The phrase "best practices" has always felt like a surprising inclusion in any discussion of mental performance. Considering the most used phrase in the field might be "it depends," one should approach the notion of "best practices" with caution. "Best practices" are not stand-alone principles that can be copied and pasted into any situation, and they are not a set of standardized instructions that can have replicated results with each deployment. However, "best practices" can be thought of as bumper lanes at a bowling alley—they provide additional structure, support, guidelines, and some metaphorical safety while exploring what works for each person. This chapter outlines information to help the reader navigate the slippery lanes of virtual mental performance delivery that exists between the metaphorical gutters.

Advantages of Virtual Service Delivery

Perhaps the greatest professional challenge we have faced has been the need to migrate an apparently idyllic system of integrated mental performance training delivery at IMG Academy—namely in person, in situ, in collaboration with sport coaches and other support staff, with relatively unfettered access to the athlete in both group and individual practice and competition environments—to a wholly online and virtual distance learning style delivery within roughly two weeks. While the COVID-19 pandemic obviously presented the world with far greater challenges than this, the need to pivot to such a delivery model allowed the continued provision of mental performance and support services to a student-athlete population in need. Of course, with the best laid plans inevitably come obstacles. The collaborative nature of IMG Academy mental performance staff was tested to the limit as collective navigation of novel technology platforms, such as Microsoft Teams, CoachNow, PowerPoint, SharePoint, OneDrive, and iMovie to name a few, became more crucial to the success of delivery that has always valued the impact of "Edutainment"—the union of education and entertainment—something that would now be tested against the likes of Netflix and online gaming.

While the shift to virtual platforms introduced significant technological challenges and tested the staff's ability to adapt, it also prompted a broader reflection on how these new methods would impact the athlete's experience. Beyond the logistical hurdles of transitioning online, the virtual space itself raised important questions about the potential benefits and limitations of delivering mental performance coaching remotely. When considering the experience of athletes in the virtual space, many first thoughts will turn to the limitations of the online experience. While there are numerous limitations to technology in both its construction and capabilities (Sadeghi, 2019), and indeed the capabilities of the practitioner to effectively harness and exploit such capabilities, there are several advantages to this coaching experience. Perhaps a more beneficial approach to understanding mental performance delivery in such a manner is to ask, "What can be done virtually that cannot be done in person?" Exploring the issue through this lens offers a solution-focused approach that benefits both athlete and practitioner and can help a coaching relationship flourish where it otherwise might not have been able.

Shrinking Time and Space

Athletes can now access coaching wherever they are. This limits the impact of geography by not having to rely on practitioner availability in the athlete's vicinity; they can receive coaching in any space (i.e., not having to travel to a practitioner's office to sit face-to-face), creating, in effect, a smaller world through greater accessibility (Wang et al., 2023). The ability to access a coach on a mobile device also means that travel time to meetings is now eliminated, allowing athletes to comfortably fit mental performance coaching into their schedules.

Short Coaching Intervention and Check-in Access

As most athletes will have constant access to their devices, this facilitates the ability for them to receive coaching "in the cracks"—the small moments that exist around performance. An example of this might be having a brief video or text chat with a practitioner in the car driving to a game, working through a self-paced exercise in the locker room, or engaging in a reflective activity before bed following a performance.

Integration of Technology and a Multimodal Delivery Approach

The integration of video and audio content, accompanied by interactive tasks and activities, allows for a multimodal approach to coaching and helps an athlete maintain their attention for greater durations. In addition, such approaches allow for the "gamification" of learning activities, leveraging additional elements of "edutainment" that create an enjoyable and engaging experience for them.

Challenges and Best Practices of Virtual Service Delivery

Developing Relationships with Deep Connection

The relationship between athlete and practitioner is vital to the success of any long-term coaching practice and is no different in the virtual space. Developing such a relationship requires intention and dedication to learn about the athlete through verbal and nonverbal cues. As a virtual platform can strip away observation of nonverbal cues, coaches must exercise additional diligence to ensure they fully understand the athlete. Practitioners can consider spending more time getting to know the athlete prior to specific interventions. Learning about athletes' interests away from sports develops an appreciation of the person rather than solely the athlete. Continually and deliberately learning about the athlete is vital to long-term success in the virtual space. As a cautionary note, practitioners working with younger athletes should consider how to frame questions in a way that does not sound like a parent questioning a child over dinner. Questions such as "how was your day?" or "what did you learn in school?" might only elicit perfunctory responses. It should be noted that virtual sessions may reduce the social awkwardness sometimes experienced during in-person interactions, as the screen can serve as a buffer, enabling athletes to express greater vulnerability (Suler, 2004).

Engagement

While harnessing young athletes' attention is a challenge to even the most skilled coaches, this is exacerbated when an athlete is appearing on the other side of a screen. Competing with open tabs, additional screens, and a distracting environment can make engagement a challenge for both practitioner and performer alike. To mitigate this, practitioners can consider how to set up their virtual environment to facilitate learning goals. Consider co-creating some "rules of engagement" with the athlete to ensure they stay on task throughout the session (e.g., turning off notifications). This practice can foster a greater sense of ownership and adherence to the rules from the athlete, rather than top-down instruction from the coach (Martens, 2012). Additionally, this conversation can be woven into the exploration of performance distractors for the athlete, providing insight into potential future work on the topic of attention, while simultaneously fostering a distraction-free learning environment.

Furthermore, practitioners can consider the integration of video, online activities and games, and virtual whiteboard collaboration alongside the more traditional use of discussion-based and PowerPoint-style delivery to continually renew and refresh the attention of the athlete throughout the session. It would be prudent for practitioners to stay up to date on technological advancements to enhance the learning experience. This might eventually include biofeedback or neurofeedback and virtual or augmented reality. However, technology integration should always seek to enhance the learning experience with purpose, not simply because it is fashionable.

The Virtual Product

Many lessons were learned during our communal "field experiment" of taking IMG Academy mental performance sessions online, and a greater understanding of what constitutes best practices for this context was reached via deliberate and intentional programming with some trial and error. As a result, IMG Academy+ was born, allowing athletes to access virtual mental performance coaching anytime, anywhere. At the time of writing, the IMG Academy+ platform has three elements to it: one-on-one coaching, one-to-many hybrid group coaching, and fully asynchronous learning. The one-on-one coaching prioritizes the person-to-person interaction that is the foundation of an effective consulting relationship (Lurey & Mahesh, 2001). Alternatively, the one-to-many hybrid group coaching solution was the closest form of interaction to established practices at IMG Academy, where one coach facilitates a session to a team or group of athletes. This provided the added benefit of social learning and social support. Additionally, to leverage the accessibility of remote coaching, both synchronous (everyone joining at the same time) and asynchronous sessions (athletes logging on at their own convenience) were included. With access and convenience in mind, a third virtual coaching option was offered: a fully asynchronous learning solution utilizing a custom-engineered phone application with self-paced learning content. This not only fostered greater accessibility to learners but also created the best option to leverage technology, multimodal delivery, and gamification in the learning process.

Future Directions

Virtual coaching will continue to be leveraged to enhance learning, access coaching, and spread the availability of mental performance sessions to a larger audience. While technology and creative delivery solutions will inevitably evolve, the advantages and challenges will be necessary considerations in the planning, execution, and effectiveness of applied mental performance in a smaller, virtual world.

IN-PERSON AND REMOTE CONSULTING IN SPORT PSYCHOLOGY: KEY DEBATES AND PERSONAL INSIGHTS

Violetta Oblinger-Peters & Ulla Geifes

It is the evening before the Olympic semifinals, when doubts start to creep in: What if she doesn't make it? Four years of preparation, her whole career, all for this moment. To clear her mind, the

athlete strolls through the Olympic Village and decides to video call her sport psychologist. Sitting by her nation's house, surrounded by the bustle of the Games, she opens her laptop and soon looks into the familiar face, which although miles away, feels comfortingly close. Reassured of what she set out to do on the Olympic stage, she ends the call, ready to chase her lifelong dream the next day.

This case example from our practice illustrates how remote consulting has become a common mode of service delivery in applied sport psychology, a shift accelerated by the COVID-19 pandemic (e.g., Oblinger-Peters, 2023). Yet, while many publications provide guidance for sport psychology practitioners (e.g., Bird & Harris, 2019), the rapid pace of digitalization makes it difficult to keep up with the evolving landscape in which applied sport psychology takes place. In this chapter, we focus on enduring parameters of in-person and remote consulting by attending to interpersonal aspects affecting how we can effectively work with our clients. Importantly, we observe that discussions in the sport psychology community are often framed around "either/or" poles, where one almost feels compelled to choose one side over the other. To stimulate a more fruitful dialogue, we hence present our (sometimes divergent) perspectives through two key debates that are currently shaping the discourse in our field. Our perspectives are rooted in our own practice, working with athletes and coaches from junior to Olympic levels, mainly in a one-to-one setting. While I (Ulla) conduct sessions with clients primarily face-to-face, I (Violetta) now deliver the majority of my consulting online. However, we both occasionally accompany clients to competitions and training camps in-person.

Key Debate 1: Boundarylessness of the Online Format

Practitioners' reservations regarding online services are often rooted in the idea that their clients may expect constant availability, while advocates emphasize the flexibility of the remote setting (Price et al., 2020).

Ulla: In my practice, I have never found availability and blurry boundaries to be an issue. Perhaps this is because all my clients initially worked with me in an in-person setting, where the parameters of practice (e.g., cancellation policy) are clearly determined. I view remote consulting as an extension of my in-person services, with similar but adaptable rules adjusted to the client's needs. For instance, I aim to schedule in-person sessions within three days of a request, and online sessions within one. For me, the key is not 24/7 availability but ensuring my clients understand that, while the rules might seem strict and somewhat insensitive, they clearly demarcate the area of practice. Precise rules (e.g., response times) are crucial for both me and my clients to establish a sense of stability and trust. As in sport, our clients need to understand the playing field if we want them to take responsibility for their own actions within its boundaries.

Violetta: Many of my clients travel for most of the year. It is only through remote counseling that I can "follow" them wherever they go and have continuity in our sessions. My practice is characterized by sessions that are tailored to the individual client's needs, such as quick check-ins before a race, debriefs at the competition venue, or evening sessions when the day's training has finished and the client has had time to recover. My youth athlete clients prefer the online setting, as their busy daily schedules prevent them from coming to see me in person. In my view, the continuity of the contact and the closeness this creates is the biggest advantage of technologically mediated service provision. In my case, it also enabled me to provide ongoing support to my clients competing in the Paris 2024 Games. The limited number of accreditations for staff at the Olympic Games meant that access to the field of play (training and competition venues) and the Olympic Village was very limited. Subsequently and paradoxically, athletes are often unable to work with their own practitioners during this important event. Connecting online, however, allowed my clients to maintain regular and flexible contact with me over the course of the Games, which would not have been feasible with an exclusive in-person approach.

Key Debate 2: In-Person is the Supreme Approach and Remote is Only Second-Best

In discussions among colleagues, the traditional face-to-face format is often portrayed as superior to the technology-mediated online setting. This is because the latter is generally associated with lower effectiveness and an inferior working alliance between practitioner and client while, as some argue, the former provides a more comprehensive or even the only genuine understanding of the client as a human being.

Ulla: My preference lies with face-to-face counseling because it feels more natural to me; I attribute this to my origins in non-sport clinical work in the hospital setting. Yet for some clients whom I see in both settings, I experience the online format as particularly helpful because these clients take the opportunity to reposition themselves or turn the camera so that I cannot establish eye contact or even see them when they address highly personal and sensitive issues. It seems to me that they explicitly seek out the "natural sense of anonymity" (Harris & Birnbaum, 2015, p. 134), often listed as a key benefit of the technology-mediated setting, as it can promote psychological safety, disinhibition, and self-disclosure (Suler, 2010).

Violetta: Many of my current clients started working with me when COVID-19 restrictions limited direct interpersonal contact. Today, although I offer both consulting formats, these clients predominantly choose the online setting for a variety of reasons (i.e. pragmatic, e.g., less travel; and psychological, e.g., feeling more comfortable and secure in their own home when disclosing difficult concerns). A closer look at the literature reveals that, contrary to the widespread reservation that online service delivery is less effective, the evidence is mixed at best (e.g., Price et al., 2020). I interpret my clients' choice as proof that we have successfully established a trusting relationship, and many of the hypothesized benefits specific to technology-mediated contact, such as less experienced vulnerability and shame among clients (Harris & Birnbaum, 2015), are part of my lived experience of delivering sport psychology services online.

Ulla: At the start of a collaboration, I find the in-person approach diagnostically more revealing. This is because it allows me to observe how my clients behave and interact in novel, unfamiliar, and for many of them, stressful situations. For me, the start mirrors challenges which they also face in their (sport) lives. Hence, I interpret how they engage in our therapeutic encounter as prototypical for how they would respond to similar demands in their sport. Unlike online sessions, where clients can more easily manage how they present themselves, I feel that in-person interactions offer a "rawer," less embellished, and ultimately holistic picture of clients.

Violetta: The Paris Olympics was a challenging experience for me as a practitioner. Although my clients specifically chose not to meet with me in person and evaluated our work positively, for the first time, I felt insufficiently connected and struggled to get a full picture of what was happening for them in the buzz of the Games. This has made me aware that it might be more the practitioner's desire to meet with clients in-person at important events rather than the clients' desire, and that we must be self-reflective enough not to project our needs onto our clients. Importantly, the in-person setting does not inherently guarantee a true encounter between practitioner and client. In the existential view from which I operate in my practice, we as human beings occupy several overlapping dimensions (i.e., physical, psychological, spiritual; e.g., Frankl, 1963) and even if we can physically attend to our clients in the in-person setting, we may not be able to fully understand their issues. For example, an athlete that displays a lack of motivation and commitment before a major competition might be questioning their very meaning in sport and life (i.e., spiritual concerns). In this case, identifying the genuine issue and meeting clients where they are is more important than the setting in which consultancy takes place.

Wrapping Things Up for the Future

While the two settings are often talked about as entirely distinct approaches, in our experience, they are already blended in many colleagues' practices, and some have based much of their daily work on remote consulting already before the COVID-19 pandemic (Oblinger-Peters, 2023). As Richards and Vigano (2013, p. 1007) stated, "In spite of criticisms and skepticism coming from professionals more so than clients, there seems to have been a tacit acknowledgment that online counseling is an inevitable branching of the field." We fully agree and argue that it would be strange not to engage with the social trends of global digitalization. The question is not whether we should consult online, but how and when. Dogmatically pitting remote against in-person setting is not helpful. Instead, our profession should focus on what is best for clients and decide on a case-to-case basis, complementing services and maintaining stability through flexibility. This will help our clients become autonomous and responsible for their own choices. Simone Biles at Paris 2024 described how she had regularly practiced visualizations and consulted with her therapist online during the entirety of the Games. While the sport psychology community was thrilled to see the superstar normalize therapy and mental health issues in the Olympics, we were also pleased to see that online sport psychology services had seamlessly integrated and played an important role in her well-being routine.

EDITORS' TAKEAWAYS

Bird and Watson noted that most research on intervention efficacy has been conducted in-person. While there's no reason to assume these interventions lose effectiveness virtually, their efficacy in online settings deserves closer examination. Revisiting foundational interventions through digital platforms offers both a methodological check and an opportunity to evolve practice for contemporary demands.

Giges and Petitpas' (2000) work on Brief Contact Interventions was seminal in my (Andrew) SEPP education; being available for spontaneous connections remains central to my practice. Young and colleagues' exploration of delivering services "in the cracks" virtually provides a compelling alternative. Technology doesn't eliminate brief contact—it reframes when and how it occurs, making it more sustainable and scalable for today's practitioners.

Oblinger-Peters and Geifes note: "It might be more the practitioner's desire to meet clients in-person rather than the clients' desire, and we must be self-reflective not to project our needs onto clients." This may be the heart of the in-person versus virtual debate: ultimately, meaningful and effective client care should remain the goal, regardless of medium.

RECOMMENDED EXERCISES

1 What factors would you consider before deciding to consult with a client virtually?
2 Which clients, service types, and presenting concerns are appropriate for virtual consulting, considering your services, philosophy, and approach? Create a mode-matching matrix (4 quadrants):

   a Top left: best suited for Virtual Only
   b Top right: best suited for In-Person Only
   c Bottom left: Hybrid
   d Bottom right: Not appropriate for virtual consultation (distinct from In-Person Only)

3 Are the same outcomes achieved virtually versus in-person? How would you ensure clients benefit from remote services and navigate the constraints of distance-based consulting?
4 Brainstorm three to four challenges or ethical dilemmas in remote consultation and how you would address them.
5 Using a current client or team, map out six-month service delivery plans for:

   a Virtual-only consultation
   b In-person-only consultation
   c Hybrid consultation

   After creating the three plans, reflect and decide which approach you would choose for this client/team and why.

REFERENCES

American Psychological Association. (2013). *Guidelines for the practice of telepsychology.* https://www.apa.org/practice/guidelines/telepsychology

Association for Applied Sport Psychology. (2024). *Association for Applied Sport Psychology ethical principles and standards* (M. Zito, C. Carter, T. Herzog, M. Kerulis, A. Muscat, T. Shigeno, L. Skvarla, T. L. Chu, S. Rose, C. Wahl, & J. Watson, Eds.). https://appliedsportpsych.org/about-the-association-for-applied-sport-psychology/ethics

Bird, M. D., & Harris, B. S. (2019). The ethical use of technology for clinical and performance enhancement services: Prevalence and perceptions among association for applied sport psychology certified consultants. *Journal of Clinical Sport Psychology, 13*(1), 56–71. https://doi.org/10.1123/jcsp.2017-0034

Frankl, V. (1963). *Man's search for meaning: An introduction to logotherapy.* Pocket Books.

Giges, B., & Petitpas, A. (2000). Brief contact interventions in sport psychology. *The Sport Psychologist, 14*(2), 176-187.

Hanley, T. (2021). Researching online counselling and psychotherapy: The past, the present and the future. *Counselling and Psychotherapy Research, 21*(3), 493–497. https://doi.org/10.1002/capr.12412

Harris, B., & Birnbaum, R. (2015). Ethical and legal implications on the use of technology in counselling. *Clinical Social Work Journal, 43*(2), 133–141. https://doi.org/10.1007/s10615-014-0515-0

International Society for Sport Psychology. (2019). *The International Society of Sport Psychology (ISSP) ethical code for sport psychology practice.* https://issponline.org/wp-content/uploads/ISSP-R_Ethics_Code.pdf

Lurey, J. S., & Mahesh, S. R. (2001). An empirical study of best practices in virtual teams. *Information & Management, 38*(8), 523–544. https://doi.org/10.1016/S0378-7206(01)00074-X

Martens, R. (2012). *Successful coaching* (4th ed.). Human Kinetics.

Oblinger-Peters, V. (2023). Lessons learned: Sport psychology practitioners' experiences of working in performance sport during the COVID-19 pandemic. *Journal of Applied Sport and Exercise Psychology, 31*(1), 1–12. https://doi.org/10.1026/2941-7597/a000001

Price, D., Wagstaff, C. R. D., & Thelwell, R. C. (2020). Opportunities and considerations of new media and technology in sport psychology service delivery. *Journal of Sport Psychology in Action, 13*(1), 4–15. https://doi.org/10.1080/21520704.2020.1846648

Rees, C. S., & Stone, S. (2005). Therapeutic alliance in face-to-face versus videoconferenced psychotherapy. *Professional Psychology: Research and Practice, 36*(6), 649–653. https://doi.org/10.1037/0735-7028.36.6.649

Richards, D., & Vigano, N. (2013). Online counseling: A narrative and critical review of the literature. *Journal of Clinical Psychology, 69*(9), 994–1011. https://doi.org/10.1002/jclp.21974

Sadeghi, M. (2019). A shift from classroom to distance learning: Advantages and limitations. *International Journal of Research in English Education, 4*(1), 80–88. https://ijreeonline.com/article-1-132-en.html

Sucala, M., Schnur, J. B., Constantino, M. J., Miller, S. J., Brackman, E. H., & Montgomery, G. H. (2012). The therapeutic relationship in e-therapy for mental health: A systematic review. *Journal of Medical Internet Research, 14*(4), e110. https://doi.org/10.2196/jmir.2084

Suler, J. (2004). The online disinhibition effect. *CyberPsychology & Behavior, 7*(3), 321–326. https://doi.org/10.1089/1094931041291295

Suler, J. (2010). Interpersonal guidelines for texting. *International Journal of Applied Psychoanalytic Studies, 7*(4), 358–361. https://doi.org/10.1002/aps.268

Wang, J., Begeny, J. C., Durling, J. M., & Newson, N. K. (2023). Adapting school-based implementation support from in-person to virtual: An experimental evaluation of a virtual coaching program to improve intervention fidelity. *Psychology in the Schools, 60*(10), 3961–3978. https://doi.org/10.1002/pits.22962

Watson, J. C., II, Harris, B. S., & Baillie, P. (2020). Ethical issues impacting the profession of sport psychology. In G. Tenenbaum & R. C. Eklund (Eds.), *Handbook of sport psychology* (4th ed., pp. 751–772). Wiley.

23 Working as an Independent or Integrated SEPP Professional

Context always matters! As professionals, in any SEPP setting, we have to consider who we serve: be that individual performers, groups, or organizations. We have to be mindful and aware of the relationships, connections, hierarchies, and systemic structure that exist around or within our client's setting. However, equally important for successful service delivery is to consider where you, as the SEPP professional, are situated: Are you working independently, are you contracted by an organization or team, are you a staff member? There are many variations in how SEPP professionals provide services to clients, and this chapter will shed some light on multiple approaches, respective implications for service delivery, and benefits as well as challenges specific scenarios involve.

BENEFITS AND DRAWBACKS TO PRACTICING INDEPENDENTLY AND AS AN EMBEDDED PRACTITIONER

Adrian Ferrera, Greg Chertok, & Joanna Foss

Depending on your perspective, sport, exercise, and performance psychology (SEPP) can be full of opportunity or challenge. Part of effective consulting is determining your values as a professional and what service delivery methods feel most effective for you. One decision you will have to make is whether you would like to systemically approach your practice as an independent consultant or embedded within an organization. In this chapter, we explore this question through the lens of our experiences. We will highlight potential benefits and drawbacks from each approach to allow you to determine what approach might fit best for you.

Operating as an Independent Consultant: Greg

"You eat what you kill!" is the motto that may ring true for the independent consultant. There is no sick leave, no paid vacation, no guaranteed paycheck every two weeks, and despite this, I have found great joy and meaning from pursuing an independent consultancy. The canvas is, as it were, largely blank; you have a choice in how, where, and with whom you construct the artwork. However, constructing a beautiful masterpiece is not possible without a few challenges along the way.

Benefits of an Independent Consultancy

Much of the joy and fulfillment as an independent consultant comes from the autonomy one is able to exert over time and decision-making. Unlike working in a team or integrated

DOI: 10.4324/9781003781479-28

setting, in which many of your professional decisions may be dictated by others, an independent consultant has the luxury to create one's own hours, decide where to invest time and attention, and determine compensation based on perceived value. An independent consultant can be involved in virtually anything—podcasts, writing books, working with various populations—without asking for an employer's permission. There are far fewer organizational politics to maneuver, less role ambiguity to unfurl, and no power hierarchies to navigate.

Another benefit of an independent consultancy is the flexibility to consult across a wide range of sports, teams, levels, and cultures. Addressing an extensive array of topics and supporting a diverse set of clients not only helps the consultant gain a broader perspective but also sustains motivation. Anything done in metronomic regularity may eventually become stale, and the varied exposure and experience an independent consultant gains can stave this off.

An additional benefit can be from the opportunities that blossom entrepreneurially. As an independent consultant, there is immense scope for growth and personal branding. Each new pursuit grants the opportunity to build new connections with other individuals and create new networking branches for future referrals (and therefore create multiple different teams).

Potential Drawbacks of an Independent Consultancy

Several drawbacks exist in the space of practicing independently. Firstly, the sword of autonomy has a clear double edge. With autonomy comes the daunting task of creating a sustainable business, likely by someone who did not receive much schooling on the art of business creation. "On one's own" often means a lack of regular peer support and mentorship, and dealing with possible ethical blind spots without a reflective network. To address this, many independent consultants have to intentionally reflect on their experiences, learn from their mistakes, and rely heavily on feedback from clients, which is not always plentiful. "On one's own" also means the onus of spreading the word about you and your service to the greater community falls on your shoulders. Many smart, driven, high-performing individuals cannot move past the discomfort of promoting themselves at the subsequent disservice to their practice. Instability is an initial natural byproduct of this struggle. Income may be irregular, especially early in one's career, which can lead to a "pressing" of sorts. The financial struggle—coupled with little to no institutional support for administration, marketing, or professional development—can discourage even the most resilient new practitioners.

As an external independent consultant, access to key stakeholders (e.g., sport science staff) may be severely limited, and insights from these populations is often critical in delivering effective work. Being external also means not always being present for day-to-day interactions, which may deprive the consultant of valuable observations—informal cues, locker room banter, or subtle changes in athletes' demeanor or mood. Relentlessly pursuing regular, informative discussions with members of the team then becomes critical.

Working within an Integrated Performance Team: Joanna

While some practitioners might prefer independent practice, you might find yourself interested in being embedded within an organization as part of the integrated performance team (IPT). This positioning allows you to be immersed in team culture and readily observe the nuances of the organization of which you are a part. The goal of an IPT is to approach service delivery from a multidisciplinary approach to make informed decisions toward optimizing performance. Members of an IPT could include: athletic trainers, physical therapists, team physicians, sport scientists, strength and conditioning, certified mental performance consultants, sport psychologists, and psychiatrists (McCalla & Fitzpatrick, 2016; Burns & Collins, 2023).

Benefits of an Integrated Performance Team

One of the primary benefits of being part of an IPT is the opportunity for collaboration and shared decision-making related to athlete health and team performance (Burns & Collins, 2023). Being a part of this team allows the consultant to develop strong working relationships with other members, gain a well-rounded picture of factors impacting the athlete, streamline access to multidisciplinary care, and make higher-quality decisions given the increased depth of information about the athlete. When these teams are functioning effectively, professionals have clear, effective communication, recognize the value of each team member, and work collectively toward mutual goals (McCalla & Fitzpatrick, 2016).

Another benefit of being part of the IPT is having a seat at the table when decisions are being made and normalizing factoring mental performance into decision-making. Additionally, athletes and staff may become more comfortable in talking to you as you become integrated within the team or organization, given there are more avenues to get to know you as a person and as a consultant. This increasing trust and respect can lead to the development of many impactful and meaningful relationships.

Potential Drawbacks of an Integrated Performance Team

There are also some potential drawbacks of being on an IPT of which you should be mindful. First and foremost, it is important to understand that, at an individual level, some athletes might have more difficulty trusting or being vulnerable with "in-house" providers. Athletes might prefer to meet with someone outside of the organization entirely because that makes it easier for them to use the mental health and performance spaces effectively. Having referral systems in place for independent mental performance and mental health practitioners, and ensuring athletes are aware that it is an option you are able to help them pursue, is helpful in building trust with athletes who prefer outside providers.

It is also recommended that you consider the political, micropolitical, and cultural factors within an organization and the high-performance team within that organization. Each IPT member has a goal of improving performance; however, each person also has their own personal goals that might be in conflict with your vision or goals as a sport psychology professional (Cruickshank et al., 2013). Being intentional about exposure and training in organizational dynamics can help you build up this skillset (McCalla & Fitzpatrick, 2016).

Finally, as part of the IPT, you need to consistently be mindful of your ethical obligations to your clients. The burden of holding to your respective ethics code is on you as the practitioner, and there might be times where you need to navigate difficult or complex ethical scenarios as part of the system. Common ethical concerns to arise include (but are not limited to): confidentiality and its limits, competence, boundaries and multiple relationships, and title usage (Sharp et al., 2021; Watson et al., 2017, 2020).

Conclusion

There is no one "right" way to approach consulting; how you approach your work may evolve over time as you advance your career. For example, I (Adrian) shifted over my career from integrated to independent and then back into an integrated setting. Both approaches provide opportunities for professional fulfillment. However, you must balance each approach's unique demands such as having less systemic information operating independently, whereas you might need to manage the challenge of balancing information from multiple competing sources in an integrated setting. Independent consulting does offer increased autonomy over your decisions, while being part of a team can foster collaborative decision-making. Overall, there are benefits and pitfalls to either working environment. As a professional in the field, it is your responsibility to find or create the environment that allows you to thrive and serve your clients. Whichever you choose, operate ethically with integrity and in a manner that allows the field to continuously expand.

FULLY INDEPENDENT OR FULLY INTEGRATED? FINDING THE SWEET SPOT FOR PRACTICING SPORT PSYCHOLOGY IN HIGH-PERFORMANCE SETTINGS

Grzegorz M. Więcław & Natalia Pawelska

In this chapter, we will—from a Polish perspective—examine professional practices of psychological consulting in high-performance environments. We will explore different collaboration setups to work with athletes along a continuum—from fully independent to integrated into a performance support team. We will discuss potential benefits, downsides, and ethical considerations.

Types of Collaboration Setups, and Similarities and Differences

Collaboration with a sport psychologist can begin as a one-on-one partnership between the athlete and the psychologist or it might be initiated within an organization. In both cases, the collaboration can be expanded to include other key individuals who will contribute to the athlete's development and performance. Factors that might influence the setup include previous experiences of both the employer and the psychologist, the interest and willingness of key actors (e.g., general manager, head coach, board members), the psychologist's philosophy of practice, finances, and the timeline. Depending on who initiates the collaboration, who finances the service, and who is informed and involved in the process, the sport psychologist's work may present various challenges, including issues of confidentiality and potential conflicts of interest (see Table 23.1).

The most significant similarity across all collaboration setups we have experienced in Poland is the sport psychologist's philosophy, knowledge, and values that form the foundation of their work. In any context, whether the collaboration is independent or integrated, the core values and ethical principles should remain consistent to ensure effective and rewarding cooperation. Additionally, regardless of the type of collaboration, it is essential to identify who the client is and prioritize their well-being and interests.

Differences in collaboration setups can be found in how services are financed. In independent setups, psychologists typically have predefined rates for specific services (e.g., consultations, presence at training sessions or competitions, preparation of materials). In integrated setups, the scope of responsibilities and rates for these services are negotiated with the organization employing or contracting the psychologist. In the Polish context, when working with a national team, where funding mostly comes from the Ministry of Sport and Tourism, certain predetermined price ranges apply for a day at a training camp/competition or for a

Table 23.1 Types of Collaborations and Considerations

Consultation without coach, support staff, and federation knowledge.	The athlete or parents of a minor athlete initiate and pay; it is fully confidential, only the athlete and parents of a minor athlete know about the process, confidentiality is respected when in contact with parents, and there can be a potential mismatch of athlete's goals with parent's goals for the collaboration.
Consultation with some key actors' (e.g., coach) knowledge, while the athlete pays for the service.	The athlete, parents of a minor athlete, or key actor (e.g., coach) may initiate, while the athlete or the parents pay for the service. The parents of a minor athlete or key actor(s) are informed and involved with the athlete's consent but know only what the athlete permits, and there can be potential pressures from parents or coaches based on their goals and agenda, confidentiality issues (i.e., what is okay to disclose?), and additional information that the psychologist cannot use because they don't have permission.
Consultation with/ or without some key actors' (e.g., coach) knowledge, while the service is paid for by the federation or sponsor.	The athlete, parents of a minor athlete, federation, or sponsor may initiate, while the federation or sponsor pays for the service. The parents of a minor athlete and key actors are informed with the athlete's consent, the federation or sponsor knows about it, the federation or sponsor may have additional requests (e.g., reports on progress or contact with coach), and there can be potential pressures from parents, coaches and/or the federation based on their goals and agenda, confidentiality issues (i.e., what is okay to disclose?), and some reporting might be necessary due to formal constraints.
Consultation for the federation, without any collaboration.	The athlete or federation may initiate, while the federation pays. The federation knows about it, only basic information might be shared with the federation though sometimes they require the coach's consent for cooperation, and there can be potential pressures from the federation based on their goals and agenda vs. the athlete's personal needs.
Consultation for the federation in collaboration with coaches and support staff.	The federation, athlete, or coaches/staff may initiate, while the federation pays. The federation, coaches, and support staff are informed and involved, some information is shared with all involved parties and thus there is a need to clarify the boundaries and gain the athlete's consent on which information might be shared, and there can be potential conflicts between the athlete's privacy and collaborative goals.

month of collaboration (in 2026 it is up to 500 PLN/day). A sports federation may increase a psychologist's remuneration by utilizing other funding sources, such as sponsorship money.

Another difference is the issue of reporting—who information may be shared with, what kind of information, and in what form (verbal vs. written). In independent work, our source of knowledge and primary point of contact is usually limited to the athlete or, in case of a minor, their parents. However, when working within an organization, we have access to a broader range of information, though its use may be restricted by lack of consent from all parties involved. One must be aware and navigate the fact that in independent collaborations, there is typically one person who serves as both the client and the payer. In integrated setups, multiple key actors require the psychologist to establish a solid contract/informed consent and ensure its terms are adhered to by all parties, including themselves.

Advantages and Limitations of Collaboration Setups

Working as a psychologist with high-performance athletes and coaches provides evident advantages and limitations for both independent (see Table 23.2) and integrated (see Table 23.3) collaborations.

Table 23.2 Advantages and Limitations of Independent Consulting

Advantages	*Limitations*
• Full autonomy, working on one's own terms • Flexibility in planning the process • Potentially better financial terms • Easier on ethical dilemmas	• Lack of knowledge and/or perspective about client's environment • Difficulty in verifying effectiveness of the interventions

Table 23.3 Advantages and Limitations of Integrated Consulting

Advantages	*Limitations*
• Easier chance to watch the client in everyday situations as well as during training and competition • Opportunity of getting a second opinion from another support staff member (physiotherapist, coach) or even a teammate	• More rigid consulting structure, depending on finances, logistics, etc. • Struggle to find the right place for consultation • Pressures to disclose information • Pressures to work on goals of other parties other than the athlete • Potential confusion between the client and the payer

Ethical Challenges and Final Considerations

Working in this profession gives a unique opportunity to work in and out of the office, which brings to life many ethical considerations. It might be especially true in Polish organizations where sport psychologists historically have not been standard staff members. Working outside the office gives practitioners additional information about the client's environment, a chance to monitor progress on mental training in real life scenarios, and the ability to provide support where it is most needed.

Thus, one of the most important ethical challenges for the sport psychologists integrated into their organizational structures is considering how to manage information in order to serve and protect often the most vulnerable parts of this system—athletes themselves. It is like walking on thin ice keeping the confidentiality of the information gained in the process of consultation with athletes and at the same time proving useful to other members of the team—coaches, medical staff, and managers. In order to do that, it is crucial to carefully craft and maintain rules and boundaries about professional conduct as a psychologist, especially in the eyes of key leadership figures in the organization—coaches, doctors, directors, and managers. At the same time, we must remember that we are often employed by these people in order to improve the performance of the athlete, team, or the organization as a whole. Therefore, some information might be considered for a release with athletes' consent and/or based on field observations. From our practical experiences in Poland, sticking to one's role might be easier when it is well-defined and communicated to everybody in the organization, including tasks, responsibilities, and ethical boundaries. It is also a good practice to discuss current ethical issues with a supervisor and/or sport psychology colleague to gain a better perspective on one's own decisions and actions.

All in all, the sport environment provides psychologists integrated into the structures of teams and organizations with many potential ethical grey zones to be considered. Each one of them will depend on the individual case, most likely on practicing philosophy of the psychologist, and demands from the employing organization.

FROM NOWHERE MAN TO GETTING BY WITH A LITTLE HELP FROM MY FRIENDS

Rich Gordin

My career in applied sport psychology started over 45 years ago when I decided to pursue a doctoral degree in the psychosocial aspects of sport. During that time period, I was able to consult in several contexts including individually and in a performance team consulting setting (Gordin, 2021). I was fortunate to have the opportunity to cooperate with a university artistic gymnastics team while I was pursuing my degree. In 1978, there were very few practicing applied sport psychology consultants in North America. Consequently, those of us who were consulting were self-taught. The gymnastics coach at my doctoral university was very interested and supportive of the psychological aspects of sport. I recruited female athletes as participants for my dissertation research; therefore, I asked each coach of a female team for permission to include their athletes in my study. All nine of the gymnasts volunteered to be in my research pool, and after the study concluded, the coach asked me to provide service delivery to his entire team. As you might expect, the support of the coach, in this instance, was crucial to the success of my delivery system. However, a consultant must also gain the support of the athletes.

The success of any consultation is driven by trust. Trust can be established in two ways: (1) the hiring team would like you to provide services that will be perceived as useful in improving performance, and (2) the provider should establish a trusting relationship with both the athletes and the coach. Trust can be earned by being available, providing meaningful and useful information, being respectful of the invitation to provide services, and doing what is necessary when it is needed. Consultants must also learn the technical aspects of the sport and all the nuances in a reasonable amount of time. It is important to speak the language of that sport and to understand the challenges as well. In gymnastics, athletes must negotiate a four-inch-wide balance beam with precision and athleticism. Most gymnastics competitions are decided on the balance beam. I had never been on a balance beam, but I needed to understand the difficulties associated with performance on that apparatus. It is important that the athlete believes that you understand these demands.

My consultations in the early part of my career were individually provided. My interactions were restricted to the coach, the athletes, and very few others. One medical provider that I found helpful, in these early years, was the team athletic trainer. The reason the trainer was so vital in gaining access to the team was that he had already established a relationship with the athletes. During these early years of my consulting practice, I had an excellent referral network to handle situations that I was not qualified to take on or was reluctant to pursue. For instance, if I had an athlete who presented with a clinical issue, I would refer them to a qualified colleague for help. In my later years, I was often paired on assignments with a clinically trained colleague to assist me with clinical cases.

My next significant consultation occurred at the national level. I attended the USA Gymnastics Championship in St. Louis in the early 1980s. I was invited to this event because of my connections with the gymnastics coaching staff at my doctoral university. The first person I sought out at the event was the national team athletic trainer. This trainer worked with the US team for many years and was trusted by all. I introduced myself and explained the services

I could provide to the national team in applied sport psychology. The trainer then introduced me to several coaches, and some were quite interested in my service provision. Likewise, I met others in attendance, who were the decision makers in that National Governing Body (NGB). Since the technology did not exist to market your services, initial entry points were conducted in person which required significant travel and time demands. Consequently, I was invited to speak at the USA Gymnastics national convention that year where I gained more exposure to the athletes and coaches. Although I would like to imply this was a smooth process, it proved difficult. Consultants should show genuine interest and commitment to the organization to remain employed within the governing body. This pathway of working alone can be lonely at times, therefore it is important to develop a cohort of colleagues to provide support and answer any questions or concerns you have regarding your service provision. I established a group of reliable and valued friends, early in my career. These colleagues still play an invaluable role for me in my professional life.

Also in the 1980s, I was invited into a consultation with the USA Track and Field NGB. The group of applied consultants consisted of Gloria Balague, Keith Henschen, Rick McGuire, Ralph Vernacchia, Jim Reardon, and me. We developed a philosophy of service delivery that we all agreed to follow. The philosophy included that our mission is about service to the athlete not self-service, it is about athlete development, not just elite level performance, and we are more educationally than clinically oriented. Although we were trained differently, we all presented a uniform approach to service delivery. We mentored each other and we allocated labor according to the demands appropriately. We provided service in various ways including speaking at national conventions, developing a coaching certification curriculum, and presenting at coaching clinics. Also, we attended and provided service at national training camps, junior development camps, and any other requested services by coaches and athletes. We presented together to develop rapport in teams so that the athletes and coaches could see our differences as well as our similarities. By doing so, we integrated ourselves into the organization by demonstrating commitment. Only after such integration did we provide our services at World Championships and the Olympic Games. While at those events, I was always accompanied by a colleague for support and comradery. It was also necessary to provide two practitioners due to the size of the delegation in track and field. It was not uncommon to have a delegation of 125 athletes and support staff including the team physicians, athletic trainers, massage therapists, chiropractors, physiotherapists in addition to the coaching staff and team managers. The advantage I found of having colleagues with me was the ability to have nightly debriefings and to provide the needed services in a timely manner. Olympic venues are often spread out geographically and having two providers was more efficient. Also, we were part of the medical staff reporting to the head team physician and we were able to coordinate care among a wide variety of service providers and make appropriate referrals when needed.

On other Olympic Games staffs, I was the only consultant due to the lack of credentials provided by the NGB. While still reporting and coordinating with the medical staff, it was difficult to have similar communication advantages. I have roomed with the Chief Medical Officers; however, because of our various schedules and duties it was difficult to communicate efficiently. I have been assigned to accompany athletes to drug testing, cleaned ice baths, and run various errands for other staff members; however, when you are the singular consultant, it can be difficult to be in places where you are always needed. The key to successful consultations is to do good work. Moreover, when working with a group of colleagues it is important to practice team building. During one Olympic experience, the coaching staff met in Houston prior to the Games for the sole purpose of developing a team approach to our efforts. My colleague and I decided to create a team code of conduct for the Games, with the help of the coaching staff. We then laminated this code on cards and distributed them to the staff. It worked well as many posted these laminated wallet sized cards on their doors in the Olympic Village or carried the card for the duration of the Games. During times of turmoil or disagreement, these cards served as a reminder and many times helped diffuse a potentially volatile situation.

Finally, near the end of my career, I am again working independently in professional golf. In professional sport, I have found that it is more efficient to do so and still provide the best service delivery environment for the athletes. Of course, I cooperate with the technical coach, the caddie, and others to keep a consistent working environment. However, my consultations are exclusively with the athlete. I am cordial with others, such as the agent, but maintaining confidentiality is essential to my working relationship. Compared to the Olympics, professional sport is a completely different context in which to work. Understanding the best working environment, whether it is alone or in cooperation with others, is essential to success. The consultant should master the ability to operate in a system that is business-like and realize that one can be fired if violations occur in this setting.

My experiences over a 45-year period have provided me with opportunities to work individually and to work in integrated working settings. While there is a certain amount of autonomy while working alone, the team approach offers many advantages that I have mentioned. Both situations offer pros and cons, which have been elucidated by other practitioners in this chapter. I hope the experiences that I have shared with you have provided a way for you to consider either structure for consultation. I wish you a successful career.

EDITORS' TAKEAWAYS

Ferrera and colleagues raise a valuable point about how some athletes may prefer to work with a practitioner outside of the in-house integrated performance team—something we are seeing more frequently in professional sport. While it is widely accepted that "fit" plays a crucial role in building a strong working alliance, in organizational settings, there is often an element of "forced pairing." For practitioners embedded within professional organizations, we would be curious to hear how they navigate these delicate dynamics and manage situations where that ideal fit may not naturally exist. This is not something that is explicitly mentioned in Więcław and Pawelska's overview of the advantages and disadvantages of working independently and as integrated in a system. And indeed, the principle of finding a "fit" then gets expanded with a discussion about who the SEPP is fitting with? What if the SEPP fits well with the coach, but not the athlete? Or with the athlete but not the governing administrator? This invites us to consider "fit" not as a single dyadic match, but as a shifting constellation of relationships that practitioners must continually and skillfully navigate, such as what was nicely exemplified by Gordin's contribution.

RECOMMENDED EXERCISES

1 Reflect on collaboration setups in your practice:
   a Who initiates the collaboration? Who funds it? Who is involved? What potential confidentiality issues or conflicts of interest exist?
   b How much can you influence the setup based on your philosophy, values, ethics, and negotiation skills?
   c How might you negotiate your next contract differently, and why?

2 Consider past group experiences:

   a What influenced group dynamics and your experience as a member?
   b What strengths and weaknesses did you show?
   c What have these experiences taught you about your preferences for operating as an independent versus integrated SEPP professional?

3 Which role—independent or integrated—aligns better with your values, skills, and career goals, and why?
4 Imagine being hired as an independent consultant for a professional team with coach-athlete communication issues, what steps would you take to build trust and establish your role? Now, imagine being embedded as an integrated consultant, how would your approach differ? What opportunities or limitations would this present?
5 How would your communication and relationship-building strategies need to adapt depending on whether you are independent or integrated?

REFERENCES

Burns, A., & Collins, D. (2023). Interdisciplinary practice in performance sport: A scoping review of evidence of collaboration. *European Journal of Sport Science, 23*(9), 1877–1891. https://doi.org/10.1080/17461391.2023.2201812

Cruickshank, A., Collins, D., & Minten, S. (2013). Culture change in a professional sports team: Shaping environmental contexts and regulating power. *International Journal of Sports Science & Coaching, 8*(2), 271–290. https://doi.org/10.1260/1747-9541.8.2.271

Gordin, R. (2021). Rich Gordin. In A. Poczwardowski & M. Aoyagi (Eds.), *Expert approaches to sport psychology: Applied theories of performance excellence* (2nd ed., pp. 85–96). Fitness Information Technology.

McCalla, T., & Fitzpatrick, S. (2016). Integrating sport psychology within a high-performance team: Potential stakeholders, micropolitics, and culture. *Journal of Sport Psychology in Action, 7*(1), 33–42. https://doi.org/10.1080/21520704.2015.1123208

Sharp, L. A., Hodge, K., & Danish, S. (2021). "I wouldn't want to operate without it": The ethical challenges faced by experienced sport psychology consultants and their engagement with supervision. *Journal of Applied Sport Psychology, 33*(3), 259–279. https://doi.org/10.1080/10413200.2019.1646838

Watson, J. C., II, Harris, B. S., & Baillie, P. (2020). Ethical issues impacting the profession of sport psychology. In G. Tenenbaum, R. C. Eklund, & N. Boiangin (Eds.), *Handbook of sport psychology: Social perspectives, cognition, and applications* (4th ed., pp. 751–772). John Wiley & Sons. https://doi.org/10.1002/9781119568124.ch36

Watson, J. C., II, Way, W. C., & Hilliard, R. C. (2017). Ethical issues in sport psychology. *Current Opinion in Psychology, 16*, 143–147. https://doi.org/10.1016/j.copsyc.2017.05.008

24 Demonstrating a Return on Investment of SEPP Practice

One of the challenges SEPPPs face in their applied work is certainly showing that their work makes a difference. Does our work actually impact and help improve performance? How do we operationalize our work, and what respective outcome and performance measures demonstrate our impact? Questions that aren't easy to answer. I (Sebastian) remember vividly my first meeting with a head coach, whose team was considering contracting with me. He wanted several questions answered first. What added benefit will you bring to the program? How will the team benefit from us working with you? What new and valuable asset do you have to offer? I was able to convince this particular coach and we did start working together, based on a very specific idea and approach that for him would provide an added benefit and return on his team's investment of resources. Clearly, then reflecting, discussing, planning, and evaluating, if we can, as well as if we did, make an impact is important—for each SEPPP individually as well as for the field of SEPP in general.

SPORT PSYCHOLOGY INTERVENTIONS AND CORRELATES OF PERFORMANCE: A SUMMARY OF PUBLISHED META-ANALYSES

Marc Lochbaum

Sport psychology, as an academic discipline, dates back at least to Carl Friedrich Koch's 1830 publication, *Calisthenics from the Viewpoint of Dietetics and Psychology* (translated). After World War II, the field grew rapidly, emerging as a recognized area of study. In the 1960s, organizations such as the *International Society for Sport Psychology* (1965), the *North American Society for the Psychology of Sport and Physical Activity* (1966), and the *European Federation of Sport Psychology* (1969) were established. These efforts were further supported by the creation of academic journals like the *International Journal of Sport Psychology* (1970) and the *Journal of Sport & Exercise Psychology* (1979), solidifying sport psychology as a distinct academic discipline.

Publications in sport psychology grew rapidly, and today they are numerous—perhaps impossible to consolidate. For example, a search conducted in October 2024 within the Web of Science Core Collection identified 6,362 publications on sport psychology, 6,995 on sport confidence, and 76,403 on mental practice. The abundance of literature can lead to confusion for both academics and practitioners regarding the relationship between sport psychology constructs or interventions and performance outcomes. Common questions include, "What works?" and "If it works, how much does it improve performance?" Summarizing key themes like confidence, flow, or mental practice is essential for better understanding these relationships.

DOI: 10.4324/9781003781479-29

Meta-Analysis Explained

Meta-analysis provides a way to summarize the vast volume of published and gray literature (e.g., conference abstracts) into concise statistical summaries, focusing on average impacts or relationships with sport performance. To guide both academics and laypeople, several sport psychology primers exist, including Martin Hagger's *Meta-Analysis* (2022). Meta-analysis involves combining quantitative or qualitative results from individual studies, identified through a systematic review, into an overall statistical analysis. This chapter highlights quantitative meta-analysis examples in sport psychology research.

The steps for conducting a meta-analysis are well-defined. Researchers begin with a specific question, such as "Does confidence improve performance?" or "What type of attentional focus is most effective for improving sport performance?" They then collect as many studies as possible from journals, databases, and credible sources that relate to this specific question. Criteria are applied to determine which studies to include, and data is extracted from each to quantify the findings. Statistical techniques are used to combine the results, often resulting in an overall effect size. Finally, researchers summarize the combined data. For example, in my coauthored confidence and sport performance meta-analysis (Lochbaum et al., 2022), we concluded that the confidence-performance relationship is small in magnitude, nearly free of bias, and moderated by factors such as sport type, performance objectivity, and athlete sex. In addition to statistical outcomes, meta-analyses identify knowledge gaps, critically appraise the state of research, reduce redundant efforts, and pinpoint moderators influencing treatment efficacy or relationships.

Sport Psychology and Performance Meta-Analyses

The first sport psychology meta-analysis was published in 1983. Feltz and Landers' study on mental practice included 98 articles dating back to 1934. Similarly, Bond and Titus' cross-disciplinary meta-analysis on social facilitation summarized 241 studies, including Triplett's often-cited 1898 study on social facilitation in cycling. Since 1983, many meta-analyses have examined sport psychology constructs (e.g., mental imagery, flow, achievement goals) and outcomes (e.g., performance, enjoyment, motivation). Performance is a primary outcome in achievement contexts like sport.

In 2022, my colleagues and I published a review of 30 meta-analyses examining common sport psychology constructs, with performance as at least one reported effect size (Lochbaum et al., 2022). This was the first comprehensive review of published meta-analyses in sport psychology with performance as a focus. Since then, I have continued researching the topic and identified nearly numerous additional meta-analyses published since our initial review or missed in our study. As of June 2025, I have cataloged 69 meta-analyses (1983–2025) covering topics such as achievement goals, anxiety, attentional focus, autonomy support, breathing techniques, cognitive functioning, cohesion, flow, goal setting, mental fatigue, mindfulness, mood, music, self-confidence, self-control, social facilitation, and stress regulation. Mental practice remains the most frequently studied topic (n = 5), with other topics such as confidence, mood, achievement goals, and cohesion receiving considerable attention (see Table 24.1 for the topics).

Questions, Interpretation, and Implications

Sport psychology and performance meta-analyses typically address one of four research questions, based on the following designs:

Table 24.1 Meta-Analyses with Participants Identified as Athletes with Sport Performance Outcomes

N	*Topics*
5	Mental practice
4	Achievement goals, Anxiety, Confidence
3	Cohesion, Mental fatigue, Mindfulness, Profile of Mood States (POMS)
2	Attentional focus, Color, Decision training, Motor cortex stimulation (tDCS), Music, Psychological interventions, Quiet eye, Self-efficacy, Self-serving attribution bias
1	Autonomy support, Biofeedback, Brain rhythms, Breathing techniques, Burnout, Coach education, Coping, Emotional intelligence, Flow, Goal setting, Home-field advantage, Interventions, Mental preparation techniques, Mental toughness, Neurofeedback training, Perceptual anticipation, Perfectionism, Personality, Pre-performance routines, Pressure training, Psychological Interventions, Self-talk, Stress regulation, Self-control

Table 24.2 LeBron James' Career Scoring with Improvement Estimates

Career Mean (SD)	*Small ES (+0.1)*	*Medium ES (+0.3)*	*Large ES (+0.5)*
28.74 (2.39)	+0.239	+0.717	+1.195

- **Intervention meta-analyses:** What is the effect of an intervention such as mindfulness on sport performance?
- **Predictive meta-analyses:** What is the relationship between pre-competition self-efficacy variables and sport performance?
- **Correlational meta-analyses:** What is the cross-sectional relationship between flow and self-reported performance in competitive athletes?
- **Group difference meta-analyses:** How do different populations, such as athletes selected for an Olympic team, differ on a construct such as vigor compared to athletes not selected for the same Olympic team?

Effect size values are essential for interpreting the magnitude of observed relationships or differences, extending beyond statistical significance. They standardize comparisons across studies, enabling researchers to evaluate practical significance. Common measures include Cohen's d for mean differences and Pearson's r for correlations, with Cohen's guidelines categorizing d as small (0.2), medium (0.5), and large (0.8), and r as small (0.1), medium (0.3), and large (0.5). However, the interpretation of these values varies by context. For example, scoring one point in a tied basketball game to win the EuroLeague finals is a small numerical difference but a monumental accomplishment. Conversely, even a large effect in a 400 m race may be negligible if the winner finishes seconds ahead of the runner-up.

Though estimating the impact of mental skills on performance against competitors is complex, practitioners can calculate within-individual effects. For example, consider LeBron James' 20-year career for points per 40 minutes. By multiplying the effect size by the standard deviation of points per 40 minutes, one can estimate potential improvements (see Table 24.2). A large effect size could raise his career average from 28.74 to 29.93 points per 40 minutes, illustrating how consistent players might benefit from mental techniques.

In conclusion, sport psychology has evolved into a robust academic discipline with a vast body of literature, including numerous meta-analyses exploring the relationship between psychological constructs and performance. By synthesizing findings through meta-analytic methods, researchers can provide clear, evidence-based insights into what works and the practical significance of interventions. While the interpretation of effect sizes varies across contexts, examples like LeBron James' scoring data demonstrate the utility of these measures in understanding individual and group performance improvements.

ASSESSING CONSULTING EFFECTIVENESS: DEMONSTRATING IMPACT AND RETURN ON INVESTMENT

Elmer A. Castillo

Due to the complex nature of applied sport psychology, a consistent definition of consultant effectiveness is imperative, yet elusive. According to Anderson and colleagues (2002), "consultant effectiveness" refers to the quality of applied services that consultants deliver to their clients. Cropley and fellow contributors (2007) added that consultant effectiveness entails the application of psychological theories, principles, and techniques to achieve stated goals and promote behavioral change in clients. The hallmark of quality work is how well clients can apply the knowledge and skills provided to them so as to improve their mental capacities, increase enjoyment, and optimize performance. Despite its obvious value, the notion of assessing consultant effectiveness is not common practice nor is it well established as a research area in the sport, exercise, and performance psychology (SEPP) field (Castillo, 2024). Paradoxically, the topic has been described as a pressing need and as a significant professional practice issue within the field. More recently, authors have noted that in spite of the limited knowledge base on consultant effectiveness, the topic requires closer examination to inform effective practice and advance the field (Gonzalez et al., 2017).

Although the literature base has not kept up with the pressing need to critically examine program and consultant effectiveness, evaluating consultant effectiveness has clear benefits that bolster professional practice and promote accountability. For instance, assessing consultant effectiveness enhances understanding of the wide array of applied sport psychology service delivery factors that might contribute to successful outcomes and robust working relationships. With increased accountability stemming from the SEPP field evolving toward professional status, mental performance consultants (MPCs) should strive to evaluate and document their effectiveness for both personal and public reasons.

Broad indicators of consultant effectiveness include (a) quality of support, (b) acquisition of mental skills that increase well-being, (c) athlete responses to services (attitude, perceptions, buy-in, etc.), and (d) enhanced performance based on both subjective and objective measures (Anderson et al., 2002). While there is no gold standard in assessing consultant effectiveness, MPCs can utilize formal methods (e.g., established standardized inventories, customized self-report surveys, direct client feedback), informal methods (e.g., collegial feedback, self-reflection, case notes, client performance journals), process approaches (i.e., adopting a case-study approach), or modified frameworks for assessing levels of client learning to measure their effectiveness across the aforementioned areas. Standardized feedback forms such as the Consultant Evaluation Form (CEF; Partington & Orlick, 1987a) and the CEF-revised (Haberl & McCann, 2012) can be useful tools for assessing quality of support.

Although several authors have previously endorsed the use of the performance profile (PP) as a useful method of determining consultant effectiveness, these recommendations have been mentioned without a clear description as to how this could happen and what it would look like in practice. To this end, Castillo (2024) introduced a novel and formal method of using the PP as a viable option for MPC evaluation. While the PP literature highlights client-facing uses and benefits, the author outlined a practitioner-focused use of leveraging the popular procedure. Aside from using the PP to monitor psychological skills acquisition over time, MPCs can leverage the technique to appraise the quality of the working alliance and its impact on client success as well as to gain insight into their current consulting skillset to identify professional strengths and growth edges.

Through a detailed case study, the author discussed how this emerging application involves MPCs crafting a fixed, consultant-based PP as a template from which clients can then assess them on evidence-based qualities of elite consultants. Largely based on the synopsis of effective consultant characteristics provided by Gonzalez et al. (2017), various qualities were presented in the predetermined PP, ranging across personal (e.g., likeable, respectful), social (trustworthy, discreet), and professional (e.g., knowledge, experience, professional philosophy) dimensions. In light of this latest adaptation to the widely used PP technique, the author suggested that just as MPCs seek to better understand and assess clients to promote awareness and more effective functioning, they must also be accountable to themselves by assessing the quality of their applied work to promote awareness and more effective practice.

In terms of assessing psychological skills acquisition and well-being, measurement options include direct athlete feedback, psychometric tools, and well-being scales. Quality of support and client responses to services can be measured through field observation (e.g., in training or competition), collegial feedback, and self-reflection. Collegial feedback involves assessing consultant effectiveness through peer mentoring, supervision, and feedback forums, typically through case studies, case note review, and video analysis. For self-evaluation, reflective practice is beneficial to MPCs at all levels, given that the goal is to assess effectiveness indicators, processes, and outcomes so as to promote self-discovery and continued development. Cropley and fellow contributors (2010) explored the relationship between effective and reflective practice in applied sport psychology and provided evidence that critical self-evaluation helps MPCs improve service delivery. Performance can be measured either subjectively with the client's personal judgments of performance or objectively through statistics and advanced analytics to quantify data regarding level of performance over time.

It is necessary to advance professional practice and promote professional development to demonstrate to coaches, sport administrators, and other stakeholders the return on investment that comes from applied sport psychology service delivery. As such, consultants of all ages and across all stages should prioritize measuring their effectiveness as applied practitioners as a quality assurance check and to demonstrate the return on investment (ROI) to clients and key stakeholders. Further documentation of this important area can help establish best practices and a stronger evidence-based approach to guide applied service provision.

SPC CONSULTANT EFFECTIVENESS: "HAVE WE MADE THE BOAT GO FASTER?"

Lee-Ann Sharp, Ken Hodge, & Peter Haberl

For many aspiring practitioners starting their journey into the applied sport psychology profession, the goal of working within high-performance sport can be inspiring. However, the reality of accessing these performance environments to gain experience of working with and alongside athletes and coaches is often challenging. One way that new or less experienced practitioners can increase their knowledge and experience of applied sport psychology practice is to observe or learn from more experienced sport psychology consultants (SPCs). Furthermore, "by understanding and communicating what professional decision makers do and how they do it well, we make valuable contributions both to our field and to the professional community at large" (Smith et al., 2004, p. 4).

Drawing upon their extensive research profiles and wide-ranging applied sport psychology experiences in high-performance sport environments, we aim to assist the reader in: (1) critically examining the characteristics of effective and ethical sport psychology practice, while (2) examining the why and when of monitoring and evaluation of practitioner effectiveness.

Characteristics of Effective Sport Psychology Practice

Sport psychology research focusing on practitioner effectiveness has built on the pioneering work of Orlick and Partington (1987) and Partington and Orlick (1987b), who explored the characteristics of effective practitioners working in Olympic sport. Effective practitioners were seen to be flexible, open, creative, likeable, and accessible enough to establish rapport with the athletes with whom they are working. Building on this seminal work, considerable progress has been made in identifying the characteristics and qualities necessary for effective sport psychology practice from the athlete's, practitioner, and coach's perspectives (Anderson et al., 2004; Orlick & Partington, 1987; Sharp & Hodge, 2011; Sharp et al., 2015). For example, elite British athletes reported perceiving effective SPCs to: (1) be personable, (2) provide practical advice, (3) be a good communicator, (4) be knowledgeable about sport psychology, (5) exhibit professional skills, and (6) be honest and trustworthy (Anderson et al., 2004). In addition to the above characteristics, New Zealand athletes identified the need for SPCs to be "friendly but not a friend"; demonstrating the need for the effective practitioner to be personable yet set clear boundaries for their professional practice (Sharp & Hodge, 2014). New Zealand athletes also reported that an SPC should be athlete-centered, where the effective practitioner is focused on meeting the needs of their athlete/client by providing them with individualized psychological support and practical solutions tailored to their specific individual needs, while also having experience working alongside clients in the sport environment (Sharp & Hodge, 2014).

Although it is important to be aware of what athletes/clients perceive to be essential for SPC effectiveness, it is also important to consider what SPCs themselves perceive as being important characteristics of effective practice. Practitioners involved in Sharp and Hodge's (2011) study reported that effective practitioners were able to: (1) build a connection with their client that enabled them to educate their client toward a positive change in behavior; (2) possess the ability, knowledge, and confidence to build a relationship with a client in a professional manner; and also (3) build a strong, balanced, collaborative relationship that met the individual needs of the client.

The elite sport environment is not only viewed as the pinnacle for athletes and their coaching teams, but also by those involved in the sport science support network who work closely with elite athletes in the buildup, preparation, and during these elite sport competitions (Sharp et al., 2014). Working within this unique environment can often be unpredictable and demanding and can therefore be a very personally challenging and uncomfortable place for a SPC to work within (Chandler et al., 2016). As McCann (2008) warned, one of the tests practitioners face while working at elite sport competitions/events is getting caught up in the same pressure and desperation as the athletes and coaches. It has been argued that to be effective within these environments, SPCs need to possess personal characteristics such as resilience, commitment, presence, authenticity, and empathy in order to be effective (Chandler et al., 2016). Kyndt and Rowell (2012) have argued that the difference between practitioners who are able to be effective under the "intense pressure" of high-performance sport, and those who are not, is more than simply their "technical prowess." Rather it is the practitioner's personal characteristics in addition to their technical expertise that allows them to be effective within this environment (Chandler et al., 2016).

Experienced practitioners with at least five years' experience supporting athletes at elite sport competitions reported that "the key to consulting effectiveness within the elite sports environment was to build a relationship with clients that had a positive impact and one which the client was both happy with and continued to develop" (Sharp et al., 2015, p. 86)—"ultimately it comes down to the relationship." Practitioners are perceived to have a positive impact on both the performance of the athlete and the athlete as a person. In elite environments, effective practitioners report having assessed the subculture in which they work (e.g., people, team members, support staff and management) and work hard at fitting in but not getting in the way (McCann, 2008; Sharp et al., 2015). Effective practitioners are also perceived to demonstrate consistent behavior, despite the pressures they may experience working at elite sport competitions, while balancing support provision to multiple clients (e.g., athletes, coaches, and organizational personnel).

Why and When to Monitor and Evaluate Practitioner Effectiveness

Scholar-practitioners have raised concerns regarding the need for the effective evaluation of the services provided by SPCs (e.g., Haberl & McCann, 2012; Sharp & Hodge, 2011; Sharp et al., 2014). Haberl and Sharp (2021) recently argued that practitioners should actively engage in both formal and informal evaluation of their applied practice not only to document their professional practice in order to facilitate improvement, but also to enable the practitioner to remain accountable to their clients, themselves, and their profession.

Formal assessments are planned, structured, and deliberately executed (Anderson et al., 2004). Program and outcome evaluations are typically undertaken using standardized psychometrics to monitor changes over time, and often utilized to examine if the services provided are achieving the desired outcomes (Sharp et al., 2014, 2015, 2021). Partington and Orlick (1987a) developed the Consultant Evaluation Form (CEF) specifically as a tool to evaluate client perceptions of SPC effectiveness. The CEF requires clients to evaluate the effectiveness of the practitioner across characteristics items, while also assessing the impact on the individual client and the team in which they are a member. More recently researchers have argued that practitioners should consider adapting the CEF to assess the specific work they have completed with their clients (Sharp et al., 2014). Haberl and McCann (2012) discussed the inclusion of additional questions that examined team building, practice attendance, the Olympic environment, as well as an open-ended item exploring, "what should the consultant stop doing, start doing, continue doing?" (p. 68).

Informal feedback regarding practitioner effectiveness is characteristically unplanned, unstructured, and spontaneous. Researchers have previously discussed that this can include: "Getting a casual comment from a coach (e.g., "You were very intense during the meeting"), an unexpected email from an athlete after a competition (e.g., "I implemented what we talked about, it worked great"), or a text from the General Manager after a team session (e.g., "Can you make the next two trips?) (Haberl & Sharp, 2021). Experienced practitioners have reported, "Effectiveness as a consultant is doing my job well… Being an effective consultant is a lot about identifying what it takes in that specific role and making sure I do those things more consistently and more effectively" (Sharp et al., 2014, p. 85). Through a reflective practice process, SPCs have the opportunity to explore and evaluate their practice decisions and experiences with the aim of increasing their personal understanding and management of themselves and their practice (Anderson et al., 2004).

When considering the "when" of assessment, practitioners should consider the natural points in their relationship and work with clients to conduct evaluation of the effectiveness of their practice (e.g., end of the season, end of an Olympic cycle, when a client wants feedback on services provided; Haberl & Sharp, 2021). However, we argue that effective and systematic monitoring and evaluation of one's applied practice is a career-long process, one which practitioners have an ethical and professional responsibility to themselves, their accrediting bodies, their funders, and especially to their clients/athletes.

CONTRIBUTING TO THE DEVELOPMENT OF SPORT PSYCHOLOGY PROGRAMS THROUGH PROGRAM EVALUATION

Charles A. Maher

The practice of sport psychology involves diverse responsibilities, being guided by psychological science, relevant contexts, and ethical codes (Keegan, 2016; American Psychological Association, 2017; British Psychological Society, 2021). In this sense, an important responsibility for practitioners is the development of programs that are intended to contribute to the mental performance, mental health, and performance of athletes, coaches, support staff, and athletic administrators (Maher, 2022). It is within this context that program evaluation is a necessary aspect of professional practice. The purpose of this chapter is to *overview* how a program evaluation approach can be used by practitioners to contribute to the development and improvement of sport psychology programs.

Relevant Context

There are a range of programs that are designed and implemented by sport psychology practitioners in specific contexts, alone and in collaboration with other stakeholders, that are candidates for program evaluation. Actual examples of a brief overview of such programs, drawn from my practice are the following:

- A program to assist major league baseball players to acquire and develop mental skills so that they can effectively prepare, perform, compete, and deal with the pressures in baseball. This program extended over the course of a calendar year in a professional baseball organization, directed by a sport psychologist. The program included the development of individual mental skills plans for each of the players and their involvement in one-on-one and group meetings with MPCs. The program was evaluated by means of goal attainment ratings of player mental plans as well as ratings from coaches on the players' application of mental skills in games.
- A mindfulness program to teach head and assistant coaches in a university setting how to manage their thoughts and emotions so that they can cope with the demands of the coaching profession. This program occurred over ten sessions during the coaches' respective off-seasons. The program was led by a sport psychologist and an assistant athletic director. For each session, the coach participants learned about and practiced non-judgmental

awareness, including methods of deep breathing and centering. The program was evaluated by means of end-of-session participant reaction forms as well as end-of-program individualized progress reports produced by each of the participants.

- A program to support the mental and emotional needs of physically injured players in a professional men's ice hockey organization so that they could engage productively in their physical rehabilitation, recovery, and return to play. This program occurred, routinely, throughout the year at the team's development complex. The program was directed by the team sport psychologist. Each injured player was involved in weekly one-on-one meetings with the psychologist, customized discussions with former players who had prior injuries, and weekly group player support meetings. The program was evaluated by means of a player reaction questionnaire, a player group meeting, and feedback from rehabilitation training staff.
- A program for a women's professional basketball team to foster an environment conducive to team mental health. The program consisted of five problem-solving meetings that included selected players, coaches, and support staff prior to the start of training camp and the season. The program was facilitated by the team sport psychologist. The program was evaluated by means of review of the clarity and appropriateness of the policies and procedures that resulted from the problem-solving sessions judged by athletic administrators, mental health staff, and players.
- A program to incorporate mental skills training for student-athletes in a large urban public high school, along with parent education. This program occurred during the fall and spring semesters of the school year, with seven education sessions each semester for student athletes, team by team. The team sessions were led by a sport psychologist, focused on actions for team members to take as people, students, and athletes. The parental aspect of the program, led by a mental performance coach, centered on how parents could support their children in balancing sport with school, family, and life responsibilities. The overall program was evaluated by means of a post-program reaction questionnaire completed by student-athletes along with an end of program group feedback discussion session that was held with parents.

In the above case examples, these programs had common features, which are relevant for program evaluation. They: (a) were provided to particular participant groups; (b) focused on intended outcome expectations; (c) involved a configuration of methods, procedures, and activities; (d) extended over prescribed periods of time; (e) were expected to add value—mentally, emotionally, or behaviorally—to the participant groups; and (f) existed in relevant cultural, ethnic, and organizational contexts. These kinds of programs, and others of similar nature and scope, demonstrate the type of programs that sport psychology practitioners can evaluate.

Nature and Scope of Program Evaluation for Practitioners

For sport psychology practitioners, program evaluation can be defined as a process (Maher, 2022) intended to gather practical, useful information so that judgments can be made about the value of a program (i.e., its strong points and areas in need of improvement) and, therefore, as an indicator of return on stakeholder investment (Didymus et al., 2018). Based on such evaluation, decisions can be made by the practitioner and other stakeholders about how to develop and improve the program. In this form, program evaluation is an essential aspect of one's professional practice of sport psychology and is described next.

Guidelines for Practitioners

As a sport psychology practitioner, you can build a practical approach to program evaluation into your operational routines by means of the following steps, in sequence:

1. *Identify the individuals who have a stake in the development* and *continued improvement of the program* (e.g., you, coordinator of sport psychology, funders of the program, athletic administrator). These are the people who desire information about the value of the program for participants. The value is reflected as the program's strong points and areas in need of improvement (Barker et al., 2011).
2. *Place the program into an "evaluable" form*, so *that its implementation can be monitored and outcomes assessed*. An evaluable program involves describing: (a) the athletes or others (e.g., coaches) who are program participants; (b) the purpose and goals of the program; (c) the methods, procedures, and activities used; and (d) the individuals who will be implementing the program (Maher, 2012, 2022).
3. *Understand the cultural, ethnic, and organizational context in which* the *program is embedded*. In this regard, such context assessment provides meaning for the program and where it occurs (Schinke & Hanrahan, 2009).
4. *Create a program evaluation plan*. This should be a plan that is: (a) *practical*, in that it can be implemented; (b) *useful*, in that it results in evaluative information that is understood; (c) *ethical*, in terms of adherence to proper codes; and (d) *technically appropriate* with respect to data gathering instruments and procedures (Maher, 2023; Tod & Eubank, 2020).
5. *Implement the program evaluation plan*. To do so, first formulate program evaluation questions. Possible example questions are: Who participated in the program? How was the program implemented? To what extent were program goals attained? What were the reactions of participants to the program? What have participants learned by their program involvement? How has the program contributed to the sport organization? Next, select the methods and procedures that will be used to answer the questions. Actual examples include interviews and discussions with stakeholders, participant reaction questionnaire, focus group of participants, observation of program sessions, and review of program documents. Then, review the data that have been collected about the program thereby allowing value judgments to be made about the program, such as *the strong points of the program (e.g.,* ease of implementation, timing, and follow through of the sessions), *areas of the program that could be improved (e.g.,* lack of clarity of program goal, miscommunication about the program with participants), and *actions that can be taken to continue to develop and improve the program* (e.g., more measurable goals, additional time between sessions, more practical discussion activities). Lastly, communicate feedback from the program evaluation to stakeholders (Spira, 2023; Anderson et al., 2004) in written report format (e.g., strengths, areas for improvement), discussions about the evaluation with client and stakeholders, and/or program planning workshop for continuation of the program.

Conclusion

The evaluation of sport psychology programs is a professional and ethical responsibility of practitioners who are involved in program design and implementation. Relatedly, evaluation of sport psychology programs is an opportunity for practitioners to provide information to clients about the value of programmatic offerings in terms of ROI. The perspectives and guidelines provided in this chapter are intended to assist practitioners to engage in sport psychology program evaluation in a practical, useful, and professional manner.

EDITORS' TAKEAWAYS

As Andrew discussed in his introduction to the chapter on basic research skills for the applied practitioner (Chapter 10), being an effective practitioner necessitates an understanding of research and statistics. While I (Lauren) also didn't understand this while I was in graduate school, I am very grateful now that I had the opportunity to get such a strong understanding of research, statistics, and program evaluation during my education. Not only have they been important for thoughtfully choosing the interventions I use with my clients, they also have been essential for speaking to the value of the services I provide—and as Sebastian mentioned in his introduction to this chapter, that we as a field collectively provide. This knowledge and skills were requisite when I had to build a four-year mental performance evaluation plan to help ensure that a team I was working with was able to receive an additional funding of several million dollars to support their Olympic efforts as well as advantageous to me now in the corporate space to support marketing and sales efforts to demonstrate the ROI of our products among a sea of competitors. Developing these skills, in my opinion and experience, is not a nice to have but rather a need to have particularly as technology offerings increase and add to the competitive landscape our field will continue to find itself in.

RECOMMENDED EXERCISES

1 How could you use meta-analyses to inform your work and create high ROI for clients? How could they help demonstrate the value of your services when pitching to prospective clients?
2 What is the most important benefit of measuring the effectiveness of your applied work? How does it impact clients, and what's in it for you?
3 How might you monitor and evaluate your effectiveness as a practitioner? How can you incorporate program evaluation into your daily practice using ideas from this chapter?
4 Reflect on a time when your work improved a client's self-regulation, well-being, or performance. How would you present this outcome to a skeptical client or stakeholder in ROI terms? Which qualitative or quantitative metrics would you use?
5 Create a table or diagram mapping sport psychology interventions (e.g., self-talk, goal setting, and attention regulation) to potential ROI indicators (e.g., performance stats, reduced burnout/injury, and team cohesion). Which ROI types are easiest or hardest to measure, and which are most meaningful to different stakeholders? What ethical considerations arise when discussing ROI, and how can you balance demonstrating value with the complexity of human behavior and performance?

REFERENCES

American Psychological Association. (2017). *Ethical principles of psychologists and code of ethics*. American Psychological Association.
Anderson, A. G., Knowles, Z., & Gilbourne, D. (2004). Reflective practice for applied sport psychologists: Concepts, models, practical implications, and thoughts on dissemination. *The Sport Psychologist, 18*(2), 188–203.
Anderson, A. G., Miles, A., Mahoney, C., & Robinson, P. (2002). Evaluating the effectiveness of applied sport psychology practice: Making the case for a case study approach. *The Sport Psychologist, 16*(4), 432–453.

Anderson, A., Miles, A., Robinson, P., & Mahoney, C. (2004). Evaluating the athlete's perception of the sport psychologist's effectiveness: What should we be assessing? *Psychology of Sport and Exercise, 5*(3), 255–277. https://doi.org/10.1016/S1469-0292(03)00005-0

Barker, J., McCarthy, L., Jones, M., & Moran, A. (2011). *Single-case research in sport and exercise.* Routledge.

Bond, C. F., & Titus, L. J. (1983). Social facilitation: A meta-analysis of 241 studies. *Psychological Bulletin, 94*(2), 265–292. https://doi.org/10.1037//0033-2909.94.2.265

British Psychological Society. (2021). *Code of ethics and conduct.* British Psychological Society.

Castillo, E. A. (2024). Using performance profiling to assess consultant effectiveness. *Journal of Sport Psychology in Action.* Advance online publication. https://doi.org/10.1080/21520704.2024.xxxxx

Chandler, C., Eubank, M. R., Nesti, M. S., & Tod, D. (2016). Personal qualities of effective sport psychologists: Coping with organisational demands in high performance sport. *International Journal of Sport Psychology, 47*(4), 297–317.

Cropley, B., Miles, A., Hanton, S., & Niven, A. (2007). Improving the delivery of applied sport psychology support through reflective practice. *The Sport Psychologist, 21*(4), 475–494.

Cropley, B., Miles, A., & Niven, A. (2010). Exploring the relationship between effective and reflective practice in applied sport psychology. *The Sport Psychologist, 24*(4), 521–541.

Didymus, F. F., Rumbold, J. L., & Staff, H. R. (2018). Promoting and protecting coach psychological well-being and performance. In R. Thelwell & M. Dicks (Eds.), *Professional advances in sports coaching: Research and practice* (pp. 261–276). Routledge.

Feltz, D. L., & Landers, D. M. (1983). The effects of mental practice on motor skill learning and performance: A meta-analysis. *Journal of Sport Psychology, 5*(1), 25–57. https://doi.org/10.1123/jsp.5.1.25

Gonzalez, S. P., Connole, I., Mugford, A., & Taylor, J. (2017). Consultant effectiveness. In J. Taylor (Ed.), *Assessment in applied sport psychology* (pp. 245–257). Human Kinetics.

Haberl, P., & McCann, S. (2012). Evaluating USOC sport psychology consultant effectiveness: A philosophical and practical imperative at the Olympic Games. *Journal of Sport Psychology in Action, 3*(1), 65–76. https://doi.org/10.1080/21520704.2012.683095

Haberl, P., & Sharp, L. (2021). Evaluation of consulting and program effectiveness. In S. Sackett, N. Durand-Bush, & L. Tashman (Eds.), *The essential guide for mental performance consultants* (Digital Resource). Human Kinetics.

Hagger, M. (2022). Meta-analysis. *International Review of Sport and Exercise Psychology, 15*(1), 120–151. https://doi.org/10.1080/1750984X.2021.1966824

Keegan, R. (2016). *Being an applied sport psychologist.* Palgrave.

Koch, C. F. (1830). *Die Gymnastik aus dem Gesichtspunkte der Diätetik und Psychologie [Callisthenics from the viewpoint of dietetics and psychology].* Creutz.

Kyndt, T., & Rowell, S. (2012). *Achieving excellence in high performance sport: The experiences and skills behind the medals.* Bloomsbury Publishing Plc.

Lochbaum, M., Stoner, E., Hefner, T., Cooper, S., Lane, A. M., & Terry, P. C. (2022). Sport psychology and performance meta-analyses: A systematic review of the literature. *Plos One, 17*(2), e0263408. https://doi.org/10.1371/journal.pone.0263408

Maher, C. A. (2012). *Planning and evaluating human services: A resource guide for practitioners.* AuthorHouse.

Maher, C. A. (2022). *Developing and sustaining sport psychology programs: A resource guide for practitioners.* Routledge.

Maher, C. A. (2023). *Fostering the mental health of athletes, coaches, and staff: A systems approach to developing a mentally healthy sport organizations.* Routledge.

McCann, S. (2008). At the Olympics, everything is a performance issue. *International Journal of Sport and Exercise Psychology, 6*(3), 267–276. https://doi.org/10.1080/1612197X.2008.9671871

Orlick, T., & Partington, J. (1987). The sport psychology consultant: Analysis of critical components as viewed by Canadian Olympic athletes. *The Sport Psychologist, 1*(1), 4–17.

Partington, J., & Orlick, T. (1987a). The sport psychology consultant evaluation form. *The Sport Psychologist, 1*(4), 309–317.

Partington, J., & Orlick, T. (1987b). The sport psychology consultant: Olympic coaches' views. *The Sport Psychologist, 1*(2), 95–102.

Schinke, R., & Hanrahn, S. J. (Eds.). (2009). *Cultural sport psychology*. Human Kinetics.

Sharp, L. A., & Hodge, K. (2011). Sport psychology consulting effectiveness: The sport psychology consultant's perspective. *Journal of Applied Sport Psychology, 23*(3), 360–376. https://doi.org/10.1080/10413200.2011.583619

Sharp, L. A., Hodge, K., & Danish, S. (2014). Sport psychology consulting at elite sport competitions. *Sport, Exercise, and Performance Psychology, 3*(2), 75–88.

Sharp, L. A., Hodge, K., & Danish, S. (2015). Ultimately it comes down to the relationship: Experienced consultants' views of effective sport psychology consulting. *The Sport Psychologist, 29*(4), 358–370.

Sharp, L. A., Hodge, K., & Danish, S. (2021). "I wouldn't want to operate without it": The ethical challenges faced by experienced sport psychology consultants and their engagement with supervision. *Journal of Applied Sport Psychology, 33*(3), 259–279. https://doi.org/10.1080/10413200.2019.1646838

Smith, K., Shanteau, J., & Johnson, P. (Eds.). (2004). *Psychological investigations of competence in decision making*. Cambridge University Press.

Spira, G. (2023). *Trust the plan: Demand management for business leaders*. J. Ross Publishing.

Tod, D., & Eubank, M. (Eds.). (2020). *Applied sport, exercise, and performance psychology: Current approaches to helping clients*. Routledge.

Section 6

The SEPP Teacher

25 Navigating Academia

So many of us in SEPP have found employment in higher education institutions. And while we might have been keen to be sport or exercise psychologists when we entered our own education, we wind up as educators and/or researchers. These are entirely different career paths from applied work. As such, these are accompanied by different competencies, values, prerequisites, and social environments. And while there might be performance psychology skills that we can draw from (e.g., goal setting or team dynamics), we are left to fend for ourselves in navigating professional life in academia. For those of us who might be freshly out of graduate school and contemplating a full career in higher education (or at least, to satisfy the immediate need for employment), or for those of us already entrenched in academia and looking for strategies to boost motivation and work efficiency, we present this chapter on "navigating academia."

HOW TO SURVIVE AND THRIVE IN ACADEMIA IN THE UNITED STATES

David W. Eccles & Kaitlin Cohen-Maher

We describe how to survive and thrive in academia in the United States in the field of sport psychology based on our experience as academics in this field, and offer our lessons learned and tips for those considering a career a sport psychology academic in the United States. Dave is in his 50s and a senior faculty member in sport psychology at a large, public research-intensive university. Kate is in her 30s and describes academia from the perspective of a recent Ph.D. graduate in Sport Psychology who has now begun working as a university instructor while also maintaining a professional powerlifting career.

Dave's Experience of Surviving and Thriving: "Never Waste a Thing You Do"

Academia is a good employment option owing to the relative stability of the profession. Bad things certainly do happen to educational institutions, but education is nearly always in demand and many academic jobs reside in the relatively stable public sector. Working in academia in the sport psychology field is also rewarding because you get to interact with athletes in your classroom, study athletes in your research, and stay up to date with trends and innovations in sport psychology research and practice. And even if your motivation in life is to consult with athletes, some academic jobs afford opportunities to engage in consultancy work. For example, a former Ph.D. student of mine has a part-time consultancy contract alongside his full-time academic job.

DOI: 10.4324/9781003781479-31

Academia typically involves teaching sport psychology to students (which can include supervising them while they learn to consult), advising students as they learn to research sport psychology topics, undertaking your own research, and doing administrative work to help the university run smoothly. There is often also an expectation to serve the profession in some way or another (e.g., with professional associations). The balance of these activities depends in large part on the type of institution. Faculty at institutions that award doctoral degrees and prioritize research and do more advising of research students, and less teaching. By comparison, faculty at less research-intensive institutions typically do more teaching and less research. Students considering a job in academia must "pick their poison"; do you want more research expectations or a higher teaching load? What are your interests, experiences, and skill sets? There is no easier option of course, because employers do not offer easy options.

If you take a job that involves any expectations for research, you will quickly notice how little time is actually available within your job to do your research. The time needed for teaching, grading, advising, and university administration can quickly squeeze out the time needed to do research. Yet, typically, your research is very important when you apply for promotion, so you absolutely must prioritize and protect time in your weekly schedule for doing your research if you are going to survive and thrive! To this aim, I offer a useful maxim: Show me your schedule and I will show you your priorities.

If you take a job that has any teaching, and especially if you are taking a job that only involves teaching (i.e., no research), then the student and peer evaluations of your teaching are typically very important. They must be at least average compared to peer instructors at the institution, and preferably good. Here are a few tips for getting good student evaluations. First, I like the adage that students do not need a perfect teacher; they need a happy teacher. Come to class happy, energetic, clearly passionate about your subject, and motivated to share this passion with your students, and it is likely that your evaluations will be good. Second, treat your students like they are people, not just "another student." They will appreciate your respect. This does not mean you cannot be firm when you need to be (e.g., with assignment deadlines), of course! Third, you cannot satisfy all of your students all of the time. If some of your student evaluations state that more group work is desired, and you run around making these changes for your class the following year, then it is highly likely that a subset of your new students will state in their evaluations that they want less group work! So, just pick some teaching activities and styles that you feel are generally effective for you and the class and make them work as best you can.

Finally, make sure that nothing you do in your work is ever completely wasted. There are many tasks that you will be required to do as an academic that can seem to involve wasted time and effort. But I have learned over the years that this is seldom true because what you have learned or produced by doing these tasks usually can be leveraged in the future if you apply a little creative thinking and strategy. My suggestion, then, is to embrace the concept of "never waste a thing." For example, your university management might ask you to teach a class you have not taught before for one semester only. While this suits them (usually financially), it leaves you frustrated because you know the overhead associated with teaching a new class, and you will not get to capitalize on this overhead the following year because you will have to teach a different class, which also might be new! But the chances are that some of the class content that you create, or some knowledge you gained by teaching the class, will be useful in the future. Whenever you are required to do anything new, be sure to think back to this course and ask yourself whether there is anything you did to develop it (e.g., ideas, approaches to group work, recorded presentations, etc.) that you can now borrow or adapt to help you complete your new work task. More generally, taking a little time to deliberately review all of your prior work will help you leverage it to make your current work so much easier.

Kate's Experience of Surviving and Thriving: Lessons Learned as a New Instructor

As you transition into your career, be sure to research during your Ph.D. what future employers value most! While "free time" is almost nonexistent during the Ph.D. journey, especially if, like me, you are juggling it with an athletic career, I wish I had dedicated more effort early in my studies to researching the academic career landscape. For example, having a high volume of publications is crucial for those aspiring to secure a professorship at a large, four-year public institution. I graduated from a university that offered opportunities to earn AASP's Certified Mental Performance Consultant credential, consult with local teams and student-athletes, and conduct research leading to publications. Given these options, I prioritized gaining consultancy experience, despite my primary goal of teaching in higher education. In hindsight, I wish I had placed more emphasis on publishing under the guidance of my mentors.

Another recommendation for those just beginning to navigate academia is to develop a strong familiarity with your student body and learn how you can most effectively relate to them. By taking the time to learn about the various sports my students are involved in, I can facilitate more meaningful and relevant discussions connected to our course materials to encourage active participation and deeper learning. For example, I might illustrate how my student Jack, a baseball player, would adopt a narrow-external focus when attending to how the pitcher grips the ball, or a broad-internal focus when evaluating the placement of his elbow while holding his bat. I may also involve my student Dylan when introducing a performance profile, asking him to share the qualities or characteristics he believes are critical for success in his sport of ultimate frisbee.

Additionally, the late Dr. Ken Ravizza, a well-known sport psychology consultant, suggested that "being in the zone is B.S." I believe that this adage applies in all avenues of performance, including teaching. As a newly appointed classroom instructor, it is not unusual to want to make the perfect impression on students and colleagues right from the start. I entered my new position expecting students to absorb every psychology-based term and theoretical concept. I was determined to ask every "right" discussion question I could creatively muster along the way. I obviously lost this all-or-nothing battle after my first 80-minute class session. Instead, I gained firsthand experience with the lesson that less is more. Not every presentation will be Nobel Prize worthy, and not every assignment will turn out exactly as you intend. As a go-getter myself, this was an unsettling feeling for me to initially accept. In fact, after the second day of classes, and coping with an influx of emotions on my drive home, I thankfully adopted an alternative perspective and found comfort in knowing that I can trust in my ability to connect with my students and in my love for teaching. If certain components of the class and its materials go as planned, great; I can use that strategy again. If not, that is fine too. I can adjust as I go and feel confident knowing that I was not afraid to try. Plus, Dave is right: students thrive off a teacher's energy and disposition more than anything else. If you are having fun while teaching, they will likely enjoy themselves while learning.

Lastly, an unfamiliar teaching environment, especially for a rookie adjunct instructor, may seem intimidating at first, but do not be scared to propose new ideas and initiatives in the workplace. In my experience, those higher up tend to respect a new employee who is eager to innovate. For instance, when I first interviewed, I advocated for the chance to pioneer the institution's first ever sport psychology course. I was confident this course would be both sought after and applicable, especially among our student-athletes. Sure enough, my administrators went for it, and my new classes in sport psychology have proved to be popular. In turn, I've been offered the opportunity to teach several more new courses related to sport psychology since. By seeking out and acting on opportunities, you remain fresh in the minds of decision-makers when emerging positions arise.

LAYING THE FOUNDATIONS FOR SPORT AND EXERCISE PSYCHOLOGY PRACTICE: A UK PERSPECTIVE

Karen Howells

On a cold, damp Monday morning in November in Wales, United Kingdom (UK), I find myself in a familiar situation. I briefly rehearse the content of the day's MSc Sport Psychology seminar on posttraumatic growth in sport delivered as part of the core module *Theory to Practice*. I am relaxed—it is my research area; my only concern is covering it in the three-hour slot available. I scan the mildly chilled classroom as the students filter in. Despite the fresh weather outside, many are wearing sporting attire I would associate with a balmy summer's day. Low-level chatter relates to events and stories of the weekend's social and sporting activities. I wonder briefly what the future holds for these young people whose personal statements were submitted to me nearly a year earlier as part of their university applications, highlighting their "lifelong desire" to help people, their passion for sport psychology, and their dreams of becoming a sport psychologist. I know from experience, six years of being a program director at Cardiff Metropolitan University, and over a decade of being involved with sport psychologist training, some will achieve their dream, while others will take alternative paths into a variety of different fields.

In the Classroom

The challenge for education providers delivering postgraduate programs is to reduce the perceived chasm between taught courses that are predominantly knowledge-based and subsequent professional training/qualifications which involve supervised practice and the development of applied skills through supervised practice (see, McCormick, 2023). In many disciplines, experiential and work-based learning approaches can be integrated with work placements, internships, or voluntary experience. In 1997, the UK National Committee of Inquiry into Higher Education (the Dearing Committee) recommended that every student should be given the opportunity to undertake a placement. Many courses use placements to develop employability skills, yet this is generally not viable in sport and exercise psychology as only those on the professional pathways or who are registered with the Health and Care Professions Council (HCPC) can *practice* sport and exercise psychology. Therefore, this challenge must be addressed by institutions delivering postgraduate qualifications in sport and exercise psychology. Programs such as an M.Sc. Sport Psychology that provide the foundations for applied practice and acceptance onto recognized professional pathways are usually accredited by the British Psychological Society (BPS). Reaccreditation by the BPS typically occurs every six years although programs are still subject to the individual academic institution requirements in the form of a periodic review. Although each program will be bespoke, designed to meet the needs of the typical demographic for that institution and to utilize the strengths of the research staff and applied practitioners delivering the curriculum, all must meet certain requirements (e.g., a set of core standards—cognitive processes, psychological skills and strategies, social processes, participation and well-being, and individual differences; BPS, 2019). To prepare students for the next step on their journey, develop employability skills, and prepare students for applied practice, providers design modules to bridge the gap between theory and practice, while not engaging in actual practice.

Returning to the mildly chilly Monday morning, I deliberate on an additional challenge: the different levels of knowledge that the students in front of me have. Discussing the cognitive aspects of posttraumatic growth, and the contrasting impact of assimilation and accommodation on the potential for growth (see Howells et al., 2017), I recognize a flicker of understanding from students on one table, they are the students who have a psychology undergraduate degree. I shift my gaze to another table where the confused looks of the students who have come through a sport and exercise science undergraduate degree transform into uncomfortable fidgeting. This contrasts with a session a few weeks earlier when the focus had been on psychological skills training and explanations of imagery, goal setting, and arousal control; this had been familiar territory for the sport and exercise science graduates but new information for the psychology students. Recognizing and managing the different levels of understanding is required by all educators; the success of the program is determined by the ability to prepare students from a variety of backgrounds for the next stage of their professional journey.

A fundamental component in the success of an academic program is the staff involved. Delivering a content-driven program to prepare for a predominantly practice-based professional qualification is challenging. To partly mitigate this, although not mandatory, the program director/lead is generally expected to be an HCPC-registered practitioner psychologist who has applied practice experience, thus providing a personal insight into the skills required to be an ethical and effective practitioner. Additionally, a proportion of the staff who deliver content will also ideally have applied experience. These individuals, as scholar-practitioners (see Howells, 2023), some who have come from psychology, and some who have come from sport and exercise science backgrounds, are ideally placed to provide links between theory and practice through the benefit of their own lenses. To be both an academic (with teaching and research responsibilities) and a practitioner, individuals must hold a Ph.D. and an applied qualification, both of which are Level 9 qualifications and each typically takes at least three years to acquire. Acquiring both qualifications in the first instance is financially challenging and time-consuming (see Howells, 2023); however, maintaining currency in both is also challenging. It is only recently that my full-time contract has included a number of hours (less than 50) over a year to provide sport psychology support to performance athletes at the University. Maintaining my currency therefore requires me to work with private clients outside my contracted role. Delivering my seminar, I recited the story of a relatively recent client who was competing at an elite level in an individual sport. Her experiences of a life-threatening illness resulted in her missing out on a place at the 2016 Rio Olympic Games, and had facilitated what we term posttraumatic growth (Tedeschi & Calhoun, 1995). Utilizing her story in my seminar enabled me to discuss the theory of growth, how it manifested in this client, and how as a practitioner I supported my client and worked with her to develop the skills to make sense of her adversity and discuss how she had the potential to benefit from her experience.

Facilitating the development of employability skills in the classroom that can be transferred to practice requires some "thinking outside the box." Counseling skills, for example, may be developed through role play facilitated by trained staff, whereby students adopt roles of practitioner and client to develop listening skills, demonstration of empathy and rapport through nonverbal communication skills, and learn to respond to unexpected disclosures and events. Dissemination of psychological knowledge is an important aspect of the sport psychologist's toolbox and a measurable competency in the professional pathways, As such, a proportion of assessments may comprise presentations to develop the skills required to present knowledge to a range of audiences. Students often report that presenting to their peers is particularly difficult due to self-comparison, self-reflection, and peer-judgment. Confidence in delivering psychological content can be developed, for example, through use of podcasts as an assessment tool—in the *Theory to Practice* module at my university, students select one of three topics and produce a 15-minute podcast. Finally, case studies provide a useful insight for students to apply their theoretical understanding to real-world examples or typical vignettes. The use of case studies in teaching and assessment facilitates the development of transferable skills such as group work, analytical thinking, and presentation and communication skills (Penn et al., 2016).

Final Thoughts

The future of sport psychology practice is bright—the stigma once associated with seeing a sport psychologist is diminishing exponentially, and the demand for sport psychology practitioner services is rising. However, it remains important that higher education institutions are proactive in developing the employability skills of future practitioners, that the gap between theory and practice is lessened within the confines of professional, statutory, and regulatory bodies' rules about legal practice, and that the innovative practice is recognized and encouraged.

NAVIGATING THE EXERCISE AND SPORT PSYCHOLOGY TEACHING PATH: AN INTERNATIONAL PERSPECTIVE FOR JUNIOR SCHOLARS

Melanie Poudevigne

As an international, first-generation, female faculty member with two decades of experience teaching at a Predominantly Black Institution (PBI) in the Southeast of the United States, my academic journey has been rich with transformative insights. I am aiming to share critical lessons learned from navigating the complex landscape of exercise and sport psychology education, with the hope of guiding emerging teaching scholars through their own professional development. My path has been shaped by a multicultural background; I grew up in one of the most diverse suburbs of Paris, in Sevran, Seine-Saint-Denis, France, and was an elite athlete who succeeded in passing the physical activity admission test at the University Paris Cité Kinesiology program, a path that will propel me forward to a fulfilling career. I had the opportunity to learn from world renown sport performance scientists, and being exposed to this level of performance fed my curiosity to continue with a doctorate at the University of Georgia (UGA) in the United States specializing in behavior change in the Exercise Psychology Laboratory founded by Drs. Patrick O'Connor and Rodney Dishman.

During my doctorate, I quickly learned to teach in English as a fourth language as I was proficient in French, German, and Spanish growing up. At UGA, my students were enrolled in the exercise science undergraduate and graduate programs. Together, we had access to the most amazing laboratory resources afforded by internal and external grants, and private and foundation contracts. After graduation, I navigated immigration requirements for an H1B visa with my personal attorney and transitioned from dedicating my time from mental and physical health research to teaching at a public regional PBI with significant budget limitations, bridging international perspectives in South Atlanta, and working within an institutional framework committed to social mobility.

Teaching at a PBI and Embracing a Pedagogy of Kindness

The PBI designation was established under the Higher Education Act in 2008 and is defined as institutions that serve at least 1,000 undergraduate students who are 50+% low income and enrolling at least 40% African American students, among other criteria (Colston, 2024). My colleagues and I play a significant role in creating equitable economic opportunity for people of color. A majority of PBI students are also non-traditional and first generation, balancing employment and family responsibilities. PBIs confer just 3.6% of all bachelor's degrees received by Black students (Colston, 2024). Prior to 2020, tenured faculty members and I were charged with diversifying our personnel to enhance belongingness within and create strong community ties. This strategic organizational effort significantly increased the inclusion of underrepresented racial groups among faculty and staff matching the local county demographics and facilitating community health initiatives tailored to addressing societal needs.

One key lesson I have learned is the importance of cultivating a "pedagogy of kindness" in the classroom. This pedagogy of kindness positively influenced the learning environment by fostering a sense of community and support among students and peer educators (Nguyen & Lee, 2025). It enhances students' retention rates, feedback, and educational achievements and encourages them to engage with social justice issues in a peaceful way (Gorny-Wegrzyn & Perry, 2021). By modeling cultural openness, acknowledging students' diverse experiences, and tailoring assignments to meet the PBI students' needs, I choose to empower culturally diverse students and colleagues (Nguyen & Lee, 2025), and create a collaborative learning environment that increases career promotions and fulfillment as well as teaching successes. The pedagogy of kindness is rooted in humanistic and philosophical principles, emphasizing the importance of personal values and emotional work in teaching. It challenges the dichotomy between emotion and reason, advocating for a more integrated approach to education that values kindness as a fundamental component of sound pedagogy (Clegg & Rowland, 2010).

Developing Intercultural Competencies Effectively

Another crucial lesson is the need to acquire intercultural competencies in teaching. As educators, we must be prepared to navigate the complex dynamics of diversity, recognizing and addressing the unique challenges faced by students, especially those from underserved backgrounds. This requires ongoing professional development, a willingness to engage in difficult conversations with peers, students, and the community, and a deep understanding of the sociocultural factors that shape our students' educational experiences. In my case, traveling the world, sharing my expertise with developing country experts in the Caribbeans and Africa, and publishing global behavior change initiatives have enhanced such knowledge and skills.

Gaining intercultural competencies means cultural openness going beyond mere tolerance; it requires curiosity, active engagement, and genuine understanding that is practiced and applied every day. Tailoring assignments to meet diverse student needs, modeling cultural sensitivity, encouraging dialogue about sociocultural experiences, and creating safer spaces for meaningful learning and conversations challenge traditional ways of teaching in the classroom and virtually. While fostering such a supportive environment, maintaining professional boundaries is a must and includes respect for students' autonomy, structured guidance without personal enmeshment, and a support system that enhances students' independent growth.

In academic contexts, the lack of diverse lived experiences can lead to inefficiencies in both research and teaching. The absence of varying perspectives may limit the scope of knowledge creation, which, in turn, can affect the development of new ideas in areas like mental flexibility, performance, and behavior change. Ensuring that talent is recognized and utilized based on merit—not solely on background—can lead to more effective and innovative outcomes in the classroom and beyond. By focusing on the value that diverse perspectives bring to research and teaching, institutions can improve efficiency in knowledge production and address the need for broader perspectives without undermining merit-based considerations. Acknowledging and tapping into the potential of individuals from different socioeconomic backgrounds can ultimately enhance the quality of research and innovation in sport psychology, driving progress in the field and ensuring that talent is allocated in ways that contribute to optimal performance and outcomes.

The Role of Continuous Learning

Statistical expertise is fundamental to understanding rigorous research in exercise and sport psychology and presenting the best information to students enrolled in our field courses. My doctoral training, supplemented by an unofficial minor in statistics, provided me with advanced analytical skills such as mixed models, linear regression, MAN(C)OVAs, and cluster analysis. These analytical competencies have allowed me to critically analyze research designs, evaluate methodological soundness, and mentor students in distinguishing between studies with robust foundations and those with methodological weaknesses. In the current era, where misinformation and poorly conducted research can proliferate, statistical literacy is indispensable. By mastering data analysis, educators can improve methodological rigor while addressing the need for more diverse participation in sampling and learning. Moreover, instilling statistical literacy in students fosters critical thinking skills that empower them to navigate the scientific literature effectively, enabling them to identify biases, understand effect sizes, and assess reproducibility in research.

My career exemplifies commitment to continuous learning. Along the way, I have expanded my expertise to include counseling, sport management, and exercise psychology. These interdisciplinary expansions to the sport performance arena have allowed me to adapt to the dynamic nature of the field, ensuring that I can address emerging challenges, identify creative or novice experts, promote their work along the way, and share opportunities while contributing to the advancement of knowledge and practice in exercise and sport psychology both in and outside the classroom.

Conclusion

These lessons represent more than academic strategies to grow through the professorial ranks in academia. They are a philosophy of education rooted in empathy, continuous growth, and genuine commitment to student success. As the educational landscape continues to evolve, they offer a compass for navigating the complex, rewarding journey of teaching and mentorship. For emerging scholars, the path is not about perfection, but about persistent learning, cultural humility, talent seeking, and an unwavering belief in the transformative power of education for all.

EDITORS' TAKEAWAYS

This chapter is beyond valuable for people pursuing academia as a career or who have found themselves on that career path. Personally, I (Lauren) spent about eight years as a full-time faculty member and several years following as an adjunct. I love teaching and being in the classroom with my students as well as the community of a department and university. I did not love all the other things that come with academia (e.g., changing priorities and leadership, financial challenges and the consequences of that, having to defend decisions about classes and class sizes, promotion requirements). The contributors in this chapter provide an essential read and roadmap for navigating life as an academic—thriving and not just surviving. What most stood out to me were: (a) Eccles' discussion about never wasting a thing you do; (b) Cohen-Maher's discussion of the importance of relating to your students; (c) Howells' discussion of teaching students who come from diverse cultural and academic backgrounds, the necessity of teaching in a way that helps them not only learn the material but more importantly be prepared to use it as a practitioner, and the importance of continuous learning as a teacher to keep up with emerging challenges and everything that changes over the years; and (d) Poudevigne's key lesson shared about cultivating a pedagogy of kindness, particularly when teaching underserved and marginalized students.

RECOMMENDED EXERCISES

1 Reflect on your academic experiences: which pedagogical practices helped your development as a practitioner? Without real-world practice, what techniques beyond storytelling, case studies, or innovative assessment can replicate professional experience?
2 Do you protect your research time? Try these exercises: create a visible mantra like "research is the most important thing"; identify your best thinking times (e.g., mornings) and prioritize them; even 15 minutes counts—schedule it in your planner; treat research time like a meeting to prevent others from interrupting.
3 Do you have a plan to switch off from work? To recover effectively, spend time after work and on days off: A. with non-work colleagues, B. in spaces free of work materials, C. without checking work emails or social media. For further guidance, see Eccles et al. (2021, 2022, in press) and Karabinski et al. (2021).
4 Document a teaching challenge from the past year. Analyze your response, then reimagine it using the pedagogy of kindness framework. Consider impacts on student engagement, actions that show kindness while maintaining rigor, and potential barriers. Include concrete examples and potential changes in approach.
5 Create a cultural competency map of your classroom: examine the diverse backgrounds in your classes, reflect on how your own culture shapes your teaching, and identify blind spots in materials or examples. Develop three strategies to make your course more culturally inclusive, and reflect on how this process has changed your awareness.

REFERENCES

British Psychological Society. (2019). *Standards for the accreditation of Masters & Doctoral programmes in sport and exercise psychology*. https://www.bps.org.uk/partnership

Clegg, S., & Rowland, S. (2010). Kindness in pedagogical practice and academic life. *British Journal of Sociology of Education, 31*, 719–735. https://doi.org/10.1080/01425692.2010.515102

Colston, J. (2024). *Issue primer: Predominantly Black institutions.* PNPI. https://pnpi.org/wp-content/uploads/2024/01/PBI_Primer_Jan24.pdf

Eccles, D. W., Balk, Y., Gretton, T., & Harris, N. (2022). "The forgotten session": Advancing research and practice concerning the psychology of rest in athletes. *Journal of Applied Sport Psychology, 34*(1), 3–24. https://doi.org/10.1080/10413200.2020.1756526

Eccles, D. W., Caviedes, G., Balk, Y., Harris, N., & Gretton, T. W. (2021). How to help athletes get the mental rest needed to perform well and stay healthy. *Journal of Sport Psychology in Action, 12*(4), 259–270. https://doi.org/10.1080/21520704.2021.1873208

Eccles, D. W., Foster, B. J., & Bean, W. (in press). Becoming an expert requires relentless commitment: A myth. In J. Coady & A. Whitehead (Eds.), *Myths of sport psychology.* Sequoia Books.

Eubank, M., Wagstaff, C., & McCarthy, P. (2022). Professional doctorates in sport and exercise psychology. In V. Shanmuganathan-Felton &Stephen Smith (Eds.) *Developing a sport psychology consultancy practice: A toolkit for students and trainees* (pp. 39–53). Routledge.

Gorny-Wegrzyn, E., & Perry, B. (2021). Exemplary educators who embrace a teaching philosophy guided by a pedagogy of kindness. *Journal of Advances in Education Research, 6*(2), 67–74. https://doi.org/10.22606/jaer.2021.62002

Howells, K. (2023). Questions of identity in sport psychology scholar practitioners. *Sports, 11*, 182. https://doi.org/10.3390/sports11090182

Howells, K., Sarkar, M., & Fletcher, D. (2017). Can athletes benefit from difficulty? A systematic review of growth following adversity in competitive sport. *Progress in Brain Research, 234*, 117–159.

Karabinski, T., Haun, V. C., Nübold, A., Wendsche, J., & Wegge, J. (2021). Interventions for improving psychological detachment from work: A meta-analysis. *Journal of Occupational Health Psychology, 26*(3), 224–242. https://doi.org/10.1037/ocp0000280

McCormick, A. (2023). Writing an excellent reflective diary: Ten suggestions from a QSEP assessor. *Sport & Exercise Psychology Review, 18*, 108–114. https://doi.org/10.53841/bpssepr.2023.18.1.108

Nguyen, T. L., & Lee, J. Y. (2025). Kindness as a public health action. *Communications Medicine, 5*(1), 122. https://doi.org/10.1038/s43856-025-00861-3

Penn, M. L., Currie, C. S., Hoad, K. A., & O'Brien, F. A. (2016). The use of case studies in OR teaching. *Higher Education Pedagogies, 1*(1), 16–25.

Tedeschi, R. G., & Calhoun, L. G. (1995). *Trauma and transformation.* Sage.

UK National Committee of Inquiry into Higher Education. (1997). *Higher education in the learning society: Summary report.* HMSO.

26 Teaching Mental Skills

When we graduate from our educational programs, many of us enter academia as university faculty. Yet curiously, few of us receive any formal training—even at a basic level—in how to teach the very content we've just mastered (to varying degrees). We are often left to rely on intuition, trial and error, or borrowed strategies from colleagues, rather than a systematic approach to pedagogy. This gap not only makes the transition into teaching more challenging but also risks limiting the impact we can have on students. Resources that support us in becoming better teachers are therefore essential if we hope to contribute to the growth of the profession. We present the following contributions from teachers around the world to help provide some insightful reflections and practical strategies for how to teach mental skills.

TEACHING MENTAL SKILLS TO FUTURE PRACTITIONERS: THE ART WITHIN THE SCIENCE

Kimberly Shaffer

Using the Scientist-Practitioner Model

The scientist-practitioner model is nothing new to the field of training and teaching novice psychology consultants. It was born in 1949 at the Boulder conference, following the end of World War II, and the surge for expanding psychological resources (Raimy, 1950). In its inception, the scientist-practitioner model provided a structure for training psychologists which merged research with applied consulting.

The sport psychology community, like its clinical counterparts, has utilized the scientist-practitioner model in training its neophyte practitioners. However, there is a need for growth, to improve the science-to-practice translation, particularly with elite performers. Lowman (2012) highlighted these sentiments when discussing the gaps between the researcher and the consultant:

> It is argued that the science-practitioner model can be differentiating in a highly competitive area of practice, that science can make its research more relevant to practice, and that practitioners have an important role to play in assuring the linkage of practice with research and theory.
>
> (p. 151)

The key for educators becomes which science to teach and how to select the appropriate resources for the classroom that will properly cater to the needs of young practitioners. While

DOI: 10.4324/9781003781479-32

peer-reviewed research is always going to be the gold standard, its accessibility from a physical perspective, and with regard to student comprehension, provides barriers.

From the educator perspective, the first step begins with doing our own homework. The more one reads, the more one knows. Knowing, not from a technical or tactical perspective, but from a sorting perspective. How to pinpoint resources that will engage and connect with students more than a 35-page meta-analysis filled with complicated statistics and methodologies they likely will never see or hear about again. Step two is trying to highlight peer-reviewed case studies. For every intervention study, balance it with a real-life case study. While case studies, of course, do not have the same methodological rigor, the exchange in internal validity is worth not only the bump in external validity, but also the buy- in from students. This becomes a delicate balancing act for educators of providing the educational backbone, while inspiring creativity and finding the individual art of being your own practitioner.

Sources of Science: Providing the Backbone for Future Practitioners

Where Does Science Come from and How Is It Taught?

Students acquire scientific knowledge from a variety of sources that collectively shape their understanding of the subject. Like any science, the foundational source of sport psychology is formal education. Students learn fundamental concepts, theories, and principles through coursework that includes textbooks, lectures, case studies, and peer-reviewed literature. While educators play a crucial role in conveying this knowledge, leading students through complex ideas, and helping them foster critical thinking and creative problem-solving, students also gain scientific knowledge from informal and self-directed learning.

Hands-on experiences, such as internships, and fieldwork, further deepen understanding by allowing students to apply theoretical teachings to real-world scenarios, helping to bring the scientist-practitioner model to life. While every educator has a treasure trove of experiential learning to pull from, behavior change projects have proved particularly effective. Have the students pick a particular health, wellness, exercise behavior they want to improve. Have them record their baseline, then have them make a plan. What theories are they going to use to make sure they actually achieve their goal (transtheoretical model, theory of planned behavior, etc.)? What mental skills need to be implemented to achieve success? How often? What time of day? Why did you select those skills, what peer-reviewed research supports this approach? Have them execute and track progress. What is working, what is not; help them to increase their own self-awareness around implementing change in their own lives so they can gain perspective on what that looks like for clients. Lastly, like all good counseling professions, include reflection. Have students connect back to the literature. Have them be critical. For example, "Article X said I should do Y and guess what, it was not that easy. It did not work. However, here is what did work." Using a project like this, students start to build a comprehensive understanding of how theory and peer-reviewed research combine with personal exploration and practical experience.

Why Is Science Important?

The science portion of the scientist-practitioner model is crucial in psychology as it ensures psychological practice is grounded in scientific evidence, and promotes effective, ethical interventions. Under the current climate of performance enhancement services (i.e., early stages of program accreditation, trouble with title oversight, differentiating between certification, licensure, or neither), there are increasing demands for legitimate performance enhancement services. The profession is currently undergoing an evolution, beyond the mere psychological skills training models of the 1980s and 1990s, which illuminates higher education and training systems for quality assurance of service delivery (Harwood, 2016). Competent service delivery outcomes require a well-regulated professional system of training, grounded in scientific underpinnings of well-researched theory, assessment, and intervention research. This formal education ultimately differentiates highly adept consultants from other less competent service providers. Additionally, the pursuit of science fosters a mindset of continuous learning and adaptation, as practitioners must stay informed about the latest research findings and incorporate them into their practice. This integration ultimately leads to better outcomes for clients and advances the field of psychology as a whole.

Inspiring Creativity: Finding the Art of Implementing Mental Skills

Where Does the "Art" Come from and How Is It Taught?

The beauty of performance psychology is centered around understanding the human experience. This understanding is why psychology is defined as a "soft science"; it is a diverse and evolving field, which encompasses multiple perspectives on understanding human behavior and mental processes (Howard, 1993). Every moment or situation in Sport, exercise, and performance psychology (SEPP) is interpreted through the lens of the consultant. Therefore, it is crucial that consultants be mindful of their theoretical orientations that guide them through these interpretive moments. Orientations arise from different foundational beliefs about the nature of the mind, how people learn and change, and what factors most significantly influence behavior (Constantine, 2001). Additionally, cultural, social, and personal experiences color a consultant's preference for mental skills approaches, as they are encouraged to seek approaches which resonate with their personal values. Through this unique blend of factors, consultants are given creative allowances which ultimately result in different approaches across both clients and practitioners.

An example of bringing this balance of science and art to life in the classroom is a book project. Have the students select a book of their choice in the sport psychology zeitgeist. This can be anything of their choosing: *Grit* by Angela Duckworth; *How Champions Think* by Bob Rotella; *Range* by David Epstein; *10 Minute Toughness* by Jason Self, the list is endless. These resources, while not peer-reviewed, are digestible, easy to read, and engageable for students. After students read the book of their choosing (yay autonomy!) have them apply those concepts to a current client. What from the book may work or not work with their client. This allows students to practice implementing skills. However, also make students find peer-reviewed literature that supports or contradicts the book. What does empirical science say about this approach? Can students triangulate this knowledge? Does the pop-culture self-help book match with applied implementation with validated science?

Why Is "Art" Important?

For educators, it is imperative to foster an environment that is psychologically safe for neophyte practitioners to explore these theoretical orientations, values, and hone their craft of psychological skills training (Giordano et al., 2018). Allowing young practitioners to explore their consulting style will ultimately encourage open communication between mentor and student, increase participation, and boost thoughtful reflection; all of which are essential for deep learning and intellectual growth (Drabick & Goldfried, 2000). Ultimately, just as clients are individual and unique, so too are the practitioners assigned to help guide them. There is no one-size-fits-all model of what sport psychology consultation should look like, therefore, this individuality needs to start in the classroom and be fostered by educators themselves.

TEACHING MENTAL SKILLS FOR TOMORROW'S GENERATIONS

Sascha Leisterer-Härtig & Barbara Halberschmidt

Mental skills are techniques that align biopsychosocial features of individuals to beneficially influence expected outcomes, such as performance or health (Lebrun et al., 2020). Today's students need (sport) psychological skills, such as emotional competencies, goal setting, imagery, recovery, and activation skills, and self-regulation to excel not only personally, socially, and academically but also athletically. Worldwide, research has shown that a foundation of sport psychological skills can be integrated into school systems by sport psychology practitioners (SPPs) (e.g., Gilbert et al., 2017). The following examples highlight how mental skills can be successfully integrated into German school settings for both regular students and student athletes.

Best Practices from Germany

In Germany, there are 43 "Elite Schools of Sport" (Deutscher Olympischer Sportbund, 2025) that train and educate aspiring elite and top-level athletes. These schools work closely with SPPs and Olympic training centers where SPPs work full-time, to support students in their mental development (among other things). Current best practice programs from three different German federal states (i.e., North Rhine-Westphalia, Lower Saxony, Saarland) demonstrate the integration of mental skill training into the school context (Halberschmidt, 2025). In North Rhine-Westphalia, the Essen network system (https://sportschuleinessen.de/) pursues an interactionist approach to talent development, complemented by systemic support mechanisms. Sport and exercise psychology modules are integrated into daily schooling and cover three content areas: motivation & mental strength, competition & recovery management, and cognitive training & team dynamics (Halberschmidt, 2025). The fundamental module "motivation & mental strength" explains motivation, applies goal-setting techniques, and highlights the influence of motivation on athletic and personal performances. Additionally, the lessons focus on self-regulation skills to cope with emotions, and on providing feedback on mistakes, and criticism.

In Lower Saxony, the Felix Klein Gymnasium (i.e., partner high school of competitive sports) in Göttingen recently launched the pilot project "Mental Training," which offers junior competitive athletes optional sport psychology support. The program includes modular workshops and individual consultations with a SPP. Similar to the concept of the Essen network system, the workshops in Göttingen introduce mental training (i.e., fundamental knowledge, goal setting, coping strategies) and additionally focus on visualization training to support individual performances. In addition, special topics, such as dealing with injuries and crises can be discussed within the mental training workshops. Due to the positive feedback from the student athletes, hybrid training for teachers is offered to disseminate this mental skills training to all students (Halberschmidt, 2025).

In Saarland, the Gymnasium am Rotenbühl (i.e., high school, Elite School of Sport) has been offering the compulsory course "Mental Training" to support students in the upper secondary school level since 2008. This course includes knowledge transfer, diagnostic methods, and practical exercises with reflection techniques to prepare athletes for the complex challenges of competitive sports (Kaiser et al., 2024). Through interactive learning arrangements and project-based approaches, the two-year course teaches basic mental skills that are further developed in individually tailored programs. Accompanying evaluations show that participants develop significantly improved stress management and self-regulation skills. The collected experiences and results underline the importance of early, structured, and long-term interventions for young athletes to minimize burnout, performance decline, and psychological stress (Halberschmidt, 2025).

According to these best practice examples, mental skills training can be included in daily schooling and provide student athletes with successful support in excelling healthily. Table 26.1 compares the three German examples. Although all three projects integrate mental skill teaching into school curricula, they follow three slightly different objectives (i.e., teaching mental skills to all students and/or to young athlete students) that are represented

Table 26.1 Comparison of Practices to Include Mental Skill Teaching in German Schools

Objective	MST for all students	MST for all but especially for young athletes	MST for young elite athletes
Format	Extracurricular	Extracurricular and curricular (in PE)	Curricular in upper secondary school
Example	Göttingen (Lower Saxony, GER)	Essen network system (North Rhine Westphalia, GER)	Rothenbühl (Saarland, GER)
Resources	SPP, teachers, administration support from schools	SPP, teachers, coaches, administration support from schools, Olympic training center	SPP as teacher, administration support from school and ministry for education
Challenges	Qualified staff (i.e., SPPs to provide MST to all students)	Maintenance of sustainable structures (e.g., personnel, school curriculum) for long-term MST	Qualified staff (i.e., SPPs to provide MST and individualized consultation)
Recommendations	offer sport and exercise psychology compulsory in university teaching for future teachers inform and collaborate with interested teachers SPP as educator and expert supervisor for teachers hybrid occupational education for teachers SPP with knowledge about school system	convince school administration to implement MST workshops in curricula specialize teachers, coaches in sport and exercise psychology via ASEP SPP with knowledge about school system	employ (PE) teachers with educational background in psychology and/or sport and exercise psychology specialize teachers, coaches in sport and exercise psychology via ASEP convince school and ministerial administration to implement MST as a subject
Evaluation	After implementation of MST programs in school, formative evaluations should assess effectiveness and inform adaptations to establish long-lasting high-quality MST programs in schools.		

Notes: MST = mental skill teaching; SPP = Sport Psychology Practitioner; PE = Physical Education; ASEP = applied sport psychology education programs in different practical formats (i.e., extracurricular, curricular, or a synthesis of both). Depending on its format, mental skill teaching programs should address different resources and challenges for successful integration in schools. To achieve long-term mental skill development in student athletes and regular students, formative evaluations are crucial so that programs can flexibly adapt to the school environment and its target groups. Moreover, further empirical evaluation is still needed to identify and recommend effective pathways for integrating mental skills training into schools.

Benefits of Mental Skills for Tomorrow's Generations

Early mental skills training lays the foundation for lifelong resilience and coping strategies, extending benefits beyond school into careers and personal life. Integrating such training into school curricula enables systematic development of these skills. Williams and Krane (2019) highlight that mental techniques are crucial in youth elite sport, and, consequently, we propose embedding mental skills training in schools as a central life domain for student athletes. Doing so enhances not only athletic and academic performance but also personal and social growth. Students can, for example, master challenging performance situations through visualization or goal setting, foster personal development by regulating emotions and applying coping strategies, and strengthen social skills through communication and team-building exercises. Empirical findings confirm that regular and repetitive programs boost both performance and transferable competences across academics and social life (Gilbert, 2017). Long-term benefits are evident when students apply these skills across contexts, thereby enhancing resilience and success (Gilbert et al., 2017).

Building on the previously discussed practice examples from Germany, school-integrated mental skills training is increasingly requested to improve, for example, focus, goal setting, and emotion regulation (Halberschmidt, 2025)—key competences for students' academic success, career readiness, and personal lives. Therefore, schools should include mental skill teaching for all students, for instance through extracurricular classes in all-day programs or embedded within physical education. Practical insights reported by Halberschmidt (2025) further suggest that early, structured, and long-term training consolidates mental skills in both student athletes and regular students, thereby supporting performance and health across the life span. Given these benefits, mental skills training should move from being optional to becoming a mandatory element of school curricula to ensure that all students develop sustainable mental skills for their future.

Concluding Recommendations for Teaching Mental Skills in Schools

Building on the program-specific recommendations from German school settings presented in Table 26.1, we offer four key recommendations to implement mental skills training in schools. First, personnel with sport psychological training (i.e., SPPs, educated teachers) are needed to offer workshops in schools. Second, transparent communication between staff, school administration, and political stakeholders is essential. Third, mental skill teaching workshops should be implemented in small student or student-athlete groups, tailored to the target group, and integrated early in the curriculum to enable individualized, long-term development of mental skills. Fourth, formative evaluation allows for flexible adaptation and ensures high-quality standards in developing the mental skills of tomorrow's generations.

ENHANCING MENTAL SKILLS FOR KINESIOLOGY STUDENTS IN A SPORT PSYCHOLOGY COURSE

Takehiro Iwatsuki

This chapter focuses specifically on how kinesiology students aspiring to enter health-related fields such as physical therapy, occupational therapy, or athletic training can benefit from learning sport psychology through their college programs. Additionally, it explores how public speaking activities can be integrated into a sport psychology class to effectively deliver various topics such as stress and anxiety management, coping with pressure, goal setting, relaxation techniques, and preparation. This will not only convey sport psychology concepts but also teach students how to enhance their presentation skills and perform better in job interviews, which are important for advancing their careers.

Teaching sport psychology courses can vary depending on the instructor's background, teaching experiences, personal values, and most importantly characteristics of learners or students. Taking different courses during my master's programs both in Japan and the United States exposed me to the ranges of ways in which sport psychology classes can be taught. Additionally, gaining experience in teaching sport psychology, exercise psychology, motor learning, and motor control courses over the past eight years has provided me with perspective as to how sport psychology content can be effectively taught to students with different career ambitions than those found in sport psychology. Different exercises using real-life examples can effectively deliver sport psychology courses. Although university courses are typically taught through lectures, psychological pressure situations can also be introduced to challenge the students.

Value of Learning Sport Psychology Concepts

Among various kinesiology courses, such as anatomy, biomechanics, exercise physiology, and motor learning and control, a sport psychology course can offer the most practical applications that students can use daily. Topics include stress management, understanding anxiety and arousal, relaxation techniques, pressure management, the importance of preparation, confidence building, and goal setting, among others. For instance, learning about stress and arousal regulation can help students handle high-pressure scenarios such as exam preparation, clinical practicum, or licensing board interviews and exams (Hufton et al., 2024). Understanding goal-setting theory can enhance their ability to design effective learning plans, whether for training cycles, academic milestones, or long-term career development. This knowledge can also be used when setting goals for their clients. Public speaking activities can teach all the topics through hands-on experiences rather than just lectures, which is crucial for effective learning.

Value of Including Public Speaking

Incorporating public speaking activities into sport psychology classes provides students with hands-on experience applying these concepts in practical settings. For kinesiology majors planning to become strength and conditioning coaches, physical therapists, or athletic trainers, the relevance is even more direct. A strength and conditioning coach engages in public speaking daily—explaining protocols to athletes, presenting progress reports to coaching staff, and motivating individuals and teams. Athletic trainers must learn to navigate confrontation with coaches when advocating for an injured athlete's health and safety. By linking psychological concepts to real scenarios and requiring students to articulate their knowledge to others, public speaking becomes a powerful tool for both learning and professional development. It enhances their ability to think critically, speak with confidence, and perform under pressure—skills that will benefit them long after graduation.

How Is Public Speech Incorporated?

Students are tasked with selecting a scholarly article related to sport psychology and preparing a three-minute presentation as if they were the researchers who conducted the study. This exercise is designed to encapsulate the essence of psychological challenges commonly faced by athletes, such as pressure, anxiety, arousal management, and the necessity of thorough preparation. Here are presentation guidelines:

Duration

Each presentation must last at least 2.5 minutes but no longer than three minutes, ensuring concise and focused content delivery. This is known as the Three-Minute Thesis Competition.

Visual Aids

Limited to three PowerPoint slides, this constraint encourages students to distill information effectively and focus on key points, mirroring the strategic focus required in sports.

Performance Assessment

After all presentations, the audience (comprising fellow students and any attending faculty) votes to determine the best presenters. The top three presenters receive extra credit, introducing a competitive element that mimics athletic competition.

Prior to the actual presentation, students are required to practice with their peers at least three times during the previous class session. As each presentation lasts only three minutes, multiple rehearsals are feasible, allowing students to notice and appreciate how their performance improves from the first to the second and third trials. They often express relief that these practice sessions are not the actual presentation day, as they can see their improvement and identify areas for further enhancement. Additionally, students provide feedback to each other, and this process, including three practice presentations and the exchange of feedback, takes only 30–40 minutes.

On the day of the presentation, students are informed that their performances will be evaluated and that the best presenter will be selected. This introduces a competitive element, although those who do not perform as well will not be explicitly critiqued. This method helps set a tone similar to that of actual competitive environments, such as those experienced by athletes during competitions.

What Educational Objectives Are Included in Public Speaking?

Public Speaking brings various learning opportunities. Not limited to these, but topics include stress and arousal management, pressure management, understanding how anxiety influences performance, the importance of preparation, how preparation increases confidence, goal setting, and others. For example, regarding stress, arousal, and pressure management, preparing and delivering a presentation under time constraints and peer evaluation mimics the stress and arousal athletes experience during competition. This exercise allows students to practice techniques like relaxation and arousal regulation under pressure. The immediate feedback loop in public speaking, where audience reactions are visible and direct, teaches speakers to manage pressure (Martiningsih et al., 2024). They learn to adapt their message on the fly, handle scrutiny, and remain poised in the face of live critiques or challenges.

In addition, public speaking provides a firsthand experience of how anxiety can impact performance, such as through nervousness or forgetfulness (Gallego et al., 2022). Speakers and audience members can study these effects in real-time and apply strategies to mitigate anxiety's negative impacts, thereby improving their overall performance. Most importantly, as students invest time in preparing, they naturally build confidence (Colbeck, 2011). They understand their material better, anticipate questions more accurately, and feel more capable of handling the spotlight. This increased confidence not only enhances their current presentation but also contributes to a more assured approach in future public speaking endeavors and other areas of life. Public speaking exercises effectively demonstrate the importance of preparation and how it can boost confidence (Alanazi et al., 2017).

Conclusion

Incorporating public speaking activities into the sport psychology class offers a unique opportunity for students to explore and understand various psychological concepts in a real-life context. By delivering presentations on topics like stress management, performance enhancement, and goal achievement, general kinesiology students not only deepen their understanding of these concepts but also develop essential communication skills vital for their future professional endeavors. Additionally, engaging in public speaking allows students to practice applying sport psychology principles to practical scenarios, fostering a deeper level of comprehension and application.

EDITORS' TAKEAWAYS

My (Lauren) first foray into the world of teaching was during my doctoral program when I was asked to teach an undergraduate Educational Psychology course. I was excited to have an opportunity to teach, yet the thought that came to mind was, "wait a minute, I'm supposed to teach students how to teach when I've not been taught how to teach?" A mind bender I know, but it was my first introduction to the idea that higher education is about knowledge and expertise in one's discipline—not in the science and art of teaching. Over the years I've had many opportunities to teach diverse audiences on many different topics. And one thing has always rang true—John Wooden's principle that you haven't taught unless people have learned. This chapter offers a lot of practical insights valuable for anyone in a teaching role—and I'd argue that since all of us in this field are meant to be teachers of the psychology of sport, exercise, and performance whether that is through conference presentations, speaking engagements, workshops, 1:1 or team sessions, podcasts, etc., there are valuable insights for all of us to take away.

RECOMMENDED EXERCISES

1 As an educator, how do you balance providing the structure of scientific theory with encouraging creative freedom?

2 How do you prepare for public speaking—class presentations, conferences, lectures, or interviews? Based on your knowledge of performance science, how would you teach others to prepare effectively?
3 Reflect on your teaching philosophy. How has this chapter shaped your views on effective teaching? Which new methods or principles are you most interested in applying, and why?
4 Recall a time as a student when you learned something exceptionally well. What made that teaching effective?
5 Imagine your ideal classroom, team meeting, presentation, or workshop. What would it look like? How would learners engage? Which teaching strategies would you prioritize, and why?

REFERENCES

Alanazi, A. A., Nicholson, N., & Thomas, S. (2017). The use of simulation training to improve knowledge, skills, and confidence among healthcare students: A systematic review. *Internet Journal of Allied Health Sciences and Practice, 15*(3), Article 2.

Colbeck, J. J. (2011). The impact of a fundamentals of speech course on public speaking anxiety. *The Journal of Undergraduate Research, 9*, 145–160.

Constantine, M. G. (2001). Theoretical orientation, empathy, and multicultural counseling competence in school counselor trainees. *Professional School Counseling, 4*(5), 342.

Deutscher Olympischer Sportbund. (2025). *Eliteschulen des Sports [Elite schools of sport]*. https://www.dosb.de/themen/leistungssport/eliteschulen-des-sports

Drabick, D. A., & Goldfried, M. R. (2000). Training the scientist–practitioner for the 21st century: Putting the bloom back on the rose. *Journal of Clinical Psychology, 56*(3), 327–340.

Gallego, A., McHugh, L., Penttonen, M., & Lappalainen, R. (2022). Measuring public speaking anxiety: Self-report, behavioral, and physiological. *Behavior Modification, 46*(4), 782–798. https://doi.org/10.1177/0145445521994308

Gilbert, J. N. (2017). Sport psychology teaching approaches for high school coaches and their student-athletes. *Journal of Physical Education, Recreation & Dance, 88*(2), 52–58. https://doi.org/10.1080/07303084.2016.1260076

Gilbert, J. N., Moore-Reed, S. D., & Clifton, A. M. (2017). Teaching sport psychology for now and the future? The psychological uniform with high school varsity athletes. *The Sport Psychologist, 31*(1), 88–100. https://doi.org/10.1123/tsp.2015-0084

Giordano, A. L., Bevly, C. M., Tucker, S., & Prosek, E. A. (2018). Psychological safety and appreciation of differences in counselor training programs: Examining religion, spirituality, and political beliefs. *Journal of Counseling & Development, 96*(3), 278–288.

Halberschmidt, B. (2025). Sportpsychologie in der Schule – Erkenntnisse aus dem Nachwuchsleistungssport [Sport psychology in school – Knowledge from youth elite sports]. In L. Kullik, T. Birnkraut, & M. Kellmann (Eds.), *Advances in stress and recovery research* (p. 43). Fifty-seventh annual convention of the German Association of Sport and Exercise Psychology (asp), Bochum, Germany. https://asp-tagung.de/wp-content/uploads/2025/05/Abstractband-57.-asp-Jahrestagung-2025.pdf

Harwood, C. G. (2016). Doing sport psychology? Critical reflections of a scientist-practitioner. In M. Raab, P. Wylleman, R. Seiler, A.-M. Elbe, A. Hatzigeorgiadis (Eds.) *Sport and Exercise Psychology Research: From Theory to Practice* (pp. 229–249). Elsevier. https://doi.org/10.1016/b978-0-12-803634-1.00011-x

Howard, G. S. (1993). When psychology looks like a "soft" science, it's for good reason! *Journal of Theoretical and Philosophical Psychology, 13*(1), 42–47. https://doi.org/10.1037/h0091107

Hufton, J. R., Vella, S. A., Goddard, S. G., & Schweickle, M. J. (2024). How do athletes perform well under pressure? A meta-study. *International Review of Sport and Exercise Psychology*, 1–24. https://doi.org/10.1080/1750984X.2024.2414442

Kaiser, J., Walter, N., Oppitz, L., Braun, B., & Schmitz, J. (2024). 2Steps4Health Project: Promotion of mental health in junior professional sports. *Sports Psychiatry, 3*(1), 23–30. https://doi.org/10.1024/2674-0052/a000066

Lebrun, F., MacNamara, À., Collins, D., & Rodgers, S. (2020). Supporting young elite athletes with mental health issues: Coaches' experience and their perceived role. *The Sport Psychologist, 34*(1), 43–53. https://doi.org/10.1123/tsp.2019-0081

Lowman, R. L. (2012). The scientist-practitioner consulting psychologist. *Consulting Psychology Journal: Practice and Research, 63*(4), 151–156.

Martiningsih, I., Susilawati, E., & Rezeki, Y. S. (2024). Students' strategies to overcome public speaking anxiety. *Inspiring: English Education Journal, 7*(1), 66–86. https://doi.org/10.35905/inspiring.v7i1.8766

Raimy, V. (Ed.). (1950). *Training in clinical psychology*. Prentice Hall.

Williams, J. M., & Krane, V. (Eds.). (2019). *Applied sport psychology: Personal growth to peak performance* (7th ed.). McGraw Hill.

27 Teaching for Today's Students

When I (Andrew) got my first teaching gig, I thought, "Great, I'll just do what my instructors did when I was a student—easy enough!" And while that did give me a wonderful starting point, I have learned that teaching today's students in SEPP requires more than just content expertise—it demands adaptability, authentic connections, and a keen understanding of how learning itself is evolving. Today's students arrive in classrooms shaped by digital immersion, heightened mental health awareness, shifting attention spans, and an expectation for active, relevant, and flexible learning experiences. SEPP instructors must balance foundational theory with applied relevance, integrate technology meaningfully, and foster a sense of connection and purpose that resonates with students' personal and professional goals. This chapter explores some pedagogical perspectives, teaching strategies, and ideas for assignments necessary to engage and prepare the next generation of SEPP professionals.

TEACHING FOR TODAY'S STUDENTS: CONNECTING IS KEY

Taryn K. Morgan, Ashwin J. Patel, & Vanessa R. Shannon

Connecting with today's students has evolved significantly but is still a central part of becoming a successful sport, exercise, and performance psychology professional (SEPPP). Connection links emotional engagement with academic and practical learning for students. It is critical to understand three points of connection: self, others, and the future.

Connecting to Self: It Starts with Self-Awareness

Connecting with oneself and gaining a firm understanding of who we are and why is the first step in connecting to others. Our values, beliefs, and worldview influence our interactions and relationships. For SEPP professionals, self-awareness is a critical component of effective teaching to enable you to understand your own strengths, deficiencies, and biases. Cultivating self-awareness helps you recognize and leverage your strengths, identify areas for improvement, and determine ways in which professional development opportunities can address these areas. Self-awareness also shows how your words and actions influence your students, which allows you to make informed and intentional instructional decisions that benefit student learning.

Developing and Implementing a Teaching Philosophy

The journey to self-awareness often begins with the development of a teaching philosophy. A teaching philosophy is a written reflection that helps professionals establish a framework for

DOI: 10.4324/9781003781479-33

their teaching and communicate their values, goals, and expectations. Your philosophy serves as a compass to guide decisions in the classroom and to ground your work in evidence-based frameworks or approaches to best serve your students (Ngene, 2023).

There are many reasons why developing a teaching philosophy is an important step for SEPP teachers. Firstly, clearly outlining your values, approach, and methods helps demonstrate that you are thoughtful and deliberate, which establishes credibility and professionalism. Secondly, it encourages you as a professional to engage in continued professional development, providing a guide by which to reflect on your experiences, learn from your work, and refine your approach. Thirdly, it provides a foundation on which to build upon. Over time, you will learn from experiences, new research, and educational trends to refine your philosophy (Ruge et al., 2021), but the foundation will remain the same allowing stability and consistency throughout your teaching career.

The process of developing a teaching philosophy can be overwhelming (Ngene, 2023). We recommend the following to help you craft a meaningful teaching philosophy including reflective questions to ask during the process:

Reflect on Personal and Institutional Values and Beliefs. First, consider your own and the institution's values and beliefs. The beliefs you have about teaching and learning influence the decisions you make. Reflect on how you want your and the institution's values and beliefs to come through in your teaching. What is/will be most important about your work as an educator? Does your philosophy align with the values and beliefs of the institution? What is your "why"?

Clarify Your Approach and Methodology. Clearly define how you plan to approach teaching, including your preferred methods, techniques, strategies, and how you plan to adapt these to varied students or situations. An effective teaching philosophy will discuss preferred teaching approaches and include instructional strategies that align. A teaching philosophy articulates how you will address diverse learning needs and inclusivity. How will you support a student with diverse learning needs? How will you create an inclusive environment?

Articulate Your Expectations. Communicating expectations is crucial for teachers to establish clear guidelines for academic performance and classroom behavior, which helps create a structured and supportive learning environment. When expectations are clearly communicated, it reduces uncertainty about what is expected, enabling students to perform to their potential and take ownership of their learning and behavior. How will you foster a classroom environment where students feel safe to learn and respected by those around them?

Connecting to Others: Building Rapport and Connection

As Theodore Roosevelt said, "They don't care how much you know until they know how much you care." This rings true when establishing rapport with students. Connecting is a central component in teaching or consulting relationships and takes focused work to understand the current generation, create sticky messages, and utilize multiple modes and styles of teaching. Connecting with today's students requires understanding and empathy. The unique characteristics of today's students, different learning preferences, and the educational landscape's evolving subtleties should all be considered. The following strategies will help you build rapport and foster connections with today's students (Sybing, 2019; Lawrence et al., 2020).

Nurture a Respectful and Inclusive Environment

Creating a classroom environment where every student feels seen and heard is foundational in connecting with today's students. Thoughtful classroom management will allow you to demonstrate respect for the identities, cultures, backgrounds, and perspectives while also holding your students accountable for doing the same. Encouraging your students to contribute to classroom discussions by expressing their opinions and sharing their experiences will foster a sense of belonging and connectedness.

Be Approachable and Accessible

Though it is important to respect students' privacy, connections come from understanding. Finding ways to learn about your students without infringing on their boundaries goes a long way to building rapport. Making yourself available for conversations before or after class, during office hours, or through scheduled meetings provides students with the ability to access you and promote additional student interactions. Learning their names as early as possible and learning about them as human beings, their motivations, and things that are important to them leads to a greater connection between teacher and student.

Use Relevant and Relatable Examples

While generational differences in experiences will exist between you and your students, we all share a common current existence. Connecting learning to current real-life and multi-modal examples is a way to overcome any generational gap; by using examples from current events and popular culture, you will demonstrate to your students that despite your differences, you can connect in the present.

Connecting to the Future: Preparing for Post-Student Life

Sport psychology has changed over the last 25 years, including the pathways that graduates can pursue for a career. The growth of the roles in various areas is exciting and inspires hope in graduates to find a path that fits their why. Faculty have the responsibility to prepare students for post-graduation by focusing on areas including integrating business concepts and literacy, providing career guidance, and highlighting transferable skills.

Integrating Business Concepts and Literacy

Within the curricular design, incorporating business-related courses or modules like entrepreneurship and financial literacy could be embedded into a sport psychology graduate program. Or, teachers could encourage students to take a cognate in marketing or business. Through guest lectures and workshops, teachers can invite industry professionals to share real-world insights and experiences so that students can understand the practical applications of starting their own business, purchasing insurance, negotiating contracts, and more.

Highlighting Transferable Skills

How can we help our students identify the skills utilized within sport psychology that can be applied in other industries? Through seminars and guest panels of professionals in parallel industries, students can learn how to apply sport psychology concepts in areas like executive coaching, performance psychology, the military, and the medical profession to enhance their marketability and service capabilities to industry professionals across various sectors.

Providing Career Guidance

There are several graduate programs that have established mentorship opportunities for students. These mentors can help students leverage their networks to create opportunities for themselves or to connect with other recent graduates who have established themselves within the industry and could provide insights on navigating graduation, how to prepare for interviews, and apply successfully for positions in the industry. By personalizing the support and not offering a one-size-fits-all approach, students can feel seen, safe, and soothed (Siegel & Bryson, 2020) and can confidently navigate their career choices and transitions.

Conclusion

Connecting with today's students is an essential component of being an effective SEPP professional. Educators can create an engaging learning environment by focusing on self-awareness, developing a strong teaching philosophy, and building meaningful relationships. Teaching and mentorship will continue to evolve, and by prioritizing connection to self, to others, and to the future, SEPP professionals can leave a lasting impact on their students.

ACTIVE, ENGAGING, AND AUTHENTIC TEACHING AND LEARNING IDEAS FOR CONTEMPORARY STUDENTS

Christopher Mesagno, Kim Encel, & Michael Spittle

Our chapter provides an understanding of the needs of today's contemporary students. By suggesting the use of engaging and active face-to-face, online, and hybrid teaching and learning environments with more practical, authentic assessments, we hope to support instructors to effectively transfer information to students so they might develop more in-depth knowledge and skills in sport and exercise psychology.

Technology for Engagement

Unlike 20 years ago, universities have transitioned away from face-to-face, lecture-type delivery to a modern learning environment, which relies on a range of technologies. The modern student integrates technology to enhance their learning, including (but not limited to) the internet, video conferencing, quiz applications, artificial intelligence, mobile phones, and online learning management systems (LMS). We as instructors can leverage these technologies to the advantage of our students (and ourselves) to promote engaging learning that entertains to maintain the attention of contemporary students. The LMS, which supplies most university online learning tools, is the first space where learners engage with the online environment. Making this learning space engaging and inviting helps to hook the learner into the education process. Many LMS have built-in "tools" that may help the instructor create a more entertaining space that includes (but is not limited to), interactive content tools (e.g., H5P and Articulate 360), mind map tools, e-Portfolios, and "Wiki". Wiki's, for example, can be used in class to promote the understanding of topics by allowing students to collaboratively explain the topic. Creating a Wiki allows the students creative license to contribute to the Wiki and introduce the topic, with the instructor facilitating the process with questions that may spur students to add more information.

The modern student may crave both an entertaining and informative educational experience to learn best, where leveraging technology effectively can add entertainment value. One method to entertain and inform during lecture-content is using video conferencing to acquire another's perspective on a particular topic. For example, within a sport psychology class, I (Mesagno) have incorporated a "live recorded interview" (video conferencing call) with a mental toughness "expert" to further enhance the content and engage students. Prior to the interview, I received permission from the expert to record the interview to share on the LMS for future classes, but I also allowed students some autonomy by asking them to share some questions for the expert prior to the session (especially if they did not want to ask questions during the session). Using music or video clips is another engaging and informative method for students to learn. Sometimes providing a short clip of carefully chosen (something the young students know) "modern" music at the beginning of a topic may help students initially understand concepts. For example, Eminem's song "Lose Yourself" is a good starter for understanding anxiety in sport because the lyrics link to nervousness and anxiety when performing publicly. TikTok, YouTube, or other video-based platforms could be used to entertain and emphasize discussion points.

Active Learning in the Classroom

Active learning opposes traditional learning, where the lecturer provides information, and the student passively receives this information. An active learning approach advocates for the instructor to facilitate engagement, with students being central in their own learning. While criticisms exist regarding active learning in higher education, evidence supports its implementation as it can enhance the retention of information due to deeper cognitive processing (Freeman et al., 2014), promote critical thinking by encouraging students to analyze and synthesize information (Smith et al., 2009), and create more inclusive learning environments allowing for more equitable learning (Theobald et al., 2020).

One active learning approach that is both engaging and effective is the "think-pair-share" approach. Think-pair-share involves the facilitator posing a question, and students proceeding through a three-step process to actively engage with that question. The "think" component involves an individual student attempting to answer a question, for example, "When have you felt highly motivated in a sports setting and were these motivations intrinsic or extrinsic motivations?" Then, once all students feel comfortable with their individual answers, students then "pair" with a partner, or group members, and discuss their answers. In the pair component, the facilitator asks students to compare their motivations with another student or small group of students. Once sufficient time has been allowed for discussion, students "share" responses with the rest of the class, where the facilitator asks pairs/groups to share one or two main differences they have in motivations and why these differences might exist.

Engaging with active learning approaches like the think-pair-share approach allows individual students to feel more comfortable with their answers before sharing them with a larger student group, which may reduce fear of judgment and increase student engagement because they have considered and possibly adjusted their answers based on other students' feedback. When students feel more comfortable with their responses, they may challenge the answers of other students, creating a critical and insightful classroom environment.

Authentic Assessment

Authentic assessment refers to assessment focused on using knowledge and skills in "real-life" situations, such as applied settings or practice, which may support active learning approaches and applied and transferable skills (McArthur, 2023). Authentic assessment is usually characterized by the simulation of professional practice and applying learned knowledge to challenging tasks (Ashford-Rowe et al., 2013). Thus, authentic assessment is more practical and performance-based such as interviews, presentations, case studies, portfolios, as opposed to more traditional assessments such as essays, multiple-choice tests, or written examinations (Wake et al., 2023). Rather than simply measuring what a student knows, authentic assessments attempt to measure how students apply that knowledge in practical ways.

Important steps in the design and implementation of authentic assessment tasks could include defining the learning outcomes, developing specific assessment criteria, creating an activity, providing marking rubrics, and providing specific, clear student instructions. In defining the learning outcomes, consider the intention of assessment and provide specific outcomes that students should acquire. After developing the learning outcomes, generate specific assessment criteria against which to assess task performance and then create an opportunity for students to use their skills and/or knowledge in a realistic or applied way through an authentic activity. To reduce subjectivity and develop more consistent and reliable assessments, use the assessment criteria to produce marking rubrics to provide students with clear expectations about how they will be evaluated. Finally, provide clear, specific instructions for students to understand the assessment task, the overall assessment process, and the assessment criteria.

Authentic assessment could incorporate a range of assessment tasks or approaches as long as the focus is on practical application and use of knowledge and skills in the "real-world" rather than recalling facts or information. Examples of the types of assessment approaches might include (but are not limited to) performance, simulated, and real-world tasks. Performance tasks require students to complete a task, or a project, usually focused on practical application related to the learning outcomes. Common examples of performance tasks may include a self-reflective task developing an intervention for themselves, field report on a site-visit, evaluation of a case study, or mind map illustrating practical understanding of a topic. Simulation tasks are activities that represent practical experiences and develop application and problem-solving skills. For example, demonstrating or presenting on a specific topic, designing a sport psychology intervention program for an athlete, or demonstrating professional tasks such as conducting an interview with a peer, or reporting the results of a mini research project. "Real-world" tasks usually mirror or simulate situations in real work-related environments to encourage exploration and application of knowledge and skills after formal education ceases. For example, assessment tasks that ask students to take on the role of a sport and exercise psychology professional and provide a case-study report on their experience and actions. Furthermore, with increased integration of technology for engagement in teaching and learning, technology such as video and virtual reality could be extended to create authentic assessment tasks and experiences.

Conclusion

In this chapter, we have described some of the engaging, real-world, and hands-on teaching methods we used to be both informative and entertaining for the modern student to enjoy, learn, and demonstrate their knowledge and skills. Essentially, in a world where student attention spans are less than previous generations, updated teaching methods are required to help students engage with learning. Adopting some of the engaging activities we have suggested will hopefully create a learning environment that helps students to explore, critically reflect on, and understand sport and exercise psychology on a deeper level.

TEACHING IN THE AGE OF ARTIFICIAL INTELLIGENCE AND TECHNOLOGICAL ADVANCES

Amber M. Shipherd & John E. Coumbe-Lilley

Teaching Generation Z (Gen Z) students requires college faculty to emphasize real-world applications and foster classroom environments that encourage relationships and empower student voices. Technological advancements continue to accelerate, pushing educators and students to explore how to integrate technology into learning. In this chapter, we outline strategies for instructors to enhance student motivation and engagement through technology.

Who are Gen Z Students in the Classroom?

Gen Z, born from 1995 to 2010, constitute the majority of students in college today (Giray, 2022; Seemiller & Grace, 2017). Gen Z students differ from previous generations in several ways: they are integrating artificial intelligence (AI) into their learning, have grown up with smartphones and constant access to the internet, are interested in studying abroad, and are still grappling with post-pandemic challenges. They also face pressures from work or family, have shorter attention spans, seek practical education, and are concerned about financial stability (Giray, 2022; Marist, 2023; McMurtrie, 2024; Seemiller & Grace, 2017). These differences are contributing to challenges for educators. Gen Z students often struggle with completing work independently, maintaining attention, and possessing weaker study skills, possibly due to emergency remote teaching during the pandemic (McMurtrie, 2024). However, educators can address these challenges by creating meaningful social interactions, providing students with a voice, ensuring relevant coursework, and guiding responsible technology use (Giray, 2022; Seemiller & Grace, 2017). Below are specific strategies educators can use, based on both literature and our own experiences teaching students in sport, exercise, and performance psychology (SEPP).

From Strangers to Collaborators: Building a Cohesive Classroom Community

Gen Z students are more engaged if their instructor cares (McMurtrie, 2024). Building rapport and fostering social connections are crucial to motivating students to succeed (Muljana & Luo, 2019). Instructors can build relationships with students by learning student names, checking in regularly, sharing personal interests or struggles, and communicating regularly with students (Shipherd et al., 2025). For example, instructors can ask students what they would prefer to be called and then use that name and preferred pronouns both in class and via electronic communication. Maintaining a document with information gathered about students can also assist instructors with fostering connections with students. For example, if a student mentions they will be starting a new job or internship, checking in with them later about how it's going will help the student feel as though their instructor is genuinely interested in them as a human being. Tools like Padlet or PollEv can help check in with student well-being in real time. For example, you can use Padlet to administer a brief check-in, asking students "How are you doing today?" at the beginning of class. Perhaps they are all reporting they are tired and overwhelmed or maybe they are excited and doing well. Instructors can enhance social interactions among students by using intentional icebreakers or small group activities, peer review, or even incorporating group tests or quizzes. When forming student groups, allow students to self-select groups and ensure students have meaningful and distinct group roles.

Classroom Design to Enhance Student Agency and Achievement

Giving Gen Z students a voice in the classroom and properly supporting and scaffolding their learning increases engagement and performance. Allowing them to choose course policies, vote on assessment weights, or create rubrics empowers students and helps them take ownership of their learning (Shipherd et al., 2025). To support learning, instructors should use strategies to help students organize their work and improve study habits, such as teaching them how to read by asking them to annotate readings using technology (e.g., Perusall, hypothesis.is) or providing them guided reading questions. For example, instructors could assist students with their study or learning skills by helping students organize their notes or showing them study strategies to use with the specific course content. To help with reading skills, instructors could use the THIEVES (title, headings, introductions, every first sentence, visuals and vocabulary, end of article/chapter questions, summarize thinking) strategy as a primer for deep reading and understanding (Manz, 2002). Breaking assignments into smaller pieces and giving feedback along the way can help students succeed (Seemiller & Grace, 2017). Similarly, keeping lectures short and varying your learning activities can keep students focused. Flexibility is also crucial with Gen Z students—offering assignment re-dos, building in assignment grace periods, or dropping the lowest grade can accommodate students' real-world challenges.

Making Learning Matter to Students

Gen Z students value relevance, so instructors should clearly explain why students need to learn concepts and how they apply to future careers. Offering opportunities like study abroad, internships, or community engagement can make learning more meaningful (Seemiller & Grace, 2017). In SEPP classes, creating partnerships with local sports or wellness organizations can give students hands-on experience. Additionally, using virtual reality (VR) and augmented reality (AR) simulations helps students practice real-world skills in a controlled setting (Asad et al., 2021). For example, simulations could include counseling athletes, conducting performance enhancement workshops, or managing team dynamics. These experiences are critical for building practical skills for a career in SEPP.

Gen Z students also value opportunities to study abroad or globalize their education. From a North American perspective, recent examples beginning in the 2010s of faculty-led programs to locations in Europe, Central America, and Australia have demonstrated student desire and commitment to engage and immerse themselves in intercultural learning in non-English-speaking and English-speaking SEPP contexts. These programs vary in duration, focus, and intensity from ten days to two months. The growing SEPP field requires students to become culturally competent and integrate various global perspectives to work as practitioners effectively across borders. Provide students with a global education through leading a study abroad course or in your classroom via international case studies and examples to help students recognize and understand cultural and societal factors that influence SEPP practice. Develop partnerships with faculty and practitioners outside of your home country who can virtually speak to and interact with your students.

Tech-Enhanced Learning: Responsible Technology Use in the Classroom

Gen Z grew up with smartphones, so integrating technology is crucial (Ingleby et al., 2019; Saienko et al., 2020). The rise of generative AI, or AI using machine learning to generate content, presents challenges, including concerns over cheating, data privacy, equitable access, diminished relationships, and a depersonalized learning experience (Saaida, 2023; Szabo, 2023; Wingard, 2023). However, educators can embrace generative AI by teaching students how to use it responsibly, knowing that employers are increasingly seeking AI proficiency (Resumebuilder.com, 2023).

Instructors can use AI to generate learning activities and teaching materials, provide students with personalized feedback, and assist in students learning. For example, instructors can teach students to use generative AI tools like ChatGPT to identify errors in their writing or create sample test questions for studying complex material. Generative AI can also be used to facilitate development of students' critical thinking skills. For example, task students with using an AI bot to generate a paper or assignment on a specific topic, then ask them to analyze the AI-generated work to determine inaccuracies or weaknesses either individually or in groups. Students could also be asked to provide empirical support for incorrect information or describe how they would improve the work.

Instructors can also incorporate technology into the classroom outside of using generative AI. Incorporating various types of multimedia into classes can provide students with different ways to learn content. Tools to administer surveys, polls, or quizzes, such as Mentimeter, Poll Everywhere, Quizizz, or Kahoot! can engage students and provide instructors an overview of student understanding. Finally, social media platforms can be integrated to extend the discussion beyond the classroom and create a sense of belonging and connection among students. However, when integrating technology into the classroom instructors should be careful to ensure they have sufficient knowledge of how to use the technology and they have carefully evaluated the limitations and challenges of the technology. Likewise, instructors should be intentional with their technology selections to ensure they are using technology purposefully.

Gen Z students are bright, value relationships, and they are interested in making a difference in the world (Giray, 2022). Working with this generation of students requires instructors to make intentional choices in designing their courses and delivering content to engage and support their learning. SEPP instructors working with Gen Z students must stay adaptable, innovative, and dedicated to creating a positive learning environment for these students. We hope that we have provided you with guidance and ideas in this chapter to help you enhance your classes and learning experience for your students.

EDITORS' TAKEAWAYS

This chapter is a must-read for any future, neophyte, or even seasoned teacher in the field. Not only is it packed with a lot of practical lessons, strategies, and approaches, but also the themes of connection, authenticity, active learning, creativity, and the time and effort needed to create quality courses and classroom environments, making learning matter, and using technology to enhance learning really resonated with me. While these principles ring true regardless of generation, they seem increasingly relevant as the world changes and thus so do the individuals growing up in it. I (Lauren) will never forget several key opportunities I had as a teacher over the years to realize how important it could be for students to feel truly connected to you as a teacher, rather than feeling like they were just another person in a seat or on the class roster. And I equally remember the impact of switching to taking more of a flipped classroom, active learning approach in my teaching. While at first the students were concerned about how they were going to manage it (i.e., no more power points, more onus on them to read the material and come to class ready to engage and participate), I could immediately see the impact in their learning. And it was always clear that the more you could make the material relate to them, the more powerful the learning, memorability, and applicability of the concepts discussed. In today's increasingly technology-supported world, it also strikes me reading this chapter that it behooves educators to find ways to leverage the technology for good (rather than focus on ways students may be using it that are ultimately unhelpful or harmful to them) as well as in service of preparing students for the future world of work, where technology use abounds and continues to grow.

RECOMMEND EXERCISES

1 What technology could supplement learning in your sport, exercise, or performance psychology classes? Choose one digital tool (e.g., Kahoot, Mentimeter) for your next session. Reflect on how it enhanced or hindered engagement and learning, and how you might adapt it in the future.
2 Do you use active learning approaches? How could they be enhanced? How would you design and implement a 'think-pair-share' activity in an upcoming class?
3 What is the difference between authentic and traditional assessment in SEPP? Develop an authentic assessment for one course and reflect on its expected impact on student learning.
4 How can you better foster relationships between yourself and your students, and among students?
5 How can you make assignments or classes more meaningful and relevant for students?

REFERENCES

Ashford-Rowe, K., Herrington, J., & Brown, C. (2013). Establishing the critical elements that determine authentic assessment. *Assessment & Evaluation in Higher Education, 39*(2), 205–222. https://doi.org/10.1080/02602938.2013.819566

Asad, M. M., Naz, A., Churi, P., & Tahanzadeh, M. M. (2021). Virtual reality as pedagogical tool to enhance experiential learning: A systematic literature review. *Education Research International, 2021*(1), 7061623.

Freeman, S., Eddy, S. L., McDonough, M., Smith, M. K., Okoroafor, N., Jordt, H., & Wenderoth, M. P. (2014). Active learning increases student performance in science, engineering, and mathematics. *Proceedings of the National Academy of Sciences, 111*(23), 8410–8415.

Giray, L. (2022). Meet the centennials: Understanding the generation Z students. *International Journal of Sociologies and Anthropologies Science Reviews, 2*(4), 9–18.

Ingleby, E., Wilford, B., & Hedges, C. (2019). Teaching with technology and higher education: A brave new world? *Practice, 1*(1), 73–87. https://doi.org/10.1080/25783858.2019.1589985

Lawrence, J., Shaw, H., Hunt, L., & Synmoie, D. (2020). Rapport and relationships: The student perspective on teaching excellence. In K. C. Thomas & A. French (Eds.), *Challenging the Teaching Excellence Framework* (pp. 129–150). Emerald Publishing. https://doi.org/10.1108/978-1-78769-533-720201006

Manz, S. L. (2002). A strategy for previewing textbooks: Teaching readers to become thieves. *The Reading Teacher, 55*(5), 434–436.

Marist. (2023, September 19). *Marist Mindset List.* https://www.marist.edu/mindset-list/2027
McArthur, J. (2023). Rethinking authentic assessment: Work, well-being, and society. *Higher Education, 85*, 85–101. https://doi.org/10.1007/s10734-022-00822-y
McMurtrie, B. (2024, August 27). Customers in the classroom. *The Chronicle of Higher Education.* https://www.chronicle.com/article/customers-in-the-classroom
Muljana, P. S., & Luo, T. (2019). Factors contributing to student retention in online learning and recommended strategies for improvement: A systematic literature review. *Journal of Information Technology Education: Research, 18*, 19–57.
Ngene, N. C. (2023). Teaching philosophy in a teaching portfolio: Domain knowledge and guidance. *Advances in Medical Education and Practice, 14*, 1231–1248. https://doi.org/10.2147/AMEP.S4s28897
Resumebuilder.com. (2023, April 10). 9 in 10 companies that are currently hiring want workers with ChatGPT experience. https://www.resumebuilder.com/9-in-10-companies-that-are-currently-hiring-want-workers-with-chatgpt-experience/
Ruge, G., Schönwetter, D. J., McCormack, C., & Kennelly, R. (2021). Teaching philosophies revalued: Beyond personal development to academic and institutional capacity building. *International Journal for Academic Development, 28*(1), 59–73. https://doi.org/10.1080/1360144X.2021.1963735
Saaida, M. B. (2023). AI-driven transformations in higher education: Opportunities and challenges. *International Journal of Educational Research and Studies, 5*(1), 29–36.
Saienko, N., Lavrysh, Y., & Lukianenko, V. (2020). The impact of educational technologies on university teachers' self-efficacy. *International Journal of Learning, Teaching and Educational Research, 19*(6), 323–336. https://doi.org/10.26803/ijlter.19.6.19
Seemiller, C., & Grace, M. (2017). Generation Z: Educating and engaging the next generation of students. *About Campus, 22*(3), 21–26.
Shipherd, A. M., Duncan, C., & O, M. P. J. (2025). Fostering social interactions in the online classroom. In A. M. Shipherd & J. E. Coumbe-Lilley (Eds.), *Equitable and Innovative Teaching Practices for Sport, Exercise, and Performance Psychology Educators.*
Siegel, D. J., & Bryson, T. P. (2020). *The power of showing up: How parental presence shapes who our kids become and how their brains get wired.* https://digitallib.pps.unj.ac.id/index.php?p=show_detail&id=92986
Smith, M. K., Wood, W. B., Adams, W. K., Wieman, C., Knight, J. K., Guild, N., & Su, T. T. (2009). Why peer discussion improves student performance on in-class concept questions. *Science, 323*(5910), 122–124.
Sybing, R. (2019). Making connections: Student-teacher rapport in higher education classrooms. *Journal of the Scholarship of Teaching and Learning, 19*(5), Article 5. https://doi.org/10.14434/josotl.v19i5.26578
Szabo, A. (2023). ChatGPT is a breakthrough in science and education but fails a test in sports and exercise psychology. *Baltic Journal of Sport & Health Sciences, 1*(128), 25–40. https://doi.org/10.33607/bjshs.v1i128.1341
Theobald, E. J., Hill, M. J., Tran, E., Agrawal, S., Arroyo, E. N., Behling, S., Chambwe, N., Cintrón, D. L., Cooper, J. D., Dunster, G., Grummer, J. A., Hennessey, K., Hsiao, J., Iranon, N., Jones, L. II, Jordt, H., Keller, M., Lacey, M. E., Littlefield, C. E.,… Freeman, S. (2020). Active learning narrows achievement gaps for underrepresented students in undergraduate science, technology, engineering, and math. *Proceedings of the National Academy of Sciences, 117*(12), 6476–6483.
Wake, S., Pownall, M., Harris, R., & Birtill, P. (2023). Balancing pedagogical innovation with psychological safety? Student perceptions of authentic assessment. *Assessment & Evaluation in Higher Education, 49*(4), 511–522. https://doi.org/10.1080/02602938.2023.2275519
Wingard, J. (2023, January 10). ChatGPT: A threat to higher education? *Forbes.* https://www.forbes.com/sites/jasonwingard/2023/01/10/chatgpt-a-threat-to-higher-education/

Section 7

The SEPP Mentor

28 Mentoring Future SEPP Practitioners

Mentoring plays a critical role in the development of professionals in SEPP. Given the complexity and nuances of all the different topics that have been so far presented in this book (e.g., ethics, the scientist-practitioner approach, entrepreneurism, self-care, navigating academia, demonstrating return on investment to stakeholders, etc.), mentorship provides emerging practitioners with guidance, feedback, and professional modeling that cannot be fully captured in textbooks or coursework. Ultimately, strong mentorship contributes not only to individual growth but also to the advancement and credibility of the field as a whole. Therefore, in the spirit of "last but not least," we present three chapters on mentoring in sport, exercise, and performance psychology. Collectively, our author groups offer an introductory overview to this very important aspect in SEPP.

MENTORING FUTURE PRACTITIONERS IN SPORT, EXERCISE, AND PERFORMANCE PSYCHOLOGY

Jack J. Lesyk, Damien Clement, & Chris Harwood

It has been widely accepted that individuals entering professions that provide human services are typically not ready to practice independently until they have gained experience utilizing applied skills under the monitoring, guidance, tutelage, and feedback of an experienced expert in the field. This has traditionally been the case in the field of sport, exercise, and performance psychology (SEPP). We shall refer to these experienced practitioners as mentors. Following the lead of several mental health professions, it is also widely accepted that effective mentoring requires an additional skill set beyond simply being an experienced practitioner. This chapter, written by three experienced, international mentors and adapted from Lesyk et al. (2020), is intended to provide practical suggestions for being an effective SEPP mentor.

Establishing the Mentor-Mentee Relationship

Although the primary purpose of the mentored experience is preparing the mentee for a professional future as a competent, ethical, and independent SEPP practitioner, two other purposes are relevant. First, the welfare of the mentee's clients; and second, gatekeeping, that is, disqualifying mentees who have demonstrated enduring personal or professional attributes that would make them unsuitable for independent practice in SEPP. Such attributes would include serious unethical behaviors, serious inability to form a professional relationship with clients, and serious deficiencies in understanding and applying basic principles of psychology. It is the mentor's responsibility to ensure that these purposes are continuously monitored and fulfilled.

DOI: 10.4324/9781003781479-35

Selection of a Mentor

Unless the mentee is a graduate student at a university program or in a work setting in which a mentor is assigned, it is the mentee's responsibility to select and establish a relationship with a mentor. The content of a mentored experience should be individualized and determined by the mentee's specific needs and goals set against the specific requirements of the accreditation or certification program. As a result, we recommend that the mentee has one, or more, informational interviews with potential mentors to ensure that this will be a good match. The mentor's expertise and experience should be consistent with the mentee's needs and interests. Some commonalities could include, but are not limited to, work setting, specific sport interests, specializations such as working with teams vs. individuals, and conceptual/philosophical framework. Additional factors which should be taken into consideration are availability for and regularity of meetings, access to mentor's networks, cultural understanding, and compatibility.

Written Agreement

We suggest that the mentor and mentee sign an agreement defining the relationship. This need not be a formal legal contract, although it could be where both parties are part of a formal practitioner accreditation program. Such a document should include topics as agreement start and end dates, conditions by which the agreement could be terminated prematurely, what the mentor commits to, what the mentee commits to, what both parties agree to, scheduling, agreement on fees, who is legally responsible for the mentee's services, commitment to adherence to relevant ethical principles depending on nationality or sport psychology organization.

Fees

In academic settings, one would not expect direct payment by the mentee since the mentor will typically be a professor or staff member at an institution where the mentee is a student on a fee-paying program. This may also occur in work settings where the mentor's job responsibilities include mentoring. Again, no payment is required by the mentee. In other scenarios where there are independent programs of accreditation (e.g., the United Kingdom), the mentee is responsible for paying the mentor for their professional services. Fees should be negotiated between the mentor and mentee and should be included in the written agreement. Some factors to consider and discuss might include the mentee's financial ability to pay, the mentor's customary fees and payment schedule, and customary fees that comparable professionals charge in the mentor's location. It is expected that, when needed, mentors will give special consideration to students and early career professionals whose financial resources may be limited. This is particularly pertinent to young professionals from emerging nations with less developed economies who may greatly benefit from an online mentorship with established international mentors.

Conflict of Interest

Mentors should not provide mentorship to individuals who may present a conflict of interest or multiple relationships such as, but not be limited to, parents, children, spouse, significant others, personal friends, business/financial partners, etc.

Relationship Between Mentees and Their Clients

It is good practice for mentees to have an agreement with their clients. Fees, when relevant, should be included in the agreement. In the interest of transparency and ethical full disclosure, mentees need to inform their clients that mentees' professional services are under the guidance of a mentor who may review case materials regarding these services. Finally, these agreements should include recognition of client confidentiality as well as the name and contact information of the mentor in the event the client believes that the services received are inadequate, inappropriate, or that there is an alleged ethical violation. Mentees should not provide professional services to individuals who may present a conflict of interest or multiple relationships such as, but not limited to, parents, children, spouse, significant others, personal friends, business/financial partners, etc.

Assessing Needs and Setting Goals for the Mentorship

Three factors are at the core of the mentored experience: (a) identifying the mentee's learning needs, (b) setting goals for the mentorship based on these needs, and (c) forming a plan for accomplishing these learning goals. The authors believe that the basic question in assessing the needs and setting goals for the mentorship process is, *What does the mentee need to learn to become a proficient, ethical, independent provider of sport psychology services?* This question can be answered through conversation between mentor and mentee discussing the mentee's current and/or prior work with clients as well as the translation of their academic learning to practical applications. Additionally, when appropriate, to meet specific competencies required for certification or accreditation by various sport psychology organizations.

The Process and Content of the Mentoring Sessions

The authors believe that several factors need to be considered regarding mentoring sessions regardless of their modality (face-to-face or virtual). These include agreeing on the content, generating agendas for each meeting, and keeping meeting records.

Mentoring sessions should primarily focus on developing the applied professional skills and competencies of the mentee. This can be achieved via the mentor sharing examples from their own work experience as well as didactic instruction and modeling to illustrate specific topics and techniques. Such examples might include the mentor's own conceptual framework, ethical dilemmas, the use of specific assessment and intervention tools and techniques, working with specific sports, a developmental model for athlete's progress, sport specific issues, the mentee's career development, and issues of developing and marketing an ethical practice. Case studies can be utilized as another modality to provide content for these sessions that would challenge the decision making of mentees when placed in certain situations.

We suggest that an agenda be established and shared prior to the meeting. This gives both parties time to prepare in advance for the meeting. Additionally, the creation of an agenda helps to keep the mentoring experience focused on the mentee's individual learning goals that were set at the beginning of the mentored experience. The authors suggest that a periodic assessment of the mentoring process itself remains part of the agenda. This assessment can lead to questions such as the extent to which the stated goals are being addressed. Should goals be modified considering the mentee's progress? Can the interactive process of the mentor and mentee be improved? How can each contribute more effectively to making sessions relevant and effective?

In order to document the mentored experience, the authors suggest that both the mentor and the mentee maintain a joint log for each mentoring session. At a minimum, each entry should contain the following: date of the session, length of the session, topics discussed, and mentee's learning goals that were addressed.

Ending the Mentor-Mentee Relationship

The final session of the mentor and mentee should be devoted to assessment and closure. To what extent is the mentee ready for independent practice? To what extent were the mentee's goals attained? Were there any deficiencies that should be addressed? How can the mentee continue their professional development? What will be the future relationship of the mentor-mentee?

Conclusion

The mentoring experience should be a very rich and rewarding experience for both mentor and mentee. It can provide an opportunity for both people to learn from one another and expand their applied sport psychology competencies. We hope the suggestions offered in this chapter will facilitate effective and successful mentorship experiences.

INTEGRATING MULTICULTURAL PRINCIPLES IN THE SUPERVISOR-SUPERVISEE RELATIONSHIP

Leilani Madrigal & Janaina L. Fogaça

This chapter will focus on the supervisor-supervisee relationship in terms of communication and expectations. Specifically, this chapter will briefly expand on how multicultural considerations can be integrated in supervision to support practitioner growth. The Association for Applied Sport Psychology (AASP) adopted the term "mentor" to avoid confusion with clinical psychology supervision, which has different legal implications (Lesyk et al., 2020). The term supervision will be used in the present chapter to refer to the supervision process that is part of mentoring future sport and performance psychology practitioners that may or may not become Certified Mental Performance Consultants (CMPCs).

A Multicultural Lens

Supervision can provide professional growth and be a source for the supervisor and supervisee to find solidarity, validation, and satisfaction (Siple et al., 2015). Ideal supervisors understand their supervisees' lived experiences and guide them through professional competence, evaluation, and gatekeeping with acceptance, worth, and affirmation (Adair et al., 2010). Beyond listening and validating the experiences of the supervisee, supervisors are needed to name, discuss, and critique the forces of oppression that exist within sport psychology, sport, and academia that might affect the performance and quality of life of the supervisee (Tibbetts & Smith, 2023). It is important to learn how factors such as ethnicity, gender, sexual orientation, age, and ability might influence applied practice and supervision processes.

The Multicultural Integrated Supervision Model (MISM; Mitchell & Butler, 2021) is a useful model to help guide supervisors in adopting a multicultural supervision approach. In this approach, supervisees progress through levels of development and supervisors can facilitate their development through interventions that are appropriate to the supervisee's developmental level. Additionally, this model considers factors such as the role of social justice, and the counselor's self-awareness, client worldview, counseling relationship, and advocacy interventions when assessing supervisees' developmental progress (Mitchell & Butler, 2021).

The strongest factor of the MISM is the supervisory alliance which is the foundation to guiding supervisees along these four levels (Mitchell & Butler, 2021). The supervisor-supervisee relationship may involve similar dynamics to the supervisee-client relationship; therefore, being able to openly discuss the relationship, power differential, and marginalized status is key to the development of a multicultural supervision approach. Importantly, having these discussions and conversations early in the supervisor-supervisee relationship is beneficial. In addition, Mitchell and Butler (2021) suggested that the use of a parallel process with more developed supervisees may help them learn how to process interpersonal dynamics in their own sessions.

In practice, supervisors working with less experienced supervisees may want to start by discussing cultural differences that could show in their relationship dynamics with their clients. For example, a supervisee who was a tennis athlete and considers swearing improper due to tennis cultural norms about etiquette might struggle with a client who likes to include swearing in their self-talk or their interactions with opponents. Discussions around the cultural influences on the view of language and respect can be valuable to increase the supervisee's awareness of their own biases and knowledge of different cultures. Similarly, the supervisor can model a discussion of identity and power in the supervisory relationship. For example, a female supervisee might struggle getting buy-in while working in a male-dominant sports environment. If her male supervisor brings up the discussion of the gender and power dynamics within their own supervisory relationship, it might help strengthen the supervisory relationship while helping her process the power dynamics in her own practice.

As supervisees develop, the supervisor can guide them through deeper explorations of their identities and how they affect their practice and supervision, in addition to building multicultural case conceptualizations (see Mittchell & Butler, 2021 for more details). Throughout this work, the supervisee develops better multicultural skills while the supervisory process becomes more culturally sensitive. We suggest two key aspects of this work will help build the supervisor-supervisee relationship: communication and clear expectations.

Communication

Although most supervisors would like to have multicultural discussions with supervisees, many report that a lack of comfort, opportunity, or time can prevent them from having these discussions (White-Davis et al., 2016). For example, Jeremy was unsure if he should bring up the impact of current immigration protests occurring on campus with his first-generation mentee Lucas because he was afraid the discussion could impact the supervisory working alliance. Lucas, on the other hand, felt acknowledged when his supervisor Jeremy had a discussion with him around current immigration events, which led to him feeling more supported by his supervisor. When supervisors do not attend to and address multicultural and social justice issues, it can weaken the supervisory relationship by instilling feelings of disappointment, invalidation, and frustration (Spowart & Robertson, 2024). Due to inherent power dynamics in a supervisory relationship, it is important that the supervisor initiate discussions surrounding multicultural issues to normalize and model this behavior for trainees (Chao et al., 2022).

Spowart and Robertson (2024) found that focusing on and discussing client-specific, rather than supervisee-specific multicultural and social justice factors and dynamics may be easier at first than addressing them within the supervisory relationship. For instance, in the case above, Jeremy could start by checking in with Lucas about his client who comes from an immigrant family then transition to see how Lucas is being affected. Chao et al. (2022) suggested that a critical first step in initiating multicultural discussion is creating a brave space in which the supervisor and supervisee(s) need to commit to providing honest feedback, accept accountability, and reflect on feedback non-defensively (see Chao et al., 2022 for scenarios and activities that can be used to facilitate discussions around identity and cultural competence with supervisees). Other ways to enhance cultural identity conversations can be to highlight and note implications of the supervisor and supervisee holding different identities, explicitly asking the supervisee if they would like support prior to any situation they might encounter, using position of privilege to lift up supervisee's voice when they might otherwise be overlooked or ignored, and checking in with supervisees after major cultural events involving racism, misogyny, or other forms of oppression (Tibbetts & Smith, 2023).

Expectations

Expectations around supervisory relationships are strongly influenced by culture (Tyler et al., 2000). For example, someone from a collaborative culture might have expectations of frequent meetings and support for various tasks that someone from an independent culture might assume to be solely the supervisee's responsibility. For this reason, discussing supervision roles and expectations for both parties should ideally be done at the beginning of the supervisory relationship (Poczwardowski et al., 2023). According to Poczwardowski et al., it is the supervisor's responsibility to clarify supervisor and supervisee roles and expectations regarding the supervisee's performance. Further, they recommended that both should discuss specific behaviors, incongruencies, and potential misunderstandings. To model multicultural considerations in this discussion, the supervisor may explore the supervisee's previous experiences with supervision and their cultural values and comfort with open communication. In this sense, building a good supervisory relationship and open communication within the dyad will be imperative (Mitchell & Butler, 2021).

Summary

The supervisory relationship is a central aspect of multicultural supervision because it allows the supervisee to be comfortable in exploring the influence of power and identity in supervision and applied work (Mitchell & Butler, 2021; Poczwardowski et al., 2023). To approach these conversations, the MISM can be a useful model that guides supervisory approaches according to the supervisee's developmental levels. Additionally, communication and clear expectations are key in the relationship. Therefore, early discussion of communication and expectations is important to build a strong supervisory relationship that will allow vulnerability as the supervisory work progresses (Mitchell & Butler, 2021). Additionally, when supervisors attend to cultural, privilege, oppression and power in the supervisee-supervisor dyad, the supervisee's ability to do the same with their clients may improve (Soheilian et al., 2014).

DEVELOPING MENTOR-MENTEE RELATIONSHIPS: SUGGESTIONS FOR INITIAL PARTNERSHIP

Michelle M. McAlarnen, Janaina L. Fogaça, & Gily Meir

Mentorship is an important factor that contributes to professional development among sport psychology practitioners (Fogaça et al., 2024). Wooding et al. (2022) interviewed 13 sport psychology graduates 5–9 years after their graduation about their transition into the job market; when asked about important factors that helped them prepare for the transition, many indicated that having a very good mentor was "invaluable" and even "the most important part of the graduate school experience." Due to this importance, mentees should choose a mentor who is a good fit and can provide the support that mentees expect to receive as well as structure the mentorship relationship so that there are clear expectations and procedures for mentor and mentee. In this chapter, we explore some key considerations for mentor selection as well as discuss how mentorship informs the mentee's initial client needs assessments.

Mentor Selection

When searching for a mentor, mentees should consider interviewing potential mentors in the same way that mentors may interview mentees to assess their potential fit. Mentees will often have several mentors during their graduate training and professional career. These mentors can provide different perspectives to service delivery, as well as mentorship. When beginning a new mentorship relationship with each mentor, the first aspect to be considered during this initial contact is assessing the mentor's qualifications. Mentorship requires a specific set of skills and knowledge that go beyond applied work skills (Bernard & Goodyear, 2019). Mentees should be proactive in asking potential mentors about their mentoring experience and training. As mentees progress in their training, they may seek out mentors whose approaches best fit their developmental stage and who challenge them, have different approaches or expertise, or provide support in different ways.

Poczwardowski et al. (2023) outlined the responsibilities of mentors and mentees and emphasized the importance of mentees also proactively engaging in conversations about roles and expectations in the mentorship. Mentees should reflect upon their goals for mentorship and for their professional development, and their expected level of mentor support. During initial conversations, mentees should ask specific questions about the mentor's expectations about what they should prepare before meetings, how to keep notes, and which situations warrant communication between meetings (e.g., emergencies). Another important area to be considered during this initial interview is the mentor's philosophy and exploring how it guides mentorship, such as setting goals, providing support, conducting mentee's evaluation, and offering guidance and autonomy (Fogaça & Madrigal, 2023).

Structure of the mentorship meetings, meeting frequency, and forms of contact between meetings can vary significantly in mentorship outside of the academic setting. Some mentors favor individual meetings while others prefer the extra layer of reflection provided by group supervision. In addition, some mentors may provide clients to their mentees or vary the frequency of meetings depending on how many clients they are currently seeing (Fogaça et al., 2023). Because of these variations, mentees should consider their own learning preferences when choosing a mentor but also consider that less experienced mentees tend to need more structure and guidance to thrive (Fogaça et al., 2018).

Lastly, feedback is an essential component of mentorship and we encourage mentees to inquire how mentors will provide feedback. Mentors can provide informal and formal feedback on mentees' competence in important areas of service delivery. Hutter et al. (2015) identified areas in which mentees desired guidance from mentors, such as using assessment, providing referrals, balancing client-led/directive counseling, and coping with boundary issues. Mentees and mentors can review Hutter and colleagues' findings or other self-assessment tools to collaboratively select areas in which to focus feedback. Mentees can also identify areas in which they would like specific feedback.

Mentorship During Initial Client Needs Assessment

Beginning applied service delivery is an exciting time in a mentee's educational journey. After learning foundational content and how professionals provide services, it is finally the mentee's chance to support performers. This moment can provide an opportunity for mentors to guide mentees as they think through how to approach, structure, and design consulting programs by asking mentees questions about their decision making, such as (a) who are important people in this organization to build rapport with and understand their needs (b) what is the important information to learn about performers in this context, why is it important, and how might you go about acquiring this information, and (c) how will you use this information to identify which interventions might fit and to design programming for the individual or group? Additionally, mentors can help support mentees with program design by discussing and modeling how they conceptualize their service delivery, rationales behind their process, and what forms and processes they use during each stage of service provision. Learning how the mentor's process has changed over the years might be of particular interest to mentees and offer an example of how professionals continue to develop and refine their work over time. Engaging in conversation about why the mentor approaches and organizes the work a certain way helps the mentee understand and practice this self-reflective process as they begin to develop their professional approach and identity.

To help guide a conversation around program design, the mentee and mentor can explore four broad categories of information gathering: (a) needs assessments, (b) mental skills assessments, (c) intake meetings, and (d) observations. Together, they can consider which approaches would fit for the performance context and practice using these approaches to inform service delivery. For example, with a new team or organization, the mentee might decide to complete a needs assessment. A needs assessment can be conducted to learn which mental skills or topics are important to performers or leaders and the goals they have for the mental skills programming (Maher, 2021). This information can help mentees plan sessions that are tailored to the client and demonstrate how the relationship is collaborative. The mentor might ask the mentee what the best method is to collect needs assessment data (e.g., survey, focus groups) and what questions and content might they include in the assessment. Additionally, a mentee may choose to use a formal mental skills assessment to understand group or individual clients' performance, coping, or use of mental skills before sessions begin and then evaluate client growth during and at the end of mental skills training (Maher, 2021). Mentors can show mentees how to effectively conduct the assessment process. Mentors might ask mentees to consider (a) which scale to select based on what they plan to assess, (b) how mentees will discuss the scale and its use with clients (along with relevant confidentiality and privacy information), (c) how the data will be collected, scored, and interpreted, and integrated into intervention design, and (d) if, and how, assessment will be used in program evaluation and shared with leadership (e.g., coaches, organizational leadership). If possible, mentees can benefit from observing leaders, groups, and individual performers in their performance context to understand the performance demands, group interactions, and performer-in-action. Mentors and mentees can discuss what and how to observe, and the insight gathered from these observations. Lastly, mentors and mentees can discuss specific approaches, paperwork, and goals of intake meetings with individual clients. During this first meeting, the mentee develops a relationship with the client, establishes clarity about services, learns about the client's performance and personal background, explores client goals and presenting concerns to inform the mental skills intervention plan, and provides an initial insight or skill for the client to use

(Chow et al., 2024). By blending needs assessment, mental skills assessment, observation, and intake meetings, mentees can design tailored service delivery and interventions with the guidance of mentors.

Conclusion

Mentorship provides opportunities for professional growth for the mentor and mentee alike. To make the most out of the relationship, mentors and mentees should have a conversation at the onset about expectations, roles, goals, logistics, and philosophical approach. A variety of mentors can demonstrate the various ways in which mentoring and consulting can occur. As mentees initiate consulting relationships, mentors can guide them through the program design process.

EDITORS' TAKEAWAYS

Lesyk, Clement, and Harwood highlight an often-overlooked purpose of the mentored experience: gatekeeping the profession by ensuring those unfit for applied SEPP practice do not continue. Nearly every faculty member or applied mentor encounters an aspiring professional who raises concern, yet the field lacks clear, ethical, and compassionate best practices for responding. Should we help the individual conduct a strengths-based analysis to explore alternative paths? How direct should feedback be, and are mechanisms in place to document concerns? These are difficult but necessary conversations, and more spaces for dialogue among mentors are needed. Madrigal and Fogaça's work on integrating multicultural principles in SEPP supervision prompted me to consider how this approach ultimately supports both athlete well-being and performance. Beyond technical outcomes, such principles may enhance confidence, engagement, and resilience, raising the question of how we define meaningful success: by performance metrics alone, or also by athletes' overall experience and identity affirmation. McAlarnen and colleagues underscore the importance of mentoring during a mentee's first SEPP client encounter. This "blank slate" moment reveals implicit beliefs and biases, making thoughtful debriefing essential for fostering professional growth, self-awareness, and reflective practice.

RECOMMENDED EXERCISES

1 What does "good mentorship" look like to you? How have your mentorship experiences shaped your identity and philosophy as a consultant and mentor/mentee?
2 What factors, needs, and preferences guide your choice of mentors or mentees? How do your values and culture affect communication with authorities or subordinates, and how can you adapt when working across cultures?
3 What are your expectations for mentor and mentee roles, and how might cultural differences influence these expectations? How could you interact differently with individuals from other cultures?
4 Reflect on a recent mentoring interaction. If you were the mentor: What strengths and areas for growth did the mentee show, and how did/would you balance challenge and support? If you were the mentee: What strengths and areas for improvement did the mentor show, and how could their approach better support you?
5 If a mentee acts incorrectly or unethically, how would you address it? How would you respond if they show common types of resistance (to self-awareness, ignorance, or change)?

REFERENCES

Adair, D., Taylor, T., & Darcy, S. (2010). Managing ethnocultural and "racial" diversity in sport: Obstacles and opportunities. *Sport Management Review, 13*(4), 307–312. https://doi.org/10.1016/j.smr.2010.06.002

Bernard, J. M., & Goodyear, R. K. (2019). *Fundamentals of clinical supervision* (6th ed.). Pearson.

Chao, D., Badwan, M., & Briceno, E. M. (2022). Addressing diversity, equity, inclusion and belonging (DEIB) in mentorship relationships. *Journal of Clinical and Experimental Neuropsychology, 44*(4), 420–440. https://doi.org/10.1080/13803395.2022.2112151

Chow, G. M., Garinger, L. M., Freeman, J., Ward, S. K., & Bird, M. D. (2024). "It's about going from good to great": Expert approaches to conducting a first sport psychology session. *Journal of Clinical Sport Psychology, 18*(1), 14–36. https://doi.org/10.1123/jcsp.2021-0107

Fogaça, J. L., & Madrigal, L. (2023). Mentoring philosophy as a guide to navigate challenges from the lens of certified mental performance consultant mentors. *Journal of Clinical Sport Psychology.* Advance online publication. https://doi.org/10.1123/jcsp.2023-0018

Fogaça, J. L., Madrigal, L., Gonzalez, B., Lerner, D., & Boyajian, S. (2023, October). Supervision in private practice: Logistics, challenges, and strategies. Poster presented at the Annual Conference of the Association for Applied Sport Psychology, Orlando, FL.

Fogaça, J. L., Quartiroli, A., & Wagstaff, C. R. D. (2024). Professional development of sport psychology practitioners: From systematic review to a model of development. *Psychology of Sport & Exercise, 70,* 102550. https://doi.org/10.1016/j.psychsport.2023.102550

Fogaça, J. L., Zizzi, S. J., & Andersen, M. B. (2018). Walking multiple paths of supervision in American sport psychology: A qualitative tale of novice supervisees' development. *The Sport Psychologist, 32*(2), 156–165. https://doi.org/10.1123/tsp.2017-0048

Hutter, R. I. (V.), Oldenhof-Veldman, T., & Oudejans, R. R. D. (2015). What trainee sport psychologists want to learn in supervision. *Psychology of Sport & Exercise, 16*(1), 101–109. https://doi.org/10.1016/j.psychsport.2014.08.003

Lesyk, J. J., Clement, D., & Maher, C. A. (2020). *CMPC mentor guidelines and best practice recommendations* [PDF]. Association for Applied Sport Psychology. https://appliedsportpsych.org/site/assets/files/30047/cmpc_guidelines_and_best_practices_recommendations-1.pdf

Maher, C. A. (2021). *Developing and sustaining sport psychology programs: A resource guide for practitioners.* Routledge.

Mitchell, M. D., & Butler, S. K. (2021). Acknowledging intersectional identity in supervision: The Multicultural Integrated Supervision Model. *Journal of Multicultural Counseling and Development, 49*(2), 101–115. https://doi.org/10.1002/jmcd.12209

Poczwardowski, A., Andersen, M. B., Van Raalte, J. L., Si, G., Harwood, C., Tshepang, T., & Noce, F. (2023). ISSP position stand: Competent supervision in sport psychology. *International Journal of Sport and Exercise Psychology, 21*(6), 931–950. https://doi.org/10.1080/1612197X.2023.2229342

Siple, B. J., Hopson, R. K., Sobehart, H. C., & Turocy, P. S. (2015). Who should mentor me? Giving a voice to Black women athletic training students. *Athletic Training Education Journal, 10*(2), 146–158. https://doi.org/10.4085/1002146

Soheilian, S. S., Inman, A. G., Klinger, R. S., Isenberg, D. S., & Kulp, L. E. (2014). Multicultural supervision: Supervisees' reflections on culturally competent supervision. *Counseling Psychology Quarterly, 27*(4), 379–392. https://doi.org/10.1080/09515070.2014.961408

Spowart, J. K. P., & Robertson, S. E. (2024). Becoming a culturally responsive and socially just clinical supervisor. *Canadian Psychology.* Advance online publication. https://doi.org/10.1037/cap0000388

Tibbetts, E., & Smith, K. P. (2023). Beyond "a good fit": Examining effective mentorship for BIPOC practitioners in a predominately white profession. *Journal of Applied Sport Psychology, 35*(1), 46–62. https://doi.org/10.1080/10413200.2022.2055221

Tyler, T. R., Allan Lind, E., & Huo, Y. J. (2000). Cultural values and authority relations: The psychology of conflict resolution across cultures. *Psychology, Public Policy, and Law, 6*(4), 1138–1163. https://doi.org/10.1037/1076-8971.6.4.1138

White-Davis, T., Stein, E., & Karasz, A. (2016). The elephant in the room: Dialogues about race within cross-cultural supervisory relationships. *The International Journal of Psychiatry in Medicine, 51*(4), 347–356. https://doi.org/10.1177/0091217416659271

Wooding, C. B., Monda, S. J., Fitzpatrick, S. J., & Statler, T. (2022). Transitioning from student to professional: Experiences of recent U.S. graduates in sport and performance psychology. *Journal of Ethnographic & Qualitative Research, 16*(4), 324–343.

29 Developing Oneself as a Mentor

A fundamental mindset we try to instill in our athletes and performers is that of "ongoing" or "lifelong" learning. This mindset supports their ability to navigate challenges, maintain motivation, and regulate emotions—among many other benefits. As such, it is equally valuable for the sport psychology mentor. As editors, we felt strongly that Developing Oneself as a Mentor deserved its own chapter because most SEPP graduate programs offer little formal training in mentorship. Often, skill development in this area is limited to occasional workshops or seminars hosted by professional associations. While some may engage in special interest groups on practitioner mentorship, these conversations can grow stagnant if confined to the same participants. To broaden and enrich the dialogue, we invited three author groups to contribute perspectives on how one might thoughtfully and intentionally grow in their role as a mentor. Collectively, the three author groups give mentors some fascinating avenues to consider for their own growth and development in this particular professional role.

MENTORSHIP IN SPORT AND EXERCISE PSYCHOLOGY: NURTURING TALENT, BUILDING SKILLS, AND EVOLVING AS A MENTOR

Moira E Lafferty, Martin Eubank, & Joanne Butt

What Do We Mean by Mentorship?

If you were to take a minute to think about your journey to date within sport and exercise psychology (SEP), you might be able to identify one person who has been instrumental in helping you; they may have been a supervisor, a colleague, or a role model who inspired you. They will have offered advice, guidance, and provided a safe space in order that you could grow and develop. In essence, they provided mentorship.

Within the wider psychology literature, mentorship has been defined by Ragins and Kram (2007) as "a developmental relationship that is embedded within the career context" (p. 13) and encapsulates two functions or strands (Kram, 1988): (1) facilitating professional development and (2) providing psychosocial support. Professional development of the mentee arises through the mentor providing a range of experiences and opportunities that allow the practitioner to develop the necessary skills to become competent within their career. For example, this may include developing ethical competence, or the skills necessary to work with multiple stakeholders and in differing cultural contexts. The psychosocial function of mentoring focuses on the interpersonal relationship between mentor and mentee, and through this both professional and personal growth occur such as the development of self-efficacy. Van Raalte and Anderson (2000) built on these functional

DOI: 10.4324/9781003781479-36

descriptions when they described mentorship within SEP as a process of protecting the client through ensuring competence in service delivery while nurturing personal and professional growth.

It is also important to acknowledge the natural mentorship life cycle. Ragins and Kram (2007) suggested that there are four distinct phases; initiation, cultivation, separation, and redefinition with cultivation being the main phase where the mentee develops their career skills. During this phase, the trainee develops, identifies, and refines their professional practice philosophy and moves from being an apprentice to an expert of their craft (Lafferty & Tod, 2023). Concurrently, with their professional development, their requirements from the mentoring relationship change (McEwan et al., 2019) and mentors need to acknowledge this change and adapt within the role to accommodate a more mutually reciprocal relationship.

Whilst we have discussed mentorship from the position of someone who directs, supervises, and supports trainees, mentors have many hats and mentorship can be both formal and informal. For example within SEP, an informal mentorship alliance might occur with peers through networking at a conference, at a continuing professional development event, within a training group, or during a graduate program. Furthermore, SEP training programs that engage with a peer mentoring model supported through meta supervision will help the field of sport psychology develop and allow the next generation of mentors to craft the skill set necessary to become formal mentors (Raabe et al., 2019).

What Are the Skills of a Good Mentor?

To optimize the mentoring process, a skilled mentor establishes an awareness of the mentee's level, assesses their psychological competencies and needs, and provides meaningful guidance and feedback on the mentee's work. The skilled mentor establishes an empathic and caring mentoring environment and provides the mentee with regular collaborative opportunities for dialogue within a psychologically safe space. Here, a skilled mentor asks questions that help the mentee to reflect on, and learn from, their experiences, and in turn manage anxieties around practitioner development. The skilled helper provides a challenge-supportive climate by intentionally creating an environment where the mentee's practitioner development is fostered through appropriate challenges to, alongside consistent mentor support for, their practice. This facilitates mentee individuation (McEwan et al., 2019) to develop their own authentic practitioner identity as a psychologist (Tod et al., 2020) and avoids them becoming a "transference clone" of their mentor.

At the heart of skilled mentorship is the quality of the mentor-mentee relationship. The skilled mentor possesses the knowledge and ability to develop a positive and power-neutral mentoring alliance. To promote an effective working alliance, the mentor and mentee may engage in the process of documenting, defining, selecting, reflecting upon, and recognizing the fundamental, deeply ingrained ideas they each hold about themselves, others, and the world. Having a reciprocal understanding of each other's beliefs and values and how they influence one's thoughts, feelings, and behaviors enables a skilled mentor to align expectations, build rapport, maintain open communication, and facilitate mentee agency to promote effective mentoring relationships. Skilled mentors are more flexible and authentic in their mentee exchanges, accepting the value of collaborative, empowering, and autonomy supportive driven interactions with their mentees. This provides the skilled mentor with an understanding of the behavioral and mindset preferences of themselves and their mentee and how they might best forge effective connections with one another.

Strategies to Improve Mentoring Skills

With such an emphasis on developing our trainees, we can unintentionally neglect the longer-term development of our own skills as mentors. One strategy we advocate to further enhance them is debriefing (cf. Byrd et al., 2022). We can use debriefing to facilitate our own skills as a practitioner, and we can use it to help our mentees process consultations and engage in training. In wearing your mentor hat, when did you last engage with a colleague to debrief one of your mentoring sessions? Using video footage to debrief the strengths and weaknesses of a mentoring session in addition to role-playing how you might provide guidance in an anticipated challenging scenario can be useful to improve your mentoring.

Research acknowledges that the mentoring process can help trainees to get to know themselves better (Sharp et al., 2021) and thus building rapport and understanding the mindset of those we mentor is a vital skill. To do this, we often engage with a profiling tool (i.e., Spotlight) that facilitates our understanding of each other's performance preferences (cf. Burnell et al., 2023) in specific contexts. Originally, Spotlight was a tool designed to enhance adaptability in that it can help individuals develop their ability to adapt how they think or behave when faced with different challenges. Spotlight comprises two distinct models that relate to an individual's *mindset* and *behavioral style* preferences, each of which, are underpinned by personality theories (cf. Burnell et al., 2023). When considering an individual's natural preferences, discussions can then take place around how one might need to adapt their mindset or behavioral style to effectively navigate different situations. For example, one strength of having a natural preference for a "prudent" mindset is being risk aware and planning for things that could go wrong. In this instance, as a mentor I am aware of the need for contingency planning with my mentee, but I am also keen to explore an alternative mindset such as "contained," knowing that on occasions it is appropriate to be confident in making a decision. With Spotlight, we can consider how our mentees might respond to setbacks and successes, encourage skills of adaptability, and highlight their key strengths. Research supports that being able to identify strengths and focus on the positives can help us to empower our trainees, it can help us to celebrate differences, and it can deepen trust—all of which contribute to building stronger relationships (Burnell et al., 2023).

Finally, it is important to note some key factors that can potentially derail effective mentoring. First, losing sight of the reasons why you are mentoring can become problematic to the nature of the relationship you have built with a trainee. For mentors, motives to supervise students training in SEP tend to be centered on professional satisfaction, the growth of the field, and achieving the common goal of developing competent and safe practitioners. However, it has been discussed in psychology supervision literature that while a natural power differential will exist (e.g., knowledge, skills, experience), it is important to avoid developing power-seeking intentions (Gardner & Moore, 2006). Second, try to avoid creating an imbalance between informal and formal mentoring opportunities for prolonged periods of time. On one perspective, practitioner development research typically acknowledges that mentees benefit from having a mentor that is "informally" available for impromptu advice (McEwan et al., 2019), perhaps at shorter notice. That said, the importance of regular, planned activities as part of formal supervision meetings has also been emphasized. For example, in helping mentees to develop professional judgment and decision-making expertise, the role of organized scenario-based training where expert feedback is available (i.e., formal supervision) has been reported as being beneficial (Smith et al., 2019). Collectively, it is important to note that service delivery in sports will often require trainees to be working in multiple environments with frequent periods of travel which can lead to changes in the mentoring process (e.g., times where structured supervision is not an option). While this flexibility in processes is crucial, an imbalance between informal or formal mentoring sessions for long periods can potentially be debilitating to effective mentoring.

To conclude, in this chapter, we discuss, highlight, and advocate for the following key areas of mentorship as it is applied to sport psychology: (1) two central elements of facilitating professional development and providing psychosocial support; (2) guiding and advising based on the mentees stage of training and development; (3) viewing the quality of the mentor-mentee relationship as a fundamental skill to being an effective mentor, maintaining a balance between formal and informal supervision meetings as well as incorporating planned activities during formal supervision meetings such as role-play and debriefing client sessions; and (4) developing an understanding of your mentees' mindset, strengths, and characteristics to further improve the effectiveness of mentoring.

A FORMER MENTOR AND MENTEE REFLECT TOGETHER ON MENTOR DEVELOPMENT

Bart Lerner & Angela Breitmeyer

Our Unique Journey to Mentorship

We offer the unique perspective of a mentor-mentee dyad coauthoring this portion of the mentorship chapter. Bart served the Association for Applied Sport Psychology (AASP) as the chair of the Recertification Committee and a member of the Certification Review Council from 2023 to 2028. He served as Angela's mentor and she was his assistant when he first served on this council. He later provided her mentorship when she worked with collegiate coaches and athletes. As Bart's mentee, Angela appreciated his commitment to providing her quality mentorship, consistency in scheduling their mentorship sessions, confidence in his sport psychology service delivery, competence in the skillset mentorship, and consultation with evidence-based resources through AASP and APA Division 47. These factors have helped to direct the mentor-mentee relationship so that the appropriate responsibilities are incorporated within the context of building a healthy and supportive relationship. Confidence in one's ability to deliver sport psychology services builds overall trust and respect when discussing issues with a mentor. This, in turn, leads one to be more consistent, committed, and competent based on prior experiences, which can be driven by evidence-based resources during current and future consultations. This emphasis on ongoing professional consultation can reinforce the importance of staying connected to the field's evolving standards of professional development. These qualities can make mentorship deeply meaningful, leaving a lasting impact on one's growth as a confident, competent, and ethically grounded practitioner.

When developing oneself as a mentor, it is essential to first understand the role, responsibilities, and expectations as a mentor; these include the ability to guide, support, and offer constructive feedback to mentees. Effective communication skills are vital, which includes techniques for active listening, providing feedback and fostering an open dialogue. Mentors must learn how to help mentees set realistic goals and create actionable plans to achieve them. Training may cover strategies for addressing and resolving conflicts that may arise during the mentoring relationship. Finally, understanding and respecting diverse backgrounds and perspectives is important for building strong, inclusive mentoring relationships.

Dimensions of Mentorship

Within the realm of SEPP mentorship, and based on our shared journey, broader experience, and published research, we have identified several key concepts relevant to mentorship for Certified Mental Performance Consultants (CMPCs), namely: (a) task dimensions of mentorship, (b) relational dimensions of mentorship, (c) self-reflective practice to develop task and relational dimensions of mentorship, (d) parallel process of mentorship, and (e) education and continuing education. For the purposes of this chapter, we will highlight the task dimensions of mentorship, parallel process of mentorship, and education and continuing education resources available to SEPP mentors.

Task Dimensions of Mentorship

When providing SEPP consultation services, there are relevant task dimensions; the same holds true for providing SEPP mentorship. These key task dimensions within mentorship include setting the agenda for mentorship sessions, considering the mentee's developmental level, modeling effective communication and SEPP service delivery, and incorporating relevant self-reflective questions for the mentee. Specifically, when Bart mentored Angela, we set a scheduled meeting for approximately 60 minutes per session, in which Angela provided an overview of her individual and team consultation sessions. Given that Angela had limited sport science knowledge with her previous clinical experience, we focused our primary attention during mentorship on sport psychology and performance enhancement services (i.e., mental skills training as opposed to Socratic questioning and active listening skills). She shared evidence-based mental skills (e.g., self-talk and team cohesion), in which Bart provided the necessary feedback and asked pertinent questions to gauge Angela's comprehension of the implementation and effectiveness of the skill. If Angela felt she needed further guidance, then she would ask Bart for suggestions as to how the skill could be implemented and taught differently in order to enhance the team's engagement and receptivity for improved retention. Some examples of self-reflective questions included:

- "How effective was your communication during your consultation?"
- "What are areas that you could improve upon?"
- "How did you connect with the team and/or athlete?"

Parallel Process of Mentorship

The concept of "parallel process" has been referenced in psychotherapy supervision literature for decades (McNeill & Worthen, 1989; Tracey et al., 2012; Zetzer et al., 2020), and not surprisingly, has parallels with SEPP mentorship as well. Rooted in the psychoanalytic tradition, the term "parallel process" essentially refers to a supervisee, or in this case, mentee, bringing in experiences from their teams/athletes/performers with whom they are consulting (e.g., anxiety) into supervision, or in this case, mentorship sessions (Zetzer et al., 2020). For example, suppose your mentee just started working with a team, and they had uncertainties as to whether they connected with the team to an appropriate degree, asked too many (or not enough) questions, and their role and professional boundaries with the team. Simultaneously, suppose your mentee just began working with you as a mentor, and you notice that they seem somewhat tentative in their interactions with you, uncertain of what to ask, and unsure about how to balance being friendly, curious and open, while simultaneously appearing professional and competent. As a mentor, you may address this dynamic with your mentee thereby, normalizing the experience of initial anxiety surrounding roles and responsibilities of being an SEPP professional. Relatedly, you may even self-disclose about some of your experiences early on in your career when you first began your SEPP work. Remember, the most seasoned SEPP professional began as a neophyte early career professional—we all start there! It is through the process of mentorship, guidance, and consultation that we evolve into competent SEPP professionals and mentors. For instance, Angela remembered Bart sharing his experiences as a young professional when working with athletes at a small Southeastern university. He shared experiences when he was uncertain in his delivery to a given team and how he sought mentorship guidance. By modeling that mentorship is a life-long process of learning as we go, you are paradoxically empowering your mentee to be "Okay" with the uncertainty, to be open to ask questions, and commit to finding answers in our discipline's resources when unsure.

Education and Continuing Education

Ideally, it is optimal for you to take a supervision/mentorship course in your degree program in order to provide the necessary mentorship to others in our field. However, if a course is not available, then it would be essential to implement lessons that you learned as a mentee when completing your graduate degree. It is also helpful to read literature that discusses models of supervision and mentorship so that you can develop your own style and method when working with mentees (Fletcher et al., 2025; Poczwardowski et al., 2023). Overall, being a competent mentor requires you to delve into your own graduate education and training, along with continuing to develop your knowledge and skills after graduation.

As you begin your journey as a mentor, you can reflect upon what you learned as a mentee and how you can apply and direct your skills as a mentor to others. With AASP's CMPC certification, you will need to obtain continuing education units (CEUs) to maintain your status as a mentor. Specifically, as of the time of this writing (2025), AASP determined that 75 continuing education hours over a five-year period is sufficient to acquire professional development activities. The required areas for recertification include 6 CEUs in Supervision/Mentorship (for those who are mentors). These hours are most often accomplished via attending workshops and/or webinars (i.e., AASP and/or APA websites). For example, we have regularly attended pre-conference workshops on mentorship at the annual AASP conference. By engaging in both initial and continuing education, mentors can enhance their effectiveness and contribute more positively to the growth and development of those they mentor.

In sum, everyone is going to have their own unique journey to mentorship. When providing mentorship, it is important to understand the roles and responsibilities, incorporating the task and relational dimensions of mentorship, as well as self-reflective practice and parallel process considerations. To assist along your mentorship journey, there are several opportunities through AASP and APA. Proper growth and development must be considered it relates to the standards of being a competent practitioner. Therefore, seek out areas that challenge you to continue to evolve as an ethical and effective SEPP mentor.

"WHAT THE HELL AM I DOING?" REFLECTIONS ON DEVELOPING ONESELF AS A MENTOR

Justine Vosloo, Shelby Anderson, & Sydney Masters

Mentoring is an opportunity to shape the profession for generations through the development of neophyte and early career mentees. Yet given the significance of the mentor role, the importance of developing oneself as a mentor is rarely explored. In this chapter, we explore mentor self-development through a lens of cultural humility, reflective practice, and psychological safety. We view these elements as interrelated concepts, with each concept influencing and enhancing the implementation of the others.

Reflective Practice and Cultural Humility in Mentor Development

Reflective practice and the development of cultural humility are key elements in any journey of self-development, and this certainly holds true for a professional journey toward effective mentorship. The nature of the mentoring relationship requires the mentor to recognize their own biases and cultural blind spots, engage in culturally humble practices, and role model cultural sensitivity and humility in the mentee. Reflective practice may aid in the development of cultural humility, as reflective practice raises awareness of the self and promotes self-development via the purposeful exploration of decision-making and knowledge during practice, which is inherently influenced by practitioner values, prejudices, and previous experiences (Anderson et al., 2004). By engaging in reflective practice, the mentor may establish a foundation on which to build on, that effectively guides the mentee's own reflective journey and cultural humility awareness.

Cultural humility is a process by which the practitioner recognizes that they are not experts, and the practitioner engages in a culturally responsive process of providing space for their clients' identities and the impact on their experiences (Curvey et al., 2022). A key element to this culturally responsive process is the practitioner bringing awareness to their own cultural presence and inviting the client to share aspects of themselves in the collaborative working space (Quartiroli et al., 2021). Similarly, the mentor-mentee relationship requires the mentor to engage in this same culturally responsive process and invite the mentee to share their own identities. However, in this mentoring context, an additional reflective element is recommended for effective mentee development, a reflective process whereby the mentor challenges the mentee to consider their own assumptions, cultural blind spots, or lack of cultural sensitivity to encourage the mentee to engage more deeply with the self-awareness journey thereby fostering further cultural humility development and implementation into practice (Curvey et al., 2022). The mentor's own cultural humility and reflective practice will influence their effectiveness as a mentor, and their abilities to challenge and guide the mentee.

Role of Mentoring and Meta-Mentoring in Training

We recommend that new mentors also engage in a meta-mentoring practice to support their own mentoring development. Meta-mentoring allows the mentor to self-reflect on the process and practice of mentoring under the guidance of an experienced mentor (see Poczwardowski et al., 2023). These experiences are most commonly available within doctoral training programs, where an advanced doctoral student is assigned to mentor an incoming doctoral or master's level student, under the guidance of a faculty member who serves as the meta-mentor. However, this is a vitally beneficial practice that we encourage all new mentors to engage in when first beginning their own mentoring practice, and the new mentor could consider connecting with former mentors or colleagues in their workplace to seek opportunities for meta-mentorship. We also recommend that the meta-mentoring process be a space where the mentor can explore their own reflective practice around the mentor-mentee dynamic and explore how the mentor is navigating issues of identity and preconceived biases within the mentoring relationship.

Goals of Mentorship

There are several areas the mentor can develop in themselves to subsequently foster their mentees' development. The effectiveness of the mentor-mentee relationship is formed in the environment the mentor establishes which ideally would consist of a psychologically safe environment. Psychological safety is an individual's belief that it is okay to express their ideas and concerns, to ask questions, seek constructive feedback, and to admit mistakes—all without fear of negative consequences (Edmondson, 1999). There is an inherent power dynamic that mentors hold over the mentees that can inhibit mentees' willingness to share challenges (Calkins, 2023). Directly addressing this power dynamic can foster a sense of psychological safety for mentees. By creating and promoting a psychologically safe environment, mentors provide a space for mentees to learn and grow by allowing both parties, particularly the mentee, to feel comfortable sharing and learning. Mentors can promote psychological safety by fostering trust and respect, encouraging open and constructive communication, and embracing mistakes and learning (Edmondson, 1999). Specific strategies for a psychologically safe mentoring space include: clarifying expectations of both parties up front by establishing a contract or working agreement; acknowledging the power differential between the mentor and mentee—such as the evaluative nature of this relationship—and establishing mentee development goals beyond this evaluation; and working toward treating the mentee as an equal by valuing the training, insights, and experiences they bring to the relationship (Calkins, 2023). Given the importance of giving feedback to the mentee, the mentee's fears of making mistakes, discomfort with negative feedback, and feelings of embarrassment may be experiences that could impede the open communication process essential to psychological safety (Edmondson, 1999). On the mentor's side, discomfort with giving feedback, or difficulty in recognizing and responding to these feelings in the mentee, could impede the mentor's ability to create a psychologically safe space.

By establishing a psychologically safe environment for mentees, mentors also set the foundation for learning and growth within the mentoring relationship. Another goal of mentorship is to foster a growth mindset in mentees. Growth mindset is the belief that our abilities can be developed and improved, whereas fixed mindset is the belief that our abilities cannot be changed nor improved (Dweck, 2006). Mentees may enter the mentoring partnership with a fixed mindset regarding their sport psychology consulting abilities. Mentors may monitor mentees for a fixed mindset by identifying when mentees: avoid challenges (e.g., teach the same skill over and over again; only willing to work with one population), get discouraged by feedback (e.g., avoid feedback from mentors, peers, and clients; don't ask questions), or are threatened by others successes (e.g., avoid co-consulting; take credit when co-consulting). Whereas a growth mindset toward consulting abilities in a mentee may present as embracing challenges (e.g., utilize different intervention approaches), sees all experiences as opportunities to learn and grow (e.g., seek feedback by asking questions during mentorship; admit and discuss failures), and demonstrating adaptability and a continued desire to learn (e.g., persevering despite setbacks, engaging in life-long learning, understanding that learning takes continuous effort). Regardless of how mentees show up to the mentorship partnership, mentors should foster a growth mindset in mentees by setting the standard that abilities can be learned and improved upon, modeling a growth mindset (e.g., ask for feedback on your mentoring style), and embrace mistakes on both ends of the relationship (e.g., share a recent challenge or struggle; encourage mentees to share challenges or failures).

Mentorship goals do not only benefit the mentee. Mentors also gain much from the mentorship experience (Bloom et al., 1998). As sport psychology professionals, we teach, guide and coach, communicate, and learn from the clients we work with; mentoring sport psychology trainees provides these same opportunities. Mentors can utilize mentorship to work on their own consulting and coaching skills. Mentorship provides the opportunity to practice effective communication skills like active listening (i.e., paying full attention to the mentee), giving constructive feedback (i.e., focusing on how to improve), and asking facilitative questions (i.e., questions that promote reflection and discussion). Mentorship can also open mentors to new ideas and practices, promote their own cultural humility via the interactions with mentees who do not share their identities, and further enhance reflective practice. An example of a goal for a mentor might consist of engaging as a continuous learner by listening to and learning from the ideas of mentees. This is not to say that the focus of mentorship should be on the self-development of mentors. We want to be clear that the focus should still be on mentees; instead, we are suggesting that mentors should also be specific and direct in how they can also benefit from the mentorship partnership. The mentor-mentee relationship is a mutually beneficial opportunity for growth and advancement. Overall, mentors should also consider what goals they have for themselves in the mentoring partnership—benefiting our mentees, our clients, and ourselves.

EDITORS' TAKEAWAYS

We really appreciated Lerner and Breitmeyer sharing insights from their personal mentoring journey. What resonated strongly with me (Sebastian) was how they point out the need to normalize uncertainties—and how both mentor and mentee can benefit from openly discussing this topic. This reminded me of how I discuss the mentoring hat with leadership coaches I work with: and how wearing it you openly share experiences you have had or how you have handled specific situations. Building on the "wearing multiple hats" idea, to me this metaphor relates also well to how Lafferty, Eubank, and Butt discuss the need for mentors to adapt and change even within one specific mentee relationship. Initially, they might use a "teacher hat" helping the mentee navigate first client meetings. Ultimately, they will embrace wearing a mentor or even a "coaching hat" more often, using more open questioning when engaging with their mentee. Lastly, the concept of psychological safety highlighted by Vosloo, Anderson, and Masters stood out to me in their contribution. Again, this is a concept that I discuss frequently in leadership coaching with clients. Being able to take risks, not having to fear failure, and sharing struggles ultimately benefits mentor, mentee and by extension also client growth and development.

RECOMMENDED EXERCISES

1 How would you describe your mentorship philosophy? I bring ____________________ to the mentoring relationship. The best advice a mentor gave me was ____________________. If you had to pick two to three words to describe your mentorship style, they would be ____________________.
2 Engage or re-engage in your cultural autobiography. Consider power, privilege, and discrimination in your experiences, and how these might create blind spots in your mentoring. How will you address them?
3 What does your ideal mentee look like? What personal or professional factors are important, and could any represent a cultural or professional limitation for you?

4 Reflect on your current strengths and areas for growth as a mentor. What steps could you take in the next six months to enhance your skills, and who or what could support you?
5 Recall a challenging mentoring experience or one where you were unsure how to act. What did it teach you, and what would you do differently? On a scale of 0–10, how willing were you to seek help, and why? What were potential solutions, and what did you decide, and why?

REFERENCES

Anderson, A. G., Knowles, Z., & Gilbourne, D. (2004). Reflective practice for sport psychologists: Concepts, models, practical implications, and thoughts on dissemination. *The Sport Psychologist, 18*(2), 188–203. https://doi.org/10.1123/tsp.18.2.188

Bloom, G., Durand-Bush, N., Schinke, R., & Salmela, J. (1998). The importance of mentoring in the development of coaches and athletes. *International Journal of Sport Psychology, 29*(3), 267–281.

Burnell, L., Ong, C. W., Pitt, T., Butt, J., & Eubank, M. (2023). Exploring the perceived benefits of engaging with spotlight personality profiling in performance domains. *Sport & Exercise Psychology Review, 18*(1), 76–95.

Byrd, B., Maurice, S., Charalambous, C., Garcia, S., & Searle, M. (2022). Bridging the gap and finding purpose: An approach for debriefing in applied sport, exercise, and performance psychology. *Journal of Sport Psychology in Action, 13*(2), 129–138. https://doi.org/10.1080/21520704.2021.2021856

Calkins, H. (2023). How to navigate the dynamics of mentorship: Knowing the best ways to handle challenges and conflict is crucial to being a good mentor. *American Psychological Association.* https://www.apa.org/monitor/2023/01/dynamics-mentorship

Curvey, R. M., White, S. C., Murphy, E. A., Scheadler, T. R., Englis, M. T., Phelps, L. L., & Hargons, C. N. (2022). Multicultural training and awareness among sport psychology practitioners. *Journal of Clinical Sport Psychology, 16*(4), 349–367. https://doi.org/10.1123/jcsp.2021-0046

Dweck, C. S. (2006). *Mindset: The new psychology of success.* Random House.

Edmondson, A. (1999). Psychological safety and learning behavior in work teams. *Administrative Science Quarterly, 44*(2), 350–383. https://doi.org/10.2307/2666999

Fletcher, T. B., Shigeno, T. C., Lauer, E. E., & DiLisio, D. C. (2025). Mentorship in applied sport psychology: The Fluid Mentorship Model. *Journal of Clinical Sport Psychology, 1*(aop), 1–15. https://doi.org/10.1123/jcsp.2025-0010

Gardner, F., & Moore, Z. (2006). *Clinical sport psychology.* Human Kinetics.

Kram, K. E. (1988). *Mentoring at work: Developmental relationships in organizational life.* University Press of America.

Lafferty, M. E., & Tod, D. (2023). Life-long learning: Life beyond training. In V. Shanmuganathan-Felton & S. Smith (Eds.), *Developing a sport psychology consultancy practice* (pp. 193–209). Routledge.

McEwan, H. E., Tod, D., & Eubank, M. (2019). The rocky road to individuation: Sport psychologists' perspectives on professional development. *Psychology of Sport and Exercise, 45,* 101542. https://doi.org/10.1016/j.psychsport.2019.101542

McNeill, B. W., & Worthen, V. (1989). The parallel process in psychotherapy supervision. *Professional Psychology: Research and Practice, 20*(5), 329–333. https://doi.org/10.1037/0735-7028.20.5.329

Poczwardowski, A., Andersen, M. B., Van Raalte, J. L., Harwood, C., Si, G., Tshube, T., & Noce, F. (2023). ISSP position stand: Competent supervision in sport psychology. *International Journal of Sport and Exercise Psychology, 21*(6), 931–950. https://doi.org/10.1080/1612197X.2023.2229342

Quartiroli, A., Vosloo, J., Schinke, R. J., Anderson, S. N., Fisher, L. A., & Giffin, C. E. (2021). Sport psychology professionals' perceptions of the roadblocks to cultural sport psychology. *Sport, Exercise, and Performance Psychology, 10*(2), 240–256. https://doi.org/10.1037/spy0000256

Raabe, J., Bejar, M. P., Bass, A. D., Lauer, E. E., Erdner, S. M., & Zakrajsek, R. A. (2019). Teach me and I may remember, involve me and I learn: Four approaches to peer mentoring in sport psychology. *Quest, 71*(4), 447–462. https://doi.org/10.1080/00336297.2019.1579859

Ragins, B. R., & Kram, K. E. (Eds.). (2007). *The handbook of mentoring at work: Theory, research, and practice.* Sage.

Sharp, L., Hodge, K., & Danish, S. (2021). "I wouldn't want to operate without it": The ethical challenges faced by experienced sport psychology consultants and their engagement with supervision. *Journal of Applied Sport Psychology, 33*(3), 259–279. https://doi.org/10.1080/10413200.2019.1646838

Smith, M., Tod, D., & Martindale, A. (2019). UK trainee sport psychologists' perspectives on developing professional judgement and decision-making expertise during training. *The Sport Psychologist, 33*(4), 334–343. https://doi.org/10.1123/tsp.2018-0102

Tod, D., McEwan, H. E., Chandler, C., Eubank, M., & Lafferty, M. (2020). The gravitational pull of identity: Professional growth in sport, exercise, and performance psychologists. *Journal of Sport Psychology in Action, 11*(4), 233–242. https://doi.org/10.1080/21520704.2020.1740762

Tracey, T. J. G., Bludworth, J., & Glidden-Tracey, C. E. (2012). Are there parallel processes in psychotherapy supervision? An empirical examination. *Psychotherapy, 49*(3), 330–343. https://doi.org/10.1037/a0026246

Van Raalte, J. L., & Andersen, M. B. (2000). Supervision I: From models to doing. In M. B. Andersen (Ed.), *Doing sport psychology* (pp. 153–165). Human Kinetics.

Zetzer, H. A., Hill, C. E., Hopsicker, R. J., Krasno, A. M., Montojo, P. C., Plumb, E. I. W., Hoffman, M. A., & Donahue, M. T. (2020). Parallel process in psychodynamic supervision: The supervisor's perspective. *Psychotherapy, 57*(2), 252–262. https://doi.org/10.1037/pst0000274

30 Peer Mentoring and Consultation

I (Andrew) remember one of my first days of graduate school—we students were in a seminar led by the late, great Prof. Terry Orlick. One of my classmates remarked that it was the first time they had ever been in the company of like-minded individuals who shared their passion. I remember thinking how odd that sounded—surely everyone had experienced a peer mentoring group like I had during my undergraduate years, no? It was then that I realized how rare and special that experience actually was. I gained a deeper appreciation for the work of my early mentors, Drs. Cal Botterill and Tom Patrick, who established SportPsychManitoba—an informal, student-led professional development group that held case studies, debriefed conferences, invited international guest speakers, and engaged in all manner of peer learning. Now, 20 years into my SEPP career, I cannot think of a single experience that had a more formative impact. That is why we felt it essential to include a chapter on peer mentoring groups in this book.

PEER MENTORING: HOW TO LEVERAGE A POWERFUL "INFORMAL" LEARNING OPPORTUNITY

Johannes Raabe & Matthew P. Bejar

Mentoring is a method of professional development that traditionally involves a dyadic interpersonal relationship with the goal of transmitting knowledge from an experienced to a less experienced individual (i.e., mentor and mentee; Tynjälä et al., 2021). While the role of mentor has conventionally been reserved for seasoned professionals with authority over their respective mentees, such as a faculty member in a university setting, peer mentoring has been proposed as a viable complement in sport, exercise, and performance psychology (SEPP) (Raabe et al., 2019). In this approach, mentor and mentee are considered peers or of equal standing with one another, such as two students or colleagues with similar levels of experience. Watson et al. (2009) found that graduate students perceived mentoring relationships with peers as more open, empathetic, trustworthy, and comfortable than with faculty. Importantly, peer mentoring not only benefits mentees but also has a positive impact on the individuals providing the mentoring by allowing them to develop leadership, teaching, and communication skills (Marshall et al., 2021).

Practical Recommendations for Peer Mentors

Seek Meta-Mentoring

While mentors in more traditional mentoring relationships (e.g., faculty-student) often have years of experience not only in their profession but also in the supervision of mentees, peer

DOI: 10.4324/9781003781479-37

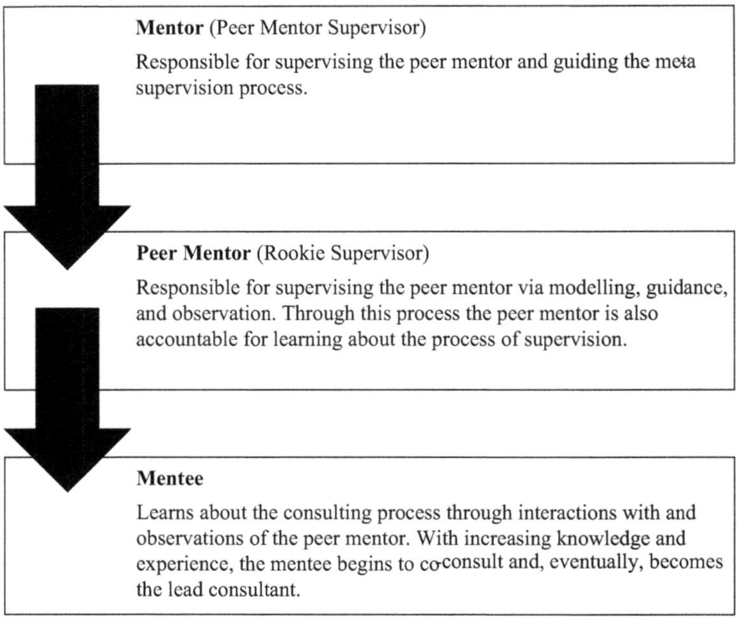

Figure 30.1 Peer mentoring and supervision training model

Source: Adapted from Vosloo et al. (2014)

mentors rarely have the same level of preparation. As a result, it is beneficial for peer mentors to seek regular supervision themselves (i.e., meta-mentoring). Vosloo et al.'s (2014) training model (see Figure 30.1) provides a framework to structure this type of mentoring approach distinguishing between what they refer to as rookies, peer mentors, and supervisors. Peer mentors' responsibilities are to structure mentees' experiences by, for example, providing and discussing relevant readings, teaching key concepts informally, and guiding rookies through relevant activities and/or observations. Simultaneously, peer mentors learn about and are trained in the process of mentoring by more experienced professionals.

(Re)define Success

Peer mentors might experience a sense of pride when their mentees follow in their "footsteps" (e.g., getting admitted into the same SEPP graduate program); however, by adhering to this narrow definition of "success," peer mentors set themselves up for disappointment and risk harming the mentor-mentee relationship. Instead, peer mentors should aim to facilitate resonance, or the alignment between an individual's internal feelings of personal fulfillment and the external environment (see Raabe et al., 2019 for a more comprehensive overview), for their mentees rather than solely focusing on outcomes. For many peer mentors, this approach requires them to critically revisit and redefine what it means to be a successful mentor. For example, a doctoral student who has invested hours mentoring an undergraduate student might feel disappointed when the mentee decides to pursue a graduate degree outside of SEPP. That peer mentor could challenge irrational beliefs about the mentoring process being a "failure" by noting how, for instance, the mentee's interpersonal or professional communication skills might have improved. It is important to recognize that success is defined differently for each individual and in each context.

Foster (Self-Determined) Motivation

Mentees might initially seek mentoring "out of necessity" because they are pursuing a certification (e.g., Certified Mental Performance Consultant) or are trying to strengthen their resume through research experiences. As a result, it is common to see varying levels of commitment among mentees. Peer mentors should, therefore, consider their role in mentees' motivation. According to self-determination theory (Ryan & Deci, 2017), mentees will experience more optimal motivation when their basic psychological needs of competence (i.e., feeling capable to successfully complete tasks and meet expectations), autonomy (i.e., having meaningful input and a sense of value), and relatedness (i.e., experiencing connection and trusting relationships) are satisfied. Peer mentors can nurture these needs in a variety of ways (see Raabe et al., 2019 for a more comprehensive overview). For example, peer mentors should offer clear directions, information about expectations, and constructive feedback (competence), provide meaningful choices (autonomy), as well as demonstrate genuine care (relatedness).

Practice Cultural Humility

Peer mentors should acknowledge and celebrate the many ways that their mentees are diverse, recognizing these as unique strengths and perspectives. Sue et al. (2022) described three components of cultural competence that can be adapted to SEPP: cultural awareness (i.e., recognition of peer mentors' own identities, backgrounds, and ways they are privileged and oppressed), cultural knowledge (i.e., important information about mentees' cultural background), and cultural skills (i.e., the application of cultural knowledge and skills into impactful strategies). In recent years, the term "cultural humility" has been used in favor of "cultural competence," which may inadvertently convey an endpoint instead of peer mentors' humbly recognizing that they always have more to learn and are fallible to mistakes. Even with the best of intentions, peer mentors will inevitably make cultural transgressions (e.g., an ableist or sexist comment) due to unavoidable implicit assumptions. Recognizing that mistakes are essential to their growth as mentors, scholars, and practitioners requires openness and continuous self-reflection.

Practical Recommendations for Peer Mentees

Be Intentional with Mentor Selection

All too often, mentees select peer mentors out of convenience because a particular individual may simply be easily accessible (e.g., be part of the same university department or have the same advisor) or the first to agree to serve in that capacity. Yet, this lack of intentionality can meaningfully decrease the effectiveness of the peer mentoring process if there are either interpersonal challenges or no match between mentors' and mentees' professional interests. While this type of misalignment will likely eventually surface, mentees should learn as much as possible about the background, experiences, and interests of possible peer mentors before making an educated decision about who to approach about a potential mentoring relationship. Students, for example, may seek advice from faculty on who may be a good fit as a peer mentor.

Communicate Effectively

Communication is a critical element of any mentoring relationship. A good peer mentor should cultivate an environment in which a mentee feels comfortable expressing any relevant concerns (e.g., unrealistic expectations or workload). Nevertheless, due to the inherent power dynamics of the mentoring process, it can still be difficult for mentees to have conversations with peer mentors that they perceive as "uncomfortable." The Describe-Express-Specify-Consequences (DESC) model (Bower & Bower, 1976) is a good heuristic for being assertive in these situations. Mentees should describe the situation (i.e., the concern they are trying to address), express their associated emotions, specify alternative behaviors, and finally convey the consequences of those alternative behaviors in an unthreatening manner. Although it is understandable for mentees to be frustrated when there is misalignment between their mentor's and their own expectations, it is important for mentees to remember that the peer mentor is a fellow student—and fellow human—who is also navigating daily hassles and major life events. Practicing empathy and building rapport should therefore be bidirectional to provide a solid foundation for open and effective communication.

Conclusion

Peer mentoring can be an extremely helpful learning opportunity for students and less experienced SEPP professionals. Nevertheless, it is an approach that is often underutilized; perhaps due to both mentors' and mentees' concerns about how to most effectively approach this type of relationship (Raabe et al., 2019). The current chapter outlines that peer mentors can enhance their effectiveness by seeking mentorship, (re)defining success, practicing cultural humility, and fostering (self-determined) motivation. Mentees are more likely to have positive peer mentoring experiences when they are intentional with their mentor selection and communicate effectively.

PUTTING PEER CONSULTATION INTO PRACTICE: TWO PROCESSES IN ACTION

Helena Schmitz, Christian Zepp, Bernadette Ramaker, & Grzegorz Więcław

This chapter will present two internationally established networks: The European Network of Young Specialists in Sport Psychology (ENYSSP) and Virtual Sport Psychology (VSP). They both offer formal and informal peer consultation and mentoring opportunities. Together, these networks demonstrate the powerful impact of professional collaboration, showing how both structured and organic peer interactions can elevate personal development and strengthen the field of SEPP.

The European Network of Young Specialists in Sport Psychology

Celebrating its 20th anniversary in 2024, ENYSSP supports (early-career) professionals, students, and researchers in SEPP in their professional development (ENYSSP, n.d.). ENYSSP's mission is to nurture growth, collaboration, and progress by fostering an environment where members from diverse cultural and academic backgrounds can connect, share knowledge, and support one another. The network provides a wide range of formal and informal engagement opportunities, promoting lifelong learning and preparing the next generation of SEPP practitioners and researchers. Visualized as a tree (see Figure 30.2), ENYSSP's structure represents its history, leadership, departments, and activities, all of which work together to support its members. The fruits at the top of the tree symbolize the resources available to members, including the Peer Consultation Sessions (PCS)—an approach to peer supervision and mentoring.

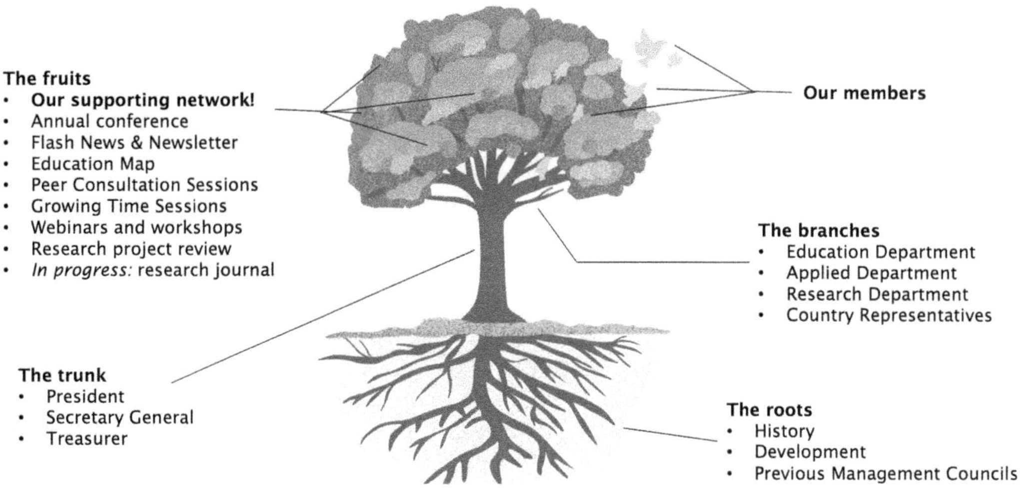

Figure 30.2 The ENYSSP tree
Source: Adapted from Dicker (2025)

Peer Consultation Sessions

The PCS were introduced to create an activity for ENYSSP members to share and experience peer feedback. In line with the first edition of this book, which already provided a detailed description of the background and philosophy behind the PCS (Bednáriková et al., 2016), the founders designed the peer mentoring process based on Vygotsky's (1962, 1978) theory of learning through interaction and communication with others. The effectiveness of this purpose-driven approach has been proven over time, as the PCS have become well-established, regular online activities (approximately every eight weeks), hosted by ENYSSP's Applied Department. The main aim of the PCS is to provide a safe space for young practitioners to share and discuss work-related questions, challenges, and cases they have encountered in their professional practice, gaining further insights into their own practice, and learning through self-reflection and in-depth peer discussions.

Since the introduction of PCS, its aims and general procedures have stayed consistent, while parts of the procedure (ENYSSP-Applied, n.d.) continuously get refined to ensure the PCS runs optimally. Before each PCS, all participating practitioners are invited to submit a case description for which they would like to receive input from their peers. If multiple case descriptions are submitted, a majority vote by the practitioners will decide which case will be discussed during the session that lasts 90 minutes. Based on Nilson's (1998) emphasis to assign small groups clear and purposeful roles, in each PCS three separate roles can be taken: Process Leader, Case Submitter, and Participants. The Process Leader is an Applied Department Coordinator, who moderates the conversation, keeps track of the time, and ensures the procedures are followed. In the first stage, the Process Leader kicks off the PCS session by introducing any new participants and reminding the Participants of the workflow. In the second stage, the chosen case will be summarized by the Case Submitter and all Participants are invited to ask the Case Submitter questions to gain more information about the case. In the third phase, the Participants analyze the situation and discuss what they interpret as the main question that should be answered to help the Case Submitter progress further. In this third stage, the Case Submitter is only listening to the conversation of the Participants and does not actively participate. During the fourth stage, all Participants get time to individually answer the determined question of the third stage and write up their suggestions and recommendations on how the Case Submitter could approach the next steps. The fifth stage is where the Participants share their suggestions for approaches with the Case Submitter and the other Participants. Afterwards, time is dedicated for the Case Submitter to react to the suggestions provided, for others to share other similar experiences and for all to reflect on the session itself. The Process Leader compiles all provided suggestions and recommendations in a report to share with the Case Submitter and Participants after the PCS. Attendees have praised the PCS for the created safe space with valuable interactions to brainstorm and the exchange of ideas and approaches that vary across countries.

Virtual Sport Psych

VSP (Zepp, n.d.) was an innovative initiative aimed at meeting the complex, evolving needs of SEPP practitioners by establishing a structured, community-driven platform. Recognizing the unique challenges that professionals in this field face, including the isolated nature of their work and the pressing need for continuous skill enhancement, VSP offered VSP+, a comprehensive and dynamic platform that provided consistent opportunities for continuing education and peer support. Central to the VSP+ initiative was a robust framework for peer mentoring, which played a pivotal role in promoting professional growth, enhancing reflective practices, and fostering a sense of shared learning among sport psychology practitioners.

The peer mentoring approach within VSP+ was intentionally multifaceted, employing diverse formats such as supervision, intervision (peer-to-peer consulting), and collaborative workshops. This structure allowed for an adaptive and engaging experience that met a variety of developmental needs. Supervision sessions provided members with an opportunity for guidance and reflective dialogue facilitated by experienced mentors, which was particularly crucial for those encountering complex ethical or professional challenges in their practice. In contrast, intervision sessions promoted an egalitarian learning environment where peers consulted each other on cases, shared experiences, and explored different perspectives while creating a non-hierarchical form of mutual support and learning. This approach was instrumental in democratizing expertise, emphasizing that every practitioner, regardless of experience, can both contribute to and benefit from shared wisdom.

VSP+ placed strong emphasis on fostering active peer learning within its community, achieved by curating diverse, peer-led initiatives such as workshops, regular peer consultations, and summits. These events served as vital platforms for facilitating in-depth discussions, practicing skills, and staying abreast of the latest research and interventions in sport psychology. By creating opportunities for informal and formal mentorship relationships to form during these gatherings, the various events significantly contributed to the culture of peer mentoring that defined VSP+.

Conclusion

Formal structures like peer mentoring and consultation sessions provide a structured setting where individuals at similar career stages collaborate, share knowledge, and work through challenges. These interactions promote teamwork, problem-solving, and continuous professional development as colleagues can systematically address challenges together and gain practical, actionable insights for their work. Furthermore, formal sessions often serve as a starting point for new connections, enabling individuals who might not have known each other to build professional relationships. Over time, these initial connections frequently evolve into informal support networks, where trust and mutual support develop organically. Informal peer interactions, such as spontaneous conversations, quick phone calls or casual discussions, allow individuals to share advice and experiences in a casual, relaxed and flexible manner. These relationships can significantly enhance the sense of community and belonging in a profession, where isolation is often experienced.

PEER MENTORING AND CONSULTATION: FROM TRAILBLAZING TO TIME-HONORED PRINCIPLES

Sari Shepphird

Tele-consultation groups (TCGs), conceived by the late Kate F. Hays and facilitated in tandem by me, create a dynamic space intending to impact numerous professional growth markers. The rationale, benefits, and utility of these group experiences will be discussed here and principles for professional development will be applied in order to serve as an example of a successful peer mentoring and consultation program.

A History of the Hays-Shepphird TCGs

Dr. Kate Hays has long been thought of as a trailblazer in sport and performance psychology (SEPP), particularly when it comes to peer mentoring and consultation. The Kate F. Hays Distinguished Mentor Award presented by the Association for Applied Sport Psychology was posthumously named in recognition of her substantial impact on peer mentoring and consultation. Dr. Hays's TCGs came to fruition in 2009 because of her creative thinking about this realm of professional development. Her intention was to provide an opportunity for guided learning and growth experiences among colleagues with shared interests. In 2016, Dr. Hays invited me to collaborate in facilitating TCGs.

Rationale for the TCGs

Prior to the development of the TCGs, there was a dearth of group peer mentoring and consultation experiences available. Knowing this and building on professional feedback from widely dispersed colleagues, Dr. Hays launched TCGs. In contrast to standard face-to-face meetings, Dr. Hays envisioned the TCGs taking place in a virtual meeting space, a format that we take for granted at the present time but was quite new to the SEPP scene in 2009 (Murphy, 2023).

Ideally, peer mentoring and consultation should serve developing and seasoned performance consultants in ways that go beyond "getting advice." As such, TCGs address varying levels of learning, interaction, and experience so that potential participants can pursue a group that seems best suited to their needs. For example, "introductory" groups provide didactic education through shared readings and discussion of concepts such as mental skills training, differentiating performance issues from clinical issues, niche practice development, and grounding in SEPP research. "Intermediate" groups provide more advanced didactic materials, along with the addition of increased discussion of professional practice issues and masked case discussion. "Advanced" groups are designed for experienced practitioners who are interested in more robust discussion of masked practice situations. Each TCG takes place in a small group setting (five to ten members) allowing for a sense of engagement for each participant in a confidential group, fostering the building of trust and relationships while obtaining peer and professional mentoring (Hays & Shepphird, 2020).

Consultant as Performer

Are SEPP consultants also "performers" themselves? Dr. Hays conceptualized them as such (Hays & Brown, 2019) and the TCG space allows consultants to receive varying kinds of support to ameliorate perceived performance pressure. In Dr. Hays's landmark text on performance psychology, Murphy (2009) elucidated five types of support, including: emotional support, tangible support (e.g., practical support to help accomplish tasks); informational support (e.g., guidance or advice); esteem support (e.g., positive feedback for efforts); and network support (e.g., the feeling of belonging to a group that shares similar interests). With such a framework in mind, TCGs attempt to meet the broad varieties of support that consultants as performers might be searching for.

Time-Honored Principles for the TCGs

Another driving guidepost for the TCG experience comes in the form of Dr. Hays's well-thought-out principles for sport psychology consulting (Shepphird, 2024), which are mindfully incorporated into the TCGs and are recommended as guiding principles for peer consultation and mentoring. These include:

- A spirit of collaborative empiricism in consultation. Dr. Hays considered every encounter to be a series of experiments in which hypotheses are formed, tested, and revised (Hays, 2021).
- Providing practical value as soon as possible. For example, including professional goal setting for TCG participants in the first meeting.
- Going in the direction the camel is already going—Dr. Hays's metaphor to convey meeting people where they are.
- Remembering you don't have to tell people everything you know, thus taking pressure off the consultant as performer.
- Maintaining an awareness of subtexts and relational factors (e.g., defenses, resistance, transference, and countertransference).
- Understanding the interaction of thought, affect, and behavior. Dr. Hays emphasized both the awareness of individual differences as well as the need for a general understanding of how people function (Hays, 2021) in order to optimize group cohesion.
- Paying attention to culture, context, systems, and domains, in addition to individuals. For Dr. Hays, this was an integral facet of meeting people where they are (Shepphird, 2024).
- Maintaining ethical boundaries. While this is the expectation for any professional relationship, TCGs are intended to be safe spaces for members, thus confidentiality and the expectation for ethical behavior within the TCG experience are paramount.
- Acting as if the world is essentially beneficent. Optimism, resilience, self-efficacy, gratitude—these are among the values that shaped Dr. Hays's professional worldview.
- Maintaining an openness to learning, growth, and change. Another of Dr. Hays's professional values, TCGs seek to contribute positively to lifelong learning through case consultations, shared readings, and from the lives and viewpoints of participants.

Fulfilling a Purpose: Feedback Received by Tele-Consultation Group Participants

Do the TCGs fulfill their intended purpose and provide "real-life" value? While both Dr. Hays and I would certainly give a resounding "yes!", we would do well to look to other data points for impact. At the time of this writing, the TCGs are in their 17th year; their longevity demonstrates their ongoing usefulness. Nearly 200 participants from 42 U.S. states, six Canadian provinces, and a few cities within Europe and the UK have joined in professional development, collaboration, mentoring, and peer consultation. Shared feedback via solicited evaluations provides the overall impression that TCG experiences are overwhelmingly positive. Selected comments from participants are included below to not only establish the effectiveness of the TCGs but to encourage readers to seek out experiences which provide similar value and support (Hays, 2019).

- "This TCG has been such an incredible experience! It helped to quiet some of my professional nagging doubts, deepened my confidence that I can make a difference, and helped me press on toward my goals."
- "My sport psychology TCG exceeded all expectations and motivated me to dive even deeper into the core competencies of this exciting area of practice."
- "This group was an excellent segue from thinking like a clinical psychologist to thinking like a sport psychologist. I am ready to take the next step in this field."
- "The meetings created an atmosphere that was structured and yet comfortable enough to openly discuss concerns, thoughts, suggestions, and questions."
- "What stands out is a 'you can do it' kind of acceptance and encouragement."
- "The TCG helped me better understand my own strengths and weaknesses and provided me with some direction—which is exactly why I signed up."
- "I really enjoy the opportunity to discuss case examples. I like the diversity of our group which makes for good input."

Beyond the TCGs

As seen in the comments above, successful peer mentoring and consultation may inspire greater professional involvement. For me, growth came full circle, from participant to facilitator to vision caster of similar peer mentoring activities, for example hosting virtual consultation experiences within the Society for Sport, Exercise, and Performance Psychology and facilitating in-person activities within the Los Angeles County Psychological Association and the California Psychological Association. Whether virtual or face-to-face in format, peer mentoring and consultation remain a vital part of ongoing professional development and growth. The outcome of that growth is further enhanced when professionals seek to reproduce the benefits derived from their peer mentoring and consultation experiences.

EDITORS' TAKEAWAYS

Honoring the aim of providing a "global perspective" to becoming an SEPP professional, we are really excited that we managed to recruit such a diverse group of authors for the peer mentoring chapter. It is exciting to read about the European peer mentoring initiative as well as the virtual option designed and implemented by our German colleague Christian Zepp. Schmitz, Zepp, Ramaker, and Więcław show how a purpose-driven, theory-based approach can be strategically implemented and sustained over time. Shepphird, of course, provides another example of a sustainable peer mentoring model, discussing the Hays-Shepphird TCGs. What struck me (Sebastian) about the TCG is how they offer peer mentoring geared specifically for "neophyte," "intermediate," and "advanced" professionals. While the format remains the same, the content is adjusted per mentees' needs. Peer mentoring, then, isn't something that is only relevant for graduate students or early-career professionals. Speaking of graduate students: Raabe and Bejar citing the finding by Watson et al. (2009) that "graduate students perceived mentoring relationships with peers as more open, empathetic, trustworthy, and comfortable than with faculty" made me pause and think! What does that say about the quality of faculty mentors and mentor development? It seems that our field has quite some learning and growing to do, if this gap that ultimately also affects client welfare and services, is to be addressed.

RECOMMENDED EXERCISES

1 What would you be trying to accomplish by engaging in peer mentoring as a mentor or mentee? What are your personal interests as they relate to the professional area that you are seeking peer mentoring for (e.g., consulting, research)?
2 List seven to ten of your identities. Represent them as a pie chart showing their relative importance (%). What do you notice about your most and least salient identities? How might these influence your interactions with peer mentors and mentees?
3 Imagine preparing for PCS within a professional network.
   a What challenges or cases from your current work would you bring, and why?
   b How would you approach giving and receiving feedback in this structured environment?
   c The TCGs always begin with participant goal sharing. What are three goals you hope to achieve from the peer mentoring experience?
4 Reflect on a time an informal conversation with a peer or colleague led to insights or solutions. What made it valuable, and how can you create more informal interactions in your professional journey?
5 Reflect on a mentor or colleague who has influenced your career path in sport psychology. What specific aspects of their support or guidance helped you the most?
6 Dr. Hays's list of principles for sport and performance consulting came from her life experiences as well as her professional ones. From your own life and professional experiences, what principles do you value for growth in sport and performance consulting?
7 Of the five different kinds of support discussed in this chapter as elucidated by Murphy (2009), which do you feel the best poised to offer in a peer mentoring experience? Which are you the most in need of for yourself?
8 What gaps do you perceive in the field when it comes to providing peer support, mentoring, and consultation? What would it look like for you to turn that perception into practical and tangible opportunities for yourself and others to benefit?

REFERENCES

Bednáriková, M., Schneider, P., & Więcław, G. (2016). Looking for guidance and support among colleagues: Peer supervision and mentoring in ENYSSP. In J. G. Cremades & L. S. Tashman (Eds.), *Global practices and training in applied sport, exercise, and performance psychology* (1st ed., pp. 298–306). Routledge.

Bower, S. A., & Bower, G. H. (1976). *Asserting yourself.* Addison-Wesley.

Dicker, S. (2025). *The tree of life: Rooted and flourishing* [Image]. Publisher.
European Network of Young Specialists in Sport Psychology. (n.d.). *ENYSSP.* https://www.enyssp.com
European Network of Young Specialists in Sport Psychology–Applied Department. (n.d.). *PCS rationale and aims.* https://drive.google.com/file/d/1slnyUHr00bAEnafzRb8kUo69zduCiCwz/view?usp=sharing
Hays, K. F. (2019, May 15). *Participants' perspectives: What participants are saying.* https://web.archive.org/web/20190515222937/https://theperformingedge.com/participants.html
Hays, K. F. (2021). Dr. Kate F. Hays. In M. W. Aoyagi & A. Poczwardowski (Eds.), *Expert approaches to sport psychology* (2nd ed., pp. 123–140). Fitness Information Technology.
Hays, K. F., & Brown, C. H. (2019). *Performance consulting competence: A description and checklist* [Unpublished manuscript].
Hays, K. F., & Shepphird, S. (2020). *Tele-consultation groups initial information* [Brochure].
Marshall, M., Dobbs-Oates, J., Kunberger, T., & Greene, J. (2021). The peer mentor experience: Benefits and challenges in undergraduate programs. *Mentoring & Tutoring: Partnership in Learning, 29*(1), 89–109. https://doi.org/10.1080/13611267.2021.1895137
Murphy, S. (2009). Isolation. In K. F. Hays (Ed.), *Performance psychology in action: A casebook for working with athletes, performing artists, business leaders, and professionals in high-risk occupations* (pp. 203–223). American Psychological Association.
Murphy, S. (2023, August 3–5). *The promise and the perils of applied technology in sport and performance psychology* [Symposium]. 131st annual meeting of the American Psychological Association, Washington, DC.
Nilson, L. B. (1998). *Teaching at its best: A research-based resource for college instructors* (1st ed.). Anker Publishing Company.
Raabe, J., Bejar, M. P., Bass, A. D., Lauer, E. E., Erdner, S. M., & Zakrajsek, R. A. (2019). Teach me and I may remember, involve me and I learn: Four approaches to peer mentoring in sport psychology. *Quest, 71*(4), 447–462. https://doi.org/10.1080/00336297.2019.1576516
Ryan, R. M., & Deci, E. L. (2017). *Self-determination theory: Basic psychological needs in motivation, development, and wellness.* Guilford Press.
Shepphird, S. (2024, August 8–10). *Principles, pearls, and a legacy* [Symposium]. 132nd annual meeting of the American Psychological Association, Seattle, WA.
Sue, D. W., Sue, D., Neville, H. A., & Smith, L. (2022). *Counseling the culturally diverse: Theory and practice* (9th ed.). John Wiley & Sons.
Tynjälä, P., Pennanen, M., Markkanen, I., & Heikkinen, H. L. (2021). Finnish model of peer-group mentoring: Review of research. *Annals of the New York Academy of Sciences, 1483*(1), 208–223. https://doi.org/10.1111/nyas.14561
Vosloo, J., Zakrajsek, R. A., & Grindley, E. (2014). From mentee to mentor: Considerations for the neophyte supervisor. In J. G. Cremades & L. S. Tashman (Eds.), *Becoming a sport, exercise, and performance psychology professional: A global perspective* (pp. 228–235). Psychology Press, Taylor & Francis Group.
Vygotsky, L. S. (1962). *Thought and language.* MIT Press.
Vygotsky, L. S. (1978). *Mind in society.* Harvard University Press.
Watson, J. C., Clement, D., Blom, L. C., & Grindley, E. (2009). Mentoring: Processes and perceptions of sport and exercise psychology graduate students. *Journal of Applied Sport Psychology, 21*(2), 231–246. https://doi.org/10.1080/10413200902777225
Zepp, C. (n.d.). *Virtual Sport Psych.* https://www.virtualsportpsych.com

For Product Safety Concerns and Information please contact our EU
representative GPSR@taylorandfrancis.com
Taylor & Francis Verlag GmbH, Kaufingerstraße 24, 80331 München, Germany

www.ingramcontent.com/pod-product-compliance
Ingram Content Group UK Ltd.
Pitfield, Milton Keynes, MK11 3LW, UK
UKHW050234200926
475702UK00020B/3024

* 9 7 8 1 0 4 1 3 1 9 4 9 8 *